ELEMENTS OF
ARGUMENT

FIFTH EDITION

ELEMENTS OF ARGUMENT
A Text and Reader

Annette T. Rottenberg

BEDFORD BOOKS   *BOSTON*

For Alex and Anna

For Bedford Books
President and Publisher: Charles H. Christensen
General Manager and Associate Publisher: Joan E. Feinberg
Managing Editor: Elizabeth M. Schaaf
Developmental Editor: Stephen A. Scipione
Editorial Assistants: Rebecca Jerman, Kate O'Sullivan
Production Editor: Karen S. Baart
Production Assistant: Stasia Zomkowski
Copyeditor: Cynthia Benn
Text Design: Claire Seng-Niemoeller
Cover Design: Night and Day Design
Cover Painting: David Park, *Two Heads,* gouache on paper. Collection of Whitney Museum of American Art. Gift of Mrs. Volney F. Righter. Photograph Copyright © 1996: Whitney Museum of American Art, New York.

Library of Congress Catalog Card Number: 96–84938

Manufactured in the United States of America.

1 0 9 8
f e

For information, write: Bedford Books, 75 Arlington Street, Boston, MA 02116 (617–426–7440)

ISBN: 0–312–13349–9

ACKNOWLEDGMENTS

Gordon Allport, "The Nature of Prejudice." From the 17th Claremont Reading Conference Yearbook, 1952. Reprinted by permission of the Claremont Reading Conference.
Jonathan Alter, "Affirmative Ambivalence." From *Newsweek,* March 27, 1995. Copyright © 1995 Newsweek, Inc. All rights reserved. Reprinted by permission.
Amtrak ® advertisement, "There's something about a train that's magic." Reprinted by permission of Amtrak®. Amtrak® is a registered service mark of the National Railroad Passenger Corporation.
"Back away. Slowly." Drawing by Mike Luckovich. Copyright © 1996 Mike Luckovich–Atlanta Constitution. Reprinted by permission of Mike Luckovich and Creators Syndicate.

Acknowledgments and copyrights are continued at the back of the book on pages 731–36, which constitute an extension of the copyright page. It is a violation of the law to reproduce these selections by any means whatsoever without the written permission of the copyright holder.

Preface
for Instructors

PURPOSE

Argumentation as the basis of a composition course should
need no defense, especially at a time of renewed pedagogical interest in critical thinking. A course in argumentation encourages practice in close analysis, use of supporting materials, and logical
organization. It encompasses all the modes of development around
which composition courses are often built. It teaches students to
read and to listen with more than ordinary care. Not least, argument
can engage the interest of students who have been indifferent or
even hostile to required writing courses. Because the subject matter
of argument can be found in every human activity, from the most
trivial to the most elevated, both students and teachers can choose
the materials that appeal to them.

Composition courses using the materials of argument are, of
course, not new. But the traditional methods of teaching argument
through mastery of the formal processes of reasoning cannot account for the complexity of arguments in practice. Even more relevant to our purposes as teachers of composition is the tenuous
relationship between learning about induction and deduction, however helpful in analysis, and the actual process of student composition. The challenge has been to find a method of teaching argument
that assists students in defending their claims as directly and efficiently as possible, a method that reflects the way people actually
go about organizing and developing claims outside the classroom.

One such method, first adapted to classroom instruction by teachers of rhetoric and speech, uses a model of argument advanced by Stephen Toulmin in *The Uses of Argument*. Toulmin was interested in producing a description of the real *process* of argument. His model was the law. "Arguments," he said, "can be compared with lawsuits, and the claims we make and argue for in extra-legal contexts with claims made in the courts."[1] Toulmin's model of argument was based on three principal elements: claim, evidence, and warrant. These elements answered the questions, "What are you trying to prove?" "What have you got to go on?" "How did you get from evidence to claim?" Needless to say, Toulmin's model of argument does not guarantee a classroom of skilled arguers, but his questions about the parts of an argument and their relationship are precisely the ones that students must ask and answer in writing their own essays and analyzing those of others. They lead students naturally into the formulation and development of their claims.

In this text I have adapted — and greatly simplified — some of Toulmin's concepts and terminology for first-year students. I have also introduced two elements of argument with which Toulmin is not directly concerned. Most rhetoricians consider them indispensable, however, to discussion of what actually happens in the defense or rejection of a claim. One is motivational appeals — warrants based on appeals to the needs and values of an audience, designed to evoke emotional responses. A distinction between logic and emotion may be useful as an analytical tool, but in producing or attacking arguments human beings find it difficult, if not impossible, to make such a separation. In this text, therefore, persuasion through appeals to needs and values is treated as a legitimate element in the argumentative process.

I have also stressed the significance of audience as a practical matter. In the rhetorical or audience-centered approach to argument, to which I subscribe in this text, success is defined as acceptance of the claim by an audience. Arguers in the real world recognize intuitively that their primary goal is not to demonstrate the purity of their logic, but to win the adherence of their audiences. To gain this adherence, students need to be reminded of the necessity for establishing themselves as credible sources for their readers.

I hope *Elements of Argument* will lead students to discover not only practical and intellectual rewards of learning how to argue but the real excitement of engaging in civilized debate.

---

[1] *The Uses of Argument* (Cambridge: Cambridge University Press, 1958), p. 7.

ORGANIZATION

In Part One, after two introductory chapters, a chapter each is devoted to the chief elements of argument — the claims that students make in their arguments, the definitions and support they must supply for their claims, the warrants that underlie their arguments, the language that they use. Popular fallacies, as well as induction and deduction, are treated in Chapter 8; because fallacies represent errors of reasoning, a knowledge of induction and deduction can make clear how and why fallacies occur. Each chapter ends with an advertisement illustrating the element of argument treated in that chapter.

I have provided examples, readings, discussion questions, and writing suggestions that are, I hope, both practical and stimulating. With the exception of several student dialogues, the examples are real, not invented; they have been taken from speeches, editorial opinions, letters to the editor, advertisements, interviews, and news reports. They reflect the liveliness and complexity that invented examples often suppress.

The forty-eight selections in Part One support the discussions in several important ways. First, they illustrate the elements of argument; in each chapter, one or more essays have been analyzed to emphasize the chapter's principles of argument. Second, they are drawn from current publications and cover as many different subjects as possible to convince students that argument is a pervasive force in the world they read about and live in. Third, some of the essays are obviously flawed and thus enable students to identify the kinds of weaknesses they should avoid in their own essays.

Part Two takes up the process of writing and researching. Chapter 9 explains how to find a topic, define the issues that it embraces, organize the information, and draft and revise an argument. Chapter 10 introduces students to the business of finding sources and using these sources effectively in research papers. The chapter concludes with two annotated student research papers, one of which employs the materials of literature and the Modern Language Association (MLA) documentation system, the other of which represents research in the social and natural sciences and uses a modified American Psychological Association (APA) documentation style.

Part Three, Opposing Viewpoints, exhibits arguers in action, using informal and formal language, debating head-on. The subjects capture headlines every day, and despite their immediacy, they are likely to arouse passions and remain controversial for a long time. Whether as matters of national policy or personal choice, they call for decisions based on familiarity with competing views.

Part Four, Classic Arguments, reprints eleven selections that have stood the tests of both time and the classroom. They are among the arguments that teachers find invaluable in any composition course.

The instructor's manual, *Resources for Teaching* Elements of Argument, provides additional suggestions for using the book, as well as for finding and using the enormous variety of materials available in a course on argument.

A briefer edition, *The Structure of Argument,* Second Edition, is available for instructors who prefer a shorter text with fewer readings. It presents only Parts One and Two and the appendix, Arguing about Literature, from the longer edition.

NEW TO THIS EDITION

This edition is substantially larger and richer than the previous edition. Revising a successful textbook — the publisher says that *Elements of Argument* is the best-selling book of its kind — presents both a challenge and an opportunity. The challenge is to avoid undoing features that have been well received in the earlier editions. The opportunity is to tap into the experiences of instructors and students who have used the earlier editions and to make use of their insights to improve what needs improvement. In Part One, for example, a simplified warrants chapter responds to instructors' suggestions by focusing on only three types of warrants. Other warrants — and a chart of types — are now discussed in the instructor's edition.

The principles and concerns of the book have not changed. Rather, I have included a greater breadth of material to increase the book's usefulness as a teaching tool. Several important new features have been added: in Part One, a chapter on responding to argument, and a short debate at the end of each chapter; in Part Two, a discussion on finding the middle ground, and a revised and expanded research chapter that now includes instructions for research using the computer; and an appendix on arguing about literature.

Chapter 2 demonstrates how students can respond to arguments as readers who annotate texts critically, writers who analyze rhetoric effectively, and listeners who think carefully about the astonishing proliferation of oral arguments that confront us daily, especially via the electronic media, on talk shows and political programs. Many students have had little education in critical listening, and even a short introduction can produce significant improvement, not only in response to oral argument but in treatment of written argument as well. In this chapter students will also find a useful guide for civil discourse in the networked classroom and on the Internet.

The short debates at the end of each chapter bring into sharp focus six familiar and timely subjects: legalization of drugs, teenage pregnancy, animal rights, capital punishment, smoking, and alien abduction. Debate on all these subjects can, of course, be enlarged with further research.

In addition to explaining the stock issues of debate, Writing an Argumentative Paper in Part Two recognizes the virtues of trying to find a middle ground between opposing viewpoints. The chapter offers examples from writers who suggest compromises in the heated abortion and pornography debates. Chapter 10, Researching an Argumentative Paper, addresses the changes in library facilities, the biggest change being the replacement of the card catalog by a computerized catalog in many schools, and the increasing use by students of computers for academic research.

Part Three, Opposing Viewpoints, retains three popular topics from the fourth edition — Euthanasia, Freedom of Speech, and Sex Education — with selections that reflect the changes in law and public opinion. The five new topics — Affirmative Action, the Digital Revolution, Immigration, Punishment, and Sex and Violence in Popular Culture — are not only among the most controversial and newsworthy subjects engaging American society today, they are also subjects that interest and affect college students at school, at work, and at home. Classic Arguments now includes the celebrated debate between Christopher Marlowe's shepherd and Sir Walter Raleigh's nymph as another example of the universality of argument in its various guises.

Finally, the appendix, Arguing about Literature, is a helpful adjunct to courses in the humanities that require analytical papers. For this section I have summarized the principal elements of fiction, drama, and poetry and added a student essay analyzing a short story.

The number of selections in the fifth edition has grown to 133 — 90 of them new, with a corresponding increase in the number of debatable issues and teaching options. Taken as a whole, the changes in the fifth edition should enhance the versatility of the book, deepen students' awareness of how pervasive argument is, and increase their ability to think critically and communicate persuasively.

This book has profited by the critiques and suggestions of reviewers and instructors who responded to a questionnaire. I appreciate the thoughtful consideration given to previous editions by Nancy E. Adams, Timothy C. Alderman, Yvonne Alexander, John V. Andersen, William Arfin, Alison K. Armstrong, Karen Arnold, Mark Edward Askren, David B. Axelrod, Peter Banland, Carol A. Barnes, Marilyn Barry, Marci Bartolotta, Dr. Bonnie C. Bedford, Frank Beesley, Don Beggs, Martine Bellen, Bruce Bennett, Chester Benson, Robert H. Bentley, Scott Bentley, Patricia Bizzell, Don Black, Kathleen Black, Stanley S. Blair, Laurel Boyd, Mary Virginia Brackett, Robert J. Branda, Dianne Brehmer, Alan Brown, Paul L. Brown, Bill

Buck, W. K. Buckley, Alison A. Bulsterbaum, Clarence Bussinger, Deborah N. Byrd, Gary T. Cage, Ruth A. Cameron, Dr. Rita Carey, Barbara R. Carlson, Eric W. Cash, Donna R. Chaney, Gail Chapman, Linda D. Chinn, Roland Christian, Gina Claywell, Dr. John O. Clemonts, Dr. Thomas S. Costello, David J. Cranmer, Edward Crothers, Sara Cutting, Jo Ann Dadisman, Sandra Dahlberg, Mimi Dane, Judy Davidson, Dr. Cynthia C. Davis, Philip E. Davis, Stephanie Demma, Julia Dietrich, Marcia B. Dinnech, Jane T. Dodge, Ellen Donovan, L. Leon Duke, P. Dunsmore, Bernard Earley, Carolyn L. Engdahl, David Estes, Kristina Faber, Lester Faigley, Faridoun Farroth, B. R. Fein, Delia Fisher, Catherine Fitzgerald, Evelyn Flores, David D. Fong, Donald Forand, Mary A. Fortner, Alice R. France, Leslye Friedberg, Sondra Frisch, Richard Fulkerson, Maureen Furniss, Diane Gabbard, Donald J. Gadow, Eric Gardner, Frieda Gardner, Gail Garloch, Darcey Garretson, Victoria Gaydosik, E. R. Gelber-Beechler, Scott Giantralley, Michael Patrick Gillespie, Paula Gillespie, Wallace Gober, Sara Gogol, Stuart Goodman, Joseph Gredler, Lucie Greenberg, Mildred Buza Gronek, Marilyn Hagans, Linda L. Hagge, Lee T. Hamilton, Carolyn Han, Phillip J. Hanse, Pat Hardré, Susan Harland, A. Leslie Harris, Carolyn G. Hartz, Theresia A. Hartz, Fredrik Hausmann, Michael Havens, William Hayes, Ursula K. Heise, Anne Helms, Peter C. Herman, Diane Price Herndl, Heidi Hobbs, William S. Hochman, Sharon E. Hockensmith, Andrew Hoffman, Joyce Hooker, Richard S. Hootman, Clarence Hundley, Patrick Hunter, Richard Ice, Mary Griffith Jackson, Ann S. Jagoe, Katherine James, Ruth Jeffries, Owen Jenkins, Ruth Y. Jenkins, Iris Jennings, Linda Johnson, Janet Jubnke, E. C. Juckett, Catherine Kaikowska, George T. Karnezis, Richard Katula, Mary Jane Kearny, Joanne Keel, Patricia Kellogg-Dennis, N. Kesinger, Susan Kincaid, Joanne Kirkland, Judith Kirscht, Nancy Klug, John H. Knight, Paul D. Knoke, Frances Kritzer, George W. Kuntzman, Barbara Ladd, M. Beardsley Land, Marlene J. Lang, Lisa Lebduska, Sara R. Lee, William Levine, Mary Levitt, Diana M. Liddle, Jack Longmale, Cynthia Lowenthal, Marjorie Lynn, Marcia MacLennan, Nancy McGee, Patrick McGuire, Ray McKerrow, Michael McKoski, Pamela J. McLagen, Suzanne McLaughlin, Dennis McMillan, Donald McQuade, Christina M. McVay, D'Ann Madewell, Beth Madison, Susan Maloney, Dan M. Manolescu, Barbara A. Manrigue, Joyce Marks, Quentin E. Martin, Michael Matzinger, Charles May, Jean-Pierre Meterean, Ekra Miezan, Carolyn R. Miller, Lisa K. Miller, Logan D. Moon, Dennis D. Moore, Dan Morgan, Karen L. Morris, Curt Mortenson, Philip A. Mottola, Thomas Mullen, Charlotte A. Myers, Michael B. Naas, Joseph Nassar, Byron Nelson, Elizabeth A. Nist, Jody Noerdlinger, Paralee F. Norman, Dr. Mary Jean Northcutt, Thomas O'Brien, James F. O'Neil, Mary O'Riordan, Arlene Okerland, Renee Olander, Amy Olsen, Richard D. Olson, Steven Olson, Lori Jo Oswald, Sushil K. Oswald, Gary Pak, Linda J.

Palumbo, Jo Patterson, Laurine Paule, Leland S. Person, Betty Peters, Nancy L. Peterson, Susan T. Peterson, Steve Phelan, Gail W. Pieper, Gloria Platzner, Mildred Postar, Ralph David Powell, Jr., Teresa Marie Purvis, Barbara E. Rees, Karen L. Regal, Pat Regel, Charles Reinhart, Thomas C. Renzi, Janice M. Reynolds, Douglas F. Rice, G. A. Richardson, Katherine M. Rogers, Marilyn Mathias Root, Judith Klinger Rose, Cathy Rosenfeld, Robert A. Rubin, Norma L. Rudinsky, Lori Ruediger, Cheryl W. Ruggiero, Richard Ruppel, Victoria Anne Sager, Joseph L. Sanders, Suzette Schlapkohl, Sybil Schlesinger, Richard Schneider, Eileen Schwartz, Esther L. Schwartz, Eugene Senff, Jeffrey Seyall, Ron Severson, Lucy Sheehey, William E. Sheidley, Sallye J. Sheppeard, Sally Bishop Shigley, John Shout, Dr. Barbara L. Siek, Thomas Simmons, Michael Simms, Jacqueline Simon, Richard Singletary, Roger L. Slakey, Thomas S. Sloane, Beth Slusser, Denzell Smith, Rebecca Smith, Margaret Smolik, Katherine Sotol, Donald L. Soucy, Minoo Southgate, Linda Spain, Richard Spilman, Sarah J. Stafford, Martha L. Stephens, Arlo Stoltenberg, Elissa L. Stuchlik, Judy Szaho, Andrew Tadie, Fernanda G. Tate-Owens, R. Terhorst, Marguerite B. Thompson, Arline R. Thorn, Mary Ann Trevathan, Sandia Tuttle, Whitney G. Vanderwerff, Jennie VerSteeg, David L. Wagner, Jeanne Walker, Linda D. Warwick, Carol Adams Watson, Roger D. Watson, Karen Webb, Raymond E. Whelan, Betty E. White, Julia Whitsitt, Toby Widdicombe, Mary Louise Willey, Heywood Williams, Matthew C. Wolfe, Alfred Wong, Bonnie B. Zitz, and Laura Zlogar. The instructor's manual is the better for the contribution of Gail Stygall of the University of Washington. Fred Kemp of Texas Tech University drafted the section on responding on-line in Chapter 2, and Debra Canale of the University of Akron revised Chapter 10's discussion of information technologies; my thanks to them both.

I am grateful to freelancers Cynthia Benn and Meg Hyre, and to the people at Bedford Books whose efforts have made the progress of the fifth edition a pleasure as well as a business: Charles Christensen, Joan Feinberg, Elizabeth Schaaf, Kate O'Sullivan, Rebecca Jerman, and Stasia Zomkowski. I especially thank Karen Baart, whose gentle but compelling arguments helped me to reach sound conclusions on many occasions, and, as always, Steve Scipione, who remains the ideal editor for all seasons.

Brief Contents

Contents

PART THREE

Opposing Viewpoints   379

A professor at Yale law school favors an affirmative action pyramid for schools, which narrows as it moves upward. Underprivileged students get a chance, but "sooner or later, talent and preparation, rather than skin color, must tell."

The author, who loathes affirmative action as a remedy for discrimination, proposes instead making discrimination a felony rather than a civil offense.

The head of a public policy institute calls on the government to tap the enormous potential of computers to solve costly problems — from traffic jams to unreliable hospital record-keeping.

Cyberspace, says a former cattle rancher and songwriter for the Grateful Dead, has become a community, as comforting — and, at times, as alienating — as suburbia, USA.

A writer weighs the damage to community and personal choice and decides not to drive the information superhighway.

Four observers of the Internet discuss the effects of the digital revolution on culture, society, and traditional modes of communication.

A professor of communication urges us to consider "what will happen to children — what they will win and what they will lose — if they enter a world in which computer technology is their chief source of motivation, authority, and . . . psychological sustenance."

An editor at *Newsweek* borrows an analogy from Senator Leahy to attack impending Congressional censorship of the Net: "I'm not going to close down a beautiful city park because periodically some idiot comes to the corner and shouts obscenities."

Having survived a life-threatening illness during which he asked to be allowed to die, a philosopher explains why he still believes that his request should have been honored.

The American Medical Association has condemned "mercy killing" but has condoned allowing a terminally ill patient to die. A philosopher of ethics asks whether it is truly kinder to watch someone yield to a slow and painful death than to hasten the patient's inevitable end.

A Harvard University law professor argues that the government should stay far away from mercy killings, which cannot be defined as crimes in any civilized country.

A doctor argues that, just as no member of our society is entitled to take a life by murder or suicide, so the burden of making life-or-death decisions in medical cases should not fall on individuals.

The controversial "Dr. Death" attacks hospitals and pharmaceutical companies who, he says, have a stake in keeping terminally ill patients alive, and justifies his career as the choice of a humanist: It's the right thing to do.

In the attempts of euthanasia proponents to substitute a "quality-of-life" ethic for a "right-to-life" ethic, a nurse perceives a covert attack on cherished American principles.

Putting the rights of the individual first should be the guiding principle of laws to reform the practice of euthanasia.

A physician and medical ethicist asks whether we really want our doctors to become "agents of death." "The dying need our presence and encouragement," not the "alleged humaneness" of assisted suicide.

14. Freedom of Speech   473

A political analyst reviews recent free-speech controversies to develop his point that censoriousness, not censorship, is an effective response to objectionable materials.

16. Punishment   535

PART FOUR

Classic Arguments   631

In this 1946 essay, the author of *Nineteen Eighty-Four* suggests why the hand that pens a stale metaphor should not be trusted with the reins of government.

In 1963, the imprisoned civil rights leader argues that nonviolent victims of unjust laws have the right to break those laws so long as they use nonviolent actions.

This stirring exhortation to marchers at a 1963 civil rights rally rings out like a church bell with rhythm, imagery, joy, hope, and deep conviction. Don't just read the words — listen to the music!

ELEMENTS OF
ARGUMENT

PART ONE

The Structure of Argument

CHAPTER ONE

Understanding Argument

THE NATURE OF ARGUMENT

A conversation overheard in the school cafeteria:

"Hey, how come you didn't order the meat loaf special? It's pretty good today."

"Well, I read this book about vegetarianism, and I've decided to give up meat. The book says meat's unhealthy and vegetarians live longer."

"Don't be silly. Americans eat lots of meat, and we're living longer and longer."

"Listen, this book tells how much healthier the Danes were during World War II because they couldn't get meat."

"I don't believe it. A lot of these health books are written by quacks. It's pretty dumb to change your diet after reading one book."

These people are having what most of us would call an argument, one that sounds dangerously close to a quarrel. There are, however, significant differences between the colloquial meaning of argument as a quarrel and its definition as a process of reasoning and advancing proof, although even the exchange reported above exhibits some of the characteristics of formal argument. The kinds of arguments we deal with in this text are not quarrels. They often resemble ordinary discourse about controversial issues. You may, for example, overhear a conversation like this one:

"This morning while I was trying to eat breakfast I heard an announcer describing the execution of that guy in Texas who raped

and murdered a teenaged couple. They gave him an injection, and it took him ten minutes to die. I almost lost my breakfast listening to it."

"Well, he deserved it. He didn't show much pity for his victims, did he?"

"Okay, but no matter what he did, capital punishment is really awful, barbaric. It's murder, even if the state does it."

"No, I'd call it justice. I don't know what else we can do to show how we feel about a cruel, pointless murder of innocent people. The punishment ought to be as terrible as we can make it."

Each speaker is defending a value judgment about an issue that tests ideas of good and evil, right and wrong, and that cannot be decided by facts.

In another kind of argument the speaker or writer proposes a solution for a specific problem. Two men, both under twenty, are engaged in a conversation.

"I'm going to be broke this week after I pay my car insurance. I don't think it's fair for males under twenty to pay such high rates. I'm a good driver, much better that my older sister. Why not consider driving experience instead of age or sex?"

"But I always thought that guys our age had the most accidents. How do you know that driving experience is the right standard to apply?"

"Well, I read a report by the Highway Commission that said it's really driving experience that counts. So I think it's unfair for us to be discriminated against. The law's behind the times. They ought to change the insurance laws."

In this case someone advocates a policy that appears to fulfill a desirable goal — making it impossible to discriminate against drivers just because they are young and male. Objections arise that the arguer must attempt to answer.

In these three dialogues, as well as in all the other arguments you will read in this book, human beings are engaged in explaining and defending their own actions and beliefs and opposing those of others. They do this for at least two reasons: to justify what they do and think both to themselves and to their opponents and, in the process, to solve problems and make decisions, especially those dependent on a consensus between conflicting views.

Unlike the examples cited so far, the arguments you will read and write will not usually take the form of dialogues, but arguments are implicit dialogues. Even when our audience is unknown, we write to persuade the unconvinced, to acquaint them with good reasons for changing their minds. As one definition has it, "Argumentation is the art of influencing others, through the medium of reasoned discourse, to believe or act as we wish them to believe or act."[1] This process is inherently dramatic; a good argument can create the kinds of tensions generated at sporting events. Who will win? What are the factors that enable a winner to emerge? One of the most popular and enduring situations on television is the courtroom debate, in which two lawyers (one, the defense attorney, the hero, unusually knowledgeable and persuasive; the other, the prosecuting attorney, bumbling and corrupt) confront each other before an audience of judge and jury that must render a heart-stopping verdict. Tensions are high because a life is in the balance. In the classroom the stakes are neither so intimidating nor so melodramatic, but even here a well-conducted argument can throw off sparks.

Of course, not all arguments end in clear victories for one side or another. Nor should they. The French philosopher Joseph Joubert said, "It is better to debate a question without settling it than to settle a question without debating it." In a democratic society of competing interests and values, a compromise between two or more extreme points of view may be the only viable solution to a vexing problem. Although formal debates under the auspices of a debating society, such as take place on many college campuses, usually end in winners and losers, real-life problems, both public and private, are often resolved through negotiation. Courtroom battles may result in compromise, and the law itself allows for exemptions and extenuating circumstances. Elsewhere in this book we speak of the importance of "trade-offs" in social and political transactions, giving up one thing in return for another.

Keep in mind, however, that some compromises will not be morally defensible. In searching for a middle ground, the thoughtful arguer must determine that the consequences of a negotiated solution will contribute to "the common good," not, in the words of one essayist, merely the good of "the sovereign self." (In Chapter 9 you will find a detailed guide for writing arguments in which you look for common ground.)

Most of the arguments in this book will deal with matters of public controversy, an area traditionally associated with the study of argument. As the word *public* suggests, these matters concern us as members of a community. "They are," according to one rhetorician, "the problems of war and peace, race and creed, poverty, wealth, and population, of democracy and communism. . . . Specific issues arise on which we must take decision from time to time. One day it is Suez, another Cuba. One week it is the Congo, another it is the plight of the American farmer or the railroads. . . . On these subjects

---

[1]J. M. O'Neill, C. Laycock, and R. L. Scale, *Argumentation and Debate* (New York: Macmillan, 1925), p. 1.

the experts as well as the many take sides."[2] Today the issues are different from the issues that writers confronted more than twenty years ago. Today we are concerned about unemployment, illegal immigration, bilingual education, gun control, gay rights, drug abuse, prayer in school, to name only a few,

Clearly, if all of us agreed about everything, if harmony prevailed everywhere, the need for argument would disappear. But given what we know about the restless, seeking, contentious nature of human beings and their conflicting interests, we should not be surprised that many controversial questions, some of them as old as human civilization itself, will not be settled nor will they vanish despite the energy we devote to settling them. Unresolved, they are submerged for a while and then reappear, sometimes in another form, sometimes virtually unchanged. Capital punishment is one such stubborn problem; abortion is another. Nevertheless, we value the argumentative process because it is indispensable to the preservation of a free society. In *Areopagitica,* his great defense of free speech, John Milton, the seventeenth-century poet, wrote, "I cannot praise a fugitive and cloistered virtue, unexercised and unbreathed, that never sallies out and sees her adversary." How can we know the truth, he asked, unless there is a "free and open encounter" between all ideas? "Give me liberty to know, to utter, and to argue freely according to conscience, above all liberties."

WHY STUDY ARGUMENT?

Perhaps the question has already occurred to you: Why *study* argument? Since you've engaged in some form of the argumentative process all your life, is there anything to be learned that experience hasn't taught you? We think there is. If you've ever felt frustration in trying to decide what is wrong with an argument, either your own or someone else's, you might have wondered if there were rules to help in the analysis. If you've ever been dissatisfied with your attempt to prove a case, you might have wondered how good arguers, the ones who succeed in persuading people, construct their cases. Good arguers do, in fact, know and follow rules. Studying and practicing these rules can provide you with some of the same skills.

You will find yourself using these skills in a variety of situations, not only in arguing important public issues. You will use them, for example, in your academic career. Whatever your major field of study — the humanities, the social sciences, the physical sciences,

---

[2]Karl R. Wallace, "Toward a Rationale for Teachers of Writing and Speaking," *English Journal,* September 1961, p. 386.

business — you will be required to defend views about materials you have read and studied.

Humanities. Why have some of the greatest novels resisted translation into great films?

Social Science. What is the evidence that upward social mobility continues to be a positive force in American life?

Physical Science. What will happen to the world climate as the amount of carbon dioxide in the atmosphere increases?

Business. Are the new tax laws beneficial or disadvantageous to the real estate investor?

For all these assignments, different as they may be, you would use the same kinds of analysis, research techniques, and evaluation. The conventions or rules for reporting results might differ from one field of study to another, but for the most part the rules for defining terms, evaluating evidence, and arriving at conclusions cross disciplinary lines. Many employers, not surprisingly, are aware of this. One sheriff in Arizona advertised for an assistant with a degree in philosophy. He had discovered, he said, that the methods used by philosophers to solve problems were remarkably similar to the methods used in law enforcement.

Whether or not you are interested in serving as sheriff's assistant, you will encounter situations in the workplace that call for the same analytical and argumentative skills employed by philosophers and law enforcement personnel. Almost everywhere — in the smallest businesses as well as the largest corporations — a worker who can articulate his or her views clearly and forcefully has an important advantage in gaining access to positions of greater interest and challenge. Even when they are primarily informative, the memorandums, reports, instructions, questions, and explanations that issue from offices and factories obey the rules of argumentative discourse.

You may not anticipate doing the kind of writing or speaking at your job that you will practice in your academic work. It is probably true that in some careers, writing constitutes a negligible part of a person's duties. But outside the office, the studio, and the salesroom, you will be called on to exhibit argumentative skills as a citizen, as a member of a community, and as a consumer of leisure. In these capacities you can contribute to decision making if you are knowledgeable and prepared. By writing or speaking to the appropriate authorities, you can argue for a change in the meal ticket plan at your school or the release of pornographic films at the neighborhood theater or against a change in automobile insurance rates. Most of us are painfully aware of opportunities we lost because we were uncertain of how to proceed, even in matters that affected us deeply.

A course in argumentation offers another invaluable dividend: It can help you to cope with the bewildering confusion of voices in the world around you. It can give you tools for distinguishing between what is true and what is false, what is valid and what is invalid, in the claims of politicians, promoters of causes, newscasters, advertisers, salespeople, teachers, parents and siblings, employers and employees, neighbors, friends, and lovers, any of whom may be engaged at some time in attempting to persuade you to accept a belief or adopt a course of action. It can even offer strategies for arguing with yourself about a personal dilemma.

So far we have treated argument as an essentially pragmatic activity that benefits the individual. But choosing argument over force or evasion has clear moral benefits for society as well. We can, in fact, defend the study of argumentation for the same reasons that we defend universal education despite its high cost and sometimes controversial results. In a democracy, widespread literacy ultimately benefits all members of society, not only those who are the immediate beneficiaries of education, because only an informed citizenry can make responsible choices. One distinguished writer explains that "democracy depends on a citizenry that can reason for themselves, on men who know whether a case has been proved, or at least made probable."[3]

It is not too much to say that argument is a civilizing influence, the very basis of democratic order. In repressive regimes, coercion, which may express itself in a number of reprehensible forms — censorship, imprisonment, exile, torture, or execution — is a favored means of removing opposition to establishment "truth." In free societies, argument and debate remain the preeminent means of arriving at consensus.

Of course, rational discourse in a democracy can and does break down. Confrontations with police at abortion clinics, shouting and heckling at a meeting to prevent a speaker from being heard, student protests against university policies — such actions have become common in recent years. The demands of the demonstrators are often passionately and sincerely held, and the protesters sometimes succeed through force or intimidation in influencing policy changes. When this happens, however, we cannot be sure that the changes are justified. History and experience teach us that reason, to a far greater degree than other methods of persuasion, ultimately determines the rightness or wrongness of our actions.

A piece of folk wisdom sums up the superiority of reasoned argument as a vehicle of persuasion: "A man convinced against his will

---

[3]Wayne C. Booth, "Boring from Within: The Art of the Freshman Essay," adapted from a speech delivered to the Illinois Council of College Teachers of English in May 1963.

is of the same opinion still." Those who accept a position after engaging in a dialogue offering good reasons on both sides will think and act with greater willingness and conviction than those who have been coerced or denied the privilege of participating in the decision.

WHY WRITE?

If we agree that studying argumentation provides important critical tools, one last question remains: Why *write*? Isn't it possible to learn the rules by reading and talking about the qualities of good and bad arguments? Not quite. All writers, both experienced and inexperienced, will probably confess that looking at what they have written, even after long thought, can produce a startled disclaimer: But that isn't what I meant to say! They know that more analysis and more hard thinking are in order. Writers are also aware that words on paper have an authority and a permanency that invite more than casual deliberation. It is one thing to make an assertion, to express an idea or a strong feeling in conversation, and perhaps even to deny it later; it is quite another to write out an extended defense of your own position or an attack on someone else's that will be read and perhaps criticized by people unsympathetic to your views.

Students are often told that they must become better thinkers if they are to become better writers. It works the other way, too. In the effort to produce a clear and convincing argument, a writer matures as a thinker and a critic. The very process of writing calls for skills that make us better thinkers. Writing argumentative essays tests and enlarges important mental skills — developing and organizing ideas, evaluating evidence, observing logical consistency, expressing ourselves clearly and economically — that we need to exercise all our lives in our various social roles, whether or not we continue to write after college.

THE TERMS OF ARGUMENT

One definition of argument, emphasizing audience, has been given earlier: "Argumentation is the art of influencing others, through the medium of reasoned discourse, to believe or act as we wish them to believe or act." A distinction is sometimes made between argument and persuasion. Argument, according to most authorities, gives primary importance to logical appeals. Persuasion introduces the element of ethical and emotional appeals. The difference is one of emphasis. In real-life arguments about social policy, the distinction is hard to measure. In this book we use the term *argument* to represent forms of discourse that attempt to persuade readers or listeners to accept a claim, whether acceptance is based on logical or on emotional appeals or, as is usually the case, on both. The following brief definition includes other elements: *An argument is a statement or statements offering support for a claim.*

An argument is composed of at least three parts: the claim, the support, and the warrant.[4]

The Claim

The claim (also called a *proposition*) answers the question "What are you trying to prove?" It may appear as the thesis statement of your essay, although in some arguments it may not be stated directly. There are three principal kinds of claim (discussed more fully in Chapter 3): claims of fact, of value, and of policy. (The three dialogues at the beginning of this chapter represent these three kinds of claim respectively.) *Claims of fact* assert that a condition has existed, exists, or will exist and are based on facts or data that the audience will accept as being objectively verifiable:

> The present cocaine epidemic is not unique. From 1885 to the 1920s, cocaine was as widely used as it is today.

> Horse racing is the most dangerous sport.

> California will experience colder, stormier weather for the next ten years.

All these claims must be supported by data. Although the last example is an inference or an educated guess about the future, a reader will probably find the prediction credible if the data seem authoritative.

Claims of value attempt to prove that some things are more or less desirable than others. They express approval or disapproval of standards of taste and morality. Advertisements and reviews of cultural events are one common source of value claims, but such claims emerge whenever people argue about what is good or bad, beautiful or ugly.

> The opera *Tannhäuser* provides a splendid viewing as well as listening experience.

> Football is one of the most dehumanizing experiences a person can face. — Dave Meggyesy

> Ending a patient's life intentionally is absolutely forbidden on moral grounds. — Presidential Commission on Medical Ethics, 1983

---

[4]Some of the terms and analyses used in this text are adapted from Stephen Toulmin's *The Uses of Argument* (Cambridge: Cambridge University Press, 1958).

Claims of policy assert that specific policies should be instituted as solutions to problems. The expression *should, must,* or *ought to* usually appears in the statement.

> Prisons should be abolished because they are crime-manufacturing concerns.

> Our first step must be to immediately establish and advertise drastic policies designed to bring our own population under control. — Paul Ehrlich, biologist

> The New York City Board of Education should make sure that qualified women appear on any new list [of candidates for Chancellor of Education].

Policy claims call for analysis of both fact and value. (A full discussion of claims follows in Chapter 3.)

The Support

Support consists of the materials used by the arguer to convince an audience that his or her claim is sound. These materials include *evidence* and *motivational appeals.* The evidence or data consist of facts, statistics, and testimony from experts. The motivational appeals are the ones that the arguer makes to the values and attitudes of the audience to win support for the claim. The word *motivational* points out that these appeals are the reasons that move an audience to accept a belief or adopt a course of action. For example, in his argument advocating population control, Ehrlich first offered statistical evidence to prove the magnitude of the population explosion. But he also made a strong appeal to the generosity of his audience to persuade them to sacrifice their own immediate interests to those of future generations. (See Chapter 5 for detailed discussion of support.)

The Warrant

The warrant is an inference or an assumption, a belief or principle that is taken for granted. A warrant is a guarantee of reliability; in argument it guarantees the soundness of the relationship between the support and the claim. It allows the reader to make the connection between the support and the claim.

Warrants or assumptions underlie all the claims we make. They may be stated or unstated. If the arguer believes that the audience shares his assumption, he may feel it unnecessary to express it. But if he thinks that the audience is doubtful or hostile, he may decide to state the assumption in order to emphasize its importance or argue for its validity.

This is how the warrant works. In the dialogue beginning this chapter, one speaker made the claim that vegetarianism was more healthful than a diet containing meat. As support he offered the evidence that the authors of a book he had read recommended vegetarianism for greater health and longer life. He did not state his warrant — that the authors of the book were trustworthy guides to theories of healthful diet. In outline form the argument looks like this:

CLAIM: Adoption of a vegetarian diet leads to healthier and longer life.

SUPPORT: The authors of *Becoming a Vegetarian Family* say so.

WARRANT: The authors of *Becoming a Vegetarian Family* are reliable sources of information on diet.

A writer or speaker may also need to offer support for the warrant. In the case cited above, the second speaker is reluctant to accept the unstated warrant, suggesting that the authors may be quacks. The first speaker will need to provide support for the assumption that the authors are trustworthy, perhaps by introducing proof of their credentials in science and medicine. Notice that although the second speaker accepts the evidence, he cannot agree that the claim has been proved unless he also accepts the warrant. If he fails to accept the warrant — that is, if he refuses to believe that the authors are credible sources of information about diet — then the evidence cannot support the claim.

The following example demonstrates how a different kind of warrant, based on values, can also lead an audience to accept a claim.

CLAIM: Laws making marijuana illegal should be repealed.

SUPPORT: People should have the right to use any substance they wish.

WARRANT: No laws should prevent citizens from exercising their rights.

Support for repeal of the marijuana laws often consists of medical evidence that marijuana is harmless. Here, however, the arguer contends that an important ethical principle is at work: Nothing should prevent people from exercising their rights, including the right to use any substance, no matter how harmful. Let us suppose that the reader agrees with the supporting statement, that individuals should have the right to use any substance. But in order to accept the claim, the reader must also agree with the principle expressed in the warrant, that government should not interfere with the individual's right. He or she can then agree that laws making marijuana illegal should be repealed. Notice that this warrant, like all warrants, certifies that the relationship between the support and the claim is sound. (For more on warrants, see Chapter 6.)

Definition, Language, Logic

In addition to the claim, the support, and the warrant, several other elements of clear, persuasive prose are crucial to good argument. For this reason we have devoted separate chapters to each of them.

One of the most important is definition. In fact, many of the controversial questions you will read or write about are primarily arguments of definition. Such terms as *abortion, pornography, racism, poverty, addiction,* and *mental illness* must be defined before useful solutions to the problems they represent can be formulated. (Chapter 4 deals with definition.)

Another important resource is the careful use of language, not only to define terms and express personal style but also to reflect clarity of thought and avoid the clichés and outworn slogans that frequently substitute for fresh ideas. (See Chapter 7 for more on language.)

Last, we have included an examination of induction and deduction, the classic elements of logic. Understanding the way in which these reasoning processes work can help you to determine the truth and validity of your own and other arguments and to identify faulty reasoning. (Induction and deduction are covered in Chapter 8.)

THE AUDIENCE

All arguments are composed with an audience in mind. We have already pointed out that an argument is an implicit dialogue or exchange. Often the writer of an argument about a public issue is responding to another writer or speaker who has made a claim that needs to be supported or opposed. In writing your own arguments, you should assume that there is a reader who may not agree with you. Throughout this book, we will continue to refer to ways of reaching such a reader.

Speechmakers are usually better informed than writers about their audience. Some writers, however, are familiar with the specific persons or groups who will read their arguments; advertising copywriters are a conspicuous example. They discover their audiences through sophisticated polling and marketing techniques and direct their messages to a well-targeted group of prospective buyers. Other professionals may be required to submit reports to persuade a specific and clearly defined audience of certain beliefs or courses of action: An engineer may be asked by an environmental interest group to defend his plans for the building of a sewage treatment plant; or a town planner may be called on to tell the town council why she believes that rent control may not work; or a sales manager may find it necessary to explain to his superior why a new product should be launched in the Midwest rather than the South.

In such cases the writer asks some or all of the following questions about the audience:

> Why has this audience requested this report? What do they want to get out of it?
>
> How much do they already know about the subject?
>
> Are they divided or agreed on the subject?
>
> What is their emotional involvement with the issues?

Assessing Credibility

Providing abundant evidence and making logical connections between the parts of an argument may not be enough to win agreement from an audience. In fact, success in convincing an audience is almost always inseparable from the writer's credibility, or the audience's belief in the writer's trustworthiness. Aristotle, the Greek philosopher who wrote a treatise on argument that has influenced its study and practice for more than two thousand years, considered credibility — what he called *ethos* — the most important element in the arguer's ability to persuade the audience to accept his or her claim.

Aristotle named "intelligence, character, and goodwill" as the attributes that produce credibility. Today we might describe these qualities somewhat differently, but the criteria for judging a writer's credibility remain essentially the same. First, the writer must convince the audience that he is knowledgeable, that he is as well informed as possible about the subject. Second, he must persuade his audience that he is not only truthful in the presentation of his evidence but also morally upright and dependable. Third, he must show that, as an arguer with good intentions, he has considered the interests and needs of others as well as his own.

As an example in which the credibility of the arguer is at stake, consider a wealthy Sierra Club member who lives on ten acres of a magnificent oceanside estate and who appears before a community planning board to argue against future development of the area. His claim is that more building will destroy the delicate ecological balance of the area. The board, acting in the interests of all the citizens of the community, will ask themselves: Has the arguer proved that his information about environmental impact is complete and accurate? Has he demonstrated that he sincerely desires to preserve the wilderness, not merely his own privacy and space? And has he also made clear that he has considered the needs and desires of those

·who might want to live in a housing development by the ocean? If the answers to all these questions are yes, then the board will hear the arguer with respect, and the arguer will have begun to establish his credibility.

A reputation for intelligence, character, and goodwill is not often won overnight. And it can be lost more quickly than it is won. Once a writer or speaker has betrayed an audience's belief in her character or judgment, she may find it difficult to persuade an audience to accept subsequent claims, no matter how sound her data and reasoning are. "We give no credit to a liar," said Cicero, "even when he speaks the truth."

Political life is full of examples of lost and squandered credibility. After it was discovered that President Lyndon Johnson had deceived the American public about U.S. conduct in the Vietnam War, he could not regain his popularity. After President Gerald Ford pardoned former President Richard Nixon for his complicity in the Watergate scandal, Ford was no longer a serious candidate for reelection. After asserting in a presidential debate that he would not raise taxes, President George Bush lost the favor of many voters — and possibly reelection — when he did.

We can see the practical consequences when an audience realizes that an arguer has been guilty of a deception — misusing facts and authority, suppressing evidence, distorting statistics, violating the rules of logic. But suppose the arguer is successful in concealing his or her manipulation of the data and can persuade an uninformed audience to take the action or adopt the idea that he or she recommends. Even supposing that the argument promotes a "good" cause, is the arguer justified in using evasive or misleading tactics?

The answer is no. To encourage another person to make a decision on the basis of incomplete or dishonestly used data is profoundly unethical. It indicates lack of respect for the rights of others — their right to know at least as much as you do about the subject, to be allowed to judge and compare, to disagree with you if they challenge your own interests. If the moral implications are still not clear, try to imagine yourself not as the perpetrator of the lie but as the victim.

There is also a danger in measuring success wholly by the degree to which audiences accept our arguments. Both as writers and readers, we must be able to respect the claim, or proposition, and what it tries to demonstrate. Toulmin has said: "To conclude that a proposition is true, it is not enough to know that this [person] or that finds it 'credible': the proposition itself must be *worthy* of credence."[5]

---

[5]*An Examination of the Place of Reason in Ethics* (Cambridge: Cambridge University Press, 1964), p. 71.

Acquiring Credibility

You may wonder how you can acquire credibility. You are not yet an expert in many of the subjects you will deal with in assignments, although you are knowledgeable about many other things, including your cultural and social activities. But there are several ways in which you can create confidence by your treatment of topics derived from academic disciplines, such as political science, psychology, economics, sociology, and art, on which most assignments will be based.

First, you can submit evidence of careful research, demonstrating that you have been conscientious in finding the best authorities, giving credit, and attempting to arrive at the truth. Second, you can adopt a thoughtful and judicious tone that reflects a desire to be fair in your conclusion. Tone expresses the attitude of the writer toward his or her subject. When the writer feels strongly about the subject and adopts a belligerent or complaining tone, for example, he or she forgets that readers who feel differently may find the tone disagreeable and unconvincing. In the following excerpt a student expresses his feelings about standard grading, that is, grading by letter or number on a scale that applies to a whole group.

> You go to school to learn, not to earn grades. To be educated, that's what they tell you. "He's educated, he graduated Magna Cum Laude." What makes a Magna Cum Laude man so much better than a man that graduates with a C? They are both still educated, aren't they? No one has a right to call someone less educated because they got a C instead of an A. Let's take both men and put them in front of a car. Each car has something wrong with it. Each man must fix his broken car. Our C man goes right to work while our Magna Cum Laude man hasn't got the slightest idea where to begin. Who's more educated now?

Probably a reader who disagreed with the claim — that standard grading should not be used — would find the tone, if not the evidence itself, unpersuasive. The writer sounds as if he is defending his own ability to do something that an honors graduate can't do, while ignoring the acknowledged purposes of standard grading in academic subjects. He sounds, moreover, as if he's angry because someone has done him an injury. Compare the preceding passage to the following one, written by a student on the same subject.

> Grades are the play money in a university Monopoly game. As long as the tokens are offered, the temptation will be largely irresistible to play for them. Students are so busy taking notes, doing tests, and getting tokens that they have forgotten to ask: Of what worth is all this? Or perhaps they ask and the grade is their answer.
>
> One certainly learns something in the passive lecture-note-read-note-test process: how to do it all more efficiently next time (in the

hope of eventually owning Boardwalk and Park Place). As Marshall McLuhan has said, we learn what we do. In this process most students come to view learning as studying and remembering what other people have learned. They assume that knowledge is logically and for practical reasons divided up into discrete pieces called "disciplines" and that the highest knowledge is achieved by specializing in a discipline. By getting good grades in a lot of disciplines they conclude they have learned a lot. They have indeed, and it is too bad.[6]

Most readers would consider this writer more credible, in part because he has adopted a tone that seems moderate and impersonal. That is, he does not convey the impression that he is interested only in defending his own grades. Notice also that the language of this passage suggests a higher level of learning and research.

Sometimes, of course, an expression of anger or even outrage is appropriate and morally justified. But if readers do not share your sense of outrage, you must try to reach them through a more moderate approach. In his autobiography, Benjamin Franklin recounted his attempts to acquire the habit of temperate language in argument:

> Retaining . . . the habit of expressing myself in terms of modest diffidence, never using when I advance anything that may possibly be disputed, the words *certainly, undoubtedly,* or any others that give the air of positiveness to an opinion; but rather say, *I conceive,* or *I apprehend* a thing to be so or so; *it appears to me,* or *I should think it so or so for such and such reasons,* or *I imagine* it to be so, or *it is so* if *I am not mistaken.* — This habit I believe has been of great advantage to me, when I have had occasion to inculcate my opinions and persuade men into measures that I have been from time to time engaged in promoting.[7]

This is not to say that the writer must hedge his or her opinions or confess uncertainty at every point. Franklin suggests that the writer must recognize that other opinions may also have validity and that, although the writer may disagree, he or she respects the other opinions. Such an attitude will also dispose the reader to be more generous in evaluating the writer's argument.

A final method of establishing credibility is to produce a clean, literate, well-organized paper, with evidence of care in writing and proofreading. Such a paper will help persuade the reader to take your efforts seriously.

Now let us turn to one of the most famous arguments in American history and examine its elements.

---

[6]Roy E. Terry in "Does Standard Grading Encourage Excessive Competitiveness?" *Change,* September 1974, p. 45.

[7]*The Autobiography of Benjamin Franklin,* ed. Louis P. Masur (Boston: Bedford Books, 1993), pp. 39–40. Italics are Franklin's.

The Declaration of Independence

THOMAS JEFFERSON

When in the course of human events, it becomes necessary for one people to dissolve the political bands which have connected them with another, and to assume among the Powers of the earth, the separate and equal station to which the Laws of Nature and Nature's God entitle them, a decent respect to the opinions of mankind requires that they should declare the causes which impel them to the separation.

We hold these truths to be self-evident, that all men are created equal, that they are endowed by their Creator with certain unalienable Rights, that among these are Life, Liberty and the pursuit of Happiness.

That to secure these rights, Governments are instituted among Men, deriving their just powers from the consent of the governed.

That whenever any Form of Government becomes destructive of these ends, it is the Right of the People to alter or to abolish it, and to institute a new Government laying its foundation on such principles and organizing its powers in such form, as to them shall seem most likely to effect their Safety and Happiness. Prudence, indeed, will dictate that Governments long established should not be changed for light and transient causes; and accordingly all experience hath shown that mankind are more disposed to suffer, while evils are sufferable, than to right themselves by abolishing the forms to which they are accustomed. But when a long train of abuses and usurpations pursuing invariably the same Object evinces a design to reduce them under absolute Despotism, it is their right, it is their duty, to throw off such government, and to provide new Guards for their future security.

Such has been the patient sufferance of these Colonies; and such 5 is now the necessity which constrains them to alter their former Systems of Government. The history of the present King of Great Britain is a history of repeated injuries and usurpations, all having in direct object the establishment of an absolute Tyranny over these States. To prove this, let Facts be submitted to a candid world.

He has refused his Assent to Laws, the most wholesome and necessary for the public good.

He has forbidden his Governors to pass Laws of immediate and pressing importance, unless suspended in their operation till his Assent should be obtained; and when so suspended, he has utterly neglected to attend to them.

He has refused to pass other Laws for the accommodation of large districts of people, unless those people would relinquish the right of Representation in the Legislature, a right inestimable to them and formidable to tyrants only.

He has called together legislative bodies at places unusual, un-comfortable, and distant from the depository of their Public Records, for the sole purpose of fatiguing them into compliance with his measures.

He has dissolved Representative Houses repeatedly, for oppos-   10
ing with manly firmness his invasions on the rights of the people.

He has refused for a long time, after such dissolutions, to cause others to be elected; whereby the Legislative Powers, incapable of Annihilation, have returned to the People at large for their exercise; the State remaining in the mean time exposed to all the danger of invasion from without, and convulsions within.

He has endeavored to prevent the population of these States; for that purpose obstructing the Laws of Naturalization of Foreigners; refusing to pass others to encourage their migration hither, and raising the conditions of new Appropriations of Lands.

He has obstructed the Administration of Justice, by refusing his Assent to Laws for establishing Judiciary Powers.

He has made Judges dependent on his Will alone, for the tenure of their offices, and the amount and payment of their salaries.

He has erected a multitude of New Offices, and sent hither   15
swarms of Officers to harass our People, and eat out their substance.

He has kept among us, in time of peace, Standing Armies without the consent of our Legislature.

He has affected to render the Military independent of and superior to the Civil Power.

He has combined with others to subject us to jurisdictions foreign to our constitution, and unacknowledged by our laws; giving his Assent to their acts of pretended Legislation:

For quartering large bodies of armed troops among us:

For protecting them, by a mock Trial, from Punishment for any   20
Murders which they should commit on the Inhabitants of these States:

For cutting off our Trade with all parts of the world:

For imposing Taxes on us without our Consent:

For depriving us in many cases, of the benefits of Trial by Jury:

For transporting us beyond Seas to be tried for pretended offenses:

For abolishing the free System of English Laws in a Neighbouring   25
Province, establishing therein an Arbitrary government, and enlarging its boundaries so as to render it at once an example and fit instrument for introducing the same absolute rule into these Colonies:

For taking away our Charters, abolishing our most valuable Laws, and altering fundamentally the Forms of our Governments:

For suspending our own legislatures, and declaring themselves invested with Power to legislate for us in all cases whatsoever.

He has abdicated Government here, by declaring us out of his Protection and waging War against us.

He has plundered our seas, ravaged our Coasts, burnt our towns and destroyed the Lives of our people.

He is at this time transporting large Armies of foreign Mercenar- 30 ies to compleat the works of death, desolation and tyranny, already begun with circumstances of Cruelty & perfidy scarcely paralleled in the most barbarous ages, and totally unworthy the Head of a civilized nation.

He has constrained our fellow Citizens taken Captive on the high Seas to bear Arms against their Country, to become the executioners of their friends and Brethren, or to fall themselves by their Hands.

He has excited domestic insurrections amongst us, and has endeavored to bring on the inhabitants of our frontiers, the merciless Indian Savages, whose known rule of warfare is an undistinguished destruction of all ages, sexes, and conditions.

In every stage of these Oppressions We Have Petitioned for Redress in the most humble terms. Our repeated petitions have been answered only by repeated injury. A Prince, whose character is thus marked by every act which may define a Tyrant, is unfit to be the ruler of a free People.

Not have We been wanting in attention to our British brethren. We have warned them from time to time of attempts by their legislature to extend an unwarrantable jurisdiction over us. We have reminded them of the circumstances of our emigration and settlement here. We have appealed to their native justice and magnanimity and we have conjured them by the ties of our common kindred to disavow these usurpations, which would inevitably interrupt our connections and correspondence. They too have been deaf to the voice of justice and of consanguinity. We must, therefore, acquiesce in the necessity, which denounces our Separation, and hold them, as we hold the rest of mankind, Enemies in War, in Peace Friends.

We, therefore, the Representatives of the United States of Amer- 35 ica, in General Congress, Assembled, appealing to the Supreme Judge of the world for the rectitude of our intentions, do, in the Name, and by Authority of the good People of these Colonies, solemnly publish and declare, That these United Colonies are, and of Right ought to be, Free and Independent States; that they are Absolved from all Allegiance to the British Crown, and that all political connection between them and the State of Great Britain, is and ought to be totally dissolved; and that as Free and Independent States, they have full power to levy War, conclude Peace, contract

Alliances, establish Commerce, and to do all other Acts and Things which Independent States may of right do. And for the support of this Declaration, with a firm reliance on the protection of Divine Providence, we mutually pledge to each other our lives, our Fortunes and our sacred Honor.

Analysis

Claim: What is Jefferson trying to prove? *The American colonies are justified in declaring their independence from British rule.* Jefferson and his fellow signers might have issued a simple statement such as appears in the last paragraph, announcing the freedom and independence of these United Colonies. Instead, however, they chose to justify their right to do so.

Support: What does Jefferson have to go on? The Declaration of Independence bases its claim on two kinds of support: *factual evidence* and *motivational appeals* or appeals to the values of the audience.

Factual Evidence: Jefferson presents a long list of specific acts of tyranny by George III, beginning with "He has refused his Assent to Laws, the most wholesome and necessary for the public good." This list constitutes more than half the text. Notice how Jefferson introduces these grievances: "The history of the present King of Great Britain is a history of repeated injuries and usurpations, all having in direct object the establishment of an absolute Tyranny over these States. *To prove this, let Facts be submitted to a candid world"* (italics for emphasis added). Jefferson hopes that a recital of these specific acts will convince an honest audience that the United Colonies have indeed been the victims of an intolerable tyranny.

Appeal to Values: Jefferson also invokes the moral values underlying the formation of a democratic state. These values are referred to throughout. In the second and third paragraphs he speaks of equality, "Life, Liberty and the pursuit of Happiness," "just powers," "consent of the governed," and in the fourth paragraph, safety. In the last paragraph he refers to freedom and independence. Jefferson believes that the people who read his appeal will, or should, share these fundamental values. Audience acceptance of these values constitutes the most important part of the support. Some historians have called the specific acts of oppression cited by Jefferson trivial, inconsequential, or distorted. Clearly, however, Jefferson felt that the list of specific grievances was vital to definition of the abstract terms in which values are always expressed.

Warrant: How does Jefferson get from support to claim? *People have a right to revolution in order to free themselves from oppression.* This warrant is explicit: "But when a long train of abuses and usurpations pursuing invariably the same Object evinces a design to reduce them under absolute Despotism, it is their right, it is their duty, to throw off such government, and to provide new Guards for their future security." Some members of Jefferson's audience, especially those whom he accuses of oppressive acts, will reject the principle that any subject people have earned the right to revolt. But Jefferson believes that the decent opinion of mankind will accept this assumption. Many of his readers will also be aware that the warrant is supported by seventeenth-century political philosophy, which defines government as a social compact between the government and the governed.

If Jefferson's readers do, in fact, accept the warrant and if they also believe in the accuracy of the factual evidence and share his moral values, then they will conclude that his claim has been proved, that Jefferson has justified the right of the colonies to separate themselves from Great Britain.

Audience: The Declaration of Independence is addressed to several audiences: to the American colonists; to the British people; to the British Parliament; to the British king, George III; and to mankind or a universal audience.

Not all the American colonists were convinced by Jefferson's argument. Large numbers remained loyal to the king and for various reasons opposed an independent nation. In the next-to-the-last paragraph, Jefferson refers to previous addresses to the British people. Not surprisingly, most of the British citizenry as well as the king also rejected the claims of the Declaration. But the universal audience, the decent opinion of mankind, found Jefferson's argument overwhelmingly persuasive. Many of the liberal reform movements of the eighteenth and nineteenth centuries were inspired by the Declaration. In basing his claim on universal principles of justice and equality, Jefferson was certainly aware that he was addressing future generations.

Definition: Several significant terms are not defined. Modern readers will ask for further definition of "all men are created equal," "Life, Liberty and the pursuit of Happiness," "Laws of Nature and Nature's God," among others. We must assume that the failure to explain these terms more strictly was deliberate, in part because Jefferson thought that his readers would understand the references — for example, to the eighteenth-century belief in freedom as the birthright of all human beings — and in part because he wished the terms to be understood as universal principles of justice, applicable in all struggles, not merely those of the colonies against the king of England. But a failure to narrow the terms of argument can have unpredictable consequences. In later years the Declaration of Independence would be used to justify other rebellions, including the secession of the South from the Union in 1861.

Language: Although some stylistic conventions of eighteenth-century writing would not be observed today, Jefferson's clear, elegant, formal prose — "a surprising mixture of simplicity and majesty," in the words of one writer — remains a masterpiece of English prose and persuades us that we are reading an important document. Several devices are worth noting:

1. *Parallelism* or balance of sentence construction gives both emphasis and rhythm to the statements in the introduction (first four paragraphs) and the list of grievances.
2. *Diction* (choice of words) supports and underlines the meaning: nouns that have positive connotations — *safety, happiness, prudence, right, duty, Supreme Judge, justice;* verbs and verbals that suggest negative actions (taken by the king) — *refused, forbidden, dissolved, obstructed, plundered, depriving, abolishing.*
3. The *tone* suggests reason and patience on the part of the author or authors (especially paragraphs 5, 33, 34).

Logic: As a logical pattern of argument, the Declaration of Independence is largely *deductive.* Deduction usually consists of certain broad general statements which we know or believe to be true and which to lead us to other statements that follow from the ones already laid down. The Declaration begins with such general statements, summarizing a philosophy of government based on the equality of men, the inalienable rights derived from the Creator, and the powers of the governed. These statements are held to be "self-evident," that is, not needing proof, and if we accept them, then it follows that a revolution is necessary to remove the oppressors and secure the safety and happiness to which the governed are entitled. The particular grievances against the king are proof that the king has oppressed the colonies, but they are not the basis for revolution.

The fact that Jefferson emphasized the universal principles underlying the right of revolution meant that the Declaration of Independence could appeal to all people everywhere, whether or not they had suffered the particular grievances in Jefferson's list.

EXERCISES

1. From the following list of claims, select the ones you consider most controversial. Tell why they are difficult to resolve. Are the underlying assumptions controversial? Is support hard to find or disputed? Can

you think of circumstances under which some of these claims might be resolved?

a. Congress should endorse the right-to-life amendment.

b. Solar power can supply 20 percent of the energy needs now satisfied by fossil and nuclear power.

c. Homosexuals should have the same job rights as heterosexuals.

d. Rapists should be treated as mentally ill rather than depraved.

e. Whale hunting should be banned by international law.

f. Violence on television produces violent behavior in children who watch more than four hours a day.

g. Both creationism and evolutionary theory should be taught in the public schools.

h. Mentally defective men and women should be sterilized or otherwise prevented from producing children.

i. History will pronounce Reggie Jackson a greater all-round baseball player than Joe DiMaggio.

j. Bilingual instruction should not be permitted in the public schools.

k. Some forms of cancer are caused by a virus.

l. Dogs are smarter than horses.

m. Curfews for teenagers will reduce the abuse of alcohol and drugs.

n. The federal government should impose a drinking age of twenty-one.

o. The United States should proceed with unilateral disarmament.

p. Security precautions at airports are out of proportion to the dangers of terrorism.

q. Bodybuilding cannot be defined as a sport; it is a form of exhibitionism.

2. Report on an argument you have heard recently. Identify the parts of that argument — claim, support, warrant — as they are defined in this chapter. What were the strengths and weaknesses in the argument you heard?

3. Choose one of the more controversial claims in the previous list and explain the reasons it is controversial. Is support lacking or in doubt? Are the warrants unacceptable to many people? Try to go as deeply as you can, exploring, if possible, systems of belief, traditions, societal customs. You may confine your discussion to personal experience with the problem in your community or group. If there has been a change over the years in the public attitude toward the claim, offer what you think may be an explanation for the change.

4. Write your own argument for or against the value of standard grading in college.

5. Discuss an occasion when a controversy arose that the opponents could not settle. Describe the problem and tell why you think the disagreement was not settled.

CHAPTER TWO

Responding to Argument

Most of us learn how to read, to listen, and to write arguments by attending critically to the arguments of those who have already mastered the important elements as well as those who have not. As we acquire skill in reading, we learn to uncover the clues that reveal meaning and to become sensitive to the kinds of organization, support, and language that experienced writers use in persuading their audiences. Listening, too, is a skill, often underrated, but increasingly important in an era when the spoken voice can be transmitted worldwide with astonishing speed. In becoming more expert listeners, we can engage in discussions with a wide and varied audience and gain proficiency in distinguishing between responsible and irresponsible speech.

A full response to any argument means more than understanding the message. It also means evaluating, deciding whether or not the message is successful and, then, determining *how* it succeeds or fails in persuading us. In making these judgments about the written and spoken arguments of others, we learn how to deliver our own. We try to avoid what we perceive to be flaws in another's arguments, and we adapt the strategies that produce clear, honest, forceful arguments.

RESPONDING AS A CRITICAL READER

You already know how essential critical reading can be to mastery of most college subjects, but its importance for reading and writing about argument, where meaning is often complex and multilayered, can hardly be overestimated. Critical, or close, reading of arguments leads to greater comprehension and more thorough evaluation. The first step is comprehension — understanding what the author is trying to prove. Then comes evaluation — careful judgment of the extent to which the author has succeeded.

Good readers are never merely passive recipients of the material. They engage in active dialogue with the author, as if he or she were present, asking questions, offering objections, expressing approval. They often write comments in the margins of the book as they read or in a notebook they reserve for this purpose. Clearly, the more information they have about the author and the subject as well as the circumstances surrounding it — an event in the news, for example — the easier and more productive their reading of any material will be. But whatever their level of preparation, they have learned to extract meaning by attending to clues both in the material itself and in their knowledge of the world around them.

Here are a few strategies for close reading of an argument.

1. Pay attention to the title — and the subtitle. They can provide a good deal of information.
   a. The title can tell you what the essay is about. It may even state the purpose of the argument in specific terms, as in "Cocaine is Even Deadlier Than We Thought," the title of one of the essays in this book.
   b. It can make reference to other writing that you will recognize. The title of the article that follows, "The Pursuit of Whining," brings to mind the phrase in the Declaration of Independence, "the pursuit of Happiness." The subtitle clinches the connection: "Affirmative Action circa 1776."
   c. It can express the author's attitude toward the subject. In the title quoted above, we realize that "whining," because it has negative connotations, will probably be attacked as a means of achieving happiness. The subtitle adds the rather surprising suggestion that the author is unfriendly to some aspects of the American Revolution.
2. As you read the essay for the first time, look for the main idea and the structure of the whole essay. Make a skeleton outline in your mind or on paper. Remember that your purpose in reading an argument is to learn what the author wants to prove and how he or she proves it, and to frame a response to it as you read. At this stage, avoid concentrating on details. Reading is a complex mental operation, and you cannot do everything at once.

   In a well-written essay, even a long one, the main idea and the organization should emerge clearly from a careful reading. Every argument, however long and complicated, has a beginning, a middle, and an end. It will offer a claim and several parts devoted to support. (Development of an important point may take two or more paragraphs.)

3. You will probably find the main idea or *thesis statement* in one of the first two or three paragraphs. Remember, however, that the beginning of an argument often has other purposes; it may lay out not the author's position but the position that the author will oppose, or background for the whole argument.

4. Pay attention to topic sentences. The topic sentence is usually but not always the first sentence of a paragraph. It is the general statement that controls the details and examples in the paragraph.

5. Don't overlook the language signposts, especially the transitional words and phrases that tell you whether the writer will change direction or offer support for a previous point — words and phrases like *but, however, nevertheless, yet, moreover, for example, at first glance, more important, the first reason,* etc.

6. Select the method for vocabulary search that suits you best: either guessing the meaning of an unfamiliar word from the context and going on or else looking it up immediately. It's true that the first method makes for more rapid reading and is sometimes recommended by teachers of reading, but guessing can be risky. Keep a good dictionary handy. If you are at all in doubt about a word that seems crucial to meaning, check your guess before you go too far in what may be the wrong direction.

7. If you use a colored marker to highlight main points, use it sparingly. Marking passages in color is meant to direct you to the major ideas and reduce the necessity for rereading the whole passage when you review.

8. Don't be timid about asking questions of the text. No author is infallible. Some authors are not always clear. Ask any questions whose answers are necessary to improve your comprehension. Disagree with the author if you feel confident of the support for your view. After you have read the whole argument, you may discover that most of your early questions have been answered. If not, this may be a signal to read the article again. Be cautious about concluding that the author hasn't proved his point.

9. Reading an assigned work is usually a solitary activity, but what follows a reading should be shared. Talk about the material with classmates or others who have read it. You probably know that discussion of a book or a movie strengthens both your memory of details and your understanding of the whole. And defending or modifying your evaluation will mean going back to the text and finding clues that you may have overlooked. Not least, it can be fun to discuss even something you didn't enjoy.

The following essay is annotated by a student as he reads. He is already familiar, as you are, with the Declaration of Independence. After reading and commenting on the essay, he adds a brief summary for his own review.

The Pursuit of Whining: Affirmative Action circa 1776

JOHN PATRICK DIGGINS

Anything to do with "the pursuit of happiness"? Who's doing the whining in 1776?

Is this about affirmative action or the Revolution? Or both?

Usually means that a second glance will show the opposite

Means it's not what it seems

So he's against aff. action because it violates the D of I?

Seems to be his thesis; is group opportunity bad?

All politics, we are now told, will not be local but universal, a struggle over values. In these "culture wars," a candidate who can touch the core nerve of American values will be sure to be elected. How will affirmative action stand up to such a contest?

At first glance, affirmative action appears to be consistent with America's commitment to egalitarianism, which derives from the Declaration of Independence and its ringing pronouncement that "all men are created equal" and are "endowed by their creator with certain unalienable rights." Actually affirmative action, as carried out, has little to do with equality and is so dependent on biology, ancestry, and history that it subverts the individualist spirit of the Declaration.

But the second part of the Declaration, which no one remembers, may affirm affirmative action as the politics of group opportunity.

The Declaration held rights to be equal and unalienable because in the state of nature, before social conventions had been formed, "Nature and Nature's God" (Jefferson's phrase) gave no person or class the authority to dominate over others. Aristocracy became such a class, and the idea of equality was not so much

John Patrick Diggins teaches history at the Graduate Center of the City University of New York. This column appeared in the *New York Times* on September 25, 1995.

Reason for the Revolution

an accurate description of the human species as it was a protest against artificial privilege and hereditary right.

Today we have a new identity politics of entitlement, and who one is depends on ethnic categories and descriptions based on either ancestry or sex. This return to a pseudo-aristocratic politics of privilege based on inherited rights by reason of birth means that equality has been replaced by diversity as the criteri[on] of governmental decisions.

Interesting point—today's affirmative action is like yesterday's aristocracy (both claim privileges of birth).

Jefferson loved diversity, but he and Thomas Paine trusted the many and suspected the few who saw themselves entitled to preferential treatment as an accident of birth. Paine was unsparing in his critique of aristocracy as a parasitic "no-ability." Speaking for the colonists, many of whom had worked their way out of conditions of indentured servitude, he insisted that hereditary privilege was "as absurd as an hereditary mathematician, or an hereditary wise man; and as ridiculous as an hereditary poet-laureate."

The founding fathers were against inherited privileges.

But if America's egalitarian critique of aristocratic privilege could be in conflict with affirmative action, the second part of the Declaration may be perfectly consistent with it. Here begins the art of protest as the Declaration turns to the colonists' grievances, and we are asked to listen to a long tale of woe. Instead of admitting that they simply had no desire to cough up taxes, even to pay for a war that drove the French out of North America and thus made possible a situation where settlers were now secure enough to demand self-government, the colonists blamed King George for every outrage conceivable.

So far, he's proved that first part of D of I argues against affirmative action.

But the second part, listing grievances, is consistent with it.

Thinks the colonists are cry-babies!

"He has erected . . . swarms of offices to harass our people and eat out their substance." Because the King, in response to the colonists' refusal to pay for the cost of protection, withdrew such protection, he is charged with abdicating "his allegiance and protection: he has plundered our seas, ravaged our coasts, burnt our towns, destroyed the lives of our people." Even Edmund Burke, the British parliamentarian and orator who supported the colonists, saw them as almost paranoid, "protestants" who protest so much that they would "snuff the approach of tyranny in every tainted breeze."

Strong language

Even Jefferson gets a few lumps!

Help! I can't find it in the D of I! (Look it up?)

The ultimate hypocrisy comes when Jefferson accuses the King of once tolerating the slave trade, only "he is now exciting those very people to rise up in arms among us, and to purchase their liberty of which he has deprived them, by murdering the people upon whom he has obtruded them." The notion that slavery was forced upon the innocent colonists, who in turn only sought to be free of "tyranny," suggests the extent to which the sentiment of the Revolution grumbles with spurious charges.

Wow!

The Declaration voiced America's first   10
proclamation of victimology. Whatever the theoretical complexities embedded in the doctrine of equality, the Declaration demonstrated that any politics that has its own interests uppermost is best put forward in the language of victimization and paranoia.

Were any of their complaints justified?

"Paranoia" seems a bit much

The very vocabulary of the document ("harass," "oppress," and so on) is consistent with affirmative action, where white racists and male chauvinists have replaced King George as the specter of complaint.

He's talking about blacks and women. Is he saying, "no justification for complaints against whites and males?" No way!

Seeing themselves as sufferers to whom awful things happen, the colonists blamed their alleged oppressors and never acknowledged that they had any responsibility for the situation in which they found themselves.

Explain a bit further

Our choices

What then is America's core value? Is it equality and civic virtue? Or is it the struggle for power that legitimizes itself in

An ending that's all questions. the more successful, and least demand-
I like it. But they're fake ques- ing, shameless politics of whining?
tions. He knows the answers
and wants us to agree with
him.

    <u>Summary</u>: Is affirmative action consistent with the Declaration of In-
dependence? On that subject the two parts of the Declaration contradict each
other. The first part says that equality and individual rights are the principles of the American Revolution. Because the founding fathers opposed privileges awarded on account of ancestry and history, they would be against
affirmative action. But in the second part of the Declaration, the grievances
of the colonists sound like the complaints of groups today that claim they
are victims of oppression and <u>want</u> special privileges because of their ancestry and history. Today America must choose between equality and privileges for special groups. Note: From <u>The Declaration of Independence</u>, a
book by Carl Becker, I found out that the excerpts in paragraph 9 come
from an earlier draft of the <u>Declaration</u>. This argument about slavery was
omitted from the final draft because Jefferson thought that it was weaker
than the others. So was it fair to include it here?

RESPONDING AS A WRITER

    The following essay is a claim of policy; that is, it offers a solu-
tion to a problem. The solution is summarized in the title. Such an
expression of the main idea of an essay is frequently used in newspaper and magazine articles as a means of capturing attention. Although the solution is baldly stated, it is controversial, and you will
see that the conclusion suggests a more limited resolution of the
problem.

    Keep in mind that an essay of this length can never do justice to
a complicated and highly debatable subject. It will probably lack sufficient evidence, as this one does, to answer all the questions and
objections of a reader opposed to orphanages. What it can do is provoke thought and initiate an intelligent discussion.

Bring Back the Orphanage
JAMES Q. WILSON

Orphanages are almost extinct in the United States, but orphans are not. More than 400,000 children now live in foster homes, and unknown thousands more live nominally at home but actually as latch-key children surviving on the mean streets of America with no fathers, crack-abusing mothers, and drug-dealers as role models.

America once provided orphanages for many children. In 1910, about 123,000 lived in such places, or about 3 out of every 1,000 persons under the age of twenty-one. Today these institutions have almost disappeared. Most people think — wrongly, as we shall see — that they vanished because they had failed. Mention "orphanage" to someone and the image that springs to mind is of Oliver Twist begging for another bowl of gruel in a bleak prison.

The negative view of orphanages has been reinforced by historians who, writing in the late 1960s, and early 1970s, reinterpreted the late nineteenth-century impulse to help children as a form of class-conscious "social control." What previously had been seen as a public-spirited effort to impart decent values was now seen as effort to impose suspect (that is, "middle-class") values.

An especially sharp-edged version of the social-control theory was set forth in Anthony Platt's 1974 book, *The Child Savers.* A more nuanced but even more influential variant on the same theory was David Rothman's 1971 *The Discovery of the Asylum.* These writings helped to convince a generation of scholars and activists that prisons, asylums, and orphanages were institutions designed by the privileged classes to ensure control over poor people.

Decent Places

Today, however, a new group of historians has produced evidence that casts great doubt on the social-control view. A particularly good example by Nurith Zmora was published this year under the title *Orphanages Reconsidered* (Temple University Press). It examines three such institutions in Baltimore (one Catholic, one Jewish, and one Protestant) out of the twenty-eight, all privately run, that existed there in 1910. 5

James Q. Wilson is professor of management and public policy at the University of California, Los Angeles. This article is from the August 22, 1994, edition of the *Wall Street Journal.*

Ms. Zmora's conclusions can be simply stated: The orphanages were decent places run by caring professionals who maintained close ties to the community. The children were housed in adequate physical facilities, offered good food and hygiene, and supplied a better education than they would have received elsewhere. Though problems existed, they were grappled with by public and private agencies that shared the view that helping children was not the same thing as indoctrinating them. Ms. Zmora was able to trace the later lives of forty-five graduates. Most did quite well, finding jobs and becoming self-supporting.

Most of the youngsters in these institutions were not literally orphans. They were, instead, children whose parents, owing to poverty or disorganization, could not adequately care for them and who were enrolled voluntarily. Half entered before they were nine years old, and several before they were six; the average stay was about five years, though a few stayed for more than ten. The orphanages did not take incorrigible children. In a sense, these institutions were not orphanages but boarding schools that charged no tuition.

Consider, for example, the Samuel Ready School, founded in the early 1870s to help orphaned girls of any religion, although most were Protestant. The school was used by impoverished single mothers as either a temporary shelter or a boarding school for their daughters.

The Ready School was a pleasant place in a parklike setting that provided its students with better surroundings than they had enjoyed at home. The food was adequate, but probably no more appealing than any institutional fare. Of the first forty girls to enter Ready, twenty-nine completed their education there and eleven were expelled or withdrawn by relatives. Of those finishing, most studied dressmaking or secretarial skills. The school devoted great efforts to finding jobs for their graduates, mostly as clerks, dressmakers, and teachers. It was not easy, because growing up in an orphanage carried a stigma. Nevertheless, Ms. Zmora reports that of twenty-six girls who entered between 1887 and 1889 and finished their vocational training, twenty-three got jobs in their fields.

Other orphanages were less devoted to vocational training. At the Dolan School for Irish youngsters, some children eventually returned to their families while others were "placed out" in foster families. It was hard to be sure that the foster parents took adequate care of their charges, and so some of the latter ran away — sometimes back to Dolan.

Some scholars, such as Michael Sherraden, have suggested that these institutions were a way of coping with an important change in the labor market. Before 1870, children, even very young ones, worked; after the 1870s, there was less demand for and much opposition to child labor, and the orphanages were an alternative to living on the street or with parents who were unable to support them. The so-called orphanages were a way for children to get the benefits of middle-class life despite having parents who had not entered that status.

These institutions did not disappear because an enlightened public was shocked by stories of abuse and neglect within their walls. On the contrary, they were destroyed by their success and the ideology of their rivals. So popular did they become, so great was the demand for places in them, that private charities could no longer afford them and public agencies refused to make up the difference. Social workers opposed them because they "broke up the family," liberal reformers because they involved "social control," fiscal conservatives because they were too expensive.

Orphanages (or free boarding schools) still exist, but in reduced numbers. Boys Town is one that has not only survived but prospered. Mary-Lou Weisman recently gave a vivid account of its successes in an *Atlantic Monthly* article. But everywhere the idea is in retreat because critics think that such places just "warehouse" children (that was never true) and that a better alternative is to provide money that will enable parents to take care of their own children (that may have been true once, but it isn't now).

Incompetent or abusive parents existed when boarding schools flourished; they exist today. But today, unlike a century ago, the ideology of "family preservation" has intervened with its plausible but overly broad message that a child is invariably better off with his parents. It is an appealing idea and an inexpensive one to boot, since supporting the child in his family or in a foster family is cheaper than caring for him in an institution.

But not all families are worth preserving. Indeed, the dramatic increase in single-parent families suggests that there is a declining number of true families worth preserving. And the main current alternative to the biological parent — namely, foster-family care — has its own problems. Many foster families simply cannot handle the kind of children they are now getting. And all foster families are hard to oversee to ensure that the best interests of the child are being served. 15

Need to Know More

We don't know as much as we should about how well institutional care might function under contemporary conditions. Such evidence as exists suggests that troubled teenagers may do well while in boarding schools but do poorly when returned to their families and communities. On the other hand, very young children placed in such schools before they become troubled may (no one knows for certain) do as well today as their predecessors did in turn-of-the-century Baltimore. Careful studies can answer these questions.

Foster care has an important role to play — for some children. But for others institutional care is necessary. At least the research of writers such as Nurith Zmora, Michael Sherraden, and Mary-Lou Weisman is making it harder to argue that boarding schools and orphanages are discredited alternatives.

Organization

While there are numerous conventional patterns of organization (see Chapter 9), it is worth pointing out that most essays of more than 750 words are rarely perfect examples of such patterns. Authors mix structures wherever it seems necessary to make a stronger case. The pattern of organization in this essay is primarily a *defense of the main idea* — that orphanages should be reestablished to take care of children who would otherwise be abused or homeless. But because the claim is highly controversial, the author must also try to *refute the opposing views* that will prevent realization of his proposal.

Having stated his claim in the title, the author can move directly to the evidence that supports it. He has divided his essay into two parts. The first part attempts to prove that orphanages have worked in the past and that views of orphanages as a form of social control are false. The second part supports the idea that such institutions can work and refutes the theory and practice of "family preservation" which governs social welfare policy today.

The essay is perfectly unified — that is, all parts of the essay contribute to the development of the main idea. But in at least one place the author has made a choice with which a reader might disagree. Another writer might have moved paragraph 11 elsewhere in the essay, perhaps after the first sentence in paragraph 5, where the author begins to discuss the favorable reports on orphanages. But its position in the essay reflects the author's decision to use it as a summary of these reports rather than an introduction to them.

You may have noticed other small departures from strict rules of organization which, nevertheless, make good sense. Paragraph 2, for example, only five sentences long, contains at least three different ideas, not the one idea that a paragraph is commonly meant to develop. In the author's mind there was no need for a conventional topic sentence. The transitions within the paragraph are smooth, and the meaning is entirely clear.

Support

The author tries to provide an answer to a question you will ask as soon as you read the title: "How are you going to prove that this is a good idea? Aren't orphanages terrible places that harmed children in the past?" As support, the author offers examples, assumptions about social theory (or ideology), and an appeal to values. Real examples are taken from history, and rejection of a prevailing theory is based on the author's knowledge of the social environment and assumptions about its impact on children.

The response to this evidence will probably be mixed. Half the essay is devoted to the historical record as it appears in three recent studies, with descriptions of the orphans and their lives both in and out of the institutions. Because these details are interesting and unfamiliar to many readers, they have a strong, immediate appeal. But the bulk of the evidence comes from research about orphanages of seventy or eighty years ago. Critics will want more evidence than examples from the work of only three authors (although a short essay can hardly provide more) and more attention to present-day institutions. (There is one reference to Boys Town.) The theory (or ideology) — that "family preservation" doesn't work for many children — is more difficult to defend or refute, especially regarding predictions of the future. The author cites data to support his own theory (paragraph 15); in addition, he brings to his argument his reputation as a widely known and respected social scientist. But critics will say that his evidence is too selective and that other theorists can effectively refute him.

The appeal to values will probably go unchallenged. It is indirect, but it pervades the essay, and all readers are likely to share with the author a concern for the welfare of children.

Style

The clear, direct prose of this essay is writing of a kind that you can aspire to as a student writer. The author makes effective use of tone, diction, transitions, sentence variety, and parenthetical insertions. Throughout he writes for an audience that he perceives as generally well-informed, interested in evidence, and socially concerned. He is also aware that some readers will disagree with his proposal and that the style, therefore, must reflect a conciliatory approach. He must give neutral or hostile readers confidence in his willingness to compromise.

The author's tone, the expression of his attitude toward his material and his audience is serious, modest, and reasonable. He gives an unemotional explanation of the opposing views, and his language makes clear that he doesn't presume to know all the answers. A number of expressions show this: "We don't know," "No one knows for certain," Such evidence as exists," "Careful studies can answer these questions."

His diction, or choice of words, is appropriate to his audience, among others, people who read the *Wall Street Journal*. It is the standard English of an educated layman, which avoids the specialized vocabulary of the academic social scientist. The choice of words is broad but accessible. The author even employs contractions here and there to reduce formality.

Transitions are the words and phrases that occur between sentences and between paragraphs to promote greater coherence or connections between ideas. It isn't necessarily true that shorter sentences without transitions make for easier reading; they may, in fact, make understanding more difficult. Transitional words and phrases help us to follow the movement of the author's thinking — words and phrases like *but, at least, indeed, on the contrary, in a sense, on the other hand, however, for example.* These expressions should not be used indiscriminately. This author limits them to what seems necessary and no more.

Varying the sentence structure is still another way to make reading and comprehension easier. For example, using complex sentences — sentences with dependent clauses — allows you to subordinate some ideas within the sentence. Compound sentences using two or more independent clauses tell the reader that the main ideas are equally important. In other words, the structure of the sentence can create emphasis. The author of this essay uses long and short sentences, simple, compound, and complex sentences, and a variety of sentence beginnings. Look at paragraphs 2 and 13 for a combination of long and short sentences; at paragraphs 6 and 9 for different kinds of sentences; at paragraphs 12 and 15 for different sentence beginnings.

Finally, there are the parenthetical insertions. They are a very small part of good style, and many writers don't use them. Student writers seldom do, but such interruptions, carefully placed, can sound like part of a thoughtful conversation.

You will find it helpful to look back over the essay to see how the examples we've cited and others work to fulfill the writer's purpose.

RESPONDING AS A CRITICAL LISTENER

Of course, not all public arguments are written. Oral arguments on radio and television now enjoy widespread popularity and influence. In fact, their proliferation means that we listen far more than we talk, read, or write. Today the art of listening has become an indispensable tool for learning about the world we live in. One informed critic predicts that the dissemination of information and opinions through the electronic media will "enable more and more Americans to participate directly in making the laws and policies by which they are governed."[1]

Because we are interested primarily in arguments about public issues — those that involve democratic decision making — we will not be concerned with the afternoon TV talk shows that are largely devoted to personal problems. (Occasionally, however, *Oprah* and *Sally Jessy Raphael* introduce topics of broad social significance.) More relevant to the kinds of written arguments you will read and write about in this course are the television and radio shows that also examine social and political problems. The most intelligent and responsible programs usually consist of a panel of experts — politicians, journalists, scholars — led by a neutral moderator (or one who, at least, allows guests to express their views). Some of these programs are decades old; others are more recent — *Meet the Press, Face the Nation, Firing Line, The McLaughlin Group, The Monday Group, The NewsHour with Jim Lehrer.* An outstanding radio show, *Talk of the Nation* on National Public Radio, invites listeners, who are generally informed and articulate, to call in and ask questions of, or comment on remarks by, experts on the topic of the day.

Several enormously popular radio talk shows are hosted by people with strong, sometimes extreme ideological positions. They may use offensive language and insult their listeners in a crude form of theater. Among the most influential shows are those of Rush Limbaugh and Howard Stern. In addition, elections and political crises bring speeches and debates on radio and TV by representatives of a variety of views. Some are long and formal, written texts that are simply read aloud, but others are short and impromptu.

Whatever the merits or shortcomings of individual programs, significant general differences exist between arguments on radio and television and arguments in the print media. These differences include the degree of organization and development and the risk of personal attacks.

First (excluding for the moment the long, prepared speeches), contributions to a panel discussion must be delivered in fragments, usually no longer than a single paragraph, weakened by time constraints, interruptions, overlapping speech, memory gaps, and real or feigned displays of derision, impatience, and disbelief by critical panelists. Even on the best programs, the result is a lack of both coherence — or connections between ideas — and solid evidence that requires development. Too often we are treated to conclusions with little indication of how they were arrived at.

---

[1] Lawrence K. Grossman, *The Electronic Republic: Reshaping Democracy in the Information Age* (New York: Viking, 1995).

The following brief passage appeared in a newspaper review of "Resolved: The flat tax is better than the income tax," a debate on *Firing Line* by an impressive array of experts. It illustrates some of the difficulties that accompany programs attempting to capture the truth of a complicated issue on TV or radio.

"It is absolutely true," says a proponent. "It is factually untrue," counters an opponent. "It's factually correct," responds a proponent. "I did my math right," says a proponent. "You didn't do your math right," says an opponent. At one point in a discussion of interest income, one of the experts says, "Oh, excuse me, I think I got it backward."

No wonder the TV critic called the exchange "disjointed and at times perplexing."[2]

In the sensational talk shows the participants rely on personal experience and vivid anecdotes which may not be sufficiently typical to prove anything.

Second, listeners and viewers of all spoken arguments are in danger of evaluating them according to criteria that are largely absent from evaluation of written texts. It is true that writers may adopt a *persona* or a literary disguise which the tone of the essay will reflect. But many readers will not be able to identify it or recognize their own response to it. Listeners and viewers, however, can hardly avoid being affected by characteristics that are clearly definable: a speaker's voice, delivery, bodily mannerisms, dress, and physical appearance. In addition, listeners may be adversely influenced by clumsy speech containing more slang, colloquialisms, and grammar and usage errors than written texts that have had the benefit of revision.

But if listeners allow consideration of physical attributes to influence their judgment of what the speaker is trying to prove, they are guilty of an *ad hominem* fallacy, that is, an evaluation of the speaker rather than the argument. This is true whether the evaluation is favorable or unfavorable. (See pp. 267–68 for a discussion of this fallacy.)

Talk shows may indeed be disjointed and perplexing, but millions of us find them both instructive and entertaining. Over time we are exposed to an astonishing variety of opinions from every corner of American life, and we also acquire information from experts who might not otherwise be available to us. Then there is the appeal of hearing the voices, seeing the faces of people engaged in earnest, sometimes passionate, discourse — a short, unrehearsed drama in which we also play a part as active listeners in a far-flung audience.

---

[2] Walter Goodman, "The Joys of the Flat Tax, Excluding the Equations," *New York Times*, December 21, 1995, Sec. C, p. 14.

Guidelines to Critical Listening

Listening is hearing with attention, a natural and immensely important human activity which, unfortunately, many people don't do very well. The good news is that listening is a skill that can be learned and, unlike some other skills, practiced every day without big investments of money and effort.

Here are some of the characteristics of critical listening most appropriate to understanding arguments.

1. Above all, listening to arguments requires concentration. If you are distracted, you cannot go back as you do with the written word to clarify a point or recover a connection. Devices such as flow sheets and outlines can be useful aids to concentration. In following a debate, for example, judges and other listeners often use flow sheets — distant cousins of baseball scorecards — to record the major points on each side and their rebuttals. For roundtable discussions or debates you can make your own simple flow chart to fill out as you listen, with columns for claims, different kinds of support, and warrants. Leave spaces in the margin for your questions and comments about the soundness of the proof. An outline is more useful for longer presentations, such as lectures. As you listen, try to avoid being distracted by facts alone. Look for the overall pattern of the speech.

2. Listeners often concentrate on the wrong things in the spoken argument. We have already noted the distractions of appearance and delivery. Research shows that listeners are likely to give greater attention to the dramatic elements of speeches than to the logical ones. But you can enjoy the sound, the appearance, and the drama of a spoken argument without allowing these elements to overwhelm what is essential to the development of a claim.

3. Good listeners try not to allow their prejudices to prevent careful evaluation of the argument. This doesn't mean accepting everything or even most of what you hear. It means trying to avoid premature judgments about what is actually said. This precaution is especially relevant when the speakers and their views are well known and the listener has already formed an opinion about them, favorable or unfavorable.

RESPONDING ON-LINE

You have learned that writers need the responses of readers and other writers to improve their writing. As the influence of computers increases in our society and more people begin using local and wide-area computer networks such as the Internet to send electronic mail ("e-mail"), it will become ever easier for writers to distribute their writing and for readers to respond to it. Only a few years ago, if you wanted feedback for your writing, you had to either read it aloud to others or copy and distribute it by hand or postal mail. Both methods were cumbersome and time-consuming, even expensive. Electronic networks now allow your writing to be distributed almost instantaneously to dozens or even thousands of readers with virtually no copying or mailing costs. Readers can respond to you just as quickly and cheaply. Even though there can be pitfalls and problems with communicating on-line, the overall ease of use can only encourage writers to seek, and readers to provide, editorial feedback.

Reading and Revising on a Word Processor

Reading text on a computer screen for the first time can be bewildering. It is difficult to get a sense of the "page," since most computer screens do not correspond to the typical fifty-line, 8½ by 11-inch typewriter page. As a reader of books and magazines, you are accustomed to taking in a whole page at a glance; as a writer, you are used to being able to spread out the pages of a draft and edit directly on them. A reader can, of course, use a *scroll bar* to scroll text up and down the screen, exposing all text in a document section by section, but even the strongest advocates of computers acknowledge that the smaller "page" of most computer monitors challenges ingrained reading practices. Still, as you grow accustomed to the screen, your difficulties in reading and editing should diminish, and you will come to appreciate the advantages of "digital text" — text that can be cut, pasted, and moved around your document far more easily than scissors, tape, liquid paper, or typewriter correction tape will allow. As one student put it, "I never realized how important it was to be able to change words and move them around so easily until I began using a word processor. It was hard at first using the mouse and scrolling, but you forget all about that once you see how easy it is to revise."

On-screen you can manipulate text in ways impossible with printed materials. By pressing a key you can increase the size of the print (the "point size") and alter the type style (the "font"; for example, Times Roman). Such options help you to focus on individual words or phrases. You can also separate out individual sentences and even clauses and phrases by using double "carriage returns" (press the <enter> or <return> key twice or click the mouse twice) at the end of each word group. (This is like hitting a return bar on a typewriter twice to double-space.) Double-spacing allows you to "spread the page" and visually isolate elements. Important words or phrases can be put in boldface or capital letters, a tactic almost certain to reveal conceptual and stylistic elements otherwise lost in a word-dense paragraph.

Most word-processing programs provide a *global search and replace* feature that allows you automatically to replace a word or term with another word or term throughout the document. This option is useful for exposing specific stylistic strengths or weaknesses in the draft you are reading. A particularly important word or phrase, for instance, or one that is habitually overused, can be globally boldfaced or capitalized, calling attention to it so that you can decide where to substitute a synonym. Globally highlighting a punctuation mark, such as an exclamation mark or colon, can graphically reveal the problem of repetitiveness of punctuation style in your own writing or that of the person whose draft you are reading on-screen.

From Word Processing to E-Mail Networks

You can anticipate that sometime during your college career — maybe even in your writing course — instructors will ask you to send drafts and comments via e-mail. On some systems this will be easy to do and on others not so easy. You may have difficulty either writing your text directly into the e-mail text editor or copying it from a word processor into an e-mail program. For example, if you are accustomed to the way word processors manipulate type size and format, you may be surprised to discover that most e-mail text editing programs do not permit text formatting. They exclude such features as underlining, boldface, and different font sizes and styles. But because the goal of most on-line responding is to improve a text's focus, development, and writing style rather than its appearance on the page, the lack of formatting is not a drawback in your drafting stage.

Some network software designed for classrooms combines a word processor with a special e-mail feature. These programs make it easy to transmit a draft, but they often limit where the e-mail can be sent — sometimes no farther than a single room or building, the limits of the local area network. (Whether or not this is a disadvantage depends mainly upon your instructor's ambitions for distributing student writing.)

Since there are so many different types of e-mail programs and text editors, specific technical information on how to use them is well beyond the scope of this discussion. The best advice is to be patient, read the instructions for your own system carefully, ask questions of your instructor and classmates, do not be afraid to experiment, and practice, practice, practice. Your patience will be rewarded once you become adept on your system.

Editing and Commenting On-Line

Before word processors, responding to a text usually meant writing comments directly on a page, squeezing suggestions into the margins or between the double-spaced lines of a draft. Such hand-editing often made a manuscript difficult to read. Electronic text, however, allows you to create as much room as necessary for a comment, simply by placing the cursor at the end of a line and pressing the return (or by clicking the mouse) several times. There are numerous typographical ways to distinguish your comments as a peer editor from the type of the original text. For example, if your response is to be delivered through e-mail, you can highlight your response by typing it in capital letters. The ease of such unrestricted interlinear note-making tends to encourage a reader to respond more fully and specifically (and legibly) than ever before.

Another instance of the handy manipulability of e-mail text (*e-text*) is the *responding template.* A responding template is a series of questions, or *prompts*, prepared by an instructor or other expert, that can be pasted close to the text being commented on in order to guide a peer responder through a critical reading session. Examples of such prompts are "Evaluate the clarity and significance of the thesis statement," or "What improvements could be made in the use of sources?" The elements of the document the instructor wishes to emphasize can be distilled into prompts and circulated to the responders as a word-processing file or e-mail message.

Guidelines for Responding On-Line

You know that in face-to-face conversation the words themselves constitute only a part of your message. Much of what you say is communicated through your body language and tone of voice. Written words provide a much narrower channel of communication, which is why you must be more careful when you write to someone than when you speak directly to them. Electronic writing, however, especially through e-mail, fosters a casualness and immediacy that often fools writers into assuming they are talking privately rather than writing publicly. On-line you may find yourself writing quickly, carelessly, and intimately; without the help of your tone and body language, you may end up being seriously misunderstood. Words written hastily are often read much differently than intended; this is especially true when the writer attempts an ironic or sarcastic tone. For example, if a classmate walks up to you with a critical comment about one of your sentences and you respond by saying "I didn't realize you were so smart," the words, if unaccompanied by a placating smile and a pleasant, jocular tone, may come across as sarcastic or hostile. In e-writing, the same words appear without the mitigating body language and may be perceived as harsh, possibly insulting. You must keep this danger in mind as you respond on-line, or risk alienating your reader.

Keep in mind, too, that electronic mail may be read not only by your addressee, but also by anyone with whom the addressee chooses to share your message. An intemperate or indiscreet message may be forwarded to other classmates or your instructor, or, depending on the limits of the system, to many other readers whom you do not know.

Experienced on-line communicators advocate a set of network etiquette guidelines called "netiquette." Here are some generally accepted netiquette rules:

- Keep your sentences short and uncomplicated.

- Separate blocks of text — which should be no more than four or five lines long — by blank lines. For those rare occasions when a comment requires more than ten or fifteen consecutive lines of text, use subheadings on separate lines to guide your reader.

- Refer specifically to the text to which you are responding. You may want to quote directly from it, cutting and pasting phrases or sentences from the document to help show exactly what you are responding to.

- Greet the person(s) to whom you are writing politely and by name.

- Be wary about attempting to be funny. Humor, as just explained, often requires a context, tone of voice, and body language to emphasize that it is not to be taken seriously. Writing witty comments that are sure to be taken humorously calls for skill and care, and e-mail messages usually are written too quickly for either.

- Avoid profanity or invective, and be wary of brusque or abrupt statements. Consider how you would feel if someone wrote to you that way.

- Avoid discussion of politics or religion unless that is the specific topic of your message.

- Do not ridicule public figures. Your reader may not share your opinions of, say, Senator Edward Kennedy or radio talk show host Rush Limbaugh.

- Frame all comments in a helpful, not critical, tone. For instance, rather than beginning a critique with "I found a number of problems in your text," you may want to start out more like this: "You have some good ideas in this paper and with a few changes, I think it will do well."

EXERCISES

Pre-Reading

1. If you haven't read "Kids in the Mall: Growing Up Controlled" (p. 57), do the following: Take note of the title of the book in which this excerpt appears. Now, write down briefly what you guess the attitude of the author will be toward his subject. Tell which words in the titles of the excerpt and the book suggest his approach. Next, read the quotation that heads the essay and the first paragraph. If you think there are further clues here, explain briefly how you interpreted them. (For example, did your own experience with malls enter into your thinking as you read?)

   Keep your notes. Refer to them after you have read the whole article (and perhaps discussed it in class). How well did your preparation help you to find the main point and understand the examples that supported it? Are there other things you might do to improve your pre-reading?

Annotating

2. Choose an editorial of at least two paragraphs in a newspaper or your school paper on a controversial subject that interests you. The title will probably reveal the subject. Annotate the editorial as you read, questioning, agreeing, objecting, offering additional ideas. (The annotation of the "The Pursuit of Whining" will suggest ways of doing this, although your personal responses are what make the annotation useful.) Then, read the editorial again. You should discover that annotating the article caused you to read more carefully, more critically, with greater comprehension and a more focused response.

Evaluating

3. Summarize the claim of the editorial in one sentence. Omit the supporting data and concentrate on the thesis. Then explain briefly your reaction to it. Has the author proved his or her point? Your annotation will show you where you expressed doubt or approval. If you already know a good deal about the subject, perhaps you will be reasonably confident of your judgment. If not, you may find that your response is tentative, that you need to read further for more information about the subject and to consult guidelines for making evaluations about the elements of argument.

Listening

4. People sometimes object to lectures as an educational tool. Think about some of the specific lectures you have listened to recently and analyze the reasons that you liked or disliked them (or liked some

aspects and disliked others). Do you think that you learned everything that the lecturer intended you to learn? If the results were doubtful, how much did your listening skills, good or bad, contribute to the result? Should the lecturer have done something differently to improve your response?

5. Watch (and *listen* to) one of the afternoon talk shows like *Oprah Winfrey* in which audiences discuss a controversial social problem. (The *TV Guide* and daily newspapers often list the subject. Recent topics on *Oprah* include the responsibility of parents for crimes committed by their children and the value of school integration.) Write a critical review of the discussion, mentioning as completely as you can the major claims, the most important evidence, and the declared or hidden warrants. (Unspoken warrants or assumptions may be easier to identify in arguments on talk shows where visual and auditory clues can reveal what participants try to hide.) How much did the oral format contribute to success or failure of the argument(s)?

6. Listen to one of the TV talk shows that feature invited experts. Write a review, telling how much you learned about the subject(s) of discussion. Be specific about the elements of the show that were either helpful or unhelpful to your understanding.

7. Listen with a friend or friends to a talk show discussion. Take notes as you listen. Then compare notes to discover if you agree on the outstanding points, the degree to which claims have been supported, and the part that seeing and/or hearing the discussion played in your evaluation. If there is disagreement about any of the elements, how do you account for it?

On-Line

8. If you are working in a networked classroom, with three or four of your classmates select an argumentative essay in this book that all of you agree to read. Each of you should draft a response to the essay, either agreeing or disagreeing with the author's position, citing evidence to support your position. Then each of you prepare a letter soliciting a response to your draft from the members of your group. For example, you may want to state what your objective was, suggest what you think are the strengths and weaknesses of the draft, and ask what sort of revisions seem appropriate. E-mail the letter and the draft to each of your peer responders. Be prepared to revise based on their comments, which should either be given to you handwritten on a printed-out copy of your draft or in an e-mailed response.

CHAPTER THREE

Claims

Claims, or propositions, represent answers to the question: "What are you trying to prove?" Although they are the conclusions of your arguments, they often appear as thesis statements. Claims can be classified as *claims of fact, claims of value,* and *claims of policy.*

CLAIMS OF FACT

Claims of fact assert that a condition has existed, exists, or will exist and their support consists of factual information — that is, information such as statistics, examples, and testimony that most responsible observers assume can be verified.

Many facts are not matters for argument: Our own senses can confirm them, and other observers will agree about them. We can agree that a certain number of students were in the classroom at a particular time, that lions make a louder sound than kittens, and that apples are sweeter than potatoes.

We can also agree about information that most of us can rarely confirm for ourselves — information in reference books, such as atlases, almanacs, and telephone directories; data from scientific resources about the physical world; and happenings reported in the media. We can agree on the reliability of such information because we trust the observers who report it.

However, the factual map is constantly being redrawn by new data in such fields as history and science that cause us to reevaluate our conclusions. For example, the discovery of the Dead Sea Scrolls in 1947 revealed that some books of the Bible — *Isaiah,* for one — were far older than we had thought. Researchers at New York Hospital–Cornell Medical Center say that many symptoms previously thought inevitable in the aging process are now believed to be treatable and reversible symptoms of depression.[1]

In your conversations with other students you probably generate claims of fact every day, some of which can be verified without much effort, others of which are more difficult to substantiate.

> CLAIM: Most of the students in this class come from towns within fifty miles of Boston.

To prove this the arguer would need only to ask the students in the class where they come from.

> CLAIM: Students who take their courses Pass/Fail make lower grades than those who take them for specific grades.

In this case the arguer would need to have access to student records showing the specific grades given by instructors. (In most schools the instructor awards a letter grade, which is then recorded as a Pass or a Fail if the student has elected this option.)

> CLAIM: The Red Sox will win the pennant this year.

This claim is different from the others because it is an opinion about what will happen in the future. But it can be verified (in the future) and is therefore classified as a claim of fact.

More complex factual claims about political and scientific matters remain controversial because proof on which all or most observers will agree is difficult or impossible to obtain.

> CLAIM: Bilingual programs are less effective than English-only programs in preparing students for higher education.
>
> CLAIM: The only life in the universe exists on this planet.

Not all claims are so neatly stated or make such unambiguous assertions. Because we recognize that there are exceptions to most generalizations, we often qualify our claims with words such as *generally, usually, probably, as a rule*. It would not be true to state flatly, for example, "College graduates earn more than high school graduates." This statement is generally true, but we know that some high school graduates who are electricians or city bus drivers or sanitation workers earn more than college graduates who are schoolteachers or nurses or social workers. In making such a claim, therefore, the writer should qualify it with a word that limits the claim.

To support a claim of fact, the writer needs to produce sufficient and appropriate data, that is, examples, statistics, and testimony

---

[1] *New York Times,* February 20, 1983, Sec. 22, p. 4.

from reliable sources. Provided this requirement is met, the task of establishing a factual claim would seem to be relatively straightforward. But as you have probably already discovered in ordinary conversation, finding convincing support for factual claims can pose a number of problems. Whenever you try to establish a claim of fact, you will need to ask at least three questions about the material you plan to use: *What are sufficient and appropriate data? Who are the reliable authorities?* and *Have I made clear whether my statements are facts or inferences?*

Sufficient and Appropriate Data

The amount and kind of data for a particular argument depend on the importance and complexity of the subject. The more controversial the subject, the more facts and testimony you will need to supply. Consider the claim "The murder rate in New York City is lower this year than last year." If you want to prove the truth of this claim, obviously you will have to provide a larger quantity of data than for a claim that says, "By following three steps, you can train your dog to sit and heel in fifteen minutes." In examining your facts and opinions, an alert reader will want to know if they are accurate, current, and typical of other facts and opinions that you have not mentioned.

The reader will also look for testimony from more than one authority, although there may be cases where only one or two experts, because they have achieved a unique breakthrough in their field, will be sufficient. These cases would probably occur most frequently in the physical sciences. The Nobel Prize winners James Watson and Francis Crick, who first discovered the structure of the DNA molecule, are an example of such experts. However, in the case of the so-called Hitler diaries that surfaced in 1983, at least a dozen experts — journalists, historians, bibliographers who could verify the age of the paper and the ink — were needed to establish that they were forgeries.

Reliable Authorities

Not all those who pronounce themselves experts are trustworthy. Your own experience has probably taught you that you cannot always believe the reports of an event by a single witness. The witness may be poorly trained to make accurate observations — about the size of a crowd, the speed of a vehicle, his distance from an object. Or his own physical conditions — illness, intoxication, disability — may prevent him from seeing or hearing or smelling accurately. The circumstances under which he observes the event — darkness, confusion, noise — may also impair his observation. In addition, the witness may be biased for or against the outcome of the event, as in a hotly contested baseball game, where the observer sees the play that he wants to see. You will find the problems associated with the biases of witnesses to be relevant to your work as a reader and writer of argumentative essays.

You will undoubtedly want to quote authors in some of your arguments. In most cases you will not be familiar with the authors. But there are guidelines for determining their reliability: the rank or title of the experts, the acceptance of their publications by other experts, their association with reputable universities, research centers, or think tanks. For example, for a paper on euthanasia, you might decide to quote from an article by Paul Ramsey, identified as the Harrington Spear Paine Professor of Religion at Princeton University. For a paper on prison reform you might want to use material supplied by Tom Murton, a professional penologist, formerly superintendent in the Arkansas prison system, now professor of criminology at the University of Minnesota. Most readers of your arguments would agree that these authors have impressive credentials in their fields.

What if several respectable sources are in conflict? What if the experts disagree? After a preliminary investigation of a controversial subject, you may decide that you have sufficient material to support your claim. But if you read further, you may discover that other material presented by equally qualified experts contradicts your original claim. In such circumstances you will find it impossible to make a definitive claim. (On pp. 152–54, in the treatment of support of a claim by evidence, you will find a more elaborate discussion of this vexing problem.)

Facts or Inferences

We have defined a fact as a statement that can be verified. An inference is "a statement about the unknown on the basis of the known."[2] The difference between facts and inferences is important to you as the writer of an argument because an inference is an *interpretation,* or an opinion reached after informed evaluation of evidence. As you and your classmates wait in your classroom on the first day of the semester, a middle-aged woman wearing a tweed jacket and a corduroy skirt appears and stands in the front of the room. You don't know who this woman is. However, based on what you do know about the appearance of many college teachers and the fact that teachers usually stand in front of the classroom, you may

---

[2]S. I. Hayakawa, *Language in Thought and Action* (New York: Harcourt, Brace, Jovanovich, 1978), p. 35.

infer that this woman is your teacher. You will probably be right. But you cannot be certain until you have more information. Perhaps you will find out that this woman has come from the department office to tell you that your teacher is sick and cannot meet the class today.

You have probably come across a statement such as the following in a newspaper or magazine: "Excessive television viewing has caused the steady decline in the reading ability of children and teenagers." Presented this way, the statement is clearly intended to be read as a factual claim that has been or can be proved. But it is an inference. The facts, which can be, and have been, verified, are (1) the reading ability of children and teenagers has declined and (2) the average child views television for six or more hours a day. (Whether this amount of time is "excessive" is also an opinion.) The cause-effect relation between the two facts is an interpretation of the investigator who has examined both the reading scores and the amount of time spent in front of the television set and *inferred* that one is the cause of the other. The causes of the decline in reading scores are probably more complex than the original statement indicates. Since we can seldom or never create laboratory conditions for testing the influence of television separate from other influences in the family and the community, any statement about the connection between reading scores and television viewing can only be a guess.

By definition, no inference can ever do more than suggest probabilities. Of course, some inferences are much more reliable than others and afford a high degree of probability. Almost all claims in science are based on inferences, interpretations of data on which most scientists agree. Paleontologists find a few ancient bones from which they make inferences about an animal that might have been alive millions of years ago. We can never be absolutely certain that the reconstruction of the dinosaur in the museum is an exact copy of the animal it is supposed to represent, but the probability is fairly high because no other interpretation works so well to explain all the observable data — the existence of the bones in a particular place, their age, their relation to other fossils, and their resemblance to the bones of existing animals with which the paleontologist is familiar.

Inferences are profoundly important, and most arguments could not proceed very far without them. But an inference is not a fact. The writer of an argument must make it clear when he or she offers an inference, an interpretation, or an opinion that it is not a fact.

Defending a Claim of Fact

Here is a summary of the guidelines that should help you to defend a factual claim. (We'll say more about support of factual claims in Chapter 5.)

1. Be sure that the claim — what you are trying to prove — is clearly stated, preferably at the beginning of your paper.
2. Define terms that may be controversial or ambiguous. For example, in trying to prove that "radicals" had captured the student government, you would have to define "radicals," distinguishing them from "liberals" or members of other ideological groups, so that your readers would understand exactly what you meant.
3. As far as possible, make sure that your evidence — facts and opinions, or interpretations of the facts — fulfills the appropriate criteria. The data should be sufficient, accurate, recent, typical; the authorities should be reliable.
4. Make clear when conclusions about the data are inferences or interpretations, not facts. For example, you might write, "The series of lectures, 'Modern Architecture,' sponsored by our fraternity, was poorly attended because the students at this college aren't interested in discussions of art." What proof could you offer that this *was* the reason, that your statement was a *fact*? Perhaps there were other reasons that you hadn't considered.
5. Arrange your evidence in order to emphasize what is most important. Place it at the beginning or the end, the most emphatic positions in an essay, and devote more space to it.

SAMPLE ANALYSIS: CLAIM OF FACT

Cocaine Is Even Deadlier Than We Thought

LOUIS L. CREGLER and HERBERT MARK

To the Editor:

In his July 3 letter about recreational cocaine use, Dr. Carl C. Pfeiffer notes that some of the toxic effects of cocaine on the heart have long been known to those versed in pharmacology. We wish to point out that cardiologists and neurologists are seeing additional complications not previously known. Indeed, little information on the cardiovascular effects of cocaine appeared until recently.

As Dr. Pfeiffer says, cocaine sensitizes the heart to the normal stimulant effects of the body's adrenaline. This ordinarily makes the

---

Louis L. Cregler, M.D., is assistant chief of medicine, and Herbert Mark, M.D., is chief of medicine at the Bronx Veterans Administration Medical Center. This article appeared in the *New York Times* on July 30, 1986.

heart beat much faster and increases blood pressure significantly. Cocaine abuse has also been associated with strokes, heart attacks (acute myocardial infarctions), and sudden deaths. Individuals with weak blood vessels (aneurysms or arteriovenous malformations) in the head are at greatest risk of having a stroke. With the sudden surge in blood pressure, a blood vessel can burst. Cocaine can also cause blood vessels supplying the heart muscle itself to undergo vasoconstriction (coronary spasm), and this can produce a heart attack.

Deaths have been reported after administration of cocaine by all routes. Most such deaths are attributed to cocaine intoxication, leading to generalized convulsions, respiratory failure, and cardiac arrhythmias, minutes to hours after administration. Much of this information is so new that it has not found its way into the medical literature or standard textbooks.

Cocaine abuse continues to escalate in American society. It is estimated that 30 million Americans have used it, and some 5 million use it regularly. As cocaine has become less expensive, its availability and purity are increasing. It has evolved from a minor problem into a major threat to public health. And as use has increased, greater numbers of emergency-room visits, cocaine-related heart problems, and sudden deaths have been reported. With so many people using cocaine, it is not unexpected that more strokes, heart attacks, and sudden cardiac deaths will be taking place.

Louis L. Cregler, M.D.
Herbert Mark, M.D.

Analysis

The authors of this letter supply data to prove that the deadly effects of cocaine exceed those that are already well known in medicine and pharmacology. Four aspects of this factual claim are noteworthy. First, it is a response to a letter that, according to the authors, ignored significant new evidence. Many factual claims originate in just this way — as answers to previous claims. Second, the authors, both physicians at a large medical center, apparently have expert knowledge of the scientific data they report. Third, the effects of cocaine use are precisely and vividly described. It is, in fact, these specific references to the damage done to heart and blood vessels that make the claim particularly convincing. Finally, the authors make this claim in order to promote a change in our attitudes toward the use of cocaine; they do not call on their readers to abstain from cocaine. This use of a factual claim as a first step in calling for changes in attitude and behavior is a familiar and often effective argumentative strategy.

CLAIMS OF VALUE

Unlike claims of fact, which attempt to prove that something is true and which can be validated by reference to the data, claims of value make a judgment. They express approval or disapproval. They attempt to prove that some action, belief, or condition is right or wrong, good or bad, beautiful or ugly, worthwhile or undesirable.

CLAIM: Democracy is superior to any other form of government.

CLAIM: Killing animals for sport is wrong.

CLAIM: The Sam Rayburn Building in Washington is an aesthetic failure.

Some claims of value are simply expressions of tastes, likes and dislikes, or preferences and prejudices. The Latin proverb "De gustibus non est disputandum" states that we cannot dispute about tastes. Suppose you express a preference for chocolate over vanilla. If your listener should ask why you prefer this flavor, you cannot refer to an outside authority or produce data or appeal to her moral sense to convince her that your preference is justified.

Many claims of value, however, can be defended or attacked on the basis of standards that measure the worth of an action, a belief, or an object. As far as possible, our personal likes and dislikes should be supported by reference to these standards. Value judgments occur in any area of human experience, but whatever the area, the analysis will be the same. We ask the arguer who is defending a claim of value: *What are the standards or criteria for deciding that this action, this belief, or this object is good or bad, beautiful or ugly, desirable or undesirable? Does the thing you are defending fulfill these criteria?*

There are two general areas in which people often disagree about matters of value: aesthetics and morality. They are also the areas that offer the greatest challenge to the writer. What follows is a discussion of some of the elements of analysis that you should consider in defending a claim of value in these areas.

Aesthetics is the study of beauty and the fine arts. Controversies over works of art — the aesthetic value of books, paintings, sculpture, architecture, dance, drama, and movies — rage fiercely among experts and laypeople alike. They may disagree on the standards for judging or, even if they agree, may disagree about how successfully the art object under discussion has met these standards.

Consider a discussion about popular music. Hearing someone praise the singing of a well-known vocalist, Sheila Jordan, you might ask why she is so highly regarded. You expect Jordan's fan to say more than "I like her" or "Man, she's great." You expect the fan to give reasons to support his claim. "She's unique," he says. He shows you a short review from a widely read newspaper that says, "Her singing is filled with fascinating phrasings, twists, and turns, and she's been compared with Billie Holiday for her emotional intensity. . . . She can be so heart-wrenching that conversations stop cold." Her fan agrees with the criteria for judging a singer given by the author of the review: uniqueness, fascinating phrasings, emotional intensity.

You may not agree that these are the only standards or even the significant ones for judging a singer. But the establishment of standards itself offers material for a discussion or an argument. You may argue about the relevance of the criteria, or, agreeing on the criteria, you may argue about the success of the singer in meeting them. Perhaps you prefer cool singers to intense ones. Or, even if you choose intensity over coolness, you may not think Sheila Jordan can be described as "expressive." Moreover, in any arguments about criteria, differences in experience and preparation acquire importance. You would probably take for granted that a writer with formal musical training who has listened carefully to dozens of singers over a period of years, who has read a good deal of musical criticism and discussed musical matters with other knowledgeable people would be a more reliable critic than someone who lacked these qualifications.

It is probably not surprising then, that, despite wide differences in taste, professional critics more often than not agree on criteria and whether an art object has met the criteria. For example, almost all movie critics agreed that *Citizen Kane* and *Gone with the Wind* were superior films. They also agreed that *Plan 9 from Outer Space,* a horror film, was terrible.

Value claims about morality express judgments about the rightness or wrongness of conduct or belief. Here disagreements are as wide and deep as in the arts. The first two examples on page 54 reveal how controversial such claims can be. Although you and your reader may share many values, among them a belief in democracy, a respect for learning, and a desire for peace, you may also disagree, even profoundly, about other values. The subject of divorce, for example, despite its prevalence in our society, can produce a conflict between differing moral standards. Some people may insist on adherence to absolute standards, arguing that the values they hold are based on immutable religious precepts derived from God and Scripture. Since marriage is sacred, divorce is always wrong, they say, whether or not the conditions of society change. Other people may argue that values are relative, based on the changing needs of societies in different places and at different times. Since marriage is an institution created by human beings at a particular time in history to serve particular social needs, they may say, it can also be dissolved when other social needs arise. The same conflicts between moral values might occur in discussions of abortion or suicide.

As a writer you cannot always know what system of values is held by your reader. Yet it might be possible to find a rule on which almost all readers agree. One such rule was expressed by the eighteenth-century German philosopher Immanuel Kant: "Man and, in general, every rational being exists as an end in itself and not merely as a means to be arbitrarily used by this or that will." Kant's prescription urges us not to subject any creature to a condition that it has not freely chosen. In other words, we cannot use other creatures, as in slavery, for our own purposes. (Some philosophers would extend this rule to the treatment of animals by human beings.) This standard of judgment has, in fact, been invoked in recent years against medical experimentation on human beings in prisons and hospitals without their consent and against the sterilization of poor or mentally defective women without their knowledge of the decision.

Nevertheless, even where there is agreement about standards for measuring behavior, you should be aware that a majority preference is not enough to confer moral value. If in a certain neighborhood a majority of heterosexual men decide to harass a few gay men and lesbians, that consensus does not make their action right. In formulating value claims, you should be prepared to ask and answer questions about the way in which your value claims and those of others have been arrived at. Lionel Ruby, an American philosopher, sums it up in these words: "The law of rationality tells us that we ought to justify our beliefs by evidence and reasons, instead of asserting them dogmatically."[3]

Of course, you will not always be able to persuade those with whom you argue that your values are superior to theirs and that they should therefore change their attitudes. Nor, on the other hand, would you want to compromise your values or pretend that they were different in order to win an argument. What you can and should do, however, as Lionel Ruby advises, is give *good reasons* why you think one thing is better than another. If as a child you asked why it was wrong to take your brother's toys, you might have been told by an exasperated parent, "Because I say so." Some adults still give such answers in defending their judgments, but such answers are not arguments and do nothing to win the agreement of others.

Defending a Claim of Value

The following suggestions are a preliminary guide to the defense of a value claim. (We discuss value claims further in Chapter 5.)

1. Try to make clear that the values or principles you are defending should have priority on any scale of values. Keep in mind that you and your readers may differ about their relative importance. For example, although your readers may agree with you that

---

[3]*The Art of Making Sense* (New York: Lippincott, 1968), p. 271.

brilliant photography is important in a film, they may think that a well-written script is even more crucial to its success. And although they may agree that freedom of the press is a mainstay of democracy, they may regard the right to privacy as even more fundamental.

2. Suggest that adherence to the values you are defending will bring about good results in some specific situation or bad results if respect for the values is ignored. You might argue, for example, that a belief in freedom of the press will make citizens better informed and the country stronger while a failure to protect this freedom will strengthen the forces of authoritarianism.

3. Since value terms are abstract, use examples and illustrations to clarify meanings and make distinctions. Comparisons and contrasts are especially helpful. If you are using the term *heroism*, can you provide examples to differentiate between *heroism* and *foolhardiness* or *exhibitionism?*

4. Use testimony of others to prove that knowledgeable or highly regarded people share your values.

SAMPLE ANALYSIS: CLAIM OF VALUE

Kids in the Mall: Growing Up Controlled

WILLIAM SEVERINI KOWINSKI

Butch heaved himself up and loomed over the group. "Like it was different for me," he piped. "My folks used to drop me off at the shopping mall every morning and leave me all day. It was like a big free baby-sitter, you know? One night they never came back for me. Maybe they moved away. Maybe there's some kind of a Bureau of Missing Parents I could check with."

— Richard Peck
Secrets of the Shopping Mall,
a novel for teenagers

From his sister at Swarthmore, I'd heard about a kid in Florida whose mother picked him up after school every day, drove him straight to the mall, and left him there until it closed — all at his in-

William Severini Kowinski is a free-lance writer who has been the book review editor and managing arts editor of the *Boston Phoenix.* This excerpt is from his book *The Malling of America: An Inside Look at the Great Consumer Paradise* (1985).

sistence. I'd heard about a boy in Washington who, when his family moved from one suburb to another, pedaled his bicycle five miles every day to get back to his old mall, where he once belonged.

These stories aren't unusual. The mall is a common experience for the majority of American youth; they have probably been going there all their lives. Some ran within their first large open space, saw their first fountain, bought their first toy, and read their first book in a mall. They may have smoked their first cigarette or first joint, or turned them down, had their first kiss or lost their virginity in the mall parking lot. Teenagers in America now spend more time in the mall than anywhere else but home and school. Mostly it is their choice, but some of that mall time is put in as the result of two-paycheck and single-parent households, and the lack of other viable alternatives. But are these kids being harmed by the mall?

I wondered first of all what difference it makes for adolescents to experience so many important moments in the mall. They are, after all, at play in the fields of its little world and they learn its ways; they adapt to it and make it adapt to them. It's here that these kids get their street sense, only it's mall sense. They are learning the ways of a large-scale, artificial environment; its subtleties and flexibilities, its particular pleasures and resonances, and the attitudes it fosters.

The presence of so many teenagers for so much time was not something mall developers planned on. In fact, it came as a big surprise. But kids became a fact of mall life very easily, and the International Council of Shopping Centers found it necessary to commission a study, which they published along with a guide to mall managers on how to handle the teenage incursion.

The study found that "teenagers in suburban centers are bored 5 and come to the shopping centers mainly as a place to go. Teenagers in suburban centers spent more time fighting, drinking, littering and walking than did their urban counterparts, but presented fewer overall problems." The report observed that "adolescents congregated in groups of two to four and predominantly at locations selected by them rather than management." This probably had something to do with the decision to install game arcades, which allow management to channel these restless adolescents into naturally contained areas away from major traffic points of adult shoppers.

The guide concluded that mall management should tolerate and even encourage the teenage presence because, in the words of the report, "The vast majority support the same set of values as does shopping center management." *The same set of values* means simply that mall kids are already preprogrammed to be consumers and that the mall can put the finishing touches to them as hard-core, lifelong shoppers just like everybody else. That, after all, is what the mall is about. So it shouldn't be surprising that in spending a lot of time there, adolescents find little that challenges the assumption that the goal of life is to make money and buy products, or that just about everything else in life is to be used to serve those ends.

Growing up in a high-consumption society already adds inestimable pressure to kids' lives. Clothes consciousness has invaded the grade schools, and popularity is linked with having the best, newest clothes in the currently acceptable styles. Even what they read has been affected. "Miss [Nancy] Drew wasn't obsessed with her wardrobe," noted the *Wall Street Journal*. "But today the mystery in teen fiction for girls is what outfit the heroine will wear next." Shopping has become a survival skill and there is certainly no better place to learn it than the mall, where its importance is powerfully reinforced and certainly never questioned.

The mall as a university of suburban materialism, where Valley Girls and Boys from coast to coast are educated in consumption, has its other lessons in this era of change in family life and sexual mores and their economic and social ramifications. The plethora of products in the mall, plus the pressure on teens to buy them, may contribute to the phenomenon that psychologist David Elkind calls "the hurried child": kids who are exposed to too much of the adult world too quickly and must respond with a sophistication that belies their still-tender emotional development. Certainly the adult products marketed for children — form-fitting designer jeans, sexy tops for preteen girls — add to the social pressure to look like an adult, along with the home-grown need to understand adult finances (why mothers must work) and adult emotions (when parents divorce).

Kids spend so much time at the mall partly because their parents allow it and even encourage it. The mall is safe, doesn't seem to harbor any unsavory activities, and there is adult supervision; it is, after all, a controlled environment. So the temptation, especially for working parents, is to let the mall be their baby-sitter. At least the kids aren't watching TV. But the mall's role as a surrogate mother may be more extensive and more profound.

Karen Lansky, a writer living in Los Angeles, has looked into the subject, and she told me some of her conclusions about the effects on its teenaged denizens of the mall's controlled and controlling environment. "Structure is the dominant idea, since true 'mall rats' lack just that in their home lives," she said, "and adolescents about to make the big leap into growing up crave more structure than our modern society cares to acknowledge." Karen pointed out some of the elements malls supply that kids used to get from their families, like warmth (Strawberry Shortcake dolls and similar cute and cuddly merchandise), old-fashioned mothering ("We do it all for you," the fast-food slogan), and even home cooking (the "homemade" treats at the food court).

The problem in all this, as Karen Lansky sees it, is that while families nurture children by encouraging growth through the assumption of responsibility and then by letting them rest in the bosom of the family from the rigors of growing up, the mall as a structural mother encourages passivity and consumption, as long as the kid doesn't make trouble. Therefore all they learn about becoming adults is how to act and how to consume.

Kids are in the mall not only in the passive role of shoppers — they also work there, especially as fast-food outlets infiltrate the mall's enclosure. There they learn how to hold a job and take responsibility, but still within the same value context. When *CBS Reports* went to Oak Park Mall in suburban Kansas City, Kansas, to tape part of their hour-long consideration of malls, "After the Dream Comes True," they interviewed a teenaged girl who worked in a fast-food outlet there. In a sequence that didn't make the final program, she described the major goal of her present life, which was to perfect the curl on top of the ice-cream cones that were her store's specialty. If she could do that, she would be moved from the lowly soft-drink dispenser to the more prestigious ice-cream division, the curl on top of the status ladder at her restaurant. These are the achievements that are important at the mall.

Other benefits of such jobs may also be overrated, according to Laurence D. Steinberg of the University of California at Irvine's social ecology department, who did a study on teenage employment. Their jobs, he found, are generally simple, mindlessly repetitive and boring. They don't really learn anything, and the jobs don't lead anywhere. Teenagers also work primarily with other teenagers; even their supervisors are often just a little older than they are. "Kids need to spend time with adults," Steinberg told me. "Although they get benefits from peer relationships, without parents and other adults it's one-side socialization. They hang out with each other, have age-segregated jobs, and watch TV."

Perhaps much of this is not so terrible or even so terribly different. Now that they have so much more to contend with in their lives, adolescents probably need more time to spend with other adolescents without adult impositions, just to sort things out. Though it is more concentrated in the mall (and therefore perhaps a clearer target), the value system there is really the dominant one of the whole society. Attitudes about curiosity, initiative, self-expression, empathy, and disinterested learning aren't necessarily made in the mall; they are mirrored there, perhaps a bit more intensely — as through a glass brightly.

Besides, the mall is not without its educational opportunities. 15
There are bookstores, where there is at least a short shelf of classics at great prices, and other books from which it is possible to learn more than how to do sit-ups. There are tools, from hammers to

VCRs, and products, from clothes to records, that can help the young find and express themselves. There are older people with stories, and places to be alone or to talk one-on-one with a kindred spirit. And there is always the passing show.

The mall itself may very well be an education about the future. I was struck with the realization, as early as my first forays into Greengate, that the mall is only one of a number of enclosed and controlled environments that are part of the lives of today's young. The mall is just an extension, say, of those large suburban schools — only there's Karmelkorn instead of chem lab, the ice rink instead of the gym: It's high school without the impertinence of classes.

Growing up, moving from home to school to the mall — from enclosure to enclosure, transported in cars — is a curiously continuous process, without much in the way of contrast or contact with unenclosed reality. Places must tend to blur into one another. But whatever differences and dangers there are in this, the skills these adolescents are learning may turn out to be useful in their later lives. For we seem to be moving inexorably into an age of preplanned and regulated environments, and this is the world they will inherit.

Still, it might be better if they had more of a choice. One teenaged girl confessed to *CBS Reports* that she sometimes felt she was missing something by hanging out at the mall so much. "But I'm here," she said, "and this is what I have."

Analysis

Kowinski has chosen to evaluate one aspect of an extraordinarily successful economic and cultural phenomenon — the commercial mall. He asks whether the influence of the mall on adolescents is good or bad. The answer seems to be a little of both. The good values may be described as exposure to a variety of experiences, a protective structure for adolescents who often live in unstable environments, and immersion in a world that may well serve as an introduction to adulthood. But the bad values, which Kowinski thinks are more influential (as the title suggests) are those of the shoppers' paradise, a society that believes in acquisition and consumption of goods as ultimate goals, and too much control over the choices available to adolescents. The tone of the judgment, however, is moderate and reflects a balanced, even scholarly, attitude. More than other arguments, the treatment of values requires such a voice, one which respects differences of opinion among readers. But serious doesn't mean heavy. His style is formal but highly readable, brightened by interesting examples and precise details. The opening paragraph is a strikingly effective lead.

Some of his observations are personal, but others are derived from studies by professional researchers, from *CBS Reports* to a well-known writer on childhood. These studies give weight and authority to his conclusions. Here and there we detect an appealing sympathy for the adolescents in their controlled environment.

Like any thoughtful social commentator, Kowinski casts a wide net. He sees the mall not only as a hangout for teens but as a good deal more, an institution that offers insights into family life and work, the changing urban culture, the nature of contemporary entertainment, even glimpses of a somewhat forbidding future.

CLAIMS OF POLICY

Claims of policy argue that certain conditions should exist. As the name suggests, they advocate adoption of policies or courses of action because problems have arisen that call for solution. Almost always *should* or *ought to* or *must* is expressed or implied in the claim.

CLAIM: Voluntary prayer should be permitted in public schools.

CLAIM: A dress code should be introduced for all public high schools.

CLAIM: A law should permit sixteen-year-olds and parents to "divorce" each other in cases of extreme incompatibility.

CLAIM: Mandatory jail terms should be imposed for drunk driving violations.

In defending such claims of policy you may find that you must first convince your audience that a problem exists. This will require that, as part of your longer argument, you make a factual claim, offering data to prove that present conditions are unsatisfactory. You may also find it necessary to refer to the values that support your claim. Then you will be ready to introduce your policy, to persuade your audience that the solution you propose will solve the problem.

We will examine a policy claim in which all these parts are at work. The claim can be stated as follows: "The time required for an undergraduate degree should be extended to five years." Immediate agreement with this policy among student readers would certainly not be universal. Some students would not recognize a problem. They would say, "The college curriculum we have now is fine. There's no need for a change. Besides, we don't want to spend more time in school." First, then, the arguer would have to persuade a skeptical audience that there is a problem, that four years of college are no longer enough because the stock of knowledge in almost all fields of study continues to increase. The arguer would provide data to show how many more choices in history, literature, and science students have now compared to the choices in the those fields a generation ago. She would also find it necessary to emphasize the value of greater knowledge and more schooling compared to the value of other goods the audience cherishes, such as earlier independence. Finally, the arguer would offer a plan for putting her policy into effect. Her plan would have to take into consideration initial psychological resistance, revision of the curriculum, the costs of more instruction, and the costs of lost production in the work force. Most important, she would point out the benefits for both individuals and society if this policy were adopted.

In this example, we assumed that the reader would disagree that a problem existed. In many cases, however, the reader may agree that there is a problem but disagree with the arguer about the way of solving it. Most of us, no doubt, will agree that we want to reduce or eliminate the following problems: misbehavior and vandalism in schools, drunk driving, crime on the streets, child abuse, pornography, pollution. But how shall we go about solving those problems? What public policy will give us well-behaved, diligent students who never destroy school property? Safe streets where no one is ever robbed or assaulted? Loving homes where no child is ever mistreated? Some members of society would choose to introduce rules or laws that punish infractions so severely that wrongdoers would be unwilling or unable to repeat their offenses. Other members of society would prefer policies that attempt to rehabilitate or reeducate offenders through training, therapy, counseling, and new opportunities.

Defending a Claim of Policy

The following steps will help you organize arguments for a claim of policy.

1. Make your proposal clear. The terms in the proposal should be precisely defined.
2. If necessary, establish that there is a need for a change. If changes have been ignored or resisted, there may be good or at least understandable reasons why this is so. (It is often wrongly assumed that people cling to cultural practices long after their significance and necessity have eroded. But rational human beings do not continue to observe practices unless those practices serve a purpose. The fact that you and I may see no value or purpose in the activities of another is irrelevant.)
3. Consider the opposing arguments. You may want to state the opposing arguments in a brief paragraph in order to answer them in the body of your argument.

4. Devote the major part of your essay to proving that your proposal is an answer to the opposing arguments and that there are distinct benefits for your readers in adopting your proposal.
5. Support your proposal with solid data, but don't neglect the moral considerations and the common-sense reasons, which may be even more persuasive.

SAMPLE ANALYSIS: CLAIM OF POLICY

The Real Victims
ALBERT SHANKER

It's increasingly clear that the biggest roadblock to improving the achievement of U.S. students is violence and disorder in our schools. Education reformers say we must set high standards for student achievement and create curriculums and assessments embodying these standards — and I agree with them. But high standards and excellent curriculums and assessments are not enough. Indeed, they will be worthless if students cannot learn because they are constantly afraid of being hit by a stray bullet or because their classes are dominated by disruptive students. This is just common sense.

A couple of weeks ago, *Washington Post* columnist Courtland Milloy told the story of a girl who had seen some classmates stab another student and was so terrified by the possibility of reprisals that she quit school ("An Education in Self-Help," January 29, 1995). This story has a relatively happy ending: The girl went on to earn a GED and is now attending college. But for every one who is motivated to continue her education the way this girl did, there are thousands and tens of thousands who are intimidated and distracted and are lost to school and learning.

Classroom disruption is more pervasive than school violence and just as fatal to learning. If there is one student in a class who constantly yells, curses out the teacher, and picks on other students who are trying to listen or participate in class, you can be sure that most of the teacher's time will not be devoted to helping the other youngsters learn math or science or English; it will be spent figuring out how to contain this student. And it does not take many

Albert Shanker was president of the American Federation of Teachers until his death in 1997. His weekly column, "Where We Stand," appeared in the *New York Times* Week in Review section for over twenty-five years. This column is from February 19, 1995.

such students to ruin the learning of the great majority of young-sters in a school.

School officials seem generally to be at a loss. In Washington, D.C., and elsewhere, students who have been caught bringing guns or drugs to school or who have hurt other students may simply be transferred to another school or suspended for a little while. There seems to be a high level of tolerance for this kind of behavior where there should be none. And when it comes to chronically disruptive students, we are even more tolerant. Little happens to kids who merely keep others from learning.

Parents are painfully aware of these problems. That's why both   5 African American and white parents put safe and orderly schools at the top of their list of things that would improve student achieve-ment. And that is undoubtedly why vouchers and tuition tax credits are so popular — especially among many parents of kids in inner-city schools. These parents are saying, "If your schools are so vio-lent and disorderly that our children can't learn — and are not even safe — let us put them in schools that won't tolerate kids who be-have that way."

Many education experts insist that our first responsibility is to the few violent and disruptive kids. They say these kids have the "right" to an education, and we need to keep them in class and in school so we can help them overcome their problems. But what about the "rights" of the twenty-five or thirty kids in every class who come to school ready to work? Why are we willing to threaten their safety and learning? I'm not advocating putting violent or disruptive kids out on the streets. We need alternative programs for these youngsters, but we also need to change a system that sacrifices the overwhelming majority of children for a handful — without even doing the handful any good.

Most children come to school believing that doing right matters, but they soon learn to question that belief. Say a youngster in kinder-garten does something that is way out of line — he knocks another kid down and kicks him. The other five-year-olds are sure something terrible is going to happen to this child, and they are very glad they're not in his place. Well, what happens? Probably the teacher gets in trouble for reporting the child. So the children's sense of jus-tice — their belief that acting naughty has consequences — begins to be eroded. The youngster who defied the teacher becomes the de facto leader of the class, and peer pressure now encourages the other children to ignore what the teacher tells them to do. At a very early age, kids are taught a bad lesson — nothing will happen if they break the rules — and whatever else they learn in English or math or science, this lesson remains consistent throughout school.

We have an irrational system, and it's no wonder that angry parents are calling for vouchers, tuition tax credits — anything that would allow them to get their kids out of schools where a few violent and disruptive kids call the shots. What this means, though, is that 98 percent of students would be leaving public schools to get away from the 2 percent. Wouldn't it make a lot more sense just to move the 2 percent?

Analysis

Shanker argues that disruptive students should be removed from their classes, but in only two places does he make the policy explicit, referring to "alternative programs" and moving "the 2 percent." Instead, he devotes almost the whole of his essay to proving that a policy to remove disruptive students is absolutely necessary. Even the title reveals the emphasis of the essay. The real victims are children who are prevented from learning by violence in the classroom, and it is their needs that must be addressed.

A reader can guess why Shanker adopts such a rhetorical strategy. Many policy claims require the arguer to first prove that a problem exists — in effect, establishing a claim of fact — and often this is the most important task. Since a policy that expels or removes students from a regular classroom, while not new, is still hotly debated, the advocate of such a policy must make a strong case for it. Shanker acknowledges the objections to his policy in paragraph 6 and answers them.

Shanker emphasizes two unfortunate consequences of a failure to adopt his policy recommendation. One is the cost imposed on children who want to learn and are prevented from doing so. Development of this idea begins in the second paragraph and occupies most of the essay. Its strength lies in its appeal to our sense of fairness. There is also an implicit appeal to fear. The withdrawal of children to safer, often private schools weakens the public school system. Shanker obviously believes that his readers will agree that public schools are worth saving.

The second consequence is more difficult to measure. It is the wrong moral lesson absorbed by children when they see that hurtful behavior goes unpunished. Although a psychological effect cannot easily be proved by numbers, unlike the exodus of children to private schools, most readers will recognize it as one common to their experience.

Despite the fact that we know little or nothing about the details of a removal policy, Shanker's argument suggests that, if the necessity for a change of policy is made sufficiently strong, the way for its adoption has been prepared.

The Landfill Excavations

WILLIAM L. RATHJE and CULLEN MURPHY

The Garbage Project began excavating landfills primarily for two reasons, both of them essentially archaeological in nature. One was to see if the data being gleaned from garbage fresh off the truck could be cross-validated by data from garbage in municipal landfills. The second, which derived from the Garbage Project's origins as an exercise in the study of formation processes, was to look into what happens to garbage after it has been interred. As it happens, the first landfill excavation got under way, in 1987, just as it was becoming clear — from persistent reports about garbage in the press that were at variance with some of the things the Garbage Project had been learning — that an adequate knowledge base about landfills and their contents did not exist. It was during this period that news of a mounting garbage crisis broke into the national consciousness. And it was during this period that two assertions were given wide currency and achieved a status as accepted fact from which they have yet to be dislodged. One is that accelerating rates of garbage generation are responsible for the rapid depletion and present shortage of landfills. The other is that, nationwide, there are few good places left to put new landfills. Whether these propositions are true or false — they happen, for the most part, to be exaggerations — it was certainly the case that however quickly landfills were being filled, the public, the press, and even most specialists had only the vaguest idea (at best) of what they were being filled up *with*. Yes, think tanks and consulting firms have done some calculations and come up with estimates of garbage quantities by commodity, based on national production figures and assumptions about rates of discard. But until 1987, when the Garbage Project's archaeologists began systematically sorting through the evidence from bucket-auger wells, no one had ever deliberately dug into landfills with a view to recording the inner reality in minute detail. . . .

One key aim of the landfill excavations was to get some idea of the volume occupied by various kinds of garbage in landfills. Although many Garbage Project studies have relied on garbage weight for comparative purposes, volume is the critical variable when it

---

William L. Rathje is a professor of anthropology at the University of Arizona, where he heads the Garbage Project. Cullen Murphy is managing editor of the *Atlantic Monthly*. This excerpt is from their book *Rubbish! The Archeology of Garbage* (1992).

comes to landfill management: Landfills close not because they are too heavy but because they are too full. And yet reliable data on the volume taken up by plastics, paper, organic material, and other kinds of garbage once it has been deposited in a landfill did not exist in 1987. The Garbage Project set out to fill the gap, applying its usual sorting and weighing procedures to excavated garbage, and then adding a final step: a volume measurement. Measuring volume was not a completely straightforward process. Because most garbage tends to puff up with air once it has been extracted from deep inside a landfill, all of the garbage exhumed was subjected to compaction, so that the data on garbage volume would reflect the volume that garbage occupies when it is squashed and under pressure inside a landfill. The compactor used by the Garbage Project is a thirty-gallon cannister with a hydraulic piston that squeezes out air from plastic bags, newspapers, cereal boxes, mowed grass, hot dogs, and everything else at a relatively gentle pressure of 0.9 pounds per square inch. The data on garbage volume that emerged from the Garbage Project's landfill excavations were the first such data in existence.

What do the numbers reveal? Briefly, that the kinds of garbage that loom largest in the popular imagination as the chief villains in the filling up and closing down of landfills — fast-food packaging, expanded polystyrene foam (the material that coffee cups are made from), and disposable diapers, to name three on many people's most-unwanted list — do not deserve the blame they have received. They may be highly visible as litter, but they are not responsible for an inordinate contribution to landfill garbage. The same goes for plastics. But one kind of garbage whose reputation has thus far been largely unbesmirched — plain old paper — merits increased attention.

Over the years, Garbage Project representatives have asked a variety of people who have never seen the inside of a landfill to estimate what percentage of a landfill's contents is made up of fast-food packaging, expanded polystyrene foam, and disposable diapers. In September of 1989, for example, this very question was asked of a group attending the biennial meeting of the National Audubon Society, and the results were generally consistent with those obtained from surveys conducted at universities, at business meetings, and at conferences of state and local government officials: Estimates at the Audubon meeting of the volume of fast-food packaging fell mainly between 20 and 30 percent of a typical landfill's contents; of expanded polystyrene foam, between 25 and 40 percent; and of disposable diapers, between 25 and 45 percent. The overall estimate, then, of the proportion of a landfill's volume that is taken up by fast-food packaging, foam in general, and disposable diapers ranged from a suspiciously high 70 percent to an obviously impossible 125 percent.

Needless to say, fast-food packaging has few friends. It is de- 5
signed to be bright, those bold reds and yellows being among the
most attention-getting colors on a marketer's palette; this, coupled
with the propensity of human beings to litter, means that fast-food
packaging gets noticed. It is also greasy and smelly, and on some
level it seems to symbolize, as do fast-food restaurants themselves,
certain attributes of modern America to which modern Americans
remain imperfectly reconciled. But is there really all that much
fast-food packaging? Is it "straining" the capacity of America's landfills, as a 1988 editorial in the *New York Times* contended?

The physical reality inside a landfill is, in fact, quite different
from the picture painted by many commentators. Of the more than
fourteen tons of garbage from landfills that the Garbage Project has
sorted, fewer than a hundred pounds was found to consist of
fast-food packaging of any kind — that is, containers or wrappers
for hamburgers, pizzas, chicken, fish, and convenience-store sandwiches, plus all the accessories, such as cups, lids, straws, sauce
containers, and so on, plus all the boxes and bags used to deliver
food and other raw materials to the fast-food restaurant. In other
words, less than one-half of 1 percent of the weight of the materials
excavated from nine municipal landfills over a period of five years
(1985–89) consisted of fast-food packaging. As for the amount of
space that fast-food packaging takes up in landfills — a more important indicator than weight — the Garbage Project estimate after
sorting is that it accounts for no more than one-third of 1 percent of
the total volume of a landfill's contents.

What about expanded polystyrene foam — the substance that
most people are referring to when they say Styrofoam (which is a
registered trademark of the Dow Chemical Corporation, and is baby
blue in color and used chiefly to insulate buildings)? Expanding polystyrene foam is, of course, used for many things. Only about 10 percent of all foam plastics that were manufactured in the period
1980–83 were used for fast-food packaging. Most foam was (and is)
blown into egg cartons, meat trays, coffee cups (the fast-food kind,
yes, but mainly the plain kind that sit stacked upside down beside
the office coffee pot), "peanuts" for packing, and the molded forms
that protect electronic appliances in their shipping cases. All the expanded polystyrene foam that is thrown away in America every
year, from the lowliest packing peanut to the most sophisticated
molded carton, accounts for no more than 1 percent of the volume
of garbage landfilled between 1980 and 1989.

Expanded polystyrene foam has been the focus of many vocal
campaigns around the country to ban it outright. It is worth remembering that if foam were banned, the relatively small amount of space
that it takes up in landfills would not be saved. Eggs, hamburgers, coffee, and stereos must still be put in *something*. The most likely re-

placement for foam is some form of coated cardboard, which can be difficult to recycle and takes up almost as much room as foam in a landfill. Indeed, in cases where cardboard replaced foam, it could often happen that a larger volume of cardboard would be needed to fulfill the same function fulfilled by a smaller volume of foam. No one burns fingers holding a foam cup filled with coffee, because the foam's insulating qualities are so effective. But people burn their fingers so frequently with plastic- or wax-coated cardboard coffee cups (and all cardboard hot-drink cups are coated) that they often put one such cup inside another for the added protection.

As for disposable diapers, the debate over their potential impact on the environment is sufficiently vociferous and complex to warrant its own chapter. . . . Suffice it to say for present purposes, though, that the pattern displayed by fast-food packaging and expanded polystyrene foam is apparent with respect to diapers, too. People *think* that disposable diapers are a big part of the garbage problem; they are not a very significant factor at all.

The three garbage categories that, as we saw, the Audubon respondents believed accounted for 70 to 125 percent of all garbage actually account, together, for only about 3 percent. The survey responses would probably have been even more skewed if respondents had also been asked to guess the proportion of a typical landfill's contents that is made up of plastic. Plastic is surrounded by a maelstrom of mythology; into the very word Americans seem to have distilled all of their guilt over the environmental degradation they have wrought and the culture of consumption they invented and inhabit. Plastic has become an object of scorn — who can forget the famous scene in *The Graduate* (or quote it properly)? — no doubt in large measure because its development corresponded chronologically with, and then powerfully reinforced, the emergence of the very consumerist ethic that is now despised. (What Mr. McGuire, a neighbor, says to Benjamin Braddock is: "I just want to say one word to you. Just one word. Are you listening? . . . Plastics. There is a great future in plastics. Think about it.") Plastic is the Great Satan of garbage. It is the apotheosis of the cheap, the inauthentic; even the attempts to replace or transform plastic — such as the recent ill-fated experiments with "biodegradable" plastic . . . — seem somehow inauthentic. . . .

[But] in landfill after landfill the volume of all plastics — foam, film, and rigid; toys, utensils, and packages — from the 1980s amounted to between 20 and 24 percent of all garbage, as sorted; when compacted along with everything else, in order to replicate actual conditions inside a landfill, the volume of plastics was reduced to under 16 percent.

Even if its share of total garbage is, at the moment, relatively low, is it not the case that plastics take up a larger proportion of landfill space with every passing year? Unquestionably a larger number of physical objects are made of plastic today than were in 1970 or 1950. But a curious phenomenon becomes apparent when garbage deposits from our own time are compared with those from strata characteristic of, say, the 1970s. While the number of individual plastic objects to be found in a deposit of garbage of a constant size has increased considerably in the course of a decade and a half — more than doubling — the proportion of landfill space taken up by these plastics has not changed; at some landfills, the proportion of space taken up by plastics was actually a little less in the 1980s than it was in the 1970s.

The explanation appears to be a strategy that is known in the plastics industry as "light-weighting" — making objects in such a way that the objects retain all the necessary functional characteristics but require the use of less resin. The concept of light-weighting is not limited to the making of plastics; the makers of glass bottles have been light-weighting their wares for decades, with the result that bottles today are 25 percent lighter than they were in 1984. (That is why bottles in landfills are likely to show up broken in the upper, more-recent, strata, whereas lower strata, holding garbage from many years ago, contain many more whole bottles.) Environmentalists might hail light-weighting as an example of source reduction. Businessmen embrace it for a different reason: sheer profit. Using fewer raw materials for a product that is lighter and therefore cheaper to transport usually translates into a competitive edge, and companies that rely heavily on plastics have been light-weighting ever since plastics were introduced. PET soda bottles had a weight of 67 grams in 1974; the weight today is 48 grams, for a reduction of 30 percent. High-density polyethylene (HDPE) milk jugs in the mid-1960s had a weight of 120 grams; the weight today is about 65 grams, for reduction of more than 45 percent. Plastic grocery bags had a thickness of 30 microns in 1976; the thickness today is at most 18 microns, for a reduction of 40 percent. Even the plastic in disposable diapers has been light-weighted, although the superabsorbent material that was added at the same time (1986) ensures that even if diapers enter the house lighter they will leave it heavier than ever. When plastic gets lighter, in most cases it also gets thinner and more crushable. The result, of course, is that many more plastic items can be squeezed into a given volume of landfill space today than could have been squeezed into it ten or twenty years ago.

This fact has frequently been met with skepticism. In 1989, Robert Krulwich, of the CBS network's *Saturday Night with Connie Chung* program, conducted a tour of the Garbage Project's operations in Tucson, and he expressed surprise when told about the light-weighting of plastics. He asked for a crushed PET soda bottle from 1989 and tried to blow it up. The light plastic container inflated easily. He was then given a crushed PET soda bottle found in a stratum dating back to 1981 — a bottle whose plastic would be considerably thicker and stiffer. Try as he might, Krulwich could not make the flattened container inflate.

Reading and Discussion Questions

1. The paragraphs in this excerpt are rather long, but while some can be divided into two or more paragraphs, others cannot. Paragraph 1, for example, can be divided. Where might it be appropriate to make a cut without violating coherence? Paragraph 2, on the other hand, seems to resist cutting. Why? Can you divide paragraph 13? Why or why not?

2. What reasons do the authors give for the importance of the Garbage Project? Do their findings seem to justify their "archeological" research?

3. Some factual claims imply a need for changes in behavior. (See the analysis of "Cocaine Is Even Deadlier Than We Thought," p. 52.) Is there any evidence that Rathje and Murphy are interested in influencing behavior?

4. How do they account for the erroneous information held by the public? Does this information reflect certain values or prejudices? Were some of your own views overturned by the authors' conclusions?

Writing Suggestions

5. Describe any changes you or your family might make in your purchases and methods of disposal as a result of reading "The Landfill Excavations." Explain how these changes would affect your life. Would they impose a hardship? If you are not persuaded to make any changes, explain why.

6. Choose another garbage or litter "problem" — one from your own experience or one you have read about — and provide the data to prove that it is or is not a problem. Newspapers and news magazines are one source of information, but remember that expert minority views may be overlooked and unreported. Like the authors of "The Landfill Excavations," select relevant statistics and examples with human interest, wherever possible.

Starving Children

FRANCINE DU PLESSIX GRAY

In the movie *Kids*, a band of teenagers forages for sex, drugs, and booze on New York City streets. The cruelty of these adolescents who taunt gay men and beat up random passersby, the callousness with which they call their girlfriends "bitches" as they paw them into submission, the subhuman grunts and epithets of their speech make the mind reel. I'm still haunted by the shot at the end of the film of their bodies sprawled over one another, like youths brought in for a Roman emperor's debauch, on the floor of a spacious Manhattan apartment. I keep recalling the remains of their daily fodder — liquor bottles and discarded joints, tacos, burritos drenched in pools of salsa — that litter the site of their orgy. It is that last detail, suggesting their feral, boorishly gulped diet, that somehow comes to mind when one of the film's characters wakes up from his all-night bender in a Manhattan apartment filled with leather furniture and abstract art, looks straight at the camera, and asks, "What happened?"

What has happened to the American family — the fraying effect of harassed working parents, the stranglehold of the media, the pressures of peer culture — is a theme much ranted about. Yet one aspect of what has happened has been overlooked: Kids like those we see in *Kids* — they come from all over the social spectrum — never seem to sit down to a proper meal at home anymore. This is not another pious harangue on "spiritual starvation"; this is about the fact that we may be witnessing the first generation in history that has not been required to participate in that primal rite of socialization, the family meal. The family meal is not only the core curriculum in the school of civilized discourse; it is also a set of protocols that curb our natural savagery and our animal greed, and cultivate a capacity for sharing and thoughtfulness.

Dinner rituals have nothing to do with class, or working women's busy lives, or any particular family structure. I've had dinners of boiled potatoes with families in Siberia, suppers of deli cold cuts with single welfare mothers in Chicago, bowls of watery gruel in the Sahara — all made memorable by the grace with which they were offered and by the sight of youngsters learning through experience the art of human companionship. The teenagers on display in *Kids* are not only physically starved — devitaminized, made hyper-

---

This essay by Francine du Plessix Gray, a journalist and novelist, appeared in *The New Yorker* on October 16, 1995.

active — by the junk food they consume as they slouch in front of the TV or lope toward their next bacchanal. Far worse, they are deprived of the main course of civilized life — the practice of sitting down at the dinner table and observing the attendant conventions. Like the Passover seder or the Communion bread, the ritual of nutrition helps to imbue families, and societies at large, with greater empathy and fellowship. However, all rituals involve, to some degree, a sacrifice, and the home meal requires genuine sacrifices of time and energy, large expenditures of those very traits it nurtures — patience, compassion, self-discipline.

Many of the teenagers in *Kids* — the more affluent ones — are the offspring of the "me generation," members of what Christopher Lasch called "the culture of narcissism." And those parents may be the most at fault. Might it be that they have stinted on the socializing of their children by focusing on their own rituals of self-improvement — enjoying their workout highs at health clubs or their learning highs in evening classes? How much more fun it is, how much less tiring, for us to enjoy a fine, quiet dinner by ourselves, or with our buddies, without the litany of questions and corrections that youngsters' company entails. But the family meal should continue to be a ceremonial, sacred time. If we don't hold on to it, we risk rearing yet more kids who wake up asking "What happened?"

Reading and Discussion Questions

1. Contrary to what Gray seems to suggest, the movie *Kids* is a fiction film, not a documentary, and the characters are actors. Does knowledge of this fact influence your appreciation of the author's argument?
2. The essay is only four paragraphs long, although it tackles a big subject. If you were asked to make this essay longer, what parts would you choose to develop?
3. In paragraphs 1 and 3, Gray offers details and examples to support her larger points. Should the essay have more of this kind of evidence?
4. How does Gray define "socialization"? Does she emphasize particular aspects of the definition?
5. Gray is a novelist and a splendid stylist. Point out places where she uses transitions, sentence variety, and other devices to embellish her prose and clarify ideas.

Writing Suggestions

6. Do the family meals you're familiar with resemble rituals that "imbue families . . . with greater empathy and fellowship"? Explain what the family meal means to you. If it has changed over time, explain why and how it has affected you. Or discuss a holiday meal — at Thanksgiving or Christmas — and what it means or should mean for you and your family.

7. One criticism of this essay might be that Gray imputes far too much importance to the family meal. Can you suggest other remedies for the alienation of these kids? Given the length of the essay you will write, the remedies should be modest. Perhaps you know of children who have been rescued from nightmarish lives. How did it happen?

Green Eggs & Ham
THE WALL STREET JOURNAL

To paraphrase Dr. Seuss, "I do like gambling, Sam-I-Am, I really like it, and I can. For I can do it in a plane, on a boat, at the track, and in the rain. I can do it in a casino, with the lottery, or with Keno." In a plane? Not quite yet, but the latest proposal is to equip airline seats with a video terminal that can eat credit cards and bankrupt you while you're still belted in, which is in many ways the opposite of what happens to a Strasbourg goose.

Some estimates suggest that gambling revenues are higher than the defense budget, and they are now poised to take a leap to the next energy level as technology threatens to bring casinos to every home and conveyance. Mayor Daley of Chicago is backing "gaming executives" who want to build a 100-acre $2 billion palace of sin in what the AP [Associated Press] calls "downtown" Chicago: Finding a 100-acre site in downtown Chicago will be only the first problem. Riverboat gambling is back on the Mississippi, and Indians are opening casinos all over the West. Thirty-three states have fallen to the lottery and more are on the way. And then there are pull-tabs; blackjack; OTB [off-track betting]; bingo; numbers; video poker; horse, dog, and insect racing (in bars); Reno; Las Vegas; Atlantic City; and Ed McMahon, the classic figure of trust, who periodically announces to every household in America that if it has won $10 million it has won $10 million. (Thank you, Ed.)

Other than littering the desert with immense, metastasized replicas of Port Said bordellos, gambling creates nothing. It reallocates resources from the desperate and the needful to the unspeakable and the inane. It, like the British royal family, is the worst possible model for the poor, being the polar opposite of thrift, discipline, hard work, and ingenuity. It violates every standard, all common sense, and every sensible equation, from ancient religious edicts to the laws of thermodynamics (at least figuratively), and it runs with almost every other form of crime and corruption.

This editorial is from the April 27, 1992, edition of the *Wall Street Journal.*

Are we for it because we favor free markets? No, in the same way that we do not favor a free market for recreational drugs, legalized prostitution, or, for that matter, the unrestricted sale of nuclear weapons. The West long ago identified gambling as a sin not because it violates some mystical equilibrium, although it does, but because it, like drunkenness or (as one might now say) spouse-beating, is destructive to society. Among other things, it is the Arnold Schwarzenegger of regressive taxation. And lotteries don't actually pay much to education, which has little to do with money anyway.

In America we once dealt wisely with gambling by isolating it in   5
the middle of a desert surrounded by unexploded practice munitions. This allowed the hardest cases to get to the roulette wheels and served as a safety valve for the ill-effects of absolutism. Now, however, the thing is spreading, and government is the sponsor. But when government substitutes gambling for taxation it relinquishes its moral authority. To the argument that if government does not play, others will, we say, in that case why not have [then New York state governor] Mario Cuomo rob jewelry stores?

Although you'd hardly know it from observing our elected officials, government's job is to resist and suppress that which is immoral and destructive, not to form a partnership with it. We would like to hear from the presidential candidates on this subject, for gambling is now almost everywhere, and has achieved a terrible hold on a people raised to think that lunch can be free.

Reading and Discussion Questions

1. Did you find any of the references to people, places, and activities unfamiliar? If so, did they prevent you from following the argument? Explain how you would go about finding out what these references mean.
2. At what point in the essay did you recognize the attitude of the writer toward gambling? Explain.
3. Why is gambling authorized or sponsored by the government more pernicious than gambling by private enterprise?
4. In the last paragraph the author summarizes his or her objections to gambling as "immoral and destructive." What is immoral about gambling? Why is it destructive?
5. The author at one point seems to advocate a solution to the gambling problem. Would that solution be workable today? Why or why not?

Writing Suggestions

6. Because gambling is widespread among all classes in the United States — and in many other societies — its appeal must be strong and universal. Some observers think it is an addiction. What is the appeal? Use your own experience as a gambler or your acquaintance with gam-

blers as well as the opinions of psychologists and other experts to explain it.

7. Find evidence from advocates of gambling to justify government sponsorship, especially in state lotteries.

8. Gambling is said to be common on college campuses. What kinds of gambling do college students engage in? Does gambling serve a useful purpose? Is it harmful in any way?

A Liberalism of Heart and Spine

HENRY LOUIS GATES, JR.

Gunmen burst into a Bahai church in a South African township, line up the few white (Iranian) members of the congregation and shoot them dead. The Bahai religion holds that all races are one, and the Azanian People's Liberation Army, which apparently dispatched the killers, explained that it wanted to send a clear message against the mixing of races.

In fact, the Azanian movement has been profoundly shaped by European racial thinking, as you might expect of a group that borrows its name from an invented place of barbarism in Evelyn Waugh's satiric novel *Black Mischief*. The truth is, the Azanians' abjuration of "race mixing" has nothing to do with indigenous local traditions and everything to do with the logic of apartheid.

"One million Arabs are not worth a Jewish fingernail," Rabbi Yaacov Perrin said in a funeral eulogy for Dr. Baruch Goldstein before a thousand sympathizers. The phrase reflects a perverse misreading of a passage from Exodus. But we have heard this voice before. It is the voice of messianic hatred. We hear it from the Balkans to the Bantustans; we hear it from Hezbollah and from Kach. We hear it in the streets of Bensonhurst.

And, of course, we hear it from some who profess to be addressing the misery of black America. "Never will I say I am not an anti-Semite," said Khalid Abdul Muhammad of the Nation of Islam. "I pray that God will kill my enemy and take him off the face of the planet Earth." He is peddling tape recordings of his speeches under the suggestive title "No Love for the Other Side."

And so it goes, with the victimized bidding to be victimizers. 5 That suffering ennobles is a lie, an old lie that has been exposed countless times, yet has proved surprisingly durable.

Henry Louis Gates, Jr., is chairman of the Afro-American Studies Department at Harvard University. This article appeared in the *New York Times* on March 27, 1994.

Messianic hatred is scarcely the province of the privileged classes. David Duke draws his support from the least affluent and most anxious of white Southerners. Similarly, if calculating demagogues find inviting prey in black America, our immediate circumstances make this unsurprising. That nearly half of African American children live in poverty is one scandal; another is simply that this fact has become an acceptable feature of our social landscape, as unremarkable as crab grass. No love for the other side?

Yet if profoundly antimodern creeds like these continue to grow, perhaps liberalism — that political tradition of individual liberty that harks back at least to the Enlightenment — must shoulder some blame.

For too long, liberalism has grown accustomed to recusing itself from other people's problems. Genital mutilation in Africa? Don't ask us to arbitrate among the mores of other cultures. Human rights abuses in China? Are we really in a position to judge? Deference to the autonomy of other beliefs, other values, other cultures has become an easy alibi for moral isolationism. When we need action, we get hand-wringing. When we need forthrightness, we get equivocation.

What we have is a rhetoric of relativism. But let's call such "moral relativism" by its real name: moral indifference. And let's admit how finite are our vaunted moral sympathies, here in the comfortable West.

According to recent reports, perhaps 100,000 people have died 10 in recent ethnic conflicts that have raged through tiny Burundi. Could any type of intervention have helped? Maybe not. But that isn't the point. The point is that nobody is asking. Not enough love for the other side. Meanwhile, the tragedy of Bosnia took on the look of the Kitty Genovese syndrome on a global scale.

We need a liberalism that has confidence in its own insights, a liberalism possessed of clarity as well as compassion. To creeds that prate of sacred fingernails, as the rabbi did, of "no love for the other side," of the sins of mixing ethnic or racial categories, we must juxtapose a muscular humanism. A humanism that is without arrogance and is unafraid to assert itself, its hard-won moral knowledge. One that neither shuns religious devotion nor mistakes itself for a religion. One that has courage as well as conviction.

There is something of a paradox here. The most heinous of deeds have always been committed in the name of future generations, of an awaiting utopia. The nature of these evils could not be concealed if they were committed in the name of our own interests in the here and now, but utopianism wraps them in the garb of virtuous "sacrifice." Accordingly, it is its stoutly anti-utopian aspect — its capacity for self-doubt — that liberalism has claimed as a moral advantage.

But the capacity to entertain uncertainly needn't entail Hamlet-like paralysis. It merely promotes a willingness to revise our beliefs in the light of experience, to extend respect to those we do not agree with. Is it, after all, unreasonable to be suspicious of Westerners who are exercised over female circumcision but whose eyes glaze over when the same women are merely facing starvation?

The Azanian, the West Bank fanatic, the American demagogue march to a single drum. There has been much talk about the politics of identity — a politics that has a collective identity as its core. One is to assert oneself in the political arena as a woman, a homosexual, a Jew, a person of color.

But while the conversation about it may seem recent, the phe- 15 nomenon itself is age-old. The politics of identity starts with the assertion of a collective allegiance. It says: This is who we are, make room for us, accommodate our special needs, confer recognition upon what is distinctive about us. It is about the priority of difference, and while it is not, by itself, undesirable, it is — by itself — dangerously inadequate.

By contrast, what I'm calling humanism starts not with the possession of identity, but with the capacity to *identify with*. It asks what we have in common with others, while acknowledging the diversity among ourselves. It is about the promise of a shared humanity.

In short, the challenge is to move from a politics of identity to a politics of identification. It was this conversion that Malcolm X underwent toward the end of his life. If Minister Farrakhan, a brilliant, charismatic man, undergoes a similar conversion, he will earn a place in the annals of our time. If not, he will just be another in a long line of racial demagogues, joining Father Coughlin, Gerald L. K. Smith, and the like.

A politics of identification doesn't enjoin us to ignore or devalue our collective identities. For it's only by exploring the multiplicity of human life in culture that we can come to terms with the commonalities that cement communitas. It is only by this route that we can move a little closer to what the poet Robert Hayden, himself a Bahai, conjured up when he urged us to "renew the vision of a human world where godliness / is possible and man / is neither god, nigger, honky, wop, nor kike / but man / permitted to be man." We may be anti-utopian, but we have dreams, too.

Reading and Discussion Questions

1. Make sure that you understand several terms in this essay that carry important ideas: relativism, messianic, humanism, liberalism, utopianism, Hamlet-like paralysis, Kitty Genovese syndrome. Were any of these terms clear from the context, or was it necessary to look them up?

   There are also references to people, groups, and places in the news: Hezbollah, Bantustans, Burundi, Bosnia, Nation of Islam, Malcolm X,

Louis Farrakhan, Father Coughlin, Gerald L. K. Smith. While it isn't necessary to know a great deal about these persons and places in order to
understand what Gates is trying to prove, knowing *something* about
them will deepen your understanding of his essay and other articles
and essays that refer to the same things.

2. Most of us can probably guess what "a liberalism of heart" means, but
   what is "a liberalism of spine"? Where does Gates explain it?

3. How can utopianism promote evil deeds? If you can, find examples from
   history to explain your answer.

4. What is the difference between the politics of identity and the politics
   of identification? Tell why Gates favors one over another.

Writing Suggestions

5. Gates denounces moral indifference. (See paragraphs 8 and 9.) Do you
   think that you are justified in condemning a custom practiced by members of another culture? You have read about such cases in the news.
   Cock-fighting is one example. Another more serious example is child
   marriage and pregnancy. (Such a case surfaced recently in Texas, concerning a couple who were living together. The male, an adult, and the
   female, a thirteen-year-old who was pregnant, were separated by the
   court, and the male was charged with violation of Texas laws. The
   couple was from a rural community in Mexico which sanctioned their
   relationship.) Choose a practice that you disapprove of and tell why
   you would or would not move to have it abolished. Make clear what
   principles would govern your decision.

6. How does religion serve either to include or to exclude other people?
   Notice that Gates makes reference to religions and religious leaders.
   This is a very large subject. Restrict your argument to development of
   one or two ideas in a religion you are familiar with.

The Right to Bear Arms
WARREN E. BURGER

Our metropolitan centers, and some suburban communities of
America, are setting new records for homicides by handguns. Many
of our large centers have up to ten times the murder rate of all of
Western Europe. In 1988, there were 9,000 handgun murders in
America. Last year, Washington, D.C., alone had more than 400
homicides — setting a new record for our capital.

The Constitution of the United States, in its Second Amendment,
guarantees a "right of the people to keep and bear arms." However,

Warren E. Burger (1907–1995) was chief justice of the United States from 1969 to
1986. This article is from the January 14, 1990, issue of *Parade* magazine.

the meaning of this clause cannot be understood except by looking to the purpose, the setting, and the objectives of the draftsmen. The first ten amendments — the Bill of Rights — were not drafted at Philadelphia in 1787; that document came two years later than the Constitution. Most of the states already had bills of rights, but the Constitution might not have been ratified in 1788 if the states had not had assurances that a national Bill of Rights would soon be added.

People of that day were apprehensive about the new "monster" national government presented to them, and this helps explain the language and purpose of the Second Amendment. A few lines after the First Amendment's guarantees — against "establishment of religion," "free exercise" of religion, free speech and free press — came a guarantee that grew out of the deep-seated fear of a "national" or "standing" army. The same First Congress that approved the right to keep and bear arms also limited the national army to 840 men; Congress in the Second Amendment then provided:

> A well regulated Militia, being necessary to the security of a free State, the right of the people to keep and bear Arms, shall not be infringed.

In the 1789 debate in Congress on James Madison's proposed Bill of Rights, Elbridge Gerry argued that a state militia was necessary:

> to prevent the establishment of a standing army, the bane of liberty. . . . Whenever governments mean to invade the rights and liberties of the people, they always attempt to destroy the militia in order to raise an army upon their ruins.

We see that the need for a state militia was the predicate of the "right" guaranteed; in short, it was declared "necessary" in order to have a state military force to protect the security of the state. That Second Amendment clause must be read as though the word "because" was the opening word of the guarantee. Today, of course, the "state militia" serves a very different purpose. A huge national defense establishment has taken over the role of the militia of 200 years ago.

Some have exploited these ancient concerns, blurring sporting guns — rifles, shotguns, and even machine pistols — with all firearms, including what are now called "Saturday night specials." There is, of course, a great difference between sporting guns and handguns. Some regulation of handguns has long been accepted as imperative; laws relating to "concealed weapons" are common. That we may be "overregulated" in some areas of life has never held us back from more regulation of automobiles, airplanes, motorboats, and "concealed weapons."

Let's look at the history.

First, many of the 3.5 million people living in the thirteen original Colonies depended on wild game for food, and a good many of them required firearms for their defense from marauding Indians — and later from the French and English. Underlying all these needs was an important concept that each able-bodied man in each of the thirteen independent states had to help or defend his state.

The early opposition to the idea of national or standing armies was maintained under the Articles of Confederation; that confederation had no standing army and wanted none. The state militia — essentially a part-time citizen army, as in Switzerland today — was the only kind of "army" they wanted. From the time of the Declaration of Independence through the victory at Yorktown in 1781, George Washington, as the commander in chief of these volunteer-militia armies, had to depend upon the states to send those volunteers.

When a company of New Jersey militia volunteers reported for duty to Washington at Valley Forge, the men initially declined to take an oath to "the United States," maintaining, "Our country is New Jersey." Massachusetts Bay men, Virginians, and others felt the same way. To the American of the eighteenth century, his state was his country, and his freedom was defended by his militia.

The victory at Yorktown — and the ratification of the Bill of Rights a decade later — did not change people's attitudes about a national army. They had lived for years under the notion that each state would maintain its own military establishment, and the seaboard states had their own navies as well. These people, and their fathers and grandfathers before them, remembered how monarchs had used standing armies to oppress their ancestors in Europe. Americans wanted no part of this. A state militia, like a rifle and powder horn, was as much a part of life as the automobile is today; pistols were largely for officers, aristocrats — and dueling.

Against this background, it was not surprising that the provision concerning firearms emerged in very simple terms with the significant predicate — basing the right on the *necessity* for a "well regulated militia," a state army.

In the two centuries since then — with two world wars and some lesser ones — it has become clear, sadly, that we have no choice but to maintain a standing national army while still maintaining a "militia" by way of the National Guard, which can be swiftly integrated into the national defense forces.

Americans also have a right to defend their homes, and we need not challenge that. Nor does anyone seriously question that the Constitution protects the right of hunters to own and keep sporting guns for hunting game any more than anyone would challenge the right to own and keep fishing rods and other equipment for fishing — or to own automobiles. To "keep and bear arms" for hunting today is essentially a recreational activity and not an imperative of survival, as it was 200 years ago; "Saturday night specials" and machine guns are not recreational weapons and surely are as much in need of regulation as motor vehicles.

Americans should ask themselves a few questions. The Constitution does not mention automobiles or motorboats, but the right to keep and own an automobile is beyond question; equally beyond question is the power of the state to regulate the purchase or the transfer of such vehicle and the right to license the vehicle and the driver with reasonable standards. In some places, even a bicycle must be registered, as must some household dogs.

If we are to stop this mindless homicidal carnage, is it unreasonable:

1. to provide that, to acquire a firearm, an application be made reciting age, residence, employment, and any prior criminal convictions?
2. to require that this application lie on the table for ten days (absent a showing for urgent need) before the license would be issued?
3. that the transfer of a firearm be made essentially as that of a motor vehicle?
4. to have a "ballistic fingerprint" of the firearm made by the manufacturer and filed with the license record so that, if a bullet is found in a victim's body, law enforcement might be helped in finding the culprit?

These are the kinds of questions the American people must answer if we are to preserve the "domestic tranquility" promised in the Constitution.

Reading and Discussion Questions

1. This essay can be divided into three or four parts. Provide headings for these parts.
2. Which part of the essay is most fully developed? What explains the author's emphasis?
3. Why does Burger recount the history of the Second Amendment so fully? Explain his reason for arguing that the Second Amendment does not guarantee the right of individuals to "bear arms."
4. Burger also uses history to argue that there is a difference between legislation against sporting guns and legislation against handguns. Summarize his argument.
5. How effective is his analogy between licensing vehicles and licensing handguns?

Writing Suggestions

6. Other people interpret "the right to bear arms" differently. Look at some of their arguments and write an essay summarizing their interpretations and defending them.

7. Burger outlines a policy for registration of handguns that would prevent criminal use. But at least one sociologist has pointed out that most guns used by criminals are obtained illegally. Examine and evaluate some of the arguments claiming that registration is generally ineffective.

8. Analyze arguments of the National Rifle Association, the nation's largest gun lobby. Do they answer Burger's claims?

Numbers don't lie.

Take goats, for example.

How many Mongolian goats do you think it takes to get enough fleece to make a single Lands' End Cashmere Sweater? The answer: from *2½ to 4* goats.

And guess how many feet of cotton yarn go into our men's Pinpoint Oxford shirts? 64,306 feet. That's a little over *12 miles* of cotton – in each shirt.

Fact is, we use lots and lots of cotton. Our Stonewashed Jeans are a tough 14¾ oz. cotton denim: a fine, honest fabric. Know how much denim we used in our jeans last year? Enough to fill *23* railroad boxcars.

Now, we're not just playing with numbers here. Numbers tell a lot about Lands' End.

Like the more than *500* crofters – cottage weavers in Scotland–who hand weave the fabric for our Harris Tweed jackets.

Or the *75* inspectors whose job is trying to make sure that everything that wears a Lands' End label deserves it.

In fact, when you consider what all the numbers say about us – and our *passion* to get things right for our customers – doesn't it make you want to see a copy of our catalog? We'd be happy to send you the latest number.

1996 Lands' End, Inc.

LANDS' END
Guaranteed. Period.©

 For a free catalog, call any time, 24 hours a day– **1-800-356-4444** Please mention ad ⬛ SJ

Name _____

Address _____ Apt. _____

City _____ State _____ Zip _____

Phone ( ) _____ Day/Night *(circle one)*

Mail to: 1 Lands' End Lane, Dodgeville, WI 53595. **E-Mail: catalogs-sj@landsend.com**

Discussion Questions

1. Notice the headline. The advertiser has supplied lots of numbers. What claim are these numbers meant to support?
2. Did you find the ad interesting to read? Do you think the advertiser was correct in thinking that people would read seven paragraphs about numbers? Explain your answer.
3. What specific aspects of the language might induce people to continue reading even if they find numbers tedious?

The initials of a friend

You will find these letters on many tools by which electricity works. They are on great generators used by electric light and power companies; and on lamps that light millions of homes.

They are on big motors that pull railway trains; and on tiny motors that make hard housework easy.

By such tools electricity dispels the dark and lifts heavy burdens from human shoulders. Hence the letters G-E are more than a trademark. They are an emblem of service—the initials of a friend.

GENERAL ELECTRIC

This advertisement first appeared in 1923. Today, you'll find our initials on many more things — from appliances, plastics, motors and lighting to financial services and medical equipment. Wherever you see our initials, we want them to mean the same thing to you — the initials of a friend.

We bring good things to life.

Discussion Questions

1. To what need does the ad make an appeal?
2. What devices in the ad — both objects and the choice of objects to discuss — contribute to the effectiveness of the message?
3. How does the company's present-day slogan compare?

A gun in the home is much more likely to kill a family member than to kill an intruder.

CEASE FIRE

Think about your family before you think about getting a handgun.

Cease Fire, Inc. P.O. Box 33424, Washington, D.C. 20033-0424.

Discussion Questions

1. Would this claim of policy be just as successful if the note were excluded? Would additional facts about guns contribute to its effectiveness?
2. Why is the gun so much larger than the printed message?
3. What is the basis of the emotional appeal? Is there more than one? Does the note go too far in exploiting our emotions?

The Case for Medicalizing Heroin

ALAN DERSHOWITZ

When *Time* magazine has a cover story on the legalization of drugs, and when Oprah Winfrey devotes an entire show to that "unthinkable" proposition, you can be sure that this is an issue whose time has come — at least for serious discussion.

But it is difficult to get politicians to *have* a serious discussion about alternatives to our currently bankrupt approach to drug abuse. Even thinking out loud about the possibility of decriminalization is seen as being soft on drugs. And no elected official can afford to be viewed as less than ferocious and uncompromising on this issue.

Any doubts about that truism were surely allayed when Vice President Bush openly broke with his president and most important supporter over whether to try to make a deal with Panamanian strongman Manuel Noriega, whom the United States has charged with drug-trafficking.

I was one of the guests on the recent Oprah Winfrey show that debated drug decriminalization. The rhetoric and emotions ran high, as politicians and audience members competed over who could be tougher in the war against drugs.

"Call out the marines," "Bomb the poppy fields," "Execute the 5 drug dealers" — these are among the "constructive" suggestions being offered to supplement the administration's simpleminded "just say no" slogan.

Proposals to medicalize, regulate, or in another way decriminalize any currently illegal drug — whether it be marijuana, cocaine, or heroin — were greeted by derision and cries of "surrender." Even politicians who *in private* recognize the virtues of decriminalization must continue to oppose it when the cameras are rolling.

That is why it is so important to outline here the politically unpopular case for an alternative approach.

Ironically, the case is easiest for the hardest drug — heroin. There can be no doubt that heroin is a horrible drug: It is highly ad-

---

Alan Dershowitz is a professor at the law school of Harvard University. This essay, originally published in 1988, is reprinted in his book *Contrary to Popular Opinion* (1992).

dictive and debilitating; taken in high, or unregulated, doses, it can kill; when administered by means of shared needles, it spreads AIDS; because of its high price and addictive quality, it makes acquisitive criminals out of desperate addicts. Few would disagree that if we could rid it from the planet through the passage of a law or the invention of a plant-specific herbicide, we should do so.

But since we can neither eliminate heroin nor the demand for it, there is a powerful case for medicalizing as much of the problem as is feasible. Under this proposal, or one of its many variants, the hard-core addict would receive the option of getting his fix in a medical setting, administered by medical personnel.

The setting could be a mobile hospital van or some other facility 10
close to where the addicts live. A doctor would determine the dosage for each addict — a maintenance dosage designed to prevent withdrawal without risking overdose. And the fix would be injected in the medical facility so the addict could not sell or barter the drug or prescription.

This will by no means solve all the problems associated with heroin addiction, but it would ameliorate some of the most serious ones. The maintained heroin addict will not immediately become a model citizen. But much of the desperation that today accounts for the victimization of innocent home-dwellers, store employees, and pedestrians — primarily in urban centers — would be eliminated, and drug-related crime would be significantly reduced.

Today's addict is simply not deterred by the law. He will get his fix by hook or by crook, or by knife or by gun, regardless of the risk. That is what heroin addiction means. Giving the desperate addict a twenty-four-hour medical alternative will save the lives of countless innocent victims of both crime and AIDS.

It will also save the lives of thousands of addicts who now kill themselves in drug shooting galleries by injecting impure street mixtures through AIDS-infected needles.

There will, of course, always be a black market for heroin, even if it were medicalized. Not every addict will accept a medically administered injection, and even some of those who do will supplement their maintenance doses with street drugs. But much of the desperate quality of the constant quest for the fix will be reduced for at least some heroin addicts. And this will have a profound impact on both the quantity and violence of inner-city crime.

Nor would new addicts be created by this medical approach. 15
Only long-term adult addicts would be eligible for the program. And the expenses would be more than offset by the extraordinary savings to our society in reduced crime.

If this program proved successful in the context of heroin addiction, variants could be considered for other illegal drugs such as cocaine and marijuana. There is no assurance that an approach which is successful for one drug will necessarily work for others. Many of the problems are different.

We have already decriminalized two of the most dangerous drugs known to humankind — nicotine and alcohol. Decriminalization of these killers, which destroy more lives than all other drugs combined, has not totally eliminated the problems associated with them.

But we have come to realize that criminalization of nicotine and alcohol causes even more problems than it solves. The time has come to consider whether that is also true of heroin and perhaps of other drugs as well.

Selling Syringes:
The Swiss Experiment

RACHEL EHRENFELD

As U.S. communities continue to experiment with programs to cut drug addiction and HIV infection spread by drug users, some have cited European experiments with the decriminalization of drug use. But before venturing further in this direction, policymakers should acquaint themselves with an elaborate new "scientific" program set in motion in 1992 in Switzerland, which has the highest per-capita rate of drug addiction and HIV infection in Europe.

Seven hundred of the 30,000 to 40,000 opiate addicts in Switzerland were targeted; nine cities participate. The experiment — in which heroin, morphine, and methadone are administered intravenously, orally, and by smoking — is scheduled to end in December 1996. Previously, the Swiss addicts were concentrated in central parts of major cities, such as "Needle Park" in Zurich. But the result was increased drug use, crime, violence, and prostitution, which quickly became intolerable. So the addicts are now in government-sponsored centers and "shooting galleries."

In analyzing this "scientific" project, I met with its administrators and evaluators and visited the major heroin distribution center, Arbeitsgemeinschaft für risikoarmen Umgang mit Drogen (ARUD), in Zurich, which currently treats seventy to eighty heroin addicts. Most have a criminal record, are unemployed, and are on social welfare. Nearly half are HIV positive. A majority of the patients are multidrug users, and many use cocaine in addition to the heroin they're

Rachel Ehrenfeld, author of *Narco-Terrorism* (1992), is preparing a book on the movement to legalize drugs. This article appeared in the *Wall Street Journal* on September 16, 1995.

given at the center. Their outside drug use, however, does not prohibit their participation in the program. Urine analysis to monitor
drug consumption is conducted once a month on a set day because
"the treatment in our center is based on trust," said Andre Seidenberg, director of ARUD.

The center is easily accessible and anyone can enter. A half-
dozen people sit in the waiting room smoking specially developed
cigarettes containing 100 milligrams of heroin, which are distributed
by the receptionist behind the window. She also provides syringes
with heroin up to nine times a day and a maximum of 300 milligrams. Each addict is listed in a computer system that monitors his
consumption. The injecting room, off the entrance, contains a large
mirror used to provide the addicts with a better view of their veins,
so they can inject more efficiently, explained the director. Why feed
heroin to the addicts? "Because the addicts prefer heroin [to
methadone]," responded Dr. Seidenberg, "and we should give them
what they want without conditions."

The design of the project calls for supervision of the injecting 5
process, to make sure the addicts don't save the drugs to sell them
later on the street, but I saw none. Although the addicts return the
syringe after the injection, they could easily inject the heroin into a
small container to be sold later. Moreover, in addition to the in-
jectable heroin, they are given twenty-six heroin cigarettes to be
used at home overnight. The heroin costs the addicts about $12.50 a
day, covered by health insurance, the City Council, the canton
(state), or the federal government. The design of the project also
calls for support services — especially psychiatric and medical
treatment, job training, occupational therapy, etc. But none of these
are available at the center.

In an emergency, the addict is sent either to a psychiatric hospital or to an emergency room. As for therapy: "There is no proof that
there is long-term effect to therapy — therapy doesn't make a difference," Dr. Seidenberg said. And as for work, "you go when you feel
like it — you really don't have to [work]," according to Ueli Locher,
the deputy director of the Department of Social Services of Zurich.

The Swiss experiment originated from a desire to reduce HIV infection among the population. Complementing this experiment are
information programs and pamphlets supplied to teenagers, young
adults and adults. This information equates homosexuality and drug
addiction and describes both as "alternative lifestyles." Both sexual
activity and drug use are described in detail with illustrations and
the motto that "if you want to experiment — do it well."

Currently, according to Mr. Locher, "cocaine is not given [to ad-
dicts] because of political reasons." But he and his comrades in drug
liberalization hope that this will change and that all drugs will be
available to those who need them. Drug supply by the government is

supposed to reduce the number of addicts, but so far there is no indication that fewer people are taking illegal drugs in Switzerland. There are no signs that crime and violence have gone down. And the Swiss taxpayer is footing the bill for a growing number of AIDS patients, more welfare recipients, and a growing police force.

Discussion Questions

1. What are the bases for Dershowitz's claim that drugs should be legalized?
2. His support consists in part of hypothetical examples of the way that legalized heroin would work. What are the strengths and weaknesses of such evidence?
3. What kinds of evidence does Ehrenfeld supply? How relevant is her argument to drug control in the United States?
4. Does Ehrenfeld's article constitute a response to Dershowitz? Explain why or why not.

EXERCISES

1. Look for personal advertisements (in which men and women advertise for various kinds of companionship) in a local or national paper or magazine. (The *Village Voice,* a New York paper, is an outstanding source.) What inferences can you draw about the people who place these particular ads? About the "facts" they choose to provide? How did you come to these conclusions? You might also try to infer the reasons that more men than women place ads and why this might be changing.
2. "I like Colonel Sanders" is the title of an article that praises ugly architecture, shopping malls, laundromats, and other symbols of "plastic" America. The author claims that these aspects of the American scene have unique and positive values. Defend or refute his claim by pointing out what the values of these things might be, giving reasons for your own assessments.
3. A psychiatrist says that in pro football personality traits determine the positions of the players. Write an essay developing this idea and providing adequate evidence for your claim. Or make inferences about the relationship between the personalities of the players and another sport that you know well.
4. At least one city in the world — Reykjavik, the capital of Iceland — bans dogs from the city. Defend or attack this policy by using both facts and values to support your claim.
5. Write a review of a movie, play, television program, concert, restaurant, or book. Make clear your criteria for judgment and their order of importance.
6. The controversy concerning seat belts and air bags in automobiles has generated a variety of proposals, one of which is mandatory use of seat belts in all the states. Make your own policy claim regarding laws about safety devices (the wearing of motorcycle helmets is another thorny

subject), and defend it by using both facts and values — facts about safety, values concerning individual freedom and responsibility.

7. Select a ritual with which you are familiar and argue for or against the value it represents. *Examples:* the high school prom, Christmas gift-giving, a fraternity initiation, a wedding, a confirmation or bar mitzvah, a funeral ceremony, a Fourth of July celebration.

8. Choose a recommended policy — from the school newspaper or elsewhere — and argue that it will or will not work to produce beneficial changes. *Examples:* expansion of core requirements, comprehensive tests as a graduation requirement, reinstitution of a physical education requirement, removal of junk food from vending machines.

Critical Listening

9. Have you ever been a member of a group which tried but failed to solve a problem through discussion? Communication theorists talk about "interference," defined by one writer as "anything that hinders or lessens the efficiency of communication."[4] Some of the elements of interference in the delivery of oral messages are fatigue, anger, inattention, vague language, personality conflict, political bias. You will probably be able to think of others. Did any of these elements prevent the group from arriving at an agreement? Describe the situation and the kinds of interference that you were aware of.

---

[4]Richard E. Crable, *One to Another* (New York: Harper and Row, 1981), p. 18.

CHAPTER FOUR

Definition

THE PURPOSES OF DEFINITION

Before we examine the other elements of argument, we need to consider definition, a component you may have to deal with early in writing an essay. Definition may be used in two ways: to clarify the meanings of vague or ambiguous terms or as a method of development for the whole essay. In some arguments your claims will contain words that need explanation before you can proceed with any discussion. But you may also want to devote an entire essay to the elaboration of a broad concept or experience that cannot be adequately defined in a shorter space.

The Roman statesman Cicero said, "Every rational discussion of anything whatsoever should begin with a definition in order to make clear what is the subject of dispute." You have probably already discovered the importance of definition in argument. If you have ever had a disagreement with your parents about using the car or drinking or dyeing your hair or going away for a weekend or staying out till three in the morning, you know that you were really arguing about the meaning of the term "adolescent freedom."

Arguments often revolve around definitions of crucial terms. For example, how does one define *democracy*? Does a democracy guarantee freedom of the press, freedom of worship, freedom of assembly, freedom of movement? In the United States, we would argue that such freedoms are essential to any definition of *democracy*. But countries in which these freedoms are nonexistent also represent themselves as democracies or governments of the people. In the words of Senator Daniel P. Moynihan, "For years now the most brutal totalitarian regimes have called themselves 'people's' or 'democratic' republics." Rulers in such governments are aware that defining their regimes as democratic may win the approval of people who would otherwise condemn them. In his formidable attack on totalitarianism, *Nineteen Eighty-Four,* George Orwell coined the slogans "War Is Peace" and "Slavery Is Freedom," phrases that represent the corrupt use of definition to distort reality.

But even where there is no intention to deceive, the snares of definition are difficult to avoid. How do you define *abortion?* Is it "termination of pregnancy"? Or is it "murder of an unborn child"? During a celebrated trial in 1975 of a physician who performed an abortion and was accused of manslaughter, the prosecution often used the word *baby* to refer to the fetus, but the defense referred to "the products of conception." These definitions of *fetus* reflected the differing judgments of those on opposite sides. Not only do judgments create definitions; definitions influence judgments. In the abortion trial, the definitions of *fetus* used by both sides were meant to promote either approval or disapproval of the doctor's action.

Definitions can indeed change the nature of an event or a "fact." How many farms are there in the state of New York? The answer to the question depends on the definition of *farm.* In 1979 the *New York Times* reported:

> Because of a change in the official definition of the word "farm," New York lost 20 percent of its farms on January 1, with numbers dropping from 56,000 to 45,000. . . .
>
> Before the change, a farm was defined as "any place from which $250 or more of agricultural products is sold" yearly or "any place of 10 acres or more from which $50 or more of agricultural products is sold" yearly. Now a farm is "any place from which $1,000 or more of agricultural products is sold" in a year.[1]

A change in the definition of poverty can have similar results. An article in the *New York Times,* whose headline reads, "A Revised Definition of Poverty May Raise Number of U.S. Poor," makes this clear.

> The official definition of poverty used by the Federal Government for three decades is based simply on cash income before taxes. But in a report to be issued on Wednesday, a panel of experts convened by the [National] Academy of Sciences three years ago at the behest of Congress says the Government should move toward a concept of poverty based on disposable income, the amount left after a family pays taxes and essential expenses.[2]

The differences are wholly a matter of definition. But such differences can have serious consequences for those being defined, most of all in the disposition of billions of federal dollars in aid of various

---

[1]*New York Times,* March 4, 1979, Sec. 1, p. 40.
[2]*New York Times,* April 10, 1995, Sec. A, p. 1.

kinds. In 1992 the Census Bureau classified 14.5 percent of Americans as poor. Under the new guidelines, at least 15 or 16 percent would be poor and, under some measures recommended by a government panel, 18 percent would be so defined.

In fact, local and federal courts almost every day redefine traditional concepts that can have a direct impact on our everyday lives. The definition of the family, for example, has undergone significant changes that acknowledge the existence of new relationships. In January 1990 the New Jersey Supreme Court ruled that a family may be defined as "one or more persons occupying a dwelling unit as a single nonprofit housekeeping unit, who are living together as a stable and permanent living unit, being a traditional family unit or the *functional equivalent* thereof" (italics for emphasis added). This meant that ten Glassboro State College students, unrelated by blood, could continue to occupy a single-family house despite the objection of the borough of Glassboro.[3] Even the legal definition of maternity has shifted. Who is the mother — the woman who contributes the egg or the woman (the surrogate) who bears the child? Several states, acknowledging the changes brought by medical technology, now recognize a difference between the "birth mother" and the "legal mother."

Defining the Terms in Your Argument

In some of your arguments you will introduce terms that require definition. We've pointed out that a definition of poverty is crucial to any debate on the existence of poverty in the United States. The same may be true in a debate about the legality of euthanasia, or mercy killing. Are the arguers referring to passive euthanasia, that is, the withdrawal of life-support systems, or to active euthanasia, in which death is hastened through the direct administration of drugs?

It is not uncommon, in fact, for arguments about controversial questions to turn into arguments about the definition of terms. If, for example, you wanted to argue in favor of the regulation of religious cults, you would first have to define *cult*. In so doing, you might discover that it is not easy to distinguish clearly between conventional religions and cults. Then you would have to define *regulation*, spelling out the legal restrictions you favored so as to make them apply only to cults, not to established religions. An argument on the subject might end almost before it began if writer and reader could not agree on definitions of these terms. While clear definitions do not guarantee agreement, they do ensure that all parties understand the nature of the argument.

---

[3]*New York Times,* February 1, 1990, Sec. B, p. 5.

Defining Vague and Ambiguous Terms

You will need to define other terms in addition to those in your claim. If you use words and phrases that have two or more meanings, they may appear vague and ambiguous to your reader. In arguments of value and policy abstract terms such as *freedom, justice, patriotism,* and *equality* require clarification. Despite their vagueness, however, they are among the most important in the language because they represent the ideals that shape our laws. When conflicts arise, the courts must define these terms to establish the legality of certain practices. Is the Ku Klux Klan permitted to make disparaging public statements about ethnic and racial groups? That depends on the court's definition of "free speech." Can execution for some crimes be considered "cruel and unusual punishment"? That, too, depends on the court's definition of "cruel and unusual punishment." In addition, such terms as *happiness, mental health, success,* and *creativity* often defy precise definition because they reflect the differing values within a society or a culture.

The definition of *success,* for example, varies not only among social groups but also among individuals within the group. One scientist has postulated five signs by which to judge the measure of success: wealth (including health), security (confidence in retaining the wealth), reputation, performance, and contentment.[4] Consider whether all of these are necessary to your own definition of *success.* If not, which may be omitted? Do you think others should be added? Notice that one of the signs — reputation — depends on definition by the community; another — contentment — can be measured only by the individual. The assessment of performance probably owes something to both the group and the individual.

Christopher Atkins, an actor, gave an interviewer an example of an externalized definition of success, that is, a definition based on the standards imposed by other people:

> Success to me is judged through the eyes of others. I mean, if you're walking around saying, "I own a green Porsche," you might meet somebody who says, "Hey, that's no big deal, I own a green Porsche and a house." So all of a sudden, you don't feel so successful. Really, it's in the eyes of others.[5]

So difficult is the formulation of a universally accepted measure for success that some scholars regard the concept as meaningless. Nevertheless, we continue to use the word as if it represented a definable concept because the idea of success, however defined, is im-

---

[4]Gwynn Nettler, *Social Concerns* (New York: McGraw-Hill, 1976), pp. 196–197.
[5]*New York Times,* August 6, 1982, Sec. III, p. 8.

portant for the identity and development of the individual and the group. It is clear, however, that when crossing subcultural boundaries, even within a small group, we need to be aware of differences in the use of the word. If "contentment" — that is, the satisfaction of achieving a small personal goal — is enough, then a person lying under a palm tree subsisting on handouts from picnickers may be a success. But you should not expect all your readers to agree that these criteria are enough to define *success.*

In arguing about aesthetic matters, whose vocabulary is almost always abstract, the criteria for judgment must be revealed, either directly or indirectly, and then the abstract terms that represent the criteria must be defined. If you want to say that a film is distinguished by great acting, have you made clear what you mean by *great?* That we do not always understand or agree on the definition of *great* is apparent, say, on the morning after the Oscar winners have been announced.

Even subjects that you feel sure you can identify may offer surprising insights when you rethink them for an extended definition. One critic, defining rock music, argued that the distinguishing characteristic of rock music was *noise* — not the beat, not the harmonies, not the lyrics, not the vocal style, but noise, "nasty, discordant irritating noise — or, to its practitioners, unfettered, liberating, expressive noise."[6] In producing this definition, the author had to give a number of examples to prove that he was justified in rejecting the most familiar criteria.

Consider the definition of race, around which so much of American history has revolved, often with tragic consequences. Currently the only categories listed in the census are white, black, Asian-Pacific, and Native American, "with the Hispanic population straddling them all." But rapidly increasing intermarriage and ethnic identity have caused a number of political and ethnic groups to demand changes in the classifications of the Census Bureau. Some Arab Americans, for example, prefer to be counted as "Middle Eastern" rather than white. Children of black-white unions are defined as black 60 percent of the time, while children of Asian-white unions are described as Asian 42 percent of the time. Research is now being conducted to discover how people feel about the terms being used to define them. As one anthropologist pointed out, "Socially and politically assigned attributes have a lot to do with access to economic resources."[7]

---

[6]Jon Pareles, "Noise Evokes Modern Chaos for a Band," *New York Times,* March 9, 1986, Sec. H, p. 26.

[7]*Wall Street Journal,* September 9, 1995, Sec. B, p. 1.

METHODS FOR DEFINING TERMS

The following strategies for defining terms in an argument are by no means mutually exclusive. You may use all of them in a single argumentative essay.

Dictionary Definition

Giving a dictionary definition is the simplest and most obvious way to define a term. An unabridged dictionary is the best source because it usually gives examples of the way a word can be used in a sentence; that is, it furnishes the proper context.

In many cases, the dictionary definition alone is not sufficient. It may be too broad or too narrow for your purpose. Suppose, in an argument about pornography, you wanted to define the word *obscene*. *Webster's New International Dictionary* (third edition, unabridged) gives the definition of *obscene* as "offensive to taste; foul; loathsome; disgusting." But these synonyms do not tell you what qualities make an object or an event or an action "foul," "loathsome," and "disgusting." In 1973 the Supreme Court, attempting to narrow the definition of *obscenity,* ruled that obscenity was to be determined by the community in accordance with local standards. One person's obscenity, as numerous cases have demonstrated, may be another person's art. The celebrated trials in the early twentieth century about the distribution of novels regarded as pornographic — D. H. Lawrence's *Lady Chatterley's Lover* and James Joyce's *Ulysses* — emphasized the problems of defining obscenity.

Another dictionary definition may strike you as too narrow. *Patriotism,* for example, is defined in one dictionary as "love and loyal or zealous support of one's country, especially in all matters involving other countries." Some readers may want to include an unwillingness to support government policies they consider wrong.

Stipulation

In stipulating the meaning of a term, the writer asks the reader to accept a definition that may be different from the conventional one. He or she does this in order to limit or control the argument. Someone has said, "Part of the task of keeping definitions in our civilization clear and pure is to keep a firm democratic rein on those with the power, or craving the power, to stipulate meaning." Perhaps this writer was thinking of a term like *national security,* which can be defined by a nation's leaders in such a way as to sanction persecution of citizens and reckless military adventures. Likewise, a term such as *liberation* can be appropriated by terrorist groups whose activities often lead to oppression rather than liberation.

Religion is usually defined as a belief in a supernatural power to be obeyed and worshiped. But in an article entitled "Civil Religion in America," a sociologist offers a different meaning.

> While some have argued that Christianity is the national faith, and others that church and synagogue celebrate only the generalized religion of "the American way of life," few have realized that there actually exists alongside of and rather clearly differentiated from the churches an elaborate and well-institutionalized civil religion in America. This article argues not only that there is such a thing, but also that this religion . . . has its own seriousness and integrity and requires the same care in understanding that any other religion does.[8]

When the author adds, "This religion — there seems no other word for it — was neither sectarian nor in any specific sense Christian," he emphasizes that he is distinguishing his definition of religion from definitions that associate religion and church.

Even the word *violence,* which the dictionary defines as "physical force used so as to injure or damage" and whose meaning seems so clear and uncompromising, can be manipulated to produce a definition different from the one normally understood by most people. Some pacifists refer to conditions in which "people are deprived of choices in a systematic way" as "institutionalized quiet violence." Even where no physical force is employed, this lack of choice in schools, in the workplace, in the black ghettos is defined as violence.[9]

In *Through the Looking-Glass* Alice asked Humpty Dumpty "whether you can make words mean so many different things."

"When I use a word," Humpty Dumpty said scornfully, "it means just what I choose it to mean, neither more nor less."[10]

A writer, however, is not free to invent definitions that no one will recognize or that create rather than solve problems between writer and reader.

Negation

To avoid confusion it is sometimes helpful to tell the reader what a term is *not.* In discussing euthanasia, a writer might say, "By euthanasia I do not mean active intervention to hasten the death of the patient."

---

[8]Robert N. Bellah, "Civil Religion in America," *Daedalus,* Winter 1967, p. 1.

[9]Newton Garver, "What Violence Is," in *Moral Choices,* edited by James Rachels (New York: Harper and Row, 1971), pp. 248–249.

[10]Lewis Carroll, *Alice in Wonderland and Through the Looking-Glass* (New York: Grosset and Dunlap, 1948), p. 238.

A negative definition may be more extensive, depending on the complexity of the term and the writer's ingenuity. The critic of rock music quoted earlier in this chapter arrived at his definition by rejecting attributes that seemed misleading. The ex-Communist Whittaker Chambers, in a foreword to a book on the spy trial of Alger Hiss, defined communism this way:

> First, let me try to say what Communism is not. It is not simply a vicious plot hatched by wicked men in a subcellar. It is not just the writings of Marx and Lenin, dialectical materialism, the Politburo, the labor theory of value, the theory of the general strike, the Red Army secret police, labor camps, underground conspiracy, the dictatorship of the proletariat, the technique of the coup d'état. It is not even those chanting, bannered millions that stream periodically, like disorganized armies, through the heart of the world's capitals: Moscow, New York, Tokyo, Paris, Rome. These are expressions, but they are not what Communism is about.[11]

This, of course, is only part of the definition. Any writer beginning a definition in the negative must go on to define what the term *is*.

Examples

One of the most effective ways of defining terms in an argument is the use of examples. Both real and hypothetical examples can bring life to abstract and ambiguous terms. The writer in the following passage defines *preferred categories* (classes of people who are meant to benefit from affirmative action policies) by invoking specific cases:

> The absence of definitions points up one of the problems with preferred categories. . . . These preferred categories take no account of family wealth or educational advantages. A black whose father is a judge or physician deserves preferential treatment over any nonminority applicant. The latter might have fought his way out of the grinding poverty of Appalachia, or might be the first member of an Italian American or a Polish American family to complete high school. But no matter.[12]

Insanity is a word that has been used and misused to describe a variety of conditions. Even psychiatrists are in dispute about its meaning. In the following anecdote, examples narrow and refine the definition.

> Dr. Zilboorg says that present-day psychiatry does not possess any satisfactory definition of mental illness or neurosis. To illustrate, he

---

[11]*Witness* (New York: Random House, 1952), p. 8.
[12]Anthony Lombardo, "Quotas Work Both Ways," *U.S. Catholic,* February 1974, p. 39.

told a story: A psychiatrist was recently asked for a definition of a "well-adjusted person" (not even slightly peculiar). The definition: "A person who feels in harmony with himself and who is not in conflict with his environment." It sounded fine, but up popped a heckler. "Would you then consider an anti-Nazi working in the underground against Hitler a maladjusted person?" "Well," the psychiatrist hemmed, "I withdraw the latter part of my definition." Dr. Zilboorg withdrew the first half for him. Many persons in perfect harmony with themselves, he pointed out, are in "distinctly pathological states."[13]

Extended Definition

When we speak of an extended definition, we usually refer not only to length but also to the variety of methods for developing the definition. Let's take the word *materialism*. A dictionary entry offers the following sentence fragments as definitions: "1. the doctrine that comfort, pleasure, and wealth are the only or highest goals or values. 2. the tendency to be more concerned with material than the spiritual goals or values." But the term *materialism* has acquired so many additional meanings, especially emotional ones, that an extended definition serves a useful purpose in clarifying the many different ideas surrounding our understanding of the term.

Below is a much longer definition of *materialism,* which appears at the beginning of an essay entitled, "People and Things: Reflections on Materialism."[14]

> There are two contemporary usages of the term, materialism, and it is important to distinguish between them. On the one hand we can talk about *instrumental materialism,* or the use of material objects to make life longer, safer, more enjoyable. By instrumental, we mean that objects act as essential means for discovering and furthering personal values and goals of life, so that the objects are instruments used to realize and further those goals. There is little negative connotation attached to this meaning of the word, since one would think that it is perfectly sensible to use things for such purposes. While it is true that the United States is the epitome of materialism in this sense, it is also true that most people in every society aspire to reach our level of instrumental materialism.
>
> On the other hand the term has a more negative connotation, which might be conveyed by the phrase *terminal materialism.* This is the sense critics use when they apply the term to Americans. What they mean is that we not only use our material resources as instruments to make life more manageable, but that we reduce our ultimate goals to the possession of things. They believe that we don't just use our cars to

---

[13]Quoted in *The Art of Making Sense,* p. 48.
[14]Mihaly Csikszentmihalyi and Eugene Rochberg-Halton, "People and Things: Reflections on Materialism," *University of Chicago Magazine,* Spring 1978, pp. 7–8.

get from place to place, but that we consider the ownership of expensive cars one of the central values in life. Terminal materialism means that the object is valued only because it indicates an end in itself, a possession. In instrumental materialism there is a sense of directionality, in which a person's goals may be furthered through the interactions with the object. A book, for example, can reveal new possibilities or widen a person's view of the world, or an old photograph can be cherished because it embodies a relationship. But in terminal materialism, there is no sense of reciprocal interaction in the relation between the object and the end. The end is valued as final, not as itself a means to further ends. And quite often it is only the status label or image associated with the object that is valued, rather than the actual object.

In the essay from which this passage is taken, the authors distinguish between two kinds of materialism and provide an extended explanation, using contrast and examples as methods of development. They are aware that the common perception of materialism, the love of things for their own sake, is a negative one. But this view, according to the authors, doesn't fully account for the attitudes of many Americans toward the things they own. There is, in fact, another more positive meaning that the authors call *instrumental materialism.* You will recognize that the authors are *stipulating* a meaning with which their readers might not be familiar. In their essay they distinguish between *terminal materialism,* in which "the object is valued only because it indicates an end in itself" and *instrumental materialism,* "the use of material objects to make life longer, safer, more enjoyable." Since *instrumental materialism* is the less familiar definition, the essay provides a great number of examples that show how people of three different generations value photographs, furniture, musical instruments, plants, and other objects for their memories and personal associations rather than as proof of the owners' ability to acquire the objects or win the approval of others.

THE DEFINITION ESSAY

The argumentative essay can take the form of an extended definition. An example of such an essay is the one from which we've just quoted, as well as the three essays at the end of this chapter. The definition essay is appropriate when the idea under consideration is so controversial or so heavy with historical connotations that even a paragraph or two cannot make clear exactly what the arguer wants his or her readers to understand. For example, if you were preparing a definition of patriotism, you would want to answer some or all of the following questions. You would probably use a number of methods to develop your definition: personal narrative, examples, stipulation, comparison and contrast, and cause and effect analysis.

1. *Dictionary Definition.* Is the dictionary definition the one I will elaborate on? Do I need to stipulate other meanings?
2. *Personal History.* Where did I first acquire my notions of patriotism? What was taught? How and by whom was it taught?
3. *Cultural Context.* Has my patriotic feeling changed in the last few years? Why or why not? Does my own patriotism reflect the mood of the country or the group to which I belong?
4. *Values.* What is the value of patriotism? Does it make me more humane, more civilized? Is patriotism consistent with tolerance of other systems and cultures? Is patriotism the highest duty of a citizen? Do any other values take precedence? What was the meaning of President Kennedy's injunction: "Ask not what your country can do for you; ask rather what you can do for your country"?
5. *Behavior.* How do I express my patriotism (or lack of it)? Can it be expressed through dissent? What sacrifice, if any, would I make for my country?

WRITING AN ESSAY OF DEFINITION

The following list suggests several important steps to be taken in writing an essay of definition.

1. Choose a term that needs definition because it is controversial or ambiguous, or because you want to offer a personal definition that differs from the accepted interpretation. Explain why an extended definition is necessary. Or choose an experience that lends itself to treatment in an extended definition. One student defined "culture shock" as she had experienced it while studying abroad in Hawaii among students of a different ethnic background.
2. Decide on the thesis — the point of view you wish to develop about the term you are defining. If you want to define "heroism," for example, you may choose to develop the idea that this quality depends on motivation and awareness of danger rather than on the specific act performed by the hero.
3. Begin by consulting the dictionary for the conventional definition, the one with which most readers will be familiar. Make clear whether you want to elaborate on the dictionary definition or take issue with it because you think it is misleading or inadequate.
4. Distinguish wherever possible between the term you are defining and other terms with which it might be confused. If you are defining "love," can you make a clear distinction between the different kinds of emotional attachments contained in the word?
5. Try to think of several methods of developing the definition — using examples, comparison and contrast, analogy, cause and ef-

fect analysis. However, you may discover that one method alone — say, use of examples — will suffice to narrow and refine your definition. See the sample essay "The Nature of Prejudice" on page 116 for an example of such a development.

6. Arrange your supporting material in an order that gives emphasis to the most important ideas.

SAMPLE ANALYSIS

Addiction Is Not a Disease
STANTON PEELE

Why Addiction Is Not a Disease

Medical schools are finally teaching about alcoholism; Johns Hopkins will require basic training for all students and clinicians. . . . Alcoholism, as a chronic disease, offers "a fantastic vehicle to teach other concepts," says Jean Kinney [of Dartmouth's Cork Institute]. . . . William Osler, Kinney remarks, coined the aphorism that "to know syphilis is to know medicine," . . . Now, she says, the same can be said of alcoholism.

— "The Neglected Disease in Medical Education," *Science*[1]

OCD (obsessive-compulsive disorder) is apparently rare in the general population.

— American Psychiatric Association, 1980[2]

The evidence is strong OCD is a common mental disorder that, like other stigmatized and hidden disorders in the past, may be ready for discovery and demands for treatment on a large scale.

— National Institute of Mental Health, 1988[3]

In America today, we are bombarded with news about drug and alcohol problems. We may ask ourselves, "How did we get here?" Alternatively, we may wonder if these problems are really worse now

---

Stanton Peele, who receive his Ph.D. in social psychology from the University of Michigan, has taught at Harvard and Columbia Universities, the University of California, and is coauthor of the bestselling *Love and Addiction* (1975). This excerpt is from *Diseasing of America* (Boston: Houghton Mifflin, 1989).

[1]C. Holden, "The Neglected Disease in Medical Education," *Science* 229 (1985), pp. 741–742.

[2]*Diagnostic and Statistical Manual of Mental Disorders,* 3rd ed. (Washington, D.C.: American Psychiatric Association, 1980).

[3]M. Karno et al., "The Epidemiology of Obsessive-Compulsive Disorder in Five US Communities," *Archives of General Psychiatry* 45 (1988), pp. 1094–1099.

than they were five or ten years ago, or fifty or one hundred. Actually, in many cases the answer is no. Estimates of the number of alcoholics requiring treatment are wildly overblown, and reputable epidemiological researchers find that as little as 1 percent of the population fits the clinical definition of alcoholism — as opposed to the 10 percent figure regularly used by the alcoholism industry. Meanwhile, cocaine use is down. All indicators are that very few young people who try drugs ever become regular users, and fewer still get "hooked."

Of course, we have real problems. The nightly news carries story after story of inner-city violence between crack gangs and of totally desolate urban environments where drugs reign supreme. The cocaine problem has resolved itself — not exclusively, but very largely — into a ghetto problem, like many that face America. A *New York Times* front-page story based on an eight-year study of young drug users showed that those who abuse drugs have a number of serious background problems, and *that these problems don't disappear from their lives when they stop using drugs.*[4] In other words, the sources — and solutions — for what is going on in our ghettos are only very secondarily a matter of drug availability and use.

America is a society broken into two worlds. The reality of the crack epidemic and of inner cities and poor environments sometimes explodes and impinges unpleasantly on our consciousness. For the most part, however, our reality is that of the middle class, which fills our magazines with health stories and warnings about family problems and the strivings of young professionals to find satisfaction. And for some time now, this other world has also focused on addiction. But this new addiction marketplace is only sometimes linked to alcohol and drugs. Even when it is, we have to redefine alcoholism as the new Betty Ford kind, which is marked by a general dull malaise, a sense that one is drinking too much, and — for many, like Betty Ford and Kitty Dukakis — relying on prescribed drugs to make life bearable.

However we define loss-of-control drinking, Betty Ford didn't experience it. But treating problems like hers and those of so many media stars is far more rewarding and profitable than trying to deal with street derelicts or ghetto addicts. At the same time, *everything can be an addiction.* This remarkable truth — which I first described in *Love and Addiction* in 1975 — has so overwhelmed us as a society that we have gone haywire. We want to pass laws to excuse compulsive gamblers when they embezzle money to gamble and to force insurance companies to pay to treat them. We want to treat people

---

[4]S. Blakeslee, "8-Year Study Finds 2 Sides to Teen-Age Drug Use," *New York Times,* July 21, 1988, p. 1, Sec. A, p. 23.

who can't find love and who instead (when they are women) go after dopey, superficial men or (when they are men) pursue endless sexual liaisons without finding true happiness. And we want to call all these things — and many, many more — addictions.

Since I was part of the movement to label non-drug-related behaviors as addictions, what am I complaining about? My entire purpose in writing *Love and Addiction* was to explain addictions as part of a larger description of people's lives. Addiction is an experience that people can get caught up in but that still expresses their values, skills at living, and personal resolve — or lack of it. The label *addiction* does not obviate either the meaning of the addictive involvement within people's lives, or their responsibility for their misbehavior or for their choices in continuing the addiction. Forty million Americans have quit smoking. What, then, are we to think about the people who do not quit but who sue a tobacco company for addicting them to cigarettes after they learn they are going to die from a smoking-related ailment?

This discrepancy between understanding addiction within the larger context of a person's life and regarding it as an *explanation* of that life underlies my opposition to the "disease theory" of addiction, which I contest throughout this book. My view of addiction explicitly refutes this theory's contentions that (1) the addiction exists *independently* of the rest of a person's life and *drives* all of his or her choices; (2) it is progressive and irreversible, so that the addiction *inevitably worsens* unless the person seeks medical treatment or joins an AA-type support group; (3) addiction means the person is incapable of controlling his or her behavior, either in relation to the addictive object itself or — when the person is intoxicated or in pursuit of the addiction — in relation to the person's dealings with the rest of the world. Everything I oppose in the disease view is represented in the passive, *1984*-ish phrase, *alcohol abuse victim,* to replace *alcohol abuser.* On the contrary, this book maintains that people are *active agents* in — not passive victims of — their addictions.

While I do believe that a host of human habits and compulsions can be understood as addictions, I think the disease version of addiction does *at least* as much harm as good. An addiction does not mean that God in heaven decided which people are alcoholics and addicts. There is no biological urge to form addictions, one that we will someday find under a microscope and that will finally make sense of all these different cravings and idiocies (such as exercising to the point of injury or having sex with people who are bad for you). No medical treatment will ever be created to excise addictions from people's lives, and support groups that convince people that they are helpless and will forever be incapable of controlling an activity are better examples of self-fulfilling prophecies than of therapy.

What is this new addiction industry meant to accomplish? More and more addictions are being discovered, and new addicts are being identified, until all of us will be locked into our own little addictive worlds with other addicts like ourselves, defined by the special interests of our neuroses. What a repugnant world to imagine, as well as a hopeless one. Meanwhile, *all of the addictions we define are increasing.* In the first place, we tell people they can never get better from their "diseases." In the second, we constantly find new addicts, looking for them in all sorts of new areas of behavior and labeling them at earlier ages on the basis of more casual or typical behaviors, such as getting drunk at holiday celebrations ("chemical-dependency disease") or checking to see whether they locked their car door ("obsessive-compulsive disorder").

We must oppose this nonsense by understanding its sources and contradicting disease ideology. . . . Our society is going wrong in excusing crime, compelling people to undergo treatment, and wildly mixing up moral responsibility with disease diagnoses. Indeed, understanding the confusion and self-defeating behavior we display in this regard is perhaps the best way to analyze the failure of many of our contemporary social policies. . . . [We must] confront the actual social, psychological, and moral issues that we face as individuals and as a society — the ones we are constantly repressing and mislabeling through widening our disease nets. It is as though we were creating distorted microscopes that actually muddy our vision and that make our problems harder to resolve into components we can reasonably hope to deal with.

What are real diseases? If we are to distinguish between addiction and other diseases, then we first need to understand what have been called diseases historically and how these differ from what are being called diseases today. To do so, let us review three generations of diseases — physical ailments, mental disorders, and addictions.

The *first* generation of diseases consists of disorders known through their physical manifestations, like malaria, tuberculosis, cancer, and AIDS. The era of medical understanding that these diseases ushered in began with the discovery of specific microbes that cause particular diseases and for which preventive inoculations — and eventually antibodies — were developed. These maladies are the ones we can unreservedly call diseases without clouding the issue. This first generation of diseases differs fundamentally from what were later called diseases in that the former are *defined by their measurable physical effects.* They are clearly connected to the functioning of the body, and our concern is with the damage the disease does to the body.

The *second* generation of diseases are the so-called mental illnesses (now referred to as emotional disorders). They are not defined in the same way as the first generation. Emotional disorders are apparent to us not because of what we measure in people's bodies but because of the feelings, thoughts, and behaviors that they produce in people, which we can only know from what the sufferers say and do. We do not diagnose emotional disorders from a brain scan; if a person cannot tell reality from fantasy, we call the person mentally ill, no matter what the person's EEG says.

The *third* generation of diseases — addictions — strays still farther from the model of physical disorder to which the name *disease* was first applied by modern medicine. That is, unlike a mental illness such as schizophrenia, which is indicated by disordered thinking, addictive disorders *are known by the goal-directed behaviors they describe.* We call a person a drug addict who consumes drugs compulsively or excessively and whose life is devoted to seeking out these substances. If an addicted smoker gives up smoking or if a habituated coffee drinker decides to drink coffee only after Sunday dinner, then each ceases to be addicted. We cannot tell whether a person is addicted or will be addicted in the absence of the ongoing behavior — the person with a hypothetical alcoholic predisposition (say, one who has an alcoholic parent or whose face flushes when drinking) but who drinks occasionally and moderately is not an alcoholic.

In order to clarify the differences between third-generation and first-generation diseases, we often have to overcome shifting definitions that have been changed solely for the purpose of obscuring crucial differences between problems like cancer and addiction. After a time, we seem not to recognize how our views have been manipulated by such gerrymandered disease criteria. For example, by claiming that alcoholics are alcoholics even if they haven't drunk for fifteen years, alcoholism is made to seem less tied to drinking behavior and more like cancer. Sometimes it seems necessary to remind ourselves of the obvious: that a person does not get over cancer by stopping a single behavior or even by changing a whole life-style, but the sole and essential indicator for successful remission of alcoholism is that the person ceases to drink.

Addictions involve appetites and behaviors. While a connection 15 can be traced between individual and cultural beliefs and first- and second-generation diseases, this connection is most pronounced for addictions. Behaviors and appetites are addictions only in particular cultural contexts — obviously, obesity matters only where people have enough to eat and think it is important to be thin. Symptoms like loss-of-control drinking depend *completely* on cultural and personal meanings, and cultural groups that don't understand how people can lose control of their drinking are almost immune to alcoholism. What is most important, however, is not how cultural beliefs affect addictions but how our defining of addictions as diseases affects our views of ourselves as individuals and as a society. . . .

What Is Addiction, and How Do People Get It?

While individual practitioners and recovering addicts — and the whole addiction movement — may believe they are helping people, they succeed principally at expanding their industry by finding more addicts and new types of addictions to treat. I too have argued — in books from *Love and Addiction* to *The Meaning of Addiction* — that addiction *can* take place with any human activity. Addiction is *not,* however, something people are born with. Nor is it a biological imperative, one that means the addicted individual is not able to consider or choose alternatives. The disease view of addiction is equally untrue when applied to gambling, compulsive sex, and everything else that it has been used to explain. Indeed, the fact that people become addicted to all these things *proves* that addiction is not *caused* by chemical or biological forces and that it is not a special disease state.

The nature of addiction. People seek specific, essential human experiences from their addictive involvement, no matter whether it is drinking, eating, smoking, loving, shopping, or gambling. People can come to depend on such an involvement for these experiences until — in the extreme — the involvement is totally consuming and potentially destructive. Addiction can occasionally veer into total abandonment, as well as periodic excesses and loss of control. Nonetheless, even in cases where addicts die from their excesses, an addiction must be understood as a human response that is motivated by the addict's desires and principles. All addictions *accomplish something for the addict.* They are ways of coping with feelings and situations with which addicts cannot otherwise cope. What is wrong with disease theories as science is that they are *tautologies;* they avoid the work of understanding *why* people drink or smoke in favor of simply declaring these activities to be addictions, as in the statement "He drinks so much because he's an alcoholic."

Addicts seek experiences that satisfy needs they cannot otherwise fulfill. Any addiction involves three components — the person, the situation or environment, and the addictive involvement or experience (see Table 1). In addition to the individual, the situation, and the experience, we also need to consider the overall cultural and social factors that affect addiction in our society.

The social and cultural milieu. We must also consider the enormous social-class differences in addiction rates. That is, the farther down the social and economic scale a person is, the more likely the person is to become addicted to alcohol, drugs, or cigarettes, to be obese, or to be a victim or perpetrator of family or sexual abuse. How does it come to be that addiction is a "disease" rooted in certain social experiences, and why in particular are drug addiction and alcoholism associated primarily with certain groups? A smaller

TABLE 1

The Person	The Situation	The Addictive Experience
Unable to fulfill essential needs	Barren and deprived: disadvantaged social groups, war zones	Creates powerful and immediate sensations; focuses and absorbs attention
Values that support or do not counteract addiction: e.g., lack of achievement motivation	Antisocial peer groups	
	Absence of supportive social groups; disturbed family structure	Provides artificial or temporary sense of self-worth, power, control, security, intimacy, accomplishment
Lack of restraint and inhibition		
Lack of self-efficacy; sense of powerlessness vis-à-vis the addiction	Life situations: adolescence, temporary isolation, deprivation, or stress	Eliminates pain, uncertainty, and other negative sensations

range of addiction and behavioral problems are associated with the middle and upper social classes. These associations must also be explained. Some addictions, like shopping, are obviously connected with the middle class. Bulimia and exercise addiction are also primarily middle-class addictions.

Finally, we must explore why addictions of one kind or another appear on our social landscape all of sudden, almost as though floodgates were released. For example, alcoholism was unknown to most colonial Americans and to most Americans earlier in this century; now it dominates public attention. This is not due to greater consumption, since we are actually drinking *less* alcohol than the colonists did. Bulimia, PMS, shopping addiction, and exercise addiction are wholly new inventions. Not that it isn't possible to go back in time to find examples of things that appear to conform to these new diseases. Yet their widespread — almost commonplace — presence in today's society must be explained, especially when the disease — like alcoholism — is supposedly biologically inbred. . . . 20

Are addicts disease victims? The development of an addictive life-style is an accumulation of patterns in people's lives of which drug use is neither a result nor a cause but another example. Sid Vicious was the consummate drug addict, an exception even among heroin users. Nonetheless, we need to understand the extremes to gain a sense of the shape of the entire phenomenon of addiction. Vicious, rather than being a passive victim of drugs, seemed intent on being and remaining addicted. He avoided opportunities to escape and turned every aspect of his life toward his addictions — booze,

Nancy, drugs — while sacrificing anything that might have rescued him — music, business interests, family, friendships, survival instincts. Vicious was pathetic; in a sense, he was a victim of his own life. But his addiction, like his life, was more an active expression of his pathos than a passive victimization.

Addiction theories have been created because it stuns us that people would hurt — perhaps destroy — themselves through drugs, drinking, sex, gambling, and so on. While people get caught up in an addictive dynamic over which they do not have full control, it is at least as accurate to say that people consciously select an addiction as it is to say an addiction has a person under its control. And this is why addiction is so hard to ferret out of the person's life — because it fits the person. The bulimic woman who has found that self-induced vomiting helps her to control her weight and who feels more attractive after throwing up is a hard person to persuade to give up her habit voluntarily. Consider the homeless man who refused to go to one of Mayor Koch's New York City shelters because he couldn't easily drink there and who said, "I don't want to give up drinking; it's the only thing I've got."

The researcher who has done the most to explore the personalities of alcoholics and drug addicts is psychologist Craig MacAndrew. MacAndrew developed the MAC scale, selected from items on the MMPI (a personality scale) that distinguish clinical alcoholics and drug abusers from normal subjects and from other psychiatric patients. This scale identifies antisocial impulsiveness and acting out: "an assertive, aggressive, pleasure-seeking character," in terms of which alcoholics and drug abusers closely "resemble criminals and delinquents."[5] These characteristics are not the *results* of substance abuse. Several studies have measured these traits in young men *prior* to [their] becoming alcoholics and in young drug and alcohol abusers.[6] This same kind of antisocial thrill-seeking characterizes most women who become alcoholic. Such women more often have disciplinary problems at school, react to boredom by "stirring up some kind of excitement," engage in more disapproved sexual practices, and have more trouble with the law.[7]

---

[5]C. MacAndrew, "What the MAC Scale Tells Us about Men Alcoholics," *Journal of Studies on Alcohol* 42 (1981), p. 617.

[6]H. Hoffman, R. G. Loper, and M. L. Kammeier, "Identifying Future Alcoholics with MMPI Alcoholism Scores," *Quarterly Journal of Studies on Alcohol* 35 (1974), pp. 490–498; M. C. Jones, "Personality Correlates and Antecedents of Drinking Patterns in Adult Males," *Journal of Consulting and Clinical Psychology* 32 (1968), pp. 2–12; R. G. Loper, M. L. Kammeier, and H. Hoffman, "MMPI Characteristics of College Freshman Males Who Later Become Alcoholics," *Journal of Abnormal Psychology* 82 (1973), pp. 159–162; C. MacAndrew, "Toward the Psychometric Detection of Substance Misuse in Young Men," *Journal of Studies on Alcohol* 47 (1986), pp. 161–166.

[7]C. MacAndrew, "Similarities in the Self-Depictions of Female Alcoholics and Psychiatric Outpatients," *Journal of Studies on Alcohol* 47 (1986), pp. 478–484.

The typical alcoholic, then, fulfills antisocial drives and pursues immediate, sensual, and aggressive rewards while having underdeveloped inhibitions. MacAndrew also found that another, smaller group comprising both men and women alcoholics — but more often women — drank to alleviate internal conflicts and feelings like depression. This group of alcoholics viewed the world, in MacAndrew's words, "primarily in terms of its potentially punishing character." For them, "alcohol functions as a palliation for a chronically fearful, distressful internal state of affairs." While these drinkers also sought specific rewards in drinking, these rewards were defined more by internal states than by external behaviors. Nonetheless, we can see that this group too did not consider normal social strictures in pursuing feelings they desperately desired.

MacAndrew's approach in this research was to identify particular personality types identified by the experiences they looked to alcohol to provide. But even for alcoholics or addicts without such distinct personalities, the purposeful dynamic is at play. For example, in *The Lives of John Lennon,* Albert Goldman describes how Lennon — who was addicted over his career to a host of drugs — would get drunk when he went out to dinner with Yoko Ono so that he could spill out his resentments of her. In many families, drinking allows alcoholics to express emotions that they are otherwise unable to express. The entire panoply of feelings and behaviors that alcohol may bring about for individual drinkers thus can be motivations for chronic intoxication. While some desire power from drinking, others seek to escape in alcohol; for some drinking is the route to excitement, while others welcome its calming effects.

25

Alcoholics or addicts may have more emotional problems or more deprived backgrounds than others, but probably they are best characterized as feeling powerless to bring about the feelings they want or to accomplish their goals without drugs, alcohol, or some other involvement. Their sense of powerlessness then translates into the belief that the drug or alcohol is extremely powerful. They see in the substance the ability to accomplish what they need or want but can't do on their own. The double edge to this sword is that the person is easily convinced that he or she cannot function without the substance or addiction, that he or she requires it to survive. This sense of personal powerlessness, on the one hand, and of the extreme power of an involvement or substance, on the other, readily translates into addiction.[8]

---

[8]G. A. Marlatt, "Alcohol, the Magic Elixir," in *Stress and Addiction,* ed. E. Gottheil et al. (New York: Brunner/Mazel, 1987); D. J. Rohsenow, "Alcoholics' Perceptions of Control," in *Identifying and Measuring Alcoholic Personality Characteristics,* ed. W. M. Cox (San Francisco: Jossey-Bass, 1983).

People don't manage to become alcoholics over years of drinking simply because their bodies are playing tricks on them — say, by allowing them to imbibe more than is good for them without realizing it until they become dependent on booze. Alcoholics' long drinking careers are motivated by their search for essential experiences they cannot gain in other ways. The odd thing is that — despite a constant parade of newspaper and magazine articles and TV programs trying to convince us otherwise — most people recognize that alcoholics drink for specific purposes. Even alcoholics, however much they spout the party line, know this about themselves. Consider, for example, . . . Monica Wright, the head of a New York City treatment center, [who] describes how she drank over the twenty years of her alcoholic marriage to cope with her insecurity and with her inability to deal with her husband and children. It is impossible to find an alcoholic who does not express similar reasons for his or her drinking, once the disease dogma is peeled away. . . .

Analysis

Peele is not the only writer to take issue with the popular practice of defining all kinds of mental and social problems as addictions. (A recent satirical newspaper article is entitled, "It's Not Me That's Guilty. My Addiction Just Took Over.") Peele's definition will be disputed by many doctors, psychologists, and a powerful industry of self-appointed healers. But definitions that attack popular opinions are often the liveliest and most interesting both to read and to write. In addition, they may serve a useful purpose, even if they are misguided, in encouraging new thinking about apparently intractable problems.

In defense of a controversial definition, an author must do at least two things: (1) make clear why a new definition is needed, that is, why the old definition does not work to explain certain conditions, and (2) argue that the new definition offers a better explanation and may even lead to more effective solutions of a problem.

The first part of Peele's argument is definition by negation. (Notice the title of this section.) Peele insists that the number of drug and alcohol addicts among both the poor and the well-to-do is not nearly so large as practitioners would have it. Next, he points out that addiction is not an explanation of a person's life, as some have insisted, nor does it mean that the addict is a victim to be absolved of responsibility for the consequences of his actions. Last, he provides the reasons that addiction is not a disease, basing his argument on the historic definition of disease as a bodily ailment whose physical effects are measurable. Defining mental illness and addiction as diseases is, Peele thinks, an evasion of the truth.

Some readers will question the narrowness of Peele's stipulation. Since the term *disease* has come to signify almost everywhere (including the dictionary) a disorder that need not be biological in origin, these readers may feel that Peele is attacking a nonexistent problem. But in the next section — "What Is Addiction?" — he elaborates on his major point: Addicts are not passive victims. Addiction is a choice, derived from the addict's desires and principles. Because this is the heart of the controversy, Peele devotes the rest of his essay to its development. In "The Nature of Addiction" he gives an overview of the motives that lead addicts to alcohol or drugs. Later, in "Are Addicts Disease Victims?" he enlarges on the descriptions of their behavior and identifies specific reasons for their actions. One of the strengths of his argument is the breadth of the analysis. In a few pages he touches on all the relevant causes of the addict's choices: the individual, the situation, the addictive experience, the social and cultural milieu.

The support for his claim is not exhaustive, but it offers a variety of evidence: examples of familiar individuals and types (Sid Vicious, John Lennon, the bulimic, the homeless man, the head of a treatment center), clear explanations of different kinds of addictive behavior, and a detailed summary of expert opinion.

All this evidence, if it is to work, must make an appeal to the common sense and experience of the reader. As Peele says, "The odd thing is that — despite a constant parade of newspaper and magazine articles and TV programs trying to convince us otherwise — most people recognize that alcoholics drink for specific purposes." Most readers, of course, will not be experts, but if they find the evidence consistent with their knowledge of and experience with addiction, they will find Peele's definition deserving of additional study.

The Nature of Prejudice

GORDON ALLPORT

Before I attempt to define prejudice, let us have in mind four instances that I think we all would agree are prejudice.

The first is the case of the Cambridge University student who said, "I despise all Americans. But," he added, a bit puzzled, "I've never met one that I didn't like."

The second is the case of another Englishman, who said to an American, "I think you're awfully unfair in your treatment to Negroes. How *do* Americans feel about Negroes?" The American replied, "Well, I suppose some Americans feel about Negroes just the way you feel about the Irish." The Englishman said, "Oh, come now. The Negroes are human beings."

Then there's the incident that occasionally takes place in various parts of the world (in the West Indies, for example, I'm told). When an American walks down the street the natives conspicuously hold their noses till the American goes by. The case of odor is always interesting. Odor gets mixed up with prejudice because odor has great associative power. We know that some Chinese deplore the odor of Americans. Some white people think Negroes have a distinctive smell and vice versa. An intrepid psychologist recently did an experiment; it went as follows. He brought to a gymnasium an equal number of white and colored students and had them take shower baths. When they were nice and clean he had them exercise vigorously for fifteen minutes. Then he brought his judges in, and each went to the sheeted figures and sniffed. They were to say "white" or "black," guessing at the identity of the subject. The experiment seemed to prove that when we are sweaty we all smell the same way. It's good to have experimental demonstration of the fact.

The fourth example I'd like to bring before you is a piece of writing that I quote. Please ask yourselves who, in your judgment, wrote it. It's a passage about the Jews. 5

> The synagogue is worse than a brothel. It's a den of scoundrels. It's a criminal assembly of Jews, a place of meeting for the assassins of

---

Gordon Allport (1897–1967) was a psychologist who taught at Harvard University from 1924 until his death. He was author of numerous books, among them *Personality: A Psychological Interpretation* (1937). Allport delivered "The Nature of Prejudice" at the Seventeenth Claremont Reading Conference in 1952. The speech was published as a paper in 1952 in the Seventeenth Claremont Reading Conference Yearbook.

Christ, a den of thieves, a house of ill fame, a dwelling of iniquity. Whatever name more horrible to be found, it could never be worse than the synagogue deserves.

I would say the same things about their souls. Debauchery and drunkenness have brought them to the level of lusty goat and pig. They know only one thing: to satisfy their stomachs and get drunk, kill, and beat each other up. Why should we salute them? We should not even have the slightest converse with them. They are lustful, rapacious, greedy, perfidious robbers.

Now who wrote that? Perhaps you say Hitler, or Goebbels, or one of our local anti-Semites? No, it was written by Saint John Chrysostom, in the fourth century A.D. Saint John Chrysostom, as you know, gave us the first liturgy in the Christian church, still used in the Orthodox churches today. From it all services of the Holy Communion derive. Episcopalians will recognize him also as the author of that exalted prayer that closes the offices of both matins and evensong in the *Book of Common Prayer*. I include this incident to show how complex the problem is. Religious people are by no means necessarily free from prejudice. In this regard be patient even with our saints.

What do these four instances have in common? You notice that all of them indicate that somebody is "down" on somebody else — a feeling of rejection, or hostility. But also, in all these four instances, there is indication that the person is not "up" on his subject — not really informed about Americans, Irish, Jews, or bodily odors.

So I would offer, first a slang definition of prejudice: *Prejudice is being down on somebody you're not up on*. If you dislike slang, let me offer the same thought in the style of St. Thomas Aquinas. Thomists have defined prejudice as *thinking ill of others without sufficient warrant.*

You notice that both definitions, as well as the examples I gave, specify two ingredients of prejudice. First there is some sort of faulty generalization in thinking about a group. I'll call this the process of *categorization*. Then there is the negative, rejective, or hostile ingredient, a *feeling* tone. "Being down on something" is the hostile ingredient; "that you're not up on" is the categorization ingredient; "thinking ill of others" is the hostile ingredient; "without sufficient warrant" is the faulty categorization.

Parenthetically I should say that of course there is such a thing as *positive* prejudice. We can be just as prejudiced *in favor of* as we are *against*. We can be biased in favor of our children, our neighborhood, or our college. Spinoza makes the distinction neatly. He says that *love prejudice* is "thinking well of others, through love, more than is right." *Hate prejudice,* he says, is "thinking ill of others, through hate, more than is right."

10

Reading and Discussion Questions

1. This was a speech, obviously not delivered extemporaneously but read to the audience. What characteristics suggest an oral presentation? If you were to revise this essay into a paper, what changes would you make? Why?
2. Allport has arranged his anecdotes carefully. What principle of organization has he used?
3. This essay was written in 1952. Are there any references or examples that seem dated? Why or why not?

Writing Suggestions

4. Some media critics claim that negative prejudice exists in the treatment of certain groups in movies and television. If you agree, select a group that seems to you to be the object of prejudice in these media, and offer evidence of the prejudice and the probable reasons for it. Or disagree with the media critics and provide evidence that certain groups are *not* the object of prejudice.
5. Can you think of examples of what Allport calls *positive prejudice*? Perhaps you can find instances that are less obvious than the ones Allport mentions. Explain in what way these prejudices represent a love that is "more than is right."

What Sexual Harassment Is — and Is Not

ELLEN BRAVO and ELLEN CASSEDY

Louette Colombano was one of the first female police officers in her San Francisco district. While listening to the watch commander, she and the other officers stood at attention with their hands behind their backs. The officer behind her unzipped his fly and rubbed his penis against her hands.

Diane, a buyer, was preparing to meet an out-of-town client for dinner when she received a message: her boss had informed the client that she would spend the night with him. Diane sent word that she couldn't make it to dinner. The next day she was fired.

Ellen Bravo is the national director of 9to5, an organization for working women. Ellen Cassedy, a founder of 9to5, writes a column for the *Philadelphia Daily News.* This article is excerpted from their book, *The 9 to 5 Guide to Combating Sexual Harassment* (New York: John Wiley & Sons, 1992). Reprinted by permission of John Wiley & Sons, Inc.

Few people would disagree that these are clear-cut examples of sexual harassment. Touching someone in a deliberately sexual way, demanding that an employee engage in sex or lose her job — such behavior is clearly out of bounds. (It's also *illegal.* . . .) But in less obvious cases, many people are confused about where to draw the line.

Is It Harassment?

Is all sexual conversation inappropriate at work? Is every kind of touching off limits? Consider the following examples. In your opinion, which, if any, constitute sexual harassment?

- A male manager asks a female subordinate to lunch to discuss a new project.
- A man puts his arm around a woman at work.
- A woman tells an off-color joke.
- These comments are made at the workplace:

  "Your hair looks terrific."

  "That outfit's a knockout."

  "Did you get any last night?"

The answer in each of these cases is, "It depends." Each one 5 *could* be an example of sexual harassment — or it could be acceptable behavior.

Take the case of the manager asking a female subordinate to lunch to discuss a new project. Suppose this manager often has such lunchtime meetings with his employees, male and female. Everyone is aware that he likes to get out of the office environment in order to get to know the associates a little better and to learn how they function — for example, whether they prefer frequent meetings or written reports, detailed instructions or more delegation of responsibility. The female subordinate in this case may feel she's being treated just like other colleagues and be glad to receive the individual attention.

On the other hand, suppose this subordinate has been trying for some time, unsuccessfully, to be assigned to an interesting project. The only woman who does get plum assignments spends a lot of time out of the office with the boss; the two of them are rumored to be sleeping together. The lunch may represent an opportunity t′ move ahead, but it could mean that the manager expects a physj relationship in return. In this case, an invitation to lunch witḥ boss is laden with unwelcome sexual overtones.

An arm around the shoulder, an off-color joke, commen′ someone's appearance, or even sexual remarks may or ꞃ offensive. What matters is the relationship between the and how each of them feels.

"Your hair looks terrific," for instance, could be an innocuous compliment if it were tossed off by one co-worker to another as they passed in the hall. But imagine this same phrase coming from a male boss bending down next to his secretary's ear and speaking in a suggestive whisper. Suddenly, these innocent-sounding words take on a different meaning. The body language and tone of voice signify something sexual. While the comment itself may not amount to much, the secretary is left to wonder *what else the boss has in mind.*

On the other hand, even words that may seem grossly inappropriate — "Did you get any last night?" — can be harmless in certain work situations. One group of male and female assembly-line workers talked like this all the time. What made it okay? They were friends and equals — no one in the group had power over any of the others. They were all comfortable with the banter. They hadn't drawn up a list specifying which words were acceptable to the group and which were not. But they had worked together for some time and knew one another well. Their remarks were made with affection and accepted as good-natured. No one intended to offend — and no one was offended. The assembly-line area was relatively isolated, so the workers weren't in danger of bothering anyone outside their group. Had a new person joined the group who wasn't comfortable with this kind of talk, the others would have stopped it. They might have thought the new person uptight, they might not have liked the new atmosphere, but they would have respected and honored any request to eliminate the remarks.

This is the essence of combating sexual harassment — creating a workplace that is built on mutual respect.

Looking at Harassment

Try assessing whether each of the following scenarios constitutes sexual harassment. Then consider the analysis that follows.

Scenario 1: Justine works in a predominantly male department. She has tried to fit in, even laughing on occasion at the frequent sexual jokes. The truth is, though, that she gets more irritated by the jokes each day. It is well known in the department that Justine has an out-of-town boyfriend whom she sees most weekends. Nonetheless, Franklin, one of Justine's co-workers, has said he has the "hots" for her and that — boyfriend or not — he's willing to do almost anything to get a date with her. One day, Sarah, another of Justine's co-workers, overheard their boss talking to Franklin in the hallway. "If you can get her to go to bed with you," the boss said, "I'll take you out to dinner. Good luck." They chuckled and went their separate ways. (From the consulting firm of Jane C. Edmonds & Associates, Inc., *Boston Globe*, 10/24/91.)

The boss is out of line. True, he probably didn't intend anyone to overhear him. But why was he having this conversation in the hallway? What was he doing having the conversation at all? The boss is responsible for keeping the workplace free of harassment. Instead, he's giving Franklin an incentive to make sexual advances to a co-worker and then to brag about it.

The conversation may constitute harassment not only of Justine   15 but also of Sarah, who overheard the conversation. A reasonable woman might easily wonder, "Who's he going to encourage to go after *me*?" Ideally, Sarah should tell the two men she was offended by their remarks. But given that one of them is her boss, it would be understandable if she were reluctant to criticize his behavior.

Franklin isn't just romantically interested in Justine; he "has the hots" for her and is willing to "do almost anything" to get a date with her. Justine could well be interested in a "fling" with Franklin. But she's irritated by the sexual remarks and innuendoes in the workplace. It's unlikely that she would be flattered by attention from one of the men responsible for this atmosphere.

Justine can just say no to Franklin. But she may well object to having to say no over and over. And most women are not pleased to be the brunt of jokes and boasts. Some may argue that whether Franklin and Justine get together is a personal matter between the two of them. The moment it becomes the subject of public boasting, however, Franklin's interest in Justine ceases to be just a private interaction.

The law doesn't say Justine should be tough enough to speak up on her own — it says the company is responsible for providing an environment free of offensive or hostile behavior. As the person in charge, the boss ought to know what kind of remarks are being made in the workplace and whether employees are offended by them. Instead of making Franklin think the way to win favor with him is to pressure a co-worker into bed, the manager might want to arrange for some training on sexual harassment.

Scenario 2:   Freda has been working for Bruce for three years. He believes they have a good working relationship. Freda has never complained to Bruce about anything and appears to be happy in her job. Bruce regularly compliments Freda on her clothing; in his opinion, she has excellent taste and a good figure. Typically, he'll make a remark like "You sure look good today." Last week, Freda was having a bad day and told Bruce that she was "sick and tired of being treated like a sex object." Bruce was stunned. (From the consulting firm of Jane C. Edmonds & Associates, Inc., *Boston Globe*, 10/24/91.)

There's really not enough information to come to any conclu-   20 sion in this case. The scenario explains how Bruce feels, but not Freda. In the past, when he said, "Hey, you look good today," did Freda usually answer, "So do you"? Or did he murmur, "Mmm, you look go-o-o-o-d," and stare at her chest while she crossed her arms and said, "Thank you, sir"? In addition to complimenting Freda's appearance, did Bruce ever praise her work? Did he compliment other women? Men?

It is plausible that Freda might have been upset earlier. She probably wouldn't say she was tired of being treated like a sex object unless she'd felt that way before. Why didn't she speak up sooner? It's not uncommon for someone in Freda's situation to be reluctant to say anything for fear of looking foolish or appearing to be a "bad sport." Remember, Bruce is her boss.

Bruce states that he was stunned when Freda blew up at him. He needs to consider whether Freda might have given him any signals he ignored. He should ask himself how his compliments fit in with the way he treats other employees. Has he really given Freda an opening to object to his remarks?

The most comfortable solution might be for Bruce and Freda to sit down and talk. Perhaps Freda doesn't really mind the compliments themselves but wants more attention paid to her work. If Freda has been upset about the compliments all along, Bruce is probably guilty only of not paying close attention to her feelings. He should let her know that he values her work *and* her feelings, listen carefully to what she has to say, and encourage her to speak up promptly about issues that may arise in the future.

Scenario 3:   Barbara is a receptionist for a printing company. Surrounding her desk are five versions of ads printed by the company for a beer distributor. The posters feature women provocatively posed with a can of beer and the slogan, "What'll you have?" On numerous occasions, male customers have walked in, looked at the posters, and commented, "I'll have you, baby." When Barbara tells her boss she wants the posters removed, he responds by saying they represent the company's work and he's proud to display them. He claims no one but Barbara is bothered by the posters.

The legal standard in this case is not how the boss feels, but whether a "reasonable woman" might object to being surrounded by such posters. The company has other products it could display. Barbara has not insisted that the company refuse this account or exclude these posters from the company portfolio. She has merely said she doesn't want the posters displayed around *her* desk. Barbara's view is substantiated by how she's been treated; the posters seem to give customers license to make suggestive remarks to her.

Scenario 4:   Therese tells Andrew, her subordinate, that she needs him to escort her to a party. She says she's selecting him because he's the most handsome guy on her staff. Andrew says he's busy. Therese responds that she expects people on her staff to be team players.

Therese may have wanted Andrew merely to accompany her to the party, not to have a sexual relationship with her. And Andrew might have been willing to go along if he hadn't been busy. Nevertheless, a reasonable employee may worry about what the boss means by such a request, particularly when it's coupled with remarks about personal appearance.

Andrew might not mind that Therese finds him handsome. But most people would object to having their job tied to their willingness to make a social appearance with the boss outside of work. The implicit threat also makes Therese's request unacceptable. The company should prohibit managers from requiring subordinates to escort them to social engagements.

Scenario 5: Darlene invites her co-worker Dan for a date. They begin a relationship that lasts several months. Then Darlene decides she is no longer interested and breaks up with Dan. He wants the relationship to continue. During the workday, he frequently calls her on the interoffice phone and stops by her desk to talk. Darlene tries to brush him off, but with no success. She asks her manager to intervene. The manager says he doesn't get involved in personal matters.

Most managers are rightly reluctant to involve themselves in 30 employees' personal relationships. Had Darlene asked for help dealing with Dan outside of work, the manager would have been justified in staying out of it. He could have referred her to the employee assistance program, if the company had one.

Once Dan starts interfering with Darlene's work, however, it's a different story. The company has an obligation to make sure the work environment is free from harassment. If Darlene finds herself less able to do her job or uncomfortable at work because of Dan and if her own efforts have failed, the manager has both the right and the responsibility to step in and tell Dan to back off.

Scenario 6: Susan likes to tell bawdy jokes. Bob objects. Although he doesn't mind when men use such language in the office, he doesn't think it's appropriate for women to do so.

An employee who objects to off-color jokes shouldn't have to listen to them at work, and management should back him up. Bob's problem, however, is restricted to jokes told by women. If he doesn't have the same problem when men tell such jokes, it's his problem — not the company's. Management can't enforce Bob's double standard.

Scenario 7: Janet is wearing a low-cut blouse and short shorts. John, her co-worker, says, "Now that I can see it, you gotta let me have some." Janet tells him to buzz off. All day, despite Janet's objections,

*John continues to make similar remarks. When Janet calls her supervi-
sor over to complain, John says, "Hey, can you blame me?"*

The company has a right to expect clothing appropriate to the   35
job. If Janet's clothes are inappropriate, management should tell her
so. But Janet's outfit doesn't give John license to say or do whatever
he likes. Once she tells him she doesn't like his comments, he
should stop — or be made to do so.

Scenario 8:   Someone posts a Hustler *magazine centerfold in the
employee men's room. No women use this room.*

Some would say that if the women aren't aware of the pinups in
the men's room, they can't be offensive. But when men walk out of the
restroom with such images in their mind's eye, how do they view their
female co-workers? And when the women find out about the pinups
— as they will — how will they feel? As the judge ruled in a 1991
Florida case involving nude posters at a shipyard, the presence of
such pictures, even if they aren't intended to offend women, "sexual-
izes the work environment to the detriment of all female employees."

A Common-Sense Definition

Sexual harassment is not complicated to define. To harass someone is to bother him or her. Sexual harassment is bothering someone in a sexual way. The harasser offers sexual attention to someone
who didn't ask for it and doesn't welcome it. The unwelcome behavior might or might not involve touching. It could just as well be spoken words, graphics, gestures, or even looks (not any look — but
the kind of leer or stare that says, "I want to undress you").

Who decides what behavior is offensive at the workplace? The
recipient does. As long as the recipient is "reasonable" and not unduly sensitive, sexual conduct that offends him or her should be
changed.

That doesn't mean there's a blueprint for defining sexual harass-   40
ment. "Reasonable" people don't always agree. Society celebrates
pluralism. Not everyone is expected to have the same standards of
morality or the same sense of humor. Still, reasonable people will
agree *much of the time* about what constitutes offensive behavior or
will recognize that certain behavior or language can be expected to
offend some others. Most people make distinctions between how
they talk to their best friends, to their children, and to their elderly
relatives. Out of respect, they avoid certain behavior in the presence
of certain people. The same distinctions must be applied at work.

Sexual harassment is different from the innocent mistake — that
is, when someone tells an off-color joke, not realizing the listener will
be offended, or gives what is meant as a friendly squeeze of the arm to
a co-worker who doesn't like to be touched. Such behavior may repre-

sent insensitivity, and that may be a serious problem, but it's usually not sexual harassment. In many cases, the person who tells the joke that misfires or who pats an unreceptive arm *knows right away* that he or she has made a mistake. Once aware or made aware, this individual will usually apologize and try not to do it again.

Do They Mean It?

Some offensive behavior stems from what University of Illinois psychologist Louise Fitzgerald calls "cultural lag." "Many men entered the workplace at a time when sexual teasing and innuendo were commonplace," Fitzgerald told the *New York Times*. "They have no idea there's anything wrong with it." Education will help such men change their behavior.

True harassers, on the other hand, *mean* to offend. Even when they know their talk or action is offensive, they continue. Sexual harassment is defined as behavior that is not only unwelcome but *repeated.* (Some kinds of behavior are *always* inappropriate, however, even if they occur only once. Grabbing someone's breast or crotch, for example, or threatening to fire a subordinate who won't engage in sexual activity does not need repetition to be deemed illegal.)

The true harasser acts not out of insensitivity but precisely because of the knowledge that the behavior will make the recipient uncomfortable. The harasser derives pleasure from the momentary or continuing powerlessness of the other individual. In some cases, the harasser presses the victim to have sex, but sexual pleasure itself is not the goal. Instead, the harasser's point is to dominate, to gain power over another. As University of Washington psychologist John Gottman puts it, "Harassment is a way for a man to make a woman vulnerable."

Some harassers target the people they consider the most likely 45 to be embarrassed and the least likely to file a charge. Male harassers are sometimes attempting to put "uppity women" in their place. In certain previously all-male workplaces, a woman who's simply attempting to do her job may be considered uppity. In this instance, the harassment is designed to make the woman feel out of place, if not to pressure her out of the job. Such harassment often takes place in front of an audience or is recounted to others afterwards ("pinch and tell").

Dr. Frances Conley, the renowned neurosurgeon who quit her job at Stanford Medical School after nearly twenty-five years of harassment, told legislators at a sexual harassment hearing in San Diego, California, that the "unsolicited touching, caressing, comments about my physical attributes" she experienced "were always for effect in front of an audience. . . ."

Part of the Job

Some harassers who don't consciously set out to offend are nevertheless unwilling to curb their behavior even after they're told it's offensive. If a woman doesn't like it, they figure that's her problem. And some harassers consider sexual favors from subordinates to be a "perk," as much a part of the job as a big mahogany desk and a private executive bathroom. A young woman on President Lyndon Johnson's staff, according to *A Sexual Profile of Men in Power* (Prentice-Hall, 1977), by Sam Janus and others, "was awakened in her bedroom on his Texas ranch in the middle of the night by a searching flashlight. Before she could scream, she heard a familiar voice: 'Move over. This is your president.'"

Men can be harassed by women, or both harasser and victim can be of the same sex. Overwhelmingly, however, sexual harassment is an injury inflicted on women by men. While the number of hard-core harassers is small, their presence is widely felt. Sexual harassment is ugly. And it's damaging — to the victims, to business, and to society as a whole.

DEFINING SEXUAL HARASSMENT

Sexual harassment means bothering someone in a sexual way.

Sexual harassment is behavior that is not only unwelcome but in most cases *repeated*.

The goal of sexual harassment is not sexual pleasure but gaining power over another.

Some male harassers want to put "uppity women" in their place.

The essence of combating sexual harassment is fostering mutual respect in the workplace.

Reading and Discussion Questions

1. What characteristics make this essay easy to read? Why do you think the authors have chosen to make their definition so accessible?
2. Most of the essay is devoted to specific examples. Where do the authors give a general definition of sexual harassment? Does the definition seem too broad or too narrow? Explain.
3. Why is the use of specific examples a particularly effective strategy for defining sexual harassment?
4. The authors say, " 'Reasonable' people will agree *much of the time* about what constitutes offensive behavior. . . ." Are there any examples of sexual harassment in this article with which you disagree? If so, explain your objection.
5. How would you characterize the tone of the article? Does it contribute to the effectiveness of the definition? Tell why or why not.

Writing Suggestions

6. Consider the reasons that sexual harassment has become a national issue. What social, political, and economic factors might account for the rise in complaints and public attention? Are some reasons more important than others?

7. The Clarence Thomas–Anita Hill case in October 1991 was a nationally televised hearing on sexual harassment which continues to reverberate. Look up the facts in several national news magazines. Then summarize them and come to a conclusion of your own about the justice of the accusations, emphasizing those areas of the debate that support your claim.

Heroes on Our Doorstep
MIKE BARNICLE

On the sidewalk outside Children's Hospital yesterday, the nurse stood in the breezy sunlight smoking a cigarette and eating an apple for lunch. As soon as she finished one Marlboro, her hand went right to the pack for another.

"Don't start," she said, "I know all about it. I've quit a hundred times. The problem is I've gone back a hundred and one."

"Maybe it's the job?" she was told.

"Nah," she laughed. "It's me. It's just me. I'm a weak individual."

She has been a nurse for a long time. She tends to children who 5 show up here looking for miracles. The kids come with cancer, a disease that does not discriminate, an often fatal illness that feeds on the human system without regard to any calendar: four or fifty-four, it doesn't matter to cancer.

She is part of a staff — doctors, nurses, even orderlies — who minister to the dying. The patients arrive from all over this country. Some buy time. Some others die on the ward.

"You see how some of these little children fight," the nurse was saying. "You see how brave they are and in its own way it is kind of thrilling to be part of the experience because you feel blessed to be among them, they are so strong."

"They are sick but they are strong. They have this spirit, you know," she said. "Certainly, it's sad but it's also uplifting because they have so much courage they make you feel good. They don't feel sorry for themselves. They deal with their situation and they make you deal with it too."

Mike Barnicle writes a thrice-weekly column in the *Boston Globe*, where this selection appeared on June 21, 1994.

O. J. Simpson made more in a month than this woman earned in the last two years. And for a week, all I have read in the paper, over and over again, is the constant reference to him as a hero, fallen now from a pedestal.

We have a horrendous problem in this country with violence 10 and disorder of every kind. We have become adept at making excuses, creating legal loopholes and avoiding any framework of individual responsibility. All this is common knowledge.

But we may have a larger problem of semantics, with the use and application of language and labels. We constantly confuse heroism with celebrity, figuring that because someone is famous or skilled at a specific task — carrying a football, hitting a baseball, acting out a scene in a movie — that they are mythic figures incapable of disappointing us with any of the evils committed by ordinary human beings. We consistently misinterpret what these people do on a field or a sound stage with who they are. But neither life nor individuals are that simple.

Yet we do it all the time: We confuse wealth with wisdom, figuring anyone worth millions must be smart. We rush to attach ourselves emotionally to people who are pretty, people who score touchdowns, sing songs on MTV, play great parts in action movies. We want to feel good about the famous so we allow them to lead make-believe lives, our very own contrivance, in the desperate hope that we will somehow feel better about ourselves because we heard or read or saw that this false idol or that creation of some political consultant was nice.

And as a result of being star-struck, we rarely notice the courage at our doorstep or heroes on the sidewalk alongside us. Firefighters rush into burning buildings seeking to save total strangers and it is only when one dies that we take the time to pay attention. Nurses labor with kids who cry from chemotherapy, holding them, hugging them, often willing life back into them and we take it for granted. Teachers act as educators, surrogate parents, and drug counselors and we resent their demand for higher pay. Police throw their bodies between the lawless and the innocent and their reward is a never-ending level of dissatisfaction because crime, like cancer, grows everywhere. There are mothers and fathers with several jobs who struggle to keep families together while their kids attend schools where others show up with handguns instead of history books.

This is an increasingly strange country, made more so by the foolish clamor over celebrity. It is a country in danger of losing what little is left of our institutional memory, a mental safeguard that allows us to establish priorities of what and who is truly important, based on performance as well as history. It is a country with the attention span of a cricket, where instant gratification is paramount: I want it now, with no effort and if I don't like it I will toss it out; doesn't matter what it is either — a marriage, a relationship, a pregnancy, a friend.

O. J. Simpson was a wonderful athlete who beat up a woman and may even have killed her. He was famous and gifted but never a hero. To find one of them, you have to stand on a city sidewalk and stare at a nurse who can't quit cigarettes because her nerves are frazzled from caring for all the dying children. 15

Reading and Discussion Questions

1. How does Barnicle make the transition from the nurse's comments to his definition of heroism? Is it effective? Why or why not?
2. Point out the use of transitional words and phrases that establish connections.
3. Barnicle changes his use of language at some point in the essay. What is the purpose of the change?
4. According to Barnicle, what is the outstanding characteristic of true heroism? Summarize his definition of heroism in one sentence.
5. Do you agree with Barnicle about our confusion of heroism with celebrity? Is he also right in arguing that our regard for celebrities "somehow [makes us] feel better about ourselves"?
6. As you read his list of the kinds of people to whom we attach ourselves emotionally, did the names of real people come to mind? Would his argument have been more persuasive if the author had mentioned real people by name?
7. In the next-to-last paragraph, Barnicle recommends establishing priorities that are truly important, "based on performance as well as history." How is this related to a discussion of a nurse and O. J. Simpson?

Writing Suggestions

8. In one class a student remarked that a man who had risked his life to save a stranger from drowning was not a hero but a fool, since the life of the rescuer, which might have been lost, was just as valuable as that of the stranger. (The sentiment expressed by the student is not new. As cited in Dixon Wecter, *The Hero in America* [Ann Arbor: Ann Arbor Paperbacks, 1963], p. 490, a 1914 antiwar poster proclaimed that anyone "who gave an arm or a leg for his country was 'a sucker'".) Write an essay agreeing or disagreeing with the student. Try to make clear a definition of heroism that would include or exclude the action of the would-be rescuer.
9. Can you think of someone you once regarded as a hero or heroine about whom you feel differently now? Is it because your own values have changed? If so, what caused the change?
10. If you have knowledge of a culture with different values from those of most Americans, describe a hero or heroine who exemplifies the virtues of that culture. Point out both the differences and the similarities.

I acquired the painting of my dreams.
Only to discover it was a brilliant forgery.

I bought stocks like they were going out of style.
And they were.

I married for love.
Then found I was being married for money.

I bought myself a Waterman.

There are some decisions one never lives to regret.

Pens write. A Waterman pen expresses. For more than a century, this distinction has remained constant. The creation shown here, for example, has been crafted from sterling silver, painstakingly tooled and balanced to absolute precision. Those who desire such an instrument of expression ⋂ will find Waterman pens in a breadth of styles, prices and lacquers.

*W*ATERMAN
— PARIS —

Discussion Questions

1. This ad is divided into two parts. The part in small print extols the distinctive attributes of the Waterman pen. Why does the advertiser relegate the description of his pen to the small print?
2. How does the advertiser define a superior "instrument of expression"? Does calling a pen an "instrument of expression" add something to the definition?
3. What contrast is the reader invited to examine in the humorous first part of the ad?

Penalize the Unwed Dad?
Fat Chance

LISA SCHIFFREN

America faces no problem more urgent than our skyrocketing illegitimacy rate. Last year, 30 percent of all babies were born out of wedlock, and the rate is expected to rise. Illegitimacy almost always sentences children to a life struggling against overwhelming odds that they will be poor and poorly educated and, for girls, prone to repeating the cycle of unwed motherhood and dependence on welfare.

For teenage mothers, completing school and acquiring marketable skills become major struggles. Marriage becomes less likely. Seventy-five percent of families headed by unmarried women live on $25,000 a year or less. The higher earners in that group are divorced; the income of most never-married mothers hovers between zero and the poverty line. In a society where work and marriage are the I-beams of a middle-class life, nothing that encourages illegitimacy can be considered in the interest of women or children.

It is important to keep these facts in mind when the Senate resumes its work on welfare reform next month. For even though all sides in the debate cite them repeatedly, few proposals actually address them.

The length of benefits and the work requirements for them may have some marginal effect on the people now receiving welfare. But considering the failure of every workfare program ever devised, tinkering is unlikely to help most of those who are in the system to transcend it.

The first goal should be to prevent girls who are not yet trapped 5 from having babies. The way to begin is to cut off the most obvious distorting incentives — cash, housing, and other subsidies — given to unwed teens for self-destructive decisions.

President Clinton recently asserted that there is a consensus not to do any such thing because it would punish innocent children.

How then would he change behavior? Like the feminist-welfare advocacy lobby, he would blame men. And along with Senator Bob

---

This article by Lisa Schiffren, a former speechwriter for Vice President Dan Quayle, appeared in the *New York Times* on August 10, 1995.

Dole, he believes that intensified efforts to get "deadbeat dads" of illegitimate children to pay child support and become involved in their children's lives will solve the problem.

The idea of punishing men for seduction and desertion is of course attractive. Unfortunately, it won't work. The nation already spends nearly $2 billion a year on child support enforcement, with state bureaucracies employing 40,000 people to collect money from divorced and never-married fathers.

Census Bureau data show that nearly 80 percent of the divorced women entitled to child support receive payments, while only 12 percent of women on Aid to Families with Dependent Children receive even negligible sums from their children's fathers.

But increased enforcement won't significantly narrow the gap. A 10
disproportionate number of unmarried fathers are unemployed, unemployable, or too young to work. Liberals were right when they argued that getting these men to pay was like squeezing blood from a stone.

Beyond that, it is bad policy for the state to enforce a contract that does not exist. We make divorced fathers support children they don't live with because marriage carries an obligation to offspring. Casual sex and teenage romance carries no such obligation. When teenagers are impregnated by older men or under coercive circumstances, the policy answers, in effect, are rape and statutory rape charges.

Blurring the distinction between legitimacy and illegitimacy undermines marriage at the very moment it most needs to be strengthened. (Notice how successfully liberals have destroyed the moral and substantive differences between divorced or widowed mothers and never-married mothers — all of whom we now call "single mothers.")

What teenage girls need most is a brutally realistic picture of what their lives will be like if they choose unwed motherhood. Society's unenforceable promise to make casual sexual partners behave like real fathers sends the wrong message. After all, as middle-class women learned during the sexual revolution, a man who indicates that he is interested in sex but not commitment should always be taken at his word.

Even granting that the men involved are scum, the inescapable fact is that women bear children. Since women and girls have sexual autonomy, they can and should be held accountable for how they use it. Before I am accused of blaming the victim, or wishing to deny women sexual freedom, recall that the women in question are not the classic victim caricature that the feminist-welfare lobby likes to cite. These are not wives bound by law or financial dependence to husbands. They are single women who control economic resources, in this case the AFDC check.

Contraception to prevent pregnancy is available — including 15
Norplant, Depo-Provera, and the pill. Abortion is an option.

Girls have the same educational opportunities and most of the economic opportunities boys have. This makes the choice of dependence less acceptable for poor women, just as it has for middle-class women.

The most useful thing we can do for girls on the verge of becoming welfare mothers is to make education, work, and marriage preferable to subsisting on a welfare check.

Sins of the Fathers

JOSEPH P. SHAPIRO and ANDREA R. WRIGHT

The problem with teen sex is not simply that teens are having sex. Adults, in disturbing numbers, are having sex with teens. It is not just Joey Buttafuoco and Amy Fisher, Woody Allen and Soon-Yi Previn or the fact that O. J. Simpson was thirty when he began dating an eighteen-year-old waitress named Nicole Brown. Federal and state surveys suggest that adult males are the fathers of some two-thirds of the babies born to teenage girls. According to the Alan Guttmacher Institute, 39 percent of fifteen-year-old mothers say the fathers of their babies are twenty years old or older. For seventeen-year-old teenage moms, 55 percent of the fathers are adults; for nineteen-year-olds, it is 78 percent.

Little inspires more national hand-wringing these days than the reality of teenage pregnancy. Americans blame impulsive kids and their raging hormones, ignoring the role of adult males. But in fact, teenage girls having sex with men is hardly a new phenomenon. In 1920, for example, 93 percent of babies born to teenagers were fathered by adults. What has changed is that more often than not, pregnant teens no longer marry the father. Today, 65 percent of teenage moms are unmarried, up from 48 percent in 1980. These teens and their children are at high risk of poverty, school failure, and welfare dependency.

Welfare reform, sex education, and teen pregnancy prevention programs are doomed to failure when they ignore the prevalence of adult-teen sex. The welfare reform bill passed by the House of Representatives would deny benefits to unmarried mothers under the age of eighteen, a provision that has become one of the most contentious points of the current debate in the Senate. But most studies suggest that curbing benefits alone will not stem the tide of teen pregnancies.

Joseph P. Shapiro is a senior editor and Andrea R. Wright a reporter-researcher at *U.S. News & World Report*, where this article appeared on August 14, 1995.

What drives teenage girls to become sexually involved with adult males is complex, and often does not follow the logic of Washington policymakers. In the minds of many teens, choosing an older boyfriend makes sense. Francisca Cativo was a sixteen-year-old high school junior when her daughter, Vanessa, was born last September. Her boyfriend, Jose Confesor, is twenty-four. To Cativo, who says she chose to get pregnant, Confesor's age was a plus; it meant he was more mature and more likely to support her child. "The boys around my age just want to be out in the streets playing around," she says. Still, on Confesor's salary as a part-time janitor, the couple is forced to live with his mother in a crowded apartment.

Older men seek out young girls for equally complex reasons — from believing there is less risk of disease to more chance of control. They often hold exaggerated power over their young companions. When teens get pregnant, for example, they are half as likely to have an abortion when their partners are twenty or older.

More disturbing, a sizable amount of teen sex is not consensual. Girls under the age of eighteen are the victims of about half of the nation's rapes each year, according to Justice Department data. When researchers Debra Boyer and David Fine surveyed poor and pregnant teens at Washington State's public health clinics, they were startled to find that two-thirds of these girls reported prior sexual abuse, almost always by parents, guardians, or relatives. Even more shocking: On average, the girls were less than ten years old at the time of the first abuse while the offending male was twenty-seven.

Other adult-teen relationships simply blur the lines between unwanted and consensual sex. Eilene Stanley, who runs a Big Sisters teen-parent program in Tacoma, Washington, says girls — particularly those from broken families or who have been abused — are easy prey for men who show the smallest kindness, even something as simple as giving flowers.

"The justice system does not take care of these girls," complains Hazel Woods-Welborne, who runs a San Diego school program for teenage mothers. Police refused her request to invoke statutory-rape laws and prosecute a fifty-one-year-old man who had a child by a supposedly willing thirteen-year-old. Woods-Welborne is also disturbed by the recent increase in relationships between very young teens and older men. "I'm talking about twelve, thirteen, fourteen-year-old girls. Most times, they cannot even spell intercourse."

The role played by older men raises doubts about pregnancy-prevention programs aimed at teens. "It's hard to teach teens about sex if one of the sexual partners is not sitting in the classroom," notes Kristin Moore of the research group Child Trends. She points to the adult-teen–sex numbers as one reason why high school sex education classes have failed to curb teen pregnancy rates, which after several years of leveling off have been climbing since 1987, fueled primarily by increases among white teens. One answer, Moore says, is to extend sex education to where the boys are — to such places as vocational schools and the military.

Similarly, welfare reform can work only if it targets both teenage moms and their adult partners. Some legislative plans, including ones put forward by Senate Majority Leader Bob Dole and President Clinton, would give cash payments to pregnant girls only if they lived with a parent or another responsible adult. But to Tina in Tacoma, getting pregnant was a conscious decision that had nothing to do with the size of her welfare check. Tina left home at fifteen when her parents objected to her twenty-one-year-old boyfriend, Rocky. She says her parents would have insisted that she give up her son, Kevin, for adoption and end her relationship with Rocky. Three years later, Rocky and Tina plan to marry soon. Her child, she says, gives her the type of bond "I never had with my mom or with my dad."

Welfare reformers have recognized that adult fathers are more likely to hold jobs and be able to pay child support. Most welfare proposals would require hospitals to establish paternity at birth and then create a national database of fathers' names, so that men who refused to support a child would have their wages withheld or lose their driver's licenses. Yet there are limits to how much money can be collected: One Baltimore study found that 32 percent of the adult male partners of teenage girls were neither working nor in school at the time of a child's birth.

Still, teenage girls have become convenient scapegoats for what are really adult problems, argues Mike Males, a graduate student at the University of California at Irvine who has written extensively on adult-teen sex. Indeed, teenage pregnancy patterns are not that different from those of adults: Rates of pregnancy among teens correlate more closely to class and ethnic background than they do to age demographics. Motherhood outside of marriage is on the rise for women of all ages. According to Child Trends, in 1991, for the first time, women over twenty accounted for more of the first births to unmarried women than did teenage girls. While single motherhood is becoming more acceptable for adult women, it remains a stigma for the unmarried teenage mother. As yet, there is little censure for the adult partners of these teenage girls.

Discussion Questions

1. A great deal has been written about the reasons that teenage girls choose to become pregnant. Do some research to discover what the experts say. Do these two debate articles address any of the reasons?
2. Schiffren suggests making "education, work and marriage preferable to subsisting on a welfare check." But she is vague about how to achieve

this. If you have ideas about solutions, write a paper defending one or two ideas.

3. The two articles take opposite sides on the question of primary responsibility for teenage pregnancy. Do you find one view more persuasive than the other? Explain why.

4. Both authors suggest reasons for the failure of attempted solutions to the problem. What explanations do they offer? Can you think of others?

EXERCISES

1. Choose one of the following statements and define the italicized term. Make the context as specific as possible (for example, by referring to the Declaration of Independence or your own experience).
   a. All men are created *equal.*
   b. I believe in *God.*
   c. This school doesn't offer a *liberal education.*
   d. The marine corps needs *good men.*
   e. *Friends* is a *better* television show than *Seinfeld.*

2. Many recent controversial movements and causes are identified by terms that have come to mean different things to different people. Choose one of the following and define it, explaining both the favorable and unfavorable connotations of the term. Use examples to clarify the meaning.
   a. comparative worth
   b. Palestinian homeland
   c. affirmative action
   d. co-dependency
   e. nationalism

3. Choose two words that are sometimes confused and define them to make their differences clear. *Examples:* authoritarianism and totalitarianism; envy and jealousy; sympathy and pity; cult and established church; justice and equality; liberal and radical; agnostic and atheist.

4. Define a good parent, a good teacher, a good husband or wife. Try to uncover the assumptions on which your definition is based. (For example, in defining a good teacher, students sometimes mention the ability of the teacher to maintain order. Does this mean that the teacher alone is responsible for classroom order?)

5. Define any popular form of entertainment, such as the soap opera, western, detective story, or science fiction story or film. Support your definition with references to specific shows or books. *Or* define an idealized type from fiction, film, the stage, advertising, or television, describing the chief attributes of that type and the principal reasons for its popularity.

6. From your own experience write an essay describing a serious misunderstanding that arose because two people had different meanings for a term they were using.

7. Write about an important or widely used term whose meaning has changed since you first learned it. Such terms often come from the

slang of particular groups: drug users, rock music fans, musicians, athletes, computer programmers or software developers.

8. Define the differences between *necessities, comforts,* and *luxuries.* Consider how they have changed over time.

Critical Listening

9. Listen for several nights to the local or national news on television or radio. Keep a record of the *kinds* of news items that are repeated. How do you think news is defined by the broadcasters? Is it relevant that radio, TV, and film have been characterized as the "dramatic media"? Is the definition of broadcast news different from that of the print media? If so, how do you account for it?

10. You and your friends have probably often argued about subjects that required definition — for example, a good teacher, a good parent, a good popular singer or band, a good movie or TV show. Think of a specific discussion. Were you able to reach agreement? How did the acts of listening and talking affect the outcome?

CHAPTER FIVE

Support

TYPES OF SUPPORT: EVIDENCE AND APPEALS TO NEEDS AND VALUES

All the claims you make — whether of fact, of value, or of policy — must be supported. Support for a claim represents the answer to the question, "What have you got to go on?"[1] There are two basic kinds of support in an argument: evidence and appeals to needs and values.

Evidence, as one dictionary defines it, is "something that tends to prove; ground for belief." When you provide evidence, you use facts, including statistics, and opinions, or interpretations of facts, both your own and those of experts. In the following conversation, the first speaker offers facts and the opinion of an expert to convince the second speaker that robots are exceptional machines.

"You know, robots do a lot more than work on assembly lines in factories."

"Like what?"

"They shear sheep, pick citrus fruit, and even assist in neurosurgery. And by the end of the century, every house will have a robot slave."

"No kidding. Who says so?"

"An engineer who's the head of the world's largest manufacturer of industrial robots."

---

[1]Stephen Toulmin, *The Uses of Argument* (Cambridge: Cambridge University Press, 1958), p. 98.

A writer often appeals to readers' needs, that is, requirements for physical and psychological survival and well-being, and values, or standards for right and wrong, good and bad. In the following conversation, the first speaker makes an appeal to the universal need for self-esteem and to the principle of helping others, a value the second speaker probably shares.

> *"I think you ought to come help us at the nursing home. We need an extra hand."*
>
> *"I'd like to, but I really don't have the time."*
>
> *"You could give us an hour a week, couldn't you? Think how good you'd feel about helping out, and the old people would be so grateful. Some of them are very lonely."*

Although they use the same kinds of support, conversations are less rigorous than arguments addressed to larger audiences in academic or public situations. In the debates on public policy that appear in the media and in the courts, the quality of support can be crucial in settling urgent matters. The following summary of a well-known court case demonstrates the critical use of both evidence and value appeals in the support of opposing claims.

On March 30, 1981, President Ronald Reagan and three other men were shot by John W. Hinckley, Jr., a young drifter from a wealthy Colorado family. Hinckley was arrested at the scene of the shooting. In his trial the factual evidence was presented first: There were dozens of reliable witnesses who had seen the shooting at close range. Hinckley's diaries, letters, and poems revealed that he had planned the shooting to impress actress Jodie Foster. Opinions, consisting of testimony by experts, were introduced by both the defense and the prosecution. This evidence was contradictory. Defense attorneys produced several psychiatrists who defined Hinckley as insane. If this interpretation of his conduct convinced the jury, then Hinckley would be confined to a mental hospital rather than a prison. The prosecution introduced psychiatrists who interpreted Hinckley's motives and actions as those of a man who knew what he was doing and knew it was wrong. They claimed he was *not* insane by legal definition. The fact that experts can make differing conclusions about the meaning of the same information indicates that interpretations are less reliable than other kinds of support.

Finally, the defense made an appeal to the moral values of the jury. Under the law, criminals judged to be insane are not to be punished as harshly as criminals judged to be sane. The laws assume that criminals who cannot be held responsible for their actions are entitled to more compassionate treatment, confinement to a mental hospital rather than prison. The jury accepted the interpretive evidence supporting the claim of the defense, and Hinckley was pronounced not guilty by reason of insanity. Clearly the moral concern for the rights of the insane proved to be decisive.

In your arguments you will advance your claims, not unlike a lawyer, with these same kinds of support. But before you begin, you should ask two questions: Which kind of support should I use in convincing an audience to accept my claim? and How do I decide that each item of support is valid and worthy of acceptance? This chapter presents the different types of evidence and appeals you can use to support your claim and examines the criteria by which you can evaluate the soundness of that support.

EVIDENCE

Factual Evidence

In Chapter 3, we defined facts as statements possessing a high degree of public acceptance. In theory, facts can be verified by experience alone. Eating too much will make us sick; we can get from Hopkinton to Boston in a half hour by car; in the Northern Hemisphere it is colder in December than in July. The experience of any individual is limited in both time and space, so we must accept as fact thousands of assertions about the world that we ourselves can never verify. Thus we accept the report that human beings landed on the moon in 1969 because we trust those who can verify it. (Country people in Morocco, however, received the news with disbelief because they had no reason to trust the reporters of the event. They insisted on trusting their senses instead. One man said, "I can see the moon very clearly. If a man were walking around up there, wouldn't I be able to see him?")

Factual evidence appears most frequently as examples and statistics, which are a numerical form of examples.

Examples

Examples are the most familiar kind of factual evidence. In addition to providing support for the truth of a generalization, examples can enliven otherwise dense or monotonous prose.

In the following paragraph the writer supports the claim in the topic sentence by offering a series of specific examples. (The article claims that most airport security is useless.)

> Meanwhile, seven hijacking incidents occurred last year (twenty-one in 1980 and eleven the year before), despite the security system. Two involved the use of flammable liquids. . . . In four other cases, hijackers claimed to have flammables or explosives but turned

out to be bluffing. In the only incident involving a gun, a man brushed past the security system and brandished the weapon on the plane before being wrestled to the ground. One other hijacking was aborted on the ground, and the remaining five were concluded after some expense, fright, and delay — but no injuries or deaths.[2]

Hypothetical examples, which create imaginary situations for the audience and encourage them to visualize what might happen under certain circumstances, can also be effective. The following paragraph, taken from the same article as the preceding paragraph, illustrates the use of hypothetical examples.

> But weapons can get through nonetheless. Some are simply overlooked; imagine being one of those 10,000 "screeners" staring at X-rayed baggage, day in and day out. Besides, a gun can be broken down into unrecognizable parts and reassembled past the checkpoint. A hand grenade can be hidden in an aerosol shaving-cream can or a photographer's lens case. The ingredients of a Molotov cocktail can be carried on quite openly; any bottle of, say, duty-free liquor or perfume can be emptied and refilled with gasoline. And the possibilities for bluffing should not be forgotten; once on board, anyone could claim that a bottle of water was really a Molotov cocktail, or that a paper bag contained a bomb.[3]

All claims about vague or abstract terms would be boring or unintelligible without examples to illuminate them. For example, if you claim that a movie contains "unusual sound effects," you will certainly have to describe some of the effects to convince the reader that your generalization can be trusted.

Statistics

Statistics express information in numbers. In the following example statistics have been used to express raw data in numerical form.

> Surveys have shown that almost half of all male high school seniors — and nearly 20 percent of all ninth grade boys — can be called "problem drinkers." . . . Over 5,000 teenagers are killed yearly in auto accidents due to drunken driving.[4]

These grim numbers probably have meaning for you, partly because you already know that alcoholism exists even among young teenagers and partly because your own experience enables you to evaluate the numbers. But if you are unfamiliar with the subject, such numbers

---

[2]Patrick Brogan, "The $310 Million Paranoia Subsidy," *Harper's,* September 1982, p. 18.

[3]Ibid.

[4]"The Kinds of Drugs Kids Are Getting Into" (Spring House, Pa.: McNeil Pharmaceutical, n.d.).

may be difficult or impossible to understand. Statistics, therefore, are more effective in comparisons that indicate whether a quantity is relatively large or small and sometimes even whether a reader should interpret the result as gratifying or disappointing. For example, if a novice gambler were told that for every dollar wagered in a state lottery, 50 percent goes back to the players as prizes, would the gambler be able to conclude that the percentage is high or low? Would he be able to choose between playing the state lottery and playing a casino game? Unless he had more information, probably not. But if he were informed that in casino games, the return to the players is over 90 percent and in slot machines and racetracks the return is around 80 percent, the comparison would enable him to evaluate the meaning of the 50 percent return in the state lottery and even to make a decision about where to gamble his money.[5]

Comparative statistics are also useful for measurements over time. A national survey by The Institute for Social Research of the University of Michigan, in which 17,000 of the nation's 2.7 million high school seniors were questioned about their use of drugs, revealed a continuing downward trend.

> 50.9 percent of those questioned in 1989 reported that they had at least tried an illicit drug like marijuana or cocaine, as against 53.9 percent in 1988 and 56.6 percent in 1987.[6]

Diagrams, tables, charts, and graphs can make clear the relations among many sets of numbers. Such charts and diagrams allow readers to grasp the information more easily than if it were presented in paragraph form. The bar graph[7] that is shown on page 143 summarizes the information produced by a poll on gambling habits. A pie chart[8] such as the one on page 144 can also clarify lists of data.

Opinions: Interpretations of the Facts

We have seen how opinions of experts influenced the verdict in the trial of John Hinckley. Facts alone were not enough to substantiate the claim that Hinckley was guilty of attempted assassination. Both the defense and the prosecution relied on experts — psychiatrists — to interpret the facts. Opinions or interpretations about the facts are the inferences discussed in Chapter 3. They are an indispensable source of support for your claims.

Suppose a nightclub for teenagers has opened in your town. That is a fact. What is the significance of it? Is the club's existence

---

[5]Curt Suphee, "Lotto Baloney," *Harper's,* July 1983, p. 201.
[6]*New York Times,* February 14, 1990, Sec. A, p. 16.
[7]*New York Times,* May 28, 1989, p. 24.
[8]*Wall Street Journal,* February 2, 1990, Sec. B, p. 1.

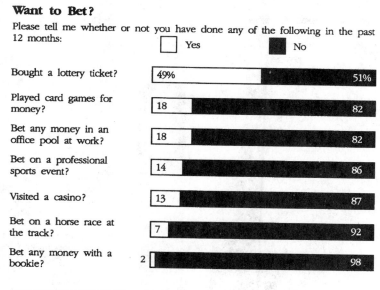

Want to Bet?

Please tell me whether or not you have done any of the following in the past 12 months:

☐ Yes   ■ No

	Yes	No
Bought a lottery ticket?	49%	51%
Played card games for money?	18	82
Bet any money in an office pool at work?	18	82
Bet on a professional sports event?	14	86
Visited a casino?	13	87
Bet on a horse race at the track?	7	92
Bet any money with a bookie?	2	98

Based on a phone survey of 1,412 people nationwide conducted April 13–16, 1989.

Bar graph

good or bad? What consequences will it have for the community? Some parents oppose the idea of a nightclub, fearing that it may allow teenagers to escape from parental control and engage in dangerous activities. Other parents approve of a club, hoping that it will serve as a substitute for unsupervised congregation in the streets. The importance of these interpretations is that they, not the fact itself, help people decide what actions they should take. If the community accepts the interpretation that the club is a source of delinquency, they may decide to revoke the owner's license and close it. As one writer puts it, "The interpretation of data becomes a struggle over power."

Opinions or interpretations of facts generally take three forms: (1) They may suggest the cause for a condition or a causal connection between two sets of data; (2) they may offer predictions about the future; (3) they may suggest solutions to a problem.

1. Causal Connection

Anorexia is a serious, sometimes fatal, disease, characterized by self-starvation. It is found largely among young women. Physicians, psychologists, and social scientists have speculated about the causes, which remain unclear. A leading researcher in the field, Hilde Bruch, believes that food refusal expresses a desire to postpone sexual development. Another authority, Joan Blumberg, be-

Plastic that Goes to Waste

Components of municipal solid waste, by volume

Types of plastic in municipal solid waste, by weight

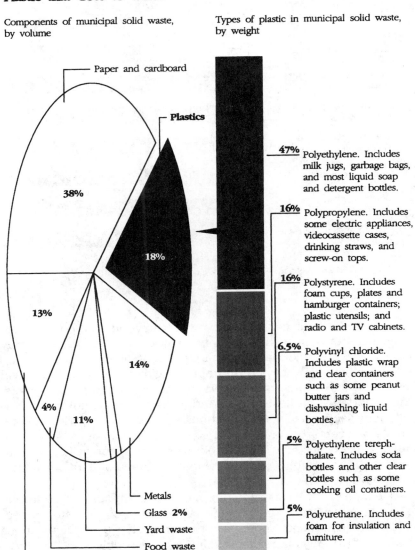

Paper and cardboard

Plastics

38%

18%

13%

14%

4%

11%

Metals

Glass 2%

Yard waste

Food waste

Other

47% Polyethylene. Includes milk jugs, garbage bags, and most liquid soap and detergent bottles.

16% Polypropylene. Includes some electric appliances, videocassette cases, drinking straws, and screw-on tops.

16% Polystyrene. Includes foam cups, plates and hamburger containers; plastic utensils; and radio and TV cabinets.

6.5% Polyvinyl chloride. Includes plastic wrap and clear containers such as some peanut butter jars and dishwashing liquid bottles.

5% Polyethylene terephthalate. Includes soda bottles and other clear bottles such as some cooking oil containers.

5% Polyurethane. Includes foam for insulation and furniture.

4.5% Other plastics.

Source: Franklin Associates Ltd.

Pie chart

lieves that one cause may be biological, a nervous dysfunction of the hypothalamus. Still others infer that the causes are cultural, a response to the admiration of the thin female body.[9]

2. Predictions about the Future

In the fall and winter of 1989–1990 extraordinary events shook Eastern Europe, toppling Communist regimes and raising more popular forms of government. Politicians and scholars offered predictions about future changes in the region. One expert, Zbigniew Brzezinski, former national security adviser under President Carter, concluded that the changes for the Soviet Union might be destructive.

> It would be a mistake to see the recent decisions as marking a breakthrough for democracy. Much more likely is a prolonged period of democratizing chaos. One will see the rise in the Soviet Union of increasingly irreconcilable conflicts between varying national political and social aspirations, all united by a shared hatred for the existing Communist nomenklatura. One is also likely to see a flashback of a nationalist type among the Great Russians, fearful of the prospective breakup of the existing Great Russian Empire.[10]

3. Solutions to Problems

How shall we solve the problems caused by young people in our cities "who commit crimes and create the staggering statistics in teenage pregnancies and the high abortion rate"? The minister emeritus of the Abyssinian Baptist Church in New York City proposes establishment of a national youth academy with fifty campuses on inactive military bases. "It is a 'parenting' institution. . . . It is not a penal institution, not a prep school, not a Job Corps Center, not a Civilian Conservation Camp, but it borrows from them." Although such an institution has not been tried before, the author of the proposal thinks that it would represent an effort "to provide for the academic, moral, and social development of young people, to cause them to become responsible and productive citizens."[11]

Expert Opinion

For many of the subjects you discuss and write about, you will find it necessary to accept and use the opinions of experts. Based on their reading of the facts, experts express opinions on a variety of

---

[9]Phyllis Rose, "Hunger Artists," *Harper's,* July 1988, p. 82.

[10]*New York Times,* February 9, 1990, Sec. A, p. 13.

[11]Samuel D. Proctor, "To the Rescue: A National Youth Academy," *New York Times,* September 16, 1989, Sec. A, p. 27.

controversial subjects: whether capital punishment is a deterrent to crime; whether legalization of marijuana will lead to an increase in its use; whether children, if left untaught, will grow up honest and cooperative; whether sex education courses will result in less sexual activity and fewer illegitimate births. The interpretations of the data are often profoundly important because they influence social policy and affect our lives directly and indirectly.

For the problems mentioned above, the opinions of people recognized as authorities are more reliable than those of people who have neither thought about nor done research on the subject. But opinions may also be offered by student writers in areas in which they are knowledgeable. If you were asked, for example, to defend or refute the statement that work has advantages for teenagers, you could call on your own experience and that of your friends to support your claim. You can also draw on your experience to write convincingly about your special interests.

One opinion, however, is not as good as another. The value of any opinion depends on the quality of the evidence and the trustworthiness of the person offering it.

EVALUATION OF EVIDENCE

Before you begin to write, you must determine whether the facts and opinions you have chosen to support your claim are sound. Can they convince your readers? A distinction between the evaluation of facts and the evaluation of opinions is somewhat artificial because many facts are verified by expert opinion, but for our analysis we discuss them separately.

Evaluation of Factual Evidence

As you evaluate factual evidence, you should keep in mind the following questions:

1. Is the evidence up to date? The importance of up-to-date information depends on the subject. If you are defending the claim that suicide is immoral, you will not need to examine new data. For many of the subjects you write about, recent research and scholarship will be important, even decisive, in proving the soundness of your data. "New" does not always mean "best," but in fields where research is ongoing — education, psychology, technology, medicine, and all the natural and physical sciences — you should be sensitive to the dates of the research.

In writing a paper a few years ago warning about the health hazards of air pollution, you would have used data referring only to outdoor pollution produced by automobile and factory emissions. But writing about air pollution today, you would have to take into account new data about indoor pollution, which has become a serious problem as a result of attempts to conserve energy. Because research studies in indoor pollution are continually being updated, recent evidence will probably be more accurate than past research.

   2. Is the evidence sufficient?   The amount of evidence you need depends on the complexity of the subject and the length of your paper. Given the relative brevity of most of your assignments, you will need to be selective. For the claim that indoor pollution is a serious problem, one example would obviously not be enough. For a 750-to-1,000-word paper, three or four examples would probably be sufficient. The choice of examples should reflect different aspects of the problem: in this case, different sources of indoor pollution — gas stoves, fireplaces, kerosene heaters, insulation — and the consequences for health.
   Indoor pollution is a fairly limited subject for which the evidence is clear. But more complex problems require more evidence. A common fault in argument is generalization based on insufficient evidence. In a 1,000-word paper you could not adequately treat the causes of conflict in the Middle East; you could not develop workable solutions for the health-care crisis; you could not predict the development of education in the next century. In choosing a subject for a brief paper, determine whether you can produce sufficient evidence to convince a reader who may not agree with you. If not, the subject may be too large for a brief paper.

   3. Is the evidence relevant?   All the evidence should, of course, contribute to the development of your argument. Sometimes the arguer loses sight of the subject and introduces examples that are wide of the claim. In defending a national health-care plan, one student offered examples of the success of health maintenance organizations, but such organizations, although subsidized by the federal government, were not the structure favored by sponsors of a national health-care plan. The examples were interesting but irrelevant.
   Also keep in mind that not all readers will agree on what is relevant. Is the unsavory private life of a politician relevant to his or her performance in office? If you want to prove that a politician is unfit to serve because of his or her private activities, you may first have to convince some members of the audience that private activities are relevant to public service.

   4. Are the examples representative?   This question emphasizes your responsibility to choose examples that are typical of all the examples you do not use. Suppose you offered Vermont's experience to support your claim that passage of a bottle bill would reduce litter. Is the experience of Vermont typical of what is happening or may happen in other states? Or is Vermont, a small, mostly rural New England state, different enough from other states to make the example unrepresentative?

5. Are the examples consistent with the experience of the audience? The members of your audience use their own experiences to judge the soundness of your evidence. If your examples are unfamiliar or extreme, they will probably reject your conclusion. Consider the following hypothetical description, which is meant to represent the thinking of your generation.

> Imagine coming to a beach at the end of a long summer of wild goings-on. The beach crowd is exhausted, the sand shopworn, hot, and full of debris — no place for walking barefoot. You step on a bottle, and some cop yells at you for littering. The sun is directly overhead and leaves no patch of shade that hasn't already been taken. You feel the glare beating down on a barren landscape devoid of secrets or innocence. You look around at the disapproving faces and can't help but sense, somehow, that the entire universe is gearing up to punish you.
>
> This is how today's young people feel, as members of the 13th generation (born 1961–1981).[12]

If most members of the audience find that such a description doesn't reflect their own expectations or those of their friends, they will probably question the validity of the claim.

Evaluation of Statistics

The questions you must ask about examples also apply to statistics. Are they recent? Are they sufficient? Are they relevant? Are they typical? Are they consistent with the experience of the audience? But there are additional questions directed specifically to evaluation of statistics.

1. Do the statistics come from trustworthy sources? Perhaps you have read newspaper accounts of very old people, some reported to be as old as 135, living in the Caucasus or the Andes, nourished by yogurt and hard work. But these statistics are hearsay; no birth records or other official documents exist to verify them. Now two anthropologists have concluded that the numbers were part of a rural mythology and that the ages of the people were actually within the normal range for human populations elsewhere.[13]

---

[12]Neil Howe and Bill Strauss, *13th GEN: Abort, Retry, Ignore, Fail?* (New York: Vintage Books, 1993), p. 13.

[13]Richard B. Mazess and Sylvia H. Forman, "Longevity and Age Exaggeration in Vilcabamba, Ecuador," *Journal of Gerontology* (1979), pp. 94–98.

Hearsay statistics should be treated with the same skepticism accorded to gossip or rumor. Sampling a population to gather statistical information is a sophisticated science; you should ask whether the reporter of the statistics is qualified and likely to be free of bias. Among the generally reliable sources are polling organizations such as Gallup, Roper, and Louis Harris and agencies of the U.S. government such as the Census Bureau and the Bureau of Labor Statistics. Other qualified sources are well-known research foundations, university centers, and insurance companies that prepare actuarial tables. Statistics from underdeveloped countries are less reliable for obvious reasons: lack of funds, lack of trained statisticians, lack of communication and transportation facilities to carry out accurate censuses.

2. Are the terms clearly defined?   In an example in Chapter 4, the reference to "poverty" (p. 95) made clear that any statistics would be meaningless unless we knew exactly how "poverty" was defined by the user. "Unemployment" is another term for which statistics will be difficult to read if the definition varies from one user to another. For example, are seasonal workers "employed" or "unemployed" during the off-season? Are part-time workers "Employed"? (In Russia they are "unemployed.") Are workers on government projects "employed"? (During the 1930s they were considered "employed" by the Germans and "unemployed" by the Americans.) The more abstract or controversial the term, the greater the necessity for clear definition.

3. Are the comparisons between comparable things?   Folk wisdom warns us that we cannot compare apples and oranges. Population statistics for the world's largest city, for example, should indicate the units being compared. Greater London is defined in one way, greater New York in another, and greater Tokyo in still another. The population numbers will mean little unless you can be sure that the same geographical units are being compared.

4. Has any significant information been omitted?   The Plain Truth, a magazine published by the World-Wide Church of God, advertises itself as follows:

> *The Plain Truth* has now topped 5,000,000 copies per issue. It is now the fastest-growing magazine in the world and one of the widest circulated mass-circulation magazines on earth. Our circulation is now greater than *Newsweek*. New subscribers are coming in at the rate of around 40,000 per week.

What the magazine neglects to mention is that it is *free*. There is no subscription fee, and the magazine is widely distributed in drugstores, supermarkets, and airports. *Newsweek* is sold on newsstands and by subscription. The comparison therefore omits significant information.

Evaluation of Opinions

When you evaluate the reliability of opinions in subjects with which you are not familiar, you will be dealing almost exclusively with opinions of experts. Most of the following questions are directed to an evaluation of authoritative sources. But you can also ask these questions of students or of others with opinions based on their own experience and research.

1. Is the source of the opinion qualified to give an opinion on the subject? The discussion on credibility in Chapter 1 (pp. 14–17) pointed out that certain achievements by the interpreter of the data — publications, acceptance by colleagues — can tell us something about his or her competence. Although these standards are by no means foolproof — people of outstanding reputations have been known to falsify their data — nevertheless they offer assurance that the source is generally trustworthy. The answers to questions you must ask are not hard to find: Is the source qualified by education? Is the source associated with a reputable institution — a university or a research organization? Is the source credited with having made contributions to the field — books, articles, research studies? Suppose that in writing a paper on organ transplants you came across an article by Peter Medawar. He is identified as follows:

> Sir Peter Medawar, British zoologist, winner of the 1960 Nobel Prize in Physiology or Medicine, for proving that the rejection by the body of foreign organs can be overcome; president of the Royal Society; head of the National Institute for Medical Research in London; a world leader in immunology.

These credentials would suggest to almost any reader that Medawar was a reliable source for information about organ transplants.

If the source is not so clearly identified, you should treat the data with caution. Such advice is especially relevant when you are dealing with popular works about such subjects as miracle diets, formulas for instant wealth, and sightings of monsters and UFOs. Do not use such data until you can verify them from other, more authoritative sources.

In addition, you should question the identity of any source listed as "spokesperson" or "reliable source" or "an unidentified authority." The mass media are especially fond of this type of attribution. Sometimes the sources are people in public life who plant stories anonymously or off the record for purposes they prefer to keep hidden.

Even when the identification is clear and genuine, you should ask if the credentials are relevant to the field in which the authority claims expertise. So specialized are areas of scientific study today that scientists in one field may not be competent to make judgments in another. William Shockley is a distinguished engineer, a Nobel Prize winner for his contribution to the invention of the electronic transistor. But when he made the claim, based on his own research, that blacks are genetically inferior to whites, geneticists accused Shockley of venturing into a field where he was unqualified to make judgments. Similarly, advertisers invite stars from the entertainment world to express opinions about products with which they are probably less familiar than members of their audience. All citizens have the right to express their views, but this does not mean that all views are equally credible or worthy of attention.

2. Is the source biased for or against his or her interpretation? Even authorities who satisfy the criteria for expertise may be guilty of bias. Bias arises as a result of economic reward, religious affiliation, political loyalty, and other interests. The expert may not be aware of the bias; even an expert can fall into the trap of ignoring evidence that contradicts his or her own intellectual preferences. A British psychologist has said:

> The search for meaning in data is bound to involve all of us in distortion to greater or lesser degree. . . . Transgression consists not so much in a clear break with professional ethics, as in an unusually high-handed, extreme or self-deceptive attempt to promote one particular view of reality at the expense of all others.[14]

Before accepting the interpretation of an expert, you should ask: Is there some reason why I should suspect the motives of this particular source?

Consider, for example, an advertisement claiming that sweetened breakfast cereals are nutritious. The advertisement, placed by the manufacturer of the cereal, provides impeccable references from scientific sources to support its claims. But since you are aware of the economic interest of the company in promoting sales, you may wonder if they have reproduced only facts that favor their claims. Are there other facts that might prove the opposite? As a careful researcher you would certainly want to look further for data about the advantages and disadvantages of sugar in our diets.

It is harder to determine bias in the research done by scientists and university members even when the research is funded by companies interested in a favorable review of their products. If you dis-

---

[14]Liam Hudson, *The Cult of the Fact* (New York: Harper and Row, 1972), p. 125.

cover that a respected biologist who advocates the use of sugar in baby food receives a consultant's fee from a sugar company, should you conclude that the research is slanted and that the scientist has ignored contrary evidence? Not necessarily. The truth may be that the scientist arrived at conclusions about the use of sugar legitimately through experiments that no other scientist would question. But it would probably occur to you that a critical reader might ask about the connection between the results of the research and the payment by a company that profits from the research. In this case you would be wise to read further to find confirmation or rejection of the claim by other scientists.

The most difficult evaluations concern ideological bias. Early in our lives we learn to discount the special interest that makes a small child brag, "My mother (or father) is the greatest!" Later we become aware that the claims of people who are avowed Democrats or Republicans or supply-side economists or Yankee fans or zealous San Franciscans or joggers must be examined somewhat more carefully than those of people who have no special commitment to a cause or a place or an activity. This is not to say that all partisan claims lack support. They may, in fact, be based on the best available support. But whenever special interest is apparent, there is always the danger that an argument will reflect this bias.

3. Has the source bolstered the claim with sufficient and appropriate evidence? In an article attacking pornography, one author wrote, "Statistics prove that the recent proliferation of porno is directly related to the increasing number of rapes and assaults on women."[15] But the author gave no further information — neither statistics nor proof that a cause-effect relation exists between pornography and violence against women. The critical reader will ask, "What are the numbers? Who compiled them?"

Even those who are reputed to be experts in the subjects they discuss must do more than simply allege that a claim is valid or that the data exist. They must provide facts to support their interpretations.

When Experts Disagree

Authoritative sources can disagree. Such disagreement is probably most common in the social sciences. They are called the "soft" sciences precisely because a consensus about conclusions in these areas is more difficult to arrive at than in the natural and physical sciences. Consider the controversy over what determines the best

---

[15]Charlotte Allen, "Exploitation for Profit," *Daily Collegian* [University of Massachusetts], October 5, 1976, p. 2.

interests of the child where both biological and foster parents are engaged in trying to secure custody. Experts are deeply divided on this issue. Dr. Daniel J. Cohen, a child psychologist and director of the Yale Child Study Center, argues that the psychological needs of the child should take precedence. If the child has a stable and loving relationship with foster parents, that is where he should stay. But Bruce Bozer and Bernadine Dohrn of the Children and Family Justice Center at Northwestern University Law School, insist that "such a solution may be overly simplistic." The child may suffer in later life when he learns that he has been prevented from returning to biological parents "who fought to get him back."[16]

But even in the natural and physical sciences, where the results of observation and experiment are more conclusive, we encounter heated differences of opinion. A popular argument concerns the extinction of the dinosaurs. Was it the effect of a comet striking the earth? Or widespread volcanic activity? Or a cooling of the planet? All these theories have their champions among the experts.

Environmental concerns also produce lively disagreements. Scientists have lined up on both sides of a debate about the importance of protecting the tropical rain forest as a source of biological, especially mammalian, diversity. Dr. Edward O. Wilson, a Harvard biologist, whose books have made us familiar with the term *biodiversity,* says, "The great majority of organisms appears to reach maximum diversity in the rain forest. There is no question that the rain forests are the world's headquarters of diversity." But in the journal *Science* another biologist, Dr. Michael Mares, a professor of zoology at the University of Oklahoma, argues that "if one could choose only a single South American habitat in which to preserve the greatest mammalian diversity, it would be the dry lands. . . . The dry lands are very likely far more highly threatened than the largely inaccessible rain forests."[17] A debate of more immediate relevance concerns possible dangers in cross-species transplants. One such transplant occurred in December 1995 when a man suffering from AIDS received bone marrow from a baboon in an experiment designed to boost the patient's immune system. Dr. Jonathan S. Allan, of the Southwest Foundation for Biomedical Research in San Antonio, is one of several doctors critical of the guidelines for these procedures, which in his opinion do not protect against possible introduction of new viruses into the general population. In an article for a medical journal, he writes:

> Once the door is opened and a new virus is unleashed, it will be a monumental task to identify a new pathogen, develop adequate screening tests and prevent the spread of that new infection.[18]

---

[16]*New York Times,* September 4, 1994, Sec. E, p. 3.
[17]*New York Times,* April 7, 1992, Sec. C, p. 4.
[18]*New York Times,* January 9, 1996, Sec. C, p. 11.

But other doctors feel that this alarm is unjustified. Dr. Frederick R. Murphy, the dean of the veterinary school at the University of California at Davis, says that "over the years unsterilized biological products derived from animals, products that differ little in risk from xenografts, have often been injected into patients" without major problems.[19]

How can you choose between authorities who disagree? If you have applied the tests discussed so far and discovered that one source is less qualified by training and experience or makes claims with little support or appears to be biased in favor of one interpretation, you will have no difficulty in rejecting that person's opinion. If conflicting sources prove to be equally reliable in all respects, then continue reading other authorities to determine whether a greater number of experts support one opinion rather than another. Although numbers alone, even of experts, don't guarantee the truth, nonexperts have little choice but to accept the authority of the greater number until evidence to the contrary is forthcoming. Finally, if you are unable to decide between competing sources of evidence, you may conclude that the argument must remain unsettled. Such an admission is not a failure; after all, such questions are considered controversial because even the experts cannot agree, and such questions are often the most interesting to consider and argue about.

APPEALS TO NEEDS AND VALUES

Good factual evidence is usually enough to convince an audience that your factual claim is sound. Using examples, statistics, and expert opinion, you can prove, for example, that women do not earn as much as men for the same work. But even good evidence may not be enough to convince your audience that unequal pay is wrong or that something should be done about it. In making value and policy claims, an appeal to the needs and values of your audience is absolutely essential to the success of your argument. If you want to persuade the audience to change their minds or adopt a course of action — in this case, to demand legalization of equal pay for equal work — you will have to show that assent to your claim will bring about what they want and care deeply about.

As a writer, you cannot always know who your audience is; it's impossible, for example, to predict exactly who will read a letter you write to a newspaper. Even in the classroom, you have only partial knowledge of your readers. You may not always know or be able to

---

[19]*New York Times,* January 9, 1996, Sec. C, p. 11.

infer what the goals and principles of your audience are. You may not know how they feel about big government, the draft, private school education, feminism, environmental protection, homosexuality, religion, or any of the other subjects you might write about. If the audience concludes that the things you care about are very different from what they care about, if they cannot identify with your goals and principles, they may treat your argument with indifference, even hostility, and finally reject it. But you can hope that decent and reasonable people will share many of the needs and values that underlie your claims.

Appeals to Needs

Suppose that you are trying to persuade Joan Doakes, a friend who is still undecided, to attend college. In your reading you have come across a report about the benefits of a college education written by Howard Bowen, a former professor of economics at Claremont (California) Graduate School, former president of Grinnell College, and a specialist in the economics of higher education. Armed with his testimony, you write to Joan. As support for your claim that she should attend college, you offer evidence that (1) college graduates earn more throughout their lifetime than high school graduates; (2) college graduates are more active and exert greater influence in their communities than high school graduates; and (3) college graduates achieve greater success as partners in marriage and as thoughtful and caring parents.[20]

Joan writes back that she is impressed with the evidence you've provided — the statistics, the testimony of economists and psychologists — and announced that she will probably enroll in college instead of accepting a job offer.

How did you succeed with Joan Doakes? If you know your friend pretty well, the answer is not difficult. Joan has needs that can be satisfied by material success; more money will enable her to enjoy the comforts and luxuries that are important to her. She also needs the esteem of her peers and the sense of achievement that political activity and service to others will give her. Finally, she needs the rootedness to be found in close and lasting family connections.

Encouraged by your success with Joan Doakes, you write the same letter to another friend, Fred Fox, who has also declined to apply for admission to college. This time, however, your argument fails. Fred, too, is impressed with your research and evidence. But college is not for him, and he repeats that he has decided not to become a student.

[20]"The Residue of Academic Learning," *Chronicle of Higher Education,* November 14, 1977, p. 13.

Why such a different response? The reason, it turns out, is that you don't know what Fred really wants. Fred Fox dreams of going to Alaska to live alone in the wilderness. Money means little to him, influence in the community is irrelevant to his goals, and at present he feels no desire to become a member of a loving family.

Perhaps if you had known Fred better, you would have offered different evidence to show that you recognized what he needed and wanted. You could have told him that Bowen's study also points out that "college-educated persons are healthier than are others," that "they also have better ability to adjust to changing times and vocations," that "going to college enhances self-discovery" and enlarges mental resources, which encourage college graduates to go on learning for the rest of their lives. This information might have persuaded Fred that college would also satisfy some of his needs.

As this example demonstrates, you have a better chance of persuading your reader to accept your claim if you know what he or she wants and what importance he or she assigns to the needs that we all share. Your reader must, in other words, see some connection between your evidence and his or her needs.

The needs to which you appealed in your letters to Joan and Fred are the requirements for physiological or psychological well-being. The most familiar classification of needs was developed by the psychologist Abraham H. Maslow in 1954.[21] These needs, said Maslow, motivate human thought and action. In satisfying our needs, we attain both long- and short-term goals. Because Maslow believed that some needs are more important than others, he arranged them in hierarchical order from the most urgent biological needs to the psychological needs that are related to our roles as members of a society.

Physiological Needs. Basic bodily requirements: food and drink; health; sex

Safety Needs. Security; freedom from harm; order and stability

Belongingness and Love Needs. Love within a family and among friends; roots within a group or a community

Esteem Needs. Material success; achievement; power, status, and recognition by others

Self-actualization Needs. Fulfillment in realizing one's potential

For most of your arguments you won't have to address the audience's basic physiological needs for nourishment or shelter. The desire for health, however, now receives extraordinary attention.

---

[21]*Motivation and Personality* (New York: Harper and Row, 1954), pp. 80–92.

Appeals to buy health foods, vitamin supplements, drugs, exercise and diet courses, and health books are all around us. Many of the claims are supported by little or no evidence, but readers are so eager to satisfy the need for good health that they often overlook the lack of facts or authoritative opinion. The desire for physical well-being, however, is not so simple as it seems; it is strongly related to our need for self-esteem and love.

Appeals to our needs to feel safe from harm, to be assured of order and stability in our lives are also common. Insurance companies, politicians who promise to rid our streets of crime, and companies that offer security services all appeal to this profound and nearly universal need. (We say "nearly" because some people are apparently attracted to risk and danger.) At this writing those who monitor global warming are attempting both to arouse fear for our safety and to suggest ways of reducing the dangers that make us fearful.

The last three needs in Maslow's hierarchy are the ones you will find most challenging to appeal to in your arguments. It is clear that these needs arise out of human relationships and participation in society. Advertisers make much use of appeals to these needs.

Belongingness and Love Needs

"Whether you are young or old, the need for companionship is universal." (ad for dating service)

"Share the Fun of High School with Your Little Girl!" (ad for a Barbie Doll)

Esteem Needs

"Enrich your home with the distinction of an Oxford library."

"Apply your expertise to more challenges and more opportunities. Here are outstanding opportunities for challenge, achievement, and growth." (Perkin-Elmer Co.)

Self-actualization Needs

"Be all that you can be." (U.S. Army)

"Are you demanding enough? Somewhere beyond the cortex is a small voice whose mere whisper can silence an army of arguments. It goes by many names: integrity, excellence, standards. And it stands alone in final judgment as to whether we have demanded enough of ourselves and, by that example, have inspired the best in those around us." (*New York Times*)

Of course, it is not only advertisers who use these appeals. We hear them from family and friends, from teachers, from employers, from editorials and letters to the editor, from people in public life.

Appeals to Values

Needs give rise to values. If we feel the need to belong to a group, we learn to value commitment, sacrifice, and sharing. And we then respond to arguments that promise to protect our values. It is hardly surprising that values, the principles by which we judge what is good or bad, beautiful or ugly, worthwhile or undesirable, should exercise a profound influence on our behavior. Virtually all claims, even those that seem to be purely factual, contain expressed or unexpressed judgments. The two scientists quoted in Chapter 3 (pp. 52–53) who presented evidence that cocaine was "deadlier than we thought," did so not for academic reasons but because they hoped to persuade people that using the drug was bad.

For our study of argument, we will speak of groups or systems of values because any single value is usually related to others. People and institutions are often defined by such systems of values. We can distinguish, for example, between those who think of themselves as traditional and those who think of themselves as modern by listing their differing values. One writer contrasts such values in this way:

> Among the values of traditionalism are: merit, accomplishment, competition, and success; self-restraint, self-discipline, and the postponement of gratification; the stability of the family; and a belief in certain moral universals. The modernist ethos scorns the pursuit of success; is egalitarian and redistributionist in emphasis; tolerates or encourages sensual gratification; values self-expression as against self-restraint; accepts alternative or deviant forms of the family; and emphasizes ethical relativism.[22]

Systems of values are neither so rigid nor so distinct from one another as this list suggests. Some people who are traditional in their advocacy of competition and success may also accept the modernist values of self-expression and alternative family structures. Values, like needs, are arranged in a hierarchy; that is, some are clearly more important than others to the people who hold them. Moreover, the arrangement may shift over time or as a result of new experiences. In 1962, for example, two speech teachers prepared a list of what they called "Relatively Unchanging Values Shared by Most Americans."[23] Included were "puritan and pioneer standards of morality" and "perennial optimism about the future." More than thirty years later, an appeal to these values might fall on a number of deaf ears.

You should also be aware of not only changes over time but also different or competing value systems that reflect a multitude of sub-

---

[22]Joseph Adelson, "What Happened to the Schools," *Commentary,* March 1981, p. 37.

[23]Edward Steele and W. Charles Redding, "The American Value System: Premises for Persuasion," *Western Speech,* Vol. 26 (Spring 1962), pp. 83–91.

cultures in our country. Differences in age, sex, race, ethnic background, social environment, religion, even in the personalities and characters of its members define the groups we belong to. Such terms as "honor," "loyalty," "justice," "patriotism," "duty," "responsibility," "equality," "freedom," and "courage" will be interpreted very differently by different groups.

All of us belong to more than one group, and the values of the several groups may be in conflict. If one group to which you belong, say, peers of your own age and class, is generally uninterested in and even scornful of religion, you may nevertheless hold to the values of your family and continue to place a high value on religious belief.

How can a knowledge of your readers' values enable you to make a more effective appeal? Suppose you want to argue in favor of a sex education program in the junior high school you attended. The program you support would not only give students information about contraception and venereal disease but also teach them about the pleasures of sex, the importance of small families, and alternatives to heterosexuality. If the readers of your argument are your classmates or your peers, you can be fairly sure that their agreement will be easier to obtain than that of their parents, especially if their parents think of themselves as conservative. Your peers are more likely to value experimentation, tolerance of alternative sexual practices, freedom, and novelty. Their parents are more likely to value restraint, conformity to conventional sexual practices, obedience to family rules, and foresight in planning for the future.

Knowing that your peers share your values and your goals will mean that you need not spell out the values supporting your claim; they are understood by your readers. Convincing their parents, however, who think that freedom, tolerance, and experimentation have been abused by their children, will be a far more challenging task. In one written piece you have little chance of changing their values, a result that might be achieved only over a longer period of time. So you might first attempt to reduce their hostility by suggesting that, even if a community-wide program were adopted, students would need parental permission to enroll. This might convince some parents that you share their values regarding parental authority and primacy of the family. Second, you might look for other values to which the parents subscribe and to which you can make an appeal. Do they prize maturity, self-reliance, responsibility in their children? If so, you could attempt to prove, with authoritative evidence, that the sex education program would promote these qualities in students who took the course.

But familiarity with the value systems of prospective readers may also lead you to conclude that winning assent to your argument will be impossible. It would probably be fruitless to attempt to persuade a group of lifelong pacifists to endorse the use of nuclear weapons. The beliefs, attitudes, and habits that support their value systems are too fundamental to yield to one or two attempts at persuasion.

EVALUATION OF APPEALS TO NEEDS AND VALUES

If your argument is based on an appeal to the needs and values of your audience, the following questions will help you evaluate the soundness of your appeal.

1. Have the values been clearly defined? If you are appealing to the patriotism of your readers, can you be sure that they agree with your definition? Does patriotism mean "Our country, right or wrong!" or does it mean dissent, even violent dissent, if you think your country is wrong? Because value terms are abstractions, you must make their meaning explicit by placing them in context and providing examples.

2. Are the needs and values to which you appeal prominent in the reader's hierarchy at the time you are writing? An affluent community, fearful of further erosion of quiet and open countryside, might resist an appeal to allow establishment of a high-technology firm, even though the firm would bring increased prosperity to the area.

3. Is the evidence in your argument clearly related to the needs and values to which you appeal? Remember that the reader must see some connection between your evidence and his or her goals. Suppose you were writing an argument to persuade a group of people to vote in an upcoming election. You could provide evidence to prove that only 20 percent of the town voted in the last election. But this evidence would not motivate your audience to vote unless you could provide other evidence to show that their needs were not being served by such a low turnout.

Single-Sex Education Benefits Men Too

CLAUDIUS E. WATTS III

Last week Virginia Military Institute, an all-male state college, got the good news from a federal judge that it can continue its single-sex program if it opens a leadership program at Mary Baldwin College, a nearby private women's school. But it is likely that the government will appeal the decision. Meanwhile, the Citadel, another such institution in Charleston, S.C., remains under attack. Unwittingly, so are some fundamental beliefs prevalent in our society: namely, the value of single-sex education, the need for diversity in education, and the freedom of choice in associating with, and not associating with, whomever one chooses.

When Shannon Faulkner received a preliminary injunction to attend day classes with the Citadel's Corps of Cadets, she was depicted as a nineteen-year-old woman fighting for her constitutional rights, while the Citadel was painted as an outdated and chauvinistic Southern school that had to be dragged into the twentieth century.

But the Citadel is not fighting to keep women out of the Corps of Cadets because there is a grandiose level of nineteenth-century machismo to protect. Rather, we at the Citadel are trying to preserve an educational environment that molds young men into grown men of good character, honor, and integrity. It is part of a single-sex educational system that has proven itself successful throughout history.

The benefits of single-sex education for men are clear: Says Harvard sociologist David Riesman, not only is single-sex education an optimal means of character development, but it also removes the distractions of the "mating-dating" game so prevalent in society and enables institutions to focus students on values and academics.

In short, the value of separate education is, simply, the fact it is 5 separate.

In October 1992, a federal appeals court ruled that "single-sex education is pedagogically justifiable." Indeed, a cursory glance at some notable statistics bears that out. For instance, the Citadel has

---

Lieutenant General Claudius E. Watts III, retired from the Air Force, is president of the Citadel in South Carolina. This selection is from the May 3, 1995, edition of the *Wall Street Journal.*

the highest retention rate for minority students of any public college in South Carolina: 67 percent of black students graduate in four years, which is more than $2\frac{1}{2}$ times the national average. Additionally, the Citadel's four-year graduation rate for all students is 70 percent, which compares with 48 percent nationally for all other public institutions and 67 percent nationally for private institutions. Moreover, many of the students come from modest backgrounds. Clearly, the Citadel is not the bastion of male privilege that the U.S. Justice Department, in briefs filed by that agency, would have us all believe.

While the Justice Department continues to reject the court's ruling affirming the values of single-sex education, others continue to argue that because the federal military academies are coeducational, so should the Citadel be. However, it is not the Citadel's primary mission to train officers for the U.S. armed forces. We currently commission approximately 30 percent of our graduates, but only 18 percent actually pursue military careers. At the Citadel, the military model is a means to an end, not the end itself.

Today there are eighty-four women's colleges scattered throughout the United States, including two that are public. These colleges defend their programs as necessary to help women overcome intangible barriers in male-dominated professions. This argument has merit; women's colleges produce only 4.5 percent of all female college graduates, but have produced one-fourth of all women board members of Fortune 500 companies and one-half of the women in Congress. However, the educational benefits of men's colleges are equally clear; and to allow women alone to benefit from single-sex education seems to perpetuate the very stereotypes that women — including Ms. Faulkner — are trying to correct.

If young women want and need to study and learn in single-sex schools, why is it automatically wrong for young men to want and need the same? Where is the fairness in this assumption?

"At what point does the insistence that one individual not be deprived of choice spill over into depriving countless individuals of choice?" asks Emory University's Elizabeth Fox Genovese in an article by Jeffrey Rosen published in the February 14 *New Republic.*   10

Yet, so it is at the Citadel. While one student maintains that she is protecting her freedom to associate, we mustn't forget that the Citadel's cadets also have a freedom — the freedom not to associate. While we have read about one female student's rights, what hasn't been addressed are the rights of the 1,900 cadets who chose the Citadel — and the accompanying discipline and drill — because it offered them the single-sex educational experience they wanted. Why do one student's rights supersede all theirs?

One might be easily tempted to argue on the grounds that Ms. Faulkner is a taxpayer and the Citadel is a tax-supported institution. But if the taxpayer argument holds, the next step is to forbid all public support for institutions that enroll students of only one sex. A draconian measure such as this would surely mean the end of private — as well as public — single-gender colleges.

Most private colleges — Columbia and Converse, the two all-female schools in South Carolina, included — could not survive without federal financial aid, tax exemptions, and state tax support in the form of tuition grants. In fact, nearly 900 of Columbia and Converse's female students receive state-funded tuition grants, a student population that is almost half the size of the Corps of Cadets. In essence, South Carolina's two private women's colleges may stand or fall with the Citadel.

Carried to its logical conclusion, then, the effort to coeducate the Citadel might mean the end of all single-sex education — for women as well as men, in private as well as public schools.

Analysis: Support

In 1993 Shannon Faulkner, a woman, was rejected for admission to the Citadel, an all-male state-supported military academy in South Carolina. In 1995, after a long court battle, she was admitted but resigned after a week of physical and emotional stress. The Court was asked to decide if an education equal to that of the Citadel could be provided for women at a nearby school.

Claudius Watts III tackles a subject that is no longer controversial in regard to women's colleges: the virtues of single-sex education. But in this essay he argues that colleges for men only deserve the same right as women's colleges to exclude the opposite sex.

The author has taken care in the limited space available to cover all the arguments that have emerged in the case of Shannon Faulkner. At the end of the opening paragraph he lays out the three ideas he will develop — the value of single-sex education, the need for diversity in education, and freedom of choice. In paragraphs 3–6 he supports his case for the benefits of separate education by first quoting a prominent sociologist and then offering statistics to prove that the Citadel population is both diverse and successful. In paragraph 7 he refutes a popular analogy — that since the service academies, like West Point and the Naval Academy, admit women, so should the Citadel. The goals of the Citadel, he says, are broader than those of the service academies. But he does more. In paragraph 8 he provides data that women's colleges produce successful graduates. This reinforces his claim that separate education has advantages over coed schooling. Perhaps it also helps to make friends of opponents who might otherwise be hostile to arguments favoring male privileges.

Notice the transition in paragraph 10. This leads the author to the defense of his last point, the far more elusive concept of freedom of choice and the rights of individuals, ideas whose validity cannot be measured in numbers. He introduces this part of his argument by quoting the words of a supporter of single-sex education, a woman professor at Emory University. He makes a strong appeal to the reader's sense of fairness and belief in the rights of the majority, represented here by the male students at the Citadel. There is also an obvious appeal to fear, an implied threat of the danger to women's colleges, in the next-to-last sentence of the essay. Finally, he invokes logic. If single-sex education cannot be defended for males, neither can it be defended for females. He assumes that against logic there can be no real defense.

Some leading advocates for women's rights have, in fact, agreed with General Watts's arguments for that reason. But those who support both Shannon Faulkner's admission to the Citadel and the sanctity of women's colleges will claim that women, as a disadvantaged group, deserve special consideration, while men do not. (One writer even insisted that the Citadel *needed* women as a civilizing influence.) General Watts's argument, however, should go some distance toward reopening the dialogue.

READINGS FOR ANALYSIS

Not Just Read and Write, but Right and Wrong
KATHLEEN KENNEDY TOWNSEND

In a suburban high school's crowded classroom, a group of juniors explained to me why drugs are difficult to control. "You see, Mrs. Townsend, what if you want a new pair of Reeboks? You could sell drugs and make $250 in an afternoon. It's a lot easier and quicker than working at McDonald's. You'd have to work there a whole week."

In my work helping teachers, I've walked into countless high schools where I could have filled a garbage bag with the trash in the halls. Yet I rarely hear teachers asking students to pick up the garbage — or telling them not to litter in the first place.

Of course, many students obey the law, stay away from drugs, and perform selfless acts: They tutor, work with the elderly, or run

---

Kathleen Kennedy Townsend is the lieutenant-governor of Maryland. This article first appeared in *The Washington Monthly,* January 1990.

antidrug campaigns. But too many lack a sense of duty to a larger community.

A survey conducted for People for the American Way asked just over 1,000 Americans between fifteen and twenty-four what goals they considered important. Three times as many selected career success as chose community service — which finished dead last. Only one-third said they could countenance joining the military or working on a political campaign. During one focus group interview for the study, some young people were asked to name qualities that make this country special. There was a long silence until one young man came up with an answer: "Cable TV."

The study concluded, "Young people have learned only half of   5 America's story. . . . [They] reveal notions of America's unique character that emphasize freedom and license almost to the complete exclusion of service or participation . . . they fail to perceive a need to reciprocate by exercising the duties and responsibilities of good citizenship."

Failure of Schools

While it is easy enough to blame this problem on the "me-ism" of the Reagan years, it's time to recognize that *it's also the result of deliberate educational policy.* One principal I know speaks for too many others. "Schools," she says, "cannot impose duties on the students. Students come from different backgrounds. They have different standards."

Twice since 1982 the Maryland Department of Education has sent out questionnaires to local education departments soliciting opinions about values education. The answers are typical of those found across the United States. Many respondents were indifferent, simply stating that values education is "inherent" in teaching. Other answers were more hostile: "Specific training in values is a new development which we do not consider essential," and "A special effort would cause trouble."

The consensus of the high school teachers and administrators participating in a curriculum workshop I ran last summer said it all: "Values — we can't get into that."

Schools across America have simply refused to take responsibility for the character of their students. They wash their hands of the teaching of virtue, doing little to create an environment that teaches children the importance of self-discipline, obligation, and civic participation. As one teacher training text says, "There is no right or wrong answer to any question of value."

Is it any surprise that students tend to agree? These days it   10 seems they're all relativists. A collection of high school interviews quotes one eleventh-grader as saying, "What one person thinks is bad or wrong, another person might think that it is good or right. I don't think morals should be taught because it would cause more conflicts and mess up the student's mind." One of her classmates adds, "Moral values cannot be taught and people must learn what works for them. In other words, 'Whatever gets you through the night, it's alright.'"

Sensitivity Needed

Now it's obvious that the public schools are a ticklish arena for instilling values. Our pluralistic society is justly worried about party lines of any kind. That means that teaching values in the schools — whether as an integral part of the traditional classes or as a separate course — requires subtle skills and real sensitivity to student and community needs. Of course, families and churches should play a part, but neither are as strong or effective as they were a generation ago. Only the schools are guaranteed to get a shot at kids. That's why their current fumbling of anything smacking of right and wrong is so disastrous.

The importance of teaching values in the schools was barely mentioned at the education summit presided over by George Bush at the University of Virginia. The meeting was dominated by talk of federal funding and drug education. The underlying valuelessness of American education — an obstacle to the intelligent use of scarce resources and a root cause of drug problems — really didn't come up.

Such a curious oversight at Thomas Jefferson's school! Jefferson fought for public education because he believed that the citizen's virtue is the foundation of democracy. Only virtuous citizens, he knew, would resist private gain for the public good. And to know the public good, you have to study literature, philosophy, history, and religion.

For many years, Jefferson's wisdom about education prevailed. James Q. Wilson attributes America's low level of crime during the nineteenth century to the efforts of educators to instill self-discipline. "In the 1830s," he explains, "crime began to rise rapidly. New York had more murders than London, even though New York was only a tiny fraction of the size of London. However, rather than relying on police forces or other government programs, the citizens concentrated on education.

"Sunday schools were started. It was an all-day effort to provide 15 education in morality, education in punctuality, in decency, in following rules, and accepting responsibility, in being generous, in being kind.

"The process was so successful that in the second half of the nineteenth century, despite urbanization, despite the enormous influx into this country of immigrants from foreign countries all over

Europe, despite the widening class cleavages, despite the beginning of an industrial proletariat, despite all those things which textbooks today teach us cause crime to go up, crime went down. And it went down insofar as I, or any historian, can tell because this effort to substitute the ethic of self-control for what appeared to be the emerging ethic of self-expression succeeded." In 1830 the average American drank ten gallons of distilled liquor a year. By 1850, it was down to two.

Basic Values

The flavor of this nineteenth-century approach to education is preserved today in many state constitutions. North Dakota's is typical in declaring that public schools should "emphasize all branches of knowledge that tend to impress upon the mind the importance of truthfulness, temperance, purity, public spirit, and respect for honest labor of every kind." In current educational jargon, this approach is called "values inculcation." . . .

In 1981 the California State Assembly considered a bill that spelled out values that should be included in public school instructional materials. Among those values were: honesty, acceptance of responsibility, respect for the individuality of others, respect for the responsibility inherent in being a parent or in a position of authority, the role of the work ethic in achieving personal goals, universal values of right and wrong, respect for property, the importance of the family unit, and the importance of respect for the law.

The bill was defeated.

How have we reached the point where a list of basic values like that is considered unsuitable for schools? . . .   20

The major criticism of not teaching values is very simple: There are some values that teachers should affirm. Not all values are the same. My daughter is the only girl on her soccer team, and recently some of the boys on the team spit at her. The coach shouldn't have the boys *justify* their actions. He should have them *stop*. He should make sure they know they were wrong. That's what he should do. What he actually did tells you a lot about the schools today. He did nothing.

Reading and Discussion Questions

1. An editorial writer has supplied three subheadings for parts of the essay. The first part lacks a heading. What do you think it should be? Is "Sensitivity Needed" an appropriate headline for the third part?
2. Mention some of the devices Townsend uses to make her essay easy to read and understand.
3. What different kinds of support does Townsend provide to establish her claim? Is the evidence sufficient to prove that instruction in values is necessary?

4. What values above all others would the author seek to promote? Why do you think she has chosen these particular values?
5. Would the nineteenth-century Sunday school effort described by James Q. Wilson work today to reduce crime? Why or why not?
6. Do you think any of the values listed in the 1981 California bill are controversial? Explain.

Writing Suggestions

7. If you have been a student in a public, private, or Sunday school where specific values were taught, directly or through literature and history, describe and evaluate the experience. Was it successful — that is, did the values taught have a meaningful influence on your life?
8. Are there some actions that are always right or wrong, regardless of the circumstances? If you think there are, choose one or two and defend your choice. (You would probably agree with Ted Koppel, who reminds us that they are the Ten Commandments, not the Ten Suggestions.) If, on the other hand, you believe that all values are relative or situational — dependent, that is, on particular circumstances — argue the proposition that any view on the rightness or wrongness of a specific action is contingent on the situation.

Talking Up Close
DEBORAH TANNEN

Fighting to Be Friends

It is frequently observed that male speakers are more likely to be confrontational by arguing, issuing commands, and taking opposing stands for the sake of argument, whereas females are more likely to avoid confrontation by agreeing, supporting, and making suggestions rather than commands. . . . Cultural linguist Walter Ong argues that "adversativeness" — a tendency to fight — is universal, but "conspicuous or expressed adversativeness is a larger element in the lives of males than of females." In other words, females may well fight, but males are more likely to fight often, openly, and for the fun of it.

But what does it mean to say that males fight more than females? One thing it does not mean is that females therefore are more connected to each other. Because status and connection are

---

Deborah Tannen, professor of Linguistics at Georgetown University, is the author of *You Just Don't Understand: Women and Men in Conversation* (1989) and *Talking from 9 to 5* (1994), from which this excerpt is taken.

mutually evocative, both fighting with each other and banding together to fight others can create strong connections among males, for example by affiliation within a team. In this regard, a man recalled that when he was young, he and his friends amused themselves after school by organizing fights among themselves. When school let out, the word would go out about who was going to fight whom in whose backyard. Yet these fights were part of the boys' friendship and did not evidence mutual animosity. (Contrast this with a group of girls banding together to pick on a low-status girl, without anyone landing a physical blow.)

I think, as well, of my eighty-five-year-old uncle who still meets yearly with his buddies from World War II, even though the members of his battalion are from vastly different cultural and geographic backgrounds. It is difficult to imagine anything other than war that could have bonded men from such different backgrounds into a group whose members feel such lasting devotion. Indeed, a man who was sent to Vietnam because of an error gave this as the reason he did not try to set the record straight and go home: "I found out I belonged in Vietnam," he said. "The bonding of men at war was the strongest thing I'd felt in my life."

Folklore provides numerous stories in which fighting precipitates friendship among men. Robert Bly recounts one such story which he identifies as Joseph Campbell's account of the Sumerian epic *Gilgamesh*. In Bly's rendition, Gilgamesh, a young king, wants to befriend a wild man named Enkidu. When Enkidu is told of Gilgamesh,

> . . . his heart grew light. He yearned for a friend. "Very well!" he said. "And I shall challenge him."

Bly paraphrases the continuation: "Enkidu then travels to the city and meets Gilgamesh; the two wrestle, Enkidu wins, and the two become inseparable friends."

A modern-day equivalent of the bonding that results from ritual   5
opposition can be found in business, where individuals may compete, argue, or even fight for their view without feeling personal enmity. Opposition as a ritualized format for inquiry is institutionalized most formally in the legal profession, and it is expected that each side will do its best to attack the other and yet retain friendly relations when the case is closed.

These examples show that aggression can be a way of establishing connection to others. Many cultures see arguing as a pleasurable sign of intimacy. Linguist Deborah Schiffrin examined conversations among lower-middle-class men *and women* of East European Jewish background in Philadelphia and found that friendly banter was one of the fundamental ways they enjoyed and reinforced their friend-ship. A similar ethic obtains among Germans, who like to engage in combative intellectual debate about such controversial topics as politics and religion, according to linguist Heidi Byrnes, who was born and raised in Germany. Byrnes points out that this has rather negative consequences in cross-cultural contact. German students try to show their friendliness to American students by provoking heated arguments about American foreign policy. But the Ameri-cans, who consider it inappropriate to argue with someone they have just met, refuse to take part. The German students conclude that Americans are uninformed and uncommitted, while the Ameri-cans go away convinced that Germans are belligerent and rude.

Linguist Christina Kakava shows that modern Greek conversa-tion is also characterized by friendly argument. She found, by taping dinner-table conversation, that members of a Greek family enjoyed opposing each other. In a study we conducted together, Kakava and I showed that modern Greek speakers routinely disagree when they actually agree, a practice that explains my own experience — and discomfort — when I lived in Greece.

I was in a suburb of Athens, talking to an older woman whom I call Ms. Stella, who had just told me about complaining to the police because a construction crew working on the house beside hers ille-gally continued drilling and pounding through the siesta hours, dis-turbing her midafternoon nap. I tried to be nice by telling her she was right, but she would not accept my agreement. She managed to maintain her independence by restating her position in different terms. Our conversation (which I taped), translated into English, went like this:

> *Deborah:*   You're right.
>
> *Stella:*   I *am* right. My dear girl, I don't know if I'm right or I'm not right. But I am watching out for my interests and my rights.

Clearly, Ms. Stella thought she was right, but she did not want the lively conversation to dissipate in so dull a way as her accepting my statement, "You're right," so she managed to disagree: "I don't know if I'm right or I'm not right." Disagreeing allowed her to amplify her position as well.

This was typical of conversations I found myself in when I lived in Greece. I vividly recall my frustration when I uttered what to me were fairly automatic expressions of agreement and support and found myself on the receiving end of what seemed like hostile re-fusal to accept my agreement. I frequently felt distanced and put down when my attempts to agree were met with contentious re-sponses. In an effort to make things right, I would try harder to be agreeable, so that my conversations became veritable litanies of

agreement: Exactly!, Absolutely!, Without a doubt! But my Greek in-
terlocutors probably were puzzled, irritated, and bored by my relentless agreement, and stepped up their contentiousness in their
efforts to liven up the interactions.

As evidence that contentious argument helps create connection 10
among Greek friends, I offer an example taken from the study by
Kakava, who was also a participant. The other two speakers were
her friends, two brothers she calls George and Alkis. George was
showing off a belt he had received as a gift, and the three friends argued animatedly about its color:

George: I've got burgundy shoes, but the belt's got black in it too.

Kakava: Does it have black in it? Let me see.

George: It has a stripe in it that's kind of black.

Alkis: Dark brown.

George: It's kind of dark.

Alkis: It's tobacco-colored, dummy! It goes with everything.

George: Tobacco-colored? What are you talking about?! Are you
color-blind?!

Conversations in this spirit often give Americans the impression
that Greeks are fighting when they are just having an animated conversation.

The discussion of fighting, silence, and interrupting is intended
to show that it is impossible to determine what a way of speaking
"really means" because the same way of speaking can create either
status differences or connection, or both at the same time.

"Is It You or Me?"

Again and again, when I have explained two different ways of
saying or doing the same thing, I am asked, "Which way is best?" or
"Which way is right?" We are all in pursuit of the right way of speaking, like the holy grail. But there is no one right way, any more than
there is a holy grail — at least not one we can hope to find. Most important, and most frustrating, the "true" intention or motive of any
utterance cannot be determined merely by considering the linguistic
strategy used.

Intentions and effects are not identical. When people have differing conversational styles, the effect of what they say may be very different from their intention. And anything that happens between two
people is the result of both their actions. Sociolinguists talk about
this by saying that all interaction is "a joint production." The double
meaning of status and connection makes every utterance potentially
ambiguous and even polysemous (meaning many things at once).

When we think we have made ourselves clear, or think we understand what someone else has said, we feel safe in the conviction that we know what words mean. When someone insists those words meant something else, we can feel like Alice trying to talk to Humpty-Dumpty, who isn't fazed by her protest that "glory doesn't mean a nice knock-down argument" but claims with aplomb, "When I use a word it means what I want it to mean, neither more nor less." If others get to make up their own rules for what words mean, the earth starts slipping beneath our feet. One of the sources of that slippage is the ambiguity and polysemy of status and connection — the fact that the same linguistic means can reflect and create one or the other or both. Understanding this makes it easier to understand the logic behind others' apparently willful misinterpretations and makes the earth feel a little more firm beneath our feet.

Reading and Discussion Questions

1. Tannen's expository strategy is to move back and forth between generalized explanations and specific examples. Does this make reading and comprehension easier or more difficult? Explain your reaction.
2. How does Tannen make a connection between the fighting of young males and the main point of the essay, which is about speech?
3. What different kinds of support does Tannen offer?
4. Point out the sentence or sentences where she summarizes her claim about language.

Writing Suggestions

5. Tannen refers to opposition as a linguistic convention among Jews, Germans, and Greeks. If you have had experiences with these or other ethnic groups in which differences in language rituals played a significant role, tell the story of the encounter and explain what it meant.
6. What have been the principal means of bonding with your friends? Did language play a role? Explain the significance of the examples you choose.

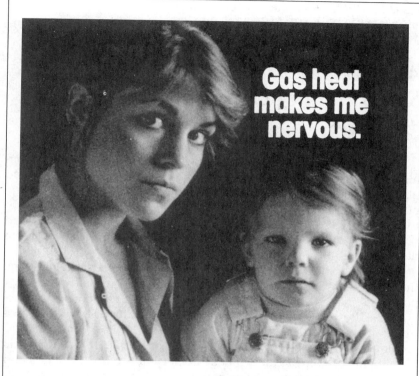

Gas heat makes me nervous.

Gas comes from the big utility.
They don't know my name.
They don't know my family.

If you need prompt service from them,
you have to say, "I smell gas."

That's what scares me most. I think gas heat
is dangerous . . . too dangerous
for my home, my kids.

I heat with oil.

Oil heat...The Intelligent Choice
Metropolitan Energy Council, Inc.

66 Morris Ave., P.O. Box 359, Springfield, NJ 07081 • (201) 379-1100

Discussion Questions

1. What strong emotional appeal does the ad make? Is it justified?
2. How would you verify the validity of the appeal?

Animal Research
Saves Human Lives

HELOISA SABIN

That scene in "Forrest Gump" in which young Forrest runs from his schoolmate tormentors so fast that his leg braces fly apart and his strong legs carry him to safety may be the only image of the polio epidemic of the 1950s etched in the minds of those too young to remember the actual devastation the disease caused. Hollywood created a scene of triumph far removed from the reality of the disease.

Some who have benefited directly from polio research, including that of my late husband, Albert, think winning the real war against polio was just as simple. They have embraced a movement that denounces the very process that enables them to look forward to continued good health and promising futures. This "animal rights" ideology — espoused by groups such as People for the Ethical Treatment of Animals, the Humane Society of the United States and the Fund for Animals — rejects the use of laboratory animals in medical research and denies the role such research played in the victory over polio.

The leaders of this movement seem to have forgotten that year after year in the early fifties, the very words "infantile paralysis" and "poliomyelitis" struck great fear in young parents that the disease would snatch their children as they slept. Each summer public beaches, playgrounds, and movie theaters were places to be avoided. Polio epidemics condemned millions of children and young adults to lives in which debilitated lungs could no longer breathe on their own and young limbs were left forever wilted and frail. The disease drafted tiny armies of children on crutches and in wheelchairs who were unable to walk, run, or jump. In the United States, polio struck down nearly 58,000 children in 1952 alone.

Unlike the braces on Forrest Gump's legs, real ones would be replaced only as the children's misshapen legs grew. Other children and young adults were entombed in iron lungs. The only view of the world these patients had was through mirrors over their heads.

Heloisa Sabin is honorary director of Americans for Medical Progress in Alexandria, Virginia. This essay appeared in the *Wall Street Journal* on October 18, 1995.

These memories, however, are no longer part of our collective cultural memory.

Albert was on the front line of polio research. In 1961, thirty years after he began studying polio, his oral vaccine was introduced in the United States and distributed widely. In the nearly forty years since, polio has been eradicated in the Western Hemisphere, the World Health Organization reports, adding that, with a full-scale effort, polio could be eliminated from the rest of the world by the year 2000.

Without animal research, polio would still be claiming thousands of lives each year. "There could have been no oral polio vaccine without the use of innumerable animals, a very large number of animals," Albert told a reporter shortly before his death in 1993. Animals are still needed to test every new batch of vaccine that is produced for today's children.

Animal activists claim that vaccines really didn't end the epidemic — that, with improvements in social hygiene, polio was dying out anyway, before the vaccines were developed. This is untrue. In fact, advanced sanitation was responsible in part for the dramatic *rise* in the number of paralytic polio cases in the fifties. Improvements in sanitation practices reduced the rate of infection, and the average age of those infected by the polio virus went up. Older children and young adults were more likely than infants to develop paralysis from their exposure to the polio virus.

Every child who has tasted the sweet sugar cube or received the drops containing the Sabin vaccine over the past four decades knows polio only as a word, or an obscure reference in a popular film. Thank heavens it's not part of their reality.

These polio-free generations have grown up to be doctors, teachers, business leaders, government officials, and parents. They have their own concerns and struggles. Cancer, heart disease, strokes, and AIDS are far more lethal realities to them now than polio. Yet, those who support an "animal rights" agenda that would cripple research and halt medical science in its tracks are slamming the door on the possibilities of new treatments and cures.

My husband was a kind man, but he was impatient with those who refused to acknowledge reality or to seek reasoned answers to the questions of life.

The pioneers of polio research included not only the scientists but also the laboratory animals that played a critical role in bringing about the end of polio and a host of other diseases for which we now have vaccines and cures. Animals will continue to be as vital as the scientists who study them in the battle to eliminate pain, suffering, and disease from our lives.

That is the reality of medical progress.

Why We Don't Need Animal Experimentation

PEGGY CARLSON

The issue of animal experimentation has become so polarized that rational thinking seems to have taken a back seat. Heloisa Sabin's October 18 editorial-page article "Animal Research Saves Lives" serves only to further misinform and polarize. She does a great disservice to science to incorrectly portray the debate about animal experimentation as occurring between "animal rights activists" and scientists. The truth is, the value of animal experimentation is being questioned by many scientists.

Mrs. Sabin uses the example of the polio vaccine developed by her husband to justify animal experimentation. However, in the case of the polio vaccine, misleading animal experiments detoured scientists away from reliable clinical studies thereby, according to Dr. Sabin himself, delaying the initial work on polio prevention. It was also unfortunate that the original polio vaccine was produced using monkey cells instead of available human cells as can be done today. The use of monkey cells resulted in viruses with the potential to cause serious disease being transferred to humans when the polio vaccine was administered.

The polio vaccine example cannot logically be used to justify the current level of animal experimentation — several billion dollars and about 30 million animals yearly. Although most people would prefer to believe that the death and suffering of all these animals is justified, the facts do not support that conclusion.

Nearly everything that medicine has learned about what substances cause human cancer and birth defects has come from human clinical and epidemiological studies because animal experiments do not accurately predict what occurs in humans. Dr. Bross, the former Director of Biostatistics at the Roswell Institute for Cancer Research states, "While conflicting animal results have often delayed and hampered advances in the war on cancer, they have never produced a single substantial advance either in the prevention or treatment of cancer." A 1990 editorial in *Stroke* notes that none of the twenty-five compounds "proven" efficacious for treating stroke in animal experiments over the preceding ten years had been effective for use in humans. From human studies alone we have learned how to lessen the risk of heart attacks. Warnings to the public that

Peggy Carlson, M.D., is research director of the Physicians Committee for Responsible Medicine in Washington, D.C. Her letter appeared in the *Wall Street Journal* on November 7, 1995.

smoking cigarettes leads to an increased risk of cancer were delayed as researchers sought, unsuccessfully, to confirm the risk by using animals.

Animal tests for drug safety, cancer-causing potential, and toxicity are unreliable, and science is leading us to more accurate methods that will offer greater protection. But if we refuse to acknowledge the inadequacies of animal tests we put a stranglehold on the very progress that will help us. Billions of precious health-care dollars have been spent to fund animal experiments that are repetitious or that have no human relevance.

An uncritical acceptance of the value of animal experiments leads to its overfunding, which, in turn, leads to the underfunding of other more beneficial areas.

Discussion Questions

1. Sabin uses the vaccine against polio as the principal example in her support of animal research. Does this limit her argument? Should she have been more specific in her references to other diseases?
2. What is the significance of Sabin's repeated references to "reality"?
3. Mention all the kinds of support that Carlson provides. Which of the supporting materials is most persuasive?
4. Does Carlson refute all the arguments in Sabin's article? Be specific.
5. Sabin makes strong emotional appeals. Describe them, and decide how large a part such appeals play in her argument. Does Carlson appeal to the emotions of her readers?

EXERCISES

1. What kind of evidence would you offer to prove to a skeptic that the moon landings — or any other space ventures — have actually occurred? What objections would you anticipate?
2. A group of heterosexual people in a middle-class community who define themselves as devout Christians have organized to keep a group of homosexuals from joining their church. What kind of support would you offer for your claim that the homosexuals should be welcomed into the church? Address your argument to the heterosexuals unwilling to admit the group of homosexuals.
3. In the summer of 1983, after an alarming rise in the juvenile crime rate, the mayor of Detroit instituted a curfew for young people under the age of eighteen. What kind of support can you provide for or against such a curfew?
4. "Racism [or sexism] is [not] a major problem on this campus [or home town or neighborhood]." Produce evidence to support your claim.
5. Write a full-page advertisement to solicit support for a project or cause that you believe in.

6. How do you account for the large and growing interest in science fiction films and literature? In addition to their entertainment value, are there other less obvious reasons for their popularity?

7. According to some researchers soap operas are influential in transmitting values, life-styles, and sexual information to youthful viewers. Do you agree? If so, what values and information are being transmitted? Be specific.

8. Choose one of the following stereotypical ideas and argue that it is true or false or partly both. Discuss the reasons for the existence of the stereotype.
   a. Jocks are stupid.
   b. The country is better than the city for bringing up children.
   c. TV is justly called "the boob tube."
   d. A dog is man's best friend.
   e. Beauty contests are degrading to women.

9. Defend or refute the view that organized sports build character.

10. The philosopher Bertrand Russell said, "Most of the work that most people have to do is not in itself interesting, but even such work has certain advantages." Defend or refute this assertion. Use your own experience as support.

Critical Listening

11. Choose a product advertised on TV by many different makers. (Cars, pain relievers, fast food, cereals, and soft drinks are some of the most popular products.) What kinds of support do the advertisers offer? Why do they choose these particular appeals? Would the support be significantly different in print?

12. From time to time advocates of causes speak on campus. The causes may be broadly based — minority rights, welfare cuts, abortion, foreign aid — or they may be local issues, having to do with harassment policy, course requirements, or tuition increases. Attend a meeting or a rally at which a speaker argues his or her cause. Write an evaluation of the speech, paying particular attention to the kinds of support. Did the speaker provide sufficient and relevant evidence? Did he or she make emotional appeals? What signs, if any, reflected the speaker's awareness of the kinds of audience he or she was addressing?

CHAPTER SIX

Warrants

We now come to the third element in the structure of the argument — the warrant. In the first chapter we defined the warrant as an *assumption,* a belief we take for granted, or a general principle. Claim and support, the other major elements we have discussed, are more familiar in ordinary discourse, but there is nothing mysterious or unusual about the warrant. All our claims, both formal and informal, are grounded in warrants or assumptions that the audience must share with us if our claims are to prove acceptable.

These warrants reflect our observations, our personal experience, and our participation in a culture. But because these observations, experiences, and cultural associations will vary, the audience may not always agree with the warrants or assumptions of the writer. The British philosopher Stephen Toulmin, who developed the concept of warrants, dismissed more traditional forms of logical reasoning in favor of a more audience-based, courtroom-derived approach to argumentation. He refers to warrants as "general, hypothetical statements, which can act as bridges" and "entitle one to draw conclusions or make claims."[1] The word *bridges* to denote the action of the warrant is crucial. One dictionary defines warrant as a "guarantee or justification." We use the word *warrant* to emphasize that in an argument it guarantees a connecting link — a bridge — between the claim and the support. This means that even if a reader agrees that the support is sound, the support cannot prove the validity of the claim unless the reader also agrees with the underlying warrant. Recall the sample argument outlined in Chapter 1 (p. 12):

---

[1]Stephen Toulmin, *The Uses of Argument* (Cambridge: Cambridge University Press, 1958), p. 98.

CLAIM: Adoption of a vegetarian diet leads to healthier and longer life.

SUPPORT: The authors of *Becoming a Vegetarian Family* say so.

WARRANT: The authors of *Becoming a Vegetarian Family* are reliable sources of information on diet.

Notice that the reader must agree with the assumption that the testimony of experts is trustworthy before he or she arrives at the conclusion that a vegetarian diet is healthy. Simply providing evidence that the authors say so is not enough to prove the claim.

The following dialogue offers another example of the relationship between the warrant and the other elements of the argument.

"I don't think that Larry can do the job. He's pretty dumb."

"Really? I thought he was smart. What makes you say he's dumb?"

"Did you know that he's illiterate — can't read above third-grade level? In my book that makes him dumb."

If we put this into outline form, the warrant or assumption in the argument becomes clear.

CLAIM: Larry is pretty dumb.

EVIDENCE: He can't read above third-grade level.

WARRANT: Anybody who can't read above third-grade level must be dumb.

We can also represent the argument in diagram form, which shows the warrant as a bridge between the claim and the support.

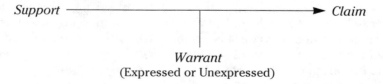

Support ————————————————➤ Claim

Warrant
(Expressed or Unexpressed)

The argument above can then be written like this:

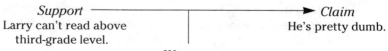

Support ————————————————➤ Claim
Larry can't read above   He's pretty dumb.
  third-grade level.

Warrant
Anybody who can't read above third-grade
level must be pretty dumb.

Is this warrant valid? We cannot answer this question until we consider the *backing*. Every warrant or assumption rests on something else that gives it authority; this is what we call backing. Backing or authority for the warrant in this example would consist of research data that prove a relationship between stupidity and illiteracy. This particular warrant, we would discover, lacks backing because we know that the failure to learn to read may be due to a number of things unrelated to intelligence. So, if the warrant is unprovable, the claim — that Larry is dumb — is also unprovable, even if the evidence is true. In this case, then, the evidence does not guarantee the soundness of the claim.

Now consider this example of a somewhat more complicated warrant: The beautiful and unspoiled Eastern Shore of Maryland is being discovered by thousands of tourists, vacationers, and developers who will, according to the residents, change the landscape and the way of life, which is now based largely on fishing and farming. In a few years the Eastern Shore may become a noisy, crowded string of resorts. Mrs. Walkup, the Kent County commissioner, says,

> Catering to the wealthy puts property back on the tax rolls, but it's going to make the Eastern Shore look like the rest of the country. Everything that made our way of life so special is being eroded. We are a fragile area. The Eastern Shore is still special, but it is feeling pressure from all directions. Lots of people don't seem to appreciate the fact that God made us to need a little peace and quiet now and then.[2]

In simplified form the argument of those opposed to development would be outlined this way:

CLAIM: Development will bring undesirable changes to the present way of life on the Eastern Shore, a life of farming and fishing, peace and quiet.

SUPPORT: Developers will build express highways, condominiums, casinos, and nightclubs.

WARRANT: A pastoral life of fishing and farming is superior to the way of life brought by expensive, fast-paced modern development.

Notice that the warrant is a broad generalization that can apply to a number of different situations, while the claim is about a specific place and time. It should be added that in other arguments the warrant may not be stated in such general terms. However, even in arguments in which the warrant makes a more specific reference to the claim, the reader can infer an extension of the warrant to other similar arguments. In the vegetarian diet example (p. 3, outlined on p. 12) the warrant mentions a specific book. But it is clear that such

---

[2]Michael Wright, "The Changing Chesapeake," *New York Times Magazine,* July 10, 1983, p. 27.

warrants can be generalized to apply to other arguments in which we accept a claim based on the credibility of the sources.

To be convinced of the validity of Mrs. Walkup's claim, you must first find that the support is true, that the developers plan to introduce drastic changes that will destroy the pastoral life of the Eastern Shore. You may, however, believe that the support is not entirely sound, that the development will be much more modest than residents fear, and that the Eastern Shore will not be seriously altered. Next, you may want to see more justification for the warrant. Is pastoral life superior to the life that will result from large-scale development? Perhaps you have always thought that a life of fishing and farming means poverty and limited opportunities for the majority of the residents. Although the superiority of a way of life is largely a matter of taste and therefore difficult to prove, Mrs. Walkup may need to produce backing for her belief that the present way of life is more desirable than one based on developing the area for new residents and summer visitors. If you find either the support or the warrant unconvincing, you cannot accept the claim.

Remember that a claim is often modified by one or more qualifiers, which limit the claim. Mrs. Walkup might have said, "Development will *probably* destroy *some aspects of* the present way of life on the Eastern Shore." Warrants can also be modified or limited by *reservations,* which remind the reader that there are conditions under which the warrants will not be relevant. Mrs. Walkup might have added, ". . . unless increased prosperity and exposure to the outside world brought by development improve some aspects of our lives."

A diagram of Mrs. Walkup's argument shows the additional elements:

Support ⟶ *Claim*

The developers will build highways, condos, casinos, nightclubs.	Development will bring undesirable changes to life on the Eastern Shore.

Warrant — *Qualifier*

A way of life devoted to farming and fishing is superior to a way of life brought by development.

Development will *most likely* bring undesirable changes.

Backing

We have experienced crowds, traffic, noise, rich strangers, high-rises, and they destroy peace and quiet.

Reservation

But increased development might improve some aspects of our lives.

Claim and support (or lack of support) are relatively easy to un-cover in most arguments. One thing that makes the warrant different is that it is often unexpressed and therefore unexamined by both writer and reader because they take it for granted. In the argument about Larry's intelligence, the warrant was stated. But in the argu-ment about development on the Eastern Shore, Mrs. Walkup did not state her warrant directly, although her meaning is perfectly clear. She probably felt that it was not necessary to be more explicit be-cause her readers would understand and supply the warrant.

We can make the discovery of warrants even clearer by examin-ing another argument, in this case a policy claim. We've looked at a factual claim — that Larry is dumb — and a value claim — that Eastern Shore development is undesirable. Now we examine a policy claim that rests on one expressed and one unexpressed warrant. Policy claims are usually more complicated than other claims be-cause the statement of policy is preceded by an array of facts and values. In addition, such claims may represent chains of reasoning in which one argument is dependent on another. These complicated arguments may be difficult or impossible to summarize in a simple diagram, but careful reading, asking the same kinds of questions that the author may have asked about his claim, can help you to find the warrant or chain of warrants that must be accepted before evi-dence and claim can be linked.

In the article we examine,[3] the author argues for a radical reform in college sports — the elimination of subprofessional intermural team sports, as practiced above all in football and basketball. The claim is clear, and evidence for the professional character of college sports not hard to find: the large salaries paid to coaches, the gener-ous perquisites offered to players, the recruitment policies which ig-nore academic standing, the virtually full-time commitment of the players, the lucrative contracts with TV. But can this evidence sup-port the author's claim that such sports do not belong on college campuses? Advocates of these sports may ask, Why not? In the con-clusion of the article the author states one warrant or assumption underlying his claim.

> Even if the money to pay college athletes could be found, though, a larger question must be answered — namely, why should a system of professional athletics be affiliated with universities at all? For the truth is that the requirements of athletics and academics operate at cross purposes, and the attempt to play both games at once serves only to re-duce the level of performance of each.

In other words, the author assumes that the goals of an academic education on the one hand and the goals of big-time college sports

---

[3]D. G. Myers, "Why College Sports?" *Commentary,* December 1990, pp. 49–51.

on the other hand are incompatible. In the article he develops the ways in which each enterprise harms the other.

But the argument clearly rests on another warrant that is not expressed because the author takes for granted that his readers will supply it: The academic goals of the university are primary and should take precedence over all other collegiate activities. This is an argument based on an authority warrant, the authority of those who define the goals of the university — scholars, public officials, university administrators, and others. (Types of warrants are discussed in the following section.)

This warrant makes clear that the evidence of the professional nature of college sports cited above supports the claim that they should be eliminated. If quasiprofessional college sports are harmful to the primary educational function of the college or university, then they must go. In the author's words, "The two are separate enterprises, to be judged by separate criteria. . . . For college sports, the university is not an educational institution at all; it is merely a locus, a means of coordinating the different aspects of the sporting enterprise."

Arguers will often neglect to state their warrants for one of two reasons: First, like Mrs. Walkup, they may believe that the warrant is obvious and need not be expressed; second, they may want to conceal the warrant in the hope that the reader will overlook its weakness.

What kinds of warrants are so obvious that they need not be expressed? Here are a few that will probably sound familiar.

Mothers love their children.

The more expensive the product, the more satisfactory it will be.

A good harvest will result in lower prices for produce.

First come, first served.

These statements seem to embody beliefs that most of us would share and that might be unnecessary to make explicit in an argument. The last statement, for example, is taken as axiomatic, an article of faith that we seldom question in ordinary circumstances. Suppose you hear someone make the claim, "I deserve to get the last ticket to the concert." If you ask why he is entitled to a ticket that you also would like to have, he may answer in support of his claim, "Because I was here first." No doubt you accept his claim without further argument because you understand and agree with the warrant that is not expressed: "If you arrive first, you deserve to be served before those who come later." Your acceptance of the warrant probably also takes into account the unexpressed backing that is based on a belief in justice: "It is only fair that those who sacrifice time and comfort to be first in line should be rewarded for their trouble."

In this case it may not be necessary to expose the warrant and examine it. Indeed, as Stephen Toulmin tells us, "If we demanded the credentials of all warrants at sight and never let one pass unchallenged, argument could scarcely begin."[4]

But even those warrants that seem to express universal truths invite analysis if we can think of claims for which these warrants might not, after all, be relevant. "First in line," for example, may justify the claim of a person who wants a concert ticket, but it cannot in itself justify the claim of someone who wants a vital medication that is in short supply. Moreover, offering a rebuttal to a long-held but unexamined warrant can often produce an interesting and original argument. If someone exclaims, "All this buying of gifts! I think people have forgotten that Christmas celebrates the birth of Christ," she need not express the assumption — that the buying of gifts violates what ought to be a religious celebration. It goes unstated by the speaker because it has been uttered so often that she knows the hearer will supply it. But one writer, in an essay titled "God's Gift: A Commercial Christmas," argued that, contrary to popular belief, the purchase of gifts, which means the expenditure of time, money, and thought on others rather than oneself, is not a violation but an affirmation of the Christmas spirit.[5]

The second reason for refusal to state the warrant lies in the arguer's intention to disarm or deceive the reader, although the arguer may not be aware of this. For instance, failure to state the warrant is common in advertising and politics, where the desire to sell a product or an idea may outweigh the responsibility to argue explicitly. The following advertisement is famous not only for what it says but for what it does not say:

> In 1918 Leona Currie scandalized a New Jersey beach with a bathing suit cut above her knees. And to irk the establishment even more, she smoked a cigarette. Leona Currie was promptly arrested.
>
> Oh, how Leona would smile if she could see you today.
>
> You've come a long way, baby. *Virginia Slims*. The taste for today's woman.

What is the unstated warrant? The manufacturer of Virginia Slims hopes we will agree that being permitted to smoke cigarettes is a significant sign of female liberation. But many readers would insist that proving "You've come a long way, baby" requires more evidence than women's freedom to smoke (or wear short bathing suits). The shaky warrant weakens the claim.

Politicians, too, conceal warrants that may not survive close scrutiny. In the 1983 mayoral election in Chicago, one candidate re-

---

[4]*The Uses of Argument* (Cambridge: Cambridge University Press, 1958), p. 106.
[5]Robert A. Sirico, *Wall Street Journal,* December 21, 1993, Sec. A, p. 12.

vealed that his opponent had undergone psychiatric treatment. He did not have to state the warrant supporting his claim. He knew that many in his audience would assume that anyone who had undergone psychiatric treatment was unfit to hold public office. This same assumption contributed to the withdrawal of a vice-presidential candidate from the 1972 campaign.

TYPES OF WARRANTS

Arguments may be classified according to the types of warrants offered as proof. Because warrants represent the reasoning process by which we establish the relationship between support and claim, analysis of the major types of warrants enables us to see the whole argument as a sum of its parts.

Warrants may be organized into three categories: "*authoritative, substantive,* and *motivational.*"[6] We have already given examples of these types of warrants in this chapter and in Chapter 1. The *authoritative warrant* (see p. 12) is based on the credibility or trustworthiness of the source. If we assume that the source of the data is authoritative, then we find that the support justifies the claim. A *substantive warrant* is based on beliefs about reliability of factual evidence. In the example on page 180 the speaker assumes, although mistakenly, that the relationship between illiteracy and stupidity is a verifiable datum, one that can be proved by objective research. A *motivational warrant,* on the other hand, is based on the needs and values of the audience. For example, the warrant on page 12 reflects a preference for individual freedom, a value that would cause a reader who held it to agree that laws against marijuana should be repealed.

Each type of warrant requires a different set of questions for testing its soundness. The following list of questions will help you to decide whether a particular warrant is valid and can justify a particular claim.

1. *Authoritative* (based on the credibility of the sources)
   Is the authority sufficiently respected to make a credible claim?
   Do other equally reputable authorities agree with the authority cited?
   Are there equally reputable authorities who disagree?

2. *Substantive* (based on beliefs about the reliability of factual evidence)
   Are sufficient examples given to convince us that a general statement is justified? That is, are the examples given representative of the whole community?

---

[6]D. Ehninger and W. Brockriede, *Decision by Debate* (New York: Dodd, Mead, 1953).

If you have argued that one event or condition can bring about another (a cause-effect argument), does the cause given seem to account entirely for the effect? Are other possible causes equally important as explanations for the effect?

If you have used comparisons, are the similarities between the two situations greater than the differences?

If you have used analogies, does the analogy explain or merely describe? Are there sufficient similarities between the two elements to make the analogy appropriate?

3. *Motivational* (based on the values of the arguer and the audience)

   Are the values ones that the audience will regard as important?
   Are the values relevant to the claim?

SAMPLE ANALYSIS

The Case for Torture

MICHAEL LEVIN

It is generally assumed that torture is impermissible, a throwback to a more brutal age. Enlightened societies reject it outright, and regimes suspected of using it risk the wrath of the United States.

I believe this attitude is unwise. There are situations in which torture is not merely permissible but morally mandatory. Moreover, these situations are moving from the realm of imagination to fact.

Suppose a terrorist has hidden an atomic bomb on Manhattan Island which will detonate at noon on July 4 unless . . . (here follow the usual demands for money and release of his friends from jail). Suppose, further, that he is caught at 10 A.M. of the fateful day, but — preferring death to failure — won't disclose where the bomb is. What do we do? If we follow due process — wait for his lawyer, arraign him — millions of people will die. If the only way to save those lives is to subject the terrorist to the most excruciating possible pain, what grounds can there be for not doing so? I suggest there are none. In any case, I ask you to face the question with an open mind.

Torturing the terrorist is unconstitutional? Probably. But millions of lives surely outweigh constitutionality. Torture is barbaric? Mass murder is far more barbaric. Indeed, letting millions of inno-

Michael Levin is a professor of philosophy at the City College of New York. This essay is reprinted from the June 7, 1982, issue of *Newsweek.*

cents die in deference to one who flaunts his guilt is moral cowardice, an unwillingness to dirty one's hands. If *you* caught the terrorist, could you sleep nights knowing that millions died because you couldn't bring yourself to apply the electrodes?

Once you concede that torture is justified in extreme cases, you have admitted that the decision to use torture is a matter of balancing innocent lives against the means needed to save them. You must now face more realistic cases involving more modest numbers. Someone plants a bomb on a jumbo jet. He alone can disarm it, and his demands cannot be met (or if they can, we refuse to set a precedent by yielding to his threats). Surely we can, we must, do anything to the extortionist to save the passengers. How can we tell 300, or 100, or 10 people who never asked to be put in danger, "I'm sorry, you'll have to die in agony, we just couldn't bring ourselves to . . ."

Here are the results of an informal poll about a third, hypothetical, case. Suppose a terrorist group kidnapped a newborn baby from a hospital. I asked four mothers if they would approve of torturing kidnappers if that were necessary to get their own newborns back. All said yes, the most "liberal" adding that she would administer it herself.

I am not advocating torture as punishment. Punishment is addressed to deeds irrevocably past. Rather, I am advocating torture as an acceptable measure for preventing future evils. So understood, it is far less objectionable than many extant punishments. Opponents of the death penalty, for example, are forever insisting that executing a murderer will not bring back his victim (as if the purpose of capital punishment were supposed to be resurrection, not deterrence or retribution). But torture, in the cases described, is intended not to bring anyone back but to keep innocents from being dispatched. The most powerful argument against using torture as a punishment or to secure confessions is that such practices disregard the rights of the individual. Well, if the individual is all that important — and he is — it is correspondingly important to protect the rights of individuals threatened by terrorists. If life is so valuable that it must never be taken, the lives of the innocents must be saved even at the price of hurting the one who endangers them.

Better precedents for torture are assassination and preemptive attack. No Allied leader would have flinched at assassinating Hitler, had that been possible. (The Allies did assassinate Heydrich.) Americans would be angered to learn that Roosevelt could have had Hitler killed in 1943 — thereby shortening the war and saving millions of lives — but refused on moral grounds. Similarly, if nation A learns that nation B is about to launch an unprovoked attack, A has a right to save itself by destroying B's military capability first. In the same way, if the police can by torture save those who would otherwise die at the hands of kidnappers or terrorists, they must.

There is an important difference between terrorists and their victims that should mute talk of the terrorists' "rights." The terrorist's victims are at risk unintentionally, not having asked to be endangered. But the terrorist knowingly initiated his actions. Unlike his victims, he volunteered for the risks of his deed. By threatening to kill for profit or idealism, he renounces civilized standards, and he can have no complaint if civilization tries to thwart him by whatever means necessary.

Just as torture is justified only to save lives (not extort confes- 10
sions or recantations), it is justifiably administered only to those *known* to hold innocent lives in their hands. Ah, but how can the authorities ever be sure they have the right malefactor? Isn't there a danger of error and abuse? Won't We turn into Them?

Questions like these are disingenuous in a world in which terrorists proclaim themselves and perform for television. The name of their game is public recognition. After all, you can't very well intimidate a government into releasing your freedom fighters unless you announce that it is your group that has seized its embassy. "Clear guilt" is difficult to define, but when 40 million people see a group of masked gunmen seize an airplane on the evening news, there is not much question about who the perpetrators are. There will be hard cases where the situation is murkier. Nonetheless, a line demarcating the legitimate use of torture can be drawn. Torture only the obviously guilty, and only for the sake of saving innocents, and the line between Us and Them will remain clear.

There is little danger that the Western democracies will lose their way if they choose to inflict pain as one way of preserving order. Paralysis in the face of evil is the greater danger. Some day soon a terrorist will threaten tens of thousands of lives, and torture will be the only way to save them. We had better start thinking about this.

Analysis

Levin's controversial essay attacks a popular assumption which most people have never thought to question — that torture is impermissible under any circumstances. Levin argues that in extreme cases torture is morally justified in order to bring about a greater good than the rights of the individual who is tortured.

Against the initial resistance that most readers may feel, Levin makes a strong case. Its strength lies in the backing he provides for the warrant that torture is sometimes necessary. This backing consists in the use of two effective argumentative strategies. One is the anticipation of objections. Unprecedented? No. Unconstitutional? No. Barbaric? No. Second, and more important, are the hypothetical examples that compel readers to rethink their positions and possibly arrive at agreement with the author. Levin chooses extreme examples — kidnapping of a newborn child, planting a bomb on a jumbo jet, detonating an atomic bomb in Manhattan — that draw a line between clear and murky cases and make agreement easier. And he bolsters his moral position by insisting that torture is not to be used as punishment or revenge but only in order to save innocent lives.

To support such an unpopular assumption the writer must convey the impression that he is a reasonable man, and this Levin attempts to do by a searching definition of terms, the careful organization and development of his argument, including references to the opinions of other people, and the expression of compassion for innocent lives.

Another strength of the article is its readability — the use of contractions, informal questions, conversational locutions. This easy, familiar style is disarming; the reader doesn't feel threatened by heavy admonitions from a writer who affects a superior, moral attitude.

READINGS FOR ANALYSIS

A Proposal to Abolish Grading
PAUL GOODMAN

Let half a dozen of the prestigious Universities — Chicago, Stanford, the Ivy League — abolish grading, and use testing only and entirely for pedagogic purposes as teachers see fit.

Anyone who knows the frantic temper of the present schools will understand the transvaluation of values that would be effected by this modest innovation. For most of the students, the competitive grade has come to be the essence. The naive teacher points to the beauty of the subject and the ingenuity of the research; the shrewd student asks if he is responsible for that on the final exam.

Let me at once dispose of an objection whose unanimity is quite fascinating. I think that the great majority of professors agree that grading hinders teaching and creates a bad spirit, going as far as cheating and plagiarizing. I have before me the collection of essays, *Examining in Harvard College,* and this is the consensus. It is uni-

Paul Goodman (1911–1972) was a college professor and writer whose outspoken views were popular with students during the 1960s. This essay is from *Compulsory Miseducation* (1964).

formly asserted, however, that the grading is inevitable; for how else will the graduate schools, the foundations, the corporations *know* whom to accept, reward, hire? How will the talent scouts know whom to tap?

By testing the applicants, of course, according to the specific task-requirements of the inducting institution, just as applicants for the Civil Service or for licenses in medicine, law, and architecture are tested. Why should Harvard professors do the testing *for* corporations and graduate schools?

The objection is ludicrous. Dean Whitla, of the Harvard Office of Tests, points out that the scholastic-aptitude and achievement tests used for *admission* to Harvard are a superexcellent index for all-around Harvard performance, better than high-school grades or particular Harvard course-grades. Presumably, these college-entrance tests are tailored for what Harvard and similar institutions want. By the same logic, would not an employer do far better to apply his own job-aptitude test rather than to rely on the vagaries of Harvard section-men? Indeed, I doubt that many employers bother to look at such grades; they are more likely to be interested merely in the fact of a Harvard diploma, whatever that connotes to them. The grades have most of their weight with the graduate schools — here, as elsewhere, the system runs mainly for its own sake.

It is really necessary to remind our academics of the ancient history of Examination. In the medieval university, the whole point of the grueling trial of the candidate was whether or not to accept him as a peer. His disputation and lecture for the Master's was just that, a masterpiece to enter the guild. It was not to make comparative evaluations. It was not to weed out and select for an extramural licensor or employer. It was certainly not to pit one young fellow against another in an ugly competition. My philosophic impression is that the medievals thought they knew what a good job of work was and that we are competitive because we do not know. But the more status is achieved by largely irrelevant competitive evaluation, the less will we ever know.

(Of course, our American examinations never did have this purely guild orientation, just as our faculties have rarely had absolute autonomy; the examining was to satisfy Overseers, Elders, distant Regents — and they as paternal superiors have always doted on giving grades, rather than accepting peers. But I submit that this set-up itself makes it impossible for the student to *become* a master, to *have* grown up, and to commence on his own. He will always be making A or B for some overseer. And in the present atmosphere, he will always be climbing on his friend's neck.)

Perhaps the chief objectors to abolishing grading would be the students and their parents. The parents should be simply disregarded; their anxiety has done enough damage already. For the students, it seems to me that a primary duty of the university is to deprive them of their props, their dependence on extrinsic valuation and motivation, and to force them to confront the difficult enterprise itself and finally lose themselves in it.

A miserable effect of grading is to nullify the various uses of testing. Testing, for both student and teacher, is a means of structuring, and also of finding out what is blank or wrong and what has been assimilated and can be taken for granted. Review — including high-pressure review — is a means of bringing together the fragments, so that there are flashes of synoptic insight.

There are several good reasons for testing, and kinds of test. But if the aim is to discover weakness, what is the point of down-grading and punishing it, and thereby inviting the student to conceal his weakness, by faking and bulling, if not cheating? The natural conclusion of synthesis is the insight itself, not a grade for having had it. For the important purpose of placement, if one can establish in the student the belief that one is testing *not* to grade and make invidious comparisons but for his own advantage, the student should normally seek his own level, where he is challenged and yet capable, rather than trying to get by. If the student dares to accept himself as he is, a teacher's grade is a crude instrument compared with a student's self-awareness. But it is rare in our universities that students are encouraged to notice objectively their vast confusion. Unlike Socrates, our teachers rely on power-drives rather than shame and ingenuous idealism.

Many students are lazy, so teachers try to goad or threaten them by grading. In the long run this must do more harm than good. Laziness is a character-defense. It may be a way of avoiding learning, in order to protect the conceit that one is already perfect (deeper, the despair that one *never* can be). It may be a way of avoiding just the risk of failing and being down-graded. Sometimes it is a way of politely saying, "I won't." But since it is the authoritarian grown-up demands that have created such attitudes in the first place, why repeat the trauma? There comes a time when we must treat people as adult, laziness and all. It is one thing courageously to fire a do-nothing out of your class; it is quite another thing to evaluate him with a lordly F.

Most important of all, it is often obvious that balking in doing the work, especially among bright young people who get to great universities, means exactly what it says: The work does not suit me, not this subject, or not at this time, or not in this school, or not in school altogether. The student might not be bookish; he might be school-tired; perhaps his development ought now to take another direction. Yet unfortunately, if such a student is intelligent and is not sure of himself, he *can* be bullied into passing, and this obscures everything. My hunch is that I am describing a common situation.

What a grim waste of young life and teacherly effort! Such a student will retain nothing of what he has "passed" in. Sometimes he must get mononucleosis to tell his story and be believed.

And ironically, the converse is also probably commonly true. A student flunks and is mechanically weeded out, who is really ready and eager to learn in a scholastic setting, but he has not quite caught on. A good teacher can recognize the situation, but the computer wreaks its will.

Reading and Discussion Questions

1. Goodman divides his argument into several parts, each of which develops a different idea. How would you subtitle these parts?
2. Are some parts of the argument stronger than others? Does Goodman indicate what points he wants to emphasize?
3. Why do you think Goodman calls on "half a dozen of the prestigious Universities" instead of all universities to abolish grading?
4. Where does the author reveal the purposes of his proposal?
5. Most professors, Goodman argues, think that grading hinders teaching. Why, then, do they continue to give grades? How does Goodman reply to their objections?
6. What does Goodman think the real purpose of testing should be? How does grading "nullify the various uses of testing"?

Writing Suggestions

7. Do you agree that grading prevents you from learning? If so, write an essay in which you support Goodman's thesis by reporting what your own experience has been.
8. If you disagree with Goodman, write an essay that outlines the benefits of grading.
9. Is there a better way than grading to evaluate the work of students — a way that would achieve the goals of education Goodman values? Suggest a method and explain why it would be superior to grading.

A Nation of Enemies

PHILIP K. HOWARD

Finding a public bathroom in New York City is not easy. Most subway toilets were closed down years ago because of vandalism and crime. Museums require people to pay admission. Restaurant bathrooms are restricted to patrons' use. As public toilets became scarce, the nooks and crannies around the city began to exude the malodorous costs of this shortage. "No one needed to be told that this was a serious problem," observed Joan Davidson, a director of a private foundation, the J. M. Kaplan Fund.

Ms. Davidson was nonetheless surprised at the outpouring of enthusiasm when, in 1991, the Kaplan Fund put forward a modest proposal to finance a test of six sidewalk toilet kiosks in different sections of the city. The coin-operated toilets would be imported from Paris, where the municipal government provides them for the convenience of residents and tourists. Perfected over years of experience in Paris, these facilities were almost too good to be true. They clean themselves with a shower of water and disinfectant after each use. The doors open automatically after fifteen minutes so they cannot be used as a place to spend the night. They are small, only five feet in diameter, which means that New York's crowded sidewalks would not be blocked. And while the City of Paris rents them, they would cost budget-strapped New York nothing: Advertising panels would be added on the outside to pay the freight. City Hall was ready to move. The six-month test, in sites from Harlem down to City Hall, would show whether they would work in New York.

Then came the glitch. Wheelchairs couldn't fit inside them. New York's antidiscrimination law provides that it is illegal to "withhold or deny" from the disabled any access to "public accommodation." Ann Emermen, the head of the Mayor's Office of the Disabled, characterized the sidewalk toilet proposal as "discrimination in its purest form." When the city's chief lawyer, Victor Kovner, whose credentials as a champion of liberal causes stretch back thirty years, sought a legislative amendment to permit the six-month test, another lobbyist for the disabled accused him of "conspiring to violate the law." Never mind that he was seeking to amend the law through the democratic process.

Suggestions that disabled-accessible bathrooms might be provided in nearby buildings or restaurants were dismissed out-of-

---

Philip K. Howard is a founding partner of the New York law firm Howard, Darby, and Levin. This selection is from his book *The Death of Common Sense: How Law Is Suffocating America* (1994).

hand: "The law requires that everyone go to the bathroom in exactly the same place." When someone had the nerve, at a public forum, to ask how many wheelchair users there might be compared with other citizens who might benefit (including blind and deaf citizens), the questioner was hooted down for asking a politically incorrect question. At stake, at least for the disabled, were their "rights." When you have a right to something, it doesn't matter what anyone thinks or whether you are, in fact, reasonable.

A kiosk accommodating wheelchairs had in fact been tried in   5
both London and Paris, but it had to be much larger and, because of its size, it could be placed only in locations where there was ample pedestrian room. Also, it was not self-cleaning. Because of the different needs of wheelchair users, it would not self-open until after thirty minutes, and experience showed that it became a refuge for prostitution and drug use. The lobby for the disabled demanded this larger kiosk or nothing.

Good-government groups and editorial boards were livid at the selfishness and intractability of the lobby. The leaders of the disabled lobby, who refer to the general public as the "temporarily abled," cast us as shortsighted bigots. Compromise was unthinkable. Politicians, ever eager to please, ducked for cover.

The ultimate resolution, while arguably legal, was undeniably silly: Two toilet kiosks would be at each of three locations, one for the general public and another, with a full-time attendant, available only for wheelchair users. Mrs. Emerman and other advocates for the disabled were still upset. Their credo is "mainstreaming": the legal right to do everything in the same way as everyone else. They still wanted the disabled to use the same toilet — not one made specifically for them — or wanted no toilet for anyone.

The test proved how great the demand was in New York. The regular units averaged over three thousand flushes per month, or 50 percent more than the average in Paris. The larger units reserved for the disabled were basically unused, the cost of the full-time attendant wasted. The test also made enemies of everyone; even liberals who had championed the cause of the disabled began to see their advocates as unreasonable zealots.

Making trade-offs in situations like this is much of what government does: Almost every government act, whether allocating use of public property, creating new programs, or granting subsidies, benefits one group more than another, and usually at the expense of everyone else. Most people expect their elected and appointed leaders to balance the pros and cons and make decisions in the public interest. The government of New York, however, lacked this power, because it had passed an innocuous-sounding law that created "rights" elevating the interests of any disabled person over any other public purpose.

Rights, almost no one needs to be told, are all around us. The lan-   10
guage of rights is used everywhere in modern America — not only in
public life, but in the workplace, in school, in welfare offices, in health
care. There are rights for children and the elderly; the disabled; the
mentally disabled; workers under twenty-five and over forty; alcoholics and the addicted; the homeless; spotted owls and snail darters.

Rights are considered as American as apple pie. This is a country where citizens have *rights*. The Bill of Rights is the best-known
part of the Constitution: Government can't tell us what to say, and
can't take away our "life, liberty or property" except by due process.
Rights are basic. Until the last few decades, however, rights were
not something to shout about. They were the bedrock of our society, something we would give our lives to defend, but not something
people thought much about as they made it through each day.
Rights were synonymous with freedom, protection against being ordered around by government or others.

Rights have taken on a new role in America. Whenever there is a
perceived injustice, new rights are created to help the victims.
These rights are different: While the rights-bearers may see them as
"protection," they don't protect so much as provide. These rights
are intended as a new, and often invisible, form of subsidy. They are
provided at everyone else's expense, but the amount of the check is
left blank. For example, in New York, the unintended consequence of
giving the disabled the "right" to do everything in the same way was
the imposition of a de facto prohibition of sidewalk toilets.

Handing out rights like land grants has become the preferred
method of staking out a place for those who feel disadvantaged.
Lawmakers and courts, confronted with evidence of past abuses,
scramble over each other to define and take credit for handing out
new rights. When refused entry to a movie because his two-year-old
son might disturb the other patrons, Rolando Acosta, then deputy
commissioner of New York City's Human Rights Commission, had an
easy fix; the commission ruled that banning children was age discrimination. In 1993, a judge in Rhode Island found rights for obese
employees. Mari Matsuda, a feminist legal scholar, has advocated
rights for those who are discriminated against on account of unusual accents — people who talk differently would be able to sue if
they feel their accent is being held against them. In 1990, the federal
government enacted a comprehensive disabled law, the Americans
with Disabilities Act (known as the ADA), to serve similar purposes
as New York's. "Let the shameful wall of exclusion finally come tum-
bling down," said President Bush on the South Lawn of the White
House upon signing the bill. The law had passed with virtually no
opposition. After all, rights cost little or nothing out of the budget.
It's only a matter of being fair. Or so we think.

Rights, however, leave no room for balance, or for looking at it
from everybody's point of view as well. Rights, as the legal philoso-

pher Ronald Dworkin has noted, are a trump card. Rights give open-ended power to one group, and it comes out of everybody else's hide. What about the three hundred other moviegoers when the two-year-old starts crying or demanding candy in a loud voice? Too bad; we gave children a right. Rights cede control to those least likely to use them wisely, usually partisans like disabled activists who have devoted their lives to remedying their own injustices. Government, for all its flaws, at least has interest in a balanced result.

This abdication has led to an inverted feudalism in which the 15 rights-bearer, by assertion of legal and moral superiority, lords it over everyone else. Rights-bearers do warfare independent of the constraints of democracy: *Give Us Our Rights.* We cringe, lacking even a vocabulary to respond.

It was only three decades ago that John F. Kennedy stirred the nation when, in his inaugural address, he said, "Ask not what your country can do for you, but what you can do for your country." Thirty years later, we have disintegrated into factions preoccupied only with our due, not what we can do.

What went wrong?

Reading and Discussion Questions

1. The organization of this essay for almost half its length is that of a narrative related as the events unfold. Is this an effective strategy? Would it have been better to state the claim at the very beginning?
2. If you were annotating this essay, are there some places where you would ask questions? How would you find the answers?
3. What is Howard's claim? Who are the enemies in the title?
4. What kinds of evidence does Howard provide to support his claim? Which evidence do you think is most convincing?
5. In one sentence summarize the warrant or assumption that underlies the claim. Is the warrant stated or merely understood? Does it seem valid?
6. What distinction does Howard make between rights as guaranteed in the Bill of Rights and rights as demanded by those with disabilities? Do you think Howard is fair to those with disabilities? Explain your answer.

Writing Suggestions

7. Do you feel that, as a student or a young person, you have been deprived of a right or rights that you can justly claim? For example, mandatory school dress codes in high school are becoming increasingly common. Are they a violation of student rights? Write a defense of your position on some relevant issue. Make clear the warrant on which you base your claim.
8. At the end of this selection, Howard asks, "What went wrong?" Do you have an answer that would explain why many of us have become preoccupied with our own rights to the exclusion of the rights of others? Perhaps some things you have learned in history or sociology classes can provide a clue.

PERHAPS THE MOST BEAUTIFUL THING ABOUT USING ENERGY
MORE EFFICIENTLY ISN'T THE FUEL IT CAN SAVE.

Use natural gas and you'll help protect the environment two ways. First, natural gas is much
cleaner than other fossil fuels. You can also take advantage of our programs to reduce natural gas use up to
30% in your home or business. And that's something that's good for the environment, too.
To find out more, call 1-800-427-3089. You'll be surprised how much you can save.

Boston gas
FOR THESE TIMES, IT'S A NATURAL.

BOS/5

Discussion Questions

1. What advantages of natural gas does this ad stress? Are butterflies superior to plants or other animals as persuasive elements?
2. What warrants or assumptions about the user underlie the advertiser's approach?
3. Contrast this ad with the ad on page 173. Which argument is stronger? Notice that one is negative, the other positive. Does that fact influence your choice?

Against the Death Penalty

JOHN P. CONRAD

Whatever the outcome of this debate in the minds of our readers, it is clear to me — and, of course, to my stern opponent as well — that at this stage of our history, capital punishment is a winning cause in America, if nowhere else in the civilized world. Abolitionists may win some of their cases in the courts, in spite of the retentionists' furious denial that the courts should have jurisdiction over the nature and quality of the punishment that the state may impose on criminals. It is still possible for abolitionists to attain high office from the electorate and subsequently to "sabotage" the executioner's craft by commuting the sentences of condemned murderers. Nevertheless, I must gloomily concede that the public opinion polls, in which the hangman now receives a handsome plurality of the respondents' votes, are corroborated in statewide referendums. If the general public has its way, Dr. van den Haag's cause is won, and without the benefit of his robust arguments.

I construe this predilection for the executioner as the outcome of the common man's yearning for a tough stand, a hard line, a crushing response to the nation's surfeit of criminals. The common man may never have met a criminal, but he knows what will deter him and what he deserves — the gallows, no less, or its local equivalent. In this certainty, the electorate is encouraged by demagogues who tell the world that the return of the executioner will signal to criminals everywhere that they can no longer expect leniency from the courts, and that the state will resume an implacable severity that prevented crimes in the old days and will soon prevent it again.

What humbug! Political candidates and their advisors know that, regardless of the deterrent value of the gallows, the death penalty has nothing to do with the nonhomicidal criminal. The arduous and costly tasks that society must undertake if crime is to be prevented still have to be defined and faced — even if we settle on an unswerving program of killing all murderers and stick to it. The signal that is really conveyed by the noose and the electric chair will be understood by thoughtful criminals and ignored by the reckless. That sig-

---

John P. Conrad has served as chief of research at the California Department of Corrections and the U.S. Bureau of Prisons. This essay is from *The Death Penalty Pro and Con: A Debate* (1983). [All notes are Conrad's.]

nal will tell those who receive it that Americans do not understand the crime problem in spite of all the exposure they have had. Whether thoughtful or reckless, criminals know that neither the gallows nor the prison awaits them, whatever their offense may be, if they are not caught, prosecuted, and convicted. They know that the police do not catch them often enough (although there is reason to suppose that most are eventually arrested), that busy prosecutors are only too willing to settle for a guilty plea to crimes less serious than those with which they are charged, and that, if they are convicted in court, the chance of probation is pretty good unless the crime is so heinous as to have become a matter of public notoriety.

Under the circumstances, how can the criminal justice system deter any man or woman desperate enough to gamble on engaging in a criminal career? The police solve a higher percentage of homicides than any other crime reported to them, but, as my well-informed opponent never tires of pointing out, the number of murders increases every year at an unacceptable rate. There are plenty of potential killers who will accept the 70-30 odds against them, perhaps because they calculate that well-planned murders by disinterested and anonymous murderers constitute most of the 30% that are uncleared. Spouse-killers and rapist-murderers are usually brought to justice, homicidal robbers and contract hit men almost never.

We distract public attention from the expensive requirements 5 of more police, more courts, and more prisons in the stentorian advocacy of capital punishment as a panacea for violent crime. The public officials responsible for this clamor know better. They also know that the execution of a contemptible killer comes cheap, compared to all the measures that must be taken to combat crime effectively.

I do not include my profoundly reflective opponent among the disingenuous office-seekers, office-holders, and editorialists who have somehow convinced the majority of the public that killing killers is the solution to the crime problem. Dr. van den Haag has for many years been a sincere believer in the efficacy of the death penalty as a deterrent of homicide, just as he has advocated more severe punishment for those who commit lesser crimes. He has not convinced me, nor has he persuaded many other abolitionists. Nevertheless, he makes what he can of a mixture of commonsense propositions about deterrence, he invokes the *lex talionis,* and he thrusts the indisputable and deplorable facts about the rising murder rate into the attention of anyone who will listen. His case for the resumption of the death penalty is rational and well argued. He is undisturbed by the overwhelming rejection of his argument by psychologists, sociologists, economists, and statisticians — with the lonely and generally discredited exception of Dr. Isaac Ehrlich.

What a stark and dismal world my bleak opponent contemplates! It is not a far cry from the world that Thomas Hobbes defined as a "time of war," when there is "continual fear and danger of violent death; and the life of man, solitary, poor, nasty, brutish, and short."[1] In this van den Haagian world, everyone must be on his guard against every neighbor, for everyone is a potential murderer, prevented from committing the most horrible of crimes only by the tenuous threat of the death penalty. Especially likely to commit such crimes are the poor, who enviously observe the comfortable classes and determine to take by force what they could not gain by merit and industry. The vertiginously rising crime rate must be attributed in very large part to the desperation of the underclasses. It follows that these people must be stringently controlled. The death penalty must be imposed on those of them who carry their crimes to the point of killing.

When pressed for evidence of the superior deterrent effect of capital punishment, as compared with life imprisonment, Dr. van den Haag will first assert that the lack of evidence does not prove that the death penalty does not deter potential killers; it merely means that statisticians and social scientists have yet to discover a methodology to prove what is self-evident to the ordinary citizen with rudimentary common sense. For those who are unimpressed with this reasoning, he invokes the ancient *lex talionis;* it is right that unlawful killers should themselves be killed.

That is a symmetry that cannot be achieved with respect to any other crime. Rapists cannot be raped; robbers cannot be robbed; burglars cannot be burglarized. The state cannot retaliate against these criminals by treating them as they treated their victims. It is nevertheless possible for the state to kill, as it must — in my righteous opponent's opinion — when a man or a woman stands convicted of murder. Only because murder, the crime of crimes, is punishable by death is it regarded with proper horror. Any lesser response would trivialize the death of an innocent victim.

I say that nothing can trivialize murder. Good men and women   10
abhor violence and particularly abhor it when it is homicidal. To suppose that ordinary citizens will accept murder as a matter of course unless the executioner impresses the horror of it upon them is to state a case for which there is not the slightest supporting evidence. It is a misanthropic fallacy that emerges from the most pessimistic misinterpretation of Freudian doctrine — that all human beings are potential killers, restrained from acting on their primitive

---

[1]Thomas Hobbes, *Leviathan; or the Matter, Forme, and Power of a Commonwealth* (London: Andrew Crooke, 1651; Penguin Books, 1975), p. 186.

and destructive urges only by the threat of extreme punishment. The truth is that in this violent country, where the punishment of criminals is more severe than in any other nation except the Soviet Union and South Africa, fewer than 20,000 murderers are found each year — less than 0.01 percent of our total population. Even if we adjust the population at risk by discounting the infants and the aged, even if we allow for the murders that take place and are not recognized as such, and even if we allow for the murderous assaults in which the victim survived, our annual crop of killers could not exceed 0.05 percent of the population. Perhaps there is another 0.05 percent of potential killers who have abstained from murder for one reason or another, and we have 0.1 percent of the population to worry about. Call for a ten-year cohort of these killers and potential killers and we can elevate the danger level to 1 percent. But what reason is there to believe that the remaining 99 percent are restrained only by the threat of the hangman? Is a society imbued with this belief about its members better than a nation of paranoids?

I insist that the murderer is an exceptional person and so is the citizen who can be persuaded only by threats to abstain from acts of violence. Let the reader consider his own experience and his observation of his friends and enemies. How many truly murderous men, women, and children does he know?

The anachronism that is capital punishment originated in an era when physical punishments were all that could be imposed on criminals. In this debate we have both alluded often to the old days when sentences of truly horrifying cruelty were imposed on men and women guilty of crimes far less grave than capital murder. It is a stain on Western civilization that children could be hanged for theft, men could be broken on the rack for robbery, and women burned to death for witchcraft and adultery as recently as the eighteenth and nineteenth centuries, when many of the brightest achievements of European and American culture flowered. It should not have taken so long for a man like Beccaria to emerge with a protest against the evils of punishment as administered in the eighteenth century, or for men like Bentham and Romilly to make their case against the idiocies of nineteenth-century criminal justice in England. Not only did it take centuries too long for such men to appear, but their opposition was intransigent to the last ditch. The only way to understand the diehards of the times is to remember the dread in the upper classes that upheavals like the French Revolution might take place in their own countries if social controls were eased. Even if a major political convulsion were to be avoided, the security of the comfortable classes required the support of the death penalty. The impassioned arguments in favor of the hangman in both the English Houses of Parliament exposed the transparent apprehensions of the privileged and their trust in the gallows as the best possible prevention of crime. Those were the days when there were over 200 offenses in the statutes that called for execution.

Romilly and his friends prevailed, as did their counterparts elsewhere in Europe. Their success may be partly laid to Yankee ingenuity, which had contributed the penitentiary to the administration of criminal justice. It was adopted with alacrity throughout Europe. The penitentiary is not the brightest gem of American social technology, but it is a feasible alternative to capital punishment. The whip was eliminated for ordinary offenders, and the gallows was reserved for murderers.

The question that I have raised so often in this debate must be confronted again. *Why should we retain capital punishment when a life sentence in prison will serve the deterrent purpose at least as well?*

Implicit in that question is my complete disbelief that there exists a population of potential murderers who would be deterred by the gallows — or the lethal needle — but would proceed with their killings if the worst they could expect was a life sentence in prison. If such extraordinary people exist, a supposition for which there is absolutely no evidence, they would be balanced by an equally extraordinary, and equally hypothetical, few who are tempted to commit murder to achieve the notoriety of public execution. There may be a few in each of these classes, but in the absence of any positive evidence of their existence in significant numbers, no debating points can be claimed for them by either side.

The adequacy of a life sentence in prison as a deterrent to murder — if deterrence is truly our aim — is obvious to those who know what that experience does to the prisoner. The term begins in ignominy. It is lived out in squalor. It ends when youth is long since gone, or, more often than most people know, in the death of the senile in a prison ward for the aged and infirm. Those who fancy that life in prison bears any resemblance to the gaiety of a resort hotel or the luxury of a country club have been beguiled by dishonest demagogues. Commitment to an American prison is a disaster for all but the most vicious human predators, men who discover a false manhood in the abuse of the weak. The unique combination of ennui and chronic dread of one's fellows, of idleness and wasted years, and of lives spent with wicked, vicious, or inane men and women should be — and for most people certainly is — a terrifyingly deterrent prospect. Those who find it tolerable are manifesting the meaninglessness of their lives before commitment.

In his now classic disquisition on punishment, the great Norwegian criminologist, Johannes Andenaes, acknowledged that "it can hardly be denied that any conclusion as to the real nature of general prevention involves a great deal of guess work. Claims based on the 'demands of general prevention,' therefore, can often be used to cloak strictly conservative demands for punishment or mere conservative resistance to change."[2]

Jack Gibbs carries this point a good deal further in his comprehensive survey of thought and rhetoric generated by the deterrence controversy:

> Hypocrisy is not likely to be a question in debates over penal policy when a protagonist either (1) opposes punishment regardless of the deterrence presumably realized or (2) advocates punishment for the sake of retribution alone. However, a party to the debate may endorse punishment, but only *insofar as it deters crime,* meaning that a value judgement at least appears to be contingent on scientific evidence. When that argument is made, hypocrisy does become an issue, and the very notion of scientific evidence becomes disputable. No scientific finding necessarily (i.e., logically) gives rise to a moral conclusion or value judgement, and the compunction to bridge the gap readily leads to personalized evidential criteria. Thus, one may believe that crimes should be punished for the sake of vengeance alone but conceal that belief by arguing that punishment deters crime and dismiss all manner of research findings as irrelevant or insufficient. At the other extreme, if one views punishment as intrinsically wrong, that value judgement can be covertly defended by invoking rigorous criteria for positive evidence of deterrence.[3]

I do not accuse my upright opponent of hypocrisy, but I think the weakness of any case to be made for the superior deterrent effect of the death penalty — as compared to long incarceration — should be apparent to the reader. It is natural in our goal-oriented culture to adopt the deterrent theory. It promises to accomplish steps toward the prevention of the worst of crimes with each cadaver hauled away from the place of execution. Some day, the retentionist hopes, science will justify the killing by showing the effectiveness of capital punishment as measured by the numbers of innocent lives saved. This is the hope that Dr. van den Haag and his friends express so ardently.

It is a hope that will not be realized. The power of the criminal justice system to prevent any category of crimes is very limited. An organized society must administer criminal justice because it cannot ignore crime. Crimes must be punished in the interests of the society's cohesion and solidarity. The methods we have devised to punish criminals will intimidate some of them, will prevent the

20

---

[2] Johannes Andenaes, *Punishment and Deterrence* (Ann Arbor: University of Michigan Press, 1974), pp. 9–10.

[3] Jack Gibbs, *Crime, Punishment and Deterrence* (New York, Oxford, and Amsterdam: Elsevier, 1975), pp. 9–10.

crimes that imprisoned criminals might commit, and may deter some potential criminals from engaging in violations of the law. To suppose that the criminal justice system can or should prevent crime is to expect too much of it and too little of the larger social system of which criminal justice is only a part.

I contend that the criminal justice system must be process-oriented, not engaged in achieving goals that are beyond its reach. The police should be efficient in apprehending criminals, the courts should be fair in trying them, and the penal system should be humane but secure. The process-oriented hanging of criminals as their just desert for the crime of murder is an archaism surviving from a bygone and primitive age. The assertion that some day it will be shown that it is a necessary deterrent to murder is, at best, a naive indulgence in wishful thinking.

Throughout this debate I have insisted on the primacy of retributivism in the administration of justice. My utilitarian opponent scorns retributivism as a theory, and in the strict sense in which that word is used by scientists, he may be right.[4] He supposes that deterrence qualifies as a theory because it may be subjected to verification tests. The reader may judge whether Professor van den Haag has cited any tests whatsoever that offer a satisfactory verification of the hypothesis on which his special case of the deterrent "theory" must rest.[5]

I take up my position somewhere between the two extremes defined by Gibbs. I do indeed hold that it is necessary to punish crimes in the interest of retribution.[6] There are enough empirical supports for the notion that punishment will deter in many situations. There are none at all for the notion that the death penalty will deter criminals more effectively than a protracted prison sentence. I do not accept the argument that punishment is intrinsically wrong, but I do

---

[4] On the usage, "theories of punishment," to which Dr. van den Haag has objected, see H. L. A. Hart, *Punishment and Responsibility* (Oxford: Clarendon Press, 1968), p. 70: "theories of punishment are not theories in any normal sense. They are not, as scientific theories are, assertions or contentions as to what is or is not the case. . . . On the contrary, those major positions concerning punishment which are called deterrent or retributive or reformative 'theories' of punishment are *moral* claims as to what justifies the practice of punishment — claims as to why, morally, it should or may be used." Hart goes on to write that if we claim that capital punishment protects society from harm, then we should call "this implicit moral claim 'the utilitarian position.'" I agree with Hart's fastidious use of terms, but the word *theory* is by now too deeply embedded in criminological discourse to be summarily uprooted.

[5] By "special case," of course, I mean the deterrence that is ascribed to capital punishment that is beyond the reach of life imprisonment.

[6] I readily concede that I am too squeamish to justify punishment for the sake of vengeance. I insist that there is a significant difference between primitive vengeance — the *lex talionis* of Hammurabi, Leviticus, and the Twelve Tables of republican Rome — and the denunciatory, reprobative functions of retribution.

hold that punishment must not be inflicted beyond simple necessity. It is not necessary to punish anyone with a sanction more severe than the gravity of the crimes committed and the criminal's record of recidivism for serious crimes. I see no great problem in achieving a consensus on the scale of sanctions, with a life term in prison for the first degree murderer at the apex of the scale.

The rule is that we should punish no more than we must. The death penalty is needless in an age when the maximum-security prison is available. Adherence to the principle of necessity as the limiting factor in determining the nature and quality of punishment will go far toward preventing our nation from ever descending to the horrible depths of degraded justice that are to be seen in Eastern Europe, in South Africa, and in Argentina.

The executioner does what he has to do in behalf of the citizens of the state that employs him. His hand is on the lever that releases the cyanide, switches on the current, or springs the trap. We, as citizens, cannot escape a full share of his responsibility. We voted into office the legislators who make killers of us all. If the deliberate killing of another human being is the most abhorrent of crimes, we are all guilty, even though we shall be scot-free from legal punishment. The pity and terror that an execution inspires in even the most callous is punishment enough for the perceptive citizen. Pity and terror, mixed with the knowledge that what has been done is futile.

As my stoical opponent has repeatedly reminded us, we must all die. Many of us will die in conditions far more painful than sudden oblivion from a whiff of gas or a lethal charge of electricity. None of us has to inflict death on another. The statutes that make such deaths occasionally possible must be repealed in the interest of decency and good conscience. The sooner the better.

For the Death Penalty

ERNEST VAN DEN HAAG

There are two basic arguments for the death penalty; they are independent of, yet consistent with, one another.

The first argument is moral: The death penalty is just; it is deserved for certain crimes. One can explain why one feels that certain crimes deserve the death penalty. But as usual with moral arguments, one cannot show this conviction to be *factually* correct (or, for that matter, incorrect) since moral arguments rest not on facts but on our evaluation of them. My evaluation leads me to believe that, e.g., premeditated murder or treason (a fact) is so grave and horrible a crime (an evaluation) as to deserve nothing less than the death penalty, that only the death penalty (a fact) is proportionate to the gravity of the crime (an evaluation).

My widely shared view is opposed by abolitionists, who claim that the death penalty is unjust for any crime, and inconsistent with human dignity. Professor Conrad's arguments in favor of this position seem unconvincing to me. Since most abolitionists believe, as I do, that punishments should be proportionate to the perceived gravity of crimes, the abolitionist claim seems to me logically precarious. It implies either that murder is not so horrible after all — not horrible enough, at any rate to deserve death — or that the death penalty is too harsh a punishment for it, and indeed for any conceivable crime. I find it hard to believe that one can hold either view seriously, let alone both. But I am wrong: Professor Conrad does, and he is by no means alone in the academic world.

I must confess that I have never understood the assorted arguments claiming that the death penalty is inconsistent with human dignity or that, somehow, society has no right to impose it. One might as well claim that death generally, or at least death from illness, is inconsistent with human dignity, or that birth is, or any suffering or any undesirable social condition. Most of these are unavoidable. At least death by execution can be avoided by not killing someone else, by not committing murder. One can preserve one's dignity in this respect if one values it. Incidentally, execution may be physically less humiliating and painful than death in a hospital. It is, however, morally more humiliating and meant to be: It indicates the extreme blame we attach to the crime of murder by deliberately expelling the murderer from among the living.

Ernest van den Haag is the retired John M. Olin Professor of Jurisprudence and Public Policy at Fordham University and a Distinguished Scholar at the Heritage Foundation. This essay is from *The Death Penalty Pro and Con: A Debate* (1983).

As for the dignity of society, it seems to me that by executing 5
murderers it tries to keep its promise to secure the lives of innocents, to vindicate the law, and to impose retribution on those who
so horribly violate it. To do anything less would be inconsistent with
the dignity of society.

I see no evidence for society somehow not having "the right" to
execute murderers. It has always done so. Traditional laws and
Scriptures have always supported the death penalty. I know of no
reasoning, even in a religious (theocratic) state, that denies the right
of secular courts to impose it. We in America have a secular republic, of course, and therefore, the suggestion that the right to punish
belongs only to God, or that the right to impose capital punishment
does, is clearly out of place. It is not a religious but a secular task to
put murderers to death. Our Constitution does provide for it
(Amendments V and XIV). However much we believe in divine justice, it is to occur after, not in, this life. As for justice here and now,
it is done by the courts, which are authorized in certain cases to impose the death penalty. A secular state cannot leave it to God. And
incidentally, no theocratic state ever has. If they make mistakes, one
can hope that God will correct the courts hereafter — but this is no
ground for depriving courts of their duty to impose the penalties
provided by law where required, nor is it a ground for depriving the
law of the ability to prescribe the punishments felt to be just, including the death penalty.

The second argument in favor of capital punishment is material,
grounded on empirical facts. They are contested, as readers of this
book know, but no one would deny that what is contested are facts.
The factual question is: Does the death penalty deter murder more
than life imprisonment, or does it make no difference?

I do not agree with Professor Conrad's wishful idea that the
work of Professor Isaac Ehrlich has been discredited. I believe that
Ehrlich's findings — that the death penalty does indeed deter more
than any other penalty currently inflicted, so that each execution
saves between seven and nine innocent lives, the lives of victims
who will not be murdered in the year of execution because of the deterrent effects of executions — have been confirmed by subsequent
studies and have stood up sturdily under criticism competent and
incompetent, which Ehrlich has convincingly refuted. However,
Ehrlich's work is controversial. Anything is, if a sufficient number of
people attack it. It is fair, therefore, to say that although the preponderance of evidence is now supporting the hypothesis that capital
punishment deters more than any other punishment, the statistical
demonstration has not been conclusive enough to convince everybody. Certainly not Professor Conrad and his friends. They have not
changed their pre-Ehrlich convictions, and indeed tend to dismiss
his work.

But Conrad's fellow abolitionists have admitted that they would want to abolish the death penalty even if it were shown statistically that each execution does reduce the homicide rate by 500 murders per year. Why then worry about statistical proof? And why take seriously people so irrational that they would sacrifice the lives of 500 innocents to preserve the life of one convicted murderer?

Statistics have their place. But here I think they scarcely are needed. Harsher penalties are more deterrent than milder ones. Not only does our whole criminal justice system accept this view; we all do to the extent to which deterrence is aimed at in our everyday life. All other things equal, we penalize our children, our friends, or our business partners the more harshly the more we feel we must deter them and others in the future from a wrong they have done. Social life would not be possible if we did not believe that we can attract people to actions we desire by giving them incentives, and deter them from actions we do not desire by disincentives. The incentives and disincentives are usually proportionate to the felt desirability or undesirability of what we want to attract to or deter from. Why should murder be an exception? Why should we not believe that the greatest disincentive — the threat of death — is most likely to be the greatest deterrent? 10

Where there is life there is hope. This certainly is one major argument in favor of the death penalty. The murderer who premeditates his crime — and crimes of passion are not subject to capital punishment — if he contemplates the risk of life imprisonment is not likely to believe that, if convicted, he will remain in prison for life. He knows, however inchoately, about parole, pardons, commutations — he believes above all that he, a smart and superior fellow, will find a way to escape. Few prisoners actually do escape. But practically all "lifers" believe that they will, at least when they start their sentence. So believing, they do not greatly fear a sentence of life imprisonment and are not deterred by it. This is why the rate of stranger-murders — murders in which victim and murderer do not know one another and to which the threat of the death penalty should apply — as a proportion of all murders has steadily climbed in the last twenty years. The murderers knew that in practice they would get away with life imprisonment, from which they would be paroled after a few years. Or they hoped they would escape. After all, we executed all of five prisoners in 1981, only one of whom was executed against his wishes. (All of them were white, to the great disappointment of the civil liberties lobby.) At this rate no murderer can foresee execution or be deterred by it.

I find it hard to believe, as Professor Conrad does, that most men are incapable of murder. I admire his optimism. But I find it hard to share. I do not see how he can cling to his faith after Stalin and Hitler, in the presence of assorted tyrants and murderers in power from Albania to Iran to China. But faith obviously is not subject to empirical verification. I am optimistic, however, in my own way, which seems more realistic to me: I believe that most men can be deterred from murder by the threat of the death penalty.

Even if Conrad were right, even if his claim that only a few men would ever become murderers in the absence of the threat of punishment were correct, I should continue to advocate the death penalty to deter these few men. And even if only some of these men need the threat of capital punishment to be deterred, while others would be deterred by the threat of life imprisonment, I should advocate the death penalty to deter the very few who, according to Conrad, do, or even just may, require it to be deterred. The lives of the innocents that will or may be spared because of the death penalty are more valuable to me, and to any civilized society, than the lives of murderers. I do not want to risk their lives for the sake of the lives of murderers.

The reader will have to decide for himself on which side he wants to be.

Discussion Questions

1. These arguments are the conclusions of a book-long debate. Do you think the debaters have omitted any significant issues?
2. Both Conrad and van den Haag accuse each other of holding views of human nature based on faulty warrants. Explain their respective views. Do they offer sufficient support for them?
3. Why does Conrad think the death penalty is unnecessary as a deterrent? Is there a contradiction in his argument that life imprisonment is just as bad as, if not worse than, capital punishment?
4. What are van den Haag's two main arguments in favor of the death penalty? How can you tell which he considers to be more important?
5. To what extent do statistics and other facts play a role in these arguments?

EXERCISES

1. What are some of the assumptions underlying the preference for *natural* foods and medicines? Can *natural* be clearly defined? Is this preference part of a broader philosophy? Try to evaluate the validity of the assumption.
2. Is plagiarism wrong? What assumptions about education are relevant to the issue of plagiarism? (Some students defend it. What kinds of arguments do they provide?)
3. Choose an advertisement and examine the warrants on which the advertiser's claim is based.
4. "Religious beliefs are (or are not) necessary to a satisfactory life." Explain the warrants underlying your claim. Define any ambiguous terms.

5. Should students be given a direct voice in the hiring of faculty members? On what warrants about education do you base your answer?

6. Discuss the validity of the warrant in this statement from *The Watch Tower* (a publication of the Jehovah's Witnesses) about genital herpes: "The sexually loose are indeed 'receiving in themselves the full recompense, which was due for their error' (Romans 1:27)."

7. Read the following passage about suicide by the Greek philosopher Aristotle (adapted from his *Ethics*). Then defend or attack his argument, being careful to make clear both Aristotle's and your own warrants.

> Just as a murderer does not have the right to take a mother from her family or a child from her parents and simultaneously to deny society the use of a productive citizen, so the suicide, even though he or she freely chooses to be his or her own victim, does not possess the right to thus diminish the welfare of so many others.

8. In view of the increasing attention to health in general, and nutrition and exercise in particular, do you think that universities and colleges should impose physical education requirements? If so, what form should they take? If not, why not? Defend your reasons.

9. In recent years both state and federal governments have been embroiled in controversies concerning the rights of citizens to engage in harmful practices. In Massachusetts, for example, a mandatory seat belt law was repealed by rebellious voters who considered the law an infringement of their freedom. What principles do you think ought to guide government regulation of dangerous practices?

10. The author of the following passage, Katherine Butler Hathaway, became a hunchback as a result of a childhood illness. Here she writes about the relationship between love and beauty from the point of view of someone who is deformed. Discuss the warrants on which the author bases her conclusion.

> I could secretly pretend that I had a lover . . . but I could never risk showing that I thought such a thing was possible for me . . . with any man. Because of my repeated encounters with the mirror and my irrepressible tendency to forget what I had seen, I had begun to force myself to believe and to remember, and especially to remember, that I would never be chosen for what I imagined to be the supreme and most intimate of all experience. I thought of sexual love as an honor that was too great and too beautiful for the body in which I was doomed to live.

Critical Listening

11. People often complain that they aren't listened to. Children complain about parents, patients about doctors, wives about husbands, citizens about government. Are the complaints to be taken literally? Or are they based on unexpressed warrants or assumptions about communication? Choose a specific situation with which you're familiar and explain the meaning of the complaint.

12. Barbara Ehrenreich, in a *Time* essay, defends "talk shows of the *Sally Jessy Raphael* variety" as highly moralistic. Listen to a few of these shows — *Ricki Lake, Geraldo, Hard Copy* — and determine what moral assumptions about personal relationships and behavior underlie the advice given to the participants by the host and the audience. Do you think Ehrenreich is correct?

CHAPTER SEVEN

Language
and Thought

THE POWER OF WORDS

Words play such a critical role in argument that they deserve special treatment. Elsewhere we have referred directly and indirectly to language: Chapter 4 discusses definitions and Part Two discusses style — the choice and arrangement of words and sentences — and shows how successful writers express arguments in language that is clear, vivid, and thoughtful. An important part of these writers' equipment is a large and active vocabulary, but no single chapter in a book can give this to you; only reading and study can widen your range of word choices. Even in a brief chapter, however, we can point out how words influence the feelings and attitudes of an audience, both favorably and unfavorably.

One kind of language responsible for shaping attitudes and feelings is *emotive language,* language that expresses and arouses emotions. Understanding it and using it effectively is indispensable to the arguer who wants to move an audience to accept a point of view or undertake an action.

Long before you thought about writing your first argument, you learned that words had the power to affect you. Endearments and affectionate and flattering nicknames evoked good feelings about the speaker and yourself. Insulting nicknames and slurs produced dislike for the speaker and bad feelings about yourself. Perhaps you were told, "Sticks and stones may break your bones, but words will never hurt you." But even to a small child it is clear that ugly words are as painful as sticks and stones and that the injuries are sometimes more lasting.

Nowhere is the power of words more obvious and more familiar than in advertising, where the success of a product may depend on the feelings that certain words produce in the prospective buyer. Even the names of products may have emotive significance. In recent years a new industry, composed of consultants who supply names for products, has emerged. Although most manufacturers agree that a good name won't save a poor product, they also recognize that the right name can catch the attention of the public and persuade people to buy a product at least once. According to an article in the *Wall Street Journal,* a product name not only should be memorable but also should "remind people of emotional or physical experiences." One consultant created the name Magnum for a malt liquor from Miller Brewing Company: "The product is aimed at students, minorities, and lower-income customers." The president of the consulting firm says that Magnum "implies strength, masculinity, and more bang for your buck."[1] This naming of products has been called the "Rumpelstiltskin effect," a phrase coined by a linguist. "The whole point," he said, "is that when you have the right name for a thing, you have control over it."[2]

Even scientists recognize the power of words to attract the attention of other scientists and the public to discoveries and theories that might otherwise remain obscure. A good name can even enable the scientist to visualize a new concept. One scientist says that "a good name," such as "quark," "black hole," "big bang," "chaos," or "great attractor," "helps in communicating a theory and can have substantial impact on financing."

It is not hard to see the connection between the use of words in conversation and advertising and the use of emotive language in the more formal arguments you will be writing. Emotive language reveals your approval or disapproval, assigns praise or blame — in other words, makes a judgment about the subject. Keep in mind that unless you are writing purely factual statements, such as scientists write, you will find it hard to avoid expressing judgments. Neutrality does not come easily, even where it may be desirable, as in news stories or reports of historical events. For this reason you need to attend carefully to the statements in your argument, making sure that you have not disguised judgments as statements of fact. Of course, in attempting to prove a claim, you will not be neutral. You will be revealing your judgment about the subject, first in the selection of facts and opinions and the emphasis you give to them and second in the selection of words.

Like the choice of facts and opinions, the choice of words can be effective or ineffective in advancing your argument, moral or im-

---

[1] *Wall Street Journal,* August 5, 1982, p. 19.
[2] *Harvard Magazine,* July–August 1995, p. 18.

moral in the honesty with which you exercise it. The following discussions offer some insights into recognizing and evaluating the use of emotive language in the arguments you read, as well as into using such language in your own arguments where it is appropriate and avoiding it where it is not.

CONNOTATION

The connotations of a word are the meanings we attach to it apart from its explicit definition. Because these added meanings derive from our feelings, connotations are one form of emotive language. For example, the word *rat* denotes or points to a kind of rodent, but the attached meanings of "selfish person," "evil-doer," "betrayer," and "traitor" reflect the feelings that have accumulated around the word.

In Chapter 4 we observed that definitions of controversial terms, such as *poverty* and *unemployment,* may vary so widely that writer and reader cannot always be sure that they are thinking of the same thing. A similar problem arises when a writer assumes that the reader shares his or her emotional response to a word. Emotive meanings originate partly in personal experience. The word *home,* defined merely as "a family's place of residence," may suggest love, warmth, and security to one person; it may suggest friction, violence, and alienation to another. The values of the groups to which we belong also influence meaning. Writers and speakers count on cultural associations when they refer to our country, our flag, and heroes and enemies we have never seen. The arguer must also be aware that some apparently neutral words trigger different responses from different groups — words such as *cult, revolution, police, beauty contest,* and *corporation.*

Various reform movements have recognized that words with unfavorable connotations have the power not only to reflect but also to shape our perceptions of things. The words *Negro* and *colored* were rejected by the civil rights movement in the 1960s because they bore painful associations with slavery and discrimination. Instead, the word *black,* which was free from such associations, became the accepted designation; more recently, the Reverend Jesse Jackson suggested another change, African American, to reflect ethnic origins. People of "Spanish-Hispanic" origin (as they are designated on the 1990 census) are now engaged in a debate about the appropriate term for a diverse population of more than 22 million American residents from Mexico, Puerto Rico, Cuba, and more than a dozen Central and South American countries. To some, the word *Hispanic* is unacceptable because it is an Anglicization and recalls the colonization of America by Spain and Portugal.

The women's liberation movement also insisted on changes that would bring about improved attitudes toward women. The movement condemned the use of *girl* for a female over the age of eighteen and the use in news stories of descriptive adjectives that emphasized the physical appearance of women. And the homosexual community succeeded in reintroducing the word *gay,* a word current centuries ago, as a substitute for words they considered offensive. Now *queer,* a word long regarded as offensive, has been adopted as a substitute for *gay* by a new generation of gays and lesbians, although it is still considered unacceptable by many members of the homosexual community.

Members of certain occupations have invented terms to confer greater respectability on their work. The work does not change, but the workers hope that public perceptions will change if janitors are called custodians, if garbage collectors are called sanitation engineers, if undertakers are called morticians, if people who sell makeup are called cosmetologists. Events considered unpleasant or unmentionable are sometimes disguised by polite terms, called *euphemisms.* During the 1992–1993 recession new terms emerged which disguised, or tried to, the grim fact that thousands of people were being dismissed from their jobs: "skill mix adjustment," "work force imbalance correction," "redundancy elimination," "downsizing," "indefinite idling," even a daring "career-change opportunity." Many people refuse to use the word *died* and choose *passed away* instead. Some psychologists and physicians use the phrase "negative patient care outcome" for what most of us would call "death." Even when referring to their pets, some people cannot bring themselves to say "put to death" but substitute "put to sleep" or "put down." In place of a term to describe an act of sexual intercourse, some people use "slept together" or "went to bed together" or "had an affair."

Polite words are not always so harmless. If a euphemism disguises a shameful event or condition, it is morally irresponsible to use it to mislead the reader into believing that the shameful condition does not exist. In his powerful essay "Politics and the English Language" George Orwell pointed out that politicians and reporters have sometimes used terms like "pacification" or "rectification of frontiers" to conceal acts that result in torture and death for millions of people. An example of such usage was cited by a member of Amnesty International, a group monitoring human rights violations throughout the world. He objected to a news report describing camps in which the Chinese were promoting "reeducation through labor." This term, he wrote, "makes these institutions seem like a cross between Police Athletic League and Civilian Conservation Corps camps." On the contrary, he went on, the reality of "reeducation through labor" was that the victims were confined to "rather unpleasant prison camps." The details he offered about the conditions under which people lived and worked gave substance to his claim.[3] More recently, when news organizations referred to the expulsion of Romanian gypsies from Germany as part of a "deportation treaty," an official of Germany's press agency objected to the use of the word "deportation." "You must know that by using words such as 'deportation' you are causing great sadness. . . . We prefer that you use the term readmission or retransfer."[4]

Some of the most interesting changes in language usage occur in modern Bible translations. The vocabulary and syntax of earlier versions have been greatly simplified in order to make the Bible more accessible to that half of the American public who cannot read above eighth-grade level. Another change responds to arguments by feminists, environmentalists, and multiculturalists for more "inclusive language." God is no longer the "Father," human beings no longer have "dominion" over creation, and even the word "blindness" as a metaphor for sin or evil has been replaced by other metaphors.

Perhaps the most striking examples of the way that connotations influence our perceptions of reality occur when people are asked to respond to questions of poll-takers. Sociologists and students of poll-taking know that the phrasing of a question, or the choice of words, can affect the answers and even undermine the validity of the poll. In one case poll-takers first asked a selected group of people if they favored continuing the welfare system. The majority answered no. But when the poll-takers asked if they favored government aid to the poor, the majority answered yes. Although the terms "welfare" and "government aid to the poor" refer to essentially the same forms of government assistance, "welfare" has acquired for many people negative connotations of corruption and shiftless recipients.

A *New York Times*/CBS News poll conducted in January 1989 asked, "If a woman wants to have an abortion and her doctor agrees to it, should she be allowed to have an abortion or not?" Sixty-one percent said yes, 25 percent said no, and 25 percent said it depended on the circumstances. But when the pollsters asked, "Should abortion be legal as it is now, or legal only in such cases as rape, incest, or to save the life of the mother, or should it not be permitted at all?" a much higher percentage said that abortion depended on the circumstances. Only 46 percent said it should be legal as it is now, and 41 percent said it should be legal only in such cases as rape, incest, or to save the life of the mother. According to polling experts, people are far more likely to say that they support abortion

---

[3]Letter to the *New York Times,* August 30, 1982, p. 25.
[4]*International Herald Tribune,* November 5, 1992.

when the question is asked in terms of the "woman's right to choose" than when the question asks about "protecting the unborn child." "How the question is framed," say the experts, "can affect the answers."[5]

This is also true in polls concerning rape, another highly charged subject. Dr. Neil Malamuth, a psychologist at the University of California at Los Angeles, says, "When men are asked if there is any likelihood they would force a woman to have sex against her will if they could get away with it, about half say they would. But if you ask them if they would rape a woman if they knew they could get away with it, only about 15 percent say they would." The men who change their answers aren't aware that "the only difference is in the words used to describe the same act."[6]

The wording of an argument is crucial. Because readers may interpret the words you use on the basis of feelings different from your own, you must support your word choices with definitions and with evidence that allows readers to determine how and why you made them.

SLANTING

Slanting, says one dictionary, is "interpreting or presenting in line with a special interest." The term is almost always used in a negative sense. It means that the arguer has selected facts and words with favorable or unfavorable connotations to create the impression that no alternative view exists or can be defended. For some questions it is true that no alternative view is worthy of presentation, and emotionally charged language to defend or attack a position that is clearly right or wrong would be entirely appropriate. We aren't neutral, nor should we be, about the tragic abuse of human rights anywhere in the world or even about less serious infractions of the law, such as drunk driving or vandalism, and we should use strong language to express our disapproval of these practices.

Most of your arguments, however, will concern controversial questions about which people of goodwill can argue on both sides. In such cases, your own judgments should be restrained. Slanting will suggest a prejudice — that is, a judgment made without regard to all the facts. Unfortunately, you may not always be aware of your bias or special interest; you may believe that your position is the only correct one. You may also feel the need to communicate a passionate belief about a serious problem. But if you are interested in persuading a reader to accept your belief and to act on it, you must

---

[5]*New York Times,* January 1, 1989, p. 21.
[6]*New York Times,* August 29, 1989, Sec. C, p. 1.

also ask: If the reader is not sympathetic, how will he or she respond? Will he or she perceive my words as "loaded" — one-sided and prejudicial — and my view as slanted?

R. D. Laing, a Scottish psychiatrist, defined prayer in this way: "Someone is gibbering away on his knees, talking to someone who is not there."[7] This description probably reflects a sincerely held belief. Laing also clearly intended it for an audience that already agreed with him. But the phrases "gibbering away" and "someone who is not there" would be offensive to people for whom prayer is sacred.

The following remark by an editor of *Penthouse* appeared in a debate on women's liberation.

> I haven't noticed that there is such a thing as a rise in the women's liberation movement. It seems to me that it's a lot of minor sound and a tiny fury. There are some bitty bitty groups of some disappointed ladies who have some objective or other.[8]

An unfriendly audience would resent the use of language intended to diminish the importance of the movement: "minor sound," "tiny fury," "bitty bitty groups of some disappointed ladies," "some objective or other." But even audiences sympathetic to the claim may be repelled or embarrassed by intense, colorful, obviously loaded words. In the mid-1980s an English environmental group, *London Greenpeace,* began to distribute leaflets accusing the McDonald's restaurants of a wide assortment of crimes. The leaflets said in part:

> McDollars, McGreedy, McCancer, McMurder, McDisease, McProfits, McDeadly, McHunger, McRipoff, McTorture, McWasteful, McGarbage.

> This leaflet is asking you to think for a moment about what lies behind McDonald's clean, bright image. It's got a lot to hide. . . .

> McDonald's and Burger King are two of the many U.S. corporations using lethal poisons to destroy vast areas of Central American rain forest to create grazing pastures for cattle to be sent back to the States as burgers and pet food. . . .

> What they don't make clear is that a diet high in fat, sugar, animal products and salt . . . and low in fiber, vitamins and minerals — which describes an average McDonald's meal — is linked with cancers of the breast and bowel, and heart disease. . . .[9]

Even readers who share the belief that McDonald's is not a reliable source of good nutrition might feel that *London Greenpeace* has gone

---

[7]"The Obvious," in *The Dialectics of Liberation,* edited by David Cooper (Penguin Books, 1968), p. 17.

[8]"Women's Liberation: A Debate" (Penthouse International Ltd., 1970).

[9]*New York Times,* August 6, 1995, Sec. E, p. 7. (In 1990 McDonald's sued the group for libel; the trial began in 1994 and will probably last until 1996, the longest libel trial in British history.)

too far, that the name-calling, loaded words, and exaggeration have damaged the credibility of the attackers more than the reputation of McDonald's.

We find slanting everywhere, not only in advertising and propaganda, where we expect to find it, but in news stories, which should be strictly neutral in their recounting of events, and in textbooks. In the field of history, for example, it is often difficult for scholars to remain impartial about significant events. Like the rest of us, they may approve or disapprove, and their choice of words will reflect their judgments.

The following passage by a distinguished Catholic historian describes the events surrounding the momentous decision by Henry VIII, king of England, to break with the Roman Catholic Church in 1534, in part because of the Pope's refusal to grant him a divorce from the Catholic princess Catherine of Aragon so that he could marry Anne Boleyn.

> The *protracted* delay in receiving an annulment was very *irritating* to the *impulsive* English king. . . . Gradually Henry's former *effusive* loyalty to Rome gave way to a settled conviction of the tyranny of the papal power, and there *rushed* to his mind the recollections of efforts of earlier English rulers to restrict that power. A few *salutary* enactments against the Church might *compel* a favorable decision from the Pope.
>
> Henry seriously opened his campaign against the Roman Church in 1531, when he *frightened* the clergy into paying a fine of over half a million dollars for violating an *obsolete* statute . . . and in the same year he *forced* the clergy to recognize himself as supreme head of the Church. . . .
>
> His *subservient* Parliament then empowered him to stop the payments of annates to the Pope and to appoint bishops in England without recourse to the papacy. *Without waiting longer* for the decision from Rome, he had Cranmer, *one of his own creatures,* whom he had just named Archbishop of Canterbury, declare his marriage null and void. . . .
>
> Yet Henry VIII encountered considerable *opposition* from the *higher clergy,* from the monks, and from many *intellectual leaders.* . . . A *popular uprising* — the Pilgrimage of Grace — was *sternly* suppressed, and such men as the *brilliant* Sir Thomas More and John Fisher, the *aged* and *saintly* bishop of Rochester, were beheaded because they retained their former belief in papal supremacy.[10] [Italics added]

In the first paragraph the italicized words help make the following points: that Henry was rash, impulsive, and insincere and that he was intent on punishing the church (the word *salutary* means healthful or beneficial and is used sarcastically). In the second paragraph the choice of words stresses Henry's use of force and the cowardly submission of his followers. In the third paragraph the adjectives de-

---

[10]Carlton J. H. Hayes, *A Political and Cultural History of Modern Europe,* Vol. 1 (New York: Macmillan Company, 1933), pp. 172–173.

scribing the opposition to Henry's campaign and those who were executed emphasize Henry's cruelty and despotism. Within the limits of this brief passage the author has offered support for his strong indictment of Henry VIII's actions, both in defining the statute as obsolete and in describing the popular opposition. In a longer exposition you would expect to find a more elaborate justification with facts and authoritative opinion from other sources.

The advocate of a position in an argument, unlike the reporter or the historian, must express a judgment, but the preceding examples demonstrate how the arguer should use language to avoid or minimize slanting and to persuade readers that he or she has come to a conclusion after careful analysis. The careful arguer must not conceal his or her judgments by presenting them as if they were statements of fact, but must offer convincing support for his or her choice of words and respect the audience's feelings and attitudes by using temperate language.

Depending on the circumstances, *exaggeration* can be defined, in the words of one writer, as "a form of lying." An essay in *Time* magazine, "Watching Out for Loaded Words," points to the danger for the arguer in relying on exaggerated language as an essential part of the argument.

> The trouble with loaded words is they tend to short-circuit thought. While they may describe something, they simultaneously try to seduce the mind into accepting a prefabricated opinion about the something described.[11]

PICTURESQUE LANGUAGE

Picturesque language consists of words that produce images in the mind of the reader. Students sometimes assume that vivid picture-making language is the exclusive instrument of novelists and poets, but writers of arguments can also avail themselves of such devices to heighten the impact of their messages.

Picturesque language can do more than render a scene. It shares with other kinds of emotive language the power to express and arouse deep feelings. Like a fine painting or photograph, it can draw readers into the picture where they partake of the writer's experience as if they were also present. Such power may be used to delight, to instruct, or to horrify. In 1741 the Puritan preacher Jonathan Edwards delivered his sermon "Sinners in the Hands of an Angry God," in which people were likened to repulsive spiders hanging over the flames of Hell to be dropped into the fire whenever a wrath-

---

[11] *Time,* May 24, 1982, p. 86.

ful God was pleased to release them. The congregation's reaction to Edwards's picture of the everlasting horrors to be suffered in the netherworld included panic, fainting, hysteria, and convulsions. Subsequently Edwards lost his pulpit in Massachusetts, in part as a consequence of his success at provoking such uncontrollable terror among his congregation.

Language as intense and vivid as Edwards's emerges from very strong emotion about a deeply felt cause. In an argument against abortion, a surgeon recounts a horrifying experience as if it were a scene in a movie.

> You walk toward the bus stop. . . . It is all so familiar. All at once you step on something soft. You feel it with your foot. Even through your shoe you may have the sense of something unusual, something marked by a special "give." It is a foreignness upon the pavement. Instinct pulls your foot away in an awkward little movement. You look down, and you see . . . a tiny naked body, its arms and legs flung apart, its head thrown back, its mouth agape, its face serious. A bird, you think, fallen from the nest. But there is no nest here on 73rd Street, no bird so big. It is rubber, then. A model, a . . . a joke. And you bend to see. Because you must. And it is no joke. Such a gray softness can be but one thing. It is a baby, and dead. You cover your mouth, your eyes. You are fixed. Horror has found its chink and crawled in, and you will never be the same as you were. Years later you will step from a sidewalk to a lawn, and you will start at its softness and think of that upon which you have just trod.[12]

Here the use of the pronoun *you* serves to draw readers into the scene and intensify their experience.

The rules governing the use of picturesque language are the same as those governing other kinds of emotive language. Is the language appropriate? Is it too strong, too colorful for the purpose of the message? Does it result in slanting or distortion? What will its impact be on a hostile or indifferent audience? Will they be angered, repelled? Will they cease to read or listen if the imagery is too disturbing?

We expect strong language in arguments about life and death. For subjects about which your feelings are not so passionate, your choice of words will be more moderate. The excerpt below, from an article arguing against repeal of Sunday closing laws, creates a sympathetic picture of a market-free Sunday. Most readers, even those who oppose Sunday closing laws, would enjoy the picture and perhaps react more favorably to the argument.

> Think of waking in the city on Sunday. Although most people no longer worship in the morning, the city itself has a reverential air. It comes to life slowly, even reluctantly, as traffic lights blink their orders

---

[12]Richard Selzer, *Mortal Lessons: Notes on the Art of Surgery* (New York: Simon and Schuster, 1974), pp. 153–154.

to empty streets. Next, joggers venture forth, people out to get the paper, families going to church or grandma's. Soon the city is its Sunday self: People cavort with their children, discuss, make repairs, go to museums, gambol. Few people go to work, and any shopping is incidental. The city on Sunday is a place outside the market. Play dominates, not the economy.[13]

CONCRETE AND ABSTRACT LANGUAGE

Writers of argument need to be aware of another use of language — the distinction between concrete and abstract. Concrete words point to real objects and real experiences. Abstract words express qualities apart from particular things and events. *Beautiful roses* is concrete; we can see, touch, and smell them. *Beauty in the eye of the beholder* is abstract; we can speak of the quality of beauty without reference to a particular object or event. *Returning money found in the street to the owner, although no one has seen the discovery* is concrete. *Honesty* is abstract. In abstracting we separate a quality shared by a number of objects or events, however different from each other the individual objects or events may be.

Writing that describes or tells a story leans heavily on concrete language. Although arguments also rely on the vividness of concrete language, they use abstract terms far more extensively than other kinds of writing. Using abstractions effectively, especially in arguments of value and policy, is important for two reasons: (1) Abstractions represent the qualities, characteristics, and values that the writer is explaining, defending, or attacking; and (2) they enable the writer to make generalizations about his or her data. Equally important is knowing when to avoid abstractions that obscure the message.

In some textbook discussions of language, abstractions are treated as inferior to concrete and specific words, but such a distinction is misleading. Abstractions allow us to make sense of our experience, to come to conclusions about the meaning of the bewildering variety of emotions and events we confront throughout a lifetime. One writer summarized his early history as follows: "My elementary school had the effect of *destroying any intellectual motivation,* of *stifling* all *creativity,* of *inhibiting personal relationships* with either my teachers or my peers" (emphasis added). Writing in the humanities and in some social and physical sciences would be impossible without recourse to abstractions that express qualities, values, and conditions.

---

[13]Robert K. Manoff, "New York City, It Is Argued, Faces 'Sunday Imperialism,'" *New York Times,* January 2, 1977, Sec. IV, p. 13.

You should not, however, expect abstract terms alone to carry the emotional content of your message. The effect of even the most suggestive words can be enhanced by details, examples, and anecdotes. One mode of expression is not superior to the other; both abstractions and concrete detail work together to produce clear, persuasive argument. This is especially true when the meanings assigned to abstract terms vary from reader to reader.

In establishing claims based on the support of values, for example, you may use such abstract terms as *religion, duty, freedom, peace, progress, justice, equality, democracy,* and *pursuit of happiness.* You can assume that some of these words are associated with the same ideas and emotions for almost all readers; others require further explanation. Suppose you write, "We have made great progress in the last fifty years." One dictionary defines *progress* as "a gradual betterment," another abstraction. How will you define "gradual betterment" for your readers? Can you be sure that they have in mind the same references for progress that you do? If not, misunderstandings are inevitable. You may offer examples: supersonic planes, computers, shopping malls, nuclear energy. Many of your readers will react favorably to the mention of these innovations, which to them represent progress; others, for whom these inventions represent change but not progress, will react unfavorably. You may not be able to convince all of your readers that "we have made great progress," but all of them will now understand what you mean by "progress." And intelligent disagreement is preferable to misunderstanding.

Abstractions tell us what conclusions we have arrived at; details tell us how we got there. But there are dangers in either too many details or too many abstractions. For example, a writer may present only concrete data without telling readers what conclusions are to be drawn from them. Suppose you read the following:

> To Chinese road-users, traffic police are part of the grass . . . and neither they nor the rules they're supposed to enforce are paid the least attention. . . . Ignoring traffic-lights is only one peculiarity of Chinese traffic. It's normal for a pedestrian to walk straight out into a stream of cars without so much as lifting his head; and goodness knows how many Chinese cyclists I've almost killed as they have shot blindly in front of me across busy main roads.[14]

These details would constitute no more than interesting gossip until we read, "It's not so much a sign of ignorance or recklessness . . . but of fatalism." The details of specific behavior have now acquired a significance expressed in the abstraction *fatalism.*

---

[14]Philip Short, "The Chinese and the Russians," *The Listener,* April 8, 1982, p. 6.

A more common problem, however, in using abstractions is omission of details. Either the writer is not a skilled observer and cannot provide the details, or he or she feels that such details are too small and quiet compared to the grand sounds made by abstract terms. These grand sounds, unfortunately, cannot compensate for the lack of clarity and liveliness. Lacking detailed support, abstract words may be misinterpreted. They may also represent ideas that are so vague as to be meaningless. Sometimes they function illegitimately as short cuts (discussed on pp. 227–34), arousing emotions but unaccompanied by good reasons for their use. The following paragraph exhibits some of these common faults. How would you translate it into clear English?

> We respectively petition, request, and entreat that due and adequate provision be made, this day and the date hereinafter subscribed, for the satisfying of these petitioners' nutritional requirements and for the organizing of such methods of allocation and distribution as may be deemed necessary and proper to assure the reception by and for said petitioners of such quantities of baked cereal products as shall, in the judgment of the aforesaid petitioners, constitute a sufficient supply thereof.[15]

If you had trouble decoding this, it was because there were almost no concrete references — the homely words *baked* and *cereal* leap out of the paragraph like English signposts in a foreign country — and too many long words or words of Latin origin when simple words would do: *requirements* instead of *needs, petition* instead of *ask.* An absence of concrete references and an excess of long Latinate words can have a depressing effect on both writer and reader. The writer may be in danger of losing the thread of the argument, the reader at a loss to discover the message.

The paragraph above, according to James B. Minor, a lawyer who teaches courses in legal drafting, is "how a federal regulation writer would probably write, 'Give us this day our daily bread.'" This brief sentence with its short, familiar words and its origin in the Lord's Prayer has a deep emotional effect. The paragraph composed by Minor deadens any emotional impact because of its preponderance of abstract terms and its lack of connection with the world of our senses.

That passage was invented to educate writers in the government bureaucracy to avoid inflated prose. But writing of this kind is not uncommon among professional writers, including academics. If the subject matter is unfamiliar and the writer an acknowledged expert, you may have to expend a special effort in penetrating the language. But you may also rightly wonder if the writer is making unreasonable demands on you.

---

[15]*New York Times,* May 10, 1977, p. 35.

The human race is now entering upon a new phase of evolutionary consciousness and progress, a phase in which, impelled by the forces of evolution itself, it must converge upon itself and convert itself into one single human organism infused by a reconciliation of knowing and being in their inner unity and destined to make a qualitative leap into a higher form of consciousness as we know it, or otherwise destroy itself. For the entire universe is one vast field, potential for incarnation, and achieving incandescence here and there of reason and spirit. And in the whole world of *quality* with which by the nature of our minds we necessarily make contact, we here and there apprehend preeminent value. This can be achieved only if we recognize that we are unable to focus our attention on the particulars of the whole, without diminishing our comprehension of the whole, and of course, conversely, we can focus on the whole only by diminishing our comprehension of the particulars which constitute the whole.[16]

You probably found this paragraph even more baffling than the previous example. Although there is some glimmer of meaning here — that mankind must attain a higher level of consciousness, or perish — you should ask whether the extraordinary overload of abstract terms is justified. In fact, most readers would be disinclined to sit still for an argument with so little reference to the real world. One critic of social science prose maintains that if preeminent thinkers like Bertrand Russell can make themselves clear but social scientists continue to be obscure, "then you can justifiably suspect that it might all be nonsense."[17]

Finally, there are the moral implications of using abstractions that conceal a disagreeable reality. George Orwell pointed them out more than forty years ago in "Politics and the English Language." Another essayist, Joseph Wood Krutch, in criticizing the attitude that cheating "doesn't really hurt anybody," observed, "'It really doesn't hurt anybody' means it doesn't do that abstraction called society any harm." The following news story reports a proposal with which Orwell and Krutch might have agreed. His intention, says the author, is to "slow the hand of any President who might be tempted to unleash a nuclear attack."

> It has long been feared that a President could be making his fateful decision while at a "psychological distance" from the victims of a nuclear barrage; that he would be in a clean, air-conditioned room, surrounded by well-scrubbed aides, all talking in abstract terms about appropriate military responses in an international crisis, and that he might well push to the back of his mind the realization that hundreds of millions of people would be exterminated.

---

[16]Ruth Nanda Anshen, "Credo Perspectives," introduction to *Two Modes of Thought* by James Bryant Conant (New York: Simon and Schuster, 1964), p. x.

[17]Stanislav Andreski, *Social Sciences as Sorcery* (New York: St. Martin's Press, 1972), p. 86.

So Roger Fisher, professor of law at Harvard University, offers a simple suggestion to make the stakes more real. He would put the codes needed to fire nuclear weapons in a little capsule, and implant the capsule next to the heart of a volunteer, who would carry a big butcher knife as he accompanied the President everywhere. If the President ever wanted to fire nuclear weapons, he would first have to kill, with his own hands, that human being.

He has to look at someone and realize what death is — what an innocent death is. "It's reality brought home," says Professor Fisher.[18]

The moral lesson is clear: It is much easier to do harm if we convince ourselves that the object of the injury is only an abstraction.

SHORT CUTS

Short cuts are arguments that depend on readers' responses to words. Short cuts, like other devices we have discussed so far, are a common use of emotive language but are often mistaken for valid argument.

Although they have power to move us, these abbreviated substitutes for argument avoid the hard work necessary to provide facts, expert opinion, and analysis of warrants. Even experts, however, can be guilty of using short cuts, and the writer who consults an authority should be alert to that authority's use of language. Two of the most common uses of short cuts are clichés and slogans.

Clichés

"I'm against sloppy, emotional thinking. I'm against fashionable thinking. I'm against the whole cliché of the moment."[19] This statement by the late Herman Kahn, the founder of the Hudson Institute, a famous think tank, serves as the text for this section. A cliché is an expression or idea grown stale through overuse. Clichés in language are tired expressions that have faded like old photographs; readers no longer see anything when clichés are placed before them. Clichés include phrases like "cradle of civilization," "few and far between," "rude awakening," "follow in the footsteps of," "fly in the ointment."

But more important to recognize and avoid are clichés of thought. A cliché of thought may be likened to a formula, which one dictionary defines as "any conventional rule or method for doing something, especially when used, applied, or repeated without thought." Clichés of thought represent ready-made answers to questions, stereotyped solutions to problems, "knee-jerk" reactions. Two writers who call these

---

[18]*New York Times,* September 7, 1982, Sec. C, p. 1.
[19]*New York Times,* July 8, 1983, Sec. B, p. 1.

forms of expression "mass language" describe it this way: "Mass language is language which presents the reader with a response he is expected to make without giving him adequate reason for having this response."[20] These "clichés of the moment" are often expressed in single words or phrases. For example, the phrase "Gen X" has been repeated so often that it has come to represent an indisputable truth for many people, one they no longer question. The acceptance of this cliché, however, conceals the fact that millions of very different kinds of people from ages eighteen to thirty-five are being thoughtlessly lumped together as apathetic and lazy.

Certain cultural attitudes encourage the use of clichés. The liberal American tradition has been governed by hopeful assumptions about our ability to solve problems. A professor of communications says that "we tell our students that for every problem there must be a solution."[21] But real solutions are hard to come by. In our haste to provide them, to prove that we can be decisive, we may be tempted to produce familiar responses that resemble solutions.

History teaches us that a solution to an old and serious problem is almost always accompanied by unexpected drawbacks. As the writer quoted in the previous paragraph warns us, "Life is not that simple. There is no one answer to a given problem. There are multiple solutions, all with advantages and disadvantages." By solving one problem, we often create another. Automobiles, advanced medical techniques, industrialization, and liberal divorce laws have all contributed to the solution of age-old problems: lack of mobility, disease, poverty, domestic unhappiness. We now see that these solutions bring with them new problems that we nevertheless elect to live with because the advantages seem greater than the disadvantages. A well-known economist puts it this way: "I don't look for solutions; I look for trade-offs. I think the person who asks, 'What is the solution to this problem?' has a fundamental misconception of the way the world works. We have trade-offs, and that's all we have."[22]

This means that we should be skeptical of solutions promising everything and ignoring limitations and criticism. Such solutions have probably gone around many times. Having heard them so often, we are inclined to believe that they have been tried and proven. Thus they escape serious analysis.

Some of these problems and their solutions represent the fashionable thinking to which Kahn objected. They confront us every-

---

[20]Richard E. Hughes and P. Albert Duhamel, *Rhetoric: Principles and Usage* (Englewood Cliffs, N.J.: Prentice-Hall, 1962), p. 161.

[21]Malcolm O. Sillars, "The New Conservatism and the Teacher of Speech," *Southern Speech Journal* 21 (1956), p. 240.

[22]Thomas Sowell, "Manhattan Report" (edited transcript of *Meet the Press*) (New York: International Center for Economic Policy Studies, 1981), p. 10.

where, like the public personalities who gaze at us week after week from the covers of magazines and tabloid newspapers at the checkout counter in the supermarket. Alarms about the failures of public education, about drug addiction or danger to the environment or teenage pregnancy are sounded throughout the media continuously. The same solutions are advocated again and again: "Back to basics"; "Impose harsher sentences"; "Offer sex education." Their popularity, however, should not prevent us from asking: Are the problems as urgent as their prominence in the media suggests? Are the solutions workable? Does sufficient evidence exist to justify their adoption?

Your arguments will not always propose solutions. They will sometimes provide interpretations of or reasons for social phenomena, especially for recurrent problems. Some explanations have acquired the status of folk wisdom, like proverbs, and careless arguers will offer them as if they needed no further support. One object of stereotyped responses is the problem of juvenile delinquency, which liberals attribute to poverty, lack of community services, meaningless education, and violence on TV. Conservatives blame parental permissiveness, decline in religious influence, lack of individual responsibility, lenient courts. Notice that the interpretations of the causes of juvenile delinquency are related to an ideology, to a particular view of the world that may prevent the arguer from recognizing any other way of examining the problem. Other stereotyped explanations for a range of social problems include inequality, competition, self-indulgence, alienation, discrimination, technology, lack of patriotism, excessive governmental regulation, and lack of sufficient governmental regulation. All of these explanations are worthy of consideration, but they must be defined and supported if they are to be used in a thoughtful, well-constructed argument.

Although formulas change with the times, some are unexpectedly hardy and survive long after critics have revealed their weaknesses. Overpopulation is an often-cited cause of poverty, disease, and war. It can be found in the writing of the ancient Greeks 2,500 years ago. "That perspective," says the editor of *Food Monitor,* a journal published by World Hunger Year, Inc., "is so pervasive that most Americans have simply stopped thinking about population and resort to inane clucking of tongues."[23] If the writer offering overpopulation as an explanation for poverty were to look further, he or she would discover that the explanation rested on shaky data. Singapore, the most densely populated country in the world (11,574 persons per square mile) is also one of the richest ($16,500 per capita income per year). Chad, one of the most sparsely populated (11 persons per square mile) is also one of the poorest ($190 per capita in-

---

[23]Letter to the *New York Times,* October 4, 1982, Sec. A, p. 18.

come per year).[24] Strictly defined, overpopulation may serve to explain some instances of poverty; obviously it cannot serve as a blanket to cover all or even most instances. "By repeating stock phrases," one columnist reminds us, "we lose the ability, finally, to hear what we are saying."

Slogans

> I have always been rather impressed by those people who wear badges stating where they stand on certain issues. The badges have to be small, and therefore the message has to be small, concise, and without elaboration. So it comes out as "I hate something" or "I love something," or ban this or ban that. There isn't space for argument, and I therefore envy the badge-wearer who is so clear-cut about his or her opinions.[25]

The word *slogan* has a picturesque origin. A slogan was the war cry or rallying cry of a Scottish or Irish clan. From that early use it has come to mean a "catchword or rallying motto distinctly associated with a political party or other group" as well as a "catch phrase used to advertise a product."

Slogans, like clichés, are short, undeveloped arguments. They represent abbreviated responses to often complex questions. As a reader you need to be aware that slogans merely call attention to a problem; they cannot offer persuasive proof for a claim in a dozen words or less. As a writer you should avoid the use of slogans that evoke an emotional response "without giving [the reader] adequate reason for having this response."

Advertising slogans are the most familiar. Some of them are probably better known than nursery rhymes: "Reach out and touch someone," "It costs more, but I'm worth it," "Don't leave home without it." Advertisements may, of course, rely for their effectiveness on more than slogans. They may also give us interesting and valuable information about products, but most advertisements give us slogans that ignore proof — short cuts substituting for argument.

The persuasive appeal of advertising slogans is heavily dependent on the connotations associated with products. In Chapter 5 (see p. 157, under "Appeals to Needs and Values"), we discussed the way in which advertisements promise to satisfy our needs and protect our values. Wherever evidence is scarce or nonexistent, the advertiser must persuade us through skillful choice of words and phrases (as well as pictures), especially those that produce pleasur-

---

[24]*World Almanac and Book of Facts,* 1995 (New York: World Almanac, 1995), pp. 754 and 818.

[25]Anthony Smith, "Nuclear Power — Why Not?" *The Listener,* October 22, 1981, p. 463.

able feelings. "Let it inspire you" is the slogan of a popular liqueur. It suggests a desirable state of being but remains suitably vague about the nature of the inspiration. Another familiar slogan — "Noxzema, clean makeup" — also emphasizes a quality that we approve of, but what is "clean" makeup? Since the advertisers are silent, we are left with warm feelings about the word and not much more.

Advertising slogans are persuasive because their witty phrasing and punchy rhythms produce an automatic "yes" response. We react to them as we might react to the lyrics of popular songs, and we treat them far less critically than we treat more straightforward and elaborate arguments. Still, the consequences of failing to analyze the slogans of advertisers are usually not serious. You may be tempted to buy a product because you were fascinated by a brilliant slogan, but if the product doesn't satisfy, you can abandon it without much loss. However, ignoring ideological slogans, coined by political parties or special interest groups, may carry an enormous price, and the results are not so easily undone.

Ideological slogans, like advertising slogans, depend on the power of connotation, the emotional associations aroused by a word or phrase. In the 1960s and 1970s, a period of well-advertised social change, slogans flourished; they appeared by the hundreds of thousands on buttons, T-shirts, and bumper stickers. One of them read, "Student Power!" To some readers of the slogan, distrustful of young people and worried about student unrest on campuses and in the streets, the suggestion was frightening. To others, mostly students, the idea of power, however undefined, was intoxicating. Notice that "Student Power!" is not an argument; it is only a claim. (It might also represent a warrant.) As a claim, for example, it might take this form: Students at this school should have the power to select the faculty. Of course, the arguer would need to provide the kinds of proof that support his or her claim, something the slogan by itself cannot do. Many people, whether they accepted or rejected the claim, supplied the rest of the argument without knowing exactly what the issues were and how a developed argument would proceed. They were accepting or rejecting the slogan largely on the basis of emotional reaction to words.

American political history is, in fact, a repository of slogans. Leaf through a history of the United States and you will come across "Tippecanoe and Tyler, too," "manifest destiny," "fifty-four forty or fight," "make the world safe for democracy," "the silent majority," "the domino theory," "the missile gap," "the window of vulnerability." Each administration tries to capture the attention and allegiance of the public by coining catchy phrases. Roosevelt's New Deal in 1932 was followed by the Square Deal and the New Frontier. Today, slogans must be carefully selected to avoid offending groups that are sensitive to the ways in which words affect their interests.

In 1983 Senator John Glenn, announcing his candidacy for president, talked about bringing "old values and new horizons" to the White House. "New horizons" apparently carried positive connotations. His staff, however, worried that "old values" might suggest racism and sexism to minorities and women.

A professor of politics and international affairs at Princeton University explains why public officials use slogans, despite their obvious shortcomings:

> Officials long have tried to capture complicated events and to dominate public discussion of foreign policy by using simple phrases and slogans. They engage in phrase-making in order to reach wide audiences. . . .
>
> Slogans and metaphors often express the tendencies of officials and academics who have a common wish to be at once sweeping, unequivocal, easily understood, and persuasive. The desire to capture complicated phenomena through slogans stems also from impatience with the particular and unwillingness or inability to master interrelationships.[26]

Over a period of time slogans, like clichés, can acquire a life of their own and, if they are repeated often enough, come to represent an unchanging truth we no longer need to examine. "Dangerously," says the writer quoted above, "policy makers become prisoners of the slogans they popularize."

The arguments you write will not, of course, be one-sentence slogans. Unfortunately, many longer arguments amount to little more than sloganeering or series of suggestive phrases strung together to imitate the process of argumentation. Following are two examples. The first is taken from a full-page magazine advertisement in 1983, urging the formation of a new political party. The second is part of the second inaugural address of George C. Wallace, governor of Alabama, in 1971. These extracts are typical of the full advertisement and the full speech.

> We can't dislodge big money from its domination over the two old parties, but we can offer the country something better: a new party that represents the people and responds to their needs. . . . How can we solve any problem without correcting the cause — the structure of the Dem/Rep machine and the power of the military-industrial establishment? . . . The power of the people could be a commanding force if only we could get together — Labor, public-interest organizations, blacks, women, antinuclear groups, and all the others.[27]

> The people of the South and those who think like the South, represent the majority viewpoint within our constitutional democracy, but they are not organized and do not speak with a loud voice. Until the day

---

[26]Henry Bienen, "Slogans Aren't the World," *New York Times,* January 16, 1983, Sec. IV, p. 19.

[27]*The Progressive,* September 1983, p. 38.

arrives when the voice of the people of the South and those who think like us is, within the law, thrust into the face of the bureaucrats, only then can the "people's power" express itself legally and ethically and get results. . . . Too long, oh, too long, has the voice of the people been silenced by their own disruptive government — by governmental bribery in quasi-governmental handouts such as H.E.W. and others that exist in America today! An aroused people can save this nation from those evil forces who seek our destruction. The choice is yours. The hour is growing late![28]

Whatever power these recommendations might have if their proposals were more clearly formulated, as they stand they are collections of slogans and loaded words. (Even the language falters: Can the voice of the people be thrust into the face of the bureaucrats?) We can visualize some of the slogans as brightly colored banners: "Dislodge Big Money!" "Power to the People!" "Save This Nation from Evil Forces!" "The Choice Is Yours!" Do all the groups mentioned share identical interests? If so, what are they? Given the vagueness of the terms, it is not surprising that arguers on opposite sides of the political spectrum — loosely characterized as liberal and conservative — sometimes resort to the same clichés and slogans: the language of populism, or a belief in the virtues of the "common people" in these examples.

Slogans have numerous shortcomings as substitutes for the development of an argument. First, their brevity presents serious disadvantages. Slogans necessarily ignore exceptions or negative instances that might qualify a claim. They usually speak in absolute terms without describing the circumstances in which a principle or idea might not work. Their claims therefore seem shrill and exaggerated. In addition, brevity prevents the sloganeer from revealing how he or she arrived at conclusions.

Second, slogans may conceal unexamined warrants. When Japanese cars were beginning to compete with American cars, the slogan "Made in America by Americans" appeared on the bumpers of thousands of American-made cars. A thoughtful reader would have discovered in this slogan several implied warrants: American cars are better than Japanese cars; the American economy will improve if we buy American; patriotism can be expressed by buying American goods. If the reader were to ask a few probing questions, he or she might find these warrants unconvincing.

Silent warrants that express values hide in other popular and influential slogans. "Pro-life," the slogan of those who oppose abortion, assumes that the fetus is a living being entitled to the same rights as individuals already born. "Pro-choice," the slogan of those

---

[28]Second Inaugural Address as governor of Alabama, January 18, 1971.

who favor abortion, suggests that the freedom of the pregnant woman to choose is the foremost or only consideration. The words *life* and *choice* have been carefully selected to reflect desirable qualities, but the words are only the beginning of the argument.

Third, although slogans may express admirable sentiments, they often fail to tell us how to achieve their objectives. They address us in the imperative mode, ordering us to take an action or refrain from it. But the means of achieving the objectives may be nonexistent or very costly. If the sloganeer cannot offer workable means for implementing his or her goals, he or she risks alienating the audience.

Sloganeering is one of the recognizable attributes of propaganda. Propaganda for both good and bad purposes is a form of slanting, of selecting language and facts to persuade an audience to take a certain action. Even a good cause may be weakened by an unsatisfactory slogan. The slogans of some organizations devoted to fundraising for the physically handicapped have come under attack for depicting the handicapped as helpless. According to one critic, the popular slogan "Jerry's kids" promotes the idea that Jerry Lewis is the sole support of children with muscular dystrophy. Perhaps increased sensitivity to the needs of the disabled will produce new words and new slogans. If you assume that your audience is sophisticated and alert, you will probably write your strongest arguments, devoid of clichés and slogans.

SAMPLE ANALYSIS

A Gen-X Rip Van Winkle

JOSHUA B. JANOFF

Ever read the story of Rip Van Winkle? These days I'd recommend it to anyone. The story is one of those uniquely American folk tales, about a work-shy gentleman farmer who falls asleep under a tree — for twenty years. When he awakes, he finds that the world is a very different place. I read the story as a young boy, and it wasn't until recently that I began to have some inkling of what poor Rip must have been feeling the day he finally opened his eyes and rejoined the world.

I'm a twenty-two-year-old freshman at a small New England liberal-arts college. I take classes in subjects like writing and sociol-

When this "My Turn" column appeared in the April 24, 1995, issue of *Newsweek*, Joshua B. Janoff was a freshman at Emerson College in Boston.

ogy. The school newspaper I write for is filled with aspiring muck-rakers, and most people here followed Teddy Kennedy's reelection bid with enthusiasm. A casual outside observer might say I fit the mold of the left-wing, out-of-touch, spotted-owl-saving, liberal-loving college student. A stereotypical Generation Xer suffering from a short bout of college-induced idealism, right?

Not so fast. I don't and never have fit such a label. When I was seventeen, I enlisted for a four-year hitch in the U.S. Navy. I entered the service as a young kid — bored, complacent, and cloistered. At the end of my completed time in the navy, I was a noncommissioned officer and Desert Storm veteran. My military service was a series of stark contrasts. I often worked for cruel idiots, scrubbed countless toilets and decks, and chipped away acres of paint. I also gazed at the hypnotic grin on the Mona Lisa, visited the birthplace of Mozart, stood inside the Roman Colosseum, climbed the Great Pyramid of Cheops and put my hand on the reputed tomb of Jesus Christ.

I'm not bragging. The day I was discharged was one of the happi-est of my life. It was also my first Rip Van Winkle experience. I turned on my car radio to begin the long drive home. I realized I was listen-ing to bands I'd never heard of. (Who the hell is Pearl Jam? Who or what is Alice in Chains?) I'd grown apart from my age group.

When I got home I told people about serving overseas, about how the pride we felt came of very hard work. My old friends just stared at me and said I sounded like their father. Or their grandfa-ther. Suddenly I felt very, very old. It seemed I now possessed values that contemporaries saw as chauvinistic, archaic, or hopelessly tra-ditional. Their reaction was odd, since people in the navy consid-ered me very liberal. 5

My first mass exposure to Generation X, which was when I hit college, accentuated my confusion. I'd never even heard the term until I got to school. I was surprised to learn that, because of my age, I was considered a member of this lazy, apathetic group of flannel-wearing misfits. At first I laughed. Then the suggestion started to bother me. I denied any complicity. Hey, I'd been away when this inane nomenclature was hatched. "No good," my fellow students said. "By virtue of your age, you are a part of it. Think about it."

So I did. But their claims just weren't true. The more I searched for common ground with my peers, the more I began to notice the habits that set me apart. When I'd tell friends I was in Desert Storm, I kept getting the same reaction. "Wow, what was it like? Were you scared? Wow, I could never have done that."

Now I'd be curious. Exactly what did that last statement mean? "Well, you know. I mean, it's not like I'd ever put on some uniform and go to war like in the movies. There's just no way."

That response disturbed me. When Desert Storm was going on, everyone I knew expressed total support and sympathy for the American servicepersons risking their safety to free Kuwait. Just a few years later, the idea of serving in such a way seems unthinkable to my generation. I don't believe it's because of an abundance of conscientious objectors among them. A true conscientious objector has strong, carefully thought out convictions and acts out of a sense of moral compulsion. I think those who told me they wouldn't go were just plain lazy.

The average age of an American combat soldier in the Korean   10 War was twenty, and in the Vietnam War, it was nineteen. I know there was a draft in effect, but besides the relative few who went to Canada, these young Americans proved that they were doers rather than talkers. Even the ones who went north *acted* on their beliefs. Today's youth, by contrast, seem willing to talk about their convictions, but not act on them.

I've seen other, more commonplace examples of my peers' laziness. Physical fitness was expected growing up in my family, and that attitude was reinforced in the navy. Now most of my friends look at me like I'm nuts when I say that I go to the gym regularly. Hell, forget the gym. To a lot of my fellow students, just walking a mile to the dining hall is unthinkable. Thank God for that shuttle bus, eh?

Sometimes, just getting out of bed is a problem. Most of the people in my college regard 8 A.M. classes as a fate between death and a world without Quentin Tarantino movies. I'm tempted to tell these people that 6 A.M. was considered "sleeping in" in the navy, but I doubt it would change anything.

Finally, there's the whole apathy thing. At first I felt certain that the idea of a generationwide sense of total indifference was crazy. It had to be an invention of the mass media. Unfortunately, the media assertions appear to be true. We as a generation have yet to produce any defining traits, except perhaps to show a defeatist belief that we will do worse than our parents.

Not that the situation is completely untenable. No living generation can honestly claim to have a general consensus on any one issue, whether the topic is politics, abortion, or health-care reform. If my age group can agree to resolve its indifference before it's too late, then maybe we can go ahead to make a more constructive future. It's time to stop channel surfing and looking for new ways to procrastinate, and to desist from blaming problems on those in authority. Perhaps what's needed is a good swift kick in the rear. Playtime is over, and there is a big bad world out there. It's waiting to see what we've got, but it's also ours for the taking. Let's lose the remote and do it.

Analysis

Most of the arguments in this book might be described as formal and objective — that is, the personality of the author is not present, and our full attention falls on the argument itself without regard to the characteristics of the individual behind it. Editorials are good examples of the formal essay, whose authors almost always remain anonymous. This is as it should be for many subjects of general interest.

But there is another way of arriving at a claim, even about these subjects, and that is through a narrative of personal experience. The essay by Janoff, a twenty-two-year-old student, is an example of such a strategy. Because the "I" is not suppressed, as in an editorial, but becomes, in fact, the central focus of the argument, the writer can exercise greater freedom in his choice of language. He can treat his idea as if it were a subject for conversation, and he can express his own feelings, which may not be appropriate or relevant in a more formal essay. (Organization is simpler because it follows the chronology of the events.)

Since he is telling a story about himself, the author uses "I" freely throughout. He adopts language that is close to colloquial speech, using contractions and sentence fragments, as well as slang and mild profanity, all of which are usually frowned on in more formal contexts. He also repeats the direct speech of fellow students, a device that emphasizes the narrative element.

There is, however, a danger in the use of "I" and the introduction of the self as part of the argument. In paragraph 7 the "I" that had previously been engaged in telling us an interesting story about events with which we might sympathize begins to change, to distance itself from the students in the story — and the readers of it — and to claim a certain superiority to them. I am a doer, not a talker; active, not lazy; involved, not apathetic; grown-up, not childish. Listening to this new and different voice, we are probably not surprised to be lectured rather severely in the last two paragraphs. And notice that here the language deteriorates, especially in the last paragraph, descending from vivid details and clear colloquial speech into cliché and vague formulas without much force. Perhaps this means that even the author felt uncomfortable speaking in this voice.

Whether or not the author is right about his moral superiority, to compare his readers unfavorably to himself is not an effective persuasive strategy. Authors often scold their readers, but by removing the subjective element — by declining to refer to themselves — they can take refuge in the defense that "It's nothing personal." Here, of course, the attack comes from someone we know, who has made himself the hero of his story. Needless to say, readers prefer modesty in their heroes. A careful writer of a personal experience essay can take advantage of the greater flexibility of language without allowing the "I" to overwhelm the argument.

The Speech the Graduates Didn't Hear

JACOB NEUSNER

We the faculty take no pride in our educational achievements with you. We have prepared you for a world that does not exist, indeed, that cannot exist. You have spent four years supposing that failure leaves no record. You have learned at Brown that when your work goes poorly, the painless solution is to drop out. But starting now, in the world to which you go, failure marks you. Confronting difficulty by quitting leaves you changed. Outside Brown, quitters are no heroes.

With us you could argue about why your errors were not errors, why mediocre work really was excellent, why you could take pride in routine and slipshod presentation. Most of you, after all, can look back on honor grades for most of what you have done. So, here grades can have meant little in distinguishing the excellent from the ordinary. But tomorrow, in the world to which you go, you had best not defend errors but learn from them. You will be ill-advised to demand praise for what does not deserve it, and abuse those who do not give it.

For four years we created an altogether forgiving world, in which whatever slight effort you gave was all that was demanded. When you did not keep appointments, we made new ones. When your work came in beyond the deadline, we pretended not to care.

Worse still, when you were boring, we acted as if you were saying something important. When you were garrulous and talked to hear yourself talk, we listened as if it mattered. When you tossed on our desks writing upon which you had not labored, we read it and even responded, as though you earned a response. When you were dull, we pretended you were smart. When you were predictable, unimaginative, and routine, we listened as if to new and wonderful things. When you demanded free lunch, we served it. And all this why?

Despite your fantasies, it was not even that we wanted to be 5 liked by you. It was that we did not want to be bothered, and the easy way out was pretense: smiles and easy Bs.

Jacob Neusner, formerly university professor at Brown University, is Distinguished Professor of Religious Studies at the University of South Florida in Tampa. His speech appeared in Brown's *The Daily Herald* on June 12, 1983.

It is conventional to quote in addresses such as these. Let me quote someone you've never heard of: Professor Carter A. Daniel, Rutgers University (*Chronicle of Higher Education,* May 7, 1979):

> College has spoiled you by reading papers that don't deserve to be read, listening to comments that don't deserve a hearing, paying attention even to the lazy, ill-informed, and rude. We had to do it, for the sake of education. But nobody will ever do it again. College has deprived you of adequate preparation for the last fifty years. It has failed you by being easy, free, forgiving, attentive, comfortable, interesting, unchallenging fun. Good luck tomorrow.

That is why, on this commencement day, we have nothing in which to take much pride.

Oh, yes, there is one more thing. Try not to act toward your co-workers and bosses as you have acted toward us. I mean, when they give you what you want but have not earned, don't abuse them, insult them, act out with them your parlous relationships with your parents. This too we have tolerated. It was, as I said, not to be liked. Few professors actually care whether or not they are liked by peer-paralyzed adolescents, fools so shallow as to imagine professors care not about education but about popularity. It was, again, to be rid of you. So go, unlearn the lies we taught you. To Life!

Reading and Discussion Questions

1. Neusner condemns students for various shortcomings. But what is he saying, both directly and indirectly, about teachers? Find places where he reveals his attitude toward them, perhaps inadvertently.
2. Pick out some of the language devices — connectives, parallel structures, sentence variety — that Neusner uses effectively.
3. Pick out some of the words and phrases — especially adjectives and verbs — used by Neusner to characterize both students and teachers. Do you think these terms are loaded? Explain.
4. Has Neusner chosen "facts" to slant his article? If so, point out where slanting occurs. If not, point out where the article seems to be truthful.
5. As a student you will probably object to Neusner's accusations. How would you defend your behavior as a student in answer to his specific charges?

Writing Suggestions

6. Rewrite Neusner's article with the same "facts" — or others from your experience — using temperate language and a tone of sadness rather than anger.
7. Write a letter to Neusner responding to his attack. Support or attack his argument by providing evidence from your own experience.
8. Write your own short commencement address. Do some things need to be said that commencement speakers seldom or never express?

9. Write an essay using the same kind of strong language as Neusner uses about some aspect of your education of which you disapprove. Or write a letter to a teacher using the same form as "The Speech the Graduates Didn't Hear."

Jack and the Beanstalk

JAMES FINN GARNER

Once upon a time, on a little farm, there lived a boy named Jack. He lived on the farm with his mother, and they were very excluded from the normal circles of economic activity. This cruel reality kept them in straits of direness, until one day Jack's mother told him to take the family cow into town and sell it for as much as he could.

Never mind the thousands of gallons of milk they had stolen from her! Never mind the hours of pleasure their bovine animal companion had provided! And forget about the manure they had appropriated for their garden! She was now just another piece of property to them. Jack, who didn't realize that nonhuman animals have as many rights as human animals — perhaps even more — did as his mother asked.

On his way to town, Jack met an old magic vegetarian, who warned Jack of the dangers of eating beef and dairy products.

"Oh, I'm not going to eat this cow," said Jack. "I'm going to take her into town and sell her."

"But by doing that, you'll just perpetuate the cultural mythos of 5 beef, ignoring the negative impact of the cattle industry on our ecology and the health and social problems that arise from meat consumption. But you look too simple to be able to make these connections, my boy. I'll tell you what I'll do: I'll offer a trade of your cow for these three magic beans, which have as much protein as that entire cow but none of the fat or sodium."

Jack made the trade gladly and took the beans home to his mother. When he told her about the deal he had made, she grew very upset. She used to think her son was merely a conceptual rather than a linear thinker, but now she was sure that he was downright differently abled. She grabbed the three magic beans and threw them out the window in disgust. Later that day, she attended her first support-group meeting with Mothers of Storybook Children.

The next morning, Jack stuck his head out the window to see if the sun had risen in the east again (he was beginning to see a pattern in

James Finn Garner is a writer and performer in Chicago who has written for the *Chicago Tribune* and appeared on Chicago Public Radio. This chapter is from *Politically Correct Bedtime Stories* (1994).

this). But outside the window, the beans had grown into a huge stalk that reached through the clouds. Because he no longer had a cow to milk in the morning, Jack climbed the beanstalk into the sky.

At the top, above the clouds, he found a huge castle. It was not only big, but it was built to larger-than-average scale, as if it were the home of someone who just happened to be a giant. Jack entered the castle and heard beautiful music wafting through the air. He followed this sound until he found its source: a golden harp that played music without being touched. Next to this self-actualized harp was a hen sitting on a pile of golden eggs.

Now, the prospect of easy wealth and mindless entertainment appealed to Jack's bourgeois sensibilities, so he picked up both the harp and the hen and started to run for the front door. Then he heard thundering footsteps and a booming voice that said:

> FEE, FIE, FOE, FUM,
> I smell the blood of an English person!
> I'd like to learn about his culture and views on life!
> And share my own perspectives in an open and generous way!

Unfortunately, Jack was too crazed with greed to accept the giant's offer of a cultural interchange. "It's only a trick," thought Jack. "Besides, what's a giant doing with such fine, delicate things? He must have stolen them from somewhere else, so I have every right to take them." His frantic justifications — remarkable for someone with his overtaxed mental resources — revealed a terrible callousness to the giant's personal rights. Jack apparently was a complete sizeist, who thought that all giants were clumsy, knowledge-impaired, and exploitable.

When the giant saw Jack with the magic harp and the hen, he asked, "Why are you taking what belongs to me?"

Jack knew he couldn't outrun the giant, so he had to think fast. He blurted out, "I'm not taking them, my friend. I am merely placing them in my stewardship so that they can be properly managed and brought to their fullest potential. Pardon my bluntness, but you giants are too simple in the head and don't know how to manage your resources properly. I'm just looking out for your interests. You'll thank me for this later."

Jack held his breath to see if the bluff would save his skin. The giant sighed heavily and said, "Yes, you are right. We giants do use our resources foolishly. Why, we can't even discover a new beanstalk before we get so excited and pick away at it so much that we pull the poor thing right out of the ground!"

Jack's heart sank. He turned and looked out the front door of the castle. Sure enough, the giant had destroyed his beanstalk. Jack grew frightened and cried, "Now I'm trapped here in the clouds with you forever!"

The giant said, "Don't worry, my little friend. We are strict vege- 15
tarians up here, and there are always plenty of beans to eat. And besides, you won't be alone. Thirteen other men of your size have
already climbed up beanstalks to visit us and stayed."

So Jack resigned himself to his fate as a member of the giant's
cloud commune. He didn't miss his mother or their farm much, because up in the sky there was less work to do and more than enough
to eat. And he gradually learned not to judge people based on their
size ever again, except for those shorter than he.

Reading and Discussion Questions

1. A comic writer often assumes a *persona*. This persona is not the author
   but a character that the author has created and whose voice he or she
   adopts. How would you describe the person that Garner pretends to be
   in this story?
2. Explain the title of the book from which this story is taken.
3. Point out the targets of Garner's satire. How did you recognize them?
   Would some readers find certain references offensive?
4. What language elements — vocabulary, sentence structure, metaphors —
   does Garner use to comic advantage? How do they reflect the character
   of the persona?

Writing Suggestions

5. Perhaps you feel that some of the things that Garner makes fun of
   should not be subjected to ridicule. Write a serious piece defending the
   politically correct attitude toward one of these targets.
6. If you are brave, write a funny piece about some subject whose absurdities have either amused or angered you. The subjects are everywhere.
   Some may even be found in the serious arguments you have been reading in this book: malls, mandatory school attendance, sexual harassment, gun control, single-sex schools. (Not surprisingly, all of these
   subjects have, in fact, been treated satirically by columnists like Russell
   Baker, Dave Barry, Mike Royko, and Maureen Dowd.) And, of course, advertisements can also be used as objects of humorous attack.

For starters,

unfortunately,
you have missed

this whole wonderful
country. ♦ You have
missed a tip of the hat

from D.W. Hunsuzker, potato
farmer, as he opens up shop
in the back of his pickup. YOU
HAVE MISSED THE CHANCE TO

WAVE BACK (it feels really good, for
some reason). ♦ You have missed
Thompson, Utah, population 40 (except
when you're passing through it). ♦ You've
missed what is *real* and *good.* You've missed a

damn nice sunset. (Remember those?) You've missed
the chance to take a few days, or even a few hours,
to *not* rush and to *not* run. ♦ You've missed the chance,
for once in your life, to go from major city to major city
AND SEE HOW LIVES ARE LIVED BETWEEN THEM. ♦ And
perhaps you've missed the one, single, dignified, civilized,
utterly relaxed form of travel left in this world. Train travel.

AMTRAK®
THERE'S SOMETHING ABOUT A TRAIN THAT'S MAGIC.

Amtrak® is a registered service mark of the National Railroad Passenger Corporation.

Discussion Questions

1. What feelings does the advertiser want to evoke? Find words that make your answer clear.
2. The words *real* and *good* are italicized. Why are they so important? Is the advertiser making a contrast with something else?
3. How does the graphic design underscore the spirit and language of the ad?

Kessler's a Drag

ALEXANDER VOLOKH

During World War II, you could unmask a Nazi soldier masquerading as an American GI by asking him, "Who won the World Series?" Today, in the nicotine debate, one question is a similar giveaway. Ask someone, "Is smoking addictive, and do people know this?"

"No" to the first part means you're talking to a tobacco company president. "No" to the second part means you're talking to Food and Drug Administration Commissioner David Kessler.

Whoever doesn't know that cigarettes are addictive and deadly has been living in a cave. People have known that cigarettes, tar and nicotine are bad at least since the 1950s. When the cancer connection was first proposed, low-tar and low-nicotine cigarettes quickly appeared on the market with no prodding from the government. Cigarette companies aggressively tried to gain market share by scaring smokers about their competitors' tar and nicotine levels — even though the Federal Trade Commission banned such advertising in 1954. From 1957 to 1959, tar and nicotine contents dropped 40 percent because of consumer demand. The FTC eventually cracked down on violators in 1959, but then it reversed course, allowing nicotine advertising in 1966 and mandating it in 1970. Today, all cigarette ads indicate tar and nicotine contents.

According to Kip Viscusi, professor of economics at Duke University, people today actually overestimate the risks of smoking. The average American estimates the risk of dying from lung cancer because of smoking at 38 percent. The true risk is between 6 percent and 13 percent. The average American estimates the total risk of dying because of smoking at 54 percent. The true risk is between 18 percent and 36 percent. Professor Viscusi calculates that if people had accurate perceptions of smoking risks, smoking actually would increase by about 7 percent.

Dr. Kessler tells us: "The public thinks of cigarettes as simply 5 blended tobacco rolled in paper. But they are much more than that. Some of today's cigarettes may, in fact, qualify as high-technology

---

This column by Alexander Volokh, a policy analyst at the Redson Foundation in Los Angeles, appeared in the *Wall Street Journal* on August 8, 1995.

nicotine delivery systems that deliver nicotine in precisely calculated quantities." But smokers don't need tobacco companies to manipulate their nicotine intake — they do it themselves all the time.
They do it by choosing which brand to smoke (nicotine contents
range from 0.05 mg to 2 mg), how often to light up, and how deeply
and often to puff. Smokers may not know exactly what secret herbs
and spices cigarette companies add to tobacco, but they're well
aware of the risk.

The surprising thing about the modern antismoking movement
isn't that it wants to regulate a personal choice. That's nothing new.
What is new is how disingenuous the movement has become. In the
early 1900s, during the first wave of anticigarette sentiment, people
at least said that they opposed smoking on moral grounds. Today,
the Kesslers of the world pretend to be scientists, acting as if their
recommendations hinged on some new evidence. They don't, and
it's dishonest to say otherwise. But while everyone sees through tobacco companies' dubious claims, Dr. Kessler's are working.

Underage smoking is a real concern, and there are probably
steps that the government should take to reduce children's access
to cigarettes. But what sort of society are the antismokers creating
for our children? Says Sam Kazman, general counsel of the Competitive Enterprise Institute, "Personally, I don't want my children to
smoke when they grow up. I also don't want them to ride motor-
cycles or fly hang-gliders. But most of all, I don't want them to grow
up thinking these aren't their decisions to make."

A Former Smoker Cheers

DAVID RAKOFF

When I quit my two-pack-a-day smoking habit three years ago, I
told myself that I would take it up again when I turned sixty-five.
Thirty-five smoke-free years and then I could resuscitate a romance
with my old habit and, as S. J. Perelman might say, go to hell my own
way.

But unless I plan to spend my retirement years in Paris or Bei-
jing, that might not be an option: New York is slowly becoming a
smoke-free zone. And you know, that's fine by me. In fact, I cheered
from my bed when I woke up Monday morning, switched on the
radio, and heard that the ban on smoking had gone into effect.

David Rakoff works for a publisher in New York. His essay appeared in the *New York Times* on April 14, 1995.

Lest you think I'm one of those zealous exsmokers, I assure you I am not. I still understand that feeling when one's next cigarette seems more important than food or shelter. I smoked through nine months of chemotherapy, after all, so why can't I just live and let live?

Well, for one thing, smoking can kill you. End of story. It's incredibly bad for you. But far more importantly, it can kill *me*. And, frankly, I'm already cranky enough without being endangered by people who are neither relatives nor friends. If we've never met and you increase the level of poison in my already toxic New York life, watch out.

Besides, we should finally have the decency to try to take care of   5
one another. There used to be a billboard at Houston and Broadway that read: "Welcome to America. The only developed country other than South Africa without universal health care!" Nelson Mandela was still in prison when that billboard was up, and here we are still grappling with people's right to universal coverage. How can we, as a society, say that we care about our citizens' health and not agree to remove this most visible and dangerous threat? Otherwise, we all put our lives at risk of being nasty, brutish and short.

I've been told that, as a nonnational (I moved to the United States thirteen years ago), I can't fully appreciate the ferocity with which Americans regard their personal freedoms, that it is a slippery slope from stopping people smoking in restaurants to installing Orwellian telescreens in their homes. But surely my right to avoid the increased risk of another bout of cancer outweighs my neighbor's right to blow smoke on my $20 entree (except, bizarrely, in a space intimate enough to contain fewer than thirty-five seats).

Finally, smoking is just not as glamorous as it used to be. It's been a long time since Jean-Paul Belmondo and Jean Seberg langorously puffed their way through Paris in the aptly titled "Breathless." And don't even mention that much touted cigar renaissance that has young and old blithely lighting up as if they had never heard the name Sigmund Freud. Smoking is somewhat passé, and surely in New York that has to count for something.

It does seem ridiculous to make Central Park smoke-free, and I feel doubly sorry for the waiters working in tiny restaurants; somehow their health has been deemed less worthy of protection under the new law, and now they're likely to see even more business from serious smokers turned away from everywhere else. But when I think of the acute nausea, pain, burned skin, side effects of medication and hair loss of cancer treatment, I can only think: "Been there. Done that." And so I cheer from my bed.

Discussion Questions

1. These two essays use different stylistic approaches to the subject. Point out examples of differences in language and appeals to an audience.

2. Both Volokh and Rakoff introduce their essay in mind-catching ways. Describe the introductions and tell how they work to lead the reader into their arguments.
3. How does Rakoff indicate the different parts of his essay? What idea does each part develop?
4. How does Rakoff try to persuade the reader that he is a reasonable fellow? Why does he think it necessary to include this declaimer in his argument? Do you find it persuasive?
5. Does Volokh offer any data that surprised you? Would they encourage you to take up or continue smoking?
6. What are Volokh's main objections to Dr. Kessler's crusade? What is the main point of the essay? Or is there more than one point?

EXERCISES

1. Select one or two related bumper stickers visible in your neighborhood. Examine the hidden warrants on which they are based and assess their validity.
2. For a slogan found on a bumper sticker or elsewhere, supply the evidence to support the claim in the slogan. Or find evidence that disproves the claim.
3. Examine a few periodicals from fifty or more years ago. Select either an advertising or a political slogan in one of them and relate it to beliefs or events of the period. Or tell why the slogan is no longer relevant.
4. Discuss the origin of a cliché or slogan. Describe, as far as possible, the backgrounds and motives of its users.
5. Make up your own slogan for a cause that you support. Explain and defend your slogan.
6. Discuss the appeal to needs and values of some popular advertising or political slogan.
7. Choose a cliché and find evidence to support or refute it. *Examples:* People were much happier in the past. Mother knows best. Life was much simpler in the past. Money can't buy happiness.
8. Choose one of the statements in exercise 7 or another statement and write a paper telling why you think such a statement has persisted as an explanation.
9. Select a passage, perhaps from a textbook, written largely in abstractions, and rewrite it using simpler and more concrete language.

Critical Listening

10. In watching TV dramas about law and medicine (*Law and Order, The Client, ER, Chicago Hope*) do you find that the professional language, some of which you may not fully understand, plays a positive or negative role in your enjoyment of the show? Explain your answer.
11. Listen to a radio or television report of a sports event. Do the announcers use a kind of language, especially jargon, that would not be used in print reports? One critic thinks that sports broadcasting has had a "destructive effect . . . on ordinary American English." Is he right or wrong?

CHAPTER EIGHT

Induction, Deduction, and Logical Fallacies

Throughout the book we have pointed out the weaknesses that cause arguments to break down. In the vast majority of cases these weaknesses represent breakdowns in logic or the reasoning process. We call such weaknesses *fallacies,* a term derived from the Latin. Sometimes these false or erroneous arguments are deliberate; in fact, the Latin word *fallere* means to deceive. But more often these arguments are either carelessly or unintentionally constructed. Thoughtful readers learn to recognize them; thoughtful writers learn to avoid them.

The reasoning process was first given formal expression by Aristotle, the Greek philosopher, almost 2,500 years ago. In his famous treatises, he described the way we try to discover the truth — observing the world, selecting impressions, making inferences, generalizing. In this process Aristotle identified two forms of reasoning: *induction* and *deduction*. Both forms, he realized, are subject to error. Our observations may be incorrect or insufficient, and our conclusions may be faulty because they have violated the rules governing the relationship between statements. The terms we've introduced may be unfamiliar, but the processes of reasoning, as well as the fallacies that violate these processes, are not. Induction and deduction are not reserved only for formal arguments about important problems; they also represent our everyday thinking about the most ordinary matters. As for the fallacies, they, too, unfortunately, may crop up anywhere, whenever we are careless in our use of the reasoning process.

In this chapter we will examine some of the most common fallacies. First, however, a closer look at induction and deduction will make clear what happens when fallacies occur.

INDUCTION

Induction is the form of reasoning in which we come to conclusions about the whole on the basis of observations of particular instances. If you notice that prices on the four items you bought in the campus bookstore are higher than similar items in the bookstore in town, you may come to the conclusion that the campus store is a more expensive place to shop. If you also noticed that all three of the instructors you saw on the first day of school were wearing faded jeans and running shoes, you might say that your teachers are generally informal in their dress. In both cases you have made an *inductive leap,* reasoning from what you have learned about a few examples to what you think is true of a whole class of things.

How safe are you in coming to these conclusions? As we've noticed in discussing data and generalization warrants, the reliability of your conclusion depends on the quantity and quality of your observations. Were four items out of the thousands available in the campus store a sufficiently large sample? Would you come to the same conclusion if you chose fifty items? Might another selection have produced a different conclusion? As for the casually dressed instructors, perhaps further investigation would disclose that the teachers wearing jeans were all teaching assistants and that associate and full professors usually wore business clothes. Or the difference might lie in the academic discipline; anthropology teachers might turn out to dress less formally than business school teachers.

In these two situations, you could come closer to verifying your conclusions by further observation and experience, that is, by buying more items at both stores over a longer period of time and by coming into contact with a greater number of professors during a whole semester. Even without pricing every item in both stores or encountering every instructor on campus, you would be more confident of your generalization as the quality and quantity of your samples increased.

In some cases you can observe all the instances in a particular situation. For example, by acquiring information about the religious beliefs of all the residents of the dormitory, you can arrive at an accurate assessment of the number of Buddhists. But since our ability to make definitive observations about everything is limited, we must also make an inductive leap about categories of things that we ourselves can never encounter in their entirety. For some generalizations, as we have learned about evidence, we rely on the testimony of reliable witnesses who report that they have experienced or observed many more instances of the phenomenon. A television documentary may give us information about unwed teenage mothers in a city neighborhood; four girls are interviewed and followed for several days by the reporter. Are these girls typical of thousands of others? A sociologist on the program assures us that, in fact, they are. She herself has consulted with hundreds of other young mothers and can vouch for the fact that a conclusion about them, based on our observation of the four, will be sound. Obviously, though, our conclusion can only be probable, not certain. The sociologist's sample is large, but she can account only for hundreds, not thousands, and there may be unexamined cases that will seriously weaken our conclusions.

In other cases, we may rely on a principle known in science as "the uniformity of nature." We assume that certain conclusions about oak trees in the temperate zone of North America, for example, will also be true for oak trees growing elsewhere under similar climatic conditions. We also use this principle in attempting to explain the causes of behavior in human beings. If we discover that institutionalization of some children from infancy results in severe emotional retardation, we think it safe to conclude that under the same circumstances all children would suffer the same consequences. As in the previous example, we are aware that certainty about every case of institutionalization is impossible. With rare exceptions, the process of induction can offer only probability, not certain truth.

SAMPLE ANALYSIS:
AN INDUCTIVE ARGUMENT

Not All Men Are Sly Foxes
ARMIN A. BROTT

If you thought your child's bookshelves were finally free of openly (and not so openly) discriminatory materials, you'd better check again. In recent years groups of concerned parents have persuaded textbook publishers to portray more accurately the roles that women and minorities play in shaping our country's history and culture. *Little Black Sambo* has all but disappeared from library and bookstore shelves; feminist fairy tales by such authors as Jack Zipes have, in many homes, replaced the more traditional (and obviously sexist) fairy tales. Richard Scarry, one of the most popular children's writers, has reissued new versions of some of his classics; now fe-

Armin A. Brott is a freelance writer. This article appeared in *Newsweek* on June 1, 1992.

male animals are pictured doing the same jobs as male animals. Even the terminology has changed: males and females are referred to as mail "carriers" or "firefighters."

There is, however, one very large group whose portrayal continues to follow the same stereotypical lines as always: fathers. The evolution of children's literature didn't end with *Goodnight Moon* and *Charlotte's Web.* My local public library, for example, previews 203 new children's picture books (for the under-five set) each *month.* Many of these books make a very conscious effort to take women characters out of the kitchen and the nursery and give them professional jobs and responsibilities.

Despite this shift, mothers are by and large still shown as the primary caregivers and, more important, as the primary nurturers of their children. Men in these books — if they're shown at all — still come home late after work and participate in the child rearing by bouncing baby around for five minutes before putting the child to bed.

In one of my two-year-old daughter's favorite books, *Mother Goose and the Sly Fox,* "retold" by Chris Conover, a single mother (Mother Goose) of seven tiny goslings is pitted against (and naturally outwits) the sly Fox. Fox, a neglectful and presumably unemployed single father, lives with his filthy, hungry pups in a grimy hovel littered with the bones of their previous meals. Mother Goose, a successful entrepreneur with a thriving lace business, still finds time to serve her goslings homemade soup in pretty porcelain cups. The story is funny and the illustrations marvelous, but the unwritten message is that women take better care of their kids and men have nothing else to do but hunt down and kill innocent, law-abiding geese.

The majority of other children's classics perpetuate the same 5 negative stereotypes of fathers. Once in a great while, people complain about *Babar*'s colonialist slant (little jungle-dweller finds happiness in the big city and brings civilization — and fine clothes — to his backward village). But I've never heard anyone ask why, after his mother is killed by the evil hunter, Babar is automatically an "orphan." Why can he find comfort only in the arms of another female? Why do Arthur's and Celeste's mothers come alone to the city to fetch their children? Don't the fathers care? Do they even have fathers? I need my answers ready for when my daughter asks.

I recently spent an entire day on the children's floor of the local library trying to find out whether these same negative stereotypes are found in the more recent classics-to-be. The librarian gave me a list of the twenty most popular contemporary picture books and I read every one of them. Of the twenty, seven don't mention a parent at all. Of the remaining thirteen, four portray fathers as much less loving and caring than mothers. In *Little Gorilla,* we are told that the little gorilla's "mother loves him" and we see Mama gorilla giving her little one a warm hug. On the next page we're also told that his "father loves him," but in the illustration, father and son aren't even touching. Six of the remaining nine books mention or portray mothers as the only parent, and only three of the twenty have what could be considered "equal" treatment of mothers and fathers.

The same negative stereotypes also show up in literature aimed at the *parents* of small children. In "What to Expect the First Year," the authors answer almost every question the parents of a newborn or toddler could have in the first year of their child's life. They are meticulous in alternating between references to boys and girls. At the same time, they refer almost exclusively to "mother" or "mommy." Men, and their feelings about parenting, are relegated to a nine-page chapter just before the recipe section.

Unfortunately, it's still true that, in our society, women do the bulk of the child care, and that thanks to men abandoning their families, there are too many single mothers out there. Nevertheless, to say that portraying fathers as unnurturing or completely absent is simply "a reflection of reality" is unacceptable. If children's literature only reflected reality, it would be like prime-time TV and we'd have books filled with child abusers, wife beaters, and criminals.

Young children believe what they hear — especially from a parent figure. And since, for the first few years of a child's life, adults select the reading material, children's literature should be held to a high standard. Ignoring men who share equally in raising their children, and continuing to show nothing but part-time or no-time fathers is only going to create yet another generation of men who have been told since boyhood — albeit subtly — that mothers are the truer parents and that fathers play, at best, a secondary role in the home. We've taken major steps to root out discrimination in what our children read. Let's finish the job.

Analysis

An inductive argument proceeds by examining particulars and arriving at a generalization that represents a probable truth. After reading a number of children's books in which the fathers, if they appear at all, are mostly portrayed as irresponsible and uncaring, Brott concludes that fathers are discriminated against in children's literature. Brott reports that he has examined twenty books. Only three of them give equal treatment to fathers and mothers. Even a book of advice for parents treats fathers with comparative indifference.

Because the subject is likely to be familiar to most readers, they will be able to participate in finding their own examples in children's literature to support — or refute — his claim. The success of Brott's argument will depend on finding that the examples in the article are sufficient, representative, and up-to-date. We know that the books he refers to are up-to-date (Brott mentions this in paragraph 6), but they may not be representative (the librarian gave him a list of the twenty "most popular contemporary picture books"), and whether twenty of 203 new books received by the library *each month* is sufficient is somewhat doubtful. Like all inductive arguments, this one too must be judged for probability, not certainty, but high probability would require a much bigger sample.

The examples in the article are not simply a list, however. Brott presents his conclusion within a broad context. In the first and second paragraphs he points out that while many negative racial and sexual stereotypes are disappearing from children's literature, one damaging stereotype remains, that of fathers. In the final paragraph he summarizes the dangers to society of allowing children — and the potential fathers among them — to believe that fathers are unimportant or indifferent to their children. One may find the latter conclusion valid, of course, even if one finds Brott's sample insufficient.

DEDUCTION

While induction attempts to arrive at the truth, deduction guarantees sound relationships between statements. If each of a series of statements, called *premises,* is true, deductive logic tells us that the conclusion must also be true. Unlike the conclusions from induction, which are only probable, the conclusions from deduction are certain. The simplest deductive argument consists of two premises and a conclusion. In outline such an argument looks like this:

MAJOR PREMISE:	All students with 3.5 averages and above for three years are invited to become members of Kappa Gamma Pi, the honor society.
MINOR PREMISE:	George has had a 3.8 average for over three years.
CONCLUSION:	Therefore, he will be invited to join Kappa Gamma Pi.

This deductive conclusion is *valid* or logically consistent because it follows necessarily from the premises. No other conclusion is possible. Validity, however, refers only to the form of the argument. The argument itself may not be satisfactory if the premises are not true — if Kappa Gamma Pi has imposed other conditions or if George has only a 3.4 average. The difference between truth and validity is important because it alerts us to the necessity for examining the truth of the premises before we decide that the conclusion is sound.

One way of discovering how the deductive process works is to look at the methods used by Sherlock Holmes, that most famous of literary detectives, in solving his mysteries. His reasoning process follows a familiar pattern. Through the inductive process — that is, observing the particulars of the world — he came to certain conclusions about those particulars. Then he applied deductive reasoning to come to a conclusion about a particular person or event.

On one occasion Holmes observed that a man sitting opposite him on a train had chalk dust on his fingers. From this observation Holmes deduced that the man was a schoolteacher. If his thinking were outlined, it would take the form of the syllogism, the classic form of deductive reasoning:

MAJOR PREMISE:	All men with chalk dust on their fingers are schoolteachers.
MINOR PREMISE:	This man has chalk dust on his fingers.
CONCLUSION:	Therefore, this man is a schoolteacher.

One dictionary defines the syllogism as "a formula of argument consisting of three propositions." The first proposition is called the major premise and offers a generalization about a large group or class. This generalization has been arrived at through inductive reasoning or observation of particulars. The second proposition is called the minor premise, and it makes a statement about a member of that group or class. The third proposition is the conclusion, which links the other two propositions, in much the same way that the warrant links the support and the claim.

If we look back at the syllogism that summarizes Holmes's thinking, we see how it represents the deductive process. The major premise, the first statement, is an inductive generalization, a statement arrived at after observation of a number of men with chalk on their fingers. The minor premise, the second statement, assigns a particular member, the man on the train, to the general class of those who have dust on their fingers.

But although the argument may be logical, it is faulty. The deductive argument is only as strong as its premises. As Lionel Ruby pointed out, Sherlock Holmes was often wrong.[1] Holmes once deduced from the size of a large hat found in the street that the owner was intelligent. He obviously believed that a large head meant a large brain and that a large brain indicated intelligence. Had he lived one hundred years later, new information about the relationship of

---

[1]*The Art of Making Sense* (Philadelphia: Lippincott, 1954), ch. 17.

brain size to intelligence would have enabled him to come to a different and better conclusion.

In this case, we might first object to the major premise, the generalization that all men with chalk dust on their fingers are schoolteachers. Is it true? Perhaps all the men with dusty fingers whom Holmes had so far observed had turned out to be schoolteachers, but was his sample sufficiently large to allow him to conclude that all dust-fingered men, even those with whom he might never have contact, were teachers? Were there no other vocations or situations that might require the use of chalk? Draftsmen or carpenters or tailors or artists might have fingers just as white as those of schoolteachers. In other words, Holmes may have ascertained that all schoolteachers have chalk dust on their fingers, but he had not determined that *only* schoolteachers can be thus identified. Sometimes it is helpful to draw circles representing the various groups in their relation to the whole.

If a large circle (see the figure below) represents all those who have chalk dust on their fingers, we see that several different groups may be contained in this universe. To be safe, Holmes should have deduced that the man on the train *might* have been a schoolteacher; he was not safe in deducing more than that. Obviously, if the inductive generalization or major premise is false, the conclusion of the particular argument is also false or invalid.

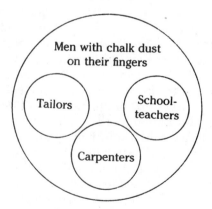

The deductive argument may also go wrong elsewhere. What if the minor premise is untrue? Could Holmes have mistaken the source of the white powder on the man's fingers? Suppose it was not chalk dust but flour or confectioner's sugar or talcum or heroin? Any of these possibilities would weaken or invalidate his conclusion.

Another example, closer to the kinds of arguments you will examine, reveals the flaw in the deductive process.

MAJOR
PREMISE: All Communists oppose organized religion.

MINOR PREMISE:	Robert Roe opposes organized religion.
CONCLUSION:	Therefore, Robert Roe is a Communist.

The common name for this fallacy is "guilt by association." The fact that two things share an attribute does not mean that they are the same thing. As in the first example, the diagram above makes clear that Robert Roe and Communists do not necessarily share all attributes. Remembering that Holmes may have misinterpreted the signs of chalk on the traveler's fingers, we may also want to question whether Robert Roe's opposition to organized religion has been misinterpreted.

An example from history shows us how such an argument may be used. In a campaign speech during the summer of 1952, Senator Joseph McCarthy, who had made a reputation as a tireless enemy of communism, said, "I do not tell you that Schlesinger, Stevenson's number one man, number one braintrust, I don't tell you he's a Communist. I have no information on that point. But I do know that if he were a Communist he would also ridicule religion as Schlesinger has done."[2] This is an argument based on a sign warrant. Clearly the sign referred to by Senator McCarthy, ridicule of religion, would not be sufficient to characterize someone as a Communist.

Some deductive arguments give trouble because one of the premises, usually the major premise, is omitted. As in the warrants we examined in Chapter 6, a failure to evaluate the truth of the unexpressed premise may lead to an invalid conclusion. When only two parts of the syllogism appear, we call the resulting form an *enthymeme.* Suppose we overhear the following snatch of conversation:

> *"Did you hear about Jean's father? He had a heart attack last week."*

---

[2]Joseph R. McCarthy, "The Red-Tinted Washington Crowd," speech delivered to a Republican campaign meeting at Appleton, Wisconsin, November 3, 1952.

"That's too bad. But I'm not surprised. I know he always refused to go for his annual physical checkups."

The second speaker has used an unexpressed major premise, the cause-effect warrant "If you have annual physical checkups, you can avoid heart attacks." He does not express it because he assumes that it is unnecessary to do so. The first speaker recognizes the unspoken warrant and may agree with it. Or the first speaker may produce evidence from reputable sources that such a generalization is by no means universally true, in which case the conclusion of the second speaker is suspect.

A knowledge of the deductive process can help guide you toward an evaluation of the soundness of your reasoning in an argument you are constructing. The syllogism is often clearer than an outline in establishing the relations between the different parts of an argument.

Suppose you wanted to argue that your former high school should introduce a dress code. You might begin by asking these questions: What would be the purpose of such a regulation? How would a dress code fulfill that purpose? What reasons could you provide to support your claim?

Then you might set down part of your argument like this:

Dressing in different styles makes students more aware of social differences among themselves.

The students in this school dress in many different styles.

Therefore, they are more aware of differences in social status among the student body.

As you diagram this first part of the argument, you should ask two sets of questions:

1. Is the major premise true? Do differences in dress cause awareness of differences in social status? Has my experience confirmed this?
2. Is the minor premise true? Has my observation confirmed this?

The conclusion, of course, represents something that you don't have to observe. You can deduce with certainty that it is true if both the major and minor premises are true.

So far the testing of your argument has been relatively easy because you have been concerned with the testing of observation and experience. Now you must examine something that does not appear in the syllogism. You have determined certain facts about perceptions of social status, but you have not arrived at the policy you want to recommend: that a dress code should be mandated. Notice that the dress code argument is based on acceptance of a moral value.

Reducing awareness of social differences is a desirable goal for the school.

A uniform dress code would help to achieve that goal.

Therefore, students should be required to dress uniformly.

The major premise in this syllogism is clearly different from the previous one. While the premise in the previous syllogism can be tested by examining sufficient examples to determine probability, this statement, about the desirability of the goal, is a value judgment and cannot be proved by counting examples. Whether equality of social status is a desirable goal depends on an appeal to other, more basic values.

Setting down your own or someone else's argument in this form will not necessarily give you the answers to questions about how to support your claim, but it should clearly indicate what your claims are and, above all, what logical connections exist between your statements.

SAMPLE ANALYSIS:
A DEDUCTIVE ARGUMENT

Advice for the Anti-Smokers: Take a Message from Garcia

ABIGAIL TRAFFORD

Long ago, I used to smoke. I was a student in Paris and I never went out without a red package of Royales and my black cigarette holder. I smoked over an espresso in the afternoon after class. I smoked over a glass of anis late at night.

I smoked because it was a prop along with long hair and poetry, a symbol of coming of age, of living on the edge. It was a year when students at the Sorbonne gathered and marched in protest. It was a year on my own, a time of hope, a celebration of freedom, symbolized by plumes of cigarette smoke.

I smoked for the same reasons my daughters and I and millions of Americans reveled in the music of the Grateful Dead and now mourn the sad end of Jerry Garcia. The Grateful Dead is about attitude, image, and lifestyle, and Jerry Garcia was the rock existentialist whose sound communicated across generations.

Abigail Trafford is health editor of the *Washington Post*. This article appeared in the *Post* on August 15, 1995.

His music was about independence and staking out your own turf and finding a comfortable personality. And so were my cigarettes. I smoked, in the words of the Grateful Dead, because *"All the years combine. . . . In the end there's just a song comes cryin' up the night."* An ashtray of half-smoked Royales. The black cigarette holder on the table. The empty glass. Paris in the sixties. *"It seems like all this life was just a dream. Stella blue. Stella blue."*

By contrast with such images of adventure and poetry, President Clinton's new crackdown on teenage smoking is going to be a tough sell. It focuses on health, but in fact is a direct intervention in the rites of passage for many teenagers. 5

The medical reasons against smoking are indisputable, and Garcia's death last week at age fifty-three gave the president a dramatic example of the consequences of unhealthy living. Captain Trips smoked three packs of cigarettes a day, lived off junk food, took all kinds of drugs and became a heroin addict, dying ignominiously in a rehab center where he was being treated for a relapse. President Clinton warned: "Young people should say: 'I'm not going to die that way.'"

But if the anti-smoking forces are to be successful, they must take a page from the Grateful Dead on how to reach the hearts and minds of young people. So far, do-not-smoke campaigns aimed at teenagers have largely missed the mark. It doesn't work to tell them to just say no.

Yet public health messages are generally written like commandments of medical virtue: Don't smoke, don't drink (too much), don't eat (too much), don't drive (too fast, without a seat belt), don't take illegal drugs, don't accept rides from strangers, don't have sex (before you're ready, before you know how to use a condom, before you're in a monogamous relationship, before you're married).

But as every parent knows, the forbidden fruit is the tastiest to young people. "Teenagers tend to rebel as a routine. The best way to get teenagers to do something is to tell them not to do it," says George D. Lundberg, editor of the *Journal of the American Medical Association.*

Compare the negative public health messages with the songs of the Grateful Dead. The group did not gloss over the fatal realities of growing up, but it talked about them in a way that struck a chord and made young people listen: *"What in the world ever became of sweet Jane. She lost her sparkle, you know she isn't the same. Livin' on reds, vitamin C and cocaine. All a friend can say is 'Ain't it a shame.'"* 10

For the most part, the Grateful Dead was about optimism. It gave fans a good feeling now, not a promise of better hearts or lungs in middle age. As the song goes: *"Dear Mr. Fantasy play us a tune. Something to make us all feel happy. Do anything to take us out of this gloom. Sing a song, play guitar, make us happy."*

To succeed, a cultural revolution that takes away smoking has to replace it with *"something to make us all feel happy . . . [and] take us out of this gloom."*

Unfortunately, cigarette advertisers have been more successful than anti-smoking forces when it comes to taking the basics of the Grateful Dead message. Billboards advertising cigarettes promise virility, power, sexuality, a message that smoking is an escape from the unbearable feelings of growing up.

The challenge of the president's attack on tobacco is to take the message away from the advertisers and turn it around so that young people will understand that their transition from teenager to adult — their demand to be recognized as an individual — does not depend on smoking. In fact, their lives depend on making this cultural shift.

After Paris, I gave up smoking. Luckily, I never learned to inhale   15 properly, which is the key to not getting addicted. Unlike most smokers, I was able to quit without a second thought.

Yet I never forgot my Paris days or the symbolism of a package of Royales. As the song goes, smoking had been for me *"A box of rain [that] will ease the pain, and Love will see you through."*

Analysis

The title is a play on words. "A Message to Garcia," written by Elbert Hubbard in 1899, is an essay extolling the heroic American army lieutenant who delivered a crucial message to a General Garcia during the Spanish-American War. It enjoyed extraordinary popularity in the early 1900s both in America and abroad.

A deductive argument proceeds from a general statement that the writer assumes to be true to a conclusion that is more specific. Deductive reasoning is commonplace, but it is seldom so pure as the definition suggests. In Trafford's article the generalization, or major premise, on which the conclusion is based, is expressed in paragraph 2: Smoking is an act that symbolizes youthful defiance and an embrace of adult freedom. The minor premise represents her belief that both the kind of life she led in Paris and the music of the Grateful Dead — especially that of the band's leader, Jerry Garcia — could give young people something that, like cigarettes, would "ease the pain." She concludes that anti-smoking advertising must concentrate not on warnings about dangers to health but on messages of optimism, like that offered by Garcia, "something to make us all feel happy."

As in any deductive argument, the validity of the claim or conclusion depends, first of all, on the soundness of the major premise. Trafford uses her own experience as a young woman in rebellion against a conventional life-style to prove that smoking is a way of establishing one's independence and individuality. Young readers will know about the bohemian life that she and others enjoyed in Paris a generation ago only from reading or movies. But Trafford's use of specific details — "the empty glass," "The black cigarette holder on the table," "an espresso in the afternoon after class" — is clear enough, and today's students can supply their own symbols. Even more appealing and original is her use of the lyrics of songs by the Grateful Dead. For her both smoking and the Grateful Dead represented "an attitude, an image, and a life-style" signifying freedom and power.

Is Trafford right, then, in concluding that warnings about health dangers alone are not enough to prevent young people from smoking? We know that cigarette smoking among the young has declined, so perhaps the warnings have taken hold, after all. But Trafford thinks that only "a cultural shift" can work. Cigarette advertisers promise virility, power, sexuality. The anti-smoking forces must somehow convince young people that adulthood can offer the satisfactions symbolized by smoking.

In logic, the conclusion of a deductive argument must be true. In real-life arguments, however, the conclusions do not fall into place quite so easily. Theoretically, Trafford's conclusion — that because of the special appeal of smoking, anti-smoking forces must find a different approach — is sound. But when we try to envision the kinds of persuasion that would produce a cultural shift, we are hard pressed to know exactly what Trafford means. Trafford herself gave up smoking as a rite of passage from teenager to adult, when youthful rebellion apparently was no longer necessary or attractive. She quit smoking easily. But we aren't told how that metamorphosis was accomplished.

A Note on the Syllogism and the Toulmin Model

In examining the classical deductive syllogism, you may have noticed the resemblance of its three-part outline to the three-part structure of claim, support, and warrant that we have used throughout the text to illustrate the elements of argument. We mentioned that the syllogism was articulated over two thousand years ago by the Greek philosopher Aristotle. By contrast, the claim-support-warrant structure is based on the model of argument proposed by the modern British philosopher Stephen Toulmin.

Now, there is every reason to think that all models of argument will share some similarities. Nevertheless, the differences between the formal syllogism and the informal Toulmin model suggest that the latter is a more effective instrument for writers who want to know which questions to ask, both before they begin and during the process of developing their arguments.

The syllogism is useful for laying out the basic elements of an argument, as we have seen in several examples. It lends itself more readily to simple arguments. The following syllogism summarizes a familiar argument.

MAJOR
PREMISE: Advertising of things harmful to our health should be legally banned.

MINOR
PREMISE: Cigarettes are harmful to our health.

CONCLUSION: Therefore, advertising of cigarettes should be legally banned.

Cast in the form of a Toulmin outline, the argument looks like this:

CLAIM: Advertising of cigarettes should be legally banned.

SUPPORT
(EVIDENCE):   Cigarettes are harmful to our health.

WARRANT: Advertising of things harmful to our health should be legally banned.

or in diagram form:

Support ——————————————————————▶ *Claim*
Cigarettes are harmful   Advertising of cigarettes
to our health.   should be legally banned.
                    Warrant
            Advertising of things harmful to our
            health should be legally banned.

In both the syllogism and the Toulmin model the principal elements of the argument are expressed in three statements. You can see that the claim in the Toulmin model is the conclusion in the syllogism — that is, the proposition that you are trying to prove. The evidence (support) in the Toulmin model corresponds to the minor premise in the syllogism. And the warrant in the Toulmin model resembles the major premise of the syllogism.

But the differences are significant. One difference is the use of language. The syllogism represents an argument "in which the validity of the assumption underlying the inference 'leap' is uncontested."[3] That is, the words "major premise" seem to suggest that the assumption has been proved. They do not emphasize that an

[3]Wayne E. Brockenreide and Douglas Ehninger, "Toulmin on Argument: An Interpretation and Application," *Contemporary Theories of Rhetoric: Selected Readings,* ed. Richard L. Johannesen (New York: Harper and Row, 1971), p. 245. This comparative analysis is indebted to Brockenreide and Ehninger's influential article.

analysis of the premise — "Advertising of things harmful to our health should be legally banned" — is necessary before we can decide that the conclusion is acceptable. Of course, a careful arguer will try to establish the truth and validity of all parts of the syllogism, but the terms in which the syllogism is framed do not encourage him or her to examine the real relationship among the three elements. Sometimes the enthymeme (see p. 256), which uses only two elements in the argument and suppresses the third, makes analyzing the relationship even more difficult.

In the Toulmin model, the use of the term *warrant* indicates that the validity of the proposition must be established in order to *guarantee* the claim, or make the crossing from support to claim. It makes clear that the arguer must ask *why* such advertising must be banned.

Nor is the term *minor premise* as useful to the arguer as "support." The word *support* instructs the arguer that he or she must take steps to provide the claim with factual evidence or an appeal to values.

A second difference is that while the syllogism is essentially static, with all three parts logically locked into place, the Toulmin model suggests that an argument is a *movement* from support to claim by way of the warrant, which acts as a bridge. Remember that Toulmin introduced the concept of warrant by asking "How do you get there?" (His first two questions, introducing the claim and support, were, "What are you trying to prove?" and "What have you got to go on?")

Lastly, recall that in addition to the three basic elements, the Toulmin model offers supplementary elements of argument. The *qualifier,* in the form of words like "probably" or "more likely," shows that the claim is not absolute. The *backing* offers support for the validity of the warrant. The *reservation* suggests that the validity of the warrant may be limited. These additional elements, which refine and expand the argument itself, reflect the real flexibility and complexity of the argumentative process.

COMMON FALLACIES

In this necessarily brief review it would be impossible to discuss all the fallacies listed by logicians, but we can examine the ones most likely to be found in the arguments you will read and write. Fallacies are difficult to classify, first, because there are literally dozens of systems for classifying, and second, because under any system there is always a good deal of overlap. Our discussion of the reasoning process, however, tells us where faulty reasoning occurs.

Inductive fallacies, as we know, result from the wrong use of evidence: That is, the arguer leaps to a conclusion on the basis of an insufficient sample, ignoring evidence that might have altered his or her conclusion. Deductive fallacies, on the other hand, result from a failure to follow the logic of a series of statements. Here the arguer neglects to make a clear connection between the parts of his or her argument. One of the commonest strategies is the introduction of an irrelevant issue, one that has little or no direct bearing on the development of the claim and serves only to distract the reader.

It's helpful to remember that, even if you cannot name the particular fallacy, you can learn to recognize it and not only refute it in the arguments of others but avoid it in your own as well.

1. Hasty Generalization

In Chapter 5 (see pp. 146–48) we discussed the dangers in drawing conclusions on the basis of insufficient evidence. Many of our prejudices are a result of hasty generalization. A prejudice is literally a judgment made before the facts are in. On the basis of experience with two or three members of an ethnic group, for example, we may form the prejudice that all members of the group share the characteristics that we have attributed to the two or three in our experience. (See Gordon Allport, "The Nature of Prejudice," on p. 116.)

Superstitions are also based in part on hasty generalization. As a result of a very small number of experiences with black cats, broken mirrors, Friday the thirteenth, or spilled salt, some people will assume a cause-effect relation between these signs and misfortunes. Superstition has been defined as "a notion maintained despite evidence to the contrary." The evidence would certainly show that, contrary to the superstitious belief, in a lifetime hundreds of such "unlucky" signs are not followed by unfortunate events. To generalize about a connection is therefore unjustified.

2. Faulty Use of Authority

The attempt to bolster claims by citing the opinions of experts was discussed in Chapter 5. Both writers and readers need to be especially aware of the testimony of authorities who may disagree with those cited. In circumstances where experts disagree, you are encouraged to undertake a careful evaluation and comparison of credentials.

3. *Post Hoc* or Doubtful Cause

The entire Latin term for this fallacy is *post hoc, ergo propter hoc,* meaning, "After this, therefore because of this." The arguer infers that because one event follows another event, the first event must be the cause of the second. But proximity of events or conditions does not guarantee a causal relation. The rooster crows every morning at 5:00 and, seeing the sun rise immediately after, decides that his crowing has caused the sun to rise. A month after A-bomb tests are concluded, tornadoes damage the area where the tests were held, and residents decide that the tests caused the tornadoes. After the school principal suspends daily prayers in the classroom, acts of vandalism increase, and some parents are convinced that failure to conduct prayer is responsible for the rise in vandalism. In each of these cases, the fact that one event follows another does not prove a causal connection. The two events may be coincidental, or the first event may be only one, and an insignificant one, of many causes that have produced the second event. The reader or writer of causal arguments must determine whether another more plausible explanation exists and whether several causes have combined to produce the effect. Perhaps the suspension of prayer was only one of a number of related causes: a decline in disciplinary action, a relaxation of academic standards, a change in school administration, and changes in family structure in the school community.

In the previous section we saw that superstitions are the result not only of hasty generalization but also of the willingness to find a cause-effect connection in the juxtaposition of two events. A belief in astrological signs also derives from erroneous inferences about cause and effect. Only a very few of the millions of people who consult the astrology charts every day in newspapers and magazines have submitted the predictions to statistical analysis. A curious reader might try this strategy: Save the columns, usually at the beginning or end of the year, in which astrologers and clairvoyants make predictions for events in the coming year, allegedly based on their reading of the stars and other signs. At the end of the year evaluate the percentage of predictions that were fulfilled. The number will be very small. But even if some of the predictions prove true, there may be other less fanciful explanations for their accuracy.

In defending simple explanations against complex ones, philosophers and scientists often refer to a maxim called *Occam's razor,* a principle of the medieval philosopher and theologian William of Occam. A modern science writer says this principle "urges a preference for the simplest hypothesis that does all we want it to do."[4] Bertrand Russell, the twentieth-century British philosopher, explained it this way:

> It is vain to do with more what can be done with fewer. That is to say, if everything in some science can be interpreted without assuming this or that hypothetical entity, there is no ground for assuming it. I have myself found this a most fruitful principle in logical analysis.[5]

---

[4]Martin Gardner, *The Whys of a Philosophical Scrivener* (New York: Quill, 1983), p. 174.
[5]*Dictionary of Mind, Matter and Morals* (New York: Philosophical Library, 1952), p. 166.

In other words, choose the simpler, more credible explanation wherever possible.

We all share the belief that scientific experimentation and research can answer questions about a wide range of natural and social phenomena: evolutionary development, hurricanes, disease, crime, poverty. It is true that repeated experiments in controlled situations can establish what seem to be solid relations suggesting cause and effect. But even scientists prefer to talk not about cause but about an extremely high probability that under controlled conditions one event will follow another.

In the social sciences cause-effect relations are especially susceptible to challenge. Human experiences can seldom be subjected to laboratory conditions. In addition, the complexity of the social environment makes it difficult, even impossible, to extract one cause from among the many that influence human behavior.

4. False Analogy

Many analogies are merely descriptive and offer no proof of the connection between the two things being compared. In recent years a debate has emerged between weight-loss professionals about the wisdom of urging overweight people to lose weight for health reasons. Susan Wooley, director of the eating disorders clinic at the University of Cincinnati and a professor of psychiatry, offered the following analogy in defense of her view that dieting is dangerous.

> We know that overweight people have a higher mortality rate than thin people. We also know that black people have a higher mortality rate than white people. Do we subject black people to torturous treatments to bleach their skin? Of course not. We have enough sense to know skin-bleaching will not eliminate sickle-cell anemia. So why do we have blind faith that weight loss will cure the diseases associated with obesity?"[6]

But it is clear that the analogy between black skin and excessive weight does not work. The color of one's skin does not cause sickle-cell anemia, but there is an abundance of proof that excess weight influences mortality.

Historians are fond of using analogical arguments to demonstrate that particular circumstances prevailing in the past are being reproduced in the present. They therefore feel safe in predicting that the present course of history will follow that of the past. British historian Arnold Toynbee argues by analogy that humans' tenure on earth may be limited.

---

[6]*New York Times,* April 12, 1992, Sec. C, p. 43.

On the evidence of the past history of life on this planet, even the extinction of the human race is not entirely unlikely. After all, the reign of man on the Earth, if we are right in thinking that man established his present ascendancy in the middle paleolithic age, is so far only about 100,000 years old, and what is that compared to the 500 million or 900 million years during which life has been in existence on the surface of this planet? In the past, other forms of life have enjoyed reigns which have lasted for almost inconceivably longer periods — and which yet at last have come to an end.[7]

Toynbee finds similarities between the limited reigns of other animal species and the possible disappearance of the human race. For this analogy, however, we need to ask whether the conditions of the past, so far as we know them, at all resemble the conditions under which human existence on earth might be terminated. Is the fact that human beings are also members of the animal kingdom sufficient support for this comparison?

5. *Ad Hominem*

The Latin term *ad hominem* means "against the man" and refers to an attack on the person rather than on the argument or the issue. The assumption in such a fallacy is that if the speaker proves to be unacceptable in some way, his or her statements must also be judged unacceptable. Attacking the author of the statement is a strategy of diversion that prevents the reader from giving attention where it is due — to the issue under discussion.

You might hear someone complain, "What can the priest tell us about marriage? He's never been married himself." This accusation ignores the validity of the advice the priest might offer. In the same way an overweight patient might reject the advice on diet by an overweight physician. In politics it is not uncommon for antagonists to attack each other for personal characteristics that may not be relevant to the tasks they will be elected to perform. They may be accused of infidelity to their partners, homosexuality, atheism, or a flamboyant social life. Even if certain accusations should be proved true, voters should not ignore the substance of what politicians do and say in their public offices.

This confusion of private life with professional record also exists in literature and the other arts. According to their biographers, the American writers Thomas Wolfe, Robert Frost, and William Saroyan — to name only a few — and numbers of film stars, including Charlie Chaplin, Joan Crawford, and Bing Crosby, made life miserable for those closest to them. Having read about their unpleasant personal characteristics, some people find it hard to separate the artist from

---

[7]*Civilization on Trial* (New York: Oxford University Press, 1948), pp. 162–163.

his or her creation, although the personality and character of the artist are often irrelevant to the content of the work.

Accusations against the person do *not* constitute a fallacy if the characteristics under attack are relevant to the argument. If the politician is irresponsible and dishonest in the conduct of his or her personal life, we may be justified in thinking that the person will also behave irresponsibly and dishonestly in public office.

6. False Dilemma

As the name tells us, the false dilemma, sometimes called the black-white fallacy, poses an either/or situation. The arguer suggests that only two alternatives exist, although there may be other explanations of or solutions to the problem under discussion. The false dilemma reflects the simplification of a complex problem. Sometimes it is offered out of ignorance or laziness, sometimes to divert attention from the real explanation or solution that the arguer rejects for doubtful reasons.

You may encounter the either/or situation in dilemmas about personal choices. "At the University of Georgia," says one writer, "the measure of a man was football. You either played it or worshiped those who did, and there was no middle ground."[8] Clearly this dilemma — "Love football or you're not a man" — ignores other measures of manhood.

Politics and government offer a wealth of examples. In an interview with the *New York Times* in 1975, the Shah of Iran was asked why he could not introduce into his authoritarian regime greater freedom for his subjects. His reply was, "What's wrong with authority? Is anarchy better?" Apparently he considered that only two paths were open to him — authoritarianism or anarchy. Of course, democracy was also an option, which, perhaps fatally, he declined to consider.

7. Slippery Slope

If an arguer predicts that taking a first step will lead inevitably to a second, usually undesirable step, he or she must provide evidence that this will happen. Otherwise, the arguer is guilty of a slippery slope fallacy.

Asked by an inquiring photographer on the street how he felt about censorship of a pornographic magazine, a man replied, "I don't think any publication should be banned. It's a slippery slope when you start making decisions on what people should be permit-

---

[8]Phil Gailey, "A Nonsports Fan," *New York Times Magazine,* December 18, 1983, Sec. VI, p. 96.

ted to read. . . . It's a dangerous precedent." Perhaps. But if questioned further, the man should have offered evidence that a ban on some things leads inevitably to a ban on everything.

Predictions based on the danger inherent in taking the first step are commonplace:

> Legalization of abortion will lead to murder of the old and the physically and mentally handicapped.

> The Connecticut law allowing sixteen-year-olds and their parents to divorce each other will mean the death of the family.

> If we ban handguns, we will end up banning rifles and other hunting weapons.

Distinguishing between probable and improbable predictions — that is, recognizing the slippery slope fallacy — poses special problems because only future developments can verify or refute predictions. For example, in 1941 the imposition of military conscription aroused some opponents to predict that the draft was a precursor of fascism in this country. Only after the war, when 10 million draftees were demobilized, did it become clear that the draft had been an insufficient sign for a prediction of fascism. In this case the slippery slope prediction of fascism might have been avoided if closer attention had been paid to other influences pointing to the strength of democracy.

Slippery slope predictions are simplistic. They ignore not only the dissimilarities between first and last steps but also the complexity of the developments in any long chain of events.

8. Begging the Question

If the writer makes a statement that assumes that the very question being argued has already been proved, the writer is guilty of begging the question. In a letter to the editor of a college newspaper protesting the failure of the majority of students to meet the writing requirement because they had failed an exemption test, the writer said, "Not exempting all students who honestly qualify for exemption is an insult." But whether the students are honestly qualified is precisely the question that the exemption test was supposed to resolve. The writer has not proved that the students who failed the writing test were qualified for exemption. She has only made an assertion *as if* she had already proved it.

In an effort to raise standards of teaching, some politicians and educators have urged that "master teachers" be awarded higher salaries. Opponents have argued that such a proposal begs the question because it assumes that the term "master teachers" can be or has already been defined.

Circular reasoning is an extreme example of begging the question: "Women should not be permitted to join men's clubs because the clubs are for men only." The question to be resolved first, of course, is whether clubs for men only should continue to exist.

9. Straw Man

This fallacy consists of an attack on a view similar to but not the same as the one your opponent holds. It is a familiar diversionary tactic. The name probably derives from an old game in which a straw man was set up to divert attention from the real target that a contestant was supposed to knock down.

One of the outstanding examples of the straw man fallacy occurred in the famous Checkers speech of Senator Richard Nixon. In 1952 during his vice-presidential campaign, Nixon was accused of having appropriated $18,000 in campaign funds for his personal use. At one point in the radio and television speech in which he defended his reputation, he said:

> One other thing I probably should tell you, because if I don't they will probably be saying this about me, too. We did get something, a gift, after the election.
>
> A man down in Texas heard Pat on the radio mention the fact that our two youngsters would like to have a dog, and, believe it or not, the day before we left on this campaign trip we got a message from Union Station in Baltimore saying they had a package for us. We went down to get it. You know what it was?
>
> It was a little cocker spaniel dog, in a crate that he had sent all the way from Texas, black and white, spotted, and our little girl, Tricia, the six-year-old, named it Checkers.
>
> And, you know, the kids, like all kids, loved the dog, and I just want to say this, right now, that regardless of what they say about it, we are going to keep it.[9]

Of course, Nixon knew that the issue was the alleged misappropriation of funds, not the ownership of the dog, which no one had asked him to return.

10. Two Wrongs Make a Right

This is another example of the way in which attention may be diverted from the question at issue.

After a speech by President Jimmy Carter in March 1977 attacking the human rights record of the Soviet Union, Russian officials responded:

---

[9]Radio and television address of Senator Nixon from Los Angeles on September 23, 1952.

As for the present state of human rights in the United States, it is characterized by the following facts: millions of unemployed, racial discrimination, social inequality of women, infringement of citizens' personal freedom, the growth of crime, and so on.[10]

The Russians made no attempt to deny the failure of *their* human rights record; instead they attacked by pointing out that the Americans are not blameless either.

11. *Non Sequitur*

The Latin term *non sequitur,* which means "it does not follow," is another fallacy of irrelevance. An advertisement for a book, *Worlds in Collision,* whose theories about the origin of the earth and evolutionary development have been challenged by almost all reputable scientists, states:

> Once rejected as "preposterous!" Critics called it an outrage! It aroused incredible antagonism in scientific and literary circles. Yet half a million copies were sold and for twenty-seven years it remained an outstanding bestseller.

We know, of course, that the popularity of a book does not bestow scientific respectability. The number of sales, therefore, is irrelevant to proof of the book's theoretical soundness.

12. *Ad Populum*

Arguers guilty of this fallacy make an appeal to the prejudices of the people (*populum* in Latin). They assume that their claim can be adequately defended without further support if they emphasize a belief or attitude that the audience shares with them. One common form of *ad populum* is an appeal to patriotism, which may allow arguers to omit evidence that the audience needs for proper evaluation of the claim. In the following advertisement the makers of Zippo lighters made such an appeal in urging readers to buy their product.

> It's a grand old lighter. Zippo — the grand old lighter that's made right here in the good old U. S. A.
> We truly make an all-American product. The raw materials used in making a Zippo lighter are all right from this great land of ours.
> Zippo windproof lighters are proud to be Americans.

13. Appeal to Tradition

In making an appeal to tradition, the arguer assumes that what has existed for a long time and has therefore become a tradition should continue to exist *because* it is a tradition. If the arguer avoids

---

[10]*New York Times,* March 3, 1977, p. 1.

telling his or her reader *why* the tradition should be preserved, he or she may be accused of failing to meet the real issue.

The following statement appeared in a letter defending the membership policy of the Century Club, an all-male club established in New York City in 1847 that was under pressure to admit women. The writer was a Presbyterian minister who opposed the admission of women.

> I am totally opposed to a proposal which would radically change the nature of the Century. . . . A club creates an ethos of its own over the years, and I would deeply deplore a step that would inevitably create an entirely different kind of place.
>
> A club like the Century should surely be unaffected by fashionable whims. . . .[11]

14. Faulty Emotional Appeals

In some discussions of fallacies, appeals to the emotions of the audience are treated as illegitimate or "counterfeit proofs." All such appeals, however, are *not* illegitimate. As we saw in Chapter 5 on support, appeals to the values and emotions of an audience are an appropriate form of persuasion. You can recognize fallacious appeals if (1) they are irrelevant to the argument or draw attention from the issues being argued or (2) they appear to conceal another purpose. Here we treat two of the most popular appeals — to pity and to fear.

Appeals to pity, compassion, and natural willingness to help the unfortunate are particularly hard to resist. The requests for aid by most charitable organizations — for hungry children, victims of disaster, stray animals — offer examples of legitimate appeals. But these appeals to our sympathetic feelings should not divert us from considering other issues in a particular case. It would be wrong, for example, to allow a multiple murderer to escape punishment because he or she had experienced a wretched childhood. Likewise, if you are asked to contribute to a charitable cause, you should try to learn how many unfortunate people or animals are being helped and what percentage of the contribution will be allocated to maintaining the organization and its officers. In some cases the financial records are closed to public review, and only a small share of the contribution will reach the alleged beneficiaries.

Appeals to fear are likely to be even more effective. But they must be based on evidence that fear is an appropriate response to the issues and that it can move an audience toward a solution to the problem. (Fear can also have the adverse effect of preventing people from taking a necessary action.) Insurance companies, for example,

---

[11]David H. C. Read, letter to the *New York Times,* January 13, 1983, p. 14.

make appeals to our fears of destitution for ourselves and our families as a result of injury, unemployment, sickness, and death. These appeals are justified if the possibilities of such destitution are real and if the insurance will provide relief. It would also be legitimate to arouse fear of the consequences of drunk driving, provided, again, that the descriptions were accurate. On the other hand, it would be wrong to induce fear that fluoridation of public water supplies causes cancer without presenting sound evidence of the probability. It would also be wrong to instill a fear of school integration unless convincing proof were offered of undesirable social consequences.

An emotional response by itself is not always the soundest basis for making decisions. Your own experience has probably taught you that in the grip of a strong emotion like love or hate or anger you often overlook good reasons for making different and better choices. Like you, your readers want to be given the opportunity to consider all the available kinds of support for an argument.

READINGS FOR ANALYSIS

On Nation and Race
ADOLF HITLER

There are some truths which are so obvious that for this very reason they are not seen or at least not recognized by ordinary people. They sometimes pass by such truisms as though blind and are most astonished when someone suddenly discovers what everyone really ought to know. Columbus's eggs lie around by the hundreds of thousands, but Columbuses are met with less frequency.

Thus men without exception wander about in the garden of Nature; they imagine that they know practically everything and yet with few exceptions pass blindly by one of the most patent principles of Nature's rule: the inner segregation of the species of all living beings on this earth.

Even the most superficial observation shows that Nature's restricted form of propagation and increase is an almost rigid basic law of all the innumerable forms of expression of her vital urge.

Adolf Hitler (1889–1945) became the Nazi dictator of Germany in the mid-1930s. "On Nation and Race" (editor's title) begins the eleventh chapter of *Mein Kampf* (*My Struggle*), vol. 1, published in 1925.

Every animal mates only with a member of the same species. The titmouse seeks the titmouse, the finch the finch, the stork the stork, the field mouse the field mouse, the dormouse the dormouse, the wolf the she-wolf, etc.

Only unusual circumstances can change this, primarily the compulsion of captivity or any other cause that makes it impossible to mate within the same species. But then Nature begins to resist this with all possible means, and her most visible protest consists either in refusing further capacity for propagation to bastards or in limiting the fertility of later offspring; in most cases, however, she takes away the power of resistance to disease or hostile attacks.

This is only too natural.   5

Any crossing of two beings not at exactly the same level produces a medium between the level of the two parents. This means: The offspring will probably stand higher than the racially lower parent, but not as high as the higher one. Consequently, it will later succumb in the struggle against the higher level. Such mating is contrary to the will of Nature for a higher breeding of all life. The precondition for this does not lie in associating superior and inferior, but in the total victory of the former. The stronger must dominate and not blend with the weaker, thus sacrificing his own greatness. Only the born weakling can view this as cruel, but he after all is only a weak and limited man; for if this law did not prevail, any conceivable higher development of organic living beings would be unthinkable.

The consequence of this racial purity, universally valid in Nature, is not only the sharp outward delimitation of the various races, but their uniform character in themselves. The fox is always a fox, the goose a goose, the tiger a tiger, etc., and the difference can lie at most in the varying measure of force, strength, intelligence, dexterity, endurance, etc., of the individual specimens. But you will never find a fox who in his inner attitude might, for example, show humanitarian tendencies toward geese, as similarly there is no cat with a friendly inclination toward mice.

Therefore, here, too, the struggle among themselves arises less from inner aversion than from hunger and love. In both cases, Nature looks on calmly, with satisfaction, in fact. In the struggle for daily bread all those who are weak and sickly or less determined succumb, while the struggle of the males for the female grants the right or opportunity to propagate only to the healthiest. And struggle is always a means for improving a species' health and power of resistance and, therefore, a cause of its higher development.

If the process were different, all further and higher development would cease and the opposite would occur. For, since the inferior always predominates numerically over the best, if both had the same possibility of preserving life and propagating, the inferior would multiply so much more rapidly that in the end the best would inevitably be driven into the background, unless a correction of this state of affairs were undertaken. Nature does just this by subjecting the weaker part to such severe living conditions that by them alone the number is limited, and by not permitting the remainder to increase promiscuously, but making a new and ruthless choice according to strength and health.

No more than Nature desires the mating of weaker with stronger 10 individuals, even less does she desire the blending of a higher with a lower race, since, if she did, her whole work of higher breeding, over perhaps hundreds of thousands of years, might be ruined with one blow.

Historical experience offers countless proofs of this. It shows with terrifying clarity that in every mingling of Aryan blood with that of lower peoples the result was the end of the cultured people. North America, whose population consists in by far the largest part of Germanic elements who mixed but little with the lower colored peoples, shows a different humanity and culture from Central and South America, where the predominantly Latin immigrants often mixed with the aborigines on a large scale. By this one example, we can clearly and distinctly recognize the effect of racial mixture. The Germanic inhabitant of the American continent, who has remained racially pure and unmixed, rose to be master of the continent; he will remain the master as long as he does not fall a victim to defilement of the blood.

The result of all racial crossing is therefore in brief always the following:

(a) Lowering of the level of the higher race;

(b) Physical and intellectual regression and hence the beginning of a slowly but surely progressing sickness.

To bring about such a development is, then, nothing else but to 15 sin against the will of the eternal creator.

And as a sin this act is rewarded.

When man attempts to rebel against the iron logic of Nature, he comes into struggle with the principles to which he himself owes his existence as a man. And this attack must lead to his own doom.

Here, of course, we encounter the objection of the modern pacifist, as truly Jewish in its effrontery as it is stupid! "Man's role is to overcome Nature!"

Millions thoughtlessly parrot this Jewish nonsense and end up by really imagining that they themselves represent a kind of conqueror of Nature; though in this they dispose of no other weapon than an idea, and at that such a miserable one, that if it were true no world at all would be conceivable.

But quite aside from the fact that man has never yet conquered 20 Nature in anything, but at most has caught hold of and tried to lift one or another corner of her immense gigantic veil of eternal riddles and secrets, that in reality he invents nothing but only discovers everything, that he does not dominate Nature, but has only risen on the basis of his knowledge of various laws and secrets of Nature to be lord over those other living creatures who lack this knowledge — quite aside from all this, an idea cannot overcome the preconditions for the development and being of humanity, since the idea itself depends only on man. Without human beings there is no human idea in this world; therefore, the idea as such is always conditioned by the presence of human beings and hence of all the laws which created the precondition for their existence.

And not only that! Certain ideas are even tied up with certain men. This applies most of all to those ideas whose content originates, not in an exact scientific truth, but in the world of emotion, or, as it is so beautifully and clearly expressed today, reflects an "inner experience." All these ideas, which have nothing to do with cold logic as such, but represent only pure expressions of feeling, ethical conceptions, etc., are chained to the existence of men, to whose intellectual imagination and creative power they owe their existence. Precisely in this case the preservation of these definite races and men is the precondition for the existence of these ideas. Anyone, for example, who really desired the victory of the pacifistic idea in this world with all his heart would have to fight with all the means at his disposal for the conquest of the world by the Germans; for, if the opposite should occur, the last pacifist would die out with the last German, since the rest of the world has never fallen so deeply as our own people, unfortunately, has for this nonsense so contrary to Nature and reason. Then, if we were serious, whether we liked it or not, we would have to wage wars in order to arrive at pacifism. This and nothing else was what Wilson, the American world savior, intended, or so at least our German visionaries believed — and thereby his purpose was fulfilled.

In actual fact the pacifistic-humane idea is perfectly all right perhaps when the highest type of man has previously conquered and subjected the world to an extent that makes him the sole ruler of this earth. Then this idea lacks the power of producing evil effects in exact proportion as its practical application becomes rare and finally impossible. Therefore, first struggle and then we shall see what can be done. Otherwise mankind has passed the high point of its development and the end is not the domination of any ethical idea but barbarism and consequently chaos. At this point someone or other may laugh, but this planet once moved through the ether for millions of years without human beings and it can do so again some day if men forget that they owe their higher existence, not to the ideas of a few crazy ideologists, but to the knowledge and ruthless application of Nature's stern and rigid laws.

Everything we admire on this earth today — science and art, technology and inventions — is only the creative product of a few peoples and originally perhaps of *one* race. On them depends the existence of this whole culture. If they perish, the beauty of this earth will sink into the grave with them.

However much the soil, for example, can influence men, the result of the influence will always be different depending on the races in question. The low fertility of a living space may spur the one race to the highest achievements; in others it will only be the cause of bitterest poverty and final undernourishment with all its consequences. The inner nature of peoples is always determining for the manner in which outward influences will be effective. What leads the one to starvation trains the other to hard work.

All great cultures of the past perished only because the origi- 25 nally creative race died out from blood poisoning.

The ultimate cause of such a decline was their forgetting that all culture depends on men and conversely; hence that to preserve a certain culture the man who creates it must be preserved. This preservation is bound up with the rigid law of necessity and the right to victory of the best and stronger in this world.

Those who want to live, let them fight, and those who do not want to fight in this world of eternal struggle do not deserve to live.

Even if this were hard — that is how it is! Assuredly, however, by far the harder fate is that which strikes the man who thinks he can overcome Nature, but in the last analysis only mocks her. Distress, misfortune, and diseases are her answer.

The man who misjudges and disregards the racial laws actually forfeits the happiness that seems destined to be his. He thwarts the triumphal march of the best race and hence also the precondition for all human progress, and remains, in consequence, burdened with all the sensibility of man, in the animal realm of helpless misery.

It is idle to argue which race or races were the original represen- 30 tative of human culture and hence the real founders of all that we sum up under the word "humanity." It is simpler to raise the question with regard to the present, and here an easy, clear answer results. All the human culture, all the results of art, science, and technology that we see before us today, are almost exclusively the creative product of the Aryan. This very fact admits of the not unfounded inference that he alone was the founder of all higher humanity, therefore representing the prototype of all that we understand by the word "man." He is the Prometheus of mankind from whose bright forehead the divine spark of genius has sprung at all times, forever kindling anew that fire of knowledge which illumined the night of silent mysteries and thus caused man to climb the path to mastery over the other beings of this earth. Exclude him

— and perhaps after a few thousand years darkness will again descend on the earth, human culture will pass, and the world turn to a desert.

Reading and Discussion Questions

1. Find places in the essay where Hitler attempts to emphasize the scientific objectivity of his theories.
2. Are there some passages which are difficult to understand? (See, for example, paragraph 13.) How do you explain the difficulty?
3. In explaining his ideology, how does Hitler misinterpret the statement that "Every animal mates only with a member of the same species"? How would you characterize this fallacy?
4. Hitler uses the theory of evolution and his interpretation of the "survival of the fittest" to justify his racial philosophy. Find the places in the text where Hitler reveals that he misunderstands the theory in its application to human beings.
5. What false evidence about race does Hitler use in his assessment of the racial experience in North America? Examine carefully the last sentence of paragraph 11: "The Germanic inhabitant of the American continent, who has remained racially pure and unmixed, rose to be master of the continent; he will remain the master as long as he does not fall a victim to defilement of the blood."
6. What criticism of Jews does Hitler offer? How does this criticism help to explain Hitler's pathological hatred of Jews?
7. Hitler believes that pacifism is a violation of "Nature and reason." Would modern scientists agree that the laws of Nature require unremitting struggle and conflict between human beings — until the master race conquers?

Writing Suggestion

8. Do some research in early human history to discover the degree of truth in this statement: "All human culture, all the results of art, science, and technology that we see before us today, are almost exclusively the creative product of the Aryan." You may want to limit your discussion to one area of human culture.

People Like Me

TONY PARKER and HANK SULLIVAN

Yeah sure I'll talk with you, like I wrote and said I would. I just hope it's interesting enough for you to feel you want to hear. My story's very simple you see, it's not at all complex, or least not the way I look at it it's not. I'm your ordinary professional criminal and there's plenty around. Some of us [are] successful, some of us aren't, you know how it goes. What's a professional criminal, what does it mean? Well all it is is someone who makes his living out of crime. Like you do with writing, it's more or less like that. You do your writing, I do my crime. Successful or unsuccessful, which one am I? Well successful of course. I must be, I'm here and still alive. I've never thought of giving up, I'm the same way as you: I just can't imagine doing anything else.

My basic facts are few, shall we start with those? You're talking to a man called Hank and his age is fifty-two. He's doing eight terms of imprisonment for life, plus six sentences consecutive totaling three hundred years. The life terms are for shootings in which people got killed, and the fixed sentences are for different offenses like attempted murder, wounding, armed robbery, possession of explosives, robbery with violence, escape, resisting arrest, and that kind of stuff. All of it straight though, nothing kinky or weird. Parole is something I'll never ever be given, no matter what, which I guess some guys'd take to mean they'd never get out. Not me though, not me my friend, myself I don't look at it that way. Because for sure if I did, well then I'd be dead.

How do I mean? Well let out and get out, they're two different things. They won't let me out ever, not from the front door, sure I know that. So what I have is the only alternative, you know what I mean? If it can't be the front then that only leaves the back. So escape's my ambition and the planning of it is all that keeps me alive. In twenty years I've made it twice so it's not an impossible dream. I'm not that sort of a man. I mean if I was I'd be frustrated wouldn't I, all disappointed and sour and eaten up inside. But I'm not. I'll get out again one day, there's no doubt about that. Believe me, do, okay?

Go back to the beginning for you, my background and childhood, you want to hear about those? Sure I'll tell you then, it won't take too much time. You see there's nothing to tell. I'm from a white middle-class Catholic family, perfectly ordinary, straight down the

---

Tony Parker is a British sociologist who has written several books on criminals and prisons, including *The Violence of Our Lives: Interviews with American Murderers* (1995) from which this interview with career criminal Hank Sullivan is excerpted.

line. As a kid I was happy and we weren't rich, but neither were we poor. We lived in a nice home, we were well raised and wanted for nothing or nothing I recall. My father was a production manager at a factory and my mother was a teacher; both of them are dead now, but they were nice people and good. They were very happy with each other, you know how some people are? They believed in family ties and values, and all that kind of thing. I've a brother and two sisters, all older than me. I've not been in contact with any of them since I was young, but as far as I know they've led conventional lives. Both my sisters are married and I couldn't tell you what their names are. That's about all I can think of that there's to say where my family's concerned. They don't really exist for me for practical purposes in any meaningful kind of way now, because that's how it goes.

Schooling, I guess that'd be interesting if I could remember any- 5 thing of it that left any mark but I'm sorry no, I can't. I went to a Catholic high school for boys and the teachers were priests. I wasn't ever beaten or sexually interfered with. There were none of those things went on you sometimes read about, so there's no interest there, just nothing at all. I think I usually got good grades. My life was not unusual and nothing occurred in it for the first ten years I'd say. No one specially influenced me either for good or for bad, you know what I mean?

The fact I was secretive and had an inner life was all that made me any different, I suppose. If you'd met me then you'd never have imagined more than anyone else what was happening inside. Exteriors conceal, right? In my case I was amusing myself from the age of ten on with stick-ups and fires. They were like kind of my hobbies, but they were much more than that: For me they were my all-consuming interests would be more correct to say. I guess to some folk that'd be unusual in a way, but if it is it didn't seem so to me. It wasn't my life was dull you know and I wanted to escape from it and fizz it up a bit; I just found it interesting to do those things and watch how people would react. Guns were easy to get like they always are, and the first one I had was like a train set for me, I'd clean it and polish it and look after it like it was a treasure or my very best friend. My very first gun, a Colt .45 automatic, gee I'll never forget that one, I loved it I did. Like the way you remember your first woman, you know how I mean?

The other part intrigued me was the psychology thing: People are always more frightened of a kid with a gun than they are of an adult armed robber, have you ever noticed that? Because they think he's not going to be so reasonable and responsible in the way he handles it like a grown-up would I suppose. Might fire a shot at them for just a trivial thing like moving too quick or something of that sort. There was a cabdriver once I stuck up when I was twelve; he'd pulled in an alley where I'd told him to go, and when I let him see the gun and told him to give me all he'd got, he got almost hysterical with fear. "Don't shoot me, don't shoot me" he went on and on. I had to really make a big effort to try and talk him down. I said "Look buddy I'm not going to shoot you" I said, "just so long as you give me all there is." . . . [H]e was so terrified. I mean can you imagine that?

As for those fires, the arson bit I mean, when I first started coming into juvenile institutions and places of that kind, it used to cause so much . . . interest among psychologists and shrinks you wouldn't believe. Very unusual and significant, least that's what they always said. Going to bed with your sister . . . that was ordinary stuff, but a fourteen-year-old who was a serial arsonist, well he really was, he was some special kind of guy. All I did actually was set fire to warehouses and stores and offices and schools and that sort of place. Just for fun you know. But they'd never accept it was that, it always had to be symbolic of something: I found that kind of weird, I really did. One center I was in a psychologist had me write down every single place I'd done. Sixteen as I recall and they divided them in groups: "masculine" and "feminine," "aggressive" and "passive" and some other categories I forget. It was a young woman who done this stuff, and I remember her better than I remember all the shit. She had a real short white overall and a pretty tight little ass, and she'd all the time lean over the table I was sitting at to mark up the blocks. So what I did naturally was I stretched it all out, then while she was arranging all the papers and covering them with marks I'd stand round in back of her and peek up her skirt or look down her front. . . . A strange kind of occupation for a young girl to have, studying someone like me. But I let her have her fun though, I didn't mind: one of us was normal and the other one was not. . . .

You know I guess the best part of all though was hearing people talk. They sure caused some chattering, those fires of mine did. "They've caught the arsonist," that I often heard, or words to the effect the owner of the premises was responsible himself, he'd done it for insurance because business was bad. You know what people say. How many I did in total I can't properly recall because I never did something stupid like keeping a list. Sixteen I told the psychologist about, but that sure was not them all; twenty-five or thirty say would be nearer the mark in around about a year. And then it all finished and came to an end. How I was caught was real stupid, no doubt at all. How it is when you're young, right, it's always the same? You want to impress some girl, and that's just what I did. I was boasting one night to her it was me who'd set the fires, and she said she didn't believe it, I was trying to pull her leg. So what did I do? I gave her a forecast: I told her wait and see, on the Saturday night I'd set alight a certain store. So when it went up like I said it would, what happened, well anyone could guess: She told her parents what I'd said. The cops were round my place in five minutes flat, and in my room they found things I'd not had time to hide. My parents were pretty shaken by it, especially my dad. He sat me down I remember and he said he knew I hadn't done such things and I must be protecting someone else, like parents always do. Finally he said he'd help me and in every way he could, but only if I'd swear on the Bible to him to tell the honest truth. I said okay I'd do that, and that's what I did: I swore on the word of God that I'd acted entirely on my own, and I guess that made him feel pretty bad. He was a good man by his lights and he just couldn't understand. It taught me a lesson though, the experience I mean and I've tried to remember it since all through my life but with varying success. What it is you'll know it, like every other man: Never trust a dame.

What happened in the end was I was sent to reform school for an 10 indefinite period, which was precisely four years. I'd say they were some of the best of my life. I mixed with guys like myself whose only aim was crime. There was a thousand juvenile offenders there of every kind you could imagine, and a lot I'm sure you couldn't, you know what I mean? That's an experience you know I'd not otherwise have had. It was good, it taught me possibilities and it opened up my eyes. Also it made me tough. You know I've often thought this since, the guys who do their time better are the ones who started early. That I honestly believe, now I've thought it out, which I've just this minute done.

I don't know what was with my parents after that, somehow we seemed to grow apart. They visited a time or two, but I never went back home; it didn't seem to have no point, we sort of lived in different worlds. I'd say from eighteen up I only associated with all my own kind. Funny, things like that, it's the way it often works. I mean some folks you fit with but others you can only say if they hadn't been your relatives you'd never have known them even for a start. Then someone else you meet and it's like you've known them all your life. That was how it was with me and my first serious girl: She was the sister of a guy I was buddy-buddy with in there. We never talked it over or arranged it any way, but as soon as I got out I went to the apartment she had, and I think all we said was "Hi there" before we then went straight to bed. That's the way it should be, so I've always found. Then you know where you are and you won't get surprised by discovering you're with a vegetarian or someone of that kind.

She was a good kid that girl was, I owe a lot to her: She was the person gave me my first proper chance. Sheila her name was or Sheena, something of the kind. She had some Irish in her you know like I do as well, and we were both brought up Catholic, which was another thing — we were ideally suited to each other in most every way there was. She wasn't much of a looker but I don't think you should let that count: What mattered was she had brains, was good with figures and intelligent. She had a job in the central cashier's office of a chain of carpet and furnishing stores, and she knew the days of the month where their different cash drops were made. That was very useful for me because she could point me to all the places where I needed to be, tell me what time the armored truck with the wages in it would arrive and all stuff like that.

Honestly I did, I learned a lot from that girl: not just where and when to make the strikes but how to plan them out so's they looked like they were at random and no one could trace a pattern in them, point a finger, you know? That stuff was very useful for a young guy like me beginning on a criminal career. I think she was hoping one day I'd make a big enough pile for us to retire and settle down. It was sad for her it didn't happen like that. My trouble was you see I had a wandering eye, something I've never come to terms with in my life. I don't attach myself to people, there's too many risks — lays you open to their moods instead of keeping them to yours. Me and her, Sheena or whatever her name was, things were going along very nice and smoothly for a couple of years till she started talking about wanting to settle down. There was nothing else for it: One night I upped and I didn't come back because you don't want discussions, you just make the break like that. Besides women can peach on you, threaten to tell, and that can lead to awkwardness. I've had it happen and it's not very nice. As soon as they say they might, the best thing to do is make for the door.

I'd say on the whole though I've been lucky with my women, they've mostly given me good times. There was one I remember, now she was one of the best, a feisty little girl; only sixteen, fast-legged and sprinty like a quarter horse. Got me to train her how to use a thirty-eight, and she was the sort to go out and pull jobs I myself'd think twice about first. She was some kid she was, red hair and not all that tall, only came up to here. You know what she'd do? What she was good at especially, it was usually hotels. She'd sit in the bar of one and when some guy propositioned her they'd go up to his room. Ten minutes flat and she'd get him stripped naked, down to his drawers. Then she'd take off all her own clothes and get him so dazzled he'd fall on the bed, and when he did that then she'd reach for her purse, pull out her gun and make him give her his last cent. Takes courage to do that you know, for a girl on her own. I used to tell her if she was my daughter I would, I'd feel real proud. . . .

Women eh, there was other ones too, plenty in my time. I met a   15
broad once, believe me she was sixty-five, she was a little old granny and she drove a big truck and suggested we go into partnership. Only let me tell you, that's something I've never ever done—take on one other guy and the risk grows three ways. One is he could let you down and not play his part; two he could get injured and captured to

follow; three if he is he could try to save his neck by telling what he knows. I'd say to any young guy to always bear that in mind: wherever it's practicable, stay on your own.

Let me tell you an example: The first time I ever came to prison, it wasn't my fault. Me and another guy, we'd held up a security truck that was taking wages to a factory. I'd done all the planning about where exactly we'd stop it which was on a bridge over a canal. Then at the last minute I heard it had four armored guards, not two like I'd been told. I always reckoned I could deal with two when I worked on my own, but four was rather different; you'd need eyes in the back of your head. So what did I do but I took on an assistant, and when the shooting started he took a bullet in his hip. He wasn't wearing body armor like I'd told him he should so of course he was caught. They beat it out of him where I was making for and they had twenty police vehicles and dogs and a helicopter too. They got me in the woods and threw a cordon round it, and all because this guy gave them knowledge so they could work out my route. I had no way out except fire power: In the confrontation I shot more accurately than they did but one against twenty's not fair odds and I surrendered in the end. I gave a good account of myself first, I think I took out a total of four, but I finished up with two life sentences plus two hundred years.

Considering for ten years I'd been working nice and steady and never once being caught, as you can imagine I felt very bitter about that result. I still think if I hadn't had that amateur along, I'd most likely have shaken off pursuit. I've learned my lesson about that, or mostly I have. I don't want to be boastful, but if someone wants to hire my services for something big when I'm out I always lay down strict conditions that they leave me alone to work the way I want to, which means on my own. I won't do nothing for anyone if I have to follow their instructions; they must follow mine.

Another thing is this: I won't do just anything, I always make it plain that there's lines. An obvious one from which I'll never deviate is I'll never hurt a woman, not for any sum at all. I don't know if it means I'm softhearted or what. I've been offered contracts and some of them were big ones, but if it's a woman, then the answer's no. I don't touch females, get somebody else. On the whole though taking individuals out, that's really not my line. I've only done two contract hits in the whole of my life, or three at the most. They're sneaky, know what I mean? I wouldn't ever touch them unless business was real bad; I'd sooner stand up and fight. I don't like killing people when they're not armed.

The excitement, you know, that's the part I like: I'm not the sort goes round shooting at random anyone I see. All of my killings they've all had a purpose, I'm a professional criminal, not a . . . psychopath. Those first two I told you about, I was trying to get away, then the next three again, they were all of men with guns who were moving me to a different state or other to face some more charges. The chances of breaching a maximum security establishment are low because you're outnumbered by the guards, so the best times are when they're moving you. Then the same thing again two years ago, there were just two prison guards. That's only seven? One two thr. . . . Oh yeah you're right, so who the hell was . . . yeah wait a minute, I've got it now, the second escape it wasn't three it was four, a state trooper turned up and thought he'd join in. Though I'll be honest with you, there's been a couple of others too that haven't come out and I think they never will. How many in total? Jeez I've no idea, more than ten it must be I guess.

Let me try and tell you how it is. Firstly I don't have to justify 20 myself, there's no need. I guess the way I'd put it would be to say it's like we are at war, me and society I mean. I see myself as a law enforcement officer — only my laws, not yours. Or another way to say it would be there's one set of guys whose uniforms are blue: They try and hang on to things like money and possessions and power. And then there'd be other ones whose uniforms are green: They want to get a slice of things themselves too. The one way they'll not do it is work from nine through five so they have to think of other ways. I've chosen one which I thoroughly enjoy: It's plotting and scheming and working out a strategy, then putting it into action and seeing if it works. And again I'm not boasting in saying this to you because it's true: I've been successful a hundred times more often than I've ever been caught for, that's certainly a fact. We're cleverer than we're given credit for, people like me, we certainly are.

I'm a professional criminal, and I take pride in my trade. An amateur, you see, he's not like that at all. How I'd define him would be a guy who makes a quick hit and relies on his luck for the amount of cash he gets: could be a few hundred bucks, might be nothing at all. But for me I need to know first what the amount is's involved, and the amount of risk I'll take's got to be commensurate with the financial reward. If it looks like it's going to be a combat situation I wouldn't go in underarmed; always at least I've got to have an automatic rifle, two pistols and at least some hand grenades. "Armed to the teeth" would be the phrase.

Obviously if it's something big other guys are going to try and stop me, right? They'll go as far as they think's necessary to do that, including killing me of course. Then I'm saying in return that to stop me that's what they'll have to do, and if they try, then I'm going to try and kill them first. That's common sense, okay? But don't get me wrong like I said before: I wouldn't kill anyone unless it was strictly necessary to get what I wanted or it was my life or theirs.

Would I ever kill you, you want an honest answer to that? Well the answer is no, probably not. I can't envisage the situation arising can you, where it would be necessary? I mean if you were a guard here and I had a gun, if I wanted your key I'd ask you for it. I'd say "Give me your key." And if you were sensible about it as I think you would be and did what I asked and stood to one side, then of course I wouldn't kill you, because there wouldn't be a need. On the other hand though if you crazily decided you wouldn't give me the key and went for your gun, then of course I'd blow your . . . head in. I'd have to wouldn't I, otherwise you might do me harm? That answer your question, do you understand? Good: no hard feelings I hope.

Oh boy Tony I've enjoyed this you know, I truly have. It's been like the kind of conversation you usually have with yourself, know what I mean? Good luck with the book.

Reading and Discussion Questions

1. Do you detect fallacious reasoning in the following statements? Examine the statements that precede or follow them in the interview in order to understand the context.
   a. "What's a professional criminal, what does it mean? Well all it is is someone who makes his living out of crime. Like you do with writing, it's more or less like that." (paragraph 1)
   b. "They got me in the woods and threw a cordon round it, and all because this guy [his accomplice, who was captured] gave them knowledge so they could work out my route. . . . In the confrontation I shot more accurately than they did but one against twenty's not fair odds and I surrendered in the end." (paragraph 16)
   c. " . . . taking individuals out, that's really not my line. I've only done two contract hits in the whole of my life, or three at the most. They're sneaky, know what I mean?" (paragraph 18)
   d. "I'm not the sort goes round shooting at random anyone I see. All my killings they've all had a purpose. I'm a professional criminal, not a . . . psychopath." (paragraph 19)
   e. "I see myself as a law enforcement officer — only my laws, not yours." (paragraph 20)
2. How does Sullivan see himself as a person? Find some of the passages where he describes himself and his personal relations. Does his self-perception strike you as strange? Why or why not?
3. When he talks about "fault," what does he mean? ("The first time I ever went to prison, it wasn't my fault. Me and another guy, we'd held up a security truck that was taking wages to a factory.")

Writing Suggestions

4. Sullivan's definitions seem perverse. Choose some of his ideas and write an analysis of the meanings he gives to them, explaining how they are different from those of most people.
5. *All God's Children: The Bosket Family and the American Tradition of Violence* by Fox Butterfield (1995) is an extraordinary documentation of one family's criminal careers over at least one hundred years. You will

probably want to read the whole book once you begin, but the story of Willie Bosket, a highly intelligent criminal who told police that he had committed 2,000 crimes by age fifteen, will give you some insight into the psychology of the criminal and his defense of his actions. He is far more articulate than Sullivan. Write an analysis of the reasons he gives for his crimes.

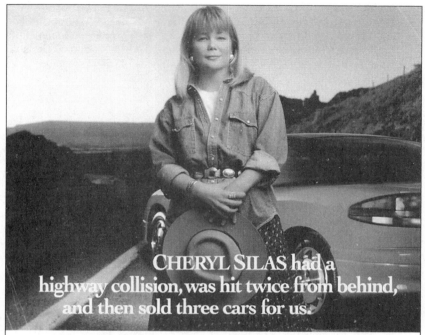

CHERYL SILAS had a highway collision, was hit twice from behind, and then sold three cars for us.

When Cheryl unbuckled her shoulder harness and lap belt, it took her a moment to realize her Saturn coupe was really a mess. And that, remarkably, she wasn't. That's when she decided to get another SC.

Several other people arrived at similar conclusions. A policeman at the accident scene came in soon after and ordered himself a sedan. As did a buddy of his, also on the force. Then Cheryl's brother, glad he still had a sister, bought yet another Saturn in Illinois.

Now, good referrals are important to any product. And we're always glad to have them. But we'd be more than happy if our customers found less dramatic ways to help spread the word.

A DIFFERENT KIND OF COMPANY. A DIFFERENT KIND OF CAR.

© 1991 Saturn Corporation. M.S.R.P. of 1992 Saturn SC shown is $12,415, including retailer prep and optional sunroof. Tax, license, transportation and other options additional. If you'd like to know more about Saturn, and our new sedans and coupe, please call us at 1-800-522-5000.

Discussion Questions

1. What example of inductive reasoning does the advertiser use? How would you evaluate the probability of the conclusion?
2. To what extent does the use of an alleged real person in a narrative contribute to the effectiveness of the advertiser's pitch? Should the ad have contained more factual information?

UFO Abductions:
An Introduction

JOHN E. MACK

In the fall of 1989, when a colleague asked me if I wished to meet Budd Hopkins, I replied, "Who's he?" She told me that he was an artist in New York who worked with people who reported being taken by alien beings into spaceships. I then said something to the effect that he must be crazy and so must they. No, no, she insisted, it was a very serious and real matter. A day came soon when I would be in New York for another purpose — it was January 10, 1990, one of those dates you remember that mark a time when everything in your life changes — and she took me to see Budd.

Nothing in my then nearly forty years of familiarity with the field of psychiatry prepared me for what Hopkins had to say. I was impressed with his warmth, sincerity, intelligence, and caring for the people with whom he had been working. But more important than that were the stories he told me from people all over the United States who had come forth to tell him about their experiences after reading one of his books or articles or hearing him on television. These corresponded, sometimes in minute detail, to those of other "abductees" or "experiencers," as they are called.

Most of the specific information that the abductees provided about the means of transport to and from the spaceships, the descriptions of the insides of the ships themselves, and the procedures carried out by the aliens during the abductions had never been written about or shown in the media. Furthermore, these individuals were from many parts of the country and had not communicated with each other. They seemed in other respects quite sane, had come forth reluctantly, fearing the discrediting of their stories or outright ridicule they had encountered in the past. They had come to see Hopkins at considerable expense, and, with rare exceptions, had nothing to gain materially from telling their stories. In one example a woman was startled when Hopkins showed her a drawing

---

John E. Mack, M.D., is a Professor of Psychiatry at the Harvard University Medical School. This selection is from *Abduction: Human Experiences with Aliens* (1994). [Bibliographic citations have been cut.]

of an alien being. She asked how he had been able to depict what she had seen when they had only just begun talking. When he explained that the drawing had been made by another person from a different part of the country she became intensely upset, for an experience that she had wanted to believe was a dream, now, she felt, must be in some way real.

My reaction was in some respects like this woman's. What Hopkins had encountered in the more than two hundred abduction cases he had seen over a fourteen-year period were reports of experiences that had the characteristics of real events: highly detailed narratives that seemed to have no obvious symbolic pattern; intense emotional and physical traumatic impact, sometimes leaving small lesions on the experiencers' bodies; and consistency of stories down to the most minute details. But if these experiences were in some sense "real," then all sorts of new questions opened up. How often was this occurring? If there were large numbers of these cases, who was helping these individuals deal with their experiences and what sort of support or treatment was called for? What was the response of the mental health profession? And, most basic of all, what was the source of these encounters? These and many other questions will be addressed in this book.

In response to my obvious but somewhat confused interest, Hopkins asked if I wished to see some of these experiencers myself. I agreed, with curiosity tinged by slight anxiety. At his home a month later Hopkins arranged for me to see four abductees, one man and three women. Each told similar stories of their encounters with alien beings and abduction experiences. None of them seemed psychiatrically disturbed except in a secondary sense; that is, they were troubled as a *consequence* of something that had apparently happened to them. There was nothing to suggest that their stories were delusional, a misinterpretation of dreams, or the product of fantasy. None of them seemed like people who would concoct a strange story for some personal purpose. Sensing my now obvious interest, Hopkins asked if I wanted him to refer cases to me in the Boston area, of which he already knew quite a few. Again I agreed, and in the spring of 1990 I began to see abductees in my home and hospital offices.

In the more than three and a half years I have been working with abductees I have seen more than a hundred individuals referred for evaluation of abductions or other "anomalous" experiences. Of these, seventy-six (ranging in age from two to fifty-seven; forty-seven females and twenty-nine males, including three boys eight and under) fulfill my quite strict criteria for an abduction case: conscious recall or recall with the help of hypnosis, of being taken by alien beings into a strange craft, reported with emotion appropriate to the experience being described and no apparent mental condition that could account for the story. I have done between one and eight several-hour modified hypnosis sessions with forty-nine of these individuals, and have evolved a therapeutic approach I will describe shortly.

Although I have a great debt and profound respect for the pioneers in this field, like Budd Hopkins, who have had the courage to investigate and report information that runs in the face of our culture's consensus reality, this book is based largely on my own clinical experience. For this is a subject that is so controversial that virtually no accepted scientific authority has evolved that I might use to bolster my arguments or conclusions. I will report, therefore, what I have learned primarily from my own cases and will make interpretations and draw conclusions on the basis of this information.

The experience of working with abductees has affected me profoundly. The intensity of the energies and emotions involved as abductees relive their experiences is unlike anything I have encountered in other clinical work. The immediacy of presence, support, and understanding that is required has influenced the way I regard the psychotherapeutic task in general. Furthermore, I have come to see that the abduction phenomenon has important philosophical, spiritual, and social implications. Above all, more than any other research I have undertaken, this work has led me to challenge the prevailing worldview or consensus reality which I had grown up believing and had always applied in my clinical/scientific endeavors. According to this view — called variously the Western, Newtonian/Cartesian, or materialist/dualist scientific paradigm — reality is fundamentally grounded in the material world or in what can be perceived by the physical senses. In this view intelligence is largely a phenomenon of the brain of human beings or other advanced species. If, on the contrary, intelligence *is* experienced as residing in the larger cosmos, this perception is an example of "subjectivity" or a projection of our mental processes.

What the abduction phenomenon had led me (I would now say inevitably) to see is that we participate in a universe or universes that are filled with intelligences from which we have cut ourselves off, having lost the senses by which we might know them. It has become clear to me also that our restricted worldview or paradigm lies behind most of the major destructive patterns that threaten the human future — mindless corporate acquisitiveness that perpetuates vast differences between rich and poor and contributes to hunger and disease; ethno-national violence resulting in mass killing which could grow into a nuclear holocaust; and ecological destruction on a scale that threatens the survival of the earth's living systems.

There are, of course, other phenomena that have led to the challenging of the prevailing materialist/dualistic worldview. These include near death experiences, meditation practices, the use of psychedelic substances, shamanic journeys, ecstatic dancing, religious rituals, and other practices that open our being to what we call in the West nonordinary states of consciousness. But none of these, I believe, speaks to us so powerfully in the language that we know best, the language of the physical world. For the abduction phenomenon reaches us, so to speak, where we live. It enters harshly into the physical world, whether or not it is *of* this world. Its power, therefore, to reach and alter our consciousness is potentially immense. All of these matters will be discussed more fully in the clinical case examples that constitute the bulk of this book, and, especially, in the concluding chapter.

One of the important questions in abduction research has been whether the phenomenon is fundamentally new — related to the sightings of "flying saucers" and other unidentified flying objects (UFOs) in the 1940s and the discovery in the 1960s that these craft had "occupants" — or is but a modern chapter in a long story of humankind's relationship to vehicles and creatures appearing from the heavens that goes back to antiquity. . . .

The most commonly debated issue, whether abductions are really taking place, leads us to the center of questions about perception and levels of consciousness. The most glaring question is whether there is any reality independent of consciousness. At the level of personal consciousness, can we apprehend reality directly, or are we by necessity bound by the restrictions of our five senses and the mind that organizes our worldview? Is there a shared, collective consciousness that operates beyond our individual consciousness? If there is a collective consciousness, how is it influenced, and what determines its content? Is UFO abduction a product of this shared consciousness? If, as in some cultures, consciousness pervades all elements of the universe, then what function do events like UFO abductions and various mystical experiences play in our psyches and in the rest of the cosmos?

These are questions that are not easily answered. Perhaps all we can do at this point in time is to acknowledge the questions as we listen to the experiences of those who have moved beyond our culturally shared ideas of "reality." The UFO abduction experience, while unique in many respects, bears resemblance to other dramatic, transformative experiences undergone by shamans, mystics, and ordinary citizens who have had encounters with the paranormal. In all of these experiential realms, the individual's ordinary consciousness is radically transformed. He or she is initiated into a non-ordinary state of being which results, ultimately, in a reintegration of the self, an immersion or entrenchment into states and/or knowledge not previously accessible. Sometimes the process is brought on by illness or a traumatic event of some kind, and sometimes the individual is simply pulled into a sequence of states of being from which he or she emerges with new powers and sensitivities. "During his initiation, the Shaman learns how to penetrate into other dimensions of reality and maintain himself there; his trials, whatever the nature of them, endow him with a sensitivity that can perceive and integrate these new experiences ... through the strangely sharpened senses of the Shaman the sacred manifests itself." . . . Like many abductees, the initiate hones his new sensibilities in the service of wisdom that can be used by his people. . . .

The UFO Abduction Phenomenon Worldwide

Another question concerns the worldwide distribution of abductions, or reports of the phenomenon, which may be quite a different matter. UFO abductions have been reported and collected most frequently in Western countries or countries dominated by Western culture and values. Insofar as the abduction phenomenon may be seen as occurring in the context of the global ecological crisis, which is an outcome of the Western materialist/dualistic worldview, it may be that its "medicine" is being administered primarily where it is most needed — in the United States and the other Western industrial countries. Related to this would be the fact that in many cultures the entry into the physical world of vehicles, and even contact with creatures, seemingly from space or another dimension, would not be as noteworthy as in societies where traffic from the spirit world or the "world beyond" into our physical existence would be considered remarkable. . . .

In some countries, where people hold all sorts of beliefs in supernatural beings, abduction experiences are confused or simply connected with other visitations. Cynthia Hind, a researcher from South Africa, reports, "Their reactions are as perhaps Westerners would react to ghosts; not necessarily terrified (or not always so) but certainly wary of what they see." . . .

Abductees overseas seem to have contact with a greater variety of entities than Americans. These range from tiny men to tall, hooded beings, and include naked individuals of both sexes and humanoid beings with every manner or shape of head, feet, and hands. A Dutch couple recently described their UFO visitors as being tiny and appearing in rainbow hues — green, orange, and purple. . . .

But universal properties of the abduction experience remain. Most often, abductees everywhere are compellingly drawn toward a powerful light, often while they are driving or asleep in their beds. Invariably, they are later unable to account for a "lost" period of time, and they frequently bear physical and psychological scars of their experience. These range from nightmares and anxiety to chronic nervous agitation, depression, and even psychosis, to actual physical scars — puncture and incision marks, scrapes, burns, and sores.

Some encounters are more sinister, traumatizing, and mysterious. Others seem to bear a healing and educational intent. Most often, say abductees, they are told or warned by the beings or people not to tell about their experiences. In Puerto Rico, Miguel Figueroa, for example, reported receiving threatening phone calls the day after he saw five little, gray men in the middle of the road. . . .

Even less well documented than the actual abductions are the consequences of the experience. In working with abductees, Gilda Moura, a Brazilian psychologist, reports on the paranormal abilities many Brazilian abductees experience after an encounter. These include increased telepathic abilities, clairvoyance, visions, and the receiving of spiritual messages which are often concerned with world ecology, the future of humankind, and social justice. Many abductees decide to change their profession after their experience. . . .

It is likely that with the publicizing of therapeutic and hypnosis   20
techniques currently being pioneered in the United States, much more information about abduction experiences overseas will be available in coming years; for the rest of the world certainly does not lack awareness of the UFO phenomenon, as is evidenced by the proliferation of UFO bureaus, offices, and research organizations abroad.

Modern-Day Abductions

The modern history of abductions begins with the experience of Barney and Betty Hill in September 1961. . . . The Hills, a stable, respectable interracial couple living in New Hampshire, had suffered from disturbing symptoms for more than two years when they reluctantly consulted Boston psychiatrist Benjamin Simon. Barney was an insomniac and Betty had frequent nightmares. Both were so persistently anxious that it became intolerable for them to continue their lives without looking into disturbing repercussions of the September night in which they could not account for two hours during the return journey from a holiday in Montreal. Except for the distresses related to the incident they described, Dr. Simon reported no psychiatric illness.

On the night of September 19, 1961, the Hills reported that their car was "flagged down" by small, gray humanoid beings with unusual eyes. Before this they had noticed an erratically moving light and then a strange craft. With binoculars Barney had been able to see the creatures inside the craft. The Hills were amnesic about what happened to them during the missing hours until undergoing repeated hypnosis sessions with Dr. Simon. In their meetings with him, Dr. Simon instructed the Hills not to tell each other details of the memories that were emerging. After being taken from their car the Hills said they were led by the beings against their wills onto a craft. Each reported that on the craft they were placed on a table and subjected to detailed medical-like examinations with taking of skin and hair "samples." A needle was inserted into Betty's abdomen and a "pregnancy test" performed. Researchers have discovered recently that a sperm sample was taken from Barney, a fact that was withheld by him and John Fuller, who later wrote about their case, because it was too humiliating at the time for Barney to admit. . . . The beings communicated with the Hills telepathically, nonverbally, "as if it were in English." The Hills were "told to" forget what had happened.

Despite Dr. Simon's belief that the Hills had experienced some sort of shared dream or fantasy, a kind of folie à deux, they persisted in their conviction that these events really happened, and that they had not communicated the corroborating details to each other during the investigation of their symptoms. Barney, who died in 1969 at the age of forty-six, had been particularly reluctant to believe in the reality of the experience lest he appear irrational. "I wish I could think it was an hallucination," he told Dr. Simon when the doctor pressed him. But in the end Barney concluded, "we had seen and been a part of something different than anything I had seen before," and "these things did happen to me." Betty, who continues to speak publicly about her experience, also believes in the reality of these events. In 1975 a film about the Hill case, *The UFO Incident,* starring James Earl Jones as Barney, was shown on television in the United States.

A number of books and articles documented abduction experiences by other individuals in the years following the Hill's testimony. . . . It has been the pioneering research of New York artist and sculptor Budd Hopkins, however, over almost two decades with hundreds of abductees, that has established the essential consistency of the abduction phenomenon. Hopkins's first book, *Missing Time,* published in 1981, documented the unaccounted-for time periods and associated symptoms that indicate that abduction experiences have taken place, as well as the characteristic details of such experiences. . . . Hopkins also found that abduction experiences were possibly associated with previously unexplainable small cuts, body scars, and scoop marks; the narratives even suggested that small objects or "implants" may have been inserted in victims' noses, legs, and other body parts. In his second book, *Intruders,* published in 1987, Hopkins defined the sexual and reproductive episodes that have come to be associated with the abduction phenomenon. . . . Temple University historian David Jacobs has further refined the basic reported pattern of an abduction experience. . . . Jacobs identifies primary phenomena such as manual or instrument examination, staring, and urological-gynecological procedures; secondary events, including machine examination, visualization, and child presentation; and ancillary events, among them miscellaneous additional physical, mental, and sexual activities and procedures.

None of this work, in my view, has come to terms with the profound implications of the abduction phenomenon for the expansion of human consciousness, the opening of perception to realities beyond the manifest physical world and the necessity of changing our place in the cosmic order if the earth's living systems are to survive the human onslaught. . . . 25

Abductions and Abductionists
CURTIS PEEBLES

This book is a chronicle of the flying saucer myth — the system of beliefs that have developed around the idea that alien spacecraft are being seen in Earth's skies. These beliefs did not suddenly spring into existence fully formed. Rather, a set of conflicting ideas originated, the myth was defined, then the beliefs evolved over nearly half a century. Moreover, the flying saucer myth is not a single, monolithic set of doctrines. As soon as the flying saucer myth was defined, schisms began to develop among "believers" — those people who accepted the idea that flying saucers were extraordinary objects. Not all believers held the same beliefs, and these schisms soon led to open warfare. This interaction between believers has been a major influence on the myth's history.

The flying saucer myth not only concerns disk-shaped spaceships and the aliens who supposedly pilot them. Because it also involves how the believers view the role and nature of government, and how the government relates to the people, the U.S. government has had to deal with the flying saucer myth. Presidents have denied their existence; they were a twenty-two-year headache for the Air Force, and were investigated by Congress and the CIA. This interaction both fed the flying saucer myth and brought about the very things the government sought to avoid.

A similar interaction has taken place between the flying saucer myth and the larger society. The flying saucer myth is a mirror to the events of postwar America — the paranoia of the 1950s, the social turmoil of the 1960s, the "me generation" of the 1970s, and the

Curtis Peebles is an aerospace historian whose books include *Watch the Skies! A Chronicle of the Flying Saucer Myth* (1994), from which this selection is taken. [Bibliographic citations have been cut.]

nihilism of the 1980s and the early 1990s. As the flying saucer myth entered popular culture, images and ideas were created which, in turn, shaped the flying saucer myth itself. . . .

Close Encounters of the Third Kind

Although many films had used flying saucer themes, *Close Encounters of the Third Kind* was the only one to fully understand the flying saucer myth. The story is one of ordinary people trying to cope with mythic experiences. Roy Neary (Richard Dreyfuss) is a power company lineman who sees a UFO. He finds himself the victim of subliminal messages which cause him to undertake obsessive, bizarre actions which cause his family to leave. Neary finally realizes he is to go to Devil's Tower, Wyoming. He embarks on an arduous cross-country journey. Overcoming obstacles, he is rewarded with a meeting with the aliens. As the multicolored mothership lifts off with Neary aboard, he rises above his own mundane, earthly existence.

In earlier films, the flying saucers were sources of danger. In *Close Encounters of the Third Kind,* the meeting with the aliens was not to be feared, but to be anticipated. It was this "sense of wonder" that was so lacking in such films as *The Thing* or *Earth vs. the Flying Saucer.*

Close Encounters of the Third Kind defined the shape of the aliens. In the film, "they" were short, with large heads, slanted dark eyes, and light gray skins. Their noses were small and their ears were only small holes. The aliens' bodies were elongated and very thin. The fingers were also long. Their overall appearance was that of a fetus. By the early 1980s, this "shape" would come to dominate abduction descriptions.

The Growth of Abduction Reports

Certain UFOlogists began to specialize in abduction cases. The first such "abductionist" was Dr. R. Leo Sprinkle, a psychologist at the University of Wyoming. Sprinkle was frequently quoted by the tabloids and was on the *National Enquirer*'s Blue Ribbon Panel. Sprinkle's role was critical in shaping both the development of the abduction myth and its acceptance. His "hypnotic sessions with UFO abductees" began in 1967 and 1968 with three cases. It was not until 1974 that Sprinkle had another abduction case (reflecting the post-Condon Report decline in interest). In 1975 there were two cases. There were three cases each in 1976 and 1977 (after *The UFO Incident*). In 1978 (after *Close Encounters of the Third Kind*), Sprinkle worked with ten subjects, while in 1979 there were eighteen abductees. In 1980 he held the first of his annual conferences for UFO abductees and investigators.

This increase in abduction reports was not limited to Sprinkle. UFOlogist David Webb noted that a 1976 search of UFO literature (covering nearly thirty years) showed only 50 abduction-type cases. Yet, over the next two years, about 100 *more* cases were reported, bringing the total to some 150. By the end of the 1970s, the total number of cases exceeded 200. . . .

Budd Hopkins

With the 1980s, a new abductionist appeared — an artist named Budd Hopkins. Long interested in UFOs, the rise in abduction reports attracted Hopkins's attention in 1976. He met "Steven Kilburn." Kilburn had a vague memory of being afraid of a stretch of road, but no UFO sighting. To this point, people claiming to have been abducted said they had seen a UFO and/or occupant. This was followed by a period of "missing time." The "abduction" itself was "remembered" under hypnosis. Kilburn had no such memory. When he was hypnotized, however, Kilburn said he was grabbed by a "big wrench" and was taken aboard a UFO.

To Hopkins, this implied a person could be an "abductee" *with-out* any overt memory. Hopkins began asking people if they had "uneasiness," recurring dreams, or "any event" which might indicate an abduction. It was no longer necessary for a person to have "missing time." *Anyone* could now be an abductee and not realize it. Hopkins believed there might be tens of thousands of abductees — what he called "an invisible multitude." 10

Hopkins published his conclusions in his 1981 book *Missing Time.* He believed "a very long-term, in-depth study is being made of a relatively large sample of humans." The "human specimens" were first abducted as young children. "Monitoring devices" would be implanted in the abductee's nose. This was described as a tiny ball on a long rod. The ball was left in the nasal cavity. The young abductees were then released with no memories of the (alleged) events. Years later, Hopkins believed, once the abductees reached puberty, they would be abducted a second time.

The aliens in Hopkins's abduction cases all followed the shape of those in *The UFO Incident* and *Close Encounters of the Third Kind* — large heads, thin bodies, slanted eyes, and gray skin. The book had several drawings of what became known as "the Grays." *Missing Time* completed the process of defining the shape of the aliens.

Hopkins also speculated on the alien's motivation. He noted several abductees had scars from childhood. He believed tissue samples were being taken. Hopkins suggested the aliens needed a specific genetic structure. Hopkins also suggested the aliens were taking sperm and ova samples. These, he continued, might be for experiments in producing human/alien hybrids.

This expanded the abduction myth; it was now much more "intrusive." In the Pascagoula case, Hickson claimed he was passively "scanned." Now, tissue samples were being taken which left scars. The alleged abductees also showed emotional scars from their supposed experiences — long-lasting anxiety and fear. The "monitoring devices" were a further intrusion. The taking of sperm and ova was, symbolically, the most intrusive of all. Humans were depicted as helpless before the aliens' overwhelming power, reduced to a lab rat.

Hopkins further developed these themes in his 1987 book *Intruders*. In September 1983, he received a letter from "Kathie Davis." She had read *Missing Time* and wrote him to describe a dream she had had in early 1978 of two small beings in her bedroom. From Davis's accounts and twelve other abductees, Hopkins came to believe the aliens had an unmistakable interest "in the process of human reproduction" going back to the Villas-Boas case.

Hopkins described the process as follows — female abductees were identified as donors during their childhood abductions. The implants allowed the aliens to "track" them. When they reached puberty, they would be reabducted. Ova would be removed, its genetic structure altered with alien characteristics, then replanted back in the human. The female abductees would carry the "baby" several months, then again be abducted. The human/alien child would be removed and brought to term.

Males were not immune to such breeding abductions, according to Hopkins. "Ed Duvall" recalled under hypnosis a sexual encounter with a hybrid alien. In this and other cases, a "suction device" was placed over the penis to remove the sperm. None of these breeding abductions could, according to Hopkins, be described as an erotic experience. "It was very perfunctory," Duvall said, "a detached, clinical procedure."

Once the hybrid children were born, the humans who had "donated" sperm or ova were (yet again) abducted and "shown" their "offspring." The aliens even encouraged the humans to hold the "babies" in a kind of bonding exercise, according to Hopkins. Four women either dreamed or remembered under hypnosis being shown a tiny baby — gray in color and oddly shaped. Kathie Davis claimed to have seen two of her *nine* hybrid children and been allowed to name them. Nor did this cycle of abductions end here. Hopkins claimed the children of abductees were themselves targets for abductions.

Some of Hopkins's abductees gave their impressions of why the aliens were doing these things. "Lucille Forman" had the impression of an alien society "millions of years old, of outstanding technology and intellect but not much individuality or warmth . . . the society was dying . . . children were being born and living to a certain age, perhaps preadolescence, and then dying." The aliens were desper-

15

ately trying to survive, through both taking new genetic material and exploiting human emotions.

Hopkins painted a progressively darker picture of the "relation- 20 ship" between humans and aliens. "The UFO phenomenon," Hopkins wrote, "seems able to exert nearly complete control over the behavior of the abductees." He continued that the "implants" had "a controlling function as receivers" and that the abductees can "be made to act as surrogates for their abductors." It is a basic tenet of the abduction myth that these alleged events were truly *alien* experiences — that they are not based on science fiction nor psychological aberrations. Hopkins said, "None of these recollections in any way suggests traditional sci-fi gods and devils . . . the aliens are described neither as all-powerful, lordly presences, nor as satanic monsters, but instead as complex, controlling, physically frail beings."

Dr. David Jacobs (a pro-UFO historian) said in a 1986 MUFON[1] paper, "Contactee stories were deeply rooted in a science fiction model of alien behavior [while] abductee stories have a profoundly alien quality to them that are strikingly devoid of cultural programmatic content."

Thomas E. Bullard said that Betty and Barney Hill had no cultural sources from which they could have derived their story, that they were "entirely unpredisposed."

Entirely Unpredisposed?

Consider the following story — a group of men are in a rural area, at night, when they are abducted. They are rendered unconscious, loaded aboard strange flying machines, and taken to a distant place. They are then programmed with false memories to hide the time they were missing. One of them is converted into a puppet of his abductors. They are then released with no overt memories of what happened. But, years later, two of the group begin having strange, surreal dreams about what was done to them.

This story has many elements of abduction stories — loss of control, loss of memory (i.e., one's soul), and loss of humanity. It is not an abduction story. It has nothing to do with UFOs. It is the plot of the 1962 film *The Manchurian Candidate.*

Despite Hopkins's and Jacobs's claims, the abductee myth has 25 numerous similarities with science fiction. Martin Kottmeyer has noted a number of these. In the film *Killers from Space* an abductee has a strange scar and missing memory. In *Invaders from Mars,* the Martians use implants to control humans. This includes not only adults, but their children as well. In the "Cold Hands, Warm Heart"

---

[1]MUFON (Mutual UFO Network) is an international organization dedicated to a scientific study of the UFO phenomenon. — ED.

episode of *The Outer Limits,* an astronaut (William Shatner) orbiting Venus loses contact with Earth for eight minutes. After returning to Earth, he has dreams that he landed on Venus and saw a Venusian approaching the ship. His body also starts changing into a Venusian.

"Dying planets" such as "Lucille Forman" described are a standard feature of science fiction — in H. G. Wells's masterpiece *War of the Worlds,* the Martians attacked because Mars was dying and Earth seemed their only hope for survival. Similar "dying planet" themes appeared in the films *This Island Earth, The 27th Day, Killers from Space,* and *Earth vs. the Flying Saucers. The Invaders* were "alien beings from a dying planet."

Crossbreeding between humans and aliens was a common science fiction film plot. They include *Devil Girl from Mars, I Married a Monster from Outer Space, The Mysterians, Village of the Damned, Mars Needs Women,* and the *Alien* film series.

The shape of aliens in abduction stories is well within the traditions of science fiction. The "bug-eyed monsters" of 1930s and 1940s pulp magazines often had large, bald heads. This was the shape of the projected image of the Wizard in the *Wizard of Oz.* The aliens in the film *Invasion of the Saucer Men* were "bald, bulgy-brained, googly-eyed, no-nosed," fitting the stereotyped image of UFO aliens. Kottmeyer noted that this "prompts worries that abductees are not only plagiarists, but have bad taste as well." In the 1960s, television series such as *The Twilight Zone* and *The Outer Limits* often featured dome-headed aliens. The original pilot for *Star Trek,* "The Cage" (telecast as the two-part episode "The Menagerie"), had short, large-headed, gray-skinned, bald, physically weak aliens with the power to control human minds.

The reasoning behind this particular shape was best expressed by an *Outer Limits* episode called "The Sixth Finger." The story involves the forced forward evolution of a human (David McCallum). As he evolves, his brain grows, his hair recedes, he becomes telepathic, and can control humans. The idea is that apes have small brains, are hairy, and strong. Modern man, in contrast, has a larger brain, has limited body hair, and is weaker. It therefore seems "right" that a future man would have a huge brain, no hair, and be physically frail.

All these similarities between science fiction concepts and the abduction myth caused Kottmeyer to write, "It seems more sensible to flip Hopkins' allegation around. He says nothing about the aliens of UFO abductions resembling 'sci-fi'. I ask, is there anything about UFO aliens that does not resemble science fiction?"

A final note — Hopkins describes a half human/half alien being lacking the ability to feel emotions. It is just such a being which is the most famous character in all of science fiction — Mr. Spock of *Star Trek.* How "logical."

Questions about Hypnosis

Hopkins's abductees had no overt memories until they were hypnotized. The question becomes whether the abduction story is only a product of being hypnotized. A controlled test of hypnotic abduction accounts was conducted in 1977 by Dr. Alvin H. Lawson, a UFOlogist and English professor at California State University, Long Beach. He and others were dissatisfied with the hypnotic regression of abductees. They decided to ask a group of people with no significant UFO knowledge to imagine an abduction under hypnosis. The hypnotic sessions were conducted by Dr. William C. McCall, an M.D. with decades of clinical hypnosis experience. Lawson and the others had expected the imaginary abductees would need prompting. The result was quite different — Lawson wrote later:

> What startled us at first was the [subject's] ease and eagerness of narrative invention. Quite often, after introducing the situation — such as, "describe the interior" — Dr. McCall would sit back and the [subject] would talk freely with no more prompting than an occasional, "what's happening, now?"

Lawson compared four imaginary abduction accounts with features of four "real" abduction stories. The chart was an exact match. He concluded:

> It is clear from the imaginary narratives that a great many apparent patterns may originate in the mind and so be available to a witness — whether imaginary or "real." If a person who is totally uninformed about UFOs suddenly finds himself in the abduction sequence, it seems safe to assume that the individual's own sensibility will be able to provide under hypnotic regression, pattern details of his encounter which he may or may not have actually experienced in a "real" sense.

The implication of the Lawson study was not that there was a massive number of covert abductions. Rather, it shows that nearly anyone can, under hypnosis, provide an abduction story. Not surprisingly, abductionists and UFO groups have criticized and ignored the Lawson test.

The typical questioning during an abduction hypnotic session 35 goes far beyond "what's happening, now." While researching the book *Mute Evidence,* Daniel Kagan was hypnotized by Dr. Sprinkle. During the session, Dr. Sprinkle said, "Imagine yourself in a spacecraft." There were no UFO images in the recurring dream Kagan was describing. Kagan was so shocked by the attempt to insert a UFO that he came out of the trance. Kagan concluded:

> Sprinkle had just demonstrated how much he had probably been responsible for the UFO imagery reported by so many of his hypnotic subjects. It meant that none of Sprinkle's case histories could be taken seriously, because his role as hypnotist could have been the single most powerful factor in introducing UFO images into the subjects' memories.

Another factor is that many of the stories originate with dreams. The dreams are real, but are they dreams of real events? One indication that they are, in fact, only dreams is the wildly irrational and contradictory nature of the stories. This includes one case in which an "abductee" reported hearing a voice from inside a UFO cry out, "I am Jimmy Hoffa!" Other psychological factors include the abductee's own mental state (even "normal" people can have hallucinations) and such organic brain disorders as temporal lobe epilepsy. Finally, there are the effects of personal experiences: under hypnosis, one abductee gave an extremely outlandish description of the aliens; when the hypnotist asked, "Are you sure?" the abductee responded, "No . . . that was something I saw in the Sunday comic section." Clearly, hypnosis is not the foolproof truth-finding technique the abductionists make it out to be.

In retrospect, it seems clear that the flying saucer myth was always an attempt to find a relationship with the aliens. Earlier myths were about contacts/interactions/struggles between humans and humanlike supernatural beings. Even the conservative Keyhoe had "Operation Lure." The contactees had their own "relationship," rooted in the worldview of the 1950s. When this faded, it was replaced, in the 1960s and 1970s, by the abduction myth, yet another attempt to find a relationship with mythological beings.

This human/alien relationship exactly mirrors society's changing attitudes toward authority, science, and sex. During the contactee era of the 1950s, the grandfatherly "Ike" was president. By the mid-1980s, authority was seen as absolutely evil. Science in the 1950s was seen as utopian. By the 1980s, this had changed into the belief science was antihuman. In 1978, Jose Inacio Alvaro described his alien sexual encounter as being pleasurable. By the 1980s, with the specter of AIDS haunting the bedroom, Hopkins was depicting it as a joyless, technological rape.

The function of mythology is to allow a society to relate to the larger world. This has not changed.

Discussion Questions

1. Does the knowledge that John Mack is a professor of psychiatry at Harvard University Medical School influence your judgment of his conclusions?
2. How would you describe the differences between the prose styles of Mack and Peebles? Dr. Mack writes very well — with grace and authority. Do you think the fact that he *sounds* like an expert is also influential? Find instances of language that conveys the idea of authority — through vocabulary, sentence structure, references to unfamiliar phenomena, etc.
3. What kind of evidence does Mack provide? (Go over his "strict criteria for an abduction case.") How much of that evidence might be considered objective or provable by scientific method?

4. Both Mack and Peebles discuss Budd Hopkins. How do you account for their very different views of him?
5. What is Peebles's principal explanation for the abduction phenomenon? Is it persuasive?
6. Mack and Peebles both mention political events and attitudes. What are they and how have they affected belief in visits by aliens?

EXERCISES

Decide whether the reasoning in the following examples is faulty. Explain your answers.

1. The presiding judge of a revolutionary tribunal, on being asked why people were being executed without trial: "Why should we put them on trial when we know that they're guilty?"
2. Since good nutrition is essential to the health of its citizens, the government should punish people who eat junk food.
3. A research study demonstrated that children who watched *Seinfeld* rather than *Friends* received higher grades in school. So it must be true that *Seinfeld* is more educational than *Friends*.
4. The meteorologist was wrong in predicting the amount of rain for May. Obviously the meteorologist is unreliable.
5. Women ought to be permitted to serve in combat. Why should men be the only ones to face death and danger?
6. If Cher uses Equal, it must taste better than Sweet 'n Low.
7. People will gamble anyway, so why not legalize gambling in this state?
8. Because so much money was spent on public education in the last decade while educational achievement declined, more money to improve education can't be the answer to reversing the decline.
9. He's a columnist for the campus newspaper, so he must be a pretty good writer.
10. We tend to exaggerate the need for standard English. You don't need much standard English for most jobs in this country.
11. It's discriminatory to mandate that police officers must conform to a certain height and weight.
12. A doctor can consult books to make a diagnosis, so a medical student should be able to consult books when being tested.
13. Because this soft drink contains so many chemicals, it must be unsafe.
14. Core requirements should be eliminated. After all, students are paying for their education, so they should be able to earn a diploma by choosing the courses they want.
15. We should encourage a return to arranged marriages in this country since marriages based on romantic love haven't been very successful.
16. I know three redheads who have terrible tempers, and since Annabel has red hair, I'll bet she has a terrible temper, too.
17. Supreme Court Justice Byron White was an All-American football player while at college, so how can you say that athletes are dumb?

18. Benjamin H. Sasway, a student at Humboldt State University in California, was indicted for failure to register for possible conscription. Barry Lynn, president of Draft Action, an antidraft group, said, "It is disgraceful that this Administration is embarking on an effort to fill the prisons with men of conscience and moral commitment."

19. You know Jane Fonda's exercise videos must be worth the money. Look at the great shape she's in.

20. James A. Harris, former president of the National Education Association: "Twenty-three percent of schoolchildren are failing to graduate, and another large segment graduate as functional illiterates. If 23 percent of anything else failed — 23 percent of automobiles didn't run, 23 percent of the buildings fell down, 23 percent of stuffed ham spoiled — we'd look at the producer."

21. A professor at Rutgers University: "The arrest rate for women is rising three times as fast as that of men. Women, inflamed by the doctrines of feminism, are pursuing criminal careers with the same zeal as business and the professions."

22. Physical education should be required because physical activity is healthful.

23. George Meany, former president of the AFL-CIO, in 1968: "To these people who constantly say you have got to listen to these younger people, they have got something to say, I just don't buy that at all. They smoke more pot than we do and if the younger generation are the hundred thousand kids that lay around a field up in Woodstock, New York, I am not going to trust the destiny of the country to that group."

24. That candidate was poor as a child, so he will certainly be sympathetic to the poor if he's elected.

25. When the federal government sent troops into Little Rock, Arkansas, to enforce integration of the public school system, the governor of Arkansas attacked the action, saying that it was as brutal an act of intervention as Russia's sending troops into Hungary to squelch the Hungarians' rebellion. In both cases, the governor said, the rights of a freedom-loving, independent people were being violated.

26. Governor Jones was elected two years ago. Since that time constant examples of corruption and subversion have been unearthed. It is time to get rid of the man responsible for this kind of corrupt government.

27. Are we going to vote a pay increase for our teachers or are we going to allow our schools to deteriorate into substandard custodial institutions?

28. You see, the priests were right. After we threw those virgins into the volcano, it quit erupting.

29. The people of Rome lost their vitality and desire for freedom when their emperors decided that the way to keep them happy was to provide them with bread and circuses. What can we expect of our own country now that the government gives people free food and there is a constant round of entertainment provided by television?

30. From Mark Clifton, "The Dread Tomato Affliction" (proving that eating tomatoes is dangerous and even deadly): "Ninety-two point four percent of juvenile delinquents have eaten tomatoes. Fifty-seven point one percent of the adult criminals in penitentiaries throughout the United

States have eaten tomatoes. Eighty-four percent of all people killed in automobile accidents during the year have eaten tomatoes."

31. "But can you doubt that air has weight when you have the clear testimony of Aristotle affirming that all elements have weight, including air, and excepting only fire?" (From Galileo, *Dialogues Concerning Two New Sciences*)

32. Robert Brustein, artistic director of the American Repertory Theatre, commenting on a threat by Congress in 1989 to withhold funding from an offensive art show: "Once we allow lawmakers to become art critics, we take the first step into the world of Ayatollah Khomeini, whose murderous review of *The Satanic Verses* still chills the heart of everyone committed to free expression." (The Ayatollah Khomeini called for the death of the author, Salman Rushdie, because he had allegedly committed blasphemy against Islam in his novel.)

Critical Listening

33. Listen carefully to a speech by a candidate for public office. Note any fallacies or lapses in logical thinking. Do some kinds of fallacies seem more common than others?

PART TWO

Writing and Researching Arguments

CHAPTER NINE

Writing an Argumentative Paper

The person who understands how arguments are constructed has an important advantage in today's world. Television commercials, political speeches, newspaper editorials, and magazine advertisements, as well as many communications between individuals, all draw on the principles we have examined in the preceding chapters. By now you should be fairly adept at picking out claims, support, and warrants (explicit or unstated) in these presentations. The next step is to apply your skills to writing an argument of your own. The process of using what you have learned will enhance your ability to analyze critically the marketing efforts with which we are all bombarded every day. Mastering the writing of arguments also gives you a valuable tool for communicating with other people in school, on the job, and even at home.

In this chapter we will move through the various stages involved in creating an argumentative paper: choosing a topic, defining the issues, organizing the material, writing the essay, and revising. We will also consider the more general question of how to use the principles already discussed in order to convince a real audience. The more carefully you follow the guidelines set out here and the more thought you give to your work at each point, the better you will be able to utilize the art of argument when this course is over.

FINDING AN APPROPRIATE TOPIC

An old British recipe for jugged hare is said to begin, "First, catch your hare." To write an argumentative paper, you first must choose your topic. This is a relatively easy task for someone writing an argument as part of his or her job — a lawyer defending a client, for example, or an advertising executive presenting a campaign. For a student, however, it can be daunting. Which of the many ideas in the world worth debating would make a good subject?

Several guidelines can help you evaluate the possibilities. Perhaps your assignment limits your choices. If you have been asked to write a research paper, you obviously must find a topic on which research is available. If your assignment is more open-ended, you need a topic that is worth the time and effort you expect to invest in it. In either case, your subject should be one that interests you. Don't feel you have to write about what you know — very often finding out what you don't know will turn out to be more satisfying. You should, however, choose a subject that is familiar enough for you to argue about without fearing you're in over your head.

Invention Strategies

As a starting point, think of conversations you've had in the past few days or weeks that have involved defending a position. Is there some current political issue you're concerned about? Some dispute with friends that would make a valid paper topic? One of the best sources is controversies in the media. Keep your project in mind as you watch TV, read, or listen to the radio. You may even run into a potential subject in your course reading assignments or classroom discussions. Fortunately for the would-be writer, nearly every human activity includes its share of disagreement.

As you consider possible topics, write them down. One that looks unlikely at first glance may suggest others or may have more appeal when you come back to it later. Further, simply putting words on paper has a way of stimulating the thought processes involved in writing. Even if your ideas are tentative, the act of converting them into phrases or sentences can often help in developing them.

Evaluating Possible Topics

Besides interesting you, your topic must interest your audience. Who is the audience? For a lawyer it is usually a judge or jury; for a columnist, anyone who reads the newspaper in which his or her column appears. For the student writer, the audience is to some extent hypothetical. You should assume that your paper is directed at readers who are reasonably intelligent and well informed, but who have no specific knowledge of the subject. It may be useful to imagine you are writing for a local or school publication — this may be the case if your paper turns out well.

Be sure, too, that you choose a topic with two sides. The purpose of an argument is to defend or refute a thesis, which means the thesis must be debatable. In evaluating a subject that looks promising, ask yourself: Can a case be made for the opposing view? If not, you have no workable ground for building your own case.

Finally, check the scope of your thesis. Consider how long your paper will be, and whether you can do justice to your topic in that amount of space. For example, suppose you want to argue in favor of worldwide nuclear disarmament. Is this a thesis you can support persuasively in a short paper? One way to find out is by listing the potential issues or points about which arguers might disagree. Consider the thesis: "The future of the world is in danger as long as nuclear weapons exist." Obviously this statement is too general. You would have to specify what you mean by the future of the world (the continuation of human life? of all life? of the earth itself?) and exactly how nuclear weapons endanger it before the claim would hold up. You could narrow it down: "Human beings are error-prone; therefore as long as nuclear weapons exist there is the chance that a large number of people will be killed accidentally." Though this statement is more specific and includes an important warrant, it still depends on other unstated warrants: that one human being (or a small group) is in the position to discharge a nuclear weapon capable of killing a large number of people; that such a weapon could, in fact, be discharged by mistake, given current safety systems. Can you expect to show sufficient evidence for these assumptions in the space available to you?

By now it should be apparent that arguing in favor of nuclear disarmament is too broad an undertaking. A more workable approach might be to defend or refute one of the disarmament proposals under consideration by the U.S. Congress, or to show that nuclear weapons pose some specific danger (such as long-term water pollution) that is sufficient reason to strive for disarmament.

Can a thesis be too narrow? Certainly. If this is true of the one you have chosen, you probably realized it when you asked yourself whether the topic was debatable. If you can prove your point convincingly in a paragraph, or even a page, you need a broader thesis.

At this preliminary stage, don't worry if you don't know exactly how to word your thesis. It's useful to write down a few possible phrasings to be sure your topic is one you can work with, but you need not be precise. The information you unearth as you do research will help you to formulate your ideas. Also, stating a thesis in final terms is premature until you know the organization and tone of your paper.

To This Point

Let's assume you have surveyed a range of possible topics and chosen one that provides you with a suitable thesis for your paper. Before you go on, check your thesis against the following questions:

1. Is this topic one that will interest both me and my audience?
2. Is the topic debatable?
3. Is my thesis appropriate in scope for a paper of this length?
4. Do I know enough about my thesis to have a rough idea of what ideas to use in supporting it and how to go about finding evidence to back up these ideas?

DEFINING THE ISSUES

Preparing an Initial Outline

An outline, like an accounting system or a computer program, is a practical device for organizing information. Nearly every elementary and high school student learns how to make an outline. What will you gain if you outline your argument? Time and an overview of your subject. The minutes you spend organizing your subject at the outset generally save at least double the time later, when you have few minutes to spare. An outline also enables you to see the whole argument at a glance.

Your preliminary outline establishes an order of priority for your argument. Which supporting points are issues to be defended, which are warrants, and which are evidence? Which supporting points are most persuasive? By constructing a map of your territory, you can identify the research routes that are likely to be most productive. You can also pinpoint any gaps in your reasoning.

List each issue as a main heading in your outline. Next, write below it any relevant support (or sources of support) that you are aware of. Then reexamine the list and consider which issues appear likely to offer the strongest support for your argument. You should number these in order of importance.

Case Study: Coed Bathrooms

To see how we raise and evaluate issues in a specific context, let's look at a controversy that surfaced recently at a large university. Students living in coed dorms elected to retain their coed bathrooms. The university administration, however, withdrew its approval, in part because of growing protests from parents and alumni.

The students raised these issues:

1. The rights of students to choose their living arrangements
2. The absence of coercion on those who did not wish to participate
3. The increase in civility between the sexes as a result of sharing accommodations

4. The practicality of coed bathrooms, which preclude the necessity for members of one sex to travel to a one-sex bathroom on another floor
5. The success of the experiment so far

On the other side, the administration introduced the following issues:

1. The role of the university *in loco parentis*
2. The necessity for the administration to retain the goodwill of parents and alumni
3. The dissatisfaction of some students with the arrangement
4. The inability of immature students to respect the right of others and resist the temptation of sexual activity

Now let's analyze these issues, comparing their strengths and weaknesses.

1. It is clear that not all the issues in this dispute were equally important. The arguers decided, therefore, to give greater emphasis to the issues that were most likely to be ultimately persuasive to their audiences and less attention to those that were difficult to prove or narrower in their appeal. The issue of convenience, for example, seemed a minor point. How much cost is imposed in being required to walk up or down a flight of stairs?

2. It was also clear that, as in several of the other cases we have examined, the support consisted of both factual data and appeals to values. In regard to the factual data, each side reported evidence to prove that

a. The experiment was or was not a success.
b. Civility had or had not increased.
c. The majority of students did or did not favor the plan.
d. Coercion had or had not been applied.

The factual data were important. If the administration could prove that the interests of some students had been injured, then the student case for coed bathrooms would be weakened.

But let us assume that the factual claims either were settled or remained in abeyance. We now turn our attention to a second set of issues, a contest over the values to be served.

3. Both sides claimed adherence to the highest principles of university life. Here the issues, while no easier to resolve, offered greater opportunity for serious and fruitful discussion.

The first question to be resolved was that of democratic control. The students asserted, "We should be permitted to have coed bathrooms because we can prove that the majority of us want them." The students hoped that the university community would agree with the implied analogy: that the university community should resemble a political democracy and that students should have full rights as citizens of that community. (This is an argument also made in regard to other areas of university life.)

The university denied that it was a democracy in which students had equal rights and insisted that it should not be. The administration offered its own analogical proof: Students are not permitted to hire their own teachers or to choose their manner of instruction, their courses of study, their grades, or the rules of admission. The university, they insisted, represented a different kind of community, like a home, in which the experienced are required to lead and instruct the inexperienced.

Students responded by pointing out that coed bathrooms or any other aspect of their living arrangements were areas in which *they* were experts and that freedom to choose living arrangements was not to be confused with a demand for equal participation in academic matters. Moreover, it was also true that in recent years the verdict had increasingly been rendered in favor of rights of special groups as against those of institutions. Students' rights have been among those that have benefited from the movement toward freedom of choice.

4. The second issue was related to the first but introduced a practical consideration, namely, the well-being of the university. The administration argued that more important than the wishes of the students in this essentially minor dispute was the necessity for retaining the support and goodwill of parents and alumni, who are ultimately responsible for the very existence of the university.

The students agreed that this support was necessary but felt that parents and alumni could be persuaded to consider the good reasons in the students' argument. Some students were inclined to carry the argument over goals even further. They insisted that if the university could maintain its existence only at the cost of sacrificing principles of democracy and freedom, then perhaps the university had forfeited its right to exist.

In making our way through this debate, we have summarized a procedure for tackling the issues in any controversial problem.

1. Raise the relevant issues and arrange them in order of importance. Plan to devote more time and space to issues you regard as crucial.
2. Produce the strongest evidence you can to support your factual claims, knowing that the opposing side or critical readers may try to produce conflicting evidence.
3. Defend your value claims by finding support in the fundamental principles with which most people in your audience would agree.
4. Argue with yourself. Try to foresee what kinds of refutation are possible. Try to anticipate and meet the opposing arguments.

ORGANIZING THE MATERIAL

Once you are satisfied that you have identified all the issues that will appear in your paper, you should begin to determine what kind of organization will be most effective for your argument. Now is the time to organize the results of your thinking into a logical and persuasive form. If you have read about your topic, answered questions, and acquired some evidence, you may already have decided on ways to approach your subject. If not, you should look closely at your outline now, recalling your purposes when you began your investigation, and develop a strategy for using the information you have gathered to achieve those purposes.

The first point to establish is what type of thesis you plan to present. Is your intention to make readers aware of some problem? To offer a solution to the problem? To defend a position? To refute a position held by others? The way you organize your material will depend to a great extent on your goal. With that goal in mind, look over your outline and reevaluate the relative importance of your issues. Which ones are most convincing? Which are backed up by the strongest support? Which ones relate to facts, and which concern values?

With these points in mind, let us look at various ways of organizing an argumentative paper. It would be foolish to decide in advance how many paragraphs a paper ought to have; however, you can and should choose a general strategy before you begin writing. If your thesis presents an opinion or recommends some course of action, you may choose simply to state your main idea and then defend it. If your thesis argues against an opposing view, you probably will want to mention that view and then refute it. Both these organizations introduce the thesis in the first or second paragraph (called the *thesis paragraph*). A third possibility is to start establishing that a problem exists and then introduce your thesis as the solution; this method is called *presenting the stock issues*. Although these three approaches sometimes overlap in practice, examining each one individually can help you structure your paper. Let's take a look at each arrangement.

Defending the Main Idea

All forms of organization will require you to defend your main idea, but one way of doing this is simple and direct. Early in the paper state the main idea that you will defend throughout your argument. You can also indicate here the two or three points you intend to develop in support of your claim; or you can raise these later as they come up. Suppose your thesis is that widespread vegetarianism would solve a number of problems. You could phrase it this way: "If the majority of people in this country adopted a vegetarian diet, we would see improvements in the economy, in the health of our people, and in moral sensitivity." You would then develop each of the claims in your list with appropriate data and warrants. Notice that the thesis statement in the first (thesis) paragraph has already outlined your organizational pattern.

Defending the main idea is effective for factual claims as well as policy claims, in which you urge the adoption of a certain policy and give the reasons for its adoption. It is most appropriate when your thesis is straightforward and can be readily supported by direct statements.

Refuting the Opposing View

Refuting an opposing view means to attack it in order to weaken, invalidate, or make it less credible to a reader. Since all arguments are dialogues or debates — even when the opponent is only imaginary — refutation of the other point of view is always implicit in your arguments. As you write, keep in mind the issues that an opponent may raise. You will be looking at your own argument as an unsympathetic reader may look at it, asking yourself the same kinds of critical questions and trying to find its weaknesses in order to correct them. In this way every argument you write becomes a form of refutation.

How do you plan a refutation? Here are some general guidelines.

1. If you want to refute the argument in a specific essay or article, read the argument carefully, noting all the points with which you disagree. This advice may seem obvious, but it cannot be too strongly emphasized. If your refutation does not indicate scrupulous familiarity with your opponent's argument, he or she has the right to say, and often does, "You haven't really read what I wrote. You haven't really answered my argument."

2. If you think that your readers are sympathetic to the opposing view or are not familiar with it, summarize it at the beginning of your paper, providing enough information to give readers an understanding of exactly what you plan to refute. When you summarize, it's important to be respectful of the opposition's views. You don't want to alienate readers who might not agree with you at first.

3. If your argument is long and complex, choose only the most important points to refute. Otherwise the reader who does not have the original argument on hand may find a detailed refutation hard to follow. If the argument is short and relatively simple — a claim supported by only two or three points — you may decide to refute all of them, devoting more space to the most important ones.

4. Attack the principal elements in the argument of your opponent.

   a. Question the evidence. (See pp. 146–52 in the text.) Question whether your opponent has proved that a problem exists.

b. Attack the warrants or assumptions that underlie the claim. (See pp. 186–87 in the text.)
c. Attack the logic or reasoning of the opposing view. (Refer to the discussion of fallacious reasoning on pp. 263–73 in the text.)
d. Attack the proposed solution to a problem, pointing out that it will not work.

5. Be prepared to do more than attack the opposing view. Supply evidence and good reasons in support of your own claim.

Finding the Middle Ground

Although an argument, by definition, assumes a difference of opinion, we know that opposing sides frequently find accommodation somewhere in the middle. As you mount your own argument about a controversial issue, you need not confine yourself to support of any of the differing positions. You may want to acknowledge that there is some justice on all sides and that you understand the difficulty of resolving the issue.

Consider these guidelines for an argument that offers a compromise between competing positions:

1. Early in your essay explain the opposing positions. Make clear the major differences separating the two (or more) sides.
2. Point out, whenever possible, that the opposing sides already agree to some exceptions to their stated positions. Such evidence may prove that the opposing sides are not so extreme as their advocates insist. Several commentators, writing about the budget conflict between Democrats and Republicans in late 1995, adopted this strategy, suggesting that compromise was possible because the differences were narrower than the public believed.
3. Make clear your own moderation and sympathy, your own willingness to negotiate. An example of this attitude appears in an essay on abortion in which the author infers how Abraham Lincoln might have treated the question of abortion rights.

> In this debate I have made my own position clear. It is a pro-life position (though it may not please all pro-lifers), and its model is Lincoln's position on slavery from 1854 until well into the Civil War: tolerate, restrict, discourage. Like Lincoln's, its touchstone is the common good of the nation, not the sovereign self. Like Lincoln's position, it accepts the legality but not the moral legitimacy of the institution that it seeks to contain. It invites argument and negotiation; it is a gambit, not a gauntlet.[1]

---

[1]George McKenna, "On Abortion: A Lincolnian Position," *The Atlantic Monthly,* September 1995, p. 68. (A gauntlet or glove is flung down in order to challenge an opponent to combat; a gambit is the opening move in a chess game, or in the words of one dictionary, "a concession that invites discussion." — ED.)

4. If you favor one side of the controversy, acknowledge that opposing views deserve to be considered. For example, in another essay on abortion, the author, who supports abortion rights, says,

> Those of us who are pro-choice must come to terms with those thoughtful pro-lifers who believe that in elevating the right to privacy above all other values, the most helpless form of humanity is left unprotected and is, in fact, defined away. They deserve to have their views addressed with sympathy and moral clarity.[2]

5. Provide evidence that accepting a middle ground can offer marked advantages for the whole society. Wherever possible, show that continued polarization can result in violence, injustice, and suffering.

6. In offering a solution that finds a common ground, be as specific as possible, emphasizing the part that you are willing to play in reaching a settlement. In an essay titled "Pro-Life and Pro-Choice? Yes!" the author concludes with this:

> Must those of us who abhor abortion, then, reconcile ourselves to seeing it spread unchecked? By no means. We can refuse to practice it ourselves — or, if we are male, beseech the women who carry our children to let them be born, and promise to support them, and mean it and do it. We can counsel and preach to others; those of us who are religious can pray. . . . What we must not do is ask the state to impose our views on those who disagree.[3]

On a different subject, a debate on pornography, the author, who is opposed to free distribution of obscene material, nevertheless refuses to endorse censorship.

> I think that, by enlarging the First Amendment to protest, in effect, freedom of expression, rather than freedom of speech and of the press, the courts made a mistake. The courts have made other mistakes, but I do not know a better way of defining the interests of the community than through legislation and through the courts. So I am willing to put up with things I think are wrong in the hope that they will be corrected. I know of no alternative that would always make the right decisions.[4]

Presenting the Stock Issues

Presenting the stock issues, or stating the problem before the solution, is a type of organization borrowed from traditional debate format. It works for policy claims when an audience must be con-

---

[2]Benjamin C. Schwarz, "Judge Ginsburg's Moral Myopia," *New York Times,* July 30, 1993, Sec. A, p. 27.

[3]George Church, *Time,* March 6, 1995, p. 108.

[4]Ernest van den Haag, *Smashing Liberal Icons: A Collection of Debates* (Washington, D.C.: The Heritage Foundation, 1981), p. 101.

vinced that a need exists for changing the status quo (present conditions) and for introducing plans to solve the problem. You begin by establishing that a problem exists (need). You then propose a solution (plan), which is your thesis. Finally, you show reasons for adopting the plan (advantages). These three elements — need, plan, and advantages — are called the stock issues.

For example, suppose you wanted to argue that measures for reducing acid rain should be introduced at once. You would first have to establish a need for such measures by defining the problem and providing evidence of damage. Then you would produce your thesis, a means for improving conditions. Finally you would suggest the benefits that would follow from implementation of your plan. Notice that in this organization your thesis paragraph usually appears toward the middle of your paper, although it may also appear at the beginning.

Ordering Material for Emphasis

Whichever way you choose to work, you should revise your outline to reflect the order in which you intend to present your thesis and supporting ideas. Not only the placement of your thesis paragraph but also the wording and arrangement of your ideas will determine what points in your paper receive the most emphasis.

Suppose your purpose is to convince the reader that cigarette smoking is a bad habit. You might decide to concentrate on three unpleasant attributes of cigarette smoking: (1) it is unhealthy; (2) it is dirty; (3) it is expensive. Obviously, these are not equally important as possible deterrents. You would no doubt consider the first reason the most compelling, accompanied by evidence to prove the relationship between cigarette smoking and cancer, heart disease, emphysema, and other diseases. This issue, therefore, should be given greater emphasis than the others.

There are several ways to achieve emphasis. One is to make the explicit statement that you consider a certain issue the most important.

> Finally, and *most importantly,* human culture is often able to neutralize or reverse what might otherwise be genetically advantageous consequences of selfish behavior.[5]

This quotation also reveals a second way — placing the material to be emphasized in an emphatic position, either first or last in the paper. The end position, however, is generally more emphatic.

A third way to achieve emphasis is to elaborate on the material to be emphasized, treating it at greater length, offering more data and reasons for it than you give for the other issues.

---

[5]Peter Singer, *The Expanding Circle* (New York: New American Library, 1982), p. 171.

Considering Scope and Audience

With a working outline in hand that indicates the order of your thesis and claims, you are almost ready to begin turning your notes into prose. First, however, it is useful to review the limits on your paper to be sure your writing time will be used to the best possible advantage.

The first limit involves scope. As mentioned earlier, your thesis should introduce a claim that can be adequately supported in the space available to you. If your research has opened up more aspects than you anticipated, you may want to narrow your thesis to one major subtopic. Or you could emphasize only the most persuasive arguments for your position (assuming these are sufficient to make your case) and omit the others. In a brief paper (three or four pages), three issues are probably all you have room to develop. On the other hand, if you suspect your thesis can be proved in one or two pages, look for ways to expand it. What additional issues might be brought in to bolster your argument? Alternatively, is there a larger issue for which your thesis could become a supporting idea?

Other limits on your paper are imposed by the need to make your points in a way that will be persuasive to an audience. The style and tone you choose depend not only on the nature of the subject, but also on how you can best convince readers that you are a credible source. *Style* in this context refers to the elements of your prose — simple versus complex sentences, active versus passive verbs, metaphors, analogies, and other literary devices. *Tone* is the approach you take to your topic — solemn or humorous, detached or sympathetic. Style and tone together compose your voice as a writer.

Many students assume that every writer has only one voice. In fact, a writer typically adapts his or her voice to the material and the audience. Perhaps the easiest way to appreciate this is to think of two or three works by the same author that are written in different voices. Or compare the speeches of two different characters in the same story, novel, or film. Every writer has individual talents and inclinations that appear in most or all of his or her work. A good writer, however, is able to amplify some stylistic elements and diminish others, as well as to change tone, by choice.

It is usually appropriate in a short paper to choose an *expository* style, which emphasizes the elements of your argument rather than your personality. You many want to appeal to your readers' emotions as well as their intellects, but keep in mind that sympathy is most effectively gained when it is supported by believable evidence. If you press your point stridently, your audience is likely to be suspicious rather than receptive. If you sprinkle your prose with jokes or metaphors, you may diminish your credibility by detracting from the substance of your case. Both humor and analogy can be useful tools, but they should be used with discretion.

You can discover some helpful pointers on essay style by reading the editorials in newspapers such as the *New York Times*, the *Washington Post*, or the *Wall Street Journal*. The authors are typically addressing a mixed audience comparable to the hypothetical readers of your own paper. Though their approaches vary, each writer is attempting to portray himself or herself as an objective analyst whose argument deserves careful attention.

Again, remember your goals. You are trying to convince your audience of something; an argument is, by its nature, directed at people who may not initially agree with its thesis. Therefore, your voice as well as the claims you make must be convincing.

To This Point

The organizing steps that come between preparation and writing are often neglected. Careful planning at this stage, however, can save much time and effort later. As you prepare to start writing, you should be able to answer the following questions:

1. Is the purpose of my paper to persuade readers to accept a potentially controversial idea, to refute someone else's position, or to propose a solution to a problem?
2. Can or should my solution also incorporate elements of compromise and negotiation?
3. Have I decided on an organization that is likely to accomplish this purpose?
4. Does my outline arrange my thesis and issues in an appropriate order to emphasize the most important issues?
5. Does my outline show an argument whose scope suits the needs of this paper?
6. What questions of style and tone do I need to keep in mind as I write to ensure that my argument will be persuasive?

WRITING

Beginning the Paper

Having found a claim you can defend and the voice you will adopt toward your audience, you must now think about how to begin. An introduction to your subject should consist of more than just the first paragraph of your paper. It should invite the reader to give attention to what you have to say. It should also point you in the direction you will take in developing your argument. You may want to begin the actual writing of your paper with the thesis paragraph. It is useful to consider the whole paragraph rather than simply the thesis statement for two reasons. First, not all theses are effectively expressed in a single sentence. Second, the rest of the paragraph will be closely related to your statement of the main idea. You may show why you have chosen this topic or why your audience will benefit from reading your paper. You may introduce your warrant, qualify your claim, and in other ways prepare for the body of your argument. Because readers will perceive the whole paragraph as a unit, it makes sense to approach it that way.

Consider first the kind of argument you intend to present. Does your paper make a factual claim? Does it address values? Does it recommend a policy or action? Is it a rebuttal of some current policy or belief? The answers to those questions will influence the way you introduce the subject.

If your thesis makes a factual claim, you may be able to summarize it in one or two opening sentences. "Whether we like it or not, money is obsolete. The currency of today is not paper or coin, but plastic." Refutations are easy to introduce in a brief statement: "Contrary to popular views on the subject, the institution of marriage is as sound today as it was a generation ago."

A thesis that defends a value is usually best preceded by an explanatory introduction. "Some wars are morally defensible" is a thesis that can be stated as a simple declarative opening sentence. However, readers who disagree may not read any further than the first line. Someone defending this claim is likely to be more persuasive if he or she first gives an example of a situation in which war is or was preferable to peace or presents the thesis less directly.

One way to keep such a thesis from alienating the audience is to phrase it as a question. "Are all wars morally indefensible?" Still better would be to prepare for the question:

> Few if any of us favor war as a solution to international problems. We are too vividly aware of the human suffering imposed by armed conflict, as well as the political and financial turmoil that inevitably result. Yet can we honestly agree that no war is ever morally defensible?

Notice that this paragraph gains appeal from use of the first person *we*. The author implies that he or she shares the readers' feelings but has good reasons for believing those feelings are not sufficient grounds for condemning all wars. Even if readers are skeptical, the conciliatory phrasing of the thesis should encourage them to continue reading.

For any subject that is highly controversial or emotionally charged, especially one that strongly condemns an existing situation or belief, you may sometimes want to express your indignation directly. Of course, you must be sure that your indignation can be justified. The author of the following introduction, a physician and writer, openly admits that he is about to make a case that may offend readers.

> Is there any polite way to introduce today's subject? I'm afraid not. It must be said plainly that the media have done about as sorry and dishonest a job of covering health news as is humanly possible, and that when the media do not fail from bias and mendacity, they fail from ignorance and laziness.[6]

If your thesis advocates a policy or makes a recommendation, it may be a good idea, as in a value claim, to provide a short background. The following paragraph introduces an argument favoring relaxation of controls in high schools.

> "Free the New York City 275,000" read a button worn by many young New Yorkers some years ago. The number was roughly the total of students enrolled in the City's high schools.
> The condition of un-freedom which is described was not, however, unique to the schools of one city. According to the Carnegie Commission's comprehensive study of American public education, *Crisis in the Classroom,* public schools across the country share a common characteristic, namely, "preoccupation with order and control." The result is that students find themselves the victims of "oppressive and petty rules which give their schools a repressive, almost prison-like atmosphere."[7]

There are also other ways to introduce your subject. One is to begin with an appropriate quotation.

> "Reading makes a full man, conversation makes a ready man, and writing makes an exact man." So Francis Bacon told us around 1600. Recently I have been wondering how Bacon's formula might apply to present-day college students.[8]

Or you may begin with an anecdote. In the following introduction to an article about the relation between cancer and mental attitude, the author recounts a personal experience.

> Shortly after I moved to California, a new acquaintance sat in my San Francisco living room drinking rose-hip tea and chainsmoking. Like so many residents of the Golden West, Cecil was "into" all things healthy, from jogging to *shiatsu* massage to kelp. Tobacco didn't seem to fit, but he told me confidently that there was no contradiction. "It all

---

[6]Michael Halberstam, "TVs Unhealthy Approach to Health News," *TV Guide,* September 20–26, 1980, p. 24.

[7]Alan Levine and Eve Carey, *The Rights of Students* (New York: Avon Books, 1977), p. 11.

[8]William Aiken, "The Conversation on Campus Today Is, Uh . . . ," *Wall Street Journal,* May 4, 1982, p. 18.

has to do with energy," he said. "Unless you have a lot of negative energy about smoking cigarettes, there's no way they can hurt you; you won't get cancer."[9]

Finally, you may introduce yourself as the author of the claim.

> I wish to argue an unpopular cause: the cause of the old, free elective system in the academic world, or the untrammeled right of the undergraduate to make his own mistakes.[10]

> My subject is the world of Hamlet. I do not of course mean Denmark, except as Denmark is given a body by the play; and I do not mean Elizabethan England, though this is necessarily close behind the scenes. I mean simply the imaginative environment that the play asks us to enter when we read it or go to see it.[11]

You should, however, use such introductions with care. They suggest an authority about the subject that you shouldn't attempt to assume unless you can demonstrate that you are entitled to it.

Guidelines for Good Writing

In general, the writer of an argument follows the same rules that govern any form of expository writing. Your style should be clear and readable, your organization logical, your ideas connected by transitional phrases and sentences, your paragraphs coherent. The main difference between an argument and other kinds of expository writing, as noted earlier, is the need to persuade an audience to adopt a belief or take an action. You should assume your readers will be critical rather than neutral or sympathetic. Therefore, you must be equally critical of your own work. Any apparent gap in reasoning or ambiguity in presentation is likely to weaken the argument.

As you read the essays in this book and elsewhere, you will discover that good style in argumentative writing shares several characteristics:

- Variety in sentence structure: a mixture of both long and short sentences, different sentence beginnings
- Rich but standard vocabulary: avoidance of specialized terms unless they are fully explained, word choice appropriate to a thoughtful argument
- Use of details and examples to illustrate and clarify abstract terms, principles, and generalizations

---

[9]Joel Guerin, "Cancer and the Mind," *Harvard Magazine,* November–December 1978, p. 11.

[10]Howard Mumford Jones, "Undergraduates on Apron Strings," *Atlantic Monthly,* October 1955, p. 45.

[11]Maynard Mack, "The World of Hamlet," *Yale Review,* June 1952, p. 502.

You should take care to avoid the following:

- Unnecessary repetition: making the same point without new data or interpretation
- Exaggeration or stridency, which can create suspicion of your fairness and powers of observation
- Short paragraphs of one or two sentences, which are common in advertising and newspaper writing to get the reader's attention but are inappropriate in a thoughtful essay

In addition to these stylistic principles, seven general points are worth keeping in mind:

1. Although *you*, like *I*, should be used judiciously, it can be found even in the treatment of weighty subjects. Here is an example from an essay by the distinguished British mathematician and philosopher, Bertrand Russell.

> Suppose you are a scientific pioneer and you make some discovery of great scientific importance and suppose you say to yourself, "I am afraid this discovery will do harm": you know that other people are likely to make the same discovery if they are allowed suitable opportunities for research; you must therefore, if you do not wish the discovery to become public, either discourage your sort of research or control publication by a board of censors.[12]

Don't be afraid to use *you* or *I* when it is useful to emphasize the presence of the person making the argument.

2. Don't pad. This point should be obvious; the word *pad* suggests the addition of unnecessary material. Many writers find it tempting, however, to enlarge a discussion even when they have little more to say. It is never wise to introduce more words into a paper that has already made its point. If the paper turns out to be shorter than you had hoped, it may mean that you have not sufficiently developed the subject or that the subject was less substantial than you thought when you selected it. Padding, which is easy to detect in its repetition and sentences empty of content, weakens the writer's credibility.

3. For any absolute generalization — a statement containing words such as *all* or *every* — consider the possibility that there may be at least one example that will weaken the generalization. Such a precaution means that you won't have to backtrack and admit that your generalization is not, after all, universal. A student who was arguing against capital punishment for the reason that all killing was wrong suddenly paused in her presentation and added, "On the

---

[12]"Science and Human Life," in *What Is Science?* edited by James R. Newman (New York: Simon and Schuster, 1955), p. 12.

other hand, if given the chance, I'd probably have been willing to kill Hitler." This admission meant that she recognized important exceptions to her rule and that she would have to qualify her generalization in some significant way.

4. When offering an explanation, especially one that is complicated or extraordinary, look first for a cause that is easier to accept, one that doesn't strain credibility. (In Chapter 8, we called attention to this principle. See pp. 265–66.) For example, a few years ago a great many people were bemused by reports about the mysterious Bermuda Triangle, which had apparently swallowed up ships and planes since the mid-nineteenth century. The forces at work were variously described as space-time warps, UFOs that transported earthlings to other planets, and sea monsters seeking revenge. But a careful investigation revealed familiar, natural causes. A reasonable person interested in the truth would have searched for more conventional explanations before accepting the bizarre stories of extraterrestrial creatures. He or she would also exercise caution when confronted by conspiracy theories that try to account for controversial political events, such as the assassination of John F. Kennedy.

5. Check carefully for questionable warrants. Your outline should specify your warrants. When necessary, these should be included in your paper to link claims with support. Many an argument has failed because it depended on an unstated warrant with which the reader did not agree. If you were arguing for a physical education requirement at your school, you might make a good case for all the physical and psychological benefits of such a requirement. But you would certainly need to introduce and develop the warrant on which your claim was based — that it is the proper function of a college or university to provide the benefits of a physical education. Many readers would agree that physical education is valuable, but they might question the assumption that an academic institution should introduce a nonintellectual enterprise into the curriculum. At any point where you draw a controversial or tenuous conclusion, be sure your reasoning is clear and logical.

6. Avoid conclusions that are merely summaries. Summaries may be needed in long technical papers, but in brief arguments they create endings that are without force or interest. In the closing paragraph you should find a new idea that emerges naturally from the development of the whole argument.

7. Strive for a paper that is unified, coherent, and emphatic where appropriate. A *unified* paper stays focused on its goal and directs each claim, warrant, and piece of evidence toward that goal. Extraneous information or unsupported claims impair unity. *Coherence* means that all ideas are fully explained and adequately connected by transitions. To ensure coherence, give especially close

attention to the beginnings and ends of your paragraphs: Is each new concept introduced in a way that shows it following naturally from the one that preceded it? *Emphasis,* as we have mentioned, is a function partly of structure and partly of language. Your most important claims should be placed where they are certain of receiving the reader's attention: key sentences at the beginning or end of a paragraph, key paragraphs at the beginning or end of your paper. Sentence structure can also be used for emphasis. If you have used several long, complex sentences, you can emphasize a significant point by stating it briefly and simply. You can also create emphasis with verbal flags, such as "The primary issue to consider . . ." or "Finally, we cannot ignore. . . ."

All clear expository prose will exhibit the qualities of unity, coherence, and emphasis. But the success of an argumentative paper is especially dependent on these qualities because the reader may have to follow a line of reasoning that is both complicated and unfamiliar. Moreover, a paper that is unified, coherent, and properly emphatic will be more readable, the first requisite of an effective argument.

REVISING

The final stage in writing an argumentative paper is revising. The first step is to read through what you have written for mistakes. Next, check your work against the guidelines listed under "Organizing the Material" and "Writing." Have you omitted any of the issues, warrants, or supporting evidence on your outline? Is each paragraph coherent in itself? Do your paragraphs work together to create a coherent paper? All the elements of the argument — the issues raised, the underlying assumptions, and the supporting material — should contribute to the development of the claim in your thesis statement. Any material that is interesting but irrelevant to that claim should be cut. Finally, does your paper reach a clear conclusion that reinforces your thesis?

Be sure, too, that the style and tone of your paper are appropriate for the topic and the audience. Remember that people choose to read an argument because they want the answer to a troubling question or the solution to a recurrent problem. Besides stating your thesis in a way that invites the reader to join you in your investigation, you must retain your audience's interest through a discussion that may be unfamiliar or contrary to their convictions. The outstanding qualities of argumentative prose style, therefore, are clarity and readability.

Style is obviously harder to evaluate in your own writing than organization. Your outline provides a map against which to check the structure of your paper. Clarity and readability, by comparison, are somewhat abstract qualities. Two procedures may be helpful. The first is to read two or three (or more) essays by authors whose style you admire and then turn back to your own writing. Awkward spots in your prose are sometimes easier to see if you get away from it and respond to someone else's perspective than if you simply keep rereading your own writing.

The second method is to read aloud. If you have never tried it, you are likely to be surprised at how valuable this can be. Again, start with someone else's work that you feel is clearly written, and practice until you achieve a smooth rhythmic delivery that satisfies you. And listen to what you are reading. Your objective is to absorb the patterns of English structure that characterize the clearest, most readable prose. Then read your paper aloud and listen to the construction of your sentences. Are they also clear and readable? Do they say what you want them to say? How would they sound to a reader? According to one theory, you can learn the rhythm and phrasing of a language as you learn the rhythm and phrasing of a melody. And you will often *hear* a mistake or a clumsy construction in your writing that has escaped your eye in proofreading.

PREPARING THE MANUSCRIPT

Type on one side of 8½-by-11-inch 20-pound white typing paper, double-spacing throughout. Leave margins of 1 to 1½ inches on all sides and indent each paragraph five spaces, or one-half inch if you are preparing your paper on a computer. Unless a formal outline is part of the paper, a separate title page is unnecessary. Instead, beginning about one inch from the top of the first page and flush with the left margin, type your name, the instructor's name, the course title, and the date, each on a separate line; then double-space and type the title, capitalizing the first letter of the first and last words of the title and all other words except articles, prepositions, and conjunctions. Double-space and type the body of the paper.

Number all pages at the top right corner, typing your last name before each page number in case pages are mislaid. If an outline is included, number its pages with lowercase roman numerals.

Proofread the paper carefully for mistakes in grammar, spelling, and punctuation. Make corrections with liquid correction fluid or, if there are only a few mistakes, cross them out and neatly write the correction above the line. If you have used a word-processing program, correct the errors and reprint the pages in question.

REVIEW CHECKLIST
FOR ARGUMENTATIVE PAPERS

A successful argumentative paper meets the following criteria:

1. It presents a thesis that is of interest to both the writer and the audience, is debatable, and can be defended in the amount of space available.
2. Each statement offered in support of the thesis is backed up with enough evidence to give it credibility. Data cited in the paper come from a variety of sources. All quotations and direct references to primary or secondary sources are fully documented.
3. The warrants linking claims to support are either specified or implicit in the author's data and line of reasoning. No claim should depend on an unstated warrant with which skeptical readers might disagree.
4. The thesis is clearly presented and adequately introduced in a thesis paragraph, which indicates the purpose of the paper.
5. Supporting statements and data are organized in a way that builds the argument, emphasizes the author's main ideas, and justifies the paper's conclusions.
6. All possible opposing arguments are anticipated and refuted.
7. The paper is written in a style and tone appropriate to the topic and the intended audience. The author's prose is clear and readable.
8. The manuscript is clean, carefully proofed, and typed in an acceptable format.

CHAPTER TEN

Researching an Argumentative Paper

The success of any argument, short or long, depends in large part on the quantity and quality of the support behind it. Research, therefore, can be crucial for any argument outside your own experience. Most papers will benefit from research in the library and elsewhere because development of the claim requires facts, examples, statistics, and informed opinions that are available only from primary and secondary research sources. This chapter offers information and advice to help you work through the steps of writing a research paper, from getting started to preparing the finished product.

GETTING STARTED

The following guidelines will help you keep your research on track:

1. Focus your investigation on building your argument, not merely on collecting information about the topic. Do follow any promising leads that turn up from the sources you consult, but don't be diverted into general reading that has no direct bearing on your thesis.

2. Look for at least two pieces of evidence to support each point you make. If you cannot find sufficient evidence, you may need to revise or abandon the point.

3. Use a variety of sources. Check not only different publications (books, magazines, journals, newspapers, and so on) but information drawn from different fields as well.

4. Be sure your sources are authoritative. We have already pointed out elsewhere the necessity for examining the credentials of sources. Although it may be difficult or impossible for those outside the field to conclude that one authority is more trustworthy than another, some guidelines are available. Articles and essays in scholarly journals are probably more authoritative than articles in college newspapers. Authors whose credentials include many publications and years of study at reputable institutions are probably more reliable than newspaper columnists and the so-called man in the street. However, we can judge reliability much more easily if we are dealing with facts and inferences than with values and emotions.

5. Don't let your sources' opinions outweigh your own. Your paper should demonstrate that the thesis and ideas you present are yours, arrived at after careful reflection and supported by research. The thesis need not be original, but your paper should be more than a collection of quotations or a report of the facts and opinions you have been reading. It should be clear to the reader that the quotations and other materials support *your* claim and that *you* have been responsible for finding and emphasizing the important issues, examining the data, and choosing between strong and weak opinions.

6. Prepare for research by learning your way around your local or university library. Locate the computerized catalog access system and practice using the system's search techniques. Identify the reference and information databases that are available electronically or on CD-ROM, noting those which index and abstract articles and those which provide full-text retrieval of the items. Know where the copy machines are and whether you need money or a key-card to use them. Finally, locate the reference center and reference librarians in case you need help.

MAPPING RESEARCH: A SAMPLE OUTLINE

To explore a range of research activities, let's suppose that you are preparing a research paper, six to ten pages long. You have chosen to defend the following thesis: *Conventional zoos should be abolished because they are cruel to animals and cannot provide the benefits to the public that they promise.* To keep your material under control and give direction to your reading, you would sketch a preliminary outline, which might look like this:

Why We Don't Need Zoos

I. Moral Objection: Animals have fundamental right to liberty
  A. Must prove animals are negatively affected by captivity
    1. research?

2. research?
B. Must refute claims that captivity is not detrimental to animals
   1. Brownlee's description of dolphin: "seeming stupor"; eating "half-heartedly"; not behaving like wild dolphins
   2. Personal experience: watching leopards running in circles in cages for hours

II. Practical Objection: Zoos can't accomplish what they claim to be their goals
   A. "Educational benefits" zoo provides are inaccurate at best: Public is not learning about wild animals at all but about domesticated descendants of same (support with research from [I.A] above)
   B. Conservation programs at zoos are ineffective
      1. It's difficult to breed animals in zoos
      2. Resultant offspring, when there is any, is victim of inbreeding. Leads to inferior stock that will eventually die out (research?)

Now you need to begin the search for the materials that will support your argument. There are two principal ways of gathering the materials — primary research and secondary research. Most writers will not want to limit themselves to one kind of research, but one method may work better than another for a particular project.

USING SOURCES: PRIMARY RESEARCH

The term *primary research* describes the search for firsthand information in the field — that is, outside the library. By firsthand we mean information taken directly from the original source. It can include interviews and conversations, surveys, questionnaires, personal observations, and experiments. If your topic relates to a local issue, one involving your school or your town, or is based on the experience of someone whose story has been unreported, firsthand information may be more useful than library research. The library, however, is also a source of original materials. For example, documents containing raw data that have not yet been interpreted — such as statistics compiled by the Census Bureau of the United States — will be most readily available in the library.

One of the rewards of primary research is that it often generates new information which in turn produces new interpretations of familiar conditions. It is a favored method for anthropologists and sociologists, and most physical and natural scientists use observation and experiment at some point as essential tools in their research. Notice that both of the student research papers at the end of this chapter used firsthand information gained from personal observation and interviews in addition to their secondary library research.

Consider the sample thesis that *zoos should be abolished.* Remember that you need to prove that *zoos are cruel to animals* and that *they cannot provide the benefits to the public that they promise.* It is possible to go directly to primary sources without consulting books or journals. For example:

- Phone the local area chapter of any animal rights group and ask to interview members on their opinions concerning zoos.

- Talk to the veterinarian on call at your local zoo and ask about animal injuries, illnesses, neuroses, and so forth.

- Search the World Wide Web for sites sponsored and developed by the groups associated with the animal rights movement. Many such informational sites will provide the text of current or proposed laws concerning this issue.

- Locate Internet newsgroups or discussion lists devoted to animal rights and identify experts in the field such as animal scientists who would be willing to provide authoritative opinions for your paper.

The information gleaned from primary research can be used directly to support your claim, or can provide a starting point for secondary research at the library.

USING SOURCES: SECONDARY RESEARCH

For freshman research papers the most common resource is still the library. If you were going to write a research paper on why we don't need zoos, you would probably want to rely on materials available in the library for most of your evidence. Although you could collect some firsthand information by visiting a zoo yourself (as did the author of the paper at the end of this chapter) and by interviewing zoo directors and other animal scientists, the published opinions of a wide range of scholars will be far more easily obtained in the library and will probably carry more weight in your argument. Having drawn up a preliminary outline to help map out your reading, how can you most effectively use the library to research the fate of wild animals in captivity?

It's a good idea to consult the librarian before starting your research; he or she will be able to direct you to specific reference works relevant to your subject, which could save you a lot of time.

Your library contains useful systems for retrieving material of all kinds, including the catalog access system; dictionaries and encyclopedias; indexes to magazines, newspapers, journals, and specialized print sources; abstracting services; and on-line and CD-ROM databases that may or may not provide full-text access to selected items.

Catalog Access Systems

Most libraries have replaced their card catalogs with computerized *on-line public access catalogs* (OPACs). These catalog systems use machine-readable cataloging (MARC) records, or bibliographic records, to provide the information traditionally shown on catalog cards. A MARC record includes

- a description of the item, including title, edition, material-specific details, content notes, publication information, and physical description
- main entry and added entry, providing alphabetic catalog access points such as subtitles, authors, series titles, and so on
- subject headings and subject added entries

Sample On-Line Catalog Record
You searched for the TITLE: animal rights movement

```
CALL #        Z7164.C45 M38 1994.
AUTHOR        Manzo, Bettina, 1943-
TITLE         The animal rights movement in the United States, 1975-
                 1990 : an annotated bibliography / by Bettina Manzo.
IMPRINT       Metuchen, N.J. : Scarecrow Press, 1994.
PHYS DESCR    xi, 296 p. ; 23 cm.
NOTE          Includes indexes.
CONTENTS      Animal rights movement -- Activists and organizations --
                 Philosophy, ethics and religion -- Law and legislation
                 -- Factory farming and vegetarianism -- Trapping and
                 fur industry -- Companion animals -- Wildlife --
                 Circuses, zoos, rodeos, dog
SUBJECT       Animal rights movement --United States --Bibliography.
              Animal rights --United States --Bibliography.
              Animal experimentation --United States --Bibliography.
OCLC #        30671149.
ISBN/ISSN     GB95-17241.
```

- call numbers, such as Dewey or Library of Congress
- shelf list information, such as the source of the book and its price

The place provided on the record for each of these pieces of information is called a *field*. The best of the computerized catalog access systems allows users to search many of these fields for selected types of information. For example, you can search for "animal rights" within the Subject or Content Notes fields, or "zoos" within the Title field. Generally, computerized library catalogs can be searched by

- author
- title
- subject, or
- words found in the titles, content notes, and subjects.

Most on-line catalogs also enable users to search efficiently by means of *Boolean logic* that combines search terms using the words AND, OR, and NOT. In Boolean logic searching, combining terms with AND means that the bibliographic record has to contain both terms. For example, when you search for the phrase "animal rights AND zoos," the computer finds MARC records that contain both the terms *animal rights* AND *zoos,* thus sparing you from having to read through many items on zoos which have nothing to say about animal rights. Searching for "dogs OR cats" provides all records that contain either the word *dogs* OR the word *cats*. Using NOT in a search limits the results to records that contain the first search term, but *not* the second one, as in "zoos NOT petting." Additionally, after your initial search, the group of resulting MARC records can also be limited by language, publication date, and so on.

On-line public access catalogs allow much more comprehensive searches for items relevant to your paper topic than were ever possible with the card catalog, because the computer can search the entire library collection at once. When you find a citation for a book or item that interests you, print the MARC record so that you can locate the item on the library shelves by using the Call Number. In addition, if the item is a good fit for your topic, identify its Subject Headings and words in the Content Notes field. By using these terms in another search, you will most likely find similar items. Ideally, a good on-line catalog and focused search will provide you with plenty of material relevant to your topic that can be used to support your claim.

Encyclopedias

General and subject-specific encyclopedias can provide useful overviews and valuable cross references of your topic area. Print versions of these sources will be on your library's shelves, but you should also check to see if the library has any on-line or CD-ROM versions.

In the nonprint versions, it is possible to search every word of the encyclopedia. By combining search terms using Boolean logic, you can quickly obtain a comprehensive collection of information on your topic. In newer on-line and multimedia CD-ROM encyclopedias, entries contain *hyperlinks* to their cross references. Hyperlinks let you click on a photo or a word within the text and instantly access that part of the encyclopedia where the linked topic is located. For example, clicking on the word *zoos* within an entry on the "animal rights movement" will instantly connect you to the "zoo" entry in the encyclopedia. In addition to general encyclopedias, others you might find useful include the following:

- *Encyclopedia of Crime and Justice*
- *Encyclopedia of Psychology*
- *Encyclopedia of Educational Research*
- *Encyclopedia of Environmental Sciences*
- *Encyclopedia of Religion*
- *Encyclopedia of Biological Sciences*
- *International Encyclopedia of Social Sciences*

Indexes and Abstracts

Indexes serve to locate information within other documents, whereas abstracts provide a summary of content. In the print version of indexes and abstracts, entries are usually organized by the author's name, title of the article, or subject of the article. Newer CD-ROM and on-line database versions have powerful search capabilities and allow focused searches on many access points by using Boolean logic to combine terms and limit the information found to the desired topic.

Many of the sources listed below are fast becoming available as full-text databases, in which the full document, paper, or article and all bibliographic citation information are provided. Many newspapers, magazines, and journals are already available in full text on CD-ROM or on-line. In order to simplify your research, ask the reference librarian at your library which databases provide full-text article retrieval, and begin your search with those.

For a controversial or current topic, look at the most recent citations first. If you are researching a specific event, start your search by limiting it to the year in which the event took place. Give yourself enough time to use your library's interlibrary loan system should you need to retrieve articles from journals not available at your university.

General Magazine Sources. In order to locate articles about your subject, you will want to use magazine indexes and abstracts which cover current events, hobbies, education, and popular culture.

- *Readers' Guide to Periodical Literature* indexes more than 200 magazines.
- *Readers' Guide Abstracts* provides summaries of many of the articles.
- *Magazine Index* indexes more than 400 popular magazines.
- *Academic Index* covers more than 400 scholarly and general interest periodicals.
- *Magazine ASAP* provides the full text of over 120 magazines.
- *Periodical Abstracts* includes 450 magazines, with full text available.
- *ArticleFirst* is an index of periodicals.
- *ABI Inform* includes full-text business articles.

Newspaper Sources. Newspaper indexes provide coverage of national, international, regional, and local news topics. Most well-known indexes are now available on CD-ROM and on-line, as well as in print. Many include comprehensive abstracts; more and more are providing the full text of the articles. These indexes are an excellent source for articles on current events and controversial topics.

- *New York Times Index*
- *National Newspaper Index*
- *Newspaper Abstracts*

Many newspapers are available in full text and searchable through on-line databases such as NEXIS, Dow Jones News Retrieval, and Data Times and also through consumer on-line services such as Compuserve, Prodigy, and America Online.

Specialized Sources. Specialized indexes and abstracts focus on more sophisticated articles from scholarly and professional journals and magazines. The articles will be more difficult to read but will be more substantial and authoritative for use as support for your claim. They include

- *Applied Science & Tech Index*
- *Art Index*
- *Biography Index*
- *Book Review Index*
- *Psychological Abstracts*

- *Sociological Abstracts*
- *Education Index*
- *Dissertation Abstracts*
- ERIC (education)
- *Essay and General Literature Index*
- *PsychInfo* (psychological literature)
- *Business Periodicals Index*
- *Biological Abstracts*
- *Chemical Abstracts*
- *Historical Abstracts*

Database Services

Many of the sources listed previously are also available through services that offer access to large collections of databases. Within these databases are millions of documents drawn from a wide array of subject areas. These one-stop-shopping services will allow you to search simultaneously, for example, *Biological Abstracts, ABI Inform,* and *Medline.* Specialized databases exist for almost any discipline you would want to search, but you should find out which services your library subscribes to and what databases are contained there before you decide to consult any one of them.

- DIALOG contains over 450 databases from a broad range of disciplines. Particularly noted for its collection of business, science, and technology databases.
- ERIC, the Educational Research Information Center, provides abstracts of educational research and indexes more than 700 journals.
- DataStar, Europe's leading on-line service, provides over 350 databases.
- LEXIS-NEXIS has 172 "libraries" containing thousands of sources. Noted for its law and business collections.
- Dow Jones News Retrieval contains more than 3,000 publications.
- OCLC, the Online Computer Library Center, provides shared cataloging.
- WorldCat is a database containing more than 26 million records from more than 15,000 libraries worldwide.
- MedLine contains thousands of sources from the medical field.
- OVID Online provides bibliographic access to more than 80 major databases in medicine, education, psychology, sociology, and business.

Internet and World Wide Web

The Internet is a fast-growing web of educational, corporate, and research computer networks around the world. The World Wide Web, a subset of the Internet, consists of millions of "pages," or small collections of text, graphics, pictures, videos, sound, and hyperlinks to other pages containing related material.

The Internet and World Wide Web can be valuable sources of primary and secondary information for your paper. Hundreds of magazines, newspapers, books, and electronic journals have Web and Internet sites that allow searching and provide citations or full-text articles. Web pages exist on practically any topic of current interest, including some of the topics addressed in this book's selections — human and animal rights issues, politics, and immigration.

Many professionals subscribe to E-Mail Discussion Lists devoted to their professional subject areas, and these lists can be used for primary research or as expert support for a claim. Usenet newsgroups are a great source of information on just about any topic. Government sites provide statistical, economic, and census information. Trade and professional associations and many consumer and human interest groups have developed informational, interactive Web pages.

One note of caution: With millions of Internet and World Wide Web sites currently up and running, the reliability of the information found on them is very much a concern. Make sure you know who sponsored or developed the site where the information resides. Most reliable sites will tell you who is updating the information and when the last update was done.

READING WITH A PURPOSE

When you begin studying your sources, read first to acquire general familiarity with your subject. Make sure that you are covering both sides of the question — in this case arguments both for and against the existence of zoos — as well as facts and opinions from a variety of sources. In investigating this subject, you will encounter data from biologists, ecologists, zoo directors, anthropologists, animal-rights activists, and ethical philosophers; their varied points of view will contribute to the strength of your claim.

As you read, look for what seem to be the major issues. They will probably be represented in all or most of your sources. For the claim about zoos the major issues may be summarized as follows: (1) the fundamental right wild animals have to liberty; (2) the harm done to animals who are denied this right and kept in captivity. On the other side, these issues will emerge: (1) the lack of concrete evidence that animals suffer or are harmed by being in zoos; (2) the benefits, in terms of entertainment, education, and conservation efforts that the public derives from zoos. The latter two, of course, are the issues you will have to refute. Your note taking should emphasize these important issues.

Record questions as they occur to you in your reading. Why do zoos exist? What are their major goals, and how well do they meet them? What happens to animals who are removed from the wild and placed in zoos? What happens to animals born and reared in captivity? How do these groups compare with their wild counterparts, who are free to live in their natural habitats? Do animals really have a right to liberty? What are the consequences of denying them this right? Are there consequences to humanity?

Taking Notes

While everyone has his or her own method for taking notes, here are a few suggestions that should be useful to any writer, including those working on a word processor.

Note Card with Quotation

> Hediger   25
>
> "The wild animal, with its marked tendency to escape, is notorious for the fact that it is never completely released from that all-important activity, avoiding enemies, even during sleep, but is constantly on the alert."

Note Card with Summary

> Hediger   25
>
> Animals who live in the wild have to be on the watch for predators constantly.

*Note
Card
with
Statistics*

> Reiger   32
>
> By end of decade, worldwide extinction rate will
> be one species per hour.
>
> Other statistics, too, in Reiger, "The Wages of
> Growth," <u>Field and Stream</u>, July 1981:32.

*Bibliography
Note
Card*

> Hediger, Heini. <u>The Psychology and Behavior
> of Animals in Zoos and Circuses</u>. Trans.
> Geoffrey Sircom. New York: Dover, 1968.

Summarize instead of quoting long passages, unless you feel the quotation is more effective than anything you can write and can provide crucial support for your argument. Summarizing as you read can save you a great deal of time.

When you do quote, make sure to quote exactly. Copy the material word for word, leaving all punctuation exactly as it appears and inserting ellipsis points if you delete material. Make sure to enclose all quotations in quotation marks and to copy complete information about your source, including page numbers and publishing information as well as the author's name and the title of the book or article. If you quote an article that appears in an anthology or collection, make sure you record complete information about the book itself.

Record complete bibliographical information for each source *as you use it*. That way you will have all the information necessary to document your paper when you need it. Some people find it useful to keep two sets of note cards: one set for the bibliographical information and one set for the notes themselves. Each source appears on one card by itself, ready to be arranged in alphabetical order for the Works Cited or References page of the paper.

If you use a word processor, you can record information in any number of ways; the best may be to open a file for each source, enter the bibliographic information, and directly type into the file a series of potentially useful quotations, paraphrases, and summaries. For each entry, make sure to note the correct page reference as you go along, and indicate clearly whether you are quoting, paraphrasing, or summarizing. The material you record can then be readily integrated into your research paper by cutting and pasting from the source files, thus eliminating the need to retype and reducing the chance of error. Resist the temptation to record nothing but direct quotations; this will only postpone the inevitable work of summarizing, paraphrasing, and composing involved in thinking critically about your topic.

As you take notes, refer to your outline frequently to ensure that you are acquiring sufficient data to support all the points you intend to use. You will also be revising your outline during the course of your research, as issues are clarified and new ones emerge. Keeping close track of your outline will prevent you from recording material that is interesting but not relevant. If you aren't sure whether you will want to use a certain piece of information later, don't copy the whole passage. Instead, make a note for future reference so that you can find it again if you need it. Taking too many notes is, however, preferable to taking too few, a problem that will force you to go back to the library for missing information. For the ideas and quotations in your notes, you should always take down enough information to enable you to find the references again as quickly as possible.

When researching your topic, you will find words and ideas put together by other people that you will want to use in your paper. Relying on the knowledge of others is an important part of doing research; expert opinions and eloquent arguments will help support your claims when your own expertise is limited. But remember, this is *your* paper. Your ideas and your insights into other people's ideas are just as important as the information you uncover at the library. Try to achieve a balance between solid information and original interpretation.

Quoting

You may want to quote passages or phrases from your sources if they express an idea in words more effective than your own. In this particular project, you might come across a statement that provides succinct, irrefutable evidence for an issue you wish to support. If the author of this statement is a professional in his or her field, someone with a great deal of authority on the subject, it would be appropriate to quote that author. Suppose, during the course of your research for the zoo paper, you find that many sources agree that zoos don't have the money or space necessary to maintain large enough animal populations to ensure successful captive breeding programs. But so far you only have opinions to that effect. You have been unable to find any concrete documentation of this fact until you come across Ulysses S. Seal's address to the National Zoological Park Symposia for the Public, September 1982. Here is how you could use Seal's words in your paper (using reference citation style of the American Psychological Association):

> Bear in mind that "none of these [zoo] budgets is allocated specifically for species preservation. Zoos have been established primarily as recreational institutions and are only secondarily developing programs in conservation, education and research" (Seal, 1982, p. 74).

Notice the use of brackets (not parentheses) in the first sentence, which enclose material that did not appear in the original source but is necessary for clarification. Brackets must be used to indicate any such changes in quoted material.

Quotations should be introduced logically and gracefully in your text. Make sure that the quoted material either supports or illustrates the point you have just made or the point you are about to make and that your writing remains grammatically correct once the quotation is introduced.

Quotations are an important tool for establishing your claims, but it is important not to overuse them. If you cannot say most of what you want to say in your own words, you probably haven't thought hard enough about what it is you want to say.

Paraphrasing

Paraphrasing involves restating the content of an original source in your own words. It is most useful when the material from your source is too long for your paper, can be made clearer to the reader by rephrasing, or is written in a style markedly different from your own.

A paraphrase should be as true to the original source as you can make it: Do not change the tone or the ideas, or even the order in which the ideas are presented. Take care not to allow your own opinions to creep into your paraphrase of someone else's argument. Your readers should always be aware of which arguments belong to you and which belong to outside sources.

Like a quotation, a paraphrase must *always* include documentation, or you will be guilty of plagiarism. Even though you are using your own words, the ideas in a paraphrase belong to someone else, and that person deserves credit for them. One final caveat: When putting a long passage into your own words, beware of picking up certain expressions and turns of phrase from your source. If you do end up using your source's exact words, make sure to enclose them in quotation marks.

Below is a passage from Shannon Brownlee's "First It Was 'Save the Whales,' Now It's 'Free the Dolphins'" (*Discover* Dec. 1986: 70–72), along with a good paraphrase of the passage and two unacceptable paraphrases.

ORIGINAL PASSAGE:

But are we being good caretakers by holding a dolphin or a sea lion in a tank? Yes, if two conditions are met: that they're given the best treatment possible and, no less important, that they're displayed in a way that educates and informs us. Captive animals must be allowed to serve as ambassadors for their species (Brownlee, 1986, p. 72).

A PARAPHRASE THAT PLAGIARIZES:

In "First It Was 'Save the Whales,' Now It's 'Free the Dolphins,'" Shannon Brownlee (1986) argues that it's all right for people to hold animals in captivity as long as (1) the animals are treated as well as possible, and (2) the animals are displayed in a way that educates the public. Brownlee insists that animals be allowed to serve as "ambassadors for their species" (p. 72).

A PARAPHRASE THAT ALTERS THE
MEANING OF THE ORIGINAL PASSAGE:

According to Shannon Brownlee (1986), a captive animal is being treated fairly as long as it's kept alive and its captivity gives people pleasure. In her essay, "First It Was 'Save the Whales,' Now It's 'Free the Dolphins,'" she argues that people who keep animals in cages are responsible to the animals in only two ways: (1) they should treat their captives as well as possible (even if a small tank is all that can be provided), and (2) they should make sure that the spectators enjoy watching them (p. 72).

A GOOD PARAPHRASE:

Shannon Brownlee (1986) holds that two criteria are necessary in order for the captivity of wild animals to be considered worthwhile. First, the animals should be treated as well as possible. Second, their captivity should have educational value for the people who come to look at them. "Captive animals," Brownlee claims, "must be allowed to serve as ambassadors for their species" (p. 72).

Summarizing

A summary is like a paraphrase, but it involves shortening the original passage as well as putting it in your own words. It gives the gist of the passage. Summarizing is useful when the material from your source is too long for the purposes of your paper. As with a paraphrase, a summary should not alter the meaning of the original passage.

In the paper at the end of this chapter, for instance, the statement, "It is generally acknowledged that there is a great deal of difficulty involved in breeding zoo animals" is not a direct quotation, but the idea comes from Jon Luoma's article in *Audubon*. The statement in the paper is both a summary and a paraphrase. Returning to the source makes it clear that neither quoting nor paraphrasing would have been suitable choices in this instance, since for the writer's purposes it was possible to reduce the following passage from Luoma's article to one sentence.

> But the successful propagation of entire captive species poses awesome management problems. . . . Sanford Friedman, the Minnesota Zoo's director of biological programs, had explained to me that long-term maintenance of a species in captivity demands solutions to these fundamental problems. "First, we have to learn *how* to breed them. Second, we have to decide *who* to breed. And third, we have to figure out *what* to do with them and their offspring once we've bred them."

This passage is far too long to include in a brief research paper, but it is easily summarized without losing any of its effectiveness.

Avoiding Plagiarism

Plagiarism is the use of someone else's words or ideas without adequate acknowledgment — that is, presenting such words or ideas as your own. Putting something in your own words is not in itself a defense against plagiarism; the source of the ideas must be identified as well. Giving credit to the sources you use serves three important purposes: (1) It reflects your own honesty and seriousness as a researcher; (2) it enables the reader to find the source of the reference and read further, sometimes to verify that the source has been correctly used; and (3) it adds the authority of experts to your argument. Deliberate plagiarism is nothing less than cheating and theft, and it is an offense that deserves serious punishment. Accidental plagiarism can be avoided if you take a little care when researching and writing your papers.

The writer of the zoo paper, for instance, uses and correctly introduces the following direct quotation by James Rachels:

As James Rachels (1976) writes:

> Humans have a right to liberty because they have various
> other interests that will suffer if their freedom is unduly
> restricted. The right to liberty--the right to be free of external
> constraints on one's actions--may then be seen as derived
> from a more basic right not to have one's interests
> needlessly harmed. (p. 210)

If the writer of the zoo paper had chosen to state this idea more briefly, in her own words, the result might have been something like this: "Human beings believe in their fundamental right to liberty because they all agree that they would suffer without it. The right to liberty, then, stems from the right not to suffer unnecessarily." Although the wording has been significantly altered, if this statement appeared as is, undocumented, the author of the paper would be guilty of plagiarism because the ideas are not original. To avoid plagiarism, the author needs to include a reference to James Rachels at the beginning of the summary and a citation of the page number at the end. Taking care to document sources is an obvious way to avoid plagiarism. You should also be careful in taking notes and, when writing your paper, indicating where your ideas end and someone else's ideas begin.

When taking notes, make sure either to quote word-for-word *or* to paraphrase: one or the other, not a little bit of both. If you quote, enclose any language that you borrow from other sources in quotation marks. That way, when you look back at your note cards weeks later, you won't mistakenly assume that the language is your own. If you know that you aren't going to use a particular writer's exact words in your paper, then take the time to summarize that person's ideas right away. That will save you time and trouble later.

When using someone else's ideas in your paper, always let the reader know where that person's ideas begin and end. Here is an example from the zoo paper:

> When zoo animals do mate successfully, the offspring is often
> weakened by inbreeding. According to geneticists, this is because a
> population of 150 breeder animals is necessary in order to "assure
> the more or less permanent survival of a species in captivity"
> (Ehrlich & Ehrlich, 1981, p. 211).

The phrase "according to geneticists" indicates that the material to follow comes from another source, cited parenthetically at the end of the borrowed material. If the student had not included the phrase "according to geneticists," it might look as if she only borrowed the passage in quotation marks, and not the information that precedes that passage.

Material that is considered common knowledge — that is, familiar or at least accessible to the general public — does not have to be documented. The author of *Hamlet,* the date the Declaration of Independence was signed, or the definition of *misfeasance,* while open to dispute (some scholars, for example, claim that William Shakespeare did not write *Hamlet*) are indisputably considered to be common knowledge in our culture. Unfortunately, it is not always clear whether a particular fact *is* common knowledge. Although too much documentation can clutter a paper and distract the reader, it's still better to cite too many sources than to cite too few and risk being accused of dishonesty. In general, if you are unsure whether or not to give your source credit, you should document the material.

Keeping Research under Control

Your preliminary outline provides guideposts for your research. You will need to revise it as you go along to make room for new ideas and evidence and for the questions that come up as you read. Rather than try to fit each new piece of information into your outline, you can use the numbering or lettering system in your outline to cross-reference your notebooks or file cards.

As much as possible, keep all materials related to the same point in the same place. You might do this by making a separate pile of file cards for each point and its support and questions or by reserving several pages in your notebook for information bearing on each point.

How do you know when you have done enough research? If you have kept your outline updated, you have a visual record of your progress. Check this against the guidelines on pages 330–31: Is each point backed by at least two pieces of support? Do your sources represent a range of authors and of types of data? If a large proportion of your support comes from one book, or if most of your references are to newspaper articles, you probably need to keep working. On the other hand, if your notes cite five different authorities making essentially the same point, you may have collected more data than you need. It can be useful to point out that more than one authority holds a given view and to make notes of examples that are notably different from one another. But it is not necessary to take down all the passages or examples expressing the same idea.

To This Point

Before you leave the library or your primary sources for your typewriter, check to make sure your research is complete.

1. Does your working outline show any gaps in your argument?
2. Have you found adequate data to support your claim?

3. Have you identified the warrants linking your claim with data and ensured that these warrants too are adequately documented?

4. If you intend to quote or paraphrase sources in your paper, do your notes include exact copies of all statements you may want to use and complete references?

5. Have you answered all the relevant questions that have come up during your research?

6. Do you have enough information about your sources to document your paper?

MLA SYSTEM FOR CITING PUBLICATIONS

One of the simplest methods of crediting sources is the Modern Language Association (MLA) in-text system, which is used in the research paper on fairy tales in this chapter. In the text of your paper, immediately after any quotation, paraphrase, or anything else you wish to document, simply insert a parenthetical mention of the author's last name and the page number on which the material appeared. You don't need a comma after the author's name or an abbreviation of the word "page." For example, the following sentence appears in the fairy tale paper:

> Famines in the seventeenth century often reduced the peasantry to a diet of "bad black bread, acorns, and roots" (Weber 96).

The parenthetical reference tells the reader that the information in this sentence came from page 96 of the book or article by Eugen Weber that appears in the Works Cited, at the end of the paper. The complete reference on the Works Cited page provides all the information readers need to locate the original source in the library:

> Weber, Eugen. "Fairies and Hard Facts: The Reality of Folktales." Journal of the History of Ideas 42 (1981): 93-113.

If the author's name is mentioned in the same sentence, it is also acceptable to place only the page numbers in parentheses; it is not necessary to repeat the author's name. For example:

> Bettelheim sees symbolic meaning in every motif and element in the story, and assumes that children interpret these symbolically as well (159-66).

The list of works cited includes all material you have used to write your research paper. This list appears at the end of your paper and always starts on a new page. Center the title Works Cited, double-space between the title and the first entry, and begin your list, which should be arranged alphabetically by author. Each entry should start at the left margin; indent all subsequent lines of the entry five spaces. Number each page, and double-space throughout.

Another method of documenting sources is to use notes, either footnotes (at the foot of the page) or endnotes (on a separate page at the end of the paper). The note method is not as commonly used today as the in-text system for two reasons: (1) Reference notes repeat almost all the information already given on the Works Cited page. (2) If footnotes are used, it requires careful calculation during typing to fit them on the page so that there is a consistent bottom margin throughout the paper.

Nevertheless, it is a valid method, so we illustrate it here. Superscript numbers go at the end of the sentence or phrase being referenced:

> Roman authors admit to borrowing frequently from earlier Greek writers for their jokes, although no joke books in the original Greek survive today.[1]

The reference note for this citation would be:

> [1]Alexander Humez and Nicholas Humez, <u>Alpha to Omega</u> (Boston: Godine, 1981) 79.

On the Works Cited page this reference would be:

> Humez, Alexander, and Nicholas Humez. <u>Alpha to Omega</u>. Boston: Godine, 1981.

Notice that the page number for a book citation is given in the note but not the reference, and that the punctuation differs. Otherwise the information is the same. Number the notes consecutively throughout your paper.

One more point: *Content notes,* which provide additional information not readily worked into a research paper, are also indicated by superscript numbers. Susan Middleton's paper on fairy tales features four such notes, included on a Notes page before the list of Works Cited.

Following are examples of the citation forms you are most likely to need as you document your research. In general, for both books and magazines, information should appear in the following order: author, title, and publication information. Each item should be followed by a period. When using as a source an essay that appears in this book, follow the citation model for "Material reprinted from another source," unless your instructor indicates otherwise. Consult the *MLA Handbook for Writers of Research Papers,* Fourth Edition, by Joseph Gibaldi (New York: Modern Language Association of America, 1995) for other documentation models and a list of acceptable shortened forms of publishers.

A BOOK BY A SINGLE AUTHOR

Kinder, Chuck. The Silver Ghost. New York: Harcourt, 1979.

AN ANTHOLOGY OR COMPILATION

Abrahams, William, ed. Prize Stories 1980: The O. Henry Awards.
    Garden City: Doubleday, 1980.

A BOOK BY TWO AUTHORS

Danzig, Richard, and Peter Szanton. National Service: What Would It
    Mean? Lexington: Lexington, 1986.

Note: This form is followed even for two authors with the same last name.

Ehrlich, Paul, and Anne Ehrlich. Extinction: The Causes and
    Consequences of the Disappearance of Species. New York:
    Random, 1981.

A BOOK BY TWO OR MORE AUTHORS

Heffernan, William A., Mark Johnston, and Frank Hodgins. Literature:
    Art and Artifact. San Diego: Harcourt, 1987.

If there are more than three authors, name only the first and add: "et al." (and others).

A BOOK BY A CORPORATE AUTHOR

Poets & Writers, Inc. The Writing Business: A Poets & Writers
    Handbook. New York: Poets & Writers, 1985.

A WORK IN AN ANTHOLOGY

Morton, Eugene S. "The Realities of Reintroducing Species to the Wild."
    Animal Extinctions: What Everyone Should Know. Ed. J. R.
    Hoage. National Zoological Park Symposia for the Public Series.
    Washington: Smithsonian Institution, 1985. 71-95.

AN INTRODUCTION, PREFACE, FOREWORD, OR AFTERWORD

Borges, Jorge Luis. Preface. New Islands. By Maria Luisa Bombal.
    Trans. Richard and Lucia Cunningham. New York: Farrar, 1982.

MATERIAL REPRINTED FROM ANOTHER SOURCE

Tannen, Deborah. "Talking Up Close." Talking from 9 to 5. New York:
Morrow, 1994. Rpt. in Elements of Argument: A Text and Reader.
Annette T. Rottenberg. 5th ed. Boston: Bedford, 1996. 168.

A MULTIVOLUME WORK

Skotheim, Robert Allen, and Michael McGiffert, eds. Since the Civil
War. Vol. 2 of American Social Thought: Sources and
Interpretations. 2 vols. Reading: Addison, 1972.

AN EDITION OTHER THAN THE FIRST

Cassill, R. V., ed. The Norton Anthology of Short Fiction, 2nd ed. New
York: Norton, 1985.

A TRANSLATION

Allende, Isabel. The House of the Spirits. Trans. Magda Bogin. New
York: Knopf, 1985.

A REPUBLISHED BOOK

Weesner, Theodore. The Car Thief. 1972. New York: Vintage-Random,
1987.

Note: The only information about original publication you need to provide is the publication date, which appears immediately after the title.

A BOOK IN A SERIES

Eady, Cornelius. Victims of the Latest Dance Craze. Omnation Press Dialogues on Dance Series 5. Chicago: Omnation, 1985.

ARTICLE FROM A DAILY NEWSPAPER

Dudar, Helen. "James Earl Jones at Bat." New York Times 22 Mar.
1987, sec. 2: 1+.

ARTICLE FROM A PERIODICAL

O'Brien, Conor Cruise. "God and Man in Nicaragua." Atlantic Monthly
Aug. 1986: 50-72.

UNSIGNED EDITORIAL

"Medium, Message." Editorial. Nation 28 Mar. 1987: 383-84.

ANONYMOUS WORKS

"The March Almanac." Atlantic Mar. 1993: 18.

Citation World Atlas. Maplewood: Hammond, 1987.

ARTICLE FROM JOURNAL WITH SEPARATE
PAGINATION FOR EACH ISSUE

Brewer, Derek. "The Battleground of Home: Versions of Fairy Tales." Encounter 54.4 (1980): 52-61.

ARTICLE IN A JOURNAL WITH CONTINUOUS
PAGINATION THROUGHOUT VOLUME

McCafferty, Janey. "The Shadders Go Away." New England Review and Bread Loaf Quarterly 9 (1987): 332-42.

Note that the issue number is not mentioned here; because the volume has continuous pagination throughout the year, only the volume number (9) is needed.

A REVIEW

Walker, David. Rev. of A Wave, by John Ashbery. Field 32 (1985): 63-71.

AN INTERVIEW

Hines, Gregory. Interview. With D. C. Denison. The Boston Globe Magazine 29 Mar. 1987: 2.

Note: An interview conducted by the author of the paper would be documented as follows:

Hines, Gregory. Personal interview. 29 Mar. 1987.

AN ARTICLE IN A REFERENCE WORK

"Bylina." The Princeton Encyclopedia of Poetry and Poetics. Ed. Alex Preminger. Enlarged ed. Princeton: Princeton UP, 1974.

GOVERNMENT DOCUMENT

United States. National Endowment for the Arts. 1989 Annual Report. Washington: Office of Public Affairs, 1990.

Frequently the Government Printing Office (GPO) is the publisher of federal government documents.

COMPUTER SOFTWARE

XyQuest. XyWrite. Vers. III Plus. Computer Software. XyQuest, 1988. PC-DOS 2.0, 384KB, disk.

Note here that the version is given in roman numerals, since it appears that way in the title; usually software versions are given in decimals (e.g., Vers. 2.1).

DATABASE SOURCE (INFORMATION SERVICE)

Gura, Mark. The Gorgeous Mosaic Project: A Work of Art by the Schoolchildren of the World. Teacher's packet. East Brunswick:
Children's Atelier, 1990. ERIC ED 347 257.

Kassebaum, Peter. Cultural Awareness Training Manual and Study
Guide. ERIC, 1992. ED 347 289.

The ERIC documentation number at the end of the entry indicates that the reader can obtain this source solely or primarily through ERIC (Educational Resources Information Center). When no other publishing information is given, treat ERIC (without a city of publication) as the publisher, as shown in the second entry. ERIC also catalogs many previously published articles with documentation numbers beginning with EJ rather than ED. Treat these simply as articles in periodicals, not as material from an information service; that is, omit the EJ number.

NTIS (National Technical Information Service) is another information service.

MATERIAL ACCESSED THROUGH A COMPUTER SERVICE

Boynton, Robert S. "The New Intellectuals." Atlantic Monthly Mar. 1995.
Atlantic Monthly Online. Online. America Online. 3 Mar. 1995.

CD-ROM

Corcoran, Mary B. "Fairy Tale." Grolier Multimedia Encyclopedia. CD-
ROM. Danbury: Grolier, 1995.

UNPUBLISHED MANUSCRIPT

Leahy, Ellen. "An Investigation of the Computerization of Information
Systems in a Family Planning Program." Unpublished master's degree project. Div. of Public Health, U of Massachusetts, Amherst,
1990.

LETTER TO THE EDITOR

Flannery, James W. Letter. New York Times Book Review 28 Feb.
1993: 34.

PERSONAL CORRESPONDENCE

Bennett, David. Letter to the author. 3 Mar. 1993.

LECTURE

Calvino, Italo. "Right and Wrong Political Uses of Literature."
Symposium on European Politics. Amherst College, Amherst. 25
Feb. 1976.

FILM

<u>The Voice of the Khalam</u>. Prod. Loretta Pauker. With Leopold Senghor, Okara, Birago Diop, Rubadiri, and Francis Parkes. Contemporary Films/McGraw-Hill, 1971. 16 mm, 29 min.

Other pertinent information to give in film references, if available, is the writer and director (see model for radio/TV program for style).

TV OR RADIO PROGRAM

<u>The Shakers: Hands to Work, Hearts to God.</u> Narr. David McCullough. Dir. Ken Burns and Amy Stechler Burns. Writ. Amy Stechler Burns, Wendy Tilghman, and Tom Lewis. PBS. WGBY, Springfield. 28 Dec. 1992.

VIDEOTAPE

<u>Style Wars!</u> Videotape. Prod. Tony Silver and Henry Chalfont. New Day Films, 1985. 69 min.

PERFORMANCE

<u>Quilters: A Musical Celebration</u>. By Molly Newman and Barbara Damashek. Dir. Joyce Devlin. Musical dir. Faith Fung. Mt. Holyoke Laboratory Theatre, South Hadley, MA. 26 Apr. 1991. Based on <u>The Quilters: Women and Domestic Art</u> by Patricia Cooper and Norma Bradley Allen.

CARTOON

Henley, Marian. "Maxine." Cartoon. <u>Valley Advocate</u> 25 Feb. 1993: 39.

SAMPLE RESEARCH PAPER (MLA STYLE)

The following paper, prepared in the MLA style, was written for an advanced composition course. Told to compose a research paper on a literary topic, Susan Middleton chose to write on fairy tales — a subject literary enough to satisfy her instructor, yet general enough to encompass her own interest in developmental psychology. But as she explored the subject, she found herself reading in a surprising array of disciplines, including folklore, anthropology, and history. Although she initially expected to report on the psychological importance of fairy tales, Middleton at last wrote an argument about the importance of their historical and cultural roots. Her paper, as is typical for literary papers, anchors its argument in the events and details of its chosen text, "Hansel and Gretel." But it also makes effective use of sources to help readers understand that there is more to the tale than a story that sends children happily off to sleep.

When a Fairy Tale Is Not Just a Fairy Tale

By
Susan Middleton

Professor Herrington
English 2A
May 1996

Include a title
page if an outline
is part of the
paper. If no
outline is
required,
include name,
instructor's name,
course name, and
date at the upper
left corner of
page 1.

Middleton   ii

Outline

Topic outline.
Some instructors
require a thesis
statement under
"Outline" heading
and before the
outline itself.

I. Introduction:

   A. Dictionary definition of "fairy tale"

   B. Thesis: "Hansel and Gretel" has historical roots

II. Origin and distribution of tale

III. Historical basis of motifs

   A. Physical and economic hardship

      1. Fear of the forest

      2. Poverty and starvation

      3. Child abandonment

      4. Fantasies of finding treasure

   B. Cruel stepmother

   C. Wicked witch

      1. Eating meat associated with cannibalism and upper classes

      2. Elderly caretaker for unwanted children

      3. Witches in community

      4. Witchcraft as remnant of ancient fertility religion

IV. Rebuttals to historical approach

   A. Motivation for telling realistic tales

   B. Psychological interpretations

      1. Fairy tales dreamlike, not literal

      2. Freudian interpretation

V. Conclusion

Middleton   1

When a Fairy Tale Is Not Just a Fairy Tale

"Hansel and Gretel" is a well-known fairy tale, beloved of many children in both Europe and North America.[1] Although it has no fairies in it, it conforms to the definition of "fairy tale" given in Merriam-Webster's Collegiate Dictionary, Tenth Edition: "a story (as for children) involving fantastic forces and beings (as fairies, wizards, and goblins)." As anyone familiar with this tale will remember, Hansel and Gretel are two children on an adventure in the woods, where they encounter a wicked witch in a gingerbread house, who plans to fatten and eat them. Through their ingenuity they outsmart her, burn her up in her own oven, and return home triumphantly with a hoard of riches found in her house.

We think of fairy tales as being lighthearted fantasies that entertain but don't have much relevance to daily life. We often borrow the word to describe a movie with an unlikely plot, or a person not quite grounded in reality: "Oh, he's living in a fairy tale world; he hasn't got his head on his shoulders." In fact, the second definition of "fairy tale" in Webster's is "a made-up story usually designed to mislead."

So what is the meaning of "Hansel and Gretel"? Is it simply a story of make-believe, or something more? Fairy tales are told, read, and heard in the context of a time and place. Today we are exposed to them through illustrated storybooks, cartoons, and film. But in Europe, before technologies in printing made mass publishing possible, folktales were passed on orally. They were told by adults mostly for adult audiences, although people often first heard them as children. They served to entertain and to relieve the boredom of repetitive work in the fields during the day and in the home in the evening (Weber 93, 113). In peasant and aboriginal communities, that is often still the case (Taggart 437).

I believe that "Hansel and Gretel" has historical meaning. Embedded in this simple narrative is a record of the experiences and events once common in the lives of the people who first told and listened to it.

Title centered

Raised, super-script number refers to notes giving information at the end to the paper.

Writer briefly summarizes tale to orient readers.

In-text citation of author and pages; citation appears at the end of the sentence before the period. Thesis with claim of fact that the writer must support

Where did "Hansel and Gretel" come from? We do not know for certain. In oral form this tale shows wide distribution. Different versions have been recorded all over Europe, India, Japan, Africa, the Caribbean, Pacific Islands, and among native North and South Americans ("Hansel and Gretel"). As with all folktales, there is no agreement among folklorists[2] about whether all these versions migrated from one place to another, sprang up independently, or derive from some combination of the two ("Hansel and Gretel"). Most oral versions of it have been recorded in Europe (Aarne 117). This does not prove that the tale originated there--it may simply reflect the eagerness of people in Europe during the nineteenth and twentieth centuries to record their own folk history--but it is the best guideline for now.

The tale may be very ancient, since folktales can be passed on faithfully from one generation to another without change. (The origins of "Cinderella," for example, can be traced back to China in the ninth century [Thompson, Folktale 126].) But we can't know that for sure. So, even though "Hansel and Gretel" may have originated hundreds or even thousands of years ago, it probably is only safe to compare a tale with the historical period when the tale was first recorded. For "Hansel and Gretel" this means Europe in the seventeenth to nineteenth centuries.[3]

Eugen Weber is one historian who sees direct parallels between the characters and motifs in "Hansel and Gretel" (and other Grimms' fairy tales), and the social and economic conditions in Europe during this period. One of the central themes in the tale is poverty and abandonment. Recall how the tale begins: Hansel and Gretel live with their parents near a huge forest; their father is a woodcutter. The family is facing starvation because there is a famine. Twice their parents abandon them in the woods to save themselves. The first time the children are able to find their way home, but the second time they get lost.

As Weber points out, until the middle of the nineteenth century, the forest, especially for northern Europeans, carried the real potential for encountering

---

Reference to dictionary article — page number not necessary

Square brackets used to represent parentheses within parentheses

Specific support from the tale cited

Consecutive references immediately following an identified source ("Weber") cite only the pages within the source without repeating the source.

danger in the form of robbers, wild animals, and getting
lost (96-97). Moreover, conditions of poverty, starvation,
early death, and danger from unknown adults were
common throughout Europe for peasants and the working
class (96). The majority of Europeans at the beginning of
the eighteenth century were farmers, and the average life
expectancy was about twenty-five years (Treasure 660,
667). Famines in the seventeenth century often reduced
the peasantry to a diet of "bad black bread, acorns, and
roots" (Weber 96). Hansel and Gretel are treated by the
witch to a dinner of pancakes and sugar, milk, nuts, and
apples (101). This may not sound particularly nourishing
to our ears because we assume a healthy dinner must have
vegetables and/or meat. But when you're starving,
anything is likely to taste good; this would have been a
sumptuous meal for Hansel and Gretel.

Narrative details
linked to histori-
cal facts

Childhood was thought of differently then than today.
"Valued as an extra pair of hands or deplored as an extra
mouth to feed, the child belonged to no privileged realm of
play and protection from life's responsibilities" (Treasure
664). Social historian John Boswell estimates that anywhere
from 10 to 40 percent of children in towns and cities were
abandoned during the eighteenth century. Parental
motivation included removing the stigma of illegitimate or
physically deformed children, being unable to support their
children and hoping to give them a better life with strangers,
desiring to promote one child's inheritance over another's,
or simply lacking interest in raising the child (48, 428).

Source cited after
direct quotation

Weber points out that peasants had very little cash
and didn't use banks. Hiding and finding treasure--gold,
silver, and jewelry--was a much more common occurrence
two centuries ago than it is today (101), a kind of lottery
for the poor. In this light, the riches the children find in
the witch's house could reflect the common person's
fantasy of striking it rich.

Writer's interpre-
tation of one as-
pect of the story

A central motif in the story is the stepmother who
wants to abandon the children to keep herself and her
husband from starving. (The father, at first reluctant,

eventually gives in to his wife's plan.) As Weber and others
have noted, stepmothers were not unusual in history. The
death rate among childbearing women was much higher in
past centuries than it is today. When women died in
childbirth, there was strong economic motivation for
fathers to remarry. In the seventeenth and eighteenth
centuries, 20 to 80 percent of widowers remarried within
the year of their wife's death. By the mid-nineteenth
century, after life expectancy rose, only 15 percent of
widowers did so (94, 112).

Reference to a newspaper

What accounts for the stereotype of the heartless
stepmother? Warner argues that mothers, not stepmothers,
actually appeared in many of the tales in their original
forms, until romantic editors, like the Grimm Brothers, "re-
belled against this desecration of motherhood and changed
mothers into wicked stepmothers" (D17). Weber suggests
that stepmothers were assigned the role of doing evil to
children for economic reasons: The family would risk losing
its good name and perhaps its land if a biological parent
killed a child (107). There is also the issue of inheritance
from the stepmother's point of view: If her husband dies,
her husband's children, not she, would inherit the land and
property. Literary and legal evidence of stepmothers
plotting to eliminate stepchildren, especially stepsons,
shows up in European literature as far back as two
millennia ago (Boswell 128).

Transition to new topic: witches

Another major theme in "Hansel and Gretel" is the
wicked witch, which also shows up in lots of other fairy
tales. Were there witches in European history, and if so,
where did the reputation for eating children come from?

Weber notes that in fairy tales only evil figures eat
meat of any kind, whether animal or human flesh. Before
the middle of the nineteenth century the peasantry rarely
ate meat, but the aristocracy and bourgeoisie did. This
discrepancy may be the origin of the motif in some fairy
tales of evil figures of upper-class background wanting to
eat children (112, 101). Weber seems to imply that

child-eating witches symbolized to the peasantry either resentment of or paranoia about the aristocracy.

Although the witch's cottage in "Hansel and Gretel" is not described as grand or large, there are other allusions to wealth and comfort. The witch puts the two children to bed between clean sheets, a luxury for much of the peasantry, who slept on straw and for whom bed lice were a common reality (Treasure 661-62). And of course there is the hoard of coin money and jewelry the children later discover there. Perhaps more significantly, the witch herself has a lot of power, just as the aristocracy was perceived to have, including the power to deceive and take away life.

David Bakan suggests that the historical basis for the witch is the unmarried elderly woman in the community who took in unwanted, illegitimate children and was often paid to do this (66-67). There is also evidence that witchcraft, ranging from white magic to sorcery (black magic), was practiced by both individual women and men among the peasantry during this time. For example, "the 'cunning folk' were at least as numerous in sixteenth-century England as the parish clergy. Moreover, in their divinatory, medical, and religious functions they were far more important in peasant society than were the official clergy" (Horsley 697). Witches were called on to influence the weather, provide love potions, find lost objects, midwife, identify thieves, and heal illnesses (698). Some services performed by witches were ambiguous: "Apparently some peasants would conjure the storms or weather spirits to avoid striking their own fields--but to strike someone else's instead," but for the most part the wisewomen and sorcerers were different people (698).

The idea that an organized witch cult, as portrayed by the Catholic Church during the Middle Ages, actually existed is dismissed today by most social historians. Jesse Nash thinks we should reconsider the possibility that some of the behavior witches were accused of, including ritual cannibalism and sexual orgies in the woods, actually

Middleton   6

occurred in some form (12). He sees witchcraft as "a surviving remnant of a religion which was concerned with the fertility of crops, animals, humans, and with the alteration of seasons and with the identification of humans with animals" (13). These practices date back to a matriarchal goddess religion which flourished in Europe 5,000 to 7,000 years ago, before invasion of the patriarchal cultures from India (Marija Gimbutas in Nash 12). This religion included human sacrifice and was based on the concept of maintaining balance in the universe: The goddess of life was at the same time the goddess of death. Wood-wives and fairies, who lived in the forest, "were mediators of sacred knowledge to their communities" (16).

Source within a source cited

Nash suggests that in Europe, although Christianity became the official way of thinking about the world, it did not replace the old beliefs entirely, despite strong attempts by the Church to eliminate them. Religious beliefs and practices can persist hidden for generations if need be.[4] The peasants were able to live with and practice both Christianity and paganism in combination for centuries (25).

So we have seen there is validity to the claim that many of the motifs of "Hansel and Gretel" have historical roots. However, one might well ask why people would want to hear stories so close to their own experiences. If oral tales during this time were meant as entertainment mostly for adults, wouldn't they want something to take their minds off their troubles? Weber suggests a couple of motivations for telling fairy tales. One was to experience "the delights of fear" (97). Fairy tales were told along with ghost stories, gossip, jokes, and fables. I suspect it was similar to the thrill some people get today watching scary movies with happy endings.

Having supported her major claim, the writer continues by anticipating and addressing possible rebuttals.

Second, fairy tales helped to explain how the world worked. To most people not able to read, the world of cause and effect was mysterious and could only be explained through symbolism and analogy. Folktales had been used in church sermons since the fourteenth century (Weber 110, Zipes 22).

Two sources cited at once

Middleton   7

But the industrial age ushered in the scientific revolution, and with it came the concept of explaining the unknown by breaking it down into working parts (Weber 113). Reading became available to large numbers of people. By this time fairy tales were no longer meaningful ways to explain the world for ordinary adults, so they became the province of children's entertainment (113).

Folklorist Alan Dundes thinks it is naive to assume fairy tales have literal meaning. In recent years he and a number of other people have looked to psychology to explain the origin of fairy tales. "Fairy tales are like dreams--can you find the historic origin of dreams?" (Dundes). In their structure and characters fairy tales do have a number of dreamlike aspects: They rarely state the feelings of the hero directly, and all inner experiences of the hero are projected outward into objects in nature and other people (Tatar 91). The other characters seem not to have separate lives of their own; all their actions and intentions relate to the hero (Brewer 55). Also, magical things happen: Elements of nature speak, granting favors to the hero or threatening success or even life. In one version of "Hansel and Gretel," for example, a white duck talks to the children and carries them across a lake on their way home.

The symbolic nature of fairy tales, however, doesn't deny the validity of examining them for historical origins. As anyone who has recorded their own dreams knows, people and objects from mundane, daily life show up regularly in them. Sometimes these elements are disguised as symbols, but other times they are transparently realistic. Similarly, the talking duck and the gingerbread house in "Hansel and Gretel" may be unreal, but other themes have more literal counterparts in history.

One of the most quoted interpreters of fairy tales is psychologist Bruno Bettelheim, whose The Uses of Enchantment analyzes fairy tales in Freudian terms. In his view, "Hansel and Gretel" represents the task each of us as children must face in coming to terms with anxiety--not the anxiety of facing starvation and being literally

Margin annotations:

Competing theories presented

Telephone interview — no page numbers

abandoned in the woods, but the ordinary fear of separating from our parents (especially mother) in the process of growing up to become independent adults. Bettelheim sees symbolic meaning in every motif and element in the story, and assumes that children interpret these symbolically as well (159-66).

Partial validity of competing theories acknowledged

Undeniably, there are themes in "Hansel and Gretel"--as in many of our most common fairy tales--that strike deep psychological chords with both children and adults. The wicked stepmother is a good example: Children often fantasize they are really stepchildren or adopted as a way to account for feeling victimized and abused by their parents. "In real life this fantasy occurs among children with a very high frequency" (Bakan 76).

Having qualified her major claim in light of other theories, student goes on to reiterate the support of her major claim in her conclusion.

These themes help to explain the enduring popularity of fairy tales among middle-class children over the last two centuries. But we cannot treat fairy tales as if they spring full-blown from the unconscious and tell us nothing about the past. For the people who told and heard "Hansel and Gretel" in the seventeenth to nineteenth centuries in Europe, the tale was describing events and phenomena that happened, if not to them, then to someone they knew. Everyone in rural communities was likely to have been exposed, whether in person or by hearsay, to some elderly woman claiming powers to alter weather patterns, heal the sick, cast spells, midwife, or take in illegitimate babies. Stepmothers were common, poverty and famine ongoing, and abandonment and child abuse very real. In addition to providing entertainment, tales like "Hansel and Gretel" reassured teller and listener alike that the ordinary physical hardships, which for most of us today are fictions, were possible to overcome.

Middleton   9

Notes

[1] We in the United States know it primarily in printed form, as it has come to us from Germany. Between 1812 and 1857, the Grimm brothers, Jacob and Wilhelm, published several editions of <u>Kinder und Hausmarchen</u> (<u>Children's and Household Tales</u>) (Zipes 6, 41, 79). In addition to "Hansel and Gretel," this book included over 200 other folktales (though not all of them were fairy tales). The anthology increased in popularity until by the turn of the twentieth century it outsold all other books in Germany except the Bible (Zipes 15). To date it has been translated into some seventy languages (Denecke).

Content notes appear at the end of the paper, before Works Cited.

[2] Folklorists collect folktales from around the world and analyze them. Tales are categorized according to <u>type</u> (basic plot line) and <u>motifs</u> (elements within the tale). Two widely used references for folklorists are Antti Aarne's <u>Types of the Folklore</u> and Stith Thompson's <u>Motif-index</u>. "Hansel and Gretel" is type 327A in the Aarne classification.

Space included between superscript number and beginning of note

[3] The Grimms were the first to record tale type 327A in 1812 (see note 1). A related tale about Tom Thumb (tale type 327B) was first recorded by Charles Perrault from France in 1697 (Thompson, <u>Folktale</u> 37, 182).

Indent five spaces to superscript number; rest of note is flush left.

[4] Consider the example of Sephardic Jews who "converted" to Christianity under duress in Spain in the fifteenth century. Some of them moved to North America, and their descendants continued to practice Christianity openly and Judaism in secret until recently ("Search for the Buried Past").

Middleton   10

Works Cited

Sources arranged alphabetically by author's last name

Aarne, Antti. The Types of the Folklore: Classification and
  Bibliography. Trans. and ed. Stith Thompson. 2nd rev.
  ed. FF Communications 184. Helsinki: Suomalainen
  Tiedeakatemia, 1964.

First line flush left in citation, rest indented five spaces

Bakan, David. Slaughter of the Innocents. Toronto:
  Canadian Broadcasting System, 1971.

Bettelheim, Bruno. The Uses of Enchantment: The Meaning
  and Importance of Fairy Tales. 1976. New York:
  Vintage, 1977.

Book

Boswell, John. The Kindness of Strangers: The
  Abandonment of Children in Western Europe from
  Late Antiquity to the Renaissance. New York:
  Pantheon, 1988.

Periodical

Brewer, Derek. "The Battleground of Home: Versions of
  Fairy Tales." Encounter 54.4 (1980): 52-61.

Encyclopedia article

Denecke, Ludwig. "Grimm, Jacob Ludwig Carl and Wilhelm
  Carl." Encyclopaedia Britannica: Micropaedia. 1992 ed.

Interview

Dundes, Alan. Telephone interview. 10 Feb. 1993.

"Fairy tale." Merriam-Webster's Collegiate Dictionary. 10th
  ed. 1993.

"Hansel and Gretel." Funk & Wagnalls Standard Dictionary
  of Folklore, Mythology, and Legend. Ed. Maria Leach.
  New York: Funk & Wagnalls, 1949.

Horsley, Richard A. "Who Were the Witches? The Social
  Roles of the Accused in the European Witch Trials."
  Journal of Interdisciplinary History 9 (1979):
  689-715.

Nash, Jesse. "European Witchcraft: The Hidden Tradition."
  Human Mosaic 21.1-2 (1987): 10-30.

Radio broadcast

"Search for the Buried Past." The Hidden Jews of New Mexico. Prod. Nan Rubin. WFCR, Amherst, MA. 13 Sept.
  1992.

Taggart, James M. " 'Hansel and Gretel' in Spain and
  Mexico." Journal of American Folklore 99 (1986):
  435-60.

Article in an edited anthology

Tatar, Maria. "Folkloristic Phantasies: Grimm's Fairy Tales
  and Freud's Family Romance." Fairy Tales as Ways of

Middleton   11

Knowing: Essays on Marchen in Psychology, Society
and Literature. Ed. Michael M. Metzger and Katharina
Mommsen. Germanic Studies in America 41. Berne:
Lang, 1981. 75-98.

Thompson, Stith. The Folktale. New York: Holt, 1946.

---. Motif-index of Folk-literature: A Classification of
Narrative Elements in Folktales, Ballads, Myths,
Fables, Mediaeval Romances, Exempla, Fabliaux,
Jest-books, and Local Legends. Rev. ed. 6 vols. plus
index. Bloomington: Indiana UP, 1957.

Treasure, Geoffrey R. R. "European History and Culture:
The Emergence of Modern Europe, 1500-1648." Encyclopaedia Britannica: Macropaedia. 1992 ed. 657-83.

Warner, Marina. "Pity the Stepmother." New York Times.
12 May 1991, late ed.: D17. New York Times Online.
On-line. Dow Jones News Retrieval. 18 Mar. 1996.

Weber, Eugen. "Fairies and Hard Facts: The Reality of Folktales." Journal of the History of Ideas 42 (1981):
93-113.

Zipes, Jack. The Brothers Grimm: From Enchanted Forests
to the Modern World. New York: Routledge, 1988.

Two consecutive
works by the
same author

Volume in a multi-
volume revised
edition

Newspaper
on-line from a
computer service

APA SYSTEM FOR CITING PUBLICATIONS

Instructors in the social sciences might prefer the citation system of the American Psychological Association (APA). Like the MLA system, the APA system calls for a parenthetical citation in the text of the paper. Unlike the MLA system, the APA system includes the year of publication in the parenthetical reference. Here is an example:

> Even though many South American countries rely on the drug trade for their economic survival, the majority of South Americans disapprove of drug use (Gorriti, 1989, p. 72).

The complete publication information for Gorriti's article will appear at the end of your paper, on a page titled "References." (Sample citations for the "References" page appear below.)

If your list of references includes more than one work written by the same author in the same year, cite the first work as *a* and the second as *b*. For example, Gorriti's second article of 1989 would be cited in your paper as (Gorriti, 1989b).

Following are examples of the citation forms you are most likely to use. If you need the format for a type of publication not listed here, consult the *Publication Manual of the American Psychological Association,* Fourth Edition (1994).

A BOOK BY A SINGLE AUTHOR

Briggs, J. (1988). Fire in the crucible: The alchemy of creative genius. New York: St. Martin's Press.

AN ANTHOLOGY OR COMPILATION

Gioseffi, D. (Ed.). (1988). Women on war. New York: Simon & Schuster.

A BOOK BY TWO OR MORE AUTHORS OR EDITORS

Atwan, R., & Roberts, J. (Eds.). (1996). Left, right, and center: Voices from across the political spectrum. Boston: Bedford Books.

Note: List the names of *all* the authors or editors, no matter how many.

A BOOK BY A CORPORATE AUTHOR

International Advertising Association. (1977). Controversy advertising: How advertisers present points of view on public affairs. New York: Hastings House.

WORK IN AN ANTHOLOGY

Mukherjee, B. (1988). The colonization of the mind. In Gioseffi, D. (Ed.) Women on war (pp. 140-142). New York: Simon & Schuster.

AN INTRODUCTION, PREFACE, FOREWORD, OR AFTERWORD

Hemenway, R. (1984). Introduction. In Z. N. Hurston, Dust tracks on a road. Urbana: University of Illinois Press, ix-xxxix.

AN EDITION OTHER THAN THE FIRST

Gumpert, G., & Cathcart, R. (Eds.). (1986). Inter/media: Interpersonal communication in a media world (3rd ed.). New York: Oxford University Press.

A TRANSLATION

Sartre, J. P. (1962). Literature and existentialism. (B. Frechtman, Trans.). New York: Citadel Press. (Original work published 1949.)

A REPUBLISHED BOOK

James, W. (1969). The varieties of religious experience: A study in human nature. London: Collier Books. (Original work published 1961.)

A BOOK IN A SERIES

Berthrong, D. J. (1976). The Cheyenne and Arapaho ordeal: Reservation and agency life in the Indian territory, 1875-1907. Vol. 136. The civilization of the American Indian series. Norman: University of Oklahoma Press.

ARTICLE FROM A DAILY NEWSPAPER

Hottelet, R. C. (1990, March 15). Germany: Why it can't happen again. Christian Science Monitor, p. 19.

ARTICLE FROM A PERIODICAL

Gorriti, G. A. (1989, July). How to fight the drug war. Atlantic Monthly, 70-76.

ARTICLE IN A JOURNAL WITH CONTINUOUS PAGINATION THROUGHOUT VOLUME

Cockburn, A. (1989). British justice, Irish victims. The Nation, 249, 554-555.

ARTICLE FROM A JOURNAL WITH SEPARATE PAGINATION FOR EACH ISSUE

Mukerji, C. Visual language in science and the exercise of power: The case of cartography in early modern Europe. Studies in Visual Communication, 10(3), 30-45.

GOVERNMENT PUBLICATION

United States Dept. of Health, Education, and Welfare. (1973). <u>Current ethical issues in mental health</u>. Washington, DC: U.S. Government Printing Office.

ABSTRACT

Fritz, M. (1990/1991). A comparison of social interactions using a friendship awareness activity. <u>Education and Training in Mental Retardation</u>, <u>25</u>, 352-359. (From <u>Psychological Abstracts</u>, 1991, <u>78</u>, Abstract No. 11474)

When the dates of the original publication and of the abstract differ, give both dates separated by a slash.

ANONYMOUS WORK

The status of women: Different but the same. (1992-1993). <u>Zontian</u>, <u>73</u>(3), 5.

MULTIPLE WORKS BY THE SAME AUTHOR IN THE SAME YEAR

Gardner, H. (1982a). <u>Art, mind, and brain: A cognitive approach to creativity</u>. New York: Basic.

Gardner, H. (1982b). <u>Developmental psychology: An introduction</u> (2nd ed.). Boston: Little, Brown.

MULTIVOLUME WORK

Mussen, Ph. H. (Ed.). (1983). <u>Handbook of child psychology</u> (4th ed., Vols. 1-4). New York: Wiley.

ARTICLE IN A REFERENCE WORK

Frisby, J. P. (1990). Direct perception. In M. W. Eysenck (Ed.), <u>Blackwell dictionary of cognitive psychology</u> (pp. 95-100). Oxford: Basil Blackwell.

COMPUTER SOFTWARE

UnionSquareware (1987). <u>Squarenote, the ideal librarian</u> [Computer program]. Somerville, MA: Author.

If the primary contributors to developing the program are known, begin the reference with those as the author(s) instead of the corporate author. If you are citing a documentation manual rather than the program itself, add the word "manual" before the closing bracket. If there is additional information needed for retrieving the program (such as report and/or acquisition numbers), add this at the end of the entry, in parentheses after the last period.

DATABASE SOURCE (INFORMATION SERVICE)

LeSourd, S. J. (1992, April). The psychology of perspective
consciousness. Paper presented at the annual meeting of the
American Educational Research Association, San Francisco. (ERIC
Document Reproduction Service No. ED 348 296)

Treat an ERIC document as a database source only if the primary or
sole place to find it is from ERIC; if the source was previously published and is readily available in printed form, treat it as a journal
article or published book.

MATERIAL ACCESSED THROUGH A COMPUTER SERVICE

Boynton, R. S. (1994, March 3). The new intellectuals [3 parts]. The
Atlantic Monthly Online: [On-line serial]. Available America
Online: Directory: The Atlantic Monthly Online: Main Menu: News-
stand: Folder: The Atlantic Monthly 40-99669: File: The New
Intellectuals: Article: The New Intellectuals Parts 1-3.

REVIEW

Harris, I. M. (1991). [Review of Rediscovering masculinity: Reason,
language, and sexuality]. Gender and Society, 5, 259-261.

Give the author of the review, not the author of the book being reviewed. Use this form for a film review also. If the review has a title,
place it before the bracketed material, and treat it like an article title.

LETTER TO THE EDITOR

Pritchett, J. T., & Kellner, C. H. (1993). Comment on spontaneous
seizure activity [Letter to the editor]. Journal of Nervous and
Mental Disease, 181, 138-139.

PERSONAL CORRESPONDENCE

B. Ehrenreich (personal communication, August 7, 1992)

(B. Ehrenreich, personal communication, August 7, 1992)

Cite all personal communications to you (such as letters, memos,
and telephone conversations) in text only, *without* listing them
among the references. The phrasing of your sentences will determine which of the two above forms to use.

UNPUBLISHED MANUSCRIPT

McIntosh, P. (1988). White privilege and male privilege: A personal
account of coming to see correspondences through work in

women's studies. Working Paper 189. Unpublished manuscript, Wellesley College, Center for Research on Women, Wellesley, MA.

LECTURE

Kagan, J. (1968, April 30). A theoretical look at child development. Albert F. Blakeslee Lecture, Smith College, Northampton, MA.

PROCEEDINGS OF A MEETING, PUBLISHED

Guerrero, R. (1972/1973). Possible effects of the periodic abstinence method. In W. A. Uricchio & M. K. Williams (Eds.), Proceedings of a Research Conference on Natural Family Planning (pp. 96-105). Washington, DC: Human Life Foundation.

If the date of the symposium or conference is different from the date of publication, give both, separated by a slash. If the proceedings are published annually, treat the reference like a periodical article.

FILM

Golden, G. (Producer). (1975). Changing images: Confronting career stereotypes [Film]. Berkeley: University of California.

VIDEOTAPE

Cambridge Video (Producer). (1987). Setting educational/vocational goals [Video]. Charleston, WV: Cambridge Career Products.

SAMPLE RESEARCH PAPER (APA STYLE)

The following paper urges a change in our attitude toward zoos. Arguing the value claim that it is morally wrong for humans to exploit animals for entertainment, the student combines expert opinion gathered from research with her own interpretations of evidence. She is always careful to anticipate and represent the claims of the opposition before going on to refute them.

The student uses the APA style, modified to suit the preferences of her writing instructor. APA style requires a title page with a centered title, author, affiliation, and a short title that can be used as a "running head" on each page. An abstract page follows the title page and includes a one-paragraph abstract or summary of the article. Amanda Repp was told she could omit the title page and abstract recommended by the APA. A full description of APA publication conventions can be found in the *Publication Manual of the American Psychological Association,* Fourth Edition (1994).

Amanda Repp   Zoos   1

English 102-G

Mr. Kennedy

Fall 1996

Why Zoos Should Be Eliminated

Zoos have come a long way from their grim beginnings. Once full of tiny cement-block steel cages, the larger zoos now boast simulated jungles, veldts, steppes, and rain forests, all in an attempt to replicate the natural habitats of the incarcerated animals. The attempt, however admirable, is misguided. It is morally wrong to keep wild animals in captivity, and no amount of replication, no matter how realistic, can compensate for the freedom these creatures are denied.

Peter Batten (1976) argues that a wild animal's life "is spent in finding food, avoiding enemies, sleeping, and in mating or other family activities. . . . Deprivation of any of these fundamentals results in irreparable damage to the individual" (p. 1). The fact that humans may be stronger or smarter than beasts does not give them the right to ambush and exploit animals for the purposes of entertainment.

We humans take our own liberty quite seriously. Indeed, we consider liberty to be one of our inalienable rights. But too many of us apparently feel no obligation to grant the same right to animals, who, because they cannot defend themselves against our sophisticated methods of capture and because they do not speak our language, cannot claim it for themselves.

But the right to liberty is not based on the ability to claim it, or even on the ability to understand what it is. As James Rachels (1976) writes:

> Humans have a right to liberty because they have various other interests that will suffer if their freedom is unduly restricted. The right to liberty--the right to be free of external constraints on one's actions--may then be seen as derived from a more basic right not to have one's interests needlessly harmed. (p. 210)

Animals, like people, have interests that are harmed if they are kept in captivity: They are separated from their families and prevented from behaving according to their

---

Margin notes:

Short title and page number, per APA style. Some instructors may prefer the student's name instead of the short title as a running head.

First paragraph ends with thesis

Citation includes author, date of publication, and page number. Ellipses (. . .) indicate omitted passage; period after ellipses indicates that the omission included the end of a sentence.

Long quotations of more than 40 words are set off as block quotations. Start a new line on a five-space indented margin, double space throughout, and put the page number of the quotations in parentheses after the final punctuation.

natural instincts by being removed from the lives they know, which are the lives they were meant to lead.

Summary of an opposing argument

Some argue that animals' interests are not being harmed when they are kept in zoos or aquariums--that no damage is being done to the individual--but their claims are highly disputable. For example, the Zurich Zoo's Dr. Heini Hediger (1985) protests that it is absurd to attribute human qualities to animals at all, but he nevertheless resorts to a human analogy: "Wild animals in the zoo rather resemble estate owners. Far from desiring to escape and regain their freedom, they are only bent on defending the space they inhabit and keeping it safe from invasion" (p. 9). How can Dr. Hediger explain the actions of the leopards and cheetahs I have seen executing figure eights off the walls and floors of their cages for hours on end? I have watched, spellbound by their grace but also horrified; it is impossible to believe that these animals do not want their freedom. An estate owner would not spend his time running frantically around the perimeters of his property. These cats know they are not lords of any estate. The senseless repetition of their actions suggests that the cats know that they are caged and that there is nothing to defend against, no "estate" to protect.

Writer suggests flaw in comparison.

Refutation of opposing argument based on evidence from personal experience

Writer summarizes, then points out a weakness in, a second opposing argument.

Shannon Brownlee (1986) also believes that there is no concrete evidence that incarcerated animals are suffering or unhappy, but she weakens her own case in her description of Jackie, a dolphin in captivity who "spends the day in a seeming stupor" and "chews on the mackerel half-heartedly" at feeding time (p. 70). Clearly there is something wrong with Jackie; this becomes apparent when Brownlee contrasts Jackie's lethargic behavior with that of wild dolphins cavorting in the bay. Brownlee points out that Jackie has never tried to escape through a hole in his enclosure, although he knows it is there. But this fact does not necessarily mean that Jackie enjoys captivity. Instead, it may mean that Jackie's spirit has been broken, and that he no longer remembers or cares what his earlier days were like. Granted we have no way of knowing what Jackie

Writer questions an unstated warrant in the argument.

is really feeling, but does that give us the right to assume
that he is not feeling anything?

To be fair, Brownlee does not go that far. She does
allow Jackie one emotional state, attributing his malaise to
boredom. But perhaps if the author were removed from
members of her family, as well as all other members of her
species, and prevented from engaging in activities that most
mattered to her, she would recognize Jackie's problems as
something more than boredom. In any case, why should we
inflict boredom on Jackie, or any other animal, just because
we happen to have the means to do so?

Having registered these basic objections to zoos--that
keeping any creature in captivity is a fundamental infringement on that creature's right to liberty and dignity--I want
to take a closer look at the zoo as an institution, in order to
assess fairly its goals and how it tries to meet them. Most
zoo professionals today maintain that zoos exist for two
main reasons: to educate humans and to conserve animal
species. These are both admirable goals, certainly, but as
Seal (1985) notes, "none of these [zoo] budgets is allocated
specifically for species preservation. Zoos have been
established primarily as recreational institutions and are
only secondarily developing programs in conservation, education, and research" (p. 74). The fact is most zoos do not
have the money, space, or equipment required to make significant contributions in this area. The bulk of their money
goes to the upkeep of the animals and exhibits--that is, to
put it crudely, to the displays.

On behalf of the education a zoo provides, a common
argument is that there is nothing like seeing the real thing.
But what you see in the zoo is not a real thing at all. Many
zoo and aquarium animals, like Jackie the dolphin, have
been domesticated to the point of lethargy, in part because
they are being exhibited alone or with only one other member of their species, when what they are used to is
traveling in groups and finding their own food, instead of
being fed. Anyone who wants to see the real thing would
be better off watching some of the excellent programming

Writer shifts to
the second half of
her argument.

Clarifying word in
square brackets

Another opposing
argument, with
refutation

Summarizes two
expert opinions
that zoos do not
help endangered
species

about nature and wildlife that appears on public television.

As for conservation, it is clearly a worthwhile effort, but zoos are not effective agents of species preservation. It is generally acknowledged that it is difficult to breed zoo animals (Luoma, 1982, p. 104). Animals often do not reproduce at all--quite possibly because of the artificial, and consequently unsettling, circumstances in which they live. When zoo animals do mate successfully, the offspring is often weakened by inbreeding. According to geneticists, this is because a population of 150 breeder animals is necessary in order to "assure the more or less permanent survival of a species in captivity" (Ehrlich & Ehrlich, 1981, p. 211). Few zoos have the resources to maintain populations that size. When zoos rely on smaller populations for breeding (as many do) the species' gene pool becomes more and more limited, "vigor and fecundity tend to decline" (Ehrlich & Ehrlich, 1981, p. 212), and this can eventually lead to extinction. In other words, we are not doing these animals any favors by trying to conserve them in zoos. Indeed, Wilson (1995) writes that "all the zoos in the world today can sustain a maximum of only 2000 species of mammals, birds, reptiles, and amphibians, out of about 24,000 known to exist" (p. 57). Reserves and preservations, which have room for the larger populations necessary for successful conservation efforts and which can concentrate on breeding animals rather than on displaying them, are much more suitable for these purposes.

For what purposes, then, are zoos suitable? Are they even necessary? At present, they must house the many generations of animals that have been bred there, since these animals have no place else to go. Most animals in captivity cannot go back to the wild for one of two reasons. The first is that the creatures would be unable to survive there, since their instincts for finding their own food and protecting themselves from predators, or even the weather, have been greatly diminished during their time spent in captivity (Morton, 1985, p. 155). Perhaps this

---

Marginal notes:

Author, date, page cited parenthetically

Source with two authors cited parenthetically

Paraphrase with source cited parenthetically

is why Jackie the dolphin chooses to remain in his
enclosure.

The other reason animals cannot return to the wild is
an even sadder one: In many cases, their natural habitats
no longer exist. Thanks to deforesting and clearing of land
for homes, highways, factories, and shopping malls--which
are continually being built with no regard for the plant and
animal life around them--ecosystems are destroyed constantly, driving increasing numbers of species from their
homes. Air and water pollution and toxic waste, results of
the ever-increasing urbanization and industrialization
throughout the world, are just some of the agents of this
change. It is a problem I wish to address in closing.

If zoos were to leave breeding programs to more
appropriate organizations and to stop collecting animals,
the zoo as an institution would eventually be phased out.
Animals would cease to be exhibits and could resume being
animals, and the money previously used to run zoos could
be put to much better use. Ideally it could be used to
investigate why endangered species <u>are</u> endangered, and
why so many of the original habitats of these species <u>have</u>
disappeared. Most important, it could be used to explore
how we can change our habits and reorient our behavior,
attitudes, and priorities, so we can begin to address these
issues.

The problem of endangered species does not exist in a
vacuum; it is a symptom of a much greater predicament.
Humankind is responsible for this predicament, and it is up
to us to recognize this before it is too late. Saving a selected
species here and there will do none of us any good if those
species can exist only in isolated, artificial environments,
where they will eventually breed themselves into extinction. The money that has been concentrated on such efforts
should be devoted instead to educating the public about the
endangered planet--not just its animals--or, like the animals,
none of us will have any place to go.

Writer closes by
proposing a solu-
tion of her own.

Zoos   6

References start
a new page

References

Batten, P. (1976). <u>Living trophies</u>. New York: Crowell.

Brownlee, S. (1986, December). First it was "save the whales," now it's "free the dolphins." <u>Discover</u>, 70-72.

A book with two authors

Ehrlich, P. & Ehrlich, A. (1981). <u>Extinction: The causes and consequences of the disappearance of species</u>. New York: Random House.

A work in an anthology

Hediger, H. (1968). From cage to territory. In R. Kirchschofer (Ed.), <u>The world of zoos: A survey and gazeteer</u> (pp. 9-20). New York: Viking.

An article from a periodical

Luoma, J. (1982, November). Prison or ark? <u>Audubon</u>, 102-109.

Morton, E. S. (1985). The realities of reintroducing species to the wild. In J. R. Hoage (Ed.), <u>Animal extinctions: What everyone should know</u> (pp. 147-158). National Zoological Park Symposia for the Public series. Washington, DC: Smithsonian Institution.

For each reference, flush left on first line, then indent three spaces on subsequent lines

Rachels, J. (1976). Do animals have a right to liberty? In T. Regan & P. Singer (Eds.), <u>Animal rights and human obligations</u> (pp. 205-223). Englewood Cliffs, NJ: Prentice-Hall.

Seal, U. S. (1985). The realities of preserving species in captivity. In J. R. Hoage (Ed.), <u>Animal extinctions: What everyone should know</u> (pp. 147-158). National Zoological Park Symposia for the Public series. Washington, DC: Smithsonian Institution.

An article on-line from a computer service

Wilson, E. (1995, October 30). Wildlife: Legions of the doomed. [On-line]. <u>Time</u>. pp. 57-62. Nexis Library: Mags.

PART THREE

Opposing Viewpoints

THE FOLLOWING SECTION contains a variety of opposing viewpoints on eight controversial questions. These questions generate conflict among experts and laypeople alike for two principal reasons. First, even when the facts are not in dispute, they may be interpreted differently by opposing sides. Example: Do the statistics prove that capital punishment is or is not a deterrent to crime? Second, and certainly more difficult to resolve, equally worthwhile values may be in conflict. Example: In dealing with harmful substances, should we decide in favor of the freedom of the individual to choose or the responsibility of the government to protect?

"Opposing Viewpoints" lends itself to classroom debates, both formal and informal. It can also serve as a useful source of informed opinions which can lead to further research. First, read all of the articles in one of the "Opposing Viewpoints." Then select a topic for your research paper, either one suggested in this book (see "Topics for Research" at the end of each chapter) or another approved by your teacher. You may wish to begin your research by choosing material to support your claim from two or three articles in the text.

In reading, analyzing, and preparing your own responses to the opposing viewpoints, you should ask the following questions about each controversy:

1. Are there two — or more — different points of view on the subject? Do all sides make clear what they are trying to prove? Summarize their claims.

2. Do all sides share the same goals? If not, how are they different?

3. How important is definition of key terms? Do all sides agree on the definitions? If so, what are they? If not, how do they differ? Does definition become a significant issue in the controversy?

4. How important is factual and opinion evidence in support of the claims? Does the support fulfill the appropriate criteria? If not, what are its weaknesses? Is the support conflicting? Do the authorities — both the arguers and the experts they quote — have convincing credentials?

5. Do the arguers base any part of their arguments on needs and values that their readers are expected to share? What are they? Do the arguers provide examples of the ways these values function? Are these values implicit or explicit in the arguments? Is there a conflict of values? If so, which seem more important?

6. What warrants or assumptions underlie the claims? Are they implicit or explicit? Do the arguers examine them for the reader? Are the warrants acceptable? If not, point out their weaknesses.

7. What are the main issues? Is there a genuine debate — that is, does each side try to respond to arguments on the other side?

8. Do the arguers propose solutions to a problem? Are the advantages of their proposals clear? Are there obvious disadvantages to implementation of their solutions?

9. Does each argument follow a clear and orderly organization, one that lends itself to a good outline? If not, what are the weaknesses?

10. Does language play a part in the argument? Are there any examples of misuse of language — slanted or loaded words, clichés, slogans, euphemisms, or other short cuts?

11. Do the arguers show an awareness of audience? How would you describe the audience(s) for whom the various arguments are presented?

12. Do you think that one side won the argument? Can you find examples of negotiation and compromise, of attempts to establish a common ground? Explain your answer in detail.

CHAPTER ELEVEN

Affirmative Action

Thirty years after the enactment of laws and rules to promote affirmative action, it is under attack on several fronts — by government, business, and education. The legal bases for affirmative action are the Civil Rights Act of 1964 and two executive orders signed by President Lyndon Johnson in 1965. (The Equal Employment Opportunities Act of 1972 was charged with enforcing their provisions.) The original objective of these actions was elimination of the barriers to employment and schooling for women and members of minority groups. To that end, government contractors and educational institutions receiving federal funds were required to set up affirmative action programs.

The earliest policies were designed to protect traditionally disadvantaged groups against discrimination. This meant *ignoring* race and gender criteria which had prevented qualified women and members of racial and ethnic groups, especially African Americans, from participating fully in American life. In the 1970s, however, affirmative action underwent significant changes with the introduction of quotas, which were intended not merely to remove barriers but to compensate for the effects of past discrimination. Employers and school officials were now compelled to hire, or show that they had made efforts to hire, a specific percentage of African Americans, Hispanics, Native Americans, or women. (Asian Americans and Jews are almost never included in these quotas.)

As a result of these changes, Americans express ambivalence about the benefits of affirmative action to the whole society. In one poll 54 percent of the respondents said that "affirmative action has been good for the country." But when affirmative action was defined as "mandatory preferences," 75 percent of respondents opposed it.

That is because most Americans believe that mandatory preferences mean quotas, a violation of the American ideal that people should be judged as individuals, not as members of a group. They are uneasy about judgments made according to criteria, such as race and gender, that may have little to do with effort or ability to perform a job.

Proponents argue that affirmative action has been successful in enlarging opportunities and increasing diversity at work and at school. And until discrimination no longer prevents minorities and women from equal access to jobs, housing, and education, affirmative action laws should remain firmly on the books.

Court actions have reflected the ambivalence of the American public. Judges, in acknowledging the claims of reverse discrimination by white plaintiffs, have struck down some affirmative action programs in employment, but they have allowed others to remain. In education, however, it seems clear that the role of affirmative action is shrinking. A federal court in March 1996 ruled against a race-based admissions policy at the University of Texas Law School. Other schools in the same federal judicial circuit will be affected. At least a dozen states, including California, Arizona, and Pennsylvania, have introduced legislation to outlaw affirmative action programs that determine college admission and financial aid. A number of colleges and universities have now moved to offer financial aid to students on the basis of family income and educational level rather than race.

Racial Justice on the Cheap
STEPHEN L. CARTER

I often feel that I should oppose all racial preferences in admission to college and professional school. But I don't. When the law school admission season rolls around during the winter, I find myself drawn to the folders of applicants who are not white, as though to something rare and precious. Those folders I give an extra bit of scrutiny, looking, perhaps, for reasons to recommend a *Yes.* I am not trying to get the numbers right and I do not believe that the standards applied by colleges or professional schools are racist; rather, I find myself wanting others to have the same leg up that I had. The question is whether I can square this instinct with what I have said

Stephen L. Carter is William Nelson Cromwell Professor of Law at Yale University and a former clerk to Supreme Court Justice Thurgood Marshall. This selection is from his book *Reflections of an Affirmative Action Baby* (1991). His other books include *Integrity* (1996) and *The Culture of Disbelief* (1993). [Bibliographic citations have been cut.]

about the damage that preferences do. One of the principal mistaken emphases (or perhaps a public relations problem) of the modern diversity movement . . . is that it often seems in its rhetoric to press toward circumventing or eradicating standards, rather than training us and pushing us until we are able to meet them. There is an important distinction between this modern approach and the more traditional understanding of affirmative action as a program that would help a critical mass of us gain the necessary training to meet the standards of our chosen fields rather than seeking to get around them. Not the least of the difficulties is that the more time we spend arguing that various standards for achievement are culturally inappropriate, the more other people are likely to think we are afraid of trying to meet them.

My own view is that, given training, given a chance, we as a people need fear no standards. That is why I want to return the special admission programs to their more innocent roots, as tools for providing that training and that chance for students who might not otherwise have it. A college or university is not fulfilling its educational missions if it fails to take a hard look at the applicant pool to be sure that it is not missing highly motivated students — some of them people of color, some of them not — who might not be "sure things" but who show good evidence of being positioned to take advantage of what the school can offer. This means taking risks, but that is what higher educational institutions ought to be doing — not to fill a quota or to look good on paper or to keep student activists quiet, and certainly not to bring into the student body a group of students who will thereafter be called upon to represent the distinctive voices of oppressed people (imagine the brouhaha were a professor to take this idea seriously in calling on students in class discussion), but because the purveying of knowledge, the reason universities exist, is a serious enterprise, and one professors should undertake joyfully, even when it isn't easy and even when there is a risk of failure.

Of course, the students who are admitted because a school has decided to take a chance on them will not look as good on paper as those who are admitted because they are sure things; and the odds are that those with the better paper records will be the better performers, too, which is why grades and test scores are considered in the first place. The school, then, is admitting more than one group of students. Many students are admitted because of their paper qualifications, and these are the ones on which the school is likely to pin its highest hopes for academic attainment. The rest are admitted because they have benefited from one preference or another: legacy (as children of alumni are sometimes called), athlete, geography, even in some places music. And some receive a preference because of race.

All the beneficiaries of preferences, not just those who have earned a place through racial preferences, would have been excluded had only a paper record been used. But although every college has its stereotypes of the dumb jock and the stupid legacy, there is a qualitative difference between these characterizations and the conscious or unconscious racial nature of similar comments about the beneficiaries of racially conscious affirmative action. For just as a different standard for admission or hiring reinforces a double standard for the measurement of success, it also reinforces a double standard for the consequence of failure. When a person admitted because of membership in a special category does not succeed, that lack of success is often attributed to others in the same category. The stereotype of the dumb jock exists because of the widespread perception (a correct one) that athletes are frequently admitted on paper records for which other students would be rejected. When people of color are admitted in the same fashion, the damage is worse, because the double standard reinforces an already existing stereotype, and because the stereotype, like the program, sorts explicitly according to race. Consequently, if our success rate at elite colleges turns out to be lower than that of white students (as, thus far, it is), we can scarcely avoid having the fact noticed and, in our racially conscious society, remembered as well.

This risk is a predictable consequence of double standards and 5 cannot be avoided. It can, however, be reduced. The best way to reduce the risk would be to eliminate racial preferences, and over time, as the competitive capacity of people of color continues to improve. A more immediate solution is for those students who are admitted as a consequence of affirmative action, while on the college campus and while in professional school and while pursuing their careers — in short, *for the rest of their professional lives* — to bend to their work with an energy that will leave competitors and detractors alike gasping in admiration. The way to turn this potential liability into a powerful asset is to make our cadre of professionals simply too good to ignore.

To accomplish this goal, the first thing that an opportunity-based affirmative action must do is to abandon the pretense that it will in any significant way compensate for present educational disadvantage. Programs of preferential admissions will not wipe away the lingering effects of struggling through the inner-city public schools about which the nation long ago ceased to care. To bring onto college campuses students whose academic abilities have been severely damaged by the conditions in which they have been forced to learn would be a recipe for failure. At best, affirmative action can take those students of color who have already shown the greatest potential and place them in environments where their minds will be tested and trained, the campuses of elite colleges and professional schools.

Besides, the evidence has long suggested, and recent studies have confirmed, that educational disadvantage is but one of a cluster of problems reducing the likelihood that students of color will attend or complete college. In the past decade, despite rising test scores, a higher rate of high school graduation, and affirmative action programs galore, college attendance by black students is down. In particular, the proportion of black youth aged eighteen to twenty-four who have been enrolled in college has plummeted. In 1976, 33.4 percent of that group were or had been enrolled in college, representing nearly half of black high school graduates; this compared very favorably with the 33.0 percent of white youth of the same age with enrollment experience, representing 40 percent of white high school graduates. Ten years later, although the high school graduation rate rose, the percentage of black youth with enrollment experience dropped to 28.6 percent, representing only 37.4 percent of high school graduates, while the equivalent percentages for white youth barely changed at all.

Debate over the causes of this decline continues, and some of the candidates — for example, the rising involvement with the drug culture, the large number of young black men caught up in the criminal justice system, and the appeal of competing career choices, such as the military — are beyond the control of educational institutions. (Besides, the drug culture and criminal justice arguments are plainly insufficient to explain why the rate of high school graduation would be *up* so sharply.) There is common agreement, however, that a principal difficulty is the high cost, especially at the nation's most exclusive universities, which makes alternative career choices more attractive. This is why preferential financial assistance (for all its obvious problems) might actually be a more logical and efficient solution than preferential admission. As this manuscript was being completed, a debate erupted over the decision (subsequently modified) by the United States Department of Education to deny federal funds to schools offering preferential financial aid packages on the basis of race.[1] This decision, defended on the ground that federal aid should be administered in a color-blind manner, created a dilemma for colleges interested in keeping both minority recruitment and academic standards at high levels. If one argues that affirmative action is impermissible, then schools are left with only the market mechanism — money — as a tool for enticing onto their campuses excellent students who are not white. A genuine believer in market solutions should allow participants in the market to bid for scarce resources — and by all accounts, first-rate students of color are such a resource. One might want to

---

[1] The compromise resolution was that schools may not use federal funds for racially preferential scholarships but may fund such scholarships from other sources.

argue that this bidding is not fair, but if colleges can rely on neither preferential admission nor bidding to attract students who are not white, they plainly can do no more than pay lip service to the ideal of "minority recruitment." . . .

With the proper goal in mind, then, a degree of racial conscious-ness *in college and perhaps professional school admission* can plausi-bly be justified — but just a degree, and just barely. The educational sphere is the place for action because the proper goal of all racial preferences is opportunity — a chance at advanced training for highly motivated people of color who, for whatever complex set of reasons, might not otherwise have it. So justified, the benefit of a racial preference carries with it the concomitant responsibility not to waste the opportunity affirmative action confers. What matters most is what happens *after* the preference.

I call this vision of professional achievement and racial prefer- 10 ence the affirmative action pyramid, and it works much as the name implies: The role of preference narrows as one moves upward. And although I do not want to say arbitrarily *This is the spot,* what is clear is that as one climbs toward professional success, at some point the preferences must fall away entirely. Possibly a slight preference is justified in college admission, not as a matter of getting the numbers right, and certainly not as a matter of finding the right set of hitherto excluded points of view, but as a matter of giving lots of people from different backgrounds the chance — only the chance — to have an education at an elite college or university. But when that opportu-nity has been exercised, when the student has shown what he or she can do, the rationale for a preference at the next level is slimmer. So an even slighter affirmative action preference for professional school admission, while possibly justified on similar grounds, is less important, and a little bit harder to defend, than a program at the college level.

And when one's training is done, when the time comes for entry to the job market, I think it is quite clear that among professionals,[2] the case for preference evaporates. The candidate has by this time had six or seven or eight years of training at the highest level; it is a bit silly, as well as demeaning, to continue to insist that one's college and professional school performance is not a very accurate barome-ter of one's professional possibilities. The time has come, finally, to stand or fall on what one has actually achieved. And, of course, as one passes the point of initial entry and moves up the ladder of one's chosen field, all of the arguments run the other way; the time

---

[2] I make no claim here about the propriety of affirmative action in labor markets demanding less in the way of educational credentials.

for preference has gone, and it is time instead to stand proudly on one's own record. The preferences cannot go on forever. Sooner or later, talent and preparation, rather than skin color, must tell.

Affirmative Action Must Go
SHELBY STEELE

There are many indications that affirmative action may soon provoke what it has never provoked before: a national debate on group preferences that will be so open and contentious that no important politician will be able to avoid a hard yea or nay position.

This has all been started by the threat of another of those California statewide initiatives in which some long-simmering public bitterness explodes onto the ballot and is then argued out in the national village of talk radio. Next year, Californians are to vote on the appropriateness of preferential treatment by sex, race, and ethnic origin as a form of social redress. What an odd opportunity: to vote in secret on the idea that some citizens should be preferred over others in public employment, contracting, and higher education.

I wish my parents had had such a vote back in the 1950s, when I was languishing in a segregated elementary school created by white preferential treatment. My guess is that Californians will vote as my parents would surely have voted then: against preferences of any kind.

Significantly, most of the new interest in affirmative action seems to be political rather than social. The buzz is all about how the issue will wedge the Democrats into white male moderates on one flank and minorities and women on the other — an ugly resegregation of America's "civil rights" party that will make President Clinton even more vulnerable than he already is.

There is little talk about affirmative action as public policy. One 5 reason, I think, is that affirmative action has always been what might be called iconographic public policy — policy that ostensibly exists to solve a social problem but actually functions as an icon for the self-image people hope to gain by supporting the policy. From the beginning, affirmative action could be cited as evidence of white social virtue and of emerging black power — the precise qualities that America's long history of racism had denied to each side.

Shelby Steele, a fellow at the Hoover Institute in California, is the author of *The Content of Our Characters: A New Vision of Race in America* (1990). This column appeared in the *New York Times* on March 1, 1995.

Had America worked from the 1960s on to educate blacks to the same standards as whites, had it truly labored to eradicate discrimination, there would be more virtue and power on both sides of the racial divide today. The disingenuousness of affirmative action — born of the black struggle for freedom — can be seen in two remarkable facts: Middle-class white women have benefited from it far more than any other group, and 46 percent of all black children live in poverty.

The perniciousness of an iconographic social policy is that you cannot be against it without seeming to be against what it purports to represent. The white who argues against affirmative action looks like a racist and the black looks like an Uncle Tom. Iconographic policies perpetuate themselves by hiding behind what they represent. This is why, after twenty-five years, affirmative action is one of the least evaluated social policies in American history. The price for accepting its illusion of virtue and power is ignorance.

Not only do we blind ourselves to the workings of a social policy that becomes an icon, but in search of a flattering self-image we justify the policy by vague ideals like "diversity." And the emptiness of these ideals makes the policy unaccountable for any result it may have, so it remains an icon whether or not it accomplishes anything in the real world.

Diversity policies (today's euphemism for affirmative action) exist in virtually every important institution even though no one really knows what diversity means. Both proportionate and disproportionate representation reflect diversity; integration is one kind of diversity and segregation another. Here is an idealism that destroys accountability in social policy, and a language of willed ignorance in which the words mean only that the speaker has good intentions.

Still, as much as I loathe affirmative action — for the indignity and Faustian bargain it presents to minorities, for the hypocrisy and shameless self-congratulation it brings out in its white supporters — I must admit that it troubles me to see its demise so glibly urged from the political right. The Republican presidential aspirants are stumbling over one another to condemn it. While they are right to do so — and right is right even when it is nothing more than right — there is also the matter of moral authority. And this is something anyone who wants to dismantle affirmative action will have to earn. 10

I would ask those who oppose preferences to acknowledge and account for the reality of black alienation. As a black, I still fear discrimination, still have the feeling that it is waiting for me in public America. Discrimination does not justify preferential treatment, but I want to know that the person who stands with me against preferences understands the problem that inspired them.

To my mind there is only one way to moral authority for those of us who want affirmative action done away with: to ask that discrimination by race, gender, or ethnicity be a criminal offense, not just civil. If someone can go to jail for stealing my car stereo, he ought to do considerably more time for stifling my livelihood and well-being by discriminating against me.

If this means there will be many trials and lawsuits, so be it. When the pressure is put precisely on the evil you want to eradicate, then individuals and institutions will quickly learn not only what discrimination is but also what fairness is — and fairness is a concept so confused by decades of affirmative action that many now believe it can be reached only through discrimination.

Ending affirmative action must involve more than bringing down an icon. It must also involve an extension of democratic principles to what might be an extreme degree in a racially homogeneous society. But in a society like ours, discrimination is the greatest and most disruptive social evil. In a multiracial democracy of individuals, you have to make it a felony.

Race, Not Class

NATHAN GLAZER

Only few months ago, affirmative action seemed sacrosanct, having survived under two Republican presidents who opposed it but were incapable of modifying it in any way. Now suddenly the policy is threatened by complete abolition. But even confirmed opponents might quail before the cold-turkey withdrawal now made possible by the massive upthrust of political opinion. Is there any alternative to extinction, and should we try to find it?

One of the most popular alternatives to complete abolition is the replacement of race-based affirmative action with class-based affirmative action. It is preference on the basis of race that arouses anger and a sense of injustice among whites, just as it arouses such feelings among blacks. When whites believe that race alone excludes them from consideration for jobs or limits their opportunities to enter selective colleges, universities, and professional schools, many will feel the same anger blacks do.

Proponents of class-based affirmative action assert it would do much of what race-based affirmative action attempts to do, and

Nathan Glazer, a professor of education and sociology at Harvard University, is the author or editor of numerous books, including *Ethnic Dilemmas* (1983). This article is reprinted from the April 5, 1995, edition of the *Wall Street Journal.*

would not arouse the same hostility. Nor is there any bar to such preference, apparently, in the Constitution or in civil rights law. Of course, it could not achieve the same results for blacks as race-based affirmative action. But since blacks are to be found disproportionately among the poor (they form 12 percent of the population, but 30 percent or more of the population in poverty), many could move up because of their poverty. Class-based affirmative action would reduce the irritation and anger of those excluded, because of the moral legitimacy of this ground of preference. It would also reduce the cases of inequity, few as they may be, in which blacks of professional and high-income backgrounds get preference on the basis of race over poorer whites.

A Bad Idea

But class-based affirmative action is a bad idea, whose weaknesses become apparent when we review the areas in which affirmative action operates. Consider the preference to government contractors on grounds of race. This was designed to increase the number of black businessmen, and it has been ineffective in doing so, because we do not know the levers that will turn people averse to entrepreneurship into eager small-business men willing to undertake the risks, long hours, and stresses. (Koreans have the highest rate of self-employment of any racial or ethnic group, but not because of any government preference in bidding for contracts, even though they are apparently eligible for preference because they are "Asian.")

How would one qualify for eligibility for preference in bidding 5 for government contracts when the racial criterion is replaced by the economic? Would it be current income, to demonstrate that the bidder is truly poor? Could a poor contractor fulfill the contract? Would it be the income of the bidder's family of origin? What sense would that make? After all, how many children of prosperous parents undertake the hard and risky life of the small-business man? And who would the new businessmen of impoverished backgrounds be replacing, but other small-business men of almost equally impoverished backgrounds?

This area of affirmative action is peculiarly afflicted by dissembling and fraud. Is the contractor truly a "minority" or a "woman"— rather than a white contractor seeking a minority cover or a woman covering for her husband? Matters in this regard would not be improved if we replaced race by class. In the case of race-based preference in government contracts, abolition is clearly preferable to class-based preference.

Class-based preference makes as little sense in another area of affirmative action, admission to colleges, universities, and professional schools. We already have a huge and expensive system of federal loans and grants, supplemented by state programs and individual institutional scholarships, to make it possible for those without parental or their own income to get higher education. These do not cover all costs, but it is the assumption in American higher education that students will work to help pay for their education, and almost all, rich or poor, do. One can imagine covering all costs for higher education for everyone, as European countries attempt to do, but the costs would be enormous, and the beneficiaries for the most part would be white and Asian.

The problem African Americans face in entering institutions of higher education is performance, and performance is affected by poverty. But then the direct answer is programs to raise performance, or to reduce poverty. We know that substantial efforts have been expended on both objectives, and how frustratingly difficult it has been to make progress on either. The only effect of preference on grounds of class could be to increase the number of poor whites and Asians in institutions of higher education, and to reduce the number of blacks.

When it comes to employment, it is also hard to see what class-based affirmative action would achieve. Those aspiring to well-paid skilled work, as electricians, plumbers, and the like; to work as policemen, firemen, sanitation workers; to teaching jobs — in all of which strong affirmative action programs exist — are not typically from well-to-do backgrounds.

In each area of employment, defined means of entry and promotion have been developed: apprenticeship and union membership for skilled work, civil-service examinations for city jobs. Endless effort has been devoted to opening apprenticeship programs, union membership, and city work forces to blacks, and there has been some modest success, particularly in police forces, but these successes could not have been achieved by class-based affirmative action. Those struggling to enter such programs do not see themselves as particularly advantaged, and would resent the notion that a preference should be given to those poorer than they are when they themselves struggle against poverty.

Affirmative action is afflicted with irrational and illogical preference categories and with fraud. Much of this can and should be stripped away. But at its heart is a reality that cannot be wished away. This is the distinctive condition of American blacks, scarred by a history of oppression no other group, save American Indians, can match. African Americans are a group still uniquely isolated and segregated.

Whatever the weight of the logic that led to the inclusion of Hispanic Americans and Asian Americans in affirmative action at its beginnings, it no longer applies. Both groups now consist in their majority of immigrants and their children. American society and institutions have no special obligation beyond nondiscrimination for these groups. Asian Americans in general already have more education and as much income as most Americans. Hispanic Americans are more poorly off, but their circumstances are explained far more by lower average education, language difficulties, and recent immigration than by discrimination. Neither group should be included in legal requirements for affirmative action. American Indians raise other issues, but their condition is already addressed by a great deal of special legislation.

A Terrible Rejection

Affirmative action was occasioned by the civil rights revolution, and was designed for blacks. The problems it was intended to address are still with us, and in some respects are more serious than they were thirty years ago. Affirmative action has done precious little to ameliorate these problems, but I am concerned that African Americans will see the abandonment of affirmative action for them as a terrible rejection by an indifferent and hostile society. It would have consequences — for example, a sharp reduction in the number of blacks in selective colleges and professional schools — that we should not accept, whatever the value of the principle that justifies them.

Just what form affirmative action for blacks should take, where it should be applied, and who should benefit require further discussion. At the very least, voluntary affirmative action, which would certainly be maintained in colleges and universities, by major corporations, and by many cities, even in the absence of federal regulations, should be encouraged. There are legal and constitutional problems here, but they should not be allowed to stand in the way of voluntary efforts to deal with our greatest domestic problem.

Affirmative Action: A Tale of Two Women
MANDALIT DEL BARCO

The issue of affirmative action is being debated across the country, having sparked such buzzwords and phrases as "angry white males," "preferential treatment," and "reverse discrimination." The policy's original intent in the late 1960s was to redress past discrimination and provide opportunities for underrepresented groups, including Latinos and women. Supporters of affirmative action say the playing fields in schools, jobs, and contracts are still not level for many minorities, and that affirmative action is still crucial for ensur-

Mandalit del Barco is a Los Angeles-based reporter for National Public Radio and the radio program "Latino USA." She is a contributing editor to *Sí*, where this article first appeared in the Fall–Winter 1995 issue.

ing equal access. Critics, meanwhile, charge that affirmative action has stigmatized the very people it was supposed to have benefited, and created new victims in those who are passed over for jobs, college admissions, and so on. Some advocate abolishing affirmative action altogether, while others call for reforms, suggesting that the best solution could be to simply recast the policy in terms of the economically disadvantaged. All sides seem to agree the problem is one of fairness, though they may disagree about what is fair. *Sí* spoke with two prominent Mexican American women, Linda Chavez and Antonia Hernández, who have opposing views on this issue, which has at times divided those within the same ethnic group, including the Latino community.

Linda Chavez is a Mexican American woman out of the mold: She is fiercely and consistently conservative in the matter of affirmative action. The articulate staff director of the Commission on Civil Rights during the Reagan administration is today the president of the Center for Equal Opportunity, a nonprofit research group in Washington, D.C. Chavez is a columnist, a TV commentator, and author of the book *Out of the Barrio: Toward a New Politics of Hispanic Assimilation.* She will soon publish her second book, *A House Divided: Race and the Politics of Multiculturalism.* Linda Chavez's views are shaped not only by an extensive education, but also by her personal experience of ethnicity in this country. She belongs to the old community of *Mexicános* in the Southwest. "The only immigrant in my family in recent memory was probably my great grandfather, who was from England," says Chavez, a native of New Mexico. "On my father's side, my family goes back to the seventeenth century. On my mother's, there were Irish and English immigrants."

Sí: What is your definition of affirmative action?

Chavez: Affirmative action was originally construed to cast a wider net or provide training opportunities to enable people to compete. Those intentions were transformed in the late sixties and early seventies into programs that emphasize race or ethnicity as qualifications to promote the ideas of diversity. Diversity for its own sake. I find that offensive and I would like to see those programs abolished.

Sí: Why?

Chavez: They are more than offensive. Racial preferences granted by the State are unconstitutional. They violate the letter as well as the spirit of the civil rights laws. The Civil Rights Act of 1964 is unequivocal in that respect. 703-J of Title Seven says, "Nothing in this Act shall be interpreted to require preferences on the basis of race, color, or national origin."

Racial preferences are also patronizing, and ultimately, a very racist concept. They imply that, somehow, you cannot apply the same standards to blacks and Hispanics as you do to whites, be-

5

cause minorities will not be able to meet them. This is a misguided notion promoted by many liberals.

Sí: What do you say to those people who feel they never would have made it to where they are had it not been for affirmation action?

Chavez: If they would not have made it because they would not have found the opportunities, that is one thing. But if they have been admitted under a separate set of standards, and then held to a different standard of performance, I find it wrong.

Another thing that concerns me about the affirmative action pro- 10 grams is that they are a perpetual motion machine: Once they start, they go on forever. A student can be admitted by a college under one of those programs. After graduation, he or she can get into law school under another affirmative action program. After law school, he or she might still use affirmative action programs to get a job. If as a professional he or she does not make it to the top, people would say that there is a glass ceiling preventing this person from succeeding. An individual who cannot stand on his or her own in any given position perhaps should not be in it at all.

Sí: Yet people who favor affirmative action say its programs are still needed to level the playing field. Students who come from a school that was economically disadvantaged, and lack opportunities available to others, need that extra help.

Chavez: I do not disagree with that, that is what affirmative action was initially. But kids of middle-class families, whose parents are sometimes college-educated, are given a preference at Berkeley or Stanford based solely on their ethnic background. My children, for example, are often recruited. I have one son who is a senior now. He has been given a book on how to apply for affirmative action and scholarships. We live in one of the most affluent communities in America. He has not faced discrimination in his life, and he is not economically or socially disadvantaged. He should not be held to a lower standard and given a preference simply on the basis of his mother's ethnicity.

That is the core of the problem: Programs do not reach out to the kids who are disadvantaged and who come from inner-city schools.

The effort should not concentrate on admissions for law or medical schools. The emphasis should be a place in education at the elementary and secondary school levels. Here, the process begins. Children are prepared to compete on their own. Four years of math, science, and a foreign language are far more important to the long-term progress of both blacks and Hispanics than anything that can be done at a later time.

Sí: What is your own experience with affirmative action? 15

Chavez: I have been chosen for jobs on the basis of being a Mexican American woman. Each time, it has been an unmitigated disaster. There was a presumption that I thought in a certain way, and that I was going to serve a certain function. When it turned out I was not interested in being the token Hispanic, things did not work out well. There have been other times when the affirmative action prejudice stigmatized me. I had to constantly demonstrate that I have earned my position.

Once, I actively went after an affirmative action program. This was in 1969. The Ford Foundation had established a series of generous fellowships for blacks, Mexican American, and American Indians. I applied for one of them. The interviewer — who happened to be Anglo — complimented me on my ability to speak English. "My, you speak English so well," he said. Well, English is my only fluent language. English is my first language, as it is for most third-generation Mexican Americans. In addition, I was then pursuing a Ph.D. in English literature. I found the comment demeaning and insulting. The interview went downhill from there.

They also found my G.R.E. scores "too high" and that somehow this meant that I could not be an authentic Mexican American. That very sour experience was caused by people who thought they were doing people like me a favor.

Sí: Do you think your position might polarize people over the issue of race, when the real problem Americans face is, as many say, disappearing jobs?

Chavez: The most vociferous opposition comes from universities, not from working-class people who have seen their income diminish because of economic restructuring. The opposition underestimates the great damage affirmative action has done to race relations in this country. Indeed, there has been an increase in racial hostility.

Sí: Do you see a connection between the issues of affirmative action and immigration?

Chavez: Yes. People for Proposition 187 — an anti-immigrant initiative on the 1994 California ballot — were worried not just about a large number of newcomers, but about an increasing number of people eligible for affirmative action. Also, a lot of the anti-immigrant sentiment is a reflection of dissatisfaction with programs such as bilingual education, and the sense that immigrants create a whole new huge clientele for programs that are draining resources. People are angry about welfare. I am convinced that 187 won by such a large margin because welfare was on the ballot.

Sí: What is your view of Latino immigration in the United States?

Chavez: I am all for immigration, and maybe for higher immigration levels than the current ones. Immigrants come with tremendous entrepreneurial spirit. They are risk takers, they invest a lot in succeeding. But historically, American immigration has worked only if immigrants do not stay outside the mainstream, and stop functioning in their own language. The problem with Latino immigration is public policy regarding bilingual education.

What could also be destructive is the apparent rush to change immigration law. A moratorium on immigration, worker registries, a national I.D. card are all bad ideas.

Affirmative action divides more neatly along conservative and liberal lines. The immigration debate is much more divided. Some of the people who are most virulently anti-immigrant are those who consider themselves liberals. We are living in interesting times.

Antonia Hernández finds her story is not unique among Mexican Americans. Her family lived in Texas, but was deported when her father was eight years old. "I also was eight when I came here," remembers Hernández. "My dad brought us to Juárez. We lived here while my father put the documents together. I remember going to the interview with the immigration officers. They told my dad that, technically, we were citizens through derivative birth. It was the month of June. We crossed the border to El Paso, and they gave us our *mica*,[1] but our uncle could not come to pick us up from Los Angeles till September. We lived in Las Cruces and worked in the cotton fields."

Hernández's memories flow with ease. "My uncle came in a beautiful Chevrolet. We all got in the car, all crunched up, and on the way to Los Angeles, they were playing on the radio two songs I will never forget: Sarah Vaughan's 'Tender Lovin'' and Connie Francis's 'Lipstick on Your Collar.' When I hear those songs, I go back to that trip from El Paso to Los Angeles. I did migrant work. My parents were industrial laborers. The usual story."

Her story, though, is not common at all. From her humble origins, Hernández has come to be a well-known leader in the defense of Latino rights. She is president and general counsel of the Mexican American Legal Defense and Education Fund (MALDEF), an organization noted for its triumphs in class actions against discrimination, including widely publicized redistricting cases. She began her advocacy career during the Chicano movement in the early seventies, and continued her passionate service to the community at the Los Angeles Center for Law and Justice, and the Legal Foundation of Los Angeles. She is currently advising on the legal challenge to California's anti-immigrant initiative, Proposition 187.

---

[1] A Mexican term for the government-issued green card allowing immigrants to work in the United States for a limited number of years. — Ed.

Sí: In your opinion, what is affirmative action?

Hernández: Affirmative action is a court-sanctioned vehicle for diversifying the work force and opening opportunities for people who have been excluded in the past. Affirmative action is not quotas. It does not allow people to get by. In colleges and universities, affirmative action programs diversify the student body by considering a variety of factors for admission. But there is no affirmative action for grades. That is up to the student.

Same thing in the work force. For example: In the past, there were height requirements for police officers. That was devastating for women, since not many of them are six feet tall, particularly Latinas. Since height has little to do with your ability to perform the job, we went to court and challenged the requirement.

After a complete review of police responsibilities and the physical ability needed to fulfill them, the height requirement was changed. The quality standards were not lowered. That is the beauty of affirmative action. It gives the flexibility to find new standards that are more relevant, more current, taking into account our past and present history of discrimination and exclusion.

Sí: In which ways do you feel affirmative action has been successful?

Hernández: All you have to do is look at the statistics. And quite frankly, I would not be here if it were not for affirmative action. I was an immigrant kid out of East Los Angeles. Without affirmative action I would not have been given an opportunity to go to UCLA and explore horizons that were never opened to my parents. "Huppies"— upwardly mobile Hispanics — do not acknowledge sometimes that affirmative action has opened doors for them. They feel uncomfortable with what they perceive as a negative tag. We need to openly say we are examples of the success of affirmative action.

Sí: Can you talk about your own experience with affirmative action?

Hernández: I am a kid out of Garfield High School in East Los Angeles. I am a pretty bright individual, and I had decent grades. I was just dirt poor. My parents lived in the projects and I dreamed of going to Cal State L.A., because it was just across the street, in the neighborhood. That was as far as my dreams would take me. While I was in college, I was exposed to UCLA. I applied and was admitted. I did relatively well at UCLA because my grades were pretty decent, and my LSAT scores were also very good. I do not know whether I got in the door through affirmative action or regular admission. But it does not matter. I was given an opportunity and, I am sure, I was judged by standards other than just grades and test scores. They saw in me the burning determination, the drive, the willingness to work. That is what made me a success. I am not the only one. It happened to thousands of Latinos who went to medical school, to architecture school, you name it.

30

35

Sí: One argument people make against affirmative action is that it brings with it the stigma of being seen as undeserving. Do people think that you were given a break, that the standards were lowered when applied to you?

Hernández: I do not know if the standards were lowered. But they did give me a break. But it is no different than the breaks other people have been given. Children of alumni are given a very special break and get admitted automatically to the best universities. The perception that this is a society based on merit is one of our biggest myths. To some degree, I think I was also less qualified than other entering students. I came from Garfield High School. If you compare what it offered in the early sixties to other public schools, I was not getting an equal opportunity education. But I will tell you: I did not get in because I was given the proper grounding. I did not get in because I was given every privilege bestowed on alumni's kids. Am I stigmatized by this? No.

Sí: Linda Chavez and others argue: Why should we continue to base jobs, hiring, promotions, admissions, on a surname or the color of your skin? 40

Hernández: There is a basic assumption people make, that race is no longer a factor in this country. Race is a more prevalent factor now, but in a much more subtle way than before. Up until the sixties, regardless of how rich you were in Texas, if you were Mexican American, you were not admitted to certain colleges and universities. Look at the census. My kids are by no means poor. Should they get "a break" because their name is Hernández? I would venture to think, probably not. But my little Ben, who looks very Mexican, is not going to be judged by how well he is prepared. Group identity is still based on gender and skin pigmentation.

Sí: You were born in Mexico. Do you see a connection between affirmative action and emerging anti-immigration policies such as Proposition 187?

Hernández: Absolutely. This country is going through a real nervous breakdown. I do not mean it in a negative way. The national complexion is changing. The dynamics of who is an American is changing. In addition to Latinos, there are high concentrations of Armenians, Koreans, Iranians, and Russian Jews in large American cities. The country is feeling uncomfortable. Being American is not about looking a certain way. It is a state of [m]ind, an ideal, an attitude. It is what we believe in: individualism, and participatory democracy.

In Defense of Joe Six-Pack

JAMES WEBB

Those who debate the impact of affirmative action and other social programs are fond of making distinctions among white Americans along professional and geographic lines while avoiding the tinderbox of ethnic distinctions among whites. But differences among white ethnic groups are huge, fed by cultural tradition, the time and geography of migrations to the country, and — not insignificantly — the tendency of white Americans to discriminate against other whites in favor of their own class and culture.

In 1974, when affirmative action was in its infancy, the University of Chicago's National Opinion Research Center published a landmark study, dividing American whites into seventeen ethnic and religious backgrounds and scoring them by educational attainment and family income. Contrary to prevailing mythology, the vaunted White Anglo Saxon Protestants were even then not at the top.

A Greater Variation

The highest WASP group — the Episcopalians — ranked only sixth, behind American Jews, then Irish, Italian, German, and Polish Catholics. WASPs — principally the descendants of those who had settled the Midwest and the South — constituted the bottom eight groups, and ten of the bottom twelve. Educational attainment and income levels did not vary geographically, as for instance among white Baptists (who scored the lowest overall) living in Arkansas or California, a further indication that these differences are culturally rather than geographically based.

Family income among white cultures in the NORC study varied by almost $5,000 dollars, from the Jewish high of $13,340 to the Baptist low of $8,693. By comparison, in the 1970 census the variance in family income between whites taken as a whole and blacks was only $3,600. In addition, white Baptists averaged only 10.7 years of education, which was almost four years less than American Jews and at the same level of black Americans in 1970. This means that, even prior to the major affirmative action programs, there was a greater variation within "white America" than there was between "white America" and black America, and the whites at the bottom were in approximately the same situation as blacks.

James Webb, former Secretary of the Navy, is a novelist and screenwriter. This article appeared in the May 5, 1995, issue of the *Wall Street Journal.*

These same less-advantaged white cultures by and large did the 5 most to lay out the infrastructure of this country, quite often suffering educational and professional regression as they tamed the wilderness, built the towns, roads, and schools, and initiated a democratic way of life that later white cultures were able to take advantage of without paying the price of pioneering. Today they have the least, socioeconomically, to show for these contributions. And if one would care to check a map, they are from the areas now evincing the greatest resistance to government practices.

It would be folly to assume that affirmative action has done anything but exacerbate these disparities. The increased stratification and economic polarization in American life since 1974 is well documented. In the technological age, with the shrinking of the industrial base, the decrease in quality of public education, and the tendency of those who "have" to protect their own and to utilize greater assets to prepare them for the future, the divergence in both expectation and reward among our citizens has grown rather than disappeared. The middle class has shrunk from 65 percent of the population in 1970 to less than 50 percent today. Its share of aggregate household income declined by 5 percent from 1968 to 1993, while the top 5 million households increased their incomes by up to 10 percent a year. A similar rift has occurred in the black culture, with dramatic declines at the bottom and significant gains among the top 5 percent.

Because America's current elites are somewhat heterogeneous and in part the product of an academically based meritocracy, they have increasingly deluded themselves regarding both the depth of this schism and the validity of their own advantages. The prevailing attitude has been to ridicule whites who have the audacity to complain about their reduced status, and to sneer at every aspect of the "redneck" way of life. In addition to rationalizing policies that hold the working-class male back from advancement in the name of an amorphous past wrong from which he himself did not benefit, the elites take great sport in debasing the man they love to call "Joe Six-Pack."

And what does "Joe Six-Pack" make of this?

He sees a president and a slew of other key luminaries who excused themselves from the dirty work of society when they were younger, feeling not remorse but "vindication" for having left him or perhaps his father to fight a war while they went on to graduate school and solidified careers.

He sees a governmental system that seems bent on belittling the 10 basis of his existence, and has established a set of laws and regulations that often keep him from competing. His ever-more-isolated leaders have mandated an "equal opportunity" bureaucracy in the military, government, and even industry that closely resembles the Soviet "political cadre" structure, whose sole function is to report "political incorrectness" and to encourage the promotion of literally everyone but him and his kind.

He sees the meaning of words like "fairness" cynically inverted in the name of "diversity," while groups who claim to have been disadvantaged by old practices, and even those who have only just arrived in the country, are immediately moved ahead of him for no reason other than his race. In one of the bitterest ironies, he is required to pay tax dollars to finance special training for recent immigrants even as he himself is held back from fair competition and the "equal opportunity" bureaucracies keep him from receiving similar training, gaining employment, or securing a promotion.

He sees cultural rites buttressed by centuries of tradition — particularly the right to use firearms and pass that skill to future generations — attacked because many who make the laws do not understand the difference between his way of life and that of criminals who are blowing people away on the streets of urban America.

He watched the Democratic Party, once a champion of the worker-producer, abandon him in favor of special interests who define their advancement mostly through the extent of his own demise. To him "diversity" is a code word used to exclude him — but seldom better-situated whites — no matter the extent of his qualifications and no matter the obstacles he has had to overcome. The Republican Party, to which he swung in the last election, has embraced him on certain social issues, but has yet to support policies that would override the tendency of elites to simply protect their own rather than reverse the travails of affirmative action and the collapse of public education.

Out of the Casualty Radius

Finally, he sees the people who erected and continue to enforce such injustices blatantly wheedling and maneuvering themselves and their children out of the casualty radius of their own policies. A smaller percentage of whites in academia and the professions is acceptable, so long as their children make it. The public school system is self-destructing, but their children go to private schools and receive special preparatory classes to elevate college board scores. International peacekeeping is a lofty goal, so long as their children are not on the firing line. Continuous scrutiny is given to minority percentages in employment, but little or none is applied to how or why one white applicant was chosen over another.

Faced as he is with such barriers, it is difficult to fault him for deciding that those who make their living running the government or commenting on it are at minimum guilty of ignorance, arrogance, and self-interest. And it is not hyperbole to say that the prospect of a class war is genuine among the very people who traditionally have been the strongest supporters of the American system. 15

Affirmative Ambivalence

JONATHAN ALTER

Affirmative action has become so hopelessly polarizing that the debate doesn't seem to have room for mushy moderates like me — and maybe you. So it's time to make some room. The squishy view might not play well politically (as Bill Clinton is likely to discover) or sound snappily resolute on television, but it happens to be the most intellectually honest. You don't believe it? You think this is a matter of "principle," that you're on the side of Abraham Lincoln and the angels, and the other view has betrayed the true meaning of fairness and the civil rights movement? Here's a little test:

Let's say you are totally in *favor* of affirmative action, and believe that compromising in the face of the right-wing onslaught will start the country on a slippery slope to the bad old days. But how about FCC rules that let a huge white-owned company like Viacom win millions in tax breaks by selling broadcasting holdings to black front groups? Or how about an admissions policy that explicitly favors the preppy daughter of a rich black doctor over a poor white boy from Appalachia? Or a set-aside system that favors, say, a wealthy Costa Rican immigrant over a struggling third-generation Latvian American? Liberals were demonstrating last week with their new slogan: "No retreat." No retreat from *that?*

Across the divide, let's say you are totally *against* affirmative action, and believe we must face up to the hard truth that group entitlement (twenty-two "protected" classes in California alone) is deeply unfair. But how about, for instance, a black city with a largely white police force that makes no effort to recruit qualified black officers? Or a computer company with no women sales representatives? Finding black cops and women sales reps requires looking beyond paper credentials and old hiring habits and at least factoring in race and gender. That's called affirmative action.

Pushed hard enough, most people turn out to be fairly conflicted on this issue, which makes the search for compromise (as opposed to ideological vindication) all the more necessary. This is especially important for supporters of affirmative action to understand. If they try to hold fast to the status quo, they'll lose it all, first in California's 1996 ballot initiative, then everywhere. Lyndon Johnson's original idea in 1965 was to help "disadvantaged" people "hobbled" by past discrimination. It was Richard Nixon who began the drift to quotas. The challenge now is to reinforce the common-sense pillars on

Jonathan Alter is a senior editor at *Newsweek* magazine, where this essay appeared on March 27, 1995.

which the old consensus can be rebuilt, before it's too late. Some possibilities:

Excellence first: If every admissions, hiring, and promotion program established this as the first principle, then complaints about affirmative-action abuses would inevitably decline. We wouldn't have to read any more horror stories like the one about the state health-department supervisor in California who was fired when he refused to fill ten clerk-typist positions with minorities who couldn't type. Stressing excellence first would also lessen the stigma that is now often attached to minority hires, and give them more confidence that they were chosen on merit.

Fewer tests: Fights over preferences routinely revolve around tests. Whites, who generally do better on exams, tend to argue that test results equal merit. Blacks tend to argue that merit should be defined broadly. The latter argument is more persuasive. White police officers who complain that they were passed over for promotion even though they did better than black colleagues on the test miss the point. Promotion shouldn't be determined by tests but by performance, which can include relating to the community better in part because you are black.

No firing on race: It's one thing to miss winning a job partly on the basis of race. It's far worse to lose a job *strictly* on the basis of race. If the layoff decision truly cannot be made on the basis of performance or seniority, as in the controversial Piscataway, New Jersey case, management should simply flip a coin. That would be arbitrary but fair.

Take pride in hairsplitting: The two big Supreme Court decisions of the last twenty years have both been attacked for ambivalence, but in both cases the court drew the right distinctions. In its 1978 *Bakke* decision, the court ruled against quotas but accepted the use of race in the admissions process to build a diverse student body. The 1989 *Richmond* ruling found that preferences in municipal hiring must be "narrowly tailored" to overcome specific examples of past discrimination. Needed next: better enforcement.

Add class: With budgets tight, schools fill affirmative action slots by admitting minority students whose families can pay, while rejecting poor applicants who really need the break. Class cannot replace race across the board. (Workplace promotions, for instance, cannot be pegged to childhood disadvantage.) But class must consistently supplement and sometimes supersede race, especially in education.

Stress success: Affirmative action has helped create a new black middle class and transform the role of women. But few recognize that it also fattens the bottom line. From newspapers to apparel, a diverse work force brings a marketing edge. Hard-headed results carry more weight than the old calls for justice.

Evaluate, evaluate, evaluate: Like any program, this one should be constantly second-guessed. Instead of whimpering about the assault, advocates of affirmative action should seize the chance to rethink, revise and reenergize their position. Enemies of the whole idea were the ones who reopened the debate. So what? Like striving for diversity, it happens to be the right thing to do.

. . . *That's My Son*

SONYA JASON

As an adult college student who had not attended high school, I toiled over the usual number of units per semester while also caring for my husband and two small boys. There was no financial aid, nor did I expect any. It was gratifying enough to edit my community college's newspaper and, one summer, to produce a weekly newspaper for a Cal State campus. I earned awards and commendations and, in 1963, a B.A. in journalism.

But after graduation, I found there were no nonclerical positions in the media for women. I was saddened that my sex was all the interviewers saw — that accomplishment was secondary. But, as any sensible person would, I set aside disappointment and put what I learned to the best possible use, accepting positions as a social worker and later as a probation officer. During those years I continued to write and be published. Above all, I believed that my children would be spared such discrimination.

But that is not the case for my two sons. One, after eighteen months of hell in Vietnam, entered a highly technical skilled field where he found a niche after a long struggle.

The other, a born scholar, spent years of fourteen-hour days in pursuit of academic excellence. He graduated from a tough university with degrees in philosophy and physics and immediately went on to earn master's degrees in computer science and philosophy and a doctorate in philosophy.

It was heartbreaking to observe him conscientiously preparing 5 for interviews for tenured positions only to have them given to [less]-qualified people, always minorities or women. How insulting to sit through the charade of an interview when the decision had already been made!

But my son did not let this defeat him. As any sensible person would, he made the most of what he'd learned. He is teaching part

---

This letter by Sonya Jason, a coal miner's daughter who is a freelance writer in Woodland Hills, California, appeared in the *Wall Street Journal* on March 27, 1995.

time and earning the bulk of his living as a business manager. And he writes and publishes, too. His two textbooks are widely used.

My parents were impoverished immigrants who knew mostly bleak oppression in their native countries. Neither they nor we, their descendants, ever oppressed anyone. Yet my sons are punished.

THINKING AND WRITING ABOUT AFFIRMATIVE ACTION

Questions for Discussion and Writing

1. Both Chavez and Carter, members of minority groups, agree on what Carter calls "the affirmative action pyramid." Explain how this might change some practices of affirmative action today.

2. Summarize the "possibilities" Alter lists in order to achieve "common ground and compromise." Do you think these would be acceptable to Hernández or Webb?

3. What does Steele mean by "iconographic public policy"? What does he see as the consequences of such policy? Does the remedy he proposes to replace affirmative action seem reasonable as a solution to the problems of discrimination?

4. Why does Glazer believe that preferences based on class and income rather than race are "a bad idea"? Which of the reasons that he defends is strongest?

5. What huge differences among white ethnic groups does Webb describe? Who or what are the objects of his attack? What different kinds of support does he provide? Do you think he has proved his point?

6. Several authors claim that affirmative action has damaged both minorities and whites in different ways. But they do not all therefore conclude that affirmative action must go. How do they reconcile these two apparently contradictory points of view?

7. Chavez, Hernández, Carter, and Jason use personal experience to defend their positions. If you have already formed an opinion about affirmative action, did any of their stories persuade you to change your mind or, at least, entertain a doubt about your position?

8. In the cartoon on page 406, identify *Brown Decision, Voting Rights Bill,* and *Emancipation Proclamation,* and explain their relevance to the point of the cartoon.

Topics for Research

The effect of affirmative action on African Americans

The effect of affirmative action on women

The birth of affirmative action in 1965

Affirmative action policies of my campus: Goals and results

Changing affirmative action policies in the nineties

CHAPTER TWELVE

The Digital Revolution

"The most transforming technological event since the capture of fire." This is the way one expert describes the revolution introduced in this century by computers. Such extravagant interpretations aside, there is no doubt that the acceleration of computer technology has produced enormous changes in all our lives. As late as the 1950s, computers were rarely seen outside university centers. Now, of course, they are everywhere, in classrooms, libraries, offices, stores, factories, research labs, and, increasingly, in our homes.

Even those who fear that it may lead to the decline of the book acknowledge what appear to be positive effects of the new technology: easier revision of writing, greater access to information, rapid solution of difficult problems, greater freedom in selection of the workplace, additional sources of entertainment, and global communication, both personal and professional.

But the number of naysayers is growing. In the words of Nicholas Negroponte, professor of media technology at the Massachusetts Institute of Technology, "Every technology or gift of science has a dark side." We have already identified some of the problems: loss of employment, invasion of privacy, unscrupulous use of the technology, isolation from the physical world and other people. In time we will undoubtedly solve some of these problems, but others will remain.

Some critics have asked if the revolution can be halted, or at least slowed, if it encounters serious resistance. But, according to one view, "It is coming, whether we like it or not." Given its inevitability, then, does the greater freedom of this medium, which enables anybody to publish his or her views, mean that our discourse will be enriched? Or are we simply creating more noise? Not least, will the development and embrace of this technology affect our human nature? Marshall McLuhan, an influential scholar, remarked, "We shape our tools and thereafter our tools shape us." Will we become different creatures — separated from nature, isolated in front of our screens, unable to distinguish between the reality and the image?

As students, you are at the center of an important controversy about the distribution and use of computers in schools. In his State of the Union address in 1996, President Clinton called for computers in every classroom and library by the year 2000. This ambitious goal is not likely to be met, and if it is not, will children in schools with access to technological innovation enjoy a significant educational advantage over children in schools without? A crucial debate is shaping up over the purpose of computers. At present, educators are deeply divided on the extent to which computers can help students develop the critical habits of mind that characterize real education.

Don't Dissect a Frog, Build One

NICHOLAS NEGROPONTE

Most American children do not know the difference between the Baltics and the Balkans, or who the Visigoths were, or when Louis XIV lived. So what? Why are those so important? Did you know that Reno is west of Los Angeles?

The heavy price paid in countries like France, South Korea, and Japan for shoving many facts into young minds is often to have students more or less dead on arrival when they enter the university system. Over the next four years they feel like marathon runners being asked to go rock climbing at the finish line.

In the 1960s, most pioneers in computers and education advocated a crummy drill-and-practice approach, using computers on a one-on-one basis, in a self-paced fashion, to teach those same God-awful facts more effectively. Now, with the rage of multimedia, we have closet drill-and-practice believers who think they can colonize the pizzazz of a Sega game to squirt a bit more information into the heads of children, with more so-called productivity.

On April 11, 1970, [Seymour] Papert held a symposium at MIT called "Teaching Children Thinking," in which he proposed using

This excerpt is from *being digital* (1995) by Nicholas Negroponte, a professor of media technology at the Massachusetts Institute of Technology and the director of the MIT Media Lab.

computers as engines that children would teach and thus learn by teaching. This astonishingly simple idea simmered for almost fifteen years before it came to life through personal computers. Today, when more than a third of all American homes contain a personal computer, the idea's time has really come.

While a significant part of learning certainly comes from teach-   5
ing — but good teaching and by good teachers — a major measure comes from exploration, from reinventing the wheel and finding out for oneself. Until the computer, the technology for teaching was limited to audiovisual devices and distance learning by television, which simply amplified the activity of teachers and the passivity of children.

The computer changed this balance radically. All of a sudden, learning by doing became the rule rather than the exception. Since computer simulation of just about anything is now possible, one need not learn about a frog by dissecting it. Instead, children can be asked to design frogs, to build an animal with froglike behavior, to modify that behavior, to simulate the muscles, to play with the frog.

By playing with information, especially abstract subjects, the material assumes more meaning. I remember when my son's third-grade teacher reported to me sadly that he could not add or subtract a pair of two- or three-digit numbers. How odd, I thought, as he was always the banker when we played Monopoly, and he seemed to do a dandy job at managing those numbers. So I suggested to the teacher that she try posing the same addition as dollars, not just numbers. And, behold, he was suddenly able to add for her three digits and more in his head. The reason is because they were not abstract and meaningless numbers; they were dollars, which related to buying Boardwalk, building hotels, and passing Go.

The computer-controllable LEGO[1] goes one step further. It allows children to endow their physical constructs with behavior. Current work with LEGOs at the Media Lab includes a computer-in-a-brick prototype, which demonstrates a further degree of flexibility and opportunity for Papert's constructivism, and includes inter-brick communications and opportunities to explore parallel processing in new ways.

Kids using LEGO/Logo today will learn physical and logical principles you and I learned in college. Anecdotal evidence and careful testing results reveal that this constructivist approach is an extraordinarily rich means of learning, across a wide range of cognitive and behavioral styles. In fact, many children said to have been learning disabled flourish in the constructionist environment.

---

[1]In its original form, the popular plastic construction set for children. — ED.

Street Smarts on the Superhighway

During the fall break, when I was in boarding school in Switzer-   10
land, a number of children including myself could not go home because home was too far away. But we could participate instead in a
concours, a truly wild goose chase.

The headmaster of the school was a Swiss general (in the reserves, as are most of the Swiss armed forces) and had both cunning
and clout. He arranged a five-day chase around the country, where
each team of four kids (twelve to sixteen years old) was equipped
with one hundred Swiss francs ($23.50 at the time) and a five-day
railroad pass.

Each team was given different clues and roamed the country,
gaining points for achieving goals along the way. These were no
mean feats. At one point we had to show up at a certain latitude and
longitude in the middle of the night, whereupon a helicopter
dropped the next message in the form of a quarter-inch tangled audiotape in Urdu, telling us to find a live pig and bring it to a location
that would be given at a certain phone number (which we had to determine by a complex number puzzle about the dates when seven
obscure events took place, whose last seven digits made up the
number to call).

This kind of challenge has always had an enormous appeal to
me, and, sorry to brag, my team did win — as I was convinced it
would. I was so taken by this experience, I did the same for my son's
fourteenth birthday. However, without the American army at my
beck and call, I made it a one-day experience in Boston for his class,
broken up into teams, with a fixed budget and an unlimited subway
pass. I spent weeks planting clues with receptionists, under park
benches, and at locations to be determined through telephone number puzzles. As you might probably guess, those who excelled in
classwork were not necessarily the winners — in fact, usually the
opposite. There has always been a real difference between street
smarts and smart smarts.

For example, to get one of the clues in my wild goose chase, you
had to solve a crossword puzzle. The smart-smart kids zoomed to
the library or called their smart friends. The street-smart kids went
up and down the subway asking people for help. Not only did they
get the answers more quickly, but they did so while moving from A
to B and gaining distance and points in the game.

Today kids are getting the opportunity to be street smart on the   15
Internet, where *children are heard and not seen*. Ironically, reading
and writing will benefit. Children will read and write on the Internet
to communicate, not just to complete some abstract and artificial exercise. What I am advocating should not be construed as anti-
intellectual or as a disdain for abstract reasonings — it is quite the

opposite. The Internet provides a new medium for reaching out to find knowledge and meaning.

A mild insomniac, I often wake up around 3:00 A.M., log in for an hour, and then go back to sleep. At one of these drowsy sessions I received a piece of e-mail from a certain Michael Schrag, who introduced himself very politely as a high school sophomore. He asked if he might be able to visit the Media Lab when he was visiting MIT later in the week. I suggested that he sit in the back of the room of my Friday "Bits Are Bits" class, and that we match him with a student guide. I also forwarded a copy of his and my e-mail to two other faculty members who agreed to see him (ironically so: they thought he was the famous columnist Michael Schrage, whose name has an *e* at the end).

When I finally met Michael, his dad was with him. He explained to me that Michael was meeting all sorts of people on the Net and really treated it the way I treated my *concours*. What startled Michael's father was that all sorts of people, Nobel Prize winners and senior executives, seemed to have time for Michael's questions. The reason is that it is so easy to reply, and (at least for the time being) most people are not drowning in gratuitous e-mail.

Over time, there will be more and more people on the Internet with the time and wisdom for it to become a web of human knowledge and assistance. The 30 million members of the American Association of Retired Persons, for example, constitute a collective experience that is currently untapped. Making just that enormous body of knowledge and wisdom accessible to young minds could close the generation gap with a few keystrokes.

Playing to Learn

In October 1981 Seymour Papert and I attended an OPEC meeting in Vienna. It was the one at which Sheik Yamani delivered his famous speech about giving a poor man a fishing rod, not fish — teach him how to make a living, not take a handout. In a private meeting with Yamani, he asked us if we knew the difference between a primitive and an uneducated person. We were smart enough to hesitate, giving him the occasion to answer his own question, which he did very eloquently.

The answer was simply that primitive people were not uneducated at all, they simply used different means to convey their knowledge from generation to generation, within a supportive and tightly knit social fabric. By contrast, he explained, an uneducated person is the product of a modern society whose fabric has unraveled and whose system is not supportive.

The great sheik's monologue was itself a primitive version of Papert's constructivist ideas. One thing led to another and both of us

20

ended up spending the next year of our lives working on the use of computers in education in developing countries.

The most complete experiment in this period was in Dakar, Senegal, where two dozen Apple computers with the programming language Logo were introduced into an elementary school. The children from this rural, poor, and underdeveloped west African nation dove into these computers with the same ease and abandon as any child from middle-class, suburban America. The Senegalese children showed no difference in adoption and enthusiasm due to the absence of a mechanistic, electronic, gadget-oriented environment in their normal life. Being white or black, rich or poor, did not have any bearing. All that counted, like learning French in France, was being a child.

Within our own society we are finding evidence of the same phenomenon. Whether it is the demographics of the Internet, the use of Nintendo and Sega, or even the penetration of home computers, the dominant forces are not social or racial or economic but generational. The haves and the have-nots are now the young and the old. Many intellectual movements are distinctly driven by national and ethnic forces, but the digital revolution is not. Its ethos and appeal are as universal as rock music.

Most adults fail to see how children learn with electronic games. The common assumption is that these mesmerizing toys turn kids into twitchy addicts and have even fewer redeeming features than the boob tube. But there is no question that many electronic games teach kids strategies and demand planning skills that they will use later in life. When you were a child, how often did you discuss strategy or rush off to learn something faster than anybody else?

Today a game like Tetris is fully understandable too quickly. All that changes is the speed. We are likely to see members of a Tetris generation who are much better at rapidly packing the trunk of a station wagon, but not much more. As games move to more powerful personal computers, we will see an increase in simulation tools (like the very popular SimCity) and more information-rich games.

Hard fun.

On Classrooms, with
and without Computers

CLIFFORD STOLL

[How well does our new technology fit into the classroom?]
Aside from the mechanical problems of using computers in classrooms, I wonder how this digital wizardry will affect the content of
schoolwork.

Certainly, college-bound students should know basic computing:
enough word-processing skills to write a paper, the ability to use
and modify a spreadsheet, and a familiarity with database programs.
Remember, though, that plenty of profs still accept handwritten
term papers.

Should computer dexterity be taught at the expense of other
skills? Hard to say, especially in a time when driver's education is
disappearing from many high schools.[1]

Maybe computing should be integrated with other classroom activities? Sounds tempting — combine computing with math, physics,
or history. In a sense, we teach students to become information
hunter-gatherers. Tell them how to access on-line resources and
make sure they're comfortable finding their way around the networks.

This assumes that most everything is available on-line and that   5
networks use simple, standardized tools. It also assumes that primary source material isn't messy and that students will know how to
use the data presented to them. I doubt that any of these assumptions are valid.

There's a deeper assumption: that gathering information is important. These teaching projects magnify the computing side, while
making the learning experience seem trivial.

In a well-publicized classroom experiment, a group of fifth-
graders from Washington State conducted an on-line survey. As a geography project, they asked the price of a twelve-inch pizza. Using
the networks, they found highs of twelve dollars in Alaska to a low of
four dollars in Ohio.

A most appealing project: These students were learning geography, handling the tools of economic research, and meeting others
over the Internet. All this from their on-line classroom.

Clifford Stoll has been involved with computer networks since their beginning.
His first book was the bestseller *The Cuckoo's Egg* (1990), which described his exposure of a German spy ring operating over the Internet. This is an excerpt from his
1995 book, *Silicon Snake Oil*. [All notes are Stoll's.]

[1] "An amusing complaint from a guy who owns five computers but no car," says
my editor.

But hold on. That pizza data could just as readily have been acquired by telephone or letter or fax. There's nothing inherent to the Internet here — it's just the data-transmission vehicle.

More damning: They were learning the wrong-most thing about geography — that data collection is an end in itself. It's usually the easy part of research, and the part requiring the least thought.

Better to hear how the fifth-graders worked with the data further, coming up with hypotheses explaining the trends in pizza prices. Is there more competition in Ohio's pizza market than in Alaska's? Are ingredients cheaper? Are these prices associated with unemployment?

Why not study Spanish, trace the flow of Pacific Rim forest products, or perform a class play? None of these have the same glamour or technological appeal as a class project over the Internet. Yet they're likely to be far more important to the students' future than a survey of pizza prices.

At the 1993 Computer-Using Educators Conference in Santa Clara, California, David Thornburg, director of the Thornburg Center of Professional Development, hooked his computer into the White House section of America Online. From there, he downloaded a dozen press releases, a presidential speech, several proposals to Congress, and hundreds of pages of governmental reports. He turned to the audience and said, "Look at all this research material that these kids now have."

In the back of the room, one teacher quietly remarked, "OK, what's next? I've got one computer and thirty kids. What can they do with this raw data? I'd have to print out a hundred pages, review what's there, then generate a lesson. As it sits, this material is worthless in a real classroom."

What do we mean by *computer literacy?* Along with buzzwords like *information superhighway, interactive multimedia,* and *paradigm,* it's a fuzzy term without fixed meaning. Defining these is like trying to nail Jell-O to the wall.[2]

To one person, computer literacy means that a student can type on a keyboard. Another sees it as the ability to use standard tools to

---

[2] Nailing Jell-O to the wall? While a grad student at Princeton, Don Alvarez tried it. I replicated his experiment and discovered that it's not so hard.

The obvious way is to freeze the Jell-O, but we're looking for something with a little more artistry than a tank of liquid nitrogen.

First nail the slab of Jell-O to a horizontal board with a grid of ten-penny nails, spaced an inch apart. Then tip the board up and nail it to the wall.

What won't work is to simply hold the Jell-O against the wall, then pound in nails. It sags under its own weight and tears as fast as you pound the nails. Not enough tensile strength.

send, copy, or delete files. A third expects students to be able to write a simple program in BASIC. One teacher showed me an exam where a student had to describe the functions of different pieces of hardware.

But what does computer literacy mean to a child who can't read at grade level and can't interpret what she reads? What does it mean to a teenager who can't write grammatically, not to mention analytically?

If a child doesn't have a questioning mind, what good does all this networked technology do?

Have we ever spoken of automobile literacy or microwave-oven literacy? Each of these is important today; yet high schools are shedding their driver's education programs and home economics classes. There's far more need for cooks, drivers, and plumbers than programmers, yet parents and school systems insist on teaching computer skills.

But what are these skills? Over the past decade, we've realized   20
that programming is of little value except to those few who take it up as a career. Word processing is plenty handy, but hardly requires a semester of teaching.

And just because students use computers doesn't mean they're computer-literate. How many couch potatoes know how their televisions work?

Slowly, the term *computer-literacy* is becoming passé, I'm told. In its place, educators speak of computer-aided education, networking, and technology seeding. If computer vendors seem filled with puffery, you haven't heard these people talk.

In physics, you measure the brightness of light with a photometer and voltages with a voltmeter. Bogosity — the degree to which something is bogus — is measured with a bogometer. When listening to these guys, I watch the needle of my bogometer.

It's usually administrators and consultants — not teachers — that give me the heebie-jeebies. Like when Frank Withrow, director of learning technology at the Council of Chief State School Officers, asserts that the network brings us virtual publishing; moreover, the ability to transmit information instantly has brought us to "a major crest of human development and symbolisms."[3]

Symbolisms? My bogometer reads midscale. Then I read David   25
Thornburg's course materials for the fall 1994 Computer-Using Educators Conference. He says that the information age is over, replaced by some sort of communications age. He wants to reshape education because "students are going to primary source materials

---

[3] At Multiple Media: The Next Step, a conference in Atlanta, Georgia, on February 16, 1994. Mr. Withrow was keynote speaker.

to research their term papers without leaving their bedrooms. The days of running through the library stacks pulling reference materials are numbered."

Not much need for books and school libraries? The bogometer needle reaches into the red zone.

Alan November, a consultant for the Glenbrook high schools in Illinois, believes that today's students are in the test-preparation business. In the May/June 1994 issue of *Electronic Learning,* he says that pupils will soon build information products that can be used by clients around the world. Teachers, in turn, will become brokers "connecting our students to others across the nets who will help them create and add to their knowledge." That one pegged my bogometer.

I'd discount such high-tech mumbo jumbo except that there are so many believers. Parents walk away from schools satisfied if they merely see computers in the classroom. Principals plead for budgets large enough to bring interactive media into their schools. Many teachers are cowed by consultants sporting fancy degrees. School board members apply for grants to bring networks into local districts. Lost in this promotion are students.

Not every kid wants to spend hours at a keyboard. Some bump into the same kind of frustrations that adults feel. Others are just bored by the experience.

Then there are the kids who can't get enough time behind the 30 screen. At first, I figured this was great . . . a lot better than television and a chance to learn useful skills. I remember spending a month learning how to solve simultaneous equations algebraically. It would have been much more fun to play with a computer instead.

"Just because children do something willingly, even eagerly, is not a sufficient reason to believe it engages their minds," writes Dr. Lillian Katz, a specialist in early education and author of *Engaging Children's Minds.* "Remember that enjoyment, per se, is not an appropriate goal for education."

You know, there are plenty of things that I'd love to do all day long that simply aren't good for me. Offhand, I'd include reading net news and eating Mars bars. Not that those chocolate bars aren't good, mind you.

Seems to me that most learning grows out of childhood curiosity, for which there is no readily installed software package. Curiosity usually begins with our physical world, not some glowing phosphorescent abstraction. Kids need to mess around with concrete materials . . . erector sets and crayons do more than filmstrips and videos.

If schools encourage inquisitiveness, exploration, and a lust for knowledge, kids won't be afraid of learning computers. They won't have a hard time with literature, science, and history, either.

But when schools pressure kids to know computers inside and 35 out, naturally some students will fail. Others will become automatons, memorizing instructions without engaging their minds.

Suppose that I accept that students should spend a lot of time behind computers. What's the limit? If computers, on-line networks, and interactive video are so important to modern classrooms, why not eliminate the classroom entirely? Students of all levels could sit behind their computers at home, and receive quality instruction from the finest teachers. Electronic correspondence courses.

A silly proposal, reminiscent of the matchbook covers that told us to enroll in their home-study course and "get a good education and step up to higher pay." Home-study dropout rates often exceed 60 percent; it's hard to believe that an electronic version would do much better, despite the gimmickry.

The Internet can probably deliver all the information taught in a university, as can a good encyclopedia. So why go to college?

Because isolated facts don't make an education. Meaning doesn't come from data alone. Creative problem solving depends on context, interrelationships, and experience. The surrounding matrix may be more important than the individual lumps of information. And only human beings can teach the connections between things.

What Are We Waiting For?

JOHN DIEBOLD

Not long ago I hurt my back while sawing up a tree. Doctors ran a series of expensive tests and advised surgery. When I checked in for the operation two days later, they had to run the same tests all over again. The earlier results had been filed away, out of reach.

Last summer, as I was driving to New York's Kennedy International Airport to catch a plane, hundreds of brake lights suddenly lit up ahead of me, and traffic slowed to a crawl. I finally realized that with the Mets playing at Shea Stadium, the toll booths ahead must be swamped. As precious minutes ticked by and tempers flared, I and hundreds of other travelers missed our flights.

We've all had similar experiences — the frustration, expense, and sometimes harmful delays that occur when the information systems we rely on aren't up to the job. That traffic jam was really an information jam — too many drivers with too few facts about the

---

This article by John Diebold, head of the Diebold Institute for Public Policy Studies, is from the April 1994 issue of *Reader's Digest*.

traffic ahead and alternative routes. My hospital tests also reflected poor information: a filing system full of data, but none at hand.

In an age of computers and instant communication, there's no excuse for such failures. We already have the technology to vastly speed the way we do things — from traffic and health care to shopping, education, emergencies, and public services. All we need is to put it to use. It's time to start building our "infostructure."

The infostructure will underlie society in the same way as a tra-   5
ditional infrastructure of roads and rails. But the infostructure isn't made of steel or concrete. Instead, it uses revolutionary new technologies to make existing systems work better. Our highways and health system are good examples of where these technologies could make our lives easier.

In the United States, 190 million vehicles jostle for room on 3.9 million miles of roads and streets. Traffic is growing almost twenty-five times faster than roads. The price tag on tie-ups is huge: The Federal Highway Administration calculates the cost of wasted time at over $100 billion a year.

The solution? Intelligent Vehicle and Highway Systems (IVHS), which increase a road's carrying capacity by letting cars and traffic signals "talk" to each other. When a traffic jam threatens — cars streaming out of a stadium parking lot, for example — the system will automatically direct traffic to swifter routes.

Simpler systems are already in use. Three years ago, street intersections in Detroit's suburban Oakland County were being paralyzed by mile-long backups. Expanding the infrastructure — the roads — would have cost $1 billion. Instead, the road commission has installed "smart signals" at one hundred intersections. Like old-time traffic cops, these signals "see" problems and respond — holding a green light longer for a bus about to cross, or keeping it green to clear out an unusual backup. You never have to wait at a red when nobody's coming; the light "reads" the empty road and turns green.

Some trucks and buses are now being equipped with instruments once seen only in fighter jets. Trucker Jimmy Kennington, fifty-five, was gingerly guiding his eighteen-wheeler over a hill outside Bakersfield, California, when thick fog enveloped him. At that moment, a new collision-avoidance radar mounted on his front grille sounded a piercing alert. Kennington braked — safely escaping a smashup with a car stalled ahead.

Radar and traffic networks are only part of IVHS. To see how a   10
complete system could work, let's take a trip downtown.

As you back your "smart" car out of the driveway after typing your destination on the keyboard on the dash, the vehicle's phone automatically calls ahead to reserve a parking space. It's a dark, wet morning, but a "slippery conditions" sign beside the road triggers an audible warning in your car. Infrared beams — probing five times farther than your eyes — alert you to a paper carrier up ahead, riding her bike without lights.

Now your car projects an illuminated arrow, pointing right, that seems to float in the air ahead of the hood. A voice directs you to turn onto Columbus Avenue. Your "navigator," a dynamic route guidance system, is constantly analyzing traffic data picked up by sensors atop many of the town's signal lights. This morning, it calculates that Columbus offers you the clearest shot to the freeway.

Once on the freeway, you click into "smart cruise." If the car in front slows down, so will yours. If it stops suddenly, your radar cuts your accelerator and hits the brakes.

There's only a beep at the toll point as you zip past a scanner that subtracts the cost from a "smart card" on your windshield. Near the city, the voice and arrow alert you to a detour, and a map on your dashboard screen shows the new route. At the touch of a button you hear the reason: "Accident at Capitol Avenue blocking northbound traffic."

You don't know this part of town, but the navigator safely directs you through it, back onto the freeway and eventually to your destination. At the parking-lot gate, a ticket pops out — stamped with the number of your reserved space. 15

Painless, on-time drives like this are not a distant dream. Many of the technical elements exist and are already being put in place in Japan and Europe. Five automakers in Japan have fitted nearly half a million navigators as add-ons, and they are standard in Toyota's top model. (Later this year General Motors will offer computerized navigation systems in one of its Oldsmobile models.) In Germany, intersections in Berlin and Stuttgart are being wired for a new "Euro-Scout" in-car information system that will start up this spring.

The benefits of building nationwide IVHS in the United States are potentially enormous. And the cost, estimated at $200 billion over twenty years, is roughly what highway inefficiency and accidents already cost the country *every year.*

There is no reason for taxpayers to foot the entire bill, however. Good information about fast-changing conditions is a marketable commodity. Drivers would pay for useful services, such as dynamic route guidance, that save time and frustration — just as they today pay bridge tolls.

State and local governments can now sell or lease property to private companies. Private firms are involved in a planned $300 million extension of the Dulles Toll Road in Virginia, for example. Besides Virginia, other states are organizing joint ventures between government and business. These changes will help make highway "infostructure" a mainstay of our lives.

While easing traffic woes means gathering thousands of bits of   20
ever-changing data, in health care the problem is the opposite: the
system is drowning in data, but doctors can't use the information effectively.

A patient's record is typically 1½ pounds of barely legible notes,
charts, and film stuffed into a folder, stored in the basement, and seldom transferred when the patient is moved. "Even in an advanced
university hospital like this," says Dr. Otto Barnett of Massachusetts
General in Boston, "there's about a one-in-ten chance your file simply can't be found when it's needed."

Doctors spend a large portion of their time writing down or looking for patient histories. Paperwork consumes at least one-third of
scarce nursing time too. My institute, undertaking a study funded by
the Alfred P. Sloan Foundation, estimated that, overall, wasteful effort in the health industry costs $90 billion a year — almost $1,000
per household.

Computer technology could lift this costly burden — but, incredibly, fewer than 1 percent of the nation's hospitals keep patient
records electronically. Sure, all hospitals have computers. But not
enough are able to share information and put it to work for patient
care.

At the Regenstrief Institute of Indianapolis, a team led by Professor Clem McDonald devised an electronic system for thirty-five
medical-care facilities. So far it has tracked more than a million patients, making their records instantly accessible from any computer
workstation in the system.

At Wishard Memorial Hospital in Indianapolis, connecting the   25
ward and emergency-room computer workstations to each other
and to the Regenstrief system cut patient charges an average of 13
percent and shortened the average hospital stay by twenty-one
hours. In Boston, a computer system allowed Beth Israel Hospital to
reduce its admitting staff even as patient admissions rose 67 percent.

But what about patient privacy? Isn't it easier to snoop electronically? Not at all. Paper files can be open to anybody wearing a white
coat and a serious expression. By contrast, Beth Israel's electronic
system controls access with passwords — and keeps an automatic
record of every inquiry so those who make one can be traced.

Electronic information also saves lives. At the LDS Hospital in
Salt Lake City, a computer system automatically checks drug prescriptions against patients' histories and symptoms. It alerted staff
to adverse drug reactions in eighty-one times as many patients as
traditional methods did.

One of the biggest weaknesses in U.S. health care comes down
to the startling fact that patients don't really know the relative merit
of different treatments. The lack of comparative information sup-

presses competition and keeps people from making knowledgeable decisions about their care.

Studies have revealed immense differences in methods of treatment. For instance, residents of New Haven, Connecticut, were found to undergo coronary-bypass operations at twice the rate of Boston patients. A hospital in Pennsylvania charged 90 percent more for cardiac surgery than one less than forty miles away, yet had a higher failure rate.

But most of us are not aware of these differences, because the 30 information is not readily accessible via computer. Doctors, too, are often in the dark about the statistics on treatments they advise. The brutal truth is, a child with a video game has more computing power in hand than the typical physician.

Political debate rages about health care, while a solution — greater competition through easier comparison — lies under our noses. As with crowded roads, we can apply information technology to make much better use of the systems we already have.

In the 1920s and '30s, American lives were transformed as households were connected by telephone and radio. In the 1950s and '60s, we were brought closer together by a network of interstate highways. Now an electronic infostructure can significantly improve our lives once more. Yet while Japan and Europe are moving ahead, U.S. progress has been disturbingly slow.

The federal government urgently needs to:

- Promote a higher vision of what information technology can do for the nation. Right now, public officials seem focused only on the "information superhighway" that will deliver more TV channels to our homes. The potential is far greater than this.

- Challenge private industry to lead the way, by funding demonstration projects and awarding prizes for significant achievement.

- Bring its own systems up to date. Government generates and controls most of the data Americans rely on. Yet it's still buying typewriters and three-by-five cards.

- Press business and local governments to agree on compatible systems so networks can work with and "talk" to one another efficiently.

Most of all, we need to recognize that information has a capital value, and encourage a free-market philosophy. The days of seemingly limitless public spending on services are gone; there simply is not enough money. But there is a huge market for smart, efficient uses of information technology. A new generation of private and public partnership can generate massive economic benefits — and help America make the leap to a new century.

Ours is an exciting time — similar to the early days of the com- 35 puter industry. We are now on the threshold of another technological adventure. Let us step boldly across.

Is There a There in Cyberspace?

JOHN PERRY BARLOW

I am often asked how I went from pushing cows around a remote Wyoming ranch to my present occupation (which *Wall Street Journal* recently described as "cyberspace cadet"). I haven't got a short answer, but I suppose I came to the virtual world looking for community.

Unlike most modern Americans, I grew up in an actual place, an entirely nonintentional community called Pinedale, Wyoming. As I struggled for nearly a generation to keep my ranch in the family, I was motivated by the belief that such places were the spiritual home of humanity. But I knew their future was not promising.

At the dawn of the twentieth century, over 40 percent of the American workforce lived off the land. The majority of us lived in towns like Pinedale. Now fewer than 1 percent of us extract a living from the soil. We just became too productive for our own good.

Of course, the population followed the jobs. Farming and ranching communities are now home to a demographically insignificant percentage of Americans, the vast majority of whom live not in ranch houses but in more or less identical split-level "ranch homes" in more or less identical suburban "communities." Generica.

In my view, these are neither communities nor homes. I believe 5 the combination of television and suburban population patterns is simply toxic to the soul. I see much evidence in contemporary America to support this view.

Meanwhile, back at the ranch, doom impended. And, as I watched community in Pinedale growing ill from the same economic forces that were killing my family's ranch, the Bar Cross, satellite dishes brought the cultural infection of television. I started looking

A former cattle rancher and songwriter for the musical group the Grateful Dead, John Perry Barlow is cofounder of the Electronic Frontier Foundation and writes frequently about cyberspace. This essay appeared in the March–April 1995 issue of *Utne Reader*.

around for evidence that community in America would not perish altogether.

I took some heart in the mysterious nomadic City of the Deadheads, the virtually physical town that follows the Grateful Dead around the country. The Deadheads lacked place, touching down briefly wherever the band happened to be playing, and they lacked continuity in time, since they had to suffer a new diaspora every time the band moved on or went home. But they had many of the other necessary elements of community, including a culture, a religion of sorts (which, though it lacked dogma, had most of the other, more nurturing aspects of spiritual practice), a sense of necessity, and, most importantly, shared adversity.

I wanted to know more about the flavor of their interaction, what they thought and felt, but since I wrote Dead songs (including "Estimated Prophet" and "Cassidy"), I was a minor icon to the Deadheads, and was thus inhibited, in some socially Heisenbergian way, from getting a clear view of what really went on among them.

Then, in 1987, I heard about a "place" where Deadheads gathered where I could move among them without distorting too much the field of observation. Better, this was a place I could visit without leaving Wyoming. It was a shared computer in Sausalito, California, called the Whole Earth 'Lectronic Link, or WELL. After a lot of struggling with modems, serial cables, init strings, and other computer arcana that seemed utterly out of phase with such notions as Deadheads and small towns, I found myself looking at the glowing yellow word "Login:" beyond which lay my future.

"Inside" the WELL were Deadheads in community. There were   10
thousands of them there, gossiping, complaining (mostly about the Grateful Dead), comforting and harassing each other, bartering, engaging in religion (or at least exchanging their totemic set lists), beginning and ending love affairs, praying for one another's sick kids. There was, it seemed, everything one might find going on in a small town, save dragging Main Street and making out on the back roads.

I was delighted. I felt I had found the new locale of human community — never mind that the whole thing was being conducted in mere words by minds from whom the bodies had been amputated. Never mind that all these people were deaf, dumb, and blind as paramecia or that their town had neither seasons nor sunsets nor smells.

Surely all these deficiencies would be remedied by richer, faster communications media. The featureless log-in handles would gradually acquire video faces (and thus expressions), shaded 3-D body puppets (and thus body language). This "space," which I recognized at once to be a primitive form of the cyberspace William Gibson predicted in his sci-fi novel *Neuromancer*, was still without apparent dimensions or vistas. But virtual reality would change all that in time.

Meanwhile, the commons, or something like it, had been rediscovered. Once again, people from the 'burbs had a place where they could encounter their friends as my fellow Pinedalians did at the post office and the Wrangler Cafe. They had a place where their hearts could remain as the companies they worked for shuffled their bodies around America. They could put down roots that could not be ripped out by forces of economic history. They had a collective stake. They had a community.

It is seven years now since I discovered the WELL. In that time, I cofounded an organization, the Electronic Frontier Foundation, dedicated to protecting its interests and those of other virtual communities like it from raids by physical government. I've spent countless hours typing away at its residents, and I've watched the larger context that contains it, the Internet, grow at such an explosive rate that. by 2004, every human on the planet will have an e-mail address unless the growth curve flattens (which it will).

My enthusiasm for virtuality has cooled. In fact, unless one 15
counts interaction with the rather too large society of those with whom I exchange electronic mail, I don't spend much time engaging in virtual community at all. Many of the near-term benefits I anticipated from it seem to remain as far in the future as they did when I first logged in. Perhaps they always will.

Pinedale works, more or less, as it is, but a lot is still missing from the communities of cyberspace, whether they be places like the WELL, the fractious news groups of USENET, the silent "auditoriums" of America Online, or even enclaves on the promising World Wide Web.

What is missing? Well, to quote Ranjit Makkuni of Xerox Corporation's Palo Alto Research Center, "the *prāna* is missing," *prāna* being the Hindu term for both breath and spirit. I think he is right about this and that perhaps the central question of the virtual age is whether or not *prāna* can somehow be made to fit through any disembodied medium.

Prāna is, to my mind, the literally vital element in the holy and unseen ecology of relationship, the dense mesh of invisible life, on whose surface carbon-based life floats like a thin film. It is at the heart of the fundamental and profound difference between information and experience. Jaron Lanier has said that "information is alienated experience," and, that being true, *prāna* is part of what is removed when you create such easily transmissible replicas of experience as, say, the evening news.

Obviously a great many other, less spiritual, things are also missing entirely, like body language, sex, death, tone of voice, clothing, beauty (or homeliness), weather, violence, vegetation, wildlife, pets, architecture, music, smells, sunlight, and that ol' harvest moon. In short, most of the things that make my life real to me.

Present, but in far less abundance than in the physical world, 20 which I call "meat space," are women, children, old people, poor people, and the genuinely blind. Also mostly missing are the illiterate and the continent of Africa. There is not much human diversity in cyberspace, which is populated, as near as I can tell, by white males under fifty with plenty of computer terminal time, great typing skills, high math SATs, strongly held opinions on just about everything, and an excruciating face-to-face shyness, especially with the opposite sex.

But diversity is as essential to healthy community as it is to healthy ecosystems (which are, in my view, different from communities only in unimportant aspects).

I believe that the principal reason for the almost universal failure of the intentional communities of the sixties and seventies was a lack of diversity in their members. It was a rare commune with any old people in it, or people who were fundamentally out of philosophical agreement with the majority.

Indeed, it is the usual problem when we try to build something that can only be grown. Natural systems, such as human communities, are simply too complex to design by the engineering principles we insist on applying to them. Like Dr. Frankenstein, Western civilization is now finding its rational skills inadequate to the task of creating and caring for life. We would do better to return to a kind of agricultural mind-set in which we humbly try to recreate the conditions from which life has sprung before. And leave the rest to God.

Given that it has been built so far almost entirely by people with engineering degrees, it is not so surprising that cyberspace has the kind of overdesigned quality that leaves out all kinds of elements nature would have provided invisibly.

Also missing from both the communes of the sixties and from 25 cyberspace are a couple of elements that I believe are very important, if not essential, to the formation and preservation of real community: an absence of alternatives and a sense of genuine adversity, generally shared. What about these?

It is hard to argue that anyone would find losing a modem literally hard to survive, while many have remained in small towns, have tolerated their intolerances and created entertainment to enliven their culturally arid lives simply because it seemed there was no choice but to stay. There are many investments — spiritual, material, and temporal — one is willing to put into a home one cannot leave. Communities are often the beneficiaries of these involuntary investments.

But when the going gets rough in cyberspace, it is even easier to move than it is in the 'burbs, where, given the fact that the average American moves some twelve times in his or her life, moving appears to be pretty easy. You can not only find another bulletin board service (BBS) or news group to hang out in, you can, with very little effort, start your own.

And then there is the bond of joint suffering. Most community is a cultural stockade erected against a common enemy that can take many forms. In Pinedale, we bore together, with an understanding needing little expression, the fact that Upper Green River Valley is the coldest spot, as measured by annual mean temperature, in the lower forty-eight states. We knew that if somebody was stopped on the road most winter nights, he would probably die there, so the fact that we might loathe him was not sufficient reason to drive on past his broken pickup.

By the same token, the Deadheads have the Drug Enforcement Administration, which strives to give them twenty-year prison terms without parole for distributing the fairly harmless sacrament of their faith. They have an additional bond in the fact that when their Microbuses die, as they often do, no one but another Deadhead is likely to stop to help them.

But what are the shared adversities of cyberspace? Lousy user interfaces? The flames of harsh invective? Dumb jokes? Surely these can all be survived without the sanctuary provided by fellow sufferers. 30

One is always free to yank the jack, as I have mostly done. For me, the physical world offers far more opportunity for *prāna*-rich connections with my fellow creatures. Even for someone whose body is in a state of perpetual motion, I feel I can generally find more community among the still-embodied.

Finally, there is that shyness factor. Not only are we trying to build community here among people who have never experienced any in my sense of the term, we are trying to build community among people who, in their lives, have rarely used the word *we* in a heartfelt way. It is a vast club, and many of the members — following Groucho Marx — wouldn't want to join a club that would have them.

And yet. . . .

How quickly physical community continues to deteriorate. Even Pinedale, which seems to have survived the plague of ranch failures, feels increasingly cut off from itself. Many of the ranches are now owned by corporate types who fly their Gulfstreams in to fish and are rarely around during the many months when the creeks are frozen over and neighbors are needed. They have kept the ranches alive financially, but they actively discourage their managers from the interdependence my former colleagues and I require. They keep agriculture on life support, still alive but lacking a functional heart.

And the town has been inundated with suburbanites who flee here, bringing all their terrors and suspicions with them. They spend their evenings as they did in Orange County, watching television or socializing in hermetic little enclaves of fundamentalist Christianity that seem to separate them from us and even, given their sectarian animosities, from one another. The town remains. The community is largely a wraith of nostalgia.

So where else can we look for the connection we need to prevent 35 our plunging further into the condition of separateness Nietzsche called sin? What is there to do but to dive further into the bramble bush of information that, in its broadcast forms, has done so much to tear us apart?

Cyberspace, for all its current deficiencies and failed promises, is not without some very real solace already.

Some months ago, the great love of my life, a vivid young woman with whom I intended to spend the rest of it, dropped dead of undiagnosed viral cardiomyopathy two days short of her thirtieth birthday. I felt as if my own heart had been as shredded as hers.

We had lived together in New York City. Except for my daughters, no one from Pinedale had met her. I needed a community to wrap around myself against colder winds than fortune had ever blown at me before. And without looking, I found I had one in the virtual world.

On the WELL, there was a topic announcing her death in one of the conferences to which I posted the eulogy I had read over her before burying her in her own small town of Nanaimo, British Columbia. It seemed to strike a chord among the disembodied living on the Net. People copied it and sent it to one another. Over the next several months I received almost a megabyte of electronic mail from all over the planet, mostly from folks whose faces I have never seen and probably never will.

They told me of their own tragedies and what they had done to 40 survive them. As humans have since words were first uttered, we shared the second most common human experience, death, with an openheartedness that would have caused grave uneasiness in physical America, where the whole topic is so cloaked in denial as to be considered obscene. Those strangers, who had no arms to put around my shoulders, no eyes to weep with mine, nevertheless saw me through. As neighbors do.

I have no idea how far we will plunge into this strange place. Unlike previous frontiers, this one has no end. It is so dissatisfying in so many ways that I suspect we will be more restless in our search for home here than in all our previous explorations. And that is one reason why I think we may find it after all. If home is where the heart is, then there is already some part of home to be found in cyberspace.

So . . . does virtual community work or not? Should we all go off to cyberspace or should we resist it as a demonic form of symbolic abstraction? Does it supplant the real or is there, in it, reality itself?

Like so many true things, this one doesn't resolve itself to a black or a white. Nor is it gray. It is, along with the rest of life, black/white. Both/neither. I'm not being equivocal or wishy-washy here. We have to get over our Manichean sense that everything is either good or bad, and the border of cyberspace seems to me a good place to leave that old set of filters.

But really it doesn't matter. We are going there whether we want to or not. In five years, everyone who is reading these words will have an e-mail address, other than the determined Luddites who also eschew the telephone and electricity.

When we are all together in cyberspace we will see what the human spirit, and the basic desire to connect, can create there. I am convinced that the result will be more benign if we go there open-minded, open-hearted, and excited with the adventure than if we are dragged into exile. 45

And we must remember that going to cyberspace, unlike previous great emigrations to the frontier, hardly requires us to leave where we have been. Many will find, as I have, a much richer appreciation of physical reality for having spent so much time in virtuality.

Despite its current (and perhaps in some areas permanent) insufficiencies, we should go to cyberspace with hope. Groundless hope, like unconditional love, may be the only kind that counts.

In Memoriam, Dr. Cynthia Horner (1964–1994).

Mega Buys

FRANKLIN SAIGE

A television ad for MCI reportedly features a child star chanting, "There will be a road. It will not connect two points. It will connect all points. It will not go from here to there. There will be no there. We will all only be here." Maybe this is actually a profound utterance, if we listen carefully, rather than the baloney it appears to be. Because even though the rumble of the bulldozers clearing the way for this information superhighway is fairly distant, perhaps it's time to listen, and then ask just where exactly is this "here" where we will all be?

This article is from the Spring 1994 issue of *Plain,* a "simple living journal" edited by Franklin Saige and published by the Center for Plain Living in Burton, Ohio. It was excerpted in this form in the March–April 1995 issue of *Utne Reader.*

One of the perils of modern technology is that it is invented to be sold, as opposed to most earlier inventions, which were made to be used by the inventor, the inventor's patron, or the community. Modern technology comes clothed in seductive imagery in order to make the sale, but it can take away our freedom once we buy into it. It takes away our freedom by reducing our ability to choose — our ability to choose not to think in terms of "organization" or having our schedules "managed," for example. It takes away our freedom by narrowing our options to a set of preprogrammed choices. It removes the sensory complexity that is the most obvious characteristic of the lived world.

Of course, there is another school of thought on this question: Most people believe that technology barely influences how we live our lives. "It's what we *do* with technology that counts," they say. In other words, it depends on our moral fitness, our will to master the machine.

I suppose that even the most seductive forms of technology can be resisted, at least for a while. People resisted using automobiles at first. Many people thought the automobile would be too noisy, too fast, too pretentious, and just too expensive to fit the existing social fabric. Initially, most people did not buy one. But even though their fears about the automobile were quickly realized, soon everyone who could afford to own one, did. Then these automobiles were used in ways that gradually led to the weakening of the family and the community, not to mention the destruction of the landscape.

If hundreds of millions of car owners supposedly could choose   5 how they would use this technology, what happened to make them choose destructive rather than supportive uses? Did they simply change their values on a whim? Or could something inherent in the technology have pulled them in a particular direction?

What does the automobile do *best:* pull families apart, cause urban sprawl, distort our sense of distance, or make travel more convenient? Only the last — convenience — is proven false every morning at rush hour, yet the car was sold to us on metaphors of speed and convenience. If we want to know where the information superhighway is leading us, maybe we should ask ourselves what *it* will do best.

To follow this road, we need to know that the term "information superhighway" is strictly the creation of the advertising muse. It was coined to piggyback onto the prestige of the "information highway" of interactive (meaning two-way) networked computers sharing text and data known as the Internet. What makes the superhighway super is that it will be a commercially run interactive video network put together by the mega telecommunication and cable television industries. "Interactive pay TV" would be a more accurate name for it, though the Internet and similar data networks will undoubtedly be incorporated and offered as incidental services. A true definition of the information superhighway would focus on its somewhat less lofty pursuits: video shopping, pay-per-view movies on demand (presently a $10 billion annual market for video rental stores), and two-way videophones.

Once the billions of dollars to build the system have been spent, every marketer will be in your living room and inside your head; your entertainment viewing choices, and especially your video shopping buying preferences, will be monitored and analyzed so that advertisers can turn around and market to you in a very targeted manner. Imagine one day using your television to purchase cloth diapers from the Virtual Wal-Mart. Then you switch to an entertainment program and *voilà!* the commercials are all for Pampers, piped to your household as a result of your latest purchasing profile. That is the commercial dream, very interactive, though not exactly in the poetic way it is being portrayed.

Whatever the specific route the superhighway takes, it is obviously going to be *best* at invading your private life. Ultimately, its best use will be driving up consumption, which appeals to marketers more than to me, concerned as I am about the condition of the planet and my soul. I don't know about you, but I need less temptation to buy things, not more. And I don't want to be constantly sold to.

In *In the Absence of the Sacred*, Jerry Mander lists "Ten Recommended Attitudes about Technology." Along with number one ("Since most of what we are told about new technology comes from its proponents, be deeply skeptical of all claims") and number two ("Assume all technology guilty until proven innocent"), my favorite is number five: "Never judge a technology by the way it benefits you personally. Seek a holistic view of its impacts. The operative question is not if it benefits you, but who benefits most? And to what end?"

Since people appear to be more enslaved in their work and home lives than ever before, we could ask whether the problems their computers and electronic media seem to alleviate can be traced to the advent of computers themselves. Have computers and television speeded up economic life and undermined the social fabric?

None of the electronic technologies would be here if not for their utility as pillars of the consuming society. An ambulance is a "good" use for an internal combustion engine, but it takes a whole society of energy-guzzling car buyers addicted to mobility and speed to provide commercial reasons to make an internal combustion engine industry happen.

We are presently being assured that stepping into the virtual reality of the information superhighway and opening our minds to it is a good thing. Doubtless there will be many examples of this good: Grandparents will be able to see the grandkids on the videophone. The disabled will have more opportunities to be included.

And we will hear more and more about "virtual communities"— an exciting concept because, after all, the real ones have nearly disappeared. Perhaps almost-real ones will suffice, but I am unwilling to be part of a technology that can only exist if it drives me to consume more, which drains my will to seek out real community.

A woman at an organic farming conference I attended told the program speaker, who was against most new technologies, that even though she, too, thought these technologies might be harmful to the social fabric, still she felt she had to keep up with them: "Since this is what's going on in the world, don't we have to participate, just to survive?" No one could answer her then, and I have only part of the answer myself. I can only say I'm unwilling to drive the superhighway, and I sense that many others are deciding whether to continue on this ride or find an exit. On the other hand, the people I glimpse in their cubicles, or sitting around their TV hearths at home, don't seem too dissatisfied. What will wake them up? How can I help them reverse direction and get back out of the machine?

I have no interest in being part of a "movement" to "ban" or "boycott." To do that, I would have to become like my friends in the ecology movement, *connected* to computer networks in order to *exchange information* and get *organized.* I see the technology encouraging in them precisely the way of relating to lived experience that has brought about the crises they seek to alleviate.

My strategy for exiting the information superhighway is simply never to enter it. The only "direct action" I can take is to live a real life, in real time, without viewing or networking or overconsuming anything. No input, no output. And I am going to tell anyone who will listen that real life, in a real community, in real reality, is better than the virtual reality of the information superhighway any day of the week.

What Are We Doing On-Line?
JOHN PERRY BARLOW, SVEN BIRKERTS,
KEVIN KELLY, and MARK SLOUKA

The following forum is based on a discussion that took place this spring in Cambridge, Massachusetts. Paul Tough, a senior editor of *Harper's Magazine,* served as moderator. John Perry Barlow is one of the founders of the Electronic Frontier Foundation, a group formed to protect civil liberties in cyberspace. He was a participant in "Is Computer Hacking a Crime?", a forum that appeared in the March 1990 issue of *Harper's Magazine.* Sven Birkerts is the author, most recently, of *The Gutenberg Elegies: The Fate of Reading in an Electronic Age,* published by Faber and Faber, an excerpt from which

This is excerpted from the August 1995 issue of *Harper's Magazine.*

appeared in the May 1994 issue of *Harper's Magazine.* Kevin Kelly is the executive director of *Wired* magazine and the author of *Out of Control: The Rise of Neo-biological Civilization,* published by Addison-Wesley, an excerpt from which appeared in the May 1994 issue of *Harper's Magazine.* Mark Slouka is the author of *War of the Worlds: Cyberspace and the Hi-tech Assault on Reality,* published by Basic Books. His short story "The Woodcarver's Tale" appeared in the March 1995 issue of *Harper's Magazine.*

Slouka: At some point do you think the virtual world is basically going to replace the world we live in? Is it going to be an alternate space?

Kelly: No, it's going to be an auxiliary space. There will be lots of things that will be similar to the physical world, and there will be lots of things that will be different. But it's going to be a space that's going to have a lot of the attributes that we like in reality — a richness, a sense of place, a place to be silent, a place to go deep.

Slouka: But the question that I keep asking myself is: Why the need? Where does the need come from to inhabit these alternate spaces? And the answer I keep coming back to is: to escape the problems and issues of the real world. I've talked to a lot of people who go on to the net and take on alternate personas. I mean, why the hell would you do that?

Barlow: Because you want to experiment.   5

Slouka: Why are you experimenting? Because you're threatened by the reality you inhabit.

Barlow: Is there something wrong with experimenting?

Slouka: There is if it distracts us from the problems at hand. One of the people I interviewed for my book was a man who posed on the net as a woman. He wanted to see what it's like to be a woman and what it's like to be hit on by another male. He wanted to get away from sexism, ageism, racism — all the collected "isms" that go along with life in the real world. Instead of dealing with those issues, though, he was sidestepping them.

Kelly: Have you ever been to Europe?

Slouka: To Europe? Yes.   10

Kelly: Why? You have your own community. Why go to Europe?

Slouka: Because I wanted to experience another physical community.

Kelly: Yes.

Slouka: I underscore the word "physical."

Kelly: Well, even though we're physical beings, we have an intel-   15
lectual sphere. It's like reading a book, one that you lose yourself in completely. Why does one do that? Do I have to be really messed up to want to lose myself in a book?

Slouka: I hope not.

Barlow: Well, why would you want to flee the physical world into a book?

Birkerts: I agree — reality is often not enough. But I think we have diverged here from the central point. If we're merely talking about this phenomenon as an interesting, valuable supplement for those who seek it, I have no problem with it. What I'm concerned by is this becoming a potentially all-transforming event that's going to change not only how I live but how my children live. I don't believe it's merely going to be auxiliary. I think it's going to be absolutely central.

Barlow: You know, it's possible that both of those things can be perfectly correct. In terms of your life span, I don't think that there's any reason you can't go on leading exactly the life you lead now, living with the technology you find most comfortable, reading your books — of which there are likely to be more over the period of your lifetime, by the way, rather than less. I see no reason why you can't personally "refuse it." But over the long haul, I'd say that society, everything that is human on this planet, is going to be profoundly transformed by this, and in many ways, some of which will probably be scary to those of us with this mind-set, some of which will be glorious and transforming.

Birkerts: But even if I've pledged myself personally, as part of my 20 "refuse it" package, to the old here and now, it still impinges on me, because it means I live in a world that I find to be increasingly attenuated, distracted, fanned-out, disembodied. Growing up in the fifties, I felt I was living in a very real place. The terms of human interchange were ones I could navigate. I could get an aura buzz from living. I can still get it, but it's harder to find. More and more of the interchanges that are being forced on me as a member of contemporary society involve me having to deal with other people though various layers of scrim, which leaves me feeling disembodied. What I'm really trying to address is a phenomenon that you don't become aware of instantly. It encroaches on you. I do believe that we gain a lot of our sense of our own reality and validity through being able to hear an echo, by getting our words back, by being mirrored. And community, in the old-world sense, was about being mirrored immediately. You know, you yell for Clem, and Clem yells back, and you understand the terms of your world. Now you type something to, say, Kiichi in Tokyo, and it comes back a few hours later. You're being mirrored in another way. Maybe it's because I'm not on-line, but it seems to me, as an adult human being living in 1995, that the signal is getting weaker. I find that more and more I navigate my days within this kind of strange landscape. People have drawn into their houses, and the shades are down. You go into a store and the clerk isn't looking at you, he's busy running bar codes. And you multiply that a thousandfold: mediation, mediation, mediation. I want an end to mediation. And I don't think I can break the membrane by going on-line.

Barlow: Sven, you and I are in absolute, complete agreement on this. But the alienating engine that I perceive in society is broadcast media, particularly television. I mean, the reason people are hermetically sealed in their homes is that they are worshiping the glass tit of fear, which is telling them that the world is too scary to go out in. I live part of the time in New York, which is widely known to be a terrifying, dangerous place. I never feel in danger there. Not ever. But if I watched television, I'd never set foot on the island of Manhattan. Nor would I ever leave my suburban home, I suspect. But this is the result of a one-way medium of communication. It's the same species of communication as your beloved book. Neither the book nor the television is face-to-face in any form.

Kelly: Sven, I think part of what you're saying is true. You're ignoring the center of the culture, and therefore you feel sort of cut off. The culture has shifted to a new medium. But it's not going to be the only medium there is. The introduction of fire produced great changes in our society. That doesn't mean that everything is on fire. Digital technologies and the net can have a great effect without meaning that everything has to *be* the net. I listen to books on tape. I have for many years. I couldn't live without them. I listen to the radio. I read books. I read magazines. I write letters. All of these things are not going to go away when the net comes.

Birkerts: But don't you think it's a push-pull model? If you send out a net that allows you to be in touch with all parts of the globe, you may well get a big bang out of doing that, but you can't do that and then turn around and look at your wife in the same way. The psyche is a closed system. If you spread yourself laterally, you sacrifice depth.

Kelly: I question that trade-off. That's my whole point about this kind of environment. It's not that we're going to deduct the book, though the book will certainly lose its preeminence. The flourishing of digital communication will enable more options, more possibilities, more diversity, more room, more frontiers. Yes, that will close off things from the past, but that is a choice I will accept.

Slouka: See, the confusion is understandable because so much 25 of the hype surrounding the digital revolution revolves around this issue of inevitability.

Kelly: But it *is* inevitable.

Slouka: Well, which is it: Is it inevitable or isn't it?

Kelly: It's inevitable that the net will continue to grow, to get bigger, to get-more complex, to become the dominant force in the culture. *That* is inevitable. What's *not* inevitable is what you choose to do about it.

Slouka: So I have the option of being marginalized?

Kelly: That's right. You can be like the Amish. Noble, but mar- 30 ginal.

Slouka: It seems to me that we have to keep a balance. The balance right now, as I see it, is tipping toward virtual technology, toward virtual reality, toward mediated worlds, and that mediation is dangerous both culturally and politically. Culturally, it sets us apart from one another. Politically, it opens us up to manipulation. Someone can manipulate the reality I'm getting on-line more easily than they can manipulate the reality I get face-to-face. So the answer is to go carefully, to take a selective look at what we're losing along the way, to discuss what's happening.

Virtual Students, Digital Classroom

NEIL POSTMAN

If one has a trusting relationship with one's students (let us say, graduate students), it is not altogether gauche to ask them if they believe in God (with a capital G). I have done this three or four times and most students say they do. Their answer is preliminary to the next question: If someone you love were desperately ill, and you had to choose between praying to God for his or her recovery or administering an antibiotic (as prescribed by a competent physician), which would you choose?

Most say the question is silly since the alternatives are not mutually exclusive. Of course. But suppose they were — which would you choose? God helps those who help themselves, some say in choosing the antibiotic, therefore getting the best of two possible belief systems. But if pushed to the wall (e.g., God does not always help those who help themselves; God helps those who pray and who believe), most choose the antibiotic, after noting that the question is asinine and proves nothing. Of course, the question was not asked, in the first place, to prove anything but to begin a discussion of the nature of belief. And I do not fail to inform the students, by the way, that there has recently emerged evidence of a "scientific" nature that when sick people are prayed for they do better than those who aren't.

This essay, which appeared in the October 9, 1995, issue of *The Nation*, is adapted from *The End of Education: Redefining the Value of School* (1995) by Neil Postman, professor of communication arts and sciences at New York University.

As the discussion proceeds, important distinctions are made among the different meanings of "belief," but at some point it becomes far from asinine to speak of the god of Technology — in the sense that people believe technology works, that they rely on it, that it makes promises, that they are bereft when denied access to it, that they are delighted when they are in its presence, that for most people it works in mysterious ways, that they condemn people who speak against it, that they stand in awe of it and that, in the "born again" mode, they will alter their life-styles, their schedules, their habits, and their relationships to accommodate it. If this be not a form of religious belief, what is?

In all strands of American cultural life, you can find so many examples of technological adoration that it is possible to write a book about it. And I would if it had not already been done so well. But nowhere do you find more enthusiasm for the god of Technology than among educators. In fact, there are those, like Lewis Perelman, who argue (for example, in his book, *School's Out*) that modern information technologies have rendered schools entirely irrelevant since there is now much more information available outside the classroom than inside it. This is by no means considered an outlandish idea. Dr. Diane Ravitch, former Assistant Secretary of Education, envisions, with considerable relish, the challenge that technology presents to the tradition that "children (and adults) should be educated in a specific place, for a certain number of hours, and a certain number of days during the week and year." In other words, that children should be educated in school. Imagining the possibilities of an information superhighway offering perhaps a thousand channels, Dr. Ravitch assures us that:

> in this new world of pedagogical plenty, children and adults will be able to dial up a program on their home television to learn whatever they want to know, at their own convenience. If Little Eva cannot sleep, she can learn algebra instead. At her home-learning station, she will tune in to a series of interesting problems that are presented in an interactive medium, much like video games. . . .
>
> Young John may decide that he wants to learn the history of modern Japan, which he can do by dialing up the greatest authorities and teachers on the subject, who will not only use dazzling graphs and illustrations, but will narrate a historical video that excites his curiosity and imagination.

In this vision there is, it seems to me, a confident and typical sense of unreality. Little Eva can't sleep, so she decides to learn a little algebra? Where does Little Eva come from? Mars? If not, it is more likely she will tune in to a good movie. Young John decides that he wants to learn the history of modern Japan? How did young John come to this point? How is it that he never visited a library up to now? Or is it that he, too, couldn't sleep and decided that a little modern Japanese history was just what he needed?

What Ravitch is talking about here is not a new technology but a new species of child, one who, in any case, no one has seen up to now. Of course, new technologies do make new kinds of people, which leads to a second objection to Ravitch's conception of the future. There is a kind of forthright determinism about the imagined world described in it. The technology is here or will be; we must use it because it is there; we will become the kind of people the technology requires us to be, and whether we like it or not, we will remake our institutions to accommodate technology. All of this must happen because it is good for us, but in any case, we have no choice. This point of view is present in very nearly every statement about the future relationship of learning to technology. And, as in Ravitch's scenario, there is always a cheery, gee-whiz tone to the prophecies. Here is one produced by the National Academy of Sciences, written by Hugh McIntosh.

> School for children of the Information Age will be vastly different than it was for Mom and Dad.
>
> Interested in biology? Design your own life forms with computer simulation.
>
> Having trouble with a science project? Teleconference about it with a research scientist.
>
> Bored with the real world? Go into a virtual physics lab and rewrite the laws of gravity.
>
> These are the kinds of hands-on learning experiences schools could be providing right now. The technologies that make them possible are already here, and today's youngsters, regardless of economic status, know how to use them. They spend hours with them every week — not in the classroom, but in their own homes and in video game centers at every shopping mall.

It is always interesting to attend to the examples of learning, and the motivations that ignite them, in the songs of love that technophiles perform for us. It is, for example, not easy to imagine research scientists all over the world teleconferencing with thousands of students who are having difficulty with their science projects. I can't help thinking that most research scientists would put a stop to this rather quickly. But I find it especially revealing that in the scenario above we have an example of a technological solution to a psychological problem that would seem to be exceedingly serious. We are presented with a student who is "bored with the real world." What does it mean to say someone is bored with the real world, especially one so young? Can a journey into virtual reality cure such a problem? And if it can, will our troubled youngster want to return to the real world? Confronted with a student who is bored with the real world, I don't think we can solve the problem so easily by making available a virtual reality physics lab.

The role that new technology should play in schools or anywhere else is something that needs to be discussed without the hyperactive fantasies of cheerleaders. In particular, the computer and its associated technologies are awesome additions to a culture, and are quite capable of altering the psychic, not to mention the sleeping, habits of our young. But like all important technologies of the past, they are Faustian bargains, giving and taking away, sometimes in equal measure, sometimes more in one way than the other. It is strange — indeed, shocking — that with the twenty-first century so close, we can still talk of new technologies as if they were unmixed blessings — gifts, as it were, from the gods. Don't we all know what the combustion engine has done for us and against us? What television is doing for us and against us? At the very least, what we need to discuss about Little Eva, Young John, and McIntosh's trio is what they will lose, and what we will lose, if they enter a world in which computer technology is their chief source of motivation, authority, and, apparently, psychological sustenance. Will they become, as Joseph Weizenbaum warns, more impressed by calculation than human judgment? Will speed of response become, more than ever, a defining quality of intelligence? If, indeed, the idea of a school will be dramatically altered, what kinds of learning will be neglected, perhaps made impossible? Is virtual reality a new form of therapy? If it is, what are its dangers?

These are serious matters, and they need to be discussed by those who know something about children from the planet Earth, and whose vision of children's needs, and the needs of society, go beyond thinking of school mainly as a place for the convenient distribution of information. Schools are not now and have never been largely about getting information to children. That has been on the schools' agenda, of course, but has always been way down on the list. For technological utopians, the computer vaults information access to the top. This reshuffling of priorities comes at a most inopportune time. The goal of giving people greater access to more information faster, more conveniently, and in more diverse forms was the main technological thrust of the nineteenth century. Some folks haven't noticed it but that problem was largely solved, so that for almost a hundred years there has been more information available to the young outside the school than inside. That fact did not make the schools obsolete, nor does it now make them obsolete. Yes, it is true that Little Eva, the insomniac from Mars, could turn on an algebra lesson, thanks to the computer, in the wee hours of the morning. She could also, if she wished, read a book or magazine, watch television, turn on the radio or listen to music. All of this she could have done before the computer. The computer does not solve any problem she has but does exacerbate one. For Little Eva's problem is not how to get access to a well-structured algebra lesson but what to do with all the information available to her during the day, as well as during sleepless nights. Perhaps this is why she couldn't sleep in the first place. Little Eva, like the rest of us, is overwhelmed by information. She lives in a culture that has 260,000 billboards, 17,000 newspapers, 12,000 periodicals, 27,000 video outlets for renting tapes, 400 million television sets, and well over 500 million radios, not including those in automobiles. There are 40,000 new book titles published every year, and each day 41 million photographs are taken. And thanks to the computer, more than 60 billion pieces of advertising junk come into our mailboxes every year. Everything from telegraphy and photography in the nineteenth century to the silicon chip in the twentieth has amplified the din of information intruding on Little Eva's consciousness. From millions of sources all over the globe, through every possible channel and medium — light waves, air waves, ticker tape, computer banks, telephone wires, television cables, satellites, and printing presses — information pours in. Behind it in every imaginable form of storage — on paper, on video, on audiotape, on disks, film, and silicon chips — is an even greater volume of information waiting to be retrieved. In the face of this we might ask, What can schools do for Little Eva besides making still more information available? If there is nothing, then new technologies will indeed make schools obsolete. But in fact, there is plenty.

One thing that comes to mind is that schools can provide her 10 with a serious form of technology education. Something quite different from instruction in using computers to process information, which, it strikes me, is a trivial thing to do, for two reasons. In the first place, approximately 35 million people have already learned how to use computers without the benefit of school instruction. If the schools do nothing, most of the population will know how to use computers in the next ten years, just as most of the population learns how to drive a car without school instruction. In the second place, what we needed to know about cars — as we need to know about computers, television, and other important technologies — is not how to use them but how they use *us*. In the case of cars, what we needed to think about in the early twentieth century was not how to drive them but what they would do to our air, our landscape, our social relations, our family life, and our cities. Suppose in 1946 we had started to address similar questions about television: What will be its effects on our political institutions, our psychic habits, our children, our religious conceptions, our economy? Would we be better positioned today to control TV's massive assault on American culture? I am talking here about making technology itself an object of inquiry so that Little Eva and Young John are more interested in asking questions about the computer than getting answers from it.

I am not arguing against using computers in school. I am arguing against our sleepwalking attitudes toward it, against allowing it to distract us from important things, against making a god of it. This is what Theodore Roszak warned against in *The Cult of Information:* "Like all cults," he wrote, "this one also has the intention of enlisting mindless allegiance and acquiescence. People who have no clear idea of what they mean by information or why they should want so much of it are nonetheless prepared to believe that we live in an Information Age, which makes every computer around us what the relics of the True Cross were in the Age of Faith: emblems of salvation." To this, I would add the sage observation of Alan Kay of Apple Computer. Kay is widely associated with the invention of the personal computer, and certainly has an interest in schools using them. Nonetheless, he has repeatedly said that any problems the schools cannot solve without computers, they cannot solve with them. What are some of those problems? There is, for example, the traditional task of teaching children how to behave in groups. One might even say that schools have never been essentially about individualized learning. It is true, of course, that groups do not learn, individuals do. But the idea of a school is that individuals must learn in a setting in which individual needs are subordinated to group interests. Unlike other media of mass communication, which celebrate individual response and are experienced in private, the classroom is intended to tame the ego, to connect the individual with others, to demonstrate the value and necessity of group cohesion. At present, most scenarios describing the uses of computers have children solving problems alone; Little Eva, Young John, and the others are doing just that. The presence of other children may, indeed, be an annoyance.

Like the printing press before it, the computer has a powerful bias toward amplifying personal autonomy and individual problem-solving. That is why educators must guard against computer technology's undermining some of the important reasons for having the young assemble (to quote Ravitch) "in a specific place, for a certain number of hours, and a certain number of days during the week and year."

Although Ravitch is not exactly against what she calls "state schools," she imagines them as something of a relic of a pretechnological age. She believes that the new technologies will offer all children equal access to information. Conjuring up a hypothetical Little Mary who is presumably from a poorer home than Little Eva, Ravitch imagines that Mary will have the same opportunities as Eva "to learn any subject, and to learn it from the same master teachers as children in the richest neighbourhood." For all of its liberalizing spirit, this scenario makes some important omissions. One is that though new technologies may be a solution to the learning of "subjects," they work against the learning of what are called "social values," including an understanding of democratic processes. If one reads the first chapter of Robert Fulghum's *All I Really Need to Know I Learned in Kindergarten,* one will find an elegant summary of a few things Ravitch's scenario has left out. They include learning the following lessons: Share everything, play fair, don't hit people, put things back where you found them, clean up your own mess, wash your hands before you eat, and, of course, flush. The only thing wrong with Fulghum's book is that no one has learned all these things at kindergarten's end. We have ample evidence that it takes many years of teaching these values in school before they have been accepted and internalized. That is why it won't do for children to learn in "settings of their own choosing." That is also why schools require children to be in a certain place at a certain time and to follow certain rules, like raising their hands when they wish to speak, not talking when others are talking, not chewing gum, not leaving until the bell rings, exhibiting patience toward slower learners, etc. This process is called making civilized people. The god of Technology does not appear interested in this function of schools. At least, it does not come up much when technology's virtues are enumerated.

The god of Technology may also have a trick or two up its sleeve about something else. It is often asserted that new technologies will equalize learning opportunities for the rich and poor. It is devoutly to be wished for, but I doubt it will happen. In the first place, it is generally understood by those who have studied the history of technology that technological change always produces winners and losers. There are many reasons for this, among them economic differences. Even in the case of the automobile, which is a commodity most people can buy (although not all), there are wide differences between the rich and poor in the quality of what is available to them. It would be quite astonishing if computer technology equalized all learning opportunities, irrespective of economic differences. One may be delighted that Little Eva's parents could afford the technology and software to make it possible for her to learn algebra at midnight. But Little Mary's parents may not be able to, may not even know such things are available. And if we say that the school could make the technology available to Little Mary (at least during the day), there may [be] something else Little Mary is lacking.

It turns out, for example, that Little Mary may be having sleep- 15 less nights as frequently as Little Eva but not because she wants to get a leg up on her algebra. Maybe because she doesn't know who her father is, or, if she does, where he is. Maybe we can understand why McIntosh's kid is bored with the real world. Or is the child confused about it? Or terrified? Are there educators who seriously believe that these problems can be addressed by new technologies?

I do not say, of course, that schools can solve the problems of poverty, alienation, and family disintegration, but schools can *respond* to them. And they can do this because there are people in them, because these people are concerned with more than algebra lessons or modern Japanese history, and because these people can identify not only one's level of competence in math but one's level of rage and confusion and depression. I am talking here about children as they really come to us, not children who are invented to show us how computers may enrich their lives. Of course, I suppose it is possible that there are children who, waking at night, want to study algebra or who are so interested in their world that they yearn to know about Japan. If there be such children, and one hopes there are, they do not require expensive computers to satisfy their hunger for learning. They are on their way, with or without computers. Unless, of course, they do not care about others or have no friends, or little respect for democracy or are filled with suspicion about those who are not like them. When we have machines that know how to do something about these problems, that is the time to rid ourselves of the expensive burden of schools or to reduce the function of teachers to "coaches" in the uses of machines (as Ravitch envisions). Until then, we must be more modest about this god of Technology and certainly not pin our hopes on it.

We must also, I suppose, be empathetic toward those who search with good intentions for technological panaceas. I am a teacher myself and know how hard it is to contribute to the making of a civilized person. Can we blame those who want to find an easy way, through the agency of technology? Perhaps not. After all, it is an old quest. As early as 1918, H. L. Mencken (although completely devoid of empathy) wrote, "There is no sure-cure so idiotic that some superintendent of schools will not swallow it. The aim seems to be to reduce the whole teaching process to a sort of automatic reaction, to discover some master formula that will not only take the place of competence and resourcefulness in the teacher but that will also create an artificial receptivity in the child."

Mencken was not necessarily speaking of technological panaceas but he may well have been. In the early 1920s a teacher wrote the following poem:

Mr. Edison says
That the radio will supplant the teacher.
Already one may learn languages by means of Victrola records.
The moving picture will visualize
What the radio fails to get across.
Teachers will be relegated to the backwoods,
With fire-horses,
And long-haired women;
Or, perhaps shown in museums.

Education will become a matter
Of pressing the button.
Perhaps I can get a position at the switchboard.

I do not go as far back as the radio and Victrola, but I am old
enough to remember when 16-millimeter film was to be the sure-
cure. Then closed-circuit television. Then 8-millimeter film. Then
teacher-proof textbooks. Now computers.

I know a false god when I see one.   20

Indecent Proposal:
Censor the Net
STEVEN LEVY

Jim Exon does not want to be known as the censor of cyberspace. The Democratic senator from Nebraska has insisted that his
aim is protecting children, not muzzling the millions of people accustomed to electronic free speech. But last Thursday his so-called
Communications Decency Act passed the Senate Commerce Committee. Despite his protestations, if this bill is made into law, the digital frontier will instantly be transformed from our most wide-open
preserve of untrammeled speech to a place where even common
forms of expression are outlawed.

Exon's bill — actually an amendment tacked to the telecommunications bill — has already undergone considerable changes. The
initial version spread the liability for "obscene, lewd, lascivious,
filthy or indecent" speech between the originator and the on-line
service that moved the message. Critics noted that it was impossible
for the service providers to read the gigabits of data that pass
through their portals; in effect, the bill would criminalize the entire
Internet. So Exon exempted them from prosecution. Responsibility
for keeping the Net clean now rests on those who post messages,
send letters, maintain web sites, and distribute documents and files.
The penalty for filth is a fine and possibly a jail term.

The heart of this matter is how our laws should apply to cyberspace. Should restrictions on electronic expression be fairly tight, as
with radio and television? Or should cyberspeech be as unrestrained as that in magazines, newspapers, and private conversations? Currently, something like the latter standard applies —
anything goes, short of obscenity, and people have been prosecuted

Steven Levy is a contributing editor at *Newsweek* magazine, where this essay appeared on April 3, 1995.

for on-line excesses. But Exon wants to apply the broadcast rule, where generally less offensive acts of indecency are also banned. The legal definition of indecency includes the "seven dirty words" that George Carlin identified as unutterable over the air.

But cyberspace doesn't work like broadcast, where a few licensed stations beam out to thousands or millions of viewers who have no idea what's coming up next. Various parts of cyberspace resemble postal mail, coffee klatches, public lectures, academic seminars, locker-room banter, and print periodicals — not broadcast. In none of these venues would we welcome regulations where fines and prison sentences would be doled out for uttering certain expletives that, though once considered scandalous, are now fairly ubiquitous in our culture.

What if the bill passes? Certain commercial servers that distrib-   5
ute pictures of unclad human beings, like those run by Penthouse or Playboy, would of course be shut down immediately, or risk prosecution. But so would any amateur web site that features nudity, sex talk, or rough language. Posting any of the seven dirty words in a Usenet discussion group — and I can verify that those words now appear routinely — could make one liable for a $50,000 fine and six months in the pokey. And if a magazine that commonly runs some of those nasty words in its pages — say, *The New Yorker* — decided to put its contents on-line, its leaders would be liable for a $100,000 fine and two years in jail. Exon's bill apparently would also "criminalize private mail," says Daniel Weitzner, deputy director of the Center of Democracy and Technology. Senator Patrick Leahy, Democrat of Vermont, agrees: "[If Exon's bill passes] I can call my brother on the phone and say anything — but if I say it on the Internet it's illegal . . :"

The phone analogy is interesting because Exon's amendment is literally an addition to previous legislation regulating the content of phone conversations. Thus it treats digital transmissions, sent to or accessed by consenting adults, with the stringent restrictions on the language used in harassing or obscene phone calls. Senator Leahy attributes the overkill to a Congress bent on acting without regard to consequences. "None of us want children to be delving into pornography, but let's not deal with it in a way that cripples one of the best communications successes in decades," he says. "I'm not going to close down a beautiful city park because periodically some idiot comes to the corner and shouts obscenities."

So how do we protect our children from the pictures of naked ladies, the discussions of bestiality, and the rough language that currently characterize the Net? Even Exon has admitted that his bill probably won't stop the smut he so urgently wants to eliminate. There are high-tech dodges around anything that the simple minds of the Senate can concoct. We would have better results by implementing some newly proposed technological solutions, ranging from software that filters out possibly objectionable material to special services that present only a bowdlerized version of the Net to junior web-surfers. And then, there's always that remedy in which censorious legislators never seem to have confidence: parental guidance.

Yes it is true — some of us who have participated in the explosive growth of the Net might have been turned off by some of the scatologies and tasteless excesses. But anyone who has spent time using this new form of communication also understands that this is a minor annoyance compared with its positive aspects. The most exciting of these is the Net's unrestrained freedom of expression. After the sound-bite smog of broadcast media, this passionate embrace of ideas and creativity is clean, fresh air. This could have been, and still can be, our legacy to the global communications infrastructure — exporting the glories of the First Amendment, granting citizens of all nations the experience of speaking without fear. Instead, in their misguided attempt to protect children, Jim Exon and company would export a vision of America based on fear, prudery, ignorance, and oppression. I find it indecent.

THINKING AND WRITING ABOUT THE DIGITAL REVOLUTION

Questions for Discussion and Writing

1. Summarize the differences between Negroponte and Stoll concerning the role of teachers in education. Have they been fair in their evaluations? Do you find any evidence that either author has slanted the argument in his own defense? If you think one author has made a more convincing argument, explain why.

2. What do Birkerts and Slouka fear about the spread of networking? Do their fears seem justified? How do Barlow and Kelly respond to their fears?

3. Postman thinks that many of the educational reforms envisioned by lovers of technology are unrealistic. List some of them and decide whether you agree with Postman. If you have had experience with computers in school, how did this influence your judgment? What are Postman's principal objections to the technological utopians in education? Do Postman and Stoll share any views?

4. Levy sees censorship of material on the Internet as a threat to our First Amendment rights of free speech. Does he make a strong case for freedom? Does he treat the problem of pornography too lightly? Is control of material on the Internet different from control of materials in other media?

5. Barlow praises the virtual community created by computers. Saige rejects it. List the main arguments on each side, affirmative and negative, and decide whether they are addressing each other's claims.

6. According to Diebold, life in America could become better and cheaper through greater use of computers. Do some of the changes seem more useful than others? Would any of these innovations bring problems as well as solutions?
7. What does the cartoonist think about the advances in communication promised by the Internet?

Topics for Research

Use of computers in the classroom

Use of computers in law enforcement

Problems on the Internet

Significance of the chess match in 1996 between Gary Kasparov, world champion, and Deep Blue, the IBM computer

Computer Power and Human Reason, by Joseph Weizenbaum (1976): Prophecy or false alarm?

Computer games: What do they teach?

CHAPTER THIRTEEN

Euthanasia

Euthanasia means "good death" or "mercy killing," that is, causing the death of one who is so ill or disabled that continued existence will produce intolerable suffering. Euthanasia may be active or passive; in the first case, death is deliberately inflicted, sometimes by a relative; in the second case, life-support systems are withdrawn and the patient dies naturally.

Controversy surrounding the morality of euthanasia has been heightened enormously in recent years because of advances in medical technology that make it possible for human beings, both newborn and old, to be kept alive almost indefinitely, even when severely impaired. As our life span lengthens, more and more people will reach an age when illness and disability create the possibility for euthanasia.

In those cases in which the patient cannot make a rational choice, decisions to prolong or terminate life must be left to families, doctors, and, not infrequently, the courts. Even the definition of *life* is at issue. A person may be declared "brain dead" while vital functions persist. Other problems of definition have become increasingly important. Where a patient has signed a living will, a physician may nevertheless refuse to remove the feeding tube, arguing that continuing to provide nourishment does not constitute "medication, artificial means, or heroic measures." In June 1990 the Supreme Court ruled that a state may pass laws allowing patients to refuse unwanted life-sustaining treatment, provided that the patient has previously expressed "clear and convincing evidence" of such a desire. Since then, legal initiatives for and against euthanasia have appeared on several state ballots. In 1992, after several doctor-assisted suicides by the inventor of a "self-execution machine," Michigan became the first state to make doctor-assisted suicide illegal.

However, neither this law, which was temporary, nor any other law has so far prevented Dr. Jack Kevorkian, the Michigan pathologist who invented the machine, from continuing to assist patients to die. He has admitted assisting at twenty-seven suicides since 1990. In the spring of 1996 he was brought to trial for the fourth time and for the fourth time was acquitted of criminal charges.

Although euthanasia continues to be deeply controversial, the right-to-die movement has recently claimed successes. In 1994 Oregon legalized physician-assisted suicide, the first state to do so. The law allows doctors "to prescribe suicide pills to a terminally ill patient with less than six months to live, who gets a second opinion, makes three requests and doesn't appear to be suffering from a mental disorder." Both this law and a similar law in New York state have been upheld by circuit courts of appeals.

On one side are those who regard the problems posed by euthanasia as essentially religious: Life is sacred, no matter how severely disabled the patient may be, and no human being can arrogate to him- or herself a decision reserved for God. On the other side are those who insist that it is the quality of life that should influence the decision and that death may be preferable to a severely impaired life. Euthanasia thus becomes an act of charity. In one widely publicized case which tested the limits of the quality-of-life criterion, parents approved denial of food and water to their severely retarded newborn son rather than allow a stomach operation for him.

One final problem confronts us in all the discussions about euthanasia. Will increasingly widespread acceptance of such deaths lead to a more relaxed attitude toward the taking of life in general and toward taking the lives of those in need of constant and lifelong attention in particular? One writer asks if the same principle of withholding food and water from a woman in a coma should be extended "to the thousands of others who fall into a coma every year, and to the many more mentally retarded or deranged, and sufferers of Alzheimer's disease who are a 'burden' on their families."

In Defense of
Voluntary Euthanasia

SIDNEY HOOK

A few short years ago, I lay at the point of death. A congestive heart failure was treated for diagnostic purposes by an angiogram that triggered a stroke. Violent and painful hiccups, uninterrupted for several days and nights, prevented the ingestion of food. My left side and one of my vocal cords became paralyzed. Some form of pleurisy set in, and I felt I was drowning in a sea of slime. At one point, my heart stopped beating; just as I lost consciousness, it was thumped back into action again. In one of my lucid intervals during those days of agony, I asked my physician to discontinue all life-supporting services or show me how to do it. He refused and predicted that someday I would appreciate the unwisdom of my request.

A month later, I was discharged from the hospital. In six months, I regained the use of my limbs, and although my voice still lacks its old resonance and carrying power I no longer croak like a frog. There remain some minor disabilities and I am restricted to a rigorous, low-sodium diet. I have resumed my writing and research.

My experience can be and has been cited as an argument against honoring requests of stricken patients to be gently eased out of their pain and life. I cannot agree. There are two main reasons. As an octogenarian, there is a reasonable likelihood that I may suffer another "cardiovascular accident" or worse. I may not even be in a position to ask for the surcease of pain. It seems to me that I have already paid my dues to death — indeed, although time has softened my memories they are vivid enough to justify my saying that I suffered enough to warrant dying several times over. Why run the risk of more?

Secondly, I dread imposing on my family and friends another grim round of misery similar to the one my first attack occasioned.

My wife and children endured enough for one lifetime. I know 5 that for them the long days and nights of waiting, the disruption of their professional duties, and their own familial responsibilities counted for nothing in their anxiety for me. In their joy at my recovery they have been forgotten. Nonetheless, to visit another prolonged spell of helpless suffering on them as my life ebbs away, or even worse, if I linger on into a comatose senility, seems altogether gratuitous.

This essay by Sidney Hook (1902–1989), former professor of philosophy at New York University and senior research fellow at the Hoover Institution on War, Revolution, and Peace, was published in the *New York Times* on March 1, 1987.

But what, it may be asked, of the joy and satisfaction of living, of basking in the sunshine, listening to music, watching one's grandchildren growing into adolescence, following the news about the fate of freedom in a troubled world, playing with ideas, writing one's testament of wisdom and folly for posterity? Is not all that one endured, together with the risk of its recurrence, an acceptable price for the multiple satisfactions that are still open even to a person of advanced years?

Apparently those who cling to life no matter what think so. I do not.

The zest and intensity of these experiences are no longer what they used to be. I am not vain enough to delude myself that I can in the few remaining years make an important discovery useful for mankind or can lead a social movement or do anything that will be historically eventful, no less event-making. My autobiography, which describes a record of intellectual and political experiences of some historical value, already much too long, could be posthumously published. I have had my fill of joys and sorrows and am not greedy for more life. I have always thought that a test of whether one had found happiness in one's life is whether one would be willing to relive it — whether, if it were possible, one would accept the opportunity to be born again.

Having lived a full and relatively happy life, I would cheerfully accept the chance to be reborn, but certainly not to be reborn again as an infirm octogenarian. To some extent, my views reflect what I have seen happen to the aged and stricken who have been so unfortunate as to survive crippling paralysis. They suffer, and impose suffering on others, unable even to make a request that their torment be ended.

I am mindful too of the burdens placed upon the community, with its rapidly diminishing resources, to provide the adequate and costly services necessary to sustain the lives of those whose days and nights are spent on mattress graves of pain. A better use could be made of these resources to increase the opportunities and qualities of life for the young. I am not denying the moral obligation the community has to look after its disabled and aged. There are times, however, when an individual may find it pointless to insist on the fulfillment of a legal and moral right.

What is required is no great revolution in morals but an enlargement of imagination and an intelligent evaluation of alternative uses of community resources.

Long ago, Seneca observed that "the wise man will live as long as he ought, not as long as he can." One can envisage hypothetical circumstances in which one has a duty to prolong one's life despite its costs for the sake of others, but such circumstances are far removed from the ordinary prospects we are considering. If wisdom is rooted in knowledge of the alternatives of choice, it must be reliably informed of the state one is in and its likely outcome. Scientific medicine is not infallible, but it is the best we have. Should a rational person be willing to endure acute suffering merely on the chance that a miraculous cure might presently be at hand? Each one should be permitted to make his own choice — especially when no one else is harmed by it.

The responsibility for the decision, whether deemed wise or foolish, must be with the chooser.

Active and Passive Euthanasia
JAMES RACHELS

The distinction between active and passive euthanasia is thought to be crucial for medical ethics. The idea is that it is permissible, at least in some cases, to withhold treatment and allow a patient to die, but it is never permissible to take any direct action designed to kill the patient. This doctrine seems to be accepted by most doctors, and it is endorsed in a statement adopted by the House of Delegates of the American Medical Association on December 4, 1973:

> The intentional termination of the life of one human being by another — mercy killing — is contrary to that for which the medical profession stands and is contrary to the policy of the American Medical Association.
>
> The cessation of the employment of extraordinary means to prolong the life of the body when there is irrefutable evidence that biological death is imminent is the decision of the patient and/or his immediate family. The advice and judgment of the physician should be freely available to the patient and/or his immediate family.

However, a strong case can be made against this doctrine. In what follows I will set out some of the relevant arguments and urge doctors to reconsider their views on this matter.

To begin with a familiar type of situation, a patient who is dying of incurable cancer of the throat is in terrible pain, which can no longer be satisfactorily alleviated. He is certain to die within a few days, even if present treatment is continued, but he does not want

James Rachels, a professor at the University of Miami, is editor of *Moral Problems*, a reader on the ethical aspects of contemporary social issues. "Active and Passive Euthanasia" was published in the *New England Journal of Medicine*, Vol. 292, in 1975.

to go on living for those days since the pain is unbearable. So he asks the doctor for an end to it, and his family joins in the request.

Suppose the doctor agrees to withhold treatment, as the conventional doctrine says he may. The justification for his doing so is that the patient is in terrible agony, and since he is going to die anyway, it would be wrong to prolong his suffering needlessly. But now notice this. If one simply withholds treatment, it may take the patient longer to die, and so he may suffer more than he would if more direct action were taken and a lethal injection given. This fact provides strong reason for thinking that, once the initial decision not to prolong his agony has been made, active euthanasia is actually preferable to passive euthanasia, rather than the reverse. To say otherwise is to endorse the option that leads to more suffering rather than less, and is contrary to the humanitarian impulse that prompts the decision not to prolong his life in the first place.

Part of my point is that the process of being "allowed to die" can be relatively slow and painful, whereas being given a lethal injection is relatively quick and painless. Let me give a different sort of example. In the United States about one in 600 babies is born with Down's syndrome. Most of these babies are otherwise healthy — that is, with only the usual pediatric care, they will proceed to an otherwise normal infancy. Some, however, are born with congenital defects such as intestinal obstructions that require operations if they are to live. Sometimes, the parents and the doctor will decide not to operate, and let the infant die. Anthony Shaw describes what happens then:

> . . . When surgery is denied [the doctor] must try to keep the infant from suffering while natural forces sap the baby's life away. As a surgeon whose natural inclination is to use the scalpel to fight off death, standing by and watching a salvageable baby die is the most emotionally exhausting experience I know. It is easy at a conference, in a theoretical discussion, to decide that such infants should be allowed to die. It is altogether different to stand by in the nursery and watch as dehydration and infection wither a tiny being over hours and days. This is a terrible ordeal for me and the hospital staff — much more so than for the parents who never set foot in the nursery.[1]

I can understand why some people are opposed to all euthanasia, and insist that such infants must be allowed to live. I think I can also understand why other people favor destroying these babies quickly and painlessly. But why should anyone favor letting "dehydration and infection wither a tiny being over hours and days"? The doctrine that says that a baby may be allowed to dehydrate and wither, but

---

[1] A. Shaw, "Doctor, Do We Have a Choice?" *New York Times Magazine,* January 30, 1972, p. 54.

may not be given an injection that would end its life without suffering, seems so patently cruel as to require no further refutation. The strong language is not intended to offend, but only to put the point in the clearest possible way.

My second argument is that the conventional doctrine leads to 5 decisions concerning life and death made on irrelevant grounds.

Consider again the case of the infants with Down's syndrome who need operations for congenital defects unrelated to the syndrome to live. Sometimes there is no operation, and the baby dies, but when there is no such defect, the baby lives on. Now, an operation such as that to remove an intestinal obstruction is not prohibitively difficult. The reason why such operations are not performed in these cases is, clearly, that the child has Down's syndrome and the parents and doctor judge that because of that fact it is better for the child to die.

But notice that this situation is absurd, no matter what view one takes of the lives and potential of such babies. If the life of such an infant is worth preserving, what does it matter if it needs a simple operation? Or, if one thinks it better that such a baby should not live on, what difference does it make that it happens to have an unobstructed intestinal tract? In either case, the matter of life and death is being decided on irrelevant grounds. It is the Down's syndrome, and not the intestines, that is the issue. The matter should be decided, if at all, on that basis, and not be allowed to depend on the essentially irrelevant question of whether the intestinal tract is blocked.

What makes this situation possible, of course, is the idea that when there is an intestinal blockage, one can "let the baby die," but when there is no such defect there is nothing that can be done, for one must not "kill" it. The fact that this idea leads to such results as deciding life or death on irrelevant grounds is another good reason why the doctrine should be rejected.

One reason why so many people think that there is an important moral difference between active and passive euthanasia is that they think killing someone is morally worse than letting someone die. But is it? Is killing, in itself, worse than letting die? To investigate this issue, two cases may be considered that are exactly alike except that one involves killing whereas the other involves letting someone die. Then, it can be asked whether this difference makes any difference to the moral assessments. It is important that the cases be exactly alike, except for this one difference, since otherwise one cannot be confident that it is this difference and not some other that accounts for any variation in the assessments of the two cases. So, let us consider this pair of cases:

In the first, Smith stands to gain a large inheritance if anything 10 should happen to his six-year-old cousin. One evening while the child is taking his bath, Smith sneaks into the bathroom and drowns the child, and then arranges things so that it will look like an accident.

In the second, Jones also stands to gain if anything should happen to his six-year-old cousin. Like Smith, Jones sneaks in planning to drown the child in his bath. However, just as he enters the bathroom Jones sees the child slip and hit his head, and fall face down in the water. Jones is delighted; he stands by, ready to push the child's head back under if it is necessary, but it is not necessary. With only a little thrashing about, the child drowns all by himself, "accidentally," as Jones watches and does nothing.

Now Smith killed the child, whereas Jones "merely" let the child die. That is the only difference between them. Did either man behave better, from a moral point of view? If the difference between killing and letting die were in itself a morally important matter, one should say that Jones's behavior was less reprehensible than Smith's. But does one really want to say that? I think not. In the first place, both men acted from the same motive, personal gain, and both had exactly the same end in view when they acted. It may be inferred from Smith's conduct that he is a bad man, although that judgment may be withdrawn or modified if certain further facts are learned about him — for example, that he is mentally deranged. But would not the very same thing be inferred about Jones from his conduct? And would not the same further considerations also be relevant to any modification of this judgment? Moreover, suppose Jones pleaded, in his own defense, "After all, I didn't do anything except just stand there and watch the child drown. I didn't kill him; I only let him die." Again, if letting die were in itself less bad than killing, this defense should have at least some weight. But it does not. Such a "defense" can only be regarded as a grotesque perversion of moral reasoning. Morally speaking, it is no defense at all.

Now, it may be pointed out, quite properly, that the cases of euthanasia with which doctors are concerned are not like this at all. They do not involve personal gain or the destruction of normal, healthy children. Doctors are concerned only with cases in which the patient's life is of no further use to him, or in which the patient's life has become or will soon become a terrible burden. However, the point is the same in these cases: The bare difference between killing and letting die does not, in itself, make a moral difference. If a doctor lets a patient die, for humane reasons, he is in the same moral position as if he had given the patient a lethal injection for humane reasons. If his decision was wrong — if, for example, the patient's illness was in fact curable — the decision would be equally regrettable no matter which method was used to carry it out. And if the doctor's decision was the right one, the method used is not in itself important.

The AMA policy statement isolates the crucial issue very well; the crucial issue is "the intentional termination of the life of one human being by another." But after identifying this issue, and forbidding "mercy killing," the statement goes on to deny that the cessation of treatment is the intentional termination of a life. This is where the mistake comes in, for what is the cessation of treatment, in these circumstances, if it is not "the intentional termination of the life of one human being by another"? Of course it is exactly that, and if it were not, there would be no point to it.

Many people will find this judgment hard to accept. One reason, I think, is that it is very easy to conflate the question of whether killing is, in itself, worse than letting die, with the very different question of whether most actual cases of killing are more reprehensible than most actual cases of letting die. Most actual cases of killing are clearly terrible (think, for example, of all the murders reported in the newspapers), and one hears of such cases every day. On the other hand, one hardly ever hears of a case of letting die, except for the actions of doctors who are motivated by humanitarian reasons. So one learns to think of killing in a much worse light than of letting die, for it is not the bare difference between killing and letting die that makes the difference in these cases. Rather, the other factors — the murderer's motive of personal gain, for example, contrasted with the doctor's humanitarian motivation — account for different reactions to the different cases.

I have argued that killing is not in itself any worse than letting die; if my contention is right, it follows that active euthanasia is not any worse than passive euthanasia. What arguments can be given on the other side? The most common, I believe, is the following:

"The important difference between active and passive euthanasia is that, in passive euthanasia, the doctor does not do anything to bring about the patient's death. The doctor does nothing, and the patient dies of whatever ills already afflict him. In active euthanasia, however, the doctor does something to bring about the patient's death: He kills him. The doctor who gives the patient with cancer a lethal injection has himself caused his patient's death; whereas if he merely ceases treatment, the cancer is the cause of the death."

A number of points need to be made here. The first is that it is not exactly correct to say that in passive euthanasia the doctor does nothing, for he does do one thing that is very important: He lets the patient die. "Letting someone die" is certainly different in some respects, from other types of action — mainly in that it is a kind of action that one may perform by way of not performing certain other actions. For example, one may let a patient die by way of not giving medication, just as one may insult someone by way of not shaking his hand. But for any purpose of moral assessment, it is a type of action nonetheless. The decision to let a patient die is subject to moral appraisal in the same way that a decision to kill him would be subject to moral appraisal: It may be assessed as wise or unwise, com-

15

passionate or sadistic, right or wrong. If a doctor deliberately let a patient die who was suffering from a routinely curable illness, the doctor would certainly be to blame for what he had done, just as he would be to blame if he had needlessly killed the patient. Charges against him would then be appropriate. If so, it would be no defense at all for him to insist that he didn't "do anything." He would have done something very serious indeed, for he let his patient die.

Fixing the cause of death may be very important from a legal point of view, for it may determine whether criminal charges are brought against the doctor. But I do not think that this notion can be used to show a moral difference between active and passive euthanasia. The reason why it is considered bad to be the cause of someone's death is that death is regarded as a great evil — and so it is. However, if it had been decided that euthanasia — even passive euthanasia — is desirable in a given case, it has also been decided that in this instance death is no greater an evil than the patient's continued existence. And if this is true, the usual reason for not wanting to be the cause of someone's death simply does not apply.

Finally, doctors may think that all of this is only of academic interest — the sort of thing that philosophers may worry about but that has no practical bearing on their own work. After all, doctors must be concerned about the legal consequences of what they do, and active euthanasia is clearly forbidden by the law. But even so, doctors should also be concerned with the fact that the law is forcing upon them a moral doctrine that may well be indefensible and has a considerable effect on their practices. Of course, most doctors are not now in the position of being coerced in this matter, for they do not regard themselves as merely going along with what the law requires. Rather, in statements such as the AMA policy statement that I have quoted, they are endorsing this doctrine as a central point of medical ethics. In that statement, active euthanasia is condemned not merely as illegal but as "contrary to that for which the medical profession stands," whereas passive euthanasia is approved. However, the preceding considerations suggest that there is really no moral difference between the two, considered in themselves (there may be important moral differences in some cases in their *consequences,* but, as I pointed out, these differences may make active euthanasia, and not passive euthanasia, the morally preferable option). So, whereas doctors may have to discriminate between active and passive euthanasia to satisfy the law, they should not do any more than that. In particular, they should not give the distinction any added authority and weight by writing it into official statements of medical ethics.

Tragic Mercy Killing Case Didn't Belong in Court

ALAN DERSHOWITZ

The dean of the law school I attended teaches a course aptly entitled "Tragic Choices." It presents the young law students with moral dilemmas that have no "good" outcomes. The choices tend to be among "worse," "worser," and "worsest." For example, how should the law decide who, among several medically eligible potential organ recipients, will receive — or be deprived of — a scarce liver or heart? Or, if only one Siamese twin can be saved by surgery, which one shall it be?

Several months ago, I received a call from a doctor who had faced a tragic choice in his own personal life. His wife was dying of a fast-spreading form of cancer. She was in excruciating pain and her doctors told her it would just get worse. Death was inevitable — within days or weeks.

The woman, who had two teenage children, decided that she did not want to die alone, suddenly, and in pain. She determined to die with dignity, surrounded by her loving family. After preparing for the end, she selected the time and the means of her death. She even appeared on television and discussed her situation, hoping to provide solace and courage to others faced with similar tragedies. She wrote letters and gave small gifts to her friends.

On the day of her scheduled death, her stepfather and half-brothers were summoned from out of town. Her family sat down to a farewell dinner. She then went to the bedroom with her husband. They drank a glass of wine, kissed, and embraced. She then asked her husband to give her pills that she had selected for a painless death. The children were given mild sedatives and put to bed, expecting to awaken only after it was all over. She swallowed the pills and drifted off, expecting to die in her sleep.

But something went wrong. She did not die immediately. In fact, 5 her coma began to lighten, and her husband could see she was in pain. He said that he then administered some painkiller to her, but still she did not die. Finally, the terminally ill woman's stepfather placed his fingers over her nose and mouth, thus cutting off her breathing. She died within minutes.

The call I received from the dead woman's husband came from jail. He was asking me to help him save his life. Nearly a year after he

---

This 1988 article by Alan Dershowitz, a professor at the Harvard University Law School, is taken from his collection of essays *Contrary to Popular Opinion* (1992).

made his tragic choice, he went on television to explain and justify it. Shortly thereafter he was arrested and charged with murder, a crime carrying the death penalty. (The woman's stepfather was given immunity, before he told the prosecutors that it was he who administered the coup de grace, in exchange for testifying against his son-in-law.)

Although the state of Florida, where this took place, has a statute punishing anyone who assists another in committing suicide, the local authorities decided to treat the husband as if he were an organized-crime hit man.

The authorities were not alone in considering his act of love to be the equivalent of the worst forms of sadistic murder. On a nationally televised talk show, the director of the International Antieuthanasia Task Force characterized this act of family devotion as akin to a "serialized gang murder."

What happened during that tragic night in Florida was neither murder nor euthanasia. It was dignified suicide. The woman died as a result of cancer. Were it not for that ravaging disease, she would be alive today. She did not choose *to die*. The cancer made that decision for her. What *she* chose was the timing and circumstances of her death. Euthanasia — mercy killing — occurs when *another* person makes the decision to take a life for humane purposes. Here, the decision was made rationally by the woman herself. It was a mercy suicide, which is no longer considered a crime in any civilized nation.

Should this terminally ill and suffering woman not have had the   10
right to avoid a few more days of painful — and, in her view, undignified — life? Could a devoted husband reject her last wish — to die in his loving arms, surrounded by family to whom she had said her farewells?

Individuals have very different views on these tragic choices. Religions provide different answers to these unanswerable questions. There is no absolute right or wrong when it comes to coping with the final days of a grievously suffering loved one's life.

But generally the government should stay far away from the deathbed of a grieving family. This prosecution, and the attitudes of some of those who were pushing it, are the best proof of the inability of most prosecutors to deal sensitively with personal tragedies of the kind experienced by this family.

Anyone who does not understand the difference between a "serialized gang murder"— indeed, any murder — and the tragic choice confronting that aggrieved family in Florida should not be in the business of telling others how to live — and how to die.

The jury in this case acquitted the doctor, but he never should have been put on trial in the first place. He did the right thing in helping his wife. The prosecutors are the guilty parties — guilty of politicizing a personal tragedy.

That Right Belongs
Only to the State

MORTIMER OSTOW

To the Editor:

Nine members of the Kennedy Institute for the Study of Human Reproduction and Bioethics commented on May 18 on your May 2 editorial "Who Shall Make the Ultimate Decision?" Their assertion that it is important to establish precise criteria to guide the judgment of reasonable people cannot be faulted.

I believe comment is called for, however, on your argument that vital decisions respecting life and death belong to the patient or, when he is incompetent to make them, to those who are presumed to have his best interests at heart. The members of the Kennedy Institute concur.

It is a basic assumption of our society that individual members possess no right to determine matters of life and death respecting other individuals, or even themselves. That right belongs only to the state. The prohibition of murder, suicide, and, until recently, abortion, has rested on this assumption. The right to determine whether life-preserving efforts are to be continued or discontinued therefore belongs neither to the physician nor to the patient or his guardian, but to the state.

In practical terms, when such a decision is called for, the decision is to be made only by some agency or agent of the state, and it is to be made only by due process. To cede the right to the individuals involved is to license murder.

Aside from the philosophic argument, which not everyone will 5 find cogent, there are two practical reasons for requiring due process in such instances. In discussion of matters of continuing or withholding life-support systems and euthanasia, the arguments usually offered relate to the best interests of the patient or to the economic cost to society. Abortion, too, is discussed in these terms. A far more important consideration, it seems to me, is what making life-and-death decisions does to the individuals who decide.

While most of us will doubt that having made a decision to terminate life support to a suffering relative will then incline one to commit murder, still, making such a decision does condition the un-

---

Dr. Ostow's letter appeared in the *New York Times* on June 1, 1971.

conditional respect for life, and does weaken the concept of the distinction between what is permitted and what is forbidden.

One can see a tendency to pass from withdrawing life support from the moribund to facilitating the death of the suffering, and from there to the neglect or even abandonment of the profoundly defective, and from there to the degradation or liquidation of any whom society might consider undesirable. The undisciplined making of life-and-death decisions tends to corrupt the individual who makes them, and corrupted individuals tend to corrupt society.

Second, it is not necessarily true that the individual himself has his own interests at heart. Afflicted with a painful and long-drawn-out illness, many individuals will wish for death, even when objectively there is a reasonable possibility of recovery. Permitting the patient to make the decision to die may amount to encouraging his suicide. Anyone familiar with the ambivalence which prevails in family relationships will not take it for granted that family members will necessarily represent the patient's best interests.

It is important for the morale and morality of our society that "the ultimate decision" be made only by a disinterested agent or agency of our society, and only by due process.

Mortimer Ostow, M.D.

A Modern Inquisition

JACK KEVORKIAN

This is probably the first time that this august body [the American Humanist Association] has been addressed by someone under indictment on two counts of first-degree murder.

The Inquisition is still alive and well. The only difference is that today it's much more dangerous and subtle. The inquisitors don't burn you at the stake anymore; they slowly sizzle you. They make sure you pay dearly for what you do. In fact, they kill you often in a subtle way. My situation is a perfect example of it.

This is not self-pity, understand. I don't regret the position I'm in. I'm not a hero, either — by my definition, anyway. To me, anyone who does what *should* be done is not a hero. And I still feel that I'm only doing what I, as a physician, should do. A license has nothing to do with it; I am a physician and therefore I will act like a physician whenever I can. That doesn't mean that I'm more compassionate

This speech by Dr. Jack Kevorkian, a proponent of physician-assisted voluntary euthanasia, first appeared in the November–December 1994 issue of *The Humanist;* this excerpt is from the March–April 1995 issue of *Utne Reader.*

than anyone else, but there is one thing I am that many aren't and that's honest.

The biggest deficiency today and the biggest problem with society is dishonesty. It underlies almost every crisis and every problem you can name. It's almost inevitable; in fact, it's unavoidable as you mature. We feel that a little dishonesty greases the wheels of society, that it makes things easier for everybody if we lie a little to each other. But all this dishonesty becomes cumulative after a while. If everyone were perfectly honest at all times, if human nature could stand that, you would find many fewer problems in the world.

When we (my lawyers, sisters, medical technologist, and myself) 5 first started this work [physician-assisted voluntary euthanasia], we didn't expect the explosion of publicity that followed. The mainstream media tried to make my work look very negative — they tried to make me look negative — so that they could denigrate the concept we're working on. They said I should not be identified with the concept, yet they strived to do just that. They insulted and denigrated me and then hoped that it would spill over onto the concept. It didn't work, however; according to the polls, people may be split 50-50 on what they think of me, but they are three-to-one in favor of the concept, and that's never changed.

Now isn't it strange that on a controversial subject of this magnitude — one that cuts across many disciplines — the entire editorial policy of the country is on one side? Even on a contentious issue like abortion, there is editorial support for both sides. And our issue — death with dignity — as far as we're concerned, is simpler than abortion. So why is every mainstream editorial writer and newspaper in the country against us on this? Not one has come out in wholehearted support of us, even though public opinion is on our side.

As I surmise it, they're in a conspiracy, which is not a revelation to many people. But with whom? Well, let's take a look at who's against this: organized religion, organized medicine, and organized big money. That's a lot of power.

Why is organized medicine against this? For a couple of reasons, I think. First, because the so-called profession — which is no longer a profession; it's really a commercial enterprise and has been for a long time — is permeated with religious overtones. The basis of so-called medical ethics is religious ethics. The Hippocratic oath is a religious manifesto. It is not medical. Hippocrates didn't write it; we don't know who did, but we think it's from the Pythagoreans. So if you meet a physician who says "Life is sacred," be careful. We didn't study sanctity in medical school. You are talking to a theologian first, probably a businessperson second, and a physician third.

The second reason that organized medicine is against physician-assisted voluntary euthanasia is the money involved. If a patient's suffering is curtailed by three weeks, can you imagine how much that adds up to in medical care? And a lot of drugs are used in the last several months and years of life, which add up to billions of dollars for the pharmaceutical industry.

This is what is so dismaying to me, what makes me cynical. You 10 have to be cynical in life when you read about a situation that's so terrible and so incorrigible. There are certain ways to deal with it: You can go along with it, which is hard to do; you can go insane, which is a refuge (and some do that); or you can face it with deep cynicism. I've opted for cynicism.

In responding to the religious issues, I ask this: Why not let all the religious underpinnings of medicine apply only to the ethics of religious hospitals and leave the secular hospitals alone? The doctors who work in religious hospitals can refuse to do abortions, they can refuse assisted suicide or euthanasia, they can do anything they want. But they have no right to impose what *they* call a universal medical ethic on secular institutions.

Besides, what is ethics? Can you define it? My definition is simple: Ethics is saying and doing what is right, at the time. And that changes. Seventy-five years ago, if I told you that for Christmas I was going to have a truck deliver ten tons of coal to your house, you would have been delighted. If I told you that today, you would be insulted. Doing the right thing changes with time.

That's true of human society also. There is a primitive society — I don't know which one exactly — whose members were shocked to learn that we embalm our dead, place them in boxes, and then bury them in the ground. Do you know what they do? They eat them. To them, it's ethical and moral and honorable to devour the corpse of your loved one. We're shocked at that, right? It's all a matter of acculturation, time, where you are, and who you are. If I visited this primitive society and I was a real humanist, I'd say, "Oh, that's interesting." And if the so-called savage in turn said "Gee, that's interesting what you do," then he or she would be a humanist. I used to define maturity as the inability to be shocked. So I guess in some ways we're still immature. But if you're truly mature, and a true humanist, you can never be shocked. If they eat their dead, so be it — that's their culture. But you know what our missionaries did, don't you? That's immoral action.

I think you get the gist of my position.

Consequences of Imposing the Quality-of-Life Ethic

EILEEN DOYLE

Under the American Constitution, all who belong to the human species *are persons* and are guaranteed the protection of their inalienable right to life (and other inalienable rights).

(The only exceptions are living human beings before birth who have unjustly been denied their right to life by the 1973 Supreme Court abortion decisions, *Roe v. Wade* and *Doe v. Bolton*.)

The Constitution adheres to the sanctity of life ethic and the theory of natural rights which state that human beings by their very nature are of intrinsic value — they do not have to earn their value; it belongs to them simply because they are human.

Therefore they are endowed with inalienable rights to life and other rights. The state cannot bestow or take away these inalienable rights because they do not belong to the state to dispose of, but rather to each individual human being. The state exists to protect these rights.

The problem for euthanasia proponents is that under our Constitution, euthanasia (killing human beings who are innocent of unjust aggression on others' lives) cannot be legalized. It is obvious that the American people would not permit them to tear up the Constitution and write a new one to fit their purposes, so they have devised a clever strategy to make it appear that we would be abiding by the Constitution even while violating it. 5

First they attack the sanctity-of-life ethic as a religious doctrine because it is based on the religious belief that human beings are created by God in His Image. They fail to realize that whatever the religious beliefs upon which it was founded, its principles embodied in our Constitution are right now held dear by the vast majority of American people.

They propose to replace this sanctity-of-life ethic with a new one which we call the quality-of-life ethic. But underlying this new ethic is another religious belief of secular humanism, which believes that human life is the result of random evolution and denies or questions the existence of God or at least God's involvement in human affairs — a remote God.

The Supreme Court has declared that secular humanism as a world view is a religion in the First Amendment sense *(Torasco v. Watkins, United States v. Seeger, Welsh v. United States)*.

Eileen Doyle, R.N., is president of New York State Nurses for Life. This selection is from *A Pro-Life Primer on Euthanasia* (1985).

Redefining Some People

This quality-of-life ethic proposes that some human beings have a quality of life so poor that they ought not be classified as legal persons with inalienable rights. To be declared a person with human rights, a human being must be able to pass certain tests. The tests vary according to who is proposing them but in general, it requires that to be declared a person (with inalienable rights) a human being must be able to: think and reason; give or receive love; be useful in some way; be capable of meaningful life, i.e., able to enjoy or appreciate life.

Those who fail the test would lose legal personhood and have 10 no inalienable rights. Therefore, these human beings could be killed without violating anyone's inalienable rights.

This is precisely what the Court did in the abortion decisions in declaring the unborn as not persons, thus allowing them to be killed. The whole idea is pure legal fiction, a subterfuge to quiet the consciences of the American people who have a horror of killing innocent people.

Killing a "nonperson" demoted to a less-than-human status by legal fiat seems then to be more like killing a dog or a cat to put it out of its misery. Then all can pretend that no evil, unjust deed has been done.

This quality-of-life ethic also holds that even among those who pass the tests of personhood, there may be many who have a quality of life so poor because of grave illness or birth defects that life itself is no longer a value to be preserved for these people. So to take these lives would not be an injustice but a benefit for them.

And finally . . . , this quality-of-life ethic allows that there is a compelling state interest sufficient to deny the inalienable right to life to a class of citizens: permanently dependent, institutionalized people who put an inordinate burden on the state to provide public funds and medical resources for their care.

The Awesome Result

If the proponents of this quality-of-life ethic succeed in having it 15 replace the sanctity-of-life ethic, what would be the consequences?

1. It would destroy the underlying principles embodied in our Constitution, reducing it to a worthless, ineffective, hypocritical document. A new constitution would have to be written to replace it.

2. It would be an injustice to the vast majority of the Americans who adhere to the principles of the Constitution and who treasure our Constitution to have those principles overridden and the Constitution destroyed by a small elite who wish to impose their own set of principles, not accepted by most people.

3. Large numbers of people whose inalienable right to life is now protected by the law of homicide would be killed without their consent because somebody else had decided they are not persons. These could include newborn infants with birth defects, autistic children, psychotic people, senile aged, comatose people, those with severe drug or alcohol addiction, and so on. All these could easily fail the tests of personhood.

Then there are the huge numbers of people who by somebody's definition other than their own have lives not worth living, who could be disposed of.

And finally there are those millions of dependent, institutionalized people on the public dole eating up the valuable resources of the powerful, so-called nondependent taxpayers. To dispose of them — the dependents — would become a "patriotic duty." 20

Equal protection of the law would become a mockery.

4. The psychological and spiritual damage to those who do the killing and to those who permit it would corrupt our entire nation. All would be a party to killing and to the lying to ourselves that we are doing good rather than admitting the crimes.

5. Inordinate power, tyrannical power, would be vested in the Supreme Court. For it would be the Court that would ultimately decide who is and who is not a legal person; who has and who has not a sufficient quality of life to give it value worth preserving; and at what point there is a compelling state interest sufficient to override the inalienable right to life of dependent citizens.

As with the concept of a constitutional right to die, the concept of a quality-of-life ethic becomes absurd as well, when analyzed to its logical conclusions. For we would literally be handing over our priceless freedom and all inalienable rights to an oligarchy of nine justices on the Supreme Court.

And for what? To give power to an elite few to create their idea 25 of a "brave new world"— for themselves, who in turn might become their own victims should misfortune make them dependent and powerless.

The Right to Die

THE ECONOMIST

Terrifying though the thought of death may be, for many people there is a greater fear: that one's final months or years may be spent in a nightmare of confusion, pain, and helplessness. It is a prospect that medical technology has made real for many in the rich West. Sustaining life in a body that is irreversibly incapacitated, and perhaps without a mind, is no longer a "miracle" but a routine procedure. Thanks to different sorts of medical advance, fewer people are dying young from heart attacks, which kill quickly, and more in old age from wasting sicknesses such as cancer. Faced with such an end, some people long for death, and beg the help they need to bring it on. Opinion polls in Europe and America find consistent majorities in support of assisted suicide and euthanasia. How, if at all, should governments respond?

As technology and opinion move, so too does the law — though much more slowly. On September 13 Germany's constitutional court ruled that doctors could withdraw treatment from terminally ill patients, and thereby hasten their death, so long as this was the patient's wish. The case concerned a seventy-two-year-old woman who had been in a coma for three years after suffering irreversible brain damage. She had earlier expressed the wish not to be left in such a condition. A lower court had fined her son for asking that her feeding tube be withdrawn.

In many other countries, "passive euthanasia" of this sort is already well-established. Increasingly, it is also accepted that for patients with only months to live, it is permissible or desirable for control of pain to take priority over prolongation of life. But rarely has this doctrine been given clear legal expression, and individual cases still arouse controversy. Assisted suicide — where the intention to end life is explicit — is even more contentious. In Holland, where it is legal, opinions are divided on whether the policy has been a success. Most countries, and forty-four of America's fifty states, ban it; the evidence suggests that the practice is not uncommon. . . .

Current thinking and current law are muddled. People suffer as a result — patients condemned to a misery they would rather end; doctors torn between law and conscience; families obliged to witness their loved ones' suffering, on penalty of prosecution or ordeal by legal process. And yet, it is argued, reform would do far greater

---

This editorial appeared in the September 17, 1994, issue of *The Economist,* a British news magazine.

harm. Society should resist any course that might diminish the reverence human beings have for life. This reverence may defy, because it is higher than, rational analysis; it is nonetheless society's best defense against an evil descent toward the disposal of inferiors and unfortunates. Therefore, draw no lines. Doctors will help people in the very direst circumstances to end their lives, as they do now; society will turn a blind eye, provided the act can be disguised. Sometimes a doctor will be prosecuted; this may be unjust, but it is useful. In this way, we can have a bit of euthanasia while retaining most of our necessary revulsion.

The slippery-slope argument deserves to be taken seriously. But some of those who advance it teeter precariously on a much more slippery slope of their own. The rights of the individual, they say, must be balanced against the interests of society: The taking of a life, at the patient's request, may seem acceptable in particular circumstances, but must be forbidden because it attacks values that bind society together. This way of thinking seems likable on the surface, but it sets the rights of the individual at nought: In that respect, it is philosophically related to the view that society should exterminate those who are a burden upon it. People who put society above the individual are indeed well-advised to be wary of assisted suicide.

Put the individual's freedoms first, and the slope looks less threatening. In a secular society it should be a man's right to take his own life. The question is, if he chooses this but is incapacitated and cannot act alone, should others be permitted (but not compelled) to help? With both parties acting freely, the presumed answer should be Yes. Nonetheless it is right that the agreement and the act should be closely supervised. The law should require the helper to be a licensed doctor, for instance; set tests to ensure that the patient's choice ("consent" is the wrong word; it implies that the initiative lies elsewhere) has been freely and persistently expressed; perhaps give a voice (but not a veto) to close relatives and others who are intimately involved. With safeguards such as these, there would be no need to restrict assisted suicide by law to the terminally ill (which is, in any case, difficult to define), though doctors would presumably be less willing to act as helpers in cases where the patient might otherwise live for years.

By similar arguments, the law should be reformed to recognize living wills (or, as they are also known, advance directives). By this means people can make choices for the future, in the event that they become unable to later — electing, for instance, to refuse life-sustaining treatment should they fall victim to severe brain damage or become incompetent due to Alzheimer's disease or other degenerative disorders. Beyond refusing treatment (which should be every patient's right), living wills could also request (not require) that active steps be taken to end life under certain circumstances.

Reverence for life is part of what it is to be human. But no less are freedom and dignity part of what gives life meaning. Let reform of laws on euthanasia and assisted suicide, now long overdue, be guided by that idea.

Death by Ballot in Oregon

LEON KASS

On November 8, watch Oregon. It may become the first U.S. jurisdiction to legalize physician-assisted suicide. The Death with Dignity Act, a ballot initiative ostensibly enhancing the freedom of dying patients, is in fact a frightful license for physicians to prescribe death, free from outside scrutiny and immune from possible prosecution — all in the name of a "humane and dignified" death.

Who doesn't want a dignified death? Dying well, never easy, is for many now harder than ever. Often worse than dying is the fear of pain, degradation, and loss of self-command; of becoming a burden or being abandoned. Relief from pain and suffering, respect for our humanity, and, above all, the comforting presence of those we love—all these we need while dying. Having a say in our terminal care, being able to avoid unwelcome machinery and to withdraw from treatment or from the hospital, gaining access to a hospice's loving care — these, too, are crucial to the possibility of dying well.

But no new law is necessary to obtain these rights and benefits. The Oregon Health Care Decisions Act of 1993 secures the right to refuse all unwanted life-prolonging treatments, including artificially supplied food and water. It also requires that patients receive effective pain control and comfort care. Living wills and advance directives have legal force in Oregon, as in nearly every other state.

The new act provides only physician-assisted suicide. Worse than unnecessary, it is very dangerous. Dignity in dying comes to mean merely a technical final solution. Relief of suffering becomes the elimination of the sufferer. Worst of all, the new law transforms the doctor, healer of human beings, into a technical dispenser of death.

Do we really want our doctors to be agents of death? Should 5 they be permitted or encouraged to prescribe poison? Common sense has always answered no. For over two millennia the medical ethic, mindful that power to cure is also power to kill, has held as an

This article by Leon Kass, a physician and medical ethicist who teaches at the University of Chicago, appeared in the *Wall Street Journal* on November 2, 1994.

inviolable rule, "Doctors must not kill." The venerable Hippocratic Oath clearly rules out physician-assisted suicide: "I will give no deadly drug if asked for it, neither will I make a suggestion to this effect." Euthanasia proponents call this taboo an irrational vestige of religious prejudice, preventing a rational, humane approach to dying. Nothing could be further from the truth.

The oath's authors — pagans, not papists — were wise students of human nature and their own frailties. They understood the need to restrain their awesome power over life and death; they protected against their own weaknesses and the temptation to do away with burdensome patients. The taboo against doctors helping to kill is thus the very embodiment of reason.

The patient's trust in the doctor's devotion to the patient's best interests will be hard to sustain once doctors can legally prescribe death. And once death becomes a "therapeutic option," how will even conscientious physicians be able to care wholeheartedly for patients? Won't they be tempted to select or encourage death as the best "treatment" for incurable patients whose care is also too costly?

It is no comfort that the proposed act provides assisted suicide only to those who request it. "Requests" made under duress rarely reveal the whole story. A demand for lethal medication is often, in fact, an angry or anxious plea for help, born of fear of abandonment, or ignorance of available comforting alternatives. Those who control information can easily engineer requests and manipulate choices of the vulnerable. Presented with a horrible prognosis and the offer of a "gentle quick release," which will the depressed or frightened patient likely choose, especially when facing spiraling hospital bills?

Nearly all patients requesting suicide assistance suffer from treatable clinical depression, alas, usually undiagnosed. But the act makes consultation to rule out depression merely optional, at the discretion of doctors who are often depression-blind. The act's failure to require family notification means that those who know the patient best will not be able to confirm that the request for death is not the work of depression — or misinformation or subtle coercion.

The act confines assistance in suicide, for the time being, to those with less than six months to live. Does this mean six months with or without other forms of treatment? Besides, such predictions are notoriously poor and easily falsified.   10

And physician-assisted suicide, once legal, will not stay confined to those who freely elect it — and its boosters do not really want it thus. Why? Because most people who "merit" "a humane and dignified death"— persons with senility, mental illness, or Alzheimer's disease; deformed infants; and retarded or dying children — are incapable of requesting death for themselves. But lawyers, encouraged by the cost containers, will sue to rectify this inequity. Why, they will argue, should the comatose or demented be denied the right to assisted suicide? Court-appointed proxy consentors will quickly erase the distinction between the right to choose one's own death and the right to request someone else's.

Clever doctors and relatives need not wait for such legal changes. Who will notice when the elderly, poor, crippled, weak, powerless, retarded, depressed, uneducated, demented, or gullible are mercifully released from the lives their doctors, nurses, and next of kin deem no longer worth living? Such elimination of "unworthy lives" is now occurring on a large scale in Holland, where physician-assisted suicide and euthanasia have been practiced for the past decade — and, note well, under "safeguards" more stringent than those proposed in the Oregon law.

The Report of the Dutch Government's Committee to Investigate the Practice of Euthanasia provides alarming figures: more than 1,000 cases per year of direct involuntary euthanasia — i.e., patients given a lethal injection without their knowledge or consent; 8,100 cases of morphine overdosage intending to terminate life, 61 percent without the patient's consent. In nearly half the cases of termination without consent, the families were not consulted or informed. Although the guidelines insist that choosing death must be informed and voluntary, more than 40 percent of Dutch physicians have performed involuntary euthanasia.

Is the average Dutch physician less committed than his American counterpart to the dignity of every life under his care? Do we really want to find out what our doctors will do, once the taboo against prescribing death is broken?

The Oregon law won't even let us find out. Its reporting require- 15
ments are inadequate. "Death by physician-assisted suicide" will not appear on death certificates. How will anyone monitor what is going on? The act's "safeguards" finally protect only physicians: "Good faith" immunizes them against all possible prosecution.

Far more than adequate morphine and the removal of burdensome machinery, the dying need our presence and our encouragement. Not the alleged humaneness of an elixir of death, but the humanness of connected living-while-dying is what medicine and the rest of us most owe the dying. The only *true* aid to dignity in dying remains company and care.

THINKING AND WRITING ABOUT EUTHANASIA

Questions for Discussion and Writing

1. Ostow argues that only the state should be allowed to make a decision concerning the lives of the terminally ill. What reasons, including analo-

"This is a surprise—he doesn't want any extraordinary measures taken to resuscitate him."

Drawing by Ed Fisher; © 1992 The New Yorker Magazine.

gies, does Ostow offer in support of his argument? In condemning euthanasia, is Ostow guilty of a slippery-slope fallacy? (Notice the reference to slippery slope in "The Right to Die.") Dershowitz opposes Ostow on the question of who should make "the ultimate decision." What was the prosecution guilty of in the case that Dershowitz describes?

2. Does Rachels prove that there is no moral difference between active and passive euthanasia? Is his attempt to meet the arguments of the op-

position a convincing tactic? Which of his arguments do you find most persuasive? Why?

3. What is Hook's principal reason for regretting that his request to discontinue the life support was denied? What qualities in the author are reflected in this article? Does the fact that the article is written by the patient himself make the argument more or less powerful? Can Hook's argument for voluntary euthanasia be used to answer Doyle?

4. Kevorkian suggests two reasons for the objections of physicians to euthanasia. Would these reasons explain the objections of Ostow, a physician? Which parts of Kevorkian's speech, if any, would opponents of euthanasia find persuasive?

5. Compare and contrast the arguments in "The Right to Die" and "Death by Ballot in Oregon." At what points do the authors disagree? Do they approach compromise on any issue?

6. Explain the disagreement between Doyle and Kevorkian about humanism. How do their definitions affect their views on euthanasia?

7. Define the "quality of life," as Doyle sees it. According to the author, how does the Constitution of the United States prevent the legalization of euthanasia? What consequences does the author foresee if euthanasia is permitted by law, as abortion is? Do you think her predictions are soundly based?

8. Readers have been familiar with Dracula for almost one hundred years, but the cartoon on page 471 might not have been so clearly understood a generation ago. What circumstances have changed?

Topics for Research

The case of Dr. Jack Kevorkian, the Michigan "suicide doctor"

The hospice solution

The Hemlock Society

Handicapped newborns: Who should decide?

Noteworthy cases involving the right to die

CHAPTER FOURTEEN

Freedom of Speech

The First Amendment to the Constitution of the United States reads, "Congress shall make no laws respecting an establishment of religion, or prohibiting the free expression thereof; or abridging the freedom of speech, or of the press; or the right of the people peaceably to assemble, and to petition the Government for a redress of grievances." (The first ten amendments were ratified on December 15, 1791, and form what is known as the "Bill of Rights.") The arguments in this section will consider primarily the issue of "abridging the freedom of speech, or of the press."

The limits of free speech in the United States are constantly being adjusted as social values change and new cases testing those limits emerge. Several prominent areas of controversy are emphasized in the following selection of essays.

One of the most hotly debated issues has been played out on college campuses. Following federal law, a number of colleges and universities have formulated codes of conduct which define the "correct" ways of naming certain persons, groups, or activities in order to avoid offense to those who have historically been most vulnerable to "hate" speech — African Americans, Jews, women, and gays and lesbians. These policies have frequently provoked opposition from members of the college community on both sides of the political spectrum. Their disagreement is based on a principle enunciated in 1929 by Justice Oliver Wendell Holmes: "the principle of free thought — not free thought for those who agree with us but freedom for the thought that we hate." A few students who have been harshly punished for using "racist, sexist, and homophobic" speech have taken their cases to court. In several cases the courts decided that the policies enforcing strict speech codes were in violation of the First Amendment. College and university officials are now drafting new codes that would define the prohibited language and conduct in narrower and more specific terms.

Probably more controversial and vastly more difficult to control is speech in cyberspace. Congress and the states have begun to enact legislation that would prohibit dissemination of material regarded as offensive. But defenders of free speech argue that cyberspace communication should be private, like posted mail and conversation.

Freedom of speech is also a central issue in arguments over the lyrics of rap songs, which have been accused of advocating violence against police officers and women. Parents have raised concerns about the effects of such lyrics on young listeners and proposed rating labels for some albums. The language in one rap song in the early 1990s, calling for murder of police officers, led to appeals for censorship and boycotts of the record company.

Even nonverbal art forms whose creators express views that offend large groups of people are not immune to issues of free speech. Controversial movies, photography, painting, and sculpture, as well as religious displays on public land, and even nude dancing have all been defended as forms of speech protected by the Constitution.

In Praise of Censure

GARRY WILLS

Rarely have the denouncers of censorship been so eager to start practicing it. When a sense of moral disorientation overcomes a society, people from the least expected quarters begin to ask, "Is nothing sacred?" Feminists join reactionaries to denounce pornography as demeaning to women. Rock musician Frank Zappa declares that when Tipper Gore, the wife of Senator Albert Gore from Tennessee, asked music companies to label sexually explicit material, she launched an illegal "conspiracy to extort." A *Penthouse* editorialist says that housewife Terry Rakolta, who asked sponsors to withdraw support from a sitcom called *Married . . . with Children,* is "yelling fire in a crowded theater," a formula that says her speech is not protected by the First Amendment.

But the most interesting movement to limit speech is directed at defamatory utterances against blacks, homosexuals, Jews, women,

Garry Wills is a journalist and educator who currently teaches at Northwestern University. He is the author of many books, among them *Lincoln at Gettysburg,* which won the Pulitzer Prize in 1993, and *Witches and Jesuits: Shakespeare's Macbeth* (1994). His essay appeared in *Time* on July 31, 1989.

or other stigmatizable groups. It took no Terry Rakolta of the left to bring about the instant firing of Jimmy the Greek and Al Campanis from sports jobs when they made racially denigrating comments. Social pressure worked far more quickly on them than on *Married . . . with Children,* which is still on the air.

The rules being considered on college campuses to punish students for making racist and other defamatory remarks go beyond social and commercial pressure to actual legal muzzling. The right-wing *Dartmouth Review* and its imitators have understandably infuriated liberals, who are beginning to take action against them and the racist expressions they have encouraged. The American Civil Liberties Union considered this movement important enough to make it the principal topic at its biennial meeting last month in Madison, Wisconsin. Ironically, the regents of the University of Wisconsin had passed their own rules against defamation just before the ACLU members convened on the university's campus. Nadine Strossen, of New York University School of Law, who was defending the ACLU's traditional position on free speech, said of Wisconsin's new rules, "You can tell how bad they are by the fact that the regents had to make an amendment at the last minute exempting classroom discussion! What is surprising is that Donna Shalala [chancellor of the university — now U.S. Secretary of Health and Human Services] went along with it." So did constitutional lawyers on the faculty.

If a similar code were drawn up with right-wing imperatives in mind — one banning unpatriotic, irreligious, or sexually explicit expressions on campus — the people framing Wisconsin-type rules would revert to their libertarian pasts. In this competition to suppress, is regard for freedom of expression just a matter of whose ox is getting gored at the moment? Does the left just get nervous about the Christian cross when Klansmen burn it, while the right will react only when Madonna flirts crucifixes between her thighs?

The cries of "un-American" are as genuine and as frequent on either side. Everyone is protecting the country. Zappa accuses Gore of undermining the moral fiber of America with the "sexual neuroses of these vigilant ladies." He argues that she threatens our freedoms with "connubial insider trading" because her husband is a senator. Apparently her marital status should deprive her of speaking privileges in public — an argument Westbrook Pegler used to make against Eleanor Roosevelt. *Penthouse* says Rakolta is taking us down the path toward fascism. It attacks her for living in a rich suburb — the old "radical chic" argument that rich people cannot support moral causes.

There is a basic distinction that cuts through this free-for-all over freedom. It is the distinction, too often neglected, between censorship and censure (the free expression of moral disapproval).

What the campuses are trying to do (at least those with state money) is use the force of government to contain freedom of speech. What Donald Wildmon, the freelance moralist from Tupelo, Mississippi, does when he gets Pepsi to cancel its Madonna ad is censure the ad by calling for a boycott. Advocating boycotts is a form of speech protected by the First Amendment. As Nat Hentoff, journalistic custodian of the First Amendment, says, "I would hate to see boycotts outlawed. Think what that would do to Cesar Chavez." Or, for that matter, to Ralph Nader. If one disapproves of a social practice, whether it is racist speech or unjust hiring in lettuce fields, one is free to denounce that and to call on others to express their disapproval. Otherwise there would be no form of persuasive speech except passing a law. This would make the law coterminous with morality.

Equating morality with legality is in effect what people do when they claim that anything tolerated by law must, in the name of freedom, be approved by citizens in all their dealings with one another. As Zappa says, "Masturbation is not illegal. If it is not illegal to do it, why should it be illegal to sing about it?" He thinks this proves that Gore, who is not trying to make raunch in rock illegal, cannot even ask distributors to label it. Anything goes, as long as it's legal. The odd consequence of this argument would be a drastic narrowing of the freedom of speech. One could not call into question anything that was not against the law — including, for instance, racist speech.

A false ideal of tolerance has not only outlawed censorship but discouraged censoriousness (another word for censure). Most civilizations have expressed their moral values by mobilization of social opprobrium. That, rather than specific legislation, is what changed the treatment of minorities in films and TV over recent years. One can now draw opprobrious attention by gay bashing, as the Beastie Boys rock group found when their distributor told them to cut out remarks about "fags" for business reasons. Or by anti-Semitism, as the just disbanded rap group Public Enemy has discovered.

It is said that only the narrow-minded are intolerant or opprobrious. Most of those who limited the distribution of Martin Scorsese's movie *The Last Temptation of Christ* had not even seen the movie. So do we guarantee freedom of speech only for the broad-minded or the better educated? Can one speak only after studying whatever one has reason, from one's beliefs, to denounce? Then most of us would be doing a great deal less speaking than we do. If one has never seen any snuff movies, is that a bar to criticizing them?

Others argue that asking people not to buy lettuce is different 10 from asking them not to buy a rocker's artistic expression. Ideas (carefully disguised) lurk somewhere in the lyrics. All the more reason to keep criticism of them free. If ideas are too important to suppress, they are also too important to ignore. The whole point of free speech is not to make ideas exempt from criticism but to expose them to it.

One of the great mistakes of liberals in recent decades has been the ceding of moral concern to right-wingers. Just because one opposes censorship, one need not be seen as agreeing with pornographers. Why should liberals, of all people, oppose Gore when she asks that labels be put on products meant for the young, to inform those entrusted by law with the care of the young? Liberals were the first to promote "healthy" television shows like *Sesame Street* and *The Electric Company.* In the 1950s and 1960s they were the leading critics of television, of its mindless violence, of the way it ravaged the attention span needed for reading. Who was keeping kids away from TV sets then? How did promoters of Big Bird let themselves be cast as champions of the Beastie Boys — not just of their *right* to perform but of their performance itself? Why should it be left to Gore to express moral disapproval of a group calling itself Dead Kennedys (sample lyric: "I kill children, I love to see them die")?

For that matter, who has been more insistent that parents should "interfere" in what their children are doing, Tipper Gore or Jesse Jackson? All through the 1970s, Jackson was traveling the high schools, telling parents to turn off TVs, make the kids finish their homework, check with teachers on their performance, get to know what the children are doing. This kind of "interference" used to be called education.

Belief in the First Amendment does not preempt other beliefs, making one a eunuch to the interplay of opinions. It is a distortion to turn "You can express any views" into the proposition "I don't care what views you express." If liberals keep equating equality with approval, they will be repeatedly forced into weak positions.

A case in point is the Corcoran Gallery's sudden cancellation of an exhibit of Robert Mapplethorpe's photographs. The whole matter was needlessly confused when the director, Christina Owr-Chall, claimed she was canceling the show to *protect* it from censorship. She meant that there might be pressure to remove certain pictures — the sadomasochistic ones or those verging on kiddie porn — if the show had gone on. But she had in mind, as well, the hope of future grants from the National Endowment for the Arts, which is under criticism for the Mapplethorpe show and for another show that contained Andres Serrano's *Piss Christ,* the photograph of a crucifix in what the title says is urine. Owr-Chall is said to be yielding to censorship, when she is clearly yielding to political and financial pressure, as Pepsi yielded to commercial pressure over the Madonna ad.

What is at issue here is not government suppression but government subsidy. Mapplethorpe's work is not banned, but showing it might have endangered federal grants to needy artists. The idea that 15 what the government does not support it represses is nonsensical, as one can see by reversing the statement to read: "No one is allowed to create anything without the government's subvention." What pussycats our supposedly radical artists are. They not only want the government's permission to create their artifacts, they want federal authorities to supply the materials as well. Otherwise they feel "gagged." If they are not given government approval (and money), they want to remain an avant-garde while being bankrolled by the Old Guard.

What is easily forgotten in this argument is the right of citizen taxpayers. They send representatives to Washington who are answerable for the expenditure of funds exacted from them. In general these voters want to favor their own values if government is going to get into the culture-subsidizing area at all (a proposition many find objectionable in itself). Politicians, insofar as they support the arts, will tend to favor conventional art (certainly not masochistic art). Anybody who doubts that has no understanding of a politician's legitimate concern for his or her constituents' approval. Besides, it is quaint for those familiar with the politics of the art world to discover, with a shock, that there is politics in politics.

Luckily, cancellation of the Mapplethorpe show forced some artists back to the flair and cheekiness of unsubsidized art. Other results of pressure do not turn out as well. Unfortunately, people in certain regions were deprived of the chance to see *The Last Temptation of Christ* in the theater. Some, no doubt, considered it a loss that they could not buy lettuce or grapes during a Chavez boycott. Perhaps there was even a buyer perverse enough to miss driving the unsafe cars Nader helped pressure off the market. On the other hand, we do not get sports analysis made by racists. These mobilizations of social opprobrium are not examples of repression but of freedom of expression by committed people who censured without censoring, who expressed the kinds of belief the First Amendment guarantees. I do not, as a result, get whatever I approve of subsidized, either by Pepsi or the government. But neither does the law come in to silence Tipper Gore or Frank Zappa or even that filthy rag, the *Dartmouth Review*.

On Racist Speech

CHARLES R. LAWRENCE III

I have spent the better part of my life as a dissenter. As a high school student, I was threatened with suspension for my refusal to participate in a civil defense drill, and I have been a conspicuous consumer of my First Amendment liberties ever since. There are very strong reasons for protecting even racist speech. Perhaps the most important of these is that such protection reinforces our society's commitment to tolerance as a value, and that by protecting bad speech from government regulation, we will be forced to combat it as a community.

But I also have a deeply felt apprehension about the resurgence of racial violence and the corresponding rise in the incidence of verbal and symbolic assault and harassment to which blacks and other traditionally subjugated and excluded groups are subjected. I am troubled by the way the debate has been framed in response to the recent surge of racist incidents on college and university campuses and in response to some universities' attempts to regulate harassing speech. The problem has been framed as one in which the liberty of free speech is in conflict with the elimination of racism. I believe this has placed the bigot on the moral high ground and fanned the rising flames of racism.

Above all, I am troubled that we have not listened to the real victims, that we have shown so little understanding of their injury, and that we have abandoned those whose race, gender, or sexual preference continues to make them second-class citizens. It seems to me a very sad irony that the first instinct of civil libertarians has been to challenge even the smallest, most narrowly framed efforts by universities to provide black and other minority students with the protection the Constitution guarantees them.

The landmark case of *Brown v. Board of Education* is not a case that we normally think of as a case about speech. But *Brown* can be broadly read as articulating the principle of equal citizenship. *Brown* held that segregated schools were inherently unequal because of the *message* that segregation conveyed — that black children were an untouchable caste, unfit to go to school with white children. If we understand the necessity of eliminating the system of signs and symbols that signal the inferiority of blacks, then we should hesitate be-

---

Charles R. Lawrence III is a professor of law at Georgetown University. His article appeared in the October 25, 1989, *Chronicle of Higher Education,* when Professor Lawrence was teaching law at Stanford University. It is adapted from a speech to a conference of the American Civil Liberties Union.

fore proclaiming that all racist speech that stops short of physical violence must be defended.

University officials who have formulated policies to respond to incidents of racial harassment have been characterized in the press as "thought police," but such policies generally do nothing more than impose sanctions against intentional face-to-face insults. When racist speech takes the form of face-to-face insults, catcalls, or other assaultive speech aimed at an individual or small group of persons, it falls directly within the "fighting words" exception to First Amendment protection. The Supreme Court has held that words which "by their very utterance inflict injury or tend to incite an immediate breach of the peace" are not protected by the First Amendment.

If the purpose of the First Amendment is to foster the greatest amount of speech, racial insults disserve that purpose. Assaultive racist speech functions as a preemptive strike. The invective is experienced as a blow, not as a proffered idea, and once the blow is struck, it is unlikely that a dialogue will follow. Racial insults are particularly undeserving of First Amendment protection because the perpetrator's intention is not to discover truth or initiate dialogue but to injure the victim. In most situations, members of minority groups realize that they are likely to lose if they respond to epithets by fighting and are forced to remain silent and submissive.

Courts have held that offensive speech may not be regulated in public forums such as streets where the listener may avoid the speech by moving on, but the regulation of otherwise protected speech has been permitted when the speech invades the privacy of the unwilling listener's home or when the unwilling listener cannot avoid the speech. Racist posters, fliers, and graffiti in dormitories, bathrooms, and other common living spaces would seem to clearly fall within the reasoning of these cases. Minority students should not be required to remain in their rooms in order to avoid racial assault. Minimally, they should find a safe haven in their dorms and in all other common rooms that are a part of their daily routine.

I would also argue that the university's responsibility for ensuring that these students receive an equal educational opportunity provides a compelling justification for regulations that ensure them safe passage in all common areas. A minority student should not have to risk becoming the target of racially assaulting speech every time he or she chooses to walk across campus. Regulating vilifying speech that cannot be anticipated or avoided would not preclude announced speeches and rallies — situations that would give minority-group members and their allies the chance to organize counterdemonstrations or avoid the speech altogether.

The most commonly advanced argument against the regulation of racist speech proceeds something like this: We recognize that minority groups suffer pain and injury as the result of racist speech, but we must allow this hate mongering for the benefit of society as a whole. Freedom of speech is the lifeblood of our democratic system. It is especially important for minorities because often it is their only vehicle for rallying support for the redress of their grievances. It will be impossible to formulate a prohibition so precise that it will prevent the racist speech you want to suppress without catching in the same net all kinds of speech that it would be unconscionable for a democratic society to suppress.

Whenever we make such arguments, we are striking a balance 10 on the one hand between our concern for the continued free flow of ideas and the democratic process dependent on that flow, and, on the other, our desire to further the cause of equality. There can be no meaningful discussion of how we should reconcile our commitment to equality and our commitment to free speech until it is acknowledged that there is real harm inflicted by racist speech and that this harm is far from trivial.

To engage in a debate about the First Amendment and racist speech without a full understanding of the nature and extent of that harm is to risk making the First Amendment an instrument of domination rather than a vehicle of liberation. We have not all known the experience of victimization by racist, misogynist, and homophobic speech, nor do we equally share the burden of the societal harm it inflicts. We are often quick to say that we have heard the cry of the victims when we have not.

The *Brown* case is again instructive because it speaks directly to the psychic injury inflicted by racist speech by noting that the symbolic message of segregation affected "the hearts and minds" of Negro children "in a way unlikely ever to be undone." Racial epithets and harassment often cause deep emotional scarring and feelings of anxiety and fear that pervade every aspect of a victim's life.

Brown also recognized that black children did not have an equal opportunity to learn and participate in the school community if they bore the additional burden of being subjected to the humiliation and psychic assault contained in the message of segregation. University students bear an analogous burden when they are forced to live and work in an environment where at any moment they may be subjected to denigrating verbal harassment and assault. The same injury was addressed by the Supreme Court when it held that sexual harassment that creates a hostile or abusive work environment violates the ban on sex discrimination in employment of Title VII of the Civil Rights Act of 1964.

Carefully drafted university regulations would bar the use of words as assault weapons and leave unregulated even the most heinous of ideas when those ideas are presented at times and places and in manners that provide an opportunity for reasoned rebuttal or escape from immediate injury. The history of the development of the right to free speech has been one of carefully evaluating the importance of free expression and its effects on other important societal interests. We have drawn the line between protected and unprotected speech before without dire results. (Courts have, for example, exempted from the protection of the First Amendment obscene speech and speech that disseminates official secrets, that defames or libels another person, or that is used to form a conspiracy or monopoly.)

Blacks and other people of color are skeptical about the argu-   15
ment that even the most injurious speech must remain unregulated because, in an unregulated marketplace of ideas, the best ones will rise to the top and gain acceptance. Our experience tells us quite the opposite. We have seen too many demagogues elected by appealing to America's racism. We have seen too many good liberal politicians shy away from the issues that might brand them as being too closely allied with us.

Whenever we decide that racist speech must be tolerated because of the importance of maintaining societal tolerance for all unpopular speech, we are asking blacks and other subordinated groups to bear the burden for the good of all. We must be careful that the ease with which we strike the balance against the regulation of racist speech is in no way influenced by the fact that the cost will be borne by others. We must be certain that those who will pay that price are fairly represented in our deliberations and that they are heard.

At the core of the argument that we should resist all government regulation of speech is the ideal that the best cure for bad speech is good, that ideas that affirm equality and the worth of all individuals will ultimately prevail. This is an empty ideal unless those of us who would fight racism are vigilant and unequivocal in that fight. We must look for ways to offer assistance and support to students whose speech and political participation are chilled in a climate of racial harassment.

Civil rights lawyers might consider suing on behalf of blacks whose right to an equal education is denied by a university's failure to ensure a nondiscriminatory educational climate or conditions of employment. We must embark upon the development of a First Amendment jurisprudence grounded in the reality of our history and our contemporary experience. We must think hard about how best to launch legal attacks against the most indefensible forms of hate speech. Good lawyers can create exceptions and narrow interpretations that limit the harm of hate speech without opening the floodgates of censorship.

Everyone concerned with these issues must find ways to engage actively in actions that resist and counter the racist ideas that we would have the First Amendment protect. If we fail in this, the victims of hate speech must rightly assume that we are on the oppressors' side.

Free Speech on the Campus

NAT HENTOFF

A flier distributed at the University of Michigan some months ago proclaimed that blacks "don't belong in classrooms, they belong hanging from trees."

At other campuses around the country, manifestations of racism are becoming commonplace. At Yale, a swastika and the words WHITE POWER! were painted on the building housing the University's Afro-American Cultural Center. At Temple University, a White Students Union has been formed with some 130 members.

Swastikas are not directed only at black students. The Nazi symbol has been spray-painted on the Jewish Student Union at Memphis State University. And on a number of campuses, women have been singled out as targets of wounding and sometimes frightening speech. At the law school of the State University of New York at Buffalo, several women students have received anonymous letters characterized by one professor as venomously sexist.

These and many more such signs of the resurgence of bigotry and know-nothingism throughout the society — as well as on campus — have to do solely with speech, including symbolic speech. There have also been physical assaults on black students and on black, white, and Asian women students, but the way to deal with physical attacks is clear: Call the police and file a criminal complaint. What is to be done, however, about speech alone — however disgusting, inflammatory, and rawly divisive that speech may be?

At more and more colleges, administrators — with the enthusiastic support of black students, women students, and liberal students — have been answering that question by preventing or punishing speech. In public universities, this is a clear violation of the First Amendment. In private colleges and universities, suppression of speech mocks the secular religion of academic freedom and free inquiry.

The Student Press Law Center in Washington, D.C. — a vital source of legal support for student editors around the country — reports, for example, that at the University of Kansas, the student host and producer of a radio news program was forbidden by school officials from interviewing a leader of the Ku Klux Klan. So much for free inquiry on that campus.

In Madison, Wisconsin, *The Capital Times* ran a story in January about Chancellor Sheila Kaplan of the University of Wisconsin

Nat Hentoff is the author of *The First Freedom* (1988) and is an editor for the *Village Voice*. This article appeared in the May 1989 issue of *The Progressive*.

branch at Parkside, who ordered her campus to be scoured of "some anonymously placed white-supremacist hate literature." Sounding like the legendary Mayor Frank ("I am the law") Hague of Jersey City, who booted "bad speech" out of town, Chancellor Kaplan said, "This institution is not a lamppost standing on the street corner. It doesn't belong to everyone."

Who decides what speech can be heard or read by everyone? Why, the chancellor, of course. That's what George III used to say, too.

University of Wisconsin political science professor Carol Tebben thinks otherwise. She believes university administrators "are getting confused when they are acting as censors and trying to protect students from bad ideas. I don't think students need to be protected from bad ideas. I think they can determine for themselves what ideas are bad."

After all, if students are to be "protected" from bad ideas, how are 10 they going to learn to identify and cope with them? Sending such ideas underground simply makes them stronger and more dangerous.

Professor Tebben's conviction that free speech means just that has become a decidedly minority view on many campuses. At the University of Buffalo Law School, the faculty unanimously adopted a "Statement Regarding Intellectual Freedom, Tolerance, and Political Harassment." Its title implies support of intellectual freedom, but the statement warned students that once they enter "this legal community," their right to free speech must become tempered "by the responsibility to promote equality and justice."

Accordingly, swift condemnation will befall anyone who engages in "remarks directed at another's race, sex, religion, national origin, age, or sex preference." Also forbidden are "other remarks based on prejudice and group stereotype."

This ukase is so broad that enforcement has to be alarmingly subjective. Yet the University of Buffalo Law School provides no due-process procedures for a student booked for making any of these prohibited remarks. Conceivably, a student caught playing a Lenny Bruce, Richard Pryor, or Sam Kinison album in his room could be tried for aggravated insensitivity by association.

When I looked into this wholesale cleansing of bad speech at Buffalo, I found it had encountered scant opposition. One protester was David Gerald Jay, a graduate of the law school and a cooperating attorney for the New York Civil Liberties Union. Said the appalled graduate: "Content-based prohibitions constitute prior restraint and should not be tolerated."

You think that the law professors and administration at this pub- 15 lic university might have known that. But hardly any professors dissented, and among the students only members of the conservative

Federalist Society spoke up for free speech. The fifty-strong chapter of the National Lawyers Guild was on the other side. After all, it was more important to go on record as vigorously opposing racism and sexism than to expose oneself to charges of insensitivity to these malignancies.

The pressures to have the "right" attitude — as proved by having the "right" language in and out of class — can be stifling. A student who opposes affirmative action, for instance, can be branded a racist.

At the University of California at Los Angeles, the student newspaper ran an editorial cartoon satirizing affirmative action. (A student stops a rooster on campus and asks how the rooster got into UCLA. "Affirmative action," is the answer.) After outraged complaints from various minority groups, the editor was suspended for violating a publications policy against running "articles that perpetuate derogatory or cultural stereotypes." The art director was also suspended.

When the opinion editor of the student newspaper at California State University at Northridge wrote an article asserting that the sanctions against the editor and art director at UCLA amounted to censorship, he was suspended too.

At New York University Law School, a student was so disturbed by the pall of orthodoxy at that prestigious institution that he wrote to the school newspaper even though, as he said, he expected his letter to make him a pariah among his fellow students.

Barry Endick described the atmosphere at NYU created by "a host of watchdog committees and a generally hostile classroom reception regarding any student comment right of center." This "can be arguably viewed as symptomatic of a prevailing spirit of academic and social intolerance of . . . any idea which is not 'politically correct.'"

He went on to say something that might well be posted on campus bulletin boards around the country, though it would probably be torn down at many of them:

> We ought to examine why students, so anxious to wield the Fourteenth Amendment, give short shrift to the First. Yes, Virginia, there are racist assholes. And you know what, the Constitution protects them, too.

Not when they engage in violence or vandalism. But when they speak or write, racist assholes fall right into this Oliver Wendell Holmes definition — highly unpopular among bigots, liberals, radicals, feminists, sexists, and college administrators:

> If there is any principle of the Constitution that more imperatively calls for attachment than any other, it is the principle of free thought — not free only for those who agree with us, but freedom for the thought we hate.

The language sounds like a pietistic Sunday sermon, but if it ever falls wholly into disuse, neither this publication nor any other journal of opinion — Right or Left — will survive.

Sometimes, college presidents and administrators sound as if they fully understand what Holmes was saying. Last year, for example, when *The Daily Pennsylvanian* — speaking for many at the University of Pennsylvania — urged that a speaking invitation to Louis Farrakhan be withdrawn, University President Sheldon Hackney disagreed.

"Open expression," said Hackney, "is the fundamental principle 25
of a university." Yet consider what the same Sheldon Hackney did to the free-speech rights of a teacher at his own university. If any story distills the essence of the current decline of free speech on college campuses, it is the Ballad of Murray Dolfman.

For twenty-two years, Dolfman, a practicing lawyer in Philadelphia, had been a part-time lecturer in the Legal Studies Department of the University of Pennsylvania's Wharton School. For twenty-two years, no complaint had ever been made against him; indeed, his student course evaluations had been outstanding. Each year students competed to get into his class.

On a November afternoon in 1984, Dolfman was lecturing about personal-service contracts. His style somewhat resembles that of Professor Charles Kingsfield in *The Paper Chase*. Dolfman insists that students he calls on be prepared — or suffer the consequences. He treats all students this way — regardless of race, creed, or sex.

This day, Dolfman was pointing out that no one can be forced to work against his or her will — even if a contract has been signed. A court may prevent the register from working for someone else so long as the contract is in effect but, Dolfman said, there can "be nothing that smacks of involuntary servitude."

Where does this concept come from? Dolfman looked around the room. Finally, a cautious hand was raised: "The Constitution?"

"Where in the Constitution?" No hands. "The Thirteenth Amend- 30
ment," said the teacher. So, what does *it* say? The students were looking everywhere but at Dolfman.

"We will lose our liberties," Dolfman often told his classes, "if we don't know what they are."

On this occasion, he told them that he and other Jews, as ex-slaves, spoke at Passover of the time when they were slaves under the Pharaohs so that they would remember every year what it was like not to be free.

"We have ex-slaves here," Dolfman continued, "who should know about the Thirteenth Amendment." He asked black students in the class if they could tell him what was in that amendment.

"I wanted them to really think about it," Dolfman told me recently, "and know its history. You're better equipped to fight racism if you know all about those post–Civil War amendments and civil-rights laws."

The Thirteenth Amendment provides that "neither slavery nor   35
involuntary servitude . . . shall exist within the United States."

The black students in his class did not know what was in that amendment, and Dolfman had them read it aloud. Later, they complained to university officials that they had been hurt and humiliated by having been referred to as ex-slaves. Moreover, they said, they had no reason to be grateful for a constitutional amendment which gave them rights which should never have been denied them — and gave them precious little else. They had not made these points in class, although Dolfman — unlike Professor Kingsfield — encourages rebuttal.

Informed of the complaint, Dolfman told the black students he had intended no offense, and he apologized if they had been offended.

That would not do — either for the black students or for the administration. Furthermore, there were mounting black-Jewish tensions on campus, and someone had to be sacrificed. Who better than a part-time Jewish teacher with no contract and no union? He was sentenced by — George Orwell would have loved this — the Committee on Academic Freedom and Responsibility.

On his way to the stocks, Dolfman told President Sheldon Hackney that if a part-time instructor "can be punished on this kind of charge, a tenured professor can eventually be booted out, then a dean, and then a president."

Hackney was unmoved. Dolfman was banished from the campus   40
for what came to be a year. But first he was forced to make a public apology to the entire university and then he was compelled to attend a "sensitivity and racial awareness" session. Sort of like a Vietnamese reeducation camp.

A few conservative professors objected to the stigmatization of Murray Dolfman. I know of no student dissent. Indeed, those students most concerned with making the campus more "sensitive" to diversity exulted in Dolfman's humiliation. So did most liberals on the faculty.

If my children were still of college age and wanted to attend the University of Pennsylvania, I would tell them this story. But where else could I encourage them to go?

In Defense of Prejudice

JONATHAN RAUCH

The war on prejudice is now, in all likelihood, the most uncontroversial social movement in America. Opposition to "hate speech," formerly identified with the liberal left, has become a bipartisan piety. In the past year, groups and factions that agree on nothing else have agreed that the public expression of any and all prejudices must be forbidden. On the left, protesters and editorialists have insisted that Francis L. Lawrence resign as president of Rutgers University for describing blacks as "a disadvantaged population that doesn't have that genetic, hereditary background to have a higher average." On the other side of the ideological divide, Ralph Reed, the executive director of the Christian Coalition, responded to criticism of the religious right by calling a press conference to denounce a supposed outbreak of "name-calling, scapegoating, and religious bigotry." Craig Rogers, an evangelical Christian student at California State University, recently filed a $2.5 million sexual-harassment suit against a lesbian professor of psychology, claiming that anti-male bias in one of her lectures violated campus rules and left him feeling "raped and trapped."

In universities and on Capitol Hill, in workplaces and newsrooms, authorities are declaring that there is no place for racism, sexism, homophobia, Christian-bashing, and other forms of prejudice in public debate or even in private thought. "Only when racism and other forms of prejudice are expunged," say the crusaders for sweetness and light, "can minorities be safe and society be fair." So sweet, this dream of a world without prejudice. But the very last thing society should do is seek to utterly eradicate racism and other forms of prejudice.

I suppose I should say, in the customary I-hope-I-don't-sound-too-defensive tone, that I am not a racist and that this is not an article favoring racism or any other particular prejudice. It is an article favoring intellectual pluralism, which permits the expression of various forms of bigotry and always will. Although we like to hope that a time will come when no one will believe that people come in types and that each type belongs with its own kind, I doubt such a day will ever arrive. By all indications, *Homo sapiens* is a tribal species for whom "us versus them" comes naturally and must be continually pushed back. Where there is genuine freedom of expression, there will be racist expression. There will also be people who believe that

---

Jonathan Rauch, author of *Kindly Inquisitors: The New Attacks on Free Thought* (1995), is a writer for *The Economist* in London. This essay is from the May 1995 issue of *Harper's Magazine.*

homosexuals are sick or threaten children or — especially among teenagers — are rightful targets of manly savagery. Homosexuality will always be incomprehensible to most people, and what is incomprehensible is feared. As for anti-Semitism, it appears to be a hardier virus than influenza. If you want pluralism, then you get racism and sexism and homophobia, and communism and fascism and xenophobia and tribalism, and that is just for a start. If you want to believe in intellectual freedom and the progress of knowledge and the advancement of science and all those other good things, then you must swallow hard and accept this: For as thickheaded and wayward an animal as us, the realistic question is how to make the best of prejudice, not how to eradicate it.

Indeed, "eradicating prejudice" is so vague a proposition as to be meaningless. Distinguishing prejudice reliably and nonpolitically from nonprejudice, or even defining it crisply, is quite hopeless. We all feel we know prejudice when we see it. But do we? At the University of Michigan, a student said in a classroom discussion that he considered homosexuality a disease treatable with therapy. He was summoned to a formal disciplinary hearing for violating the school's policy against speech that "victimizes" people based on "sexual orientation." Now, the evidence is abundant that this particular hypothesis is wrong, and any American homosexual can attest to the harm that the student's hypothesis has inflicted on many real people. But was it a statement of prejudice or of misguided belief? Hate speech or hypothesis? Many Americans who do not regard themselves as bigots or haters believe that homosexuality is a treatable disease. They may be wrong, but are they all bigots? I am unwilling to say so, and if you are willing, beware. The line between a prejudiced belief and a merely controversial one is elusive, and the harder you look the more elusive it becomes. "God hates homosexuals" is a statement of fact, not of bias, to those who believe it; "American criminals are disproportionately black" is a statement of bias, not of fact, to those who disbelieve it.

Who is right? You may decide, and so may others, and there is no need to agree. That is the great innovation of intellectual pluralism (which is to say, of post-Enlightenment science, broadly defined). We cannot know in advance or for sure which belief is prejudice and which is truth, but to advance knowledge we don't need to know. The genius of intellectual pluralism lies not in doing away with prejudices and dogmas but in channeling them — making them socially productive by pitting prejudice against prejudice and dogma against dogma, exposing all to withering public criticism. What survives at the end of the day is our base of knowledge.

What they told us in high school about this process is very largely a lie. The Enlightenment tradition taught us that science is orderly, antiseptic, rational, the province of detached experimenters and high-minded logicians. In the popular view, science stands for reason against prejudice, open-mindedness against dogma, calm consideration against passionate attachment — all personified by pop-science icons like the magisterially deductive Sherlock Holmes, the coolly analytic Mr. Spock, the genially authoritative Mr. Science (from our junior-high science films). Yet one of science's dirty secrets is that although science as a whole is as unbiased as anything human can be, scientists are just as biased as anyone else, sometimes more so. "One of the strengths of science," writes the philosopher of science David L. Hull, "is that it does not require that scientists be unbiased, only that different scientists have different biases." Another dirty secret is that, no less than the rest of us, scientists can be dogmatic and pigheaded. "Although this pigheadedness often damages the careers of individual scientists," says Hull, "it is beneficial for the manifest goal of science," which relies on people to invest years in their ideas and defend them passionately. And the dirtiest secret of all, if you believe in the antiseptic popular view of science, is that this most ostensibly rational of enterprises depends on the most irrational of motives — ambition, narcissism, animus, even revenge. "Scientists acknowledge that among their motivations are natural curiosity, the love of truth, and the desire to help humanity, but other inducements exist as well, and one of them is to 'get that son of a bitch,'" says Hull. "Time and again, scientists whom I interviewed described the powerful spur that 'showing that son of a bitch' supplied to their own research."

Many people, I think, are bewildered by this unvarnished and all too human view of science. They believe that for a system to be unprejudiced, the people in it must also be unprejudiced. In fact, the opposite is true. Far from eradicating ugly or stupid ideas and coarse or unpleasant motives, intellectual pluralism relies upon them to excite intellectual passion and redouble scientific effort. I know of no modern idea more ugly and stupid than that the Holocaust never happened, nor any idea more viciously motivated. Yet the deniers' claims that the Auschwitz gas chambers could not have worked led to closer study and, in 1993, research showing, at last, how they actually did work. Thanks to prejudice and stupidity, another opening for doubt has been shut.

An enlightened and efficient intellectual regime lets a million prejudices bloom, including many that you or I may regard as hateful or grotesque. It avoids any attempt to stamp out prejudice, because stamping out prejudice really means forcing everyone to share the same prejudice, namely that of whoever is in authority. The great American philosopher Charles Sanders Peirce wrote in 1877: "When complete agreement could not otherwise be reached, a general massacre of all who have not thought in a certain way has proved a very effective means of settling opinion in a country." In speaking of "settling opinion," Peirce was writing about one of the two or three most fundamental problems that any human society must confront and solve. For most societies down through the centuries, this problem was dealt with in the manner he described: errors were identified by the authorities — priests, politburos, dictators — or by mass opinion, and then the error-makers were eliminated along with their putative mistakes. "Let all men who reject the established belief be terrified into silence," wrote Peirce, describing this system. "This method has, from the earliest times, been one of the chief means of upholding correct theological and political doctrines."

Intellectual pluralism substitutes a radically different doctrine: We kill our mistakes rather than each other. Here I draw on another great philosopher, the late Karl Popper, who pointed out that the critical method of science "consists in letting our hypotheses die in our stead." Those who are in error are not (or are not supposed to be) banished or excommunicated or forced to sign a renunciation or required to submit to "rehabilitation" or sent for psychological counseling. It is the error we punish, not the errant. By letting people make errors — even mischievous, spiteful errors (as, for instance, Galileo's insistence on Copernicanism was taken to be in 1633) — pluralism creates room to challenge orthodoxy, think imaginatively, experiment boldly. Brilliance and bigotry are empowered in the same stroke.

Pluralism is the principle that protects and makes a place in 10 human company for that loneliest and most vulnerable of all minorities, the minority who is hounded and despised among blacks and whites, gays and straights, who is suspect or criminal among every tribe and in every nation of the world, and yet on whom progress depends: the dissident. I am not saying that dissent is always or even usually enlightened. Most of the time it is foolish and self-serving. No dissident has the right to be taken seriously, and the fact that Aryan Nation racists or Nation of Islam anti-Semites are unorthodox does not entitle them to respect. But what goes around comes around. As a supporter of gay marriage, for example, I reject the majority's view of family, and as a Jew I reject its view of God. I try to be civil, but the fact is that most Americans regard my views on marriage as a reckless assault on the most fundamental of all institutions, and many people are more than a little discomfited by the statement "Jesus Christ was no more divine than anybody else" (which is why so few people ever say it). Trap the racists and anti-Semites, and you lay a trap for me too. Hunt for them with eradication in your mind, and you have brought dissent itself within your sights.

The new crusade against prejudice waves aside such warnings. Like earlier crusades against antisocial ideas, the mission is fueled by good (if cocksure) intentions and a genuine sense of urgency. Some kinds of error are held to be intolerable, like pollutants that even in small traces poison the water for a whole town. Some errors are so pernicious as to damage real people's lives, so wrongheaded that no person of right mind or goodwill could support them. Like their forebears of other stripe — the Church in its campaigns against heretics, the McCarthyites in their campaigns against Communists — the modern antiracist and antisexist and antihomophobic campaigners are totalists, demanding not that misguided ideas and ugly expressions be corrected or criticized but that they be eradicated. They make war not on errors but on error, and like other totalists they act in the name of public safety — the safety, especially, of minorities.

The sweeping implications of this challenge to pluraism are not, I think, well enough understood by the public at large. Indeed, the new brand of totalism has yet even to be properly named. "Multiculturalism," for instance, is much too broad. "Political correctness" comes closer but is too trendy and snide. For lack of anything else, I will call the new antipluralism "purism," since its major tenet is that society cannot be just until the last traces of invidious prejudice have been scrubbed away. Whatever you call it, the purists' way of seeing things has spread through American intellectual life with remarkable speed, so much so that many people will blink at you uncomprehendingly or even call you a racist (or sexist or homophobe, etc.) if you suggest that expressions of racism should be tolerated or that prejudice has its part to play.

The new purism sets out, to begin with, on a campaign against words, for words are the currency of prejudice, and if prejudice is hurtful then so must be prejudiced words. "We are not safe when these violent words are among us," wrote Mari Matsuda, then a UCLA law professor. Here one imagines gangs of racist words swinging chains and smashing heads in back alleys. To suppress bigoted language seems, at first blush, reasonable, but it quickly leads to a curious result. A peculiar kind of verbal shamanism takes root, as though certain expressions, like curses or magical incantations, carry in themselves the power to hurt or heal — as though words were bigoted rather than people. "Context is everything," people have always said. The use of the word "nigger" in *Huckleberry Finn* does not make the book an "act" of hate speech — or does it? In the new view, this is no longer so clear. The very utterance of the word "nigger" (at least by a nonblack) is a racist act. When a *Sacramento Bee* cartoonist put the word "nigger" mockingly in the mouth of a white supremacist, there were howls of protest and 1,400 canceled subscriptions and an editorial apology, even though the word was plainly being invoked against racists, not against blacks.

Faced with escalating demands of verbal absolutism, newspapers issue lists of forbidden words. The expressions "gyp" (derived from "Gypsy") and "Dutch treat" were among the dozens of terms stricken as "offensive" in a much-ridiculed (and later withdrawn) *Los Angeles Times* speech code. The University of Missouri journalism school issued a *Dictionary of Cautionary Words and Phrases,* which included "*Buxom:* Offensive reference to a woman's chest. Do not use. See 'Woman.' *Codger:* Offensive reference to a senior citizen."

As was bound to happen, purists soon discovered that chasing around after words like "gyp" or "buxom" hardly goes to the roots of the problem. As long as they remain bigoted, bigots will simply find other words. If they can't call you a kike then they will say Jewboy, Judas, or Hebe, and when all those are banned they will press words like "oven" and "lampshade" into their service. The vocabulary of hate is potentially as rich as your dictionary, and all you do by banning language used by cretins is to let them decide what the rest of us may say. The problem, some purists have concluded, must therefore go much deeper than laws: It must go to the deeper level of ideas. Racism, sexism, homophobia, and the rest must be built into the very structure of American society and American patterns of thought, so pervasive yet so insidious that, like water to a fish, they are both omnipresent and unseen. The mere existence of prejudice constructs a society whose very nature is prejudiced. 15

This line of thinking was pioneered by feminists, who argued that pornography, more than just being expressive, is an act by which men construct an oppressive society. Racial activists quickly picked up the argument. Racist expressions are themselves acts of oppression, they said. "All racist speech constructs the social reality that constrains the liberty of nonwhites because of their race," wrote Charles R. Lawrence III, then a law professor at Stanford. From the purist point of view, a society with even one racist is a racist society, because the idea itself threatens and demeans its targets. They cannot feel wholly safe or wholly welcome as long as racism is present. Pluralism says: There will always be some racists. Marginalize them, ignore them, exploit them, ridicule them, take pains to make their policies illegal, but otherwise leave them alone. Purists say: That's not enough. Society cannot be just until these pervasive and oppressive ideas are searched out and eradicated.

And so what is now under way is a growing drive to eliminate prejudice from every corner of society. I doubt that many people have noticed how far-reaching this antipluralist movement is becoming.

In universities: Dozens of universities have adopted codes proscribing speech or other expression that (this is from Stanford's policy, which is more or less representative) "is intended to insult or stigmatize an individual or a small number of individuals on the basis of their sex, race, color, handicap, religion, sexual orientation or national and ethnic origin." Some codes punish only persistent harassment of a targeted individual, but many, following the purist doctrine that even one racist is too many, go much further. At Penn, an administrator declared: "We at the University of Pennsylvania have guaranteed students and the community that they can live in a community free of sexism, racism, and homophobia." Here is the purism that gives "political correctness" its distinctive combination of puffy high-mindedness and authoritarian zeal.

In school curricula: "More fundamental than eliminating racial segregation has to be the removal of racist thinking, assumptions, symbols, and materials in the curriculum," writes theorist Molefi Kete Asante. In practice, the effort to "remove racist thinking" goes well beyond striking egregious references from textbooks. In many cases it becomes a kind of mental engineering in which students are encouraged to see prejudice everywhere; it includes teaching identity politics as an antidote to internalized racism; it rejects mainstream science as "white male" thinking; and it tampers with history, installing such dubious notions as that the ancient Greeks stole their culture from Africa or that an ancient carving of a bird is an example of "African experimental aeronautics."

In criminal law: Consider two crimes. In each, I am beaten bru-   20
tally; in each, my jaw is smashed and my skull is split in just the same way. However, in the first crime my assailant calls me an "asshole"; in the second he calls me a "queer." In most states, in many localities, and, as of September 1994, in federal cases, these two crimes are treated differently: the crime motivated by bias — or deemed to be so motivated by prosecutors and juries — gets a stiffer punishment. "Longer prison terms for bigots," shrilled Brooklyn Democratic Congressman Charles Schumer, who introduced the federal hate-crimes legislation, and those are what the law now provides. Evidence that the assailant holds prejudiced beliefs, even if he doesn't actually express them while committing an offense, can serve to elevate the crime. Defendants in hate-crimes cases may be grilled on how many black friends they have and whether they have told racist jokes. To increase a prison sentence only because of the defendant's "prejudice" (as gauged by prosecutor and jury) is, of course, to try minds and punish beliefs. Purists say, Well, they are dangerous minds and poisonous beliefs.

In the workplace: Though government cannot constitutionally suppress bigotry directly, it is now busy doing so indirectly by requiring employers to eliminate prejudice. Since the early 1980s, courts and the Equal Employment Opportunity Commission have moved to bar workplace speech deemed to create a hostile or abusive working environment for minorities. The law, held a federal court in 1988, "does require that an employer take prompt action to prevent . . . bigots from expressing their opinions in a way that abuses or offends their co-workers," so as to achieve "the goal of eliminating prejudices and biases from our society." So it was, as UCLA law professor Eugene Volokh notes, that the EEOC charged that a manufacturer's ads using admittedly accurate depictions of samurai, kabuki, and sumo were "racist" and "offensive to people to Japanese origin"; that a Pennsylvania court found that an employer's printing Bible verses on paychecks was religious harassment of Jewish employees; that an employer had to desist using gender-based job titles like "foreman" and "draftsman" after a female employee sued.

On and on the campaign goes, darting from one outbreak of prejudice to another like a cat chasing flies. In the American Bar Association, activists demand that lawyers who express "bias or prejudice" be penalized. In the Education Department, the civil rights office presses for a ban on computer bulletin board comments that "show hostility toward a person or group based on sex, race or color, including slurs, negative stereotypes, jokes or pranks." In its security checks for government jobs, the FBI takes to asking whether applicants are "free of biases against any class of citizens," whether, for instance, they have told racist jokes or indicated other "prejudices." Joke police! George Orwell, grasping the close relationship of jokes to dissent, said that every joke is a tiny revolution. The purists will have no such rebellions.

The purist campaign reaches, in the end, into the mind itself. In a lecture at the University of New Hampshire, a professor compared writing to sex ("You and the subject become one"); he was suspended and required to apologize, but what was most insidious was the order to undergo university-approved counseling to have his mind straightened out. At the University of Pennsylvania, a law lecturer said, "We have ex-slaves here who should know about the Thirteenth Amendment"; he was banished from campus for a year and required to make a public apology, and he, too, was compelled to attend a "sensitivity and racial awareness" session. Mandatory reeducation of alleged bigots is the natural consequence of intellectual purism. Prejudice must be eliminated!

Ah, but the task of scouring minds clean is Augean. "Nobody escapes," said a Rutgers University report on campus prejudice. Bias and prejudice, it found, cross every conceivable line, from sex to race to politics: "No matter who you are, no matter what the color of your skin, no matter what your gender or sexual orientation, no matter what you believe, no matter how you behave, there is somebody out there who doesn't like people of your kind." Charles Lawrence writes: "Racism is ubiquitous. We are all racists." If he means that most of us think racist thoughts of some sort at one time or another, he is right. If we are going to "eliminate prejudices and biases from our society," then the work of the prejudice police is unending. They are doomed to hunt and hunt and hunt, scour and scour and scour.

What is especially dismaying is that the purists pursue prejudice 25 in the name of protecting minorities. In order to protect people like me (homosexual), they must pursue people like me (dissident). In order to bolster minority self-esteem, they suppress minority opinion. There are, of course, all kinds of practical and legal problems with the purists' campaign: the incursions against the First Amendment; the inevitable abuses by prosecutors and activists who define as "hateful" or "violent" whatever speech they dislike or can score points off of; the lack of any evidence that repressing prejudice eliminates rather than inflames it. But minorities, of all people, ought to remember that by definition we cannot prevail by numbers, and we generally cannot prevail by force. Against the power of ignorant mass opinion and group prejudice and superstition, we have only our voices. If you doubt that minorities' voices are powerful weapons, think of the lengths to which Southern officials went to silence the Reverend Martin Luther King, Jr. (recall that the city commissioner of Montgomery, Alabama, won a $500,000 libel suit, later overturned in *New York Times v. Sullivan* [1964], regarding an advertisement in the *Times* placed by civil rights leaders who denounced the Montgomery police). Think of how much gay people have improved their lot over twenty-five years simply by refusing to remain silent. Recall the Michigan student who was prosecuted for saying that homosexuality is a treatable disease, and notice that he was black. Under that Michigan speech code, more than twenty blacks were charged with racist speech, while no instance of racist speech by whites was punished. In Florida, the hate-speech law was invoked against a black man who called a policeman a "white cracker"; not so surprisingly, in the first hate-crimes case to reach the Supreme Court, the victim was white and the defendant black.

In the escalating war against "prejudice," the right is already learning to play by the rules that were pioneered by the purist activists of the left. Last year leading Democrats, including the president, criticized the Republican Party for being increasingly in the thrall of the Christian right. Some of the rhetoric was harsh ("fire-breathing Christian radical right"), but it wasn't vicious or even clearly wrong. Never mind: When Democratic Representative Vic Fazio said Republicans were "being forced to the fringes by the aggressive political tactics of the religious right," the chairman of the Republican National Committee, Haley Barbour, said, "Christian-bashing" was "the left's preferred form of religious bigotry." Bigotry! Prejudice! "Christians active in politics are now on the receiving end of an extraordinary campaign of bias and prejudice," said the conservative leader William J. Bennett. One discerns, here, where the new purism leads. Eventually, any criticism of any group will be "prejudice."

Here is the ultimate irony of the new purism: Words, which pluralists hope can be substituted for violence, are redefined by purists as violence. "The experience of being called 'nigger,' 'spic,' 'Jap,' or 'kike' is like receiving a slap in the face," Charles Lawrence wrote in 1990. "Psychic injury is no less an injury than being struck in the face, and it often is far more severe." This kind of talk is commonplace today. Epithets, insults, often even polite expressions of what's taken to be prejudice are called by purists "assaultive speech," "words that wound," "verbal violence." "To me, racial epithets are not speech," one University of Michigan law professor said. "They are bullets." In her speech accepting the 1993 Nobel Prize for Literature in Stockholm, Sweden, the author Toni Morrison said this: "Oppressive language does more than represent violence; it is violence."

It is not violence. I am thinking back to a moment on the subway in Washington, a little thing. I was riding home late one night and a squad of noisy kids, maybe seventeen or eighteen years old, noisily piled into the car. They yelled across the car and a girl said, "Where do we get off?"

A boy said, "Farragut North."

The girl: "*Faggot* North!"   30

The boy: "Yeah! Faggot North!"

General hilarity.

First, before the intellect resumes control, there is a moment of fear, an animal moment. Who are they? How many of them? How dangerous? Where is the way out? All of these things are noted preverbally and assessed by the gut. Then the brain begins an assessment: They are sober, this is probably too public a place for them to do it, there are more girls than boys, they were just talking, it is probably nothing.

They didn't notice me and there was no incident. The teenage babble flowed on, leaving me to think. I became interested in my own reaction: the jump of fear out of nowhere like an alert animal, the sense for a brief time that one is naked and alone and should hide or run away. For a time, one ceases to be a human being and becomes instead a faggot.

The fear engendered by these words is real. The remedy is as   35 clear and as imperfect as ever: protect citizens against violence. This, I grant, is something that American society has never done very well and now does quite poorly. It is no solution to define words as violence or prejudice as oppression, and then by cracking down on words or thoughts pretend that we are doing something about violence and oppression. No doubt it is easier to pass a speech code or hate-crimes law and proclaim the streets safer than actually to make the streets safer, but the one must never be confused with the other. Every cop or prosecutor chasing words is one fewer chasing criminals. In a world rife with real violence and oppression, full of Rwandas and Bosnias and eleven-year-olds spraying bullets at children in Chicago and in turn being executed by gang lords, it is odious of Toni Morrison to say that words are violence.

Indeed, equating "verbal violence" with physical violence is a treacherous, mischievous business. Not long ago a writer was charged with viciously and gratuitously wounding the feelings and dignity of millions of people. He was charged, in effect, with exhibiting flagrant prejudice against Muslims and outrageously slandering their beliefs. "What is freedom of expression?" mused Salman Rushdie a year after the ayatollahs sentenced him to death and put a price on his head. "Without the freedom to offend, it ceases to exist." I can think of nothing sadder than that minority activists, in their haste to make the world better, should be the ones to forget the lesson of Rushdie's plight: For minorities, pluralism, not purism, is the answer. The campaigns to eradicate prejudice — all of them, the speech codes and workplace restrictions and mandatory therapy for accused bigots and all the rest — should stop, now. The whole objective of eradicating prejudice, as opposed to correcting and criticizing it, should be repudiated as a fool's errand. Salman Rushdie is right, Toni Morrison wrong, and minorities belong at his side, not hers.

The First Amendment under Fire from the Left

CATHARINE A. MacKINNON
and FLOYD ABRAMS

"Congress shall make no law ... abridging the freedom of speech, or of the press." The late Justice Hugo L. Black wrote memorably about that proposition: "First in the catalogue of human liberties essential to the life and growth of a government of, for and by the people are those liberties written into the First Amendment to our Constitution."

Are those guarantees in trouble? That is the question put by the *Times Magazine* to two quite different authorities: Floyd Abrams, the prominent First Amendment lawyer, and Professor Catharine A. MacKinnon, the scholar and author of *Only Words* and an advocate of sex equality laws against harms of pornography. They met at the

This selection is excerpted from the March 13, 1994, issue of the *New York Times Magazine*.

New York Times for the discussion excerpted here. Anthony Lewis, a columnist for the *New York Times,* was the moderator.

Lewis: In your book you suggest that the First Amendment has been of use primarily to those who hold power. But isn't it true that since the 1920s, when the First Amendment began to be seriously enforced in this country, it has been primarily of use in protecting the free speech and press rights of the dissident — the Seventh-day Adventists, the Communists, the Ku Klux Klan, the civil rights movement? Not the powerful. The First Amendment is of use to the nonpowerful. Is that wrong?

MacKinnon: It's partly wrong and it's partly right. It's not that there haven't been dissidents who have found that the First Amendment is helpful. It's that the First Amendment only protects that speech that can manage to get itself expressed, and often that is the speech of power. Only that speech that can be expressed is speech that the government can attempt to silence; in the name of dissent one can then attempt to use the First Amendment to defend that speech. But what about those layers of society that have been deeply silenced, among them sexually violated women, including prostituted women, including groups who are kept illiterate and thus not given access to speech from slavery times through the present. Those groups the First Amendment doesn't help. They need equality to get access to speech — to get to the point where the First Amendment could help them by keeping the government from interfering with their speech. We have barely heard from those groups.

Lewis: Why aren't *you* a representative of the women you say   5 have been voiceless? It seems to me that in terms of First Amendment expression, the women's movement is one of the most successful and admirable reform movements in American history.

MacKinnon: Yes, and one of our jobs is to keep talking to you about all the women you're not listening to, all the women who can't speak, instead of getting bought off by some illusion of preeminence. We are here to talk not only about all the things that haven't been said, but also about all the women who haven't been heard and are still unheard. . . . I am no substitute for them.

Abrams: I agree with Professor MacKinnon insofar as what she's saying is that our society rewards power and to a large extent rewards wealth. People who have money have a lot more say about how our society is run than people who don't. People who are powerful by definition have a lot more say about what happens in our society than people of the underclass. There are ways to try to deal with that if one chooses to. One way is to speak about it. Another way is to legislate about it. But one way that I would oppose trying to deal with it is to suppress speech with which we disagree.

MacKinnon: What about the film, *Deep Throat*, which Linda "Lovelace" was coerced into making? Is that what you call the expression of ideas I disagree with?

Abrams: Well, I think first of all it is the expression of ideas —

MacKinnon: So is the rape of women.   10

Abrams: The rape of women is handled by rape laws.

MacKinnon: And *Deep Throat* — how should that be handled?

Abrams: Judged by obscenity laws.

MacKinnon: It's been judged obscene in some places and not in others. You think Linda "Lovelace" should have no equality rights in relation to that film? How does that film give rise to a speech interest you want to protect?

Abrams: I don't even know what you mean in this case about   15
equality rights. She has a perfect right not to be raped.

MacKinnon: I mean that, as a woman, Linda was sexually subordinated to make it and that — as she puts it — "every time someone watches that film they are watching me be raped." She has an equality right not to have that done. And to stop the film that is doing it, and whose profit is an incentive to keep doing it.

Lewis: Am I right in thinking that coercion as you would define it in the law you drafted with Andrea Dworkin — that is, graphic, sexually explicit materials that subordinate women through pictures and words — disallows voluntarily engaging in a pornographic film since it says that a written consent shall not be proof that there was no coercion?

MacKinnon: No, you're not. If you can force a woman to have sex with a dog, you can force her to sign a contract. The mere fact of a contract being signed doesn't in itself negate a finding of coercion. The coercion itself would have to be proven under our ordinance.

Abrams: Look, your statute provides in part that graphic, sexually explicit subordination of women in which women are presented as sexual objects for domination, conquest, violation, exploitation, possession or use, etc., can give rise to a private cause of action. The Court of Appeals in holding the statute unconstitutional — a decision affirmed by the Supreme Court — indicated that books like Joyce's *Ulysses,* Homer's *Iliad,* poems by Yeats, novels by D. H. Lawrence, and the like could all be subject to a finding of violation of the statute that you have drafted.

MacKinnon: And that's just simply false.   20

Abrams: Well, I don't think it *is* false.

MacKinnon: Those materials are not even sexually explicit. They don't even get in the door.

Lewis: Why don't you just repeat your definition of pornography?

MacKinnon: Professor Abrams just quoted the definition. Andrea Dworkin's and my approach to pornography is to define it in terms of what it does, not in terms of what it says, not by its ideas, not by whether someone is offended by it, not by whether somebody doesn't like it. None of that has anything to do with our definition. Our definition, and our legal causes of action, all have to do with what it *does* to the women in it, to the children in it, and to other people who can *prove* that as a direct result of these materials they were assaulted or made second-class citizens on the basis of sex.

Abrams: You mean because people will think less of women on 25 account of how they're portrayed?

MacKinnon: No, because people will *do* things to them like not hiring them, like sexualizing them and not taking them seriously as students, the entire array of violent and nonviolent civil subordination, when they can prove it comes from pornography.

Abrams: That is why your legislation is so frontal an attack on the First Amendment. When the Court of Appeals said that the impact of your statute is such that it could apply to everything from hard-core films to the collected works of James Joyce, D. H. Lawrence, and John Cleland, it was entirely correct. It is correct because what you have drafted as a definition of actionable pornography is "graphic sexual explicit subordination of women, in which women are presented as sexual objects for domination." Lots of great art as well as cheap and vile productions have depicted women in just that way — *The Rape of the Sabine Women,* for example. And my point is not that your definition is vague, but that it is clear. It includes any art, whether it is good or bad, art or nonart, that you have concluded may do harm. That's an unacceptable basis and it should be.

MacKinnon: O.K., there are several things wrong with this. No. 1, those materials are not sexually explicit. The court was told exactly what sexually explicit means in law and in ordinary use, and it should have known better. No. 2, these materials have never yet been shown in any study to have produced any of the effects that pornography produces. So no one could prove that women are subordinated as a result of them. This statute does not cover those materials, period. It is false as a matter of statutory construction. The statute could potentially cover something like a film in which somebody was actually killed but claims are made that it has artistic value — an artistic snuff film — or in which someone is raped but the film has interesting camera angles. That does raise a conflict between existing law and our statute. The examples you cite do not.

Lewis: Professor MacKinnon, we do have a concrete example of what your view of the law might result in. The Canadian Supreme Court adopted your view. Since then, there has been an intensification of gay and lesbian books' being intercepted at the border. That seems to be the result of a country actually adopting your standard.

MacKinnon: That's disinformation. Canada customs has singled 30 out those materials for years, and customs law was not involved in the case I was part of in Canada. What happened was, the Supreme Court of Canada rejected its morality-based standard for obscenity and held that when pornography hurts equality it can be stopped. Customs has not reviewed its standards since. I think that if Canada customs is still stopping materials because they are gay or lesbian, on a moral ground not a harm ground, they have lost their constitutional authority to do it under this ruling. If the materials hurt women or men or their equality, they can still stop them. But Andrea Dworkin and I do not favor addressing pornography through criminal law, especially obscenity law, so in that way Canada has not adopted our approach.

Lewis: Professor MacKinnon, there's an assumption explicitly stated in your book that pornography as you define it results in antisocial, abusive activity by the customers.

MacKinnon: There's overwhelming documentation of it.

Lewis: But it is a fact that in countries in which pornography is lawful and there are no legal restraints whatever on sexually explicit materials the incidence of sexual crimes is much lower than in this country.

MacKinnon: Actually, that isn't true. It's urban legend.

Lewis: In Denmark, in Germany, in Japan —   35

MacKinnon: In Denmark, data on reported rape after liberalization is inconclusive. It did not drop, though. Also, the definitions and categories of sexual offenses were changed at the same time that pornography was decriminalized. Also, reporting may well have dropped. If your government supports pornography, reporting sexual abuse seems totally pointless to women. So, too, Germany and Sweden. Once pornography is legitimized throughout society, you get an explosion in sexual abuse, but women don't report it anymore because they know that nothing will be done about it. Feminists and sex educators in Denmark are beginning to say that selling twelve-year-old children on street corners is not what they mean by sexual liberation. What's happened in Japan and other places is that much of sexual abuse is just part of the way women are normally treated. If you're still essentially chattel, what is it to rape you? In Sweden there aren't any rape-crisis centers. All there is is battered-women's shelters. So the battered-women's movement has been pushing the government to look at the reality of rape there, which is massive.

Abrams: But those countries that are harshest on what you would call pornography are also harshest on women. In China promulgation of pornography leads to capital punishment. In Iran it leads to the harshest and most outrageous physical torture. These are not good countries for women to live in. If you look at countries like Sweden and Japan and Holland and Germany, which have allowed more rather than less free expression in this area of sexually explicit speech, you'll find that these are the countries in which sexual abuse of women is not particularly prevalent. It's one thing for you to advocate a statute such as you have proposed in Sweden, but I daresay it has not been seriously suggested that Swedish women as a group have been victimized by their free press and free-speech laws.

MacKinnon: Swedish women have seriously supported our law, against the legalized victimization of pornography. But it's hard to know what the reality is. It's wrong to base how much rape there is on reported rape. It's also very hard to know how much pornography is actually available. You could look at the United States laws and get the impression that pornography was being taken seriously as a problem in this country.

Abrams: But when you cite, for example, the Balkans as a place where there's been a vast amount of rape and infer that it has something to do with the existence of sexually explicit materials, you don't tell us that in 1913 there was an orgy of rapes at a time when such material didn't exist at all. It puts into question the validity of the whole thesis.

MacKinnon: It is not an exclusive thesis. There are lots of ways of sexualizing subordination — religion, veiling, clitoridectomies. Pornography is one way, and some of the abuses it is connected to we can do something about. In countries where women have recently got more voice, like the United States and Sweden, women are becoming more able to identify the sources of our subordination. The United States is a mass culture, media-saturated and capitalistic. In asking how women are subordinated in the United States, it would be wrong to eliminate the capitalistic mass media of the pornography industry. At other times and places, the ways in which women are subordinated are different. But now, the United States is exporting this form of subordination to the rest of the world.

Ice-T: The Issue
Is Creative Freedom

BARBARA EHRENREICH

Ice-T's song "Cop Killer" is as bad as they come. This is black anger — raw, rude, and cruel — and one reason the song's so shocking is that in postliberal America, black anger is virtually taboo. You won't find it on TV, not on the *McLaughlin Group* or *Crossfire,* and certainly not in the placid features of Arsenio Hall or Bernard Shaw. It's been beaten back into the outlaw subcultures of rap and rock, where, precisely because it is taboo, it sells. And the nastier it is, the faster it moves off the shelves. As Ice-T asks in another song on the same album, "Goddamn what a brotha gotta do / To get a message through / To the red, white, and blue?"

But there's a gross overreaction going on, building to a veritable paroxysm of white denial. A national boycott has been called, not just of the song or Ice-T, but of all Time Warner products. The president himself has denounced Time Warner as "wrong" and Ice-T as "sick." Ollie North's Freedom Alliance has started a petition drive aimed at bringing Time Warner executives to trial for "sedition and anarchy."

Much of this is posturing and requires no more courage than it takes to stand up in a VFW hall and condemn communism or crack. Yes, "Cop Killer" is irresponsible and vile. But Ice-T is as right about some things as he is righteous about the rest. And ultimately, he's not even dangerous — least of all to the white power structure his songs condemn.

The "danger" implicit in all the uproar is of empty-headed, suggestible black kids, crouching by their boom boxes, waiting for the word. But what Ice-T's fans know and his detractors obviously don't is that "Cop Killer" is just one more entry in pop music's long history of macho hyperbole and violent boast. Flip to the classic-rock station, and you might catch the Rolling Stones announcing "the time is right for violent revoloo-shun!" from their 1968 hit "Street Fighting Man." And where were the defenders of our law-enforcement officers when a white British group, the Clash, taunted its fans with the lyrics: "When they kick open your front door / How you gonna come / With your hands on your head / Or on the trigger of your gun?"

"Die, Die, Die Pig" is strong speech, but the Constitution protects 5 strong speech, and it's doing so this year more aggressively than ever. The Supreme Court has just downgraded cross burnings to the

Barbara Ehrenreich, cochair of Democratic Socialists of America, is the author of *The Snarling Citizen: Essays* (1995). This article is from the July 20, 1992, issue of *Time.*

level of bonfires and ruled that it's no crime to throw around verbal grenades like "nigger" and "kike." Where are the defenders of decorum and social stability when prime-time demagogues like Howard Stern deride African Americans as "spear chuckers"?

More to the point, young African Americans are not so naive and suggestible that they have to depend on a compact disc for their sociology lessons. To paraphrase another song from another era, you don't need a rap song to tell which way the wind is blowing. Black youths know that the police are likely to see them through a filter of stereotypes as miscreants and potential "cop killers." They are aware that a black youth is seven times as likely to be charged with a felony as a white youth who has committed the same offense, and is much more likely to be imprisoned.

They know, too, that in a shameful number of cases, it is the police themselves who indulge in "anarchy" and violence. The U.S. Justice Department has received 47,000 complaints of police brutality in the past six years, and Amnesty International has just issued a report on police brutality in Los Angeles, documenting forty cases of "torture or cruel, inhuman, or degrading treatment."

Menacing as it sounds, the fantasy in "Cop Killer" is the fantasy of the powerless and beaten down — the black man who's been hassled once too often ("A pig stopped me for nothin'!"), spread-eagled against a police car, pushed around. It's not a "responsible" fantasy (fantasies seldom are). It's not even a very creative one. In fact, the sad thing about "Cop Killer" is that it falls for the cheapest, most conventional image of rebellion that our culture offers: the lone gunman spraying fire from his AK-47. This is not "sedition"; it's the familiar, all-American, Hollywood-style pornography of violence.

Which is why Ice-T is right to say he's no more dangerous than George Bush's pal Arnold Schwarzenegger, who wasted an army of cops in *Terminator 2*. Images of extraordinary cruelty and violence are marketed every day, many of far less artistic merit than "Cop Killer." This is our free market of ideas and images, and it shouldn't be any less free for a black man than for other purveyors of "irresponsible" sentiments, from David Duke to Andrew Dice Clay.[1]

Just, please, don't dignify Ice-T's contribution with the word 10 *sedition*. The past masters of sedition — men like George Washington, Toussaint L'Ouverture, Fidel Castro, or Mao Zedong, all of whom led and won armed insurrections — would be unimpressed by "Cop Killer" and probably saddened. They would shake their heads and mutter words like "infantile" and "adventurism." They might point out that the cops are hardly a noble target, being, for

---

[1]David Duke, an advocate of white supremacy, was defeated in his bid for governor of Louisiana in 1991. Andrew Dice Clay is a stand-up comedian known for his use of offensive language against women and minorities.

the most part, honest working stiffs who've got stuck with the job of patrolling ghettos ravaged by economic decline and official neglect.

There is a difference, the true seditionist would argue, between a revolution and a gesture of macho defiance. Gestures are cheap. They feel good, they blow off some rage. But revolutions, violent or otherwise, are made by people who have learned how to count very slowly to ten.

Freedom of Speech and Holocaust Revisionism

DAVID M. OSHINSKY and MICHAEL CURTIS

College newspapers are facing a dilemma that pits free speech against historical deception. A group calling itself the Committee for Open Debate on the Holocaust has sent an advertisement to at least a dozen leading campus dailies. The ad contends that the Holocaust never occurred.

Newspapers at Harvard, Yale, Brown, the University of Pennsylvania, and the University of Southern California have refused to run it. Those at Northwestern, Cornell, Duke, and the University of Michigan have published it amid protests from students, faculty, and members of their own editorial boards. At Rutgers, the ad was printed free of charge on December 3 as a "guest commentary," surrounded by rebuttals.

The ad attempts to prey on students' ignorance about the Holocaust. It insists, without evidence, that there were no mass killings of Jews and no "execution gas chambers in any camp in Europe that was under German control." It claims the so-called execution chambers were "fumigation chambers," used "to delouse clothing . . . and prevent disease." It is "from this life-*saving* procedure," the ad says, "that the myth of extermination gas chambers emerged."

The slickly done ad does not use the violent language common to the literature of racist and nativist groups. It wraps itself in concepts of free speech and open inquiry, arguing that all points of view deserve to be heard. Timed to exploit the controversy about political correctness, the ad says, "elitist" and "Zionist" groups have stifled debate on the Holocaust in order "to drum up world sympathy" for Jewish causes and Israel.

David M. Oshinsky is a professor of history at Rutgers University. Michael Curtis, also at Rutgers, is a professor of political science. Their article was published in the *New York Times* on December 11, 1991.

The ad was written by Bradley R. Smith, a political soulmate of 5
the California-based institute for Historical Review, the principal
promoter of "Holocaust revisionism." Its founder, Willis A. Carto,
was described by the Anti-Defamation League last year as "perhaps
the leading anti-Semite in the United States." He has been associated
with the Populist Party, whose presidential candidate in 1988 was
David Duke; the Liberty Lobby, a hate group; and the Noontide
Press, which distributes such tracts as "The Testing of Negro Intelligence" and "The International Jew."

In 1980, Mr. Carto's institute offered $50,000 to anyone who could
"prove" that Jews were exterminated at Auschwitz. Mel Mermelstein,
a Holocaust survivor, submitted sworn declarations from people who
had been in the camp. When the institute refused to pay up, he took
its officers to court in Los Angeles. That Jews were gassed to death at
Auschwitz "is not reasonably subject to dispute," the presiding judge
declared. "It is simply a fact." In 1985, Mr. Mermelstein was awarded
the $50,000, plus $40,000 for pain and suffering.

Bradley Smith's committee apparently believes that its theories
will be tolerated by some on First Amendment grounds and accepted by others out of ignorance or worse. The Duke student newspaper naively repeated the committee's description of itself as a
group of revisionist scholars. Duke's history department was appalled and responded with a statement that distinguished between
those who revise history and those who deny it.

Most college editors seem aware of the committee's intentions.
Their decision to print its ad is based on principle: an aversion to
censorship or a belief that hate material should be aired and publicly refuted. Surely their right to publish such ads should not be
questioned. They alone must decide what good purpose, if any, is
served by printing ads that are intentionally hurtful and obviously
false.

The ads should be rejected. If one group advertises that the
Holocaust never happened, another can buy space to insist that
American blacks were never enslaved. The stakes are high because
college newspapers may soon be flooded with ads that present discredited assertions as if they were part of normal historical debate.
If the Holocaust is not a fact, then nothing is a fact, and truth itself
will be diminished.

Net.Censor: Who's to Say
What We Should See or Hear?

EDMUND B. (PETER) BURKE

Green: Free speech, academic freedom, privacy, and the right to be left alone, the right to not listen — all traditional issues of academic communication, and all relevant to the uses (and misuses) of the Internet in colleges and universities. We may have new media, but we have old problems.

White: To me, the most perplexing legal and policy problems can arise when well-recognized and wholly legitimate rights come into conflict with each other. Our law often requires a "balancing" of rights, based on the fundamental values of which the rights are mere expressions. We often find this balancing process troubling, but such is life in our complex, and pluralistic, society.

Green: The Net only makes things more complicated, if that is possible.

Brown: Green, you mention free speech. . . . What do you mean by that anyway?

Green: It clearly doesn't mean that anyone can say or write any-   5
thing that he or she wants at any given time. Think of laws prohibiting false advertising or regulating the sale of stocks and bonds on the securities markets. Or laws prohibiting you from calling me nasty names and provoking me to violence.

White: I would like to submit that there is no free speech. There are innumerable ways in which my speech is limited every day. Some of these ways are quite important. For instance, I'd like to tell my boss what I think of her — but if I did, I'd be looking for a new job. And I can't afford that right now (although the time is drawing near for a showdown). I can't speak my mind in that arena.

Brown: Well, I'd like to set up a booth at that new shopping mall down the street, to tell the shoppers how the construction of the mall has ruined our neighborhood, but the management of the mall wouldn't allow it.

Green: But these are not problems of free speech. The government doesn't compel you to shut up in these cases. White, you choose to keep silent for your own best interest. And Brown, the mall manager chooses not to provide you with a forum; but it's a matter of indifference to the government whether you are allowed to

---

Edmund B. (Peter) Burke is a practicing attorney in Atlanta, Georgia. This article is from the November–December 1995 issue of *Educom Review.*

speak at the mall. To your chagrin, bosses and mall owners have rights as well. As I understand the principle of free speech, it's only a restraint on the ability of the government to shut us up. If I control a Web site on the Internet, I don't violate your rights of free speech by declining to include your views. You can create your own Web site if you like.

Brown: I could, but I think your site would probably be more interesting.

Green: Let's take a question from real life. I noted a posting on the Internet from someone at a small, private college with a church affiliation. The school wants to restrict students from gaining access to Web sites which are deemed (in the school's estimation) to contain pornography. If the school does that, is it restricting the students' rights?

White: Of course it is. And it is discriminating as well. Our question is whether the discrimination and these restrictions are unlawful. The college wants to restrict the students' rights, because it wants to define itself as having a certain purpose and meaning which distinguish it from *Roseanne* and MTV.

Brown: I'd like to understand what the college means by "restrict" here. Would a student be expelled, or suspended, or warned for gaining access to these forbidden sites? Or does the school just want to ensure that no one can use its computers and software as a means of approach?

Green: Not clear. Let's suppose that the school's main concern is to keep its own computers free from pornographic bits. Can the college set up a "software screening" mechanism that prohibits access to specified Web sites?

White: Why not, if it's a private school?

Brown: What if it receives grants or funding from the state?

Green: That shouldn't matter in my opinion. Lots of people and businesses receive government subsidies, but that doesn't make them government actors.

Brown: Could the government make a rule that, if a private college takes the money, it must allow unrestricted Internet access? Sort of a free speech contract?

White: If the federal government has the power to make detailed laws that protect and advance the values embodied in the First Amendment, then that kind of rule would seem to be permitted in our system.

Brown: But wouldn't such a rule injure the free speech rights of the college, because it forces the college to permit activities that it considers to be wrong?

Green: The school doesn't have to take the money, any more than the student has to attend the school. But let's take a less speculative example. Suppose the school discovers some renegade students who, feeling challenged by the software-imposed restrictions and rising to confront it in the best student tradition, figure out a way to circumvent the restrictions.

Brown: That seems a very likely scenario, students being students.

White: I don't see why we should stop the school from expelling the students if the Internet access regulations are well-understood parts of the institution's rules. The students aren't required to attend the college. If they don't like the college rules, let them leave and find some place more to their liking.

Green: Censorship, love it or leave it. Is that your view, White?

White: No, but I think a part of my right of freedom of expression is my right to refrain from supporting causes or activities that I find offensive. My freedom of speech is just the logical complement of your freedom to not listen.

Brown: I think that's a freedom that I'm about ready to exercise, 25 if you two don't mind. Green, you can e-mail me with the names of any alt.news.groups you want me to avoid for my own good.

Green: All three of us know that the paternalism of such a "forbidden" list would only encourage you to use those groups, Brown.

White: Given Brown's rebellious tendencies, that goes without saying. We'll see how well the trustees of the private college appreciate that fundamental, and intriguing, aspect of human behavior.

THINKING AND WRITING ABOUT FREEDOM OF SPEECH

Questions for Discussion and Writing

1. According to Garry Wills, "censure" is superior to censorship. Summarize his argument. (Look up or ask about the specific references in his essay if you aren't familiar with them.)
2. Can you think of circumstances in which creative freedom should bow to social responsibility? What evidence does Ehrenreich use to prove that "Cop Killer" is not dangerous? Is it convincing?
3. How does Lawrence relate *Brown v. Board of Education* to issues of free speech? What principle does he invoke in defense of restrictive speech codes on campus?
4. Hentoff argues for exposure of students to bad ideas as well as good ones. (See p. 6 for a quotation from *Areopagitica,* in which John Milton makes the same point.) What bad ideas does Hentoff have in mind? Spell out the educational advantages of such exposure. What is Hentoff's main criticism of university officials? Do you think it is justified?
5. In the discussion among White, Green, and Brown about censorship of the Net, several different views of free speech are expressed. Which one is closest to your own? Explain why. With which views do you think

Lawrence and Hentoff would agree? Do you know of any incidents on your campus that have involved the issues debated here? If so, how were they resolved?

6. Oshinsky and Curtis raise the question of media responsibility to the truth. Does a belief in freedom of speech mean that newspapers have a right to publish "discredited assertions as if they were part of normal historical debate"? Why or why not? Are "discredited assertions" the same as Hentoff's "bad ideas"? Has the college newspaper on your campus ever been guilty of publishing nontruths?

7. MacKinnon offers a controversial definition of pornography, a description of the industry by herself and feminist writer Andrea Dworkin. What does she mean by "a moral ground, not a harm ground"? Explain this and tell why Abrams considers it a violation of the First Amendment. Does he address the Fourteenth Amendment equality issues she raises?

8. Summarize the debate between Abrams and MacKinnon on the effect of pornography laws on sexual abuse of women in other parts of the world. Did some parts of the argument seem stronger than others? If so, tell why.

9. Why does Rauch think that "eradicating prejudice" is probably impossible? Explain what he means by "the new purism." Examine his examples. Could Rauch have proved his claims without them? According to Rauch, what are the advantages of "intellectual pluralism," which

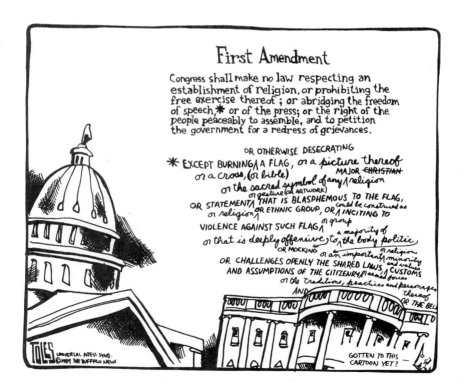

permits the expression of prejudice and ignorance? Which authors in this chapter would agree with him? Which authors would disagree?

10. Summarize the cartoonist's wry claim about the First Amendment. Is the same point expressed in any of the essays in this chapter?

Topics for Research

Lyrics in rock music: How dangerous are they?

Codes of speech conduct at some colleges and universities: Goals and effect

Religious displays on public land

Public funds for offensive art. (Look up the cases of Robert Mapplethorpe and Andres Serrano, whose works scandalized some members of Congress in the summer and fall of 1989.) Is withdrawal of public funds a "regulation of the imagination"?

Freedom of speech on the Internet

Prayer in public schools

CHAPTER FIFTEEN

Immigration

The United States is a nation of immigrants. Between 1820 and 1920 more than 33 million immigrants, fleeing poverty and oppression, arrived in this country from parts of Europe, China, and Japan. Today millions of additional immigrants, escaping similar conditions, are entering the United States, both legally and illegally, from Latin America and Asia. According to the 1990 Census, there are now 19 million immigrants in the United States, including 8.9 million legal immigrants and at least 2 million illegal ones who entered during the 1980s alone. The United States today accepts more immigrants than all other countries of the world combined.

Anti-immigration sentiment arises periodically in this country as a result of cultural differences and changing economic conditions. In the past we have found it easier to accept those who assimilated more readily into mainstream culture, such as white northern Europeans. It is worth noting that the term "melting pot," coined in 1908, was once widely held to be an accurate metaphor for the process of assimilation. Now some observers suggest that in the 1990s a mosaic, each of whose separate parts retains its distinct identity, is a more appropriate figure of speech. The most recent arrivals may also have greater difficulty in finding employment than those at the turn of the century, a time of booming industry and unmechanized farms.

On one side of the controversy are the advocates of a liberal immigration policy; they argue not only that our humanity should encourage us to open our doors to refugees but that immigrants contribute to the social and economic enrichment of the country. On the other side, advocates of a tighter immigration policy argue that new waves of immigrants are straining our resources and changing the cultural character of our country. Policies will be

513

based on definitions of the American dream and reassessment of our historic role as a haven for the oppressed. But they will not be easy to formulate. Even the facts — the statistics of immigration and whether there is a crisis at all — are matters of dispute.

Proposals to limit immigration are now being debated. In 1995 California voted for Proposition 187, which deprives illegal immigrants of certain public services. (It is presently under court review.) Welfare reform bills in Congress would deny some services to legal immigrants for five years after arrival in this country; other bills would limit the family-reunification quotas that permit relatives of an immigrant to enter the country.

We Should Always Lift Our Lamp to the World

SUSAN ROOSEVELT WELD and WILLIAM F. WELD

From the building of the railroads to the building of space age technology, immigrants have left their imprint on our nation and our commonwealth. They have contributed to our art, religion, science, education, medicine, business, theater, and every aspect of the culture that is known throughout the world as American. There can be no question that the story of the United States is the story of immigration.

Lately, we have been amazed at the amount of confusion that surrounds immigration. Almost all Americans recognize the value of past immigration; however, many are uncertain of the value of immigration today. They point with pride to ancestors who came here with full hearts and empty pockets, who prospered and contributed mightily to the quality of life that all Americans enjoy today.

At the same time, many of them wonder if changing times have modified America's needs. Several bills before Congress reflect the idea that immigrants are no longer a tremendous national advantage but instead are a liability [that] must be controlled.

Is the United States now so self-sufficient, so rich, and so powerful that we no longer need immigrants?

We do not think so. We look at an economy that is rapidly becoming global, and we recognize the value of speaking more than

Susan Roosevelt Weld is a research fellow in East Asian Legal Studies at Harvard University Law School. William F. Weld is governor of Massachusetts. This essay appeared in the *Boston Globe* on January 11, 1996.

one language. We look at the information highway, and we recognize that the world is getting smaller and the distances among continents are shrinking. More than ever, we see the need for new ideas, new problem-solving skills, new Americans.

But, we are asked, do immigrants impose an intolerable burden on our economy? Are we looking at an increase in immigration that is unprecedented in the history of our nation? Studies say otherwise. Census data show that immigrants were nearly 15 percent of our population in 1910; today they are 8 percent. Although the U.S. population has tripled during that time, the immigrant population has not doubled.

Other generally accepted "facts" about immigration are not supported by the figures. For example:

- A 1993 poll indicates that 70 percent of Americans think that "most of the people who have moved to the United States in the last few years are here illegally." The Urban Institute, however, estimates that in 1993 there were about 11 million aliens, of whom 2.5 million were undocumented.

- Many people believe that today's immigrants are not as well educated as native-born Americans. According to census figures, however, while more immigrants have not completed high school than natives, they are twice as likely to hold a Ph.D.

- Although it is widely believed that immigrants put people out of work, the Manhattan Institute tells us that of the ten states with the highest immigrant populations, only one — Illinois — is among the ten highest unemployment states. Immigrants start businesses, pay taxes, purchase goods and services, and create jobs.

- Nor are immigrants overloading our state prisons. A 1991 survey by the National Institute of Corrections showed that 4 percent of state prison populations are aliens. Federal prisons do have a higher percentage (25 percent) of aliens, but most are international drug smugglers and other border-hopping felons, not immigrants.

- There is a persistent belief that immigrants use far more welfare than the native-born. Actually, according to the Urban Institute, 2.3 percent of immigrants use these services, as opposed to 3.3 percent of natives. Only if you factor in refugees escaping intolerable conditions in their home countries does the percentage go higher, and refugees and asylum-seekers are allowed public benefits for eight months only. Immigrants generate $285 billion in income and pay more than $70 billion in taxes — far greater sums than the $5.7 billion they use in public assistance.

Any way you look at it, the economic evidence is overwhelming: Newcomers support themselves through work, not welfare.

We therefore question the wisdom of provisions in Congress's welfare compromise that would make legal immigrants ineligible for most federal social services for five years after their arrival. Legal immigrants should enjoy rights and protections that are not available to those who break the law to come here. We believe that denying ordinary citizen benefits to future American citizens is not only ungenerous and unwelcoming, but also unnecessary.

Those who sponsor immigrants pledge to take financial respon- 10
sibility for them through a process called "deeming." If deeming were enforced, there would be little need to yank away the social safety net from legal arrivals. And, except in cases when it would tie immigrants to sponsors who batter them or when the sponsor is in financial distress, deeming should be enforced.

Another proposal before Congress would eliminate the "national interest waiver" that eases immigration for those with special skills and would make it much more difficult and expensive for employers to hire recent graduates of American universities. Right now, the best of these students are often hired by the best of our high-tech firms. If we start telling MIT Ph.D's that their employment future in the United States is uncertain, we're not improving the economy for the native-born, we're sending badly needed talent straight to our global competitors; we're depriving our businesses of the whizzes that can help them grow; and we're shrinking opportunities for everyone. We believe this proposal should be dumped into the "cutting off your nose to spite your face" file and promptly forgotten.

Many people believe that unlike the hard-working, eager-to-learn, grateful immigrants of the past, today's newcomers do not want to speak English, that they cling to their old cultures and tend to reject American society and culture. Our experience has been the opposite. We find that despite differences in culture and language, today's immigrants quickly recognize that they must learn English if they want to get ahead.

We also find that to an amazing degree, they share the most traditional of American values: a disciplined work ethic, strong family ties, religious values, an inclination toward entrepreneurship, respect for education, personal independence, appreciation of democracy and a determination that — whatever it takes, whatever sacrifices may be called for, whatever deprivations must be endured — their children will have a better life.

They share with other Americans a conviction that they and their children are smart enough, tough enough, and brave enough to answer questions, solve problems, avert disasters, and ultimately not only flourish and thrive themselves, but help bring prosperity and honor to their new country.

And they are right. Immigrants are not helpless victims relying 15
on our charity and good will — far from it! They are survivors. It

takes courage, creativity, determination, and commitment to abandon cherished possessions and people, leave the known for the unknown, cross unfamiliar territory, and set up a new life in a new land. It is a tribute to the indomitable human spirit that so many people continue to do this so well.

To those who say that the time has come to extinguish Lady Liberty's lamp and to slam shut the golden door, we say nonsense. Did you ever notice how, in the Olympic Games, the Norwegians look like Norwegians, the Chinese look like Chinese, the Ethiopians look like Ethiopians, the Spaniards look like Spaniards, and the Americans look like everybody?

There is a reason for this: Americans are everybody. America is still a young country, somewhat brash perhaps, occasionally prone to stumble and recover, and then stumble and recover again. But the United States possesses a vigor and a record for accomplishment that has prompted many an Old World aristocrat to drop his monocle and say, "Wow!"

Diversity has played a significant role in our success. We believe, as surely as we believe anything, that immigration is good for the United States and Massachusetts. We welcome new Americans and the legacy they bring with them. We firmly believe that with the help of our new Americans, the United States will do far more than survive: We will grow and mature, and we will witness the unfolding of a nation that is stronger, wiser, fairer, braver, kinder, and more prosperous than anything heretofore seen. We will be honored to be part of it.

A Growing Burden

DONALD L. HUDDLE

In 1962, two major studies reported that immigrants used up a lot more public money — for education, medical care, welfare, and other social benefits — than they paid in taxes that year.

In a Los Angeles County government report, the gap for 2.3 million immigrants, both legal and illegal, was $808 million in county costs. A study of San Diego by the auditor general of California found that the net cost of state and county services for 200,000 illegals was $145.9 million.

Both studies emphasized that while the county governments were bearing a large share of these costs, the federal government col-

Donald L. Huddle is professor emeritus of economics at Rice University. This article appeared in the *New York Times* on September 3, 1993.

lected the lion's share of immigrants' tax revenues and returned little to the counties. State governments may be in a similar position. Last month, Governor Pete Wilson of California said that illegal immigrants and their U.S.-born children (who are citizens) were costing the state $2.9 billion a year for only four services: welfare, education, health care, and — if it can be called a service — incarceration.

A study I conducted for the Carrying Capacity Network, a non-profit educational organization, was the first comprehensive assessment of the costs of immigration at the federal, state, and county levels. Do immigrants as a group contribute enough in federal taxes to cancel out the burden they pose at the county and state levels? Or does government spending on immigrants outweigh their tax revenues? The answers have obvious implications for immigration policy.

Our nationwide study assessed the net costs to taxpayers of immigrants who have arrived since 1970 and projected spending on those expected to arrive from 1993 to 2002. It examined twenty-three categories of federal, state, and local assistance, including county health and welfare services. 5

In three previous field studies, I found that for every hundred unskilled immigrants who were working, twenty-five or more unskilled native-born Americans were displaced or unable to get jobs. The Carrying Capacity Network study calculated the costs of public assistance for 2.1 million American workers displaced by immigrants, using the 25 percent displacement rate.

According to 1990 Census data, the poverty rate of immigrants is 42.8 percent higher than that of the native-born. On average, immigrant households receive 44.2 percent more public assistance dollars than do native households.

Public assistance costs in 1992 at the county, state, and national levels were $42.5 billion for the 19.3 million legal and illegal immigrants who have settled in the United States since 1970. These are net costs, after deducting the $20.2 billion in taxes paid by immigrants and including the $11.9 billion for public assistance for the 2.1 million displaced U.S.-born workers. The biggest expense was for primary and secondary public education, followed by Medicaid.

And these costs are projected to rise, assuming that laws and their enforcement don't change. Our estimate is that 11.1 million immigrants, legal and illegal, will enter the country in the next decade. The bill for supporting all immigrants and the American workers they displace for those ten years will total $951.7 billion. We estimated that the immigrants will pay $283.2 billion in taxes.

Thus there will be a net cost to U.S. taxpayers of $668.5 billion over the decade. Legal immigrants will account for almost three-quarters of the total cost; illegal aliens will account for $186.4 billion. 10

The costs over the next decade may increase if, as some project, the number of immigrants rises above the 11.1 million our study estimates. And the number may rise even more because spending is being increased for programs such as the earned-income tax credit and other services that act as magnets for potential immigrants.

The Clinton administration's anticipated plan for universal health coverage would significantly raise medical costs for immigrants, a larger percentage of whom tend to be uninsured. Indeed, access to public health care alone might be enough to attract new immigrants, particularly those with difficult medical conditions.

How can the United States reduce this growing burden? It should not single out legal immigrants for cuts in entitlements because that would be discriminatory. But it should tighten financial responsibility requirements for families and other sponsors of immigrants.

A better way of cutting the costs would be to reduce immigration and select entrants more carefully.

Current law incorporates a preference for family reunification and   15
for political asylum seekers and refugees. Aliens who received amnesty under the 1986 immigration act are becoming eligible to bring in their families. World events could encourage an even greater number of refugees, most of whom will be low-skilled and dependent.

If the policies were changed, however, to accept only skilled or professional legal immigrants — 38 percent of the current flow — we would avoid a projected cost of $171.8 billion, while netting a modest revenue gain of $13.7 billion by 2002.

Curbing illegal immigration could save $186 billion by 2002. Stricter control of the border, enforcement of sanctions against employers who hire illegals, and better programs to screen immigrant welfare applications could help stem the flow.

Get Out of Dodge!
WANDA COLEMAN

I am terrorized by the murder of a child. Intermittently, dramatic images of her death unreel. Two years after it happened, I'm still enraged, upset, unable to sleep. I'm haunted by her murder and by the thousands of murders of black youths since 1955, when a brutally bludgeoned Emmett Till rose from the autumn waters of Mississippi's Tallahatchie River. Each afternoon, as I wait for my fourteen-year-old son to return from school, I pray. I'm not a religious woman. But when I hear him coming through that door, I'm overjoyed. How long, I wonder, will America allow him to live?

Wanda Coleman is a poet who writes regularly for the *Los Angeles Times*. This selection originally appeared in the February 15, 1993, issue of *The Nation*, and was then excerpted in this form in the May–June 1994 issue of *Utne Reader*.

It allowed Latasha Harlins barely fifteen years. In March and April 1991, a year before South Central Los Angeles erupted, local residents repeatedly witnessed news broadcasts of the videotaped Empire Liquor Market killing of fifteen-year-old Latasha Harlins by fifty-one-year-old Soon Ja Du. Central to the black-Korean tensions that fueled the riots, this incident was scarcely a footnote in national media coverage of the riots.

The video, filmed by an in-store camera, is painfully graphic: Latasha approaches Du, alone behind the counter, with money in her hand. Du accuses her of stealing a $1.79 bottle of orange juice. Latasha turns to show Du the juice in her knapsack, then waves the $2. After a heated verbal exchange, Latasha throws the orange juice down on the counter. The angry Du grabs for Latasha's pack, then catches the flap of her jacket. Latasha slaps Du, who immediately lets go. Latasha turns and walks away. Du fumbles for the .38 caliber, fires once. Latasha pitches forward and drops to the floor as the bullet strikes the back of her head.

Initial newspaper accounts of the incident were careful to describe Latasha as "studious and self-assured." But the slant of so-called objective coverage betrayed tacit sympathy for Du. She had lived every bigot's fantasy. She had shot *one of them.*

The fear that motivated Soon Ja Du was couched in statistics designed to justify her killing of Latasha: "In the surrounding 32 blocks, 936 felonies reported last year . . . 5 murders . . . 9 rapes . . . 184 robberies and 254 assaults." The fact that Du's son was the victim in one of those assaults was subtly emphasized. The nasties of ghetto life were responsible, not the "feeble and overwhelmed" grocer forced to work fourteen-hour days, at the mercy of shoplifters, street hoodlums, and chronic migraines, and certainly not white society. 5

Local protests over the Harlins shooting were swift and raucous, the culmination of complaints by black community leaders about "the Korean invasion" and lack of dialogue between the two groups. For nearly a decade the local media, alternative and mainstream, had refused to investigate the problem initially brought to their attention by a handful of concerned black writers, including me.

During that period, I had had three especially infuriating run-ins with Korean merchants. One was a fight at a hamburger stand, when the Koreans across the counter refused to accept my newly minted $20 bill. They'd been burned before, and they thought the bill was bogus. I was guilty of the crime someone else, also black, had committed. Using my own stubby fuse and lofty blood pressure as a gauge seemed unfair. But when even my demure sixty-year-old mother complained of abuse by "some Koreans because I'm black," I saw that violence was inevitable in my community.

Black protest over the Harlins-Du incident increased, but was unexpectedly dissipated when attorney Charles Lloyd was hired for

Du's defense. Lloyd is black. As in the Hill versus Thomas fiasco, many were reluctant to go against one of our own. A "wait and see" attitude was adopted toward the previously hotly disputed case. When Soon Ja Du's bail was set at $250,000 and her release made imminent, the courtroom, crowded with Korean Americans, broke into applause. The black community was virtually silent. It would remain so until after the verdict in the Rodney King beating trial.

The socioeconomic reversals and unchecked discrimination of the Nixon/Ford/Reagan/Bush years stymied progress for most African Americans. And the high expectations many had for President Carter were gradually deflated. One year into the Carter administration, NAACP executive director Benjamin Hooks told 3,000 Urban League delegates. "Nearly 80 percent of the white people in America feel that enough has been done for black people." Since then, study after study has documented his gloomy insight: Blacks still disproportionately live in substandard and segregated housing; attend inferior public schools staffed by underpaid, underencouraged teachers; confront corporate America's glass ceiling; make do with lower wages as skilled labor devolves into low-paid service jobs; populate worsening neighborhoods plagued by unfettered drug traffic, increased violent crimes, overflowing prisons; battle homelessness. Factor in the unacceptably high rate of premature death due to hypertension and stroke, murder, and AIDS. While the richest 20 percent of America got richer, the largely disenfranchised fifteenth-generation African Americans struggled to "keep hope alive."

Blacks squeezed out of the L.A. economy were likewise being squeezed out nationally. Economic statistics repeatedly illuminated the concurrence of events that have conspired to marginalize struggling blacks. The increasing influx of immigrants exacerbated our crisis. While blacks were being pushed out of the marketplace by recession and widespread apathy, that same American marketplace was accommodating a groundswell of immigrants, privileged and underprivileged, from as far away as the former Soviet Union, the Middle East, Vietnam, and Korea. Their presence pushed blacks out of the marketplace altogether. Only lucky exceptions remained.

In his October 1992 *Atlantic* article "Blacks vs. Browns," Jack Miles sidesteps black-Korean conflicts to trace black-Latino clashes underscoring "Watts II." (A June 1983 issue of *Time* estimated that 90 percent of illegal immigrants come from Mexico. The Census Bureau reported a 16 percent increase in America's Latino population between 1981 and 1986, making one out of fourteen Americans Latino.) Miles observes that Latinos, even when they're foreign, seem native and safe while blacks, who are native, seem foreign and dangerous. Miles implies that blacks are so "nihilistic, so utterly alienated" that white Americans cannot "make a connection" with us. It's "just easier with the Mexicans." But the point is that the prejudice of white

America has promoted the very attitude among blacks that whites like Miles find so discomforting. No matter how many immigrants white America puts between itself and blacks, this national dilemma will persist.

Furthermore, as a price of entry, the majority of immigrants buy into the lie of American apartheid: Black people are inferior. To fail to accept this tenet of American life is to jeopardize what is already a tenuous existence for the newly arrived. When merchants like Soon Ja Du mimic whites' fear of blacks, their behavior is condoned, if not rewarded, by our society. Alliances between blacks and immigrants are troubled because the two groups profoundly misunderstand each other: While the immigrant populations (Koreans, Latinos, et al.) expect rational behavior from blacks driven mad by poverty and racism, blacks expect immigrants to emphathize with our plight the minute they set foot on our turf — when too many of us don't grasp it ourselves. Newly arrived immigrants often do not understand that what may be interpreted as a mere inconvenience or slight by whites may be interpreted as disrespectful, even life-threatening, by blacks. "Objectivity" is impossible because racism prevents it.

Cooked under the pressures of the penal system, Latino-black conflicts have steadily worsened and are emphasized by the media. Violence on local campuses makes the front pages. Two black families in the Boyle Heights barrio of Ramona Gardens were fire-bombed. I got my taste of these tensions when I parked my car across the street from a liquor store and dashed in to play the lottery. Pulling up, I noticed about a dozen Latino men in a nearby alley and on the stoop next door, drinking and hanging out. My car is dilapidated and rusty, so I trusted no one would bother it. I left it open, windows down. When I returned the entire interior was wet. Not a Latino in sight. I wiped it down, sniffing to see if it was urine. It was water. And the message was clear: *Get out of Dodge.*

Immigration Straight-Talk

WILLIAM RASPBERRY

America, as Jim Sleeper of the *New York Daily News* once noted, is one of the few places where a charge of racial or ethnic bigotry is a serious indictment.

Even when Americans are being unfair to one group or another, they are at pains to protest that their objective is inclusion, not exclusion — that they believe in America as a welcoming place for all who share her ideals.

This desire not to be seen as bigoted has helped to change perceptions, laws, and attitudes. It has also kept at least one issue virtually off the table: immigration.

We have been worried about the deleterious effects of uncontrolled immigration for a long time, yet we've been fearful of speaking plainly about it lest we be viewed as bigots. We have seen the social costs of immigration (overcrowding and depressed wages, to name two). At least one poll found that some two-thirds of Hispanics — the category usually evoked by the phrase "immigration problem"— believe we're admitting too many immigrants.

Why is straight talk on the subject so difficult? One explanation 5 may lie in the reaction to California's recent passage of Proposition 187 — a decision by the voters there that they will no longer pay for the health, education, and welfare of *illegal* aliens.

A fair number of liberals have attacked the vote as "immigrant bashing," and at least two conservatives — Jack Kemp and Bill Bennett — called it "an ugly antipathy toward all immigrants."

As William B. Dickinson of the Biocentric Institute put it: "Those who favor open borders have long tried — with considerable success — to blur the distinction between legal and illegal immigrants. America's tradition as an immigrant nation, its congenital sympathy for underdogs, and its less-principled desire for an endless supply of cheap labor make it easy to excuse poor people who slip across our borders in the dead of night. Those of us who support an orderly immigration policy based on law find ourselves demonized as bigots, racists or nativists."

Even that quintessential liberal Barbara Jordan came in for her share of knocks when the commission she headed called for an end to public aid for illegal immigrants aside from immunizations and emergency food and health care.

This column by William Raspberry, a syndicated columnist, appeared in the *Boston Globe* on December 13, 1995.

It's easy enough to see what drove the Californians. The presence of the illegals in California (and in dozens of other cities) is the result of the failure of the federal government to keep them out. This same government, through the federal courts, has ruled that the state has the duty to provide services (including health, education, and welfare) for people whose very presence here is a violation of the law. But the states get little help from Washington in paying for these services, and the feds, though recently better at enforcing the borders, seem unable to deport the illegals they arrest here.

But passing Proposition 187 isn't the end of the matter. In the 10 first place, unless the Supreme Court overturns its earlier ruling, California state law will not relieve Californians of the burden of educating the children of illegals (or undocumented workers, as the gentler, less accurate phrase has it). More importantly, it's not clear, upon sober reflection, that California has an interest in keeping large numbers of its residents poor and hungry and ignorant.

A counter argument is used by antiwelfare advocates: Harsh treatment of present illegals will seem inhumane, but generosity will only increase their numbers.

Dickinson, like Mortimer Zuckerman of *U.S. News,* argues that it's time to revamp American immigration law across the board — including those bedeviling questions of which country's immigrants should be favored, what skills should be required of those admitted, and how many immigrants are too many.

Certainly it seems reasonable to rethink the 1990 liberalization of the rules that allow immigrants to send home for members of their families, very broadly defined — and to reconsider as well the notion (unique to the United States?) that anyone born here is automatically a U.S. citizen.

But for now, I'd be happy to hear serious and candid discussion of the one problem that everybody acknowledges is a problem: illegal immigration.

As Zuckerman noted, these are the people who "have, by defini- 15 tion, broken the law, and they are guilty of an ethical breach as well: They have jumped the line of people patiently waiting for years for their visas."

Does it really make sense for the federal government to reward these violaters of law and civility with mandated services for themselves and their children, paid for by money-short states with no choice in the matter?

Can't we put aside our charges of bigotry and at least talk about it?

The Americanization Ideal

BARBARA JORDAN

Congress is considering legislation to curb illegal immigration and set priorities for legal admissions. Several presidential candidates have made immigration a keystone of their campaigns. Newspapers carry immigration-related articles almost daily, in contrast to just a few years ago when hardly any appeared.

This attention is not misplaced. Reform is needed in policies that permit the continued entry of hundreds of thousands of illegal aliens and blur distinctions between what is legal and beneficial and what is illegal and harmful. The Commission on Immigration Reform issued a report last year on illegal immigration and will release its second report, on legal migrants, tomorrow. These two reports outline a rational set of principles that will restore credibility to our policies while setting priorities for the future.

Legitimate concern about weaknesses in our immigration policy should not, however, obfuscate what remains the essential point: The United States has been and should continue to be a nation of immigrants. A well-regulated system of legal immigration is in our national interest.

There have always been those who despised the newcomers. The history of American immigration policy is full of racism and ethnic prejudice. The Know-Nothings. The Chinese Exclusion Acts. Even before the Revolution, as eminent a person as Benjamin Franklin feared that Germans coming to Pennsylvania would not become English.

Of course, German immigrants to Pennsylvania did not become English, nor did they make Pennsylvanians into Germans. Instead, they became *Americans.* So did the Chinese, Japanese, and Koreans who came, despite prejudice. So do the Mexicans, Cubans, and Haitians who come today.   5

The United States has united immigrants and their descendants around a commitment to democratic ideals and constitutional principles. People from an extraordinary range of ethnic and religious backgrounds have embraced these ideals.

There is a word for this process: Americanization. That word earned a bad reputation when it was stolen by racists and xenophobes in the 1920s. But it is our word, and we are taking it back.

Barbara Jordan (1937–1996), the first African American woman from the South since Reconstruction to serve in the House of Representatives, was chair of the United States Commission on Immigration Reform. This article appeared in the September 11, 1995, issue of the *New York Times.*

Americanization means becoming a part of the polity — becoming one of us. But that does not mean conformity. We are more than a melting pot; we are a kaleidoscope, where every turn of history refracts new light on the old promise.

Immigration imposes mutual obligations. Those who choose to come here must embrace the common core of American civic culture. We must assist them in learning our common language: American English. We must renew civic education in the teaching of American history for all Americans. We must vigorously enforce the laws against hate crimes and discrimination. We must remind ourselves, as we illustrate for newcomers, what makes us America.

Naturalization is a vital step in this process. Interest in naturalization has never been greater; applications for citizenship exceed in number and proportion any previous period in our history. But would-be citizens must wait too long to be processed, as much as two years in some cities. The Immigration and Naturalization Service must make timely naturalization a strategic goal while maintaining rigorous standards.

Reforming our immigration policy is the best way to revitalize 10 our commitment to immigration and to immigrants. It is literally a matter of who we are as a nation, and who we become as a people.

Unchecked Immigration
PETER BRIMELOW

I am not at all relaxed . . . about problems posed to the American national project by what the editors call, quite accurately, "unchecked immigration." The facts here are compelling. But they are not widely understood because of the romantic haze, intellectual inertia, and downright dishonesty that surrounds the subject.

The 1965 Immigration Act triggered an influx of historically high proportions, particularly compared to current U.S. birth rates. Thus the Census Bureau projects that Americans, left to themselves, are stabilizing their population around 250 to 260 million. But the government is in effect second-guessing them through immigration policy. If present trends continue, the U.S. population will reach 390 million by 2050. More than 130 million will be post-1970 immigrants and their descendants. Because the 1965 Act arbitrarily choked off

Peter Brimelow is a senior editor of *National Review* and *Forbes* magazine. This excerpt is from the November 1995 edition of *Commentary*.

immigration from Europe, this influx has been almost all from the Third World. So by 2050, whites, who were 90 percent of the population as recently as 1960, will be on the verge of becoming a minority.

This is a demographic transformation without precedent in the history of the world. It is incumbent on those who favor it to explain what makes them think it is going to work — and why they want to transform the American nation as it had evolved by 1965.

Because the new arrangements are clearly not working at the moment. The 1990 Census revealed that native-born Americans, both black and white, were fleeing the immigrant-favored areas, where they were being replaced on an almost one-for-one basis by immigrants, and going to entirely separate sections of the country — whites to the white heartland of the Midwest, the Pacific Northwest, and so on; blacks to the black areas of the South, Atlanta, Washington, D.C., and so on.

The country is coming apart ethnically under the impact of the 5 enormous influx. This must ultimately raise what might be called the National Question: Is America still that interlacing of ethnicity and culture that we call a nation — and can the American nation-state, the political expression of that nation, survive?

All of the unraveling that the editors instance — multiculturalism, dissolution of shared values, increased stratification — is exacerbated, at the very least, by immigration. This is not to say that immigration necessarily caused these policies, a point immigration enthusiasts invariably miss. "The fault, dear Peter, lies not in our immigrants but in ourselves," *New York Post* columnist Maggie Gallagher wrote in what was one of the nicer reactions to my arguments. But here's the rub: If there is a rainstorm when you have a cold, you stay indoors.

Unless there is another pause for assimilation, as there have been many times in the past, immigration will add to America's latent sectionalism and ultimately break the country up like the late Roman empire — a crisis as utterly unexpected as World War I by the American political elite, both Left and Right.

Illegal immigration should be ended with a second Operation Wetback, as the Eisenhower administration ended the similar illegal-immigration crisis of the 1950s: Seal the borders, deport the illegals already here. Legal immigration should be halted with a five- or ten-year moratorium: no net immigration, with admissions for hardship cases or needed skills balancing the 200,000 legal residents who leave each year. During that moratorium, there should be a debate in which Americans would be asked what they want — as they have not yet been. Immigration might then be resumed, at moderate levels, with an emphasis on skills, and on evidence of cultural compatibility such as speaking English.

Geniuses from Abroad

GEORGE GILDER

The current immigration debate founders on ignorance of one huge fact: Without immigration, the United States would not exist as a world power. Without immigration, the United States could not have produced the computerized weapons that induced the Soviet Union to surrender in the arms race. Without immigration, the United States could not have built the atomic bomb during World War II, or the hydrogen bomb in the early 1950s, or intercontinental missiles in the 1960s, or MIRVs in the 1970s, or cruise missiles for the Gulf War in the 1990s.

Today, immigrants are vital not only for targeted military projects but also for the wide range of leading-edge ventures in an information-age economy. No less than military superiority in previous eras, U.S. industrial dominance and high standards of living today depend on outsiders.

Every high-technology company, big or small, is like a Manhattan Project. All must mobilize the personnel best trained and most able to perform a specific function, and deliver a product within a window of opportunity as fateful and remorseless as a war deadline. This requires access to the small elite of human beings in the world capable of pioneering these new scientific and engineering frontiers. For many specialized high-technology tasks, the pool of potential talent around the world numbers around ten people, or even fewer.

The Right People

If you are running such a technology company, you will quickly discover that the majority of this cognitive elite are not citizens of your country. Unless you can find the right people wherever they may be, you will not be able to launch the exotic innovation that changes the world. Unless you can fill the key technology jobs, you will not create any other jobs at all, and your country will forgo the cycle of new products, skills, and businesses that sustain a world-leading standard of living.

Discussing the impact of immigration, economists and their followers are beady-eyed gnatcatchers, expert on the movements of cabbage pickers and au pair girls and the possible impact of Cubans on Miami wage levels. But like hunters in a cartoon, they ignore the tyrannosaurus rex crouching behind them. Thus sophisticated ana-

5

George Gilder is a fellow at Seattle's Discovery Institute. This column appeared in the *Wall Street Journal* on December 18, 1995.

lysts, such as George Borjas of the University of California, San Diego, and artful writers, such as Peter Brimelow, conclude that the impact of immigration on the U.S. economy is slight or negligible.

In fact, the evidence is overwhelming and undeniable; it is all around us, in a spate of inventions and technical advances, from microwaves and air bags to digital cable and satellite television, from home computers and air conditioners to cellular phones and lifesaving pharmaceuticals and medical devices. Without immigration over the last fifty years, I would estimate that U.S. real living standards would be at least 40 percent lower.

The underplaying of immigration as an economic force stems from a basic flaw in macroeconomic analysis. Economists fail to account for the indispensable qualitative effects of genius. Almost by definition, genius is the ability to generate unique products and concepts and bring them to fruition. Geniuses are literally thousands of times more productive than the rest of us. We all depend on them for our livelihoods and opportunities.

The feats of genius are necessarily difficult to identify or predict, except in retrospect. But judging from the very rough metric of awards of mathematical doctorates and other rigorous scientific and engineering degrees, prizes, patents, and publications, about a third of the geniuses in the United States are foreign born, and another 20 percent are the offspring of immigrants. A third of all American Nobel Prize winners, for example, were born overseas.

A stellar example of these elites in action is Silicon Valley in California. Silicon Valley companies have reduced the price of computer MIPs and memory bits by a factor of some 10,000 in 2 1/2 decades. Although mainstream economists neglect to measure the qualitative impact of these innovations, most of the new value in the world economy over the last decade has stemmed, directly or indirectly, from the semiconductor and computer industries, both hardware and software.

Consider Intel Corporation. Together with its parent, Fairchild 10 Semiconductor, Intel developed the basic processes of microchip manufacture and created dynamic and static random access memory, the microprocessor, and the electrically programmable read-only memory. In other words, Intel laid the foundations for the personal computer revolution and scores of other chip-based industries that employ the vast bulk of U.S. engineers today.

Two American-born geniuses, Robert Noyce and Gordon Moore, were key founders of Fairchild and Intel. But their achievements would have been impossible without the help of Jean Hourni, inventor of planar processing; Dov Frohmann-Benchkowski, inventor of electrically erasable programmable ROMs; Federico Faggin, inventor of silicon gate technology and builder of the first microprocessor; Mayatoshi Shima, layout designer of key 8086 family devices; and of course Andrew Grove, the company's now revered CEO who solved several intractable problems of the metal oxide silicon technology at the heart of Intel's growth. All these Intel engineers — and hundreds of other key contributors — were immigrants.

The pattern at Intel was repeated throughout Silicon Valley, from National Semiconductor and Advanced Micro Devices to Applied Materials, LSI Logic, Actel, Atmel, Integrated Device Technologies, Xicor, Cypress, Sun Microsystems and Hewlett-Packard, all of which from the outset heavily depended on immigrants in the laboratories and on engineering workbenches. LSI, IDT, Actel, Atmel, Xicor, and Sun were all founded or led by immigrants. Today, fully one-third of all the engineers in Silicon Valley are foreign born.

Now, with Silicon Valleys proliferating throughout the U.S. economy, with Silicon Deserts, Prairies, Mountains, and even Alleys being hopefully launched from Manhattan to Oregon, immigration becomes ever more vital to the future of the U.S. economy. And microchips are just the beginning. On the foundation of silicon have arisen world-leading software and medical equipment industries almost equally dependent on immigrants. As spearhead of the fastest growing U.S. industry, software, Microsoft offers some of the most coveted jobs in the U.S. economy. But for vital functions, it still must turn to immigrants for 5 percent of its domestic work force, despite the difficult and expensive legal procedures required to import an alien.

Freedom of Enterprise

In recent congressional testimony, Ira Rubenstein, a Microsoft attorney, declared that immigration bars could jeopardize the 58 percent of its revenue generated overseas, threaten American dominance of advanced "client-server" business applications, and render "stillborn" the information superhighway. In particular, Corning and other producers of fiber-optic technology have faced a severe shortage of native engineers equipped to pursue this specialty crucial to both telecommunications and medical instruments.

With U.S. high school students increasingly shunning mathemat- 15 ics and the hard sciences, America is the global technology and economic leader in spite of, not because of, any properties of the American gene pool or dominant culture. America prevails only because it offers the freedom of enterprise and innovation to people from around the world.

A decision to cut back legal immigration today, as Congress is contemplating, is a decision to wreck the key element of the American technological miracle. After botching the issues of telecom deregulation and tax rate reduction, and wasting a year on Hooverian myths about the magic of a balanced budget, the Republican Congress now proposes to issue a deadly body blow to the intellectual heart of U.S. growth. Congress must not cripple the new Manhattan Projects of the U.S. economy in order to pursue some xenophobic and archaic dream of ethnic purity and autarky.

How about Home-Grown Geniuses?

MARK KRIKORIAN, NORMAN MATLOFF,
EDWARD SHUCK, JOHN KRUSTINS,
RICHARD J. JOHNSON, and MARK W. NOWAK

The move in Congress to rationalize our nation's Rube-Goldberg immigration policy, which Mr. Gilder tars as "some xenophobic and archaic dream of ethnic purity and autarky," would not, as he appears to think, cut the number of skills-tested immigrants. The bill approved by the Senate immigration subcommittee more than covers current demand for such visas, while the bill soon to be debated on the House floor actually increases the number of available visas.

Like other amateur opponents of a sustainable immigration policy, Mr. Gilder offers no solutions to the real problems we face in this area: millions of people on waiting lists, a large and growing education gap between natives and immigrants, a politicized and racialized visa lottery, a refugee system which admits few genuine refugees, and a political asylum policy which is metastasizing to cover virtually everyone on the planet. Perhaps instead of waxing poetic about the role of genius in economic growth, Mr. Gilder could have made some useful suggestions for managing these real problems.

Mark Krikorian
Executive Director
Center for Immigration Studies

Congress's concern is that many employers are hiring not "the best and the brightest," but rather the cheapest. The 1990 Census data show, for instance, that immigrant engineers in Silicon Valley are paid an average of $7,000 less than natives of the same age and education. Sun Microsystems, one of the companies cited by Mr. Gilder, has even boasted publicly that it hired Russian engineers "at bargain prices." Mr. Gilder's own numbers show that high levels of immigration are not needed by the high-tech sector: He says one-

These letters in response to George Gilder's "Geniuses from Abroad" appeared in the December 27, 1995, issue of the *Wall Street Journal.*

third of the technical work force in Silicon Valley is foreign-born, yet his corresponding figure is only 5 percent for Microsoft, the company he cites as the industry leader.

Norman Matloff

The sentimental hyperbole carved in stone on the Statue of Liberty when we were a nation of 50 million in need of a larger unskilled and semiskilled population to manage our vacant continent needs review. That we can use, and will continue to need and welcome, intelligent and properly motivated people from abroad for refreshment of our population is an axiom. That we can continue to be a dumping ground for Third World population surpluses who are lacking in skills and motivation to contribute to the American technological society is questionable.

Edward Shuck

Mr. Gilder pronounces that immigration control will "wreck the key element of the American technological miracle." The technical geniuses he is talking about are a drop in the bucket of the total immigration picture. They will always be able to come here if we need them. Instead we are flooding areas of the country with millions of uneducated immigrants who then take over, impose their culture, and don't even try to assimilate. Witness bilingualism and multiculturalism.

John Krustins

Gilderians believe in the dogma of "Universal Man." That dogma proposes that when products, capital and humanity are free to flow to circumstances of advantage, the world will achieve higher levels of prosperity. Universal Man will stand astride the world propelling mankind to wondrous destinies. This is blatant materialism. Gilderians never entertain the possibility that people function from motives other than economic.

If immigration is so valuable, then surely Mr. Gilder would not hesitate to permit 300,000,000 Hindus (or Chinese, Africans, etc.) to become immigrants to America. For this would of course change America into a Hindi-speaking Hindu nation resembling Bombay more than Boston. In democracies, demography is political destiny, and America would no longer be a Western nation. The Gilders of the world apparently don't care.

Richard J. Johnson

The overwhelming majority of immigrants arrive solely because one or more family members are already here, regardless of whether they possess any marketable skills or promise of genius. In fact, of the 804,000 immigrants in 1994, only 140,000 arrived under employment provisions, and of those, about half were family members of the skilled individual.

The result: a flooded unskilled labor market. In fact, immigration economist George Borjas estimates that our current immigration policy results in wage depression and job displacement costs to U.S. workers of $133 billion a year. Foreign-born skilled workers have contributed to this declining wage, as well. Labor Department statistics reveal that foreign-born workers are generally paid less than comparably skilled native-born, revealing the real reason companies like Microsoft have been railing against proposed changes in immigration law that would make it more expensive to hire immigrants.

Mr. Gilder's "genius requirement" would be more effectively met 10 through targeted skill requirements and dramatically reduced immigration than through the current de facto human lottery he advocates.

Mark W. Nowak
Executive Director
Population-Environment Balance

THINKING AND WRITING ABOUT IMMIGRATION

1. To what extent should immigrants be expected to assimilate into the majority culture — by learning English, attending public schools, adopting the cultural practices of mainstream groups? Be specific in pointing out the degree of acculturation that you think desirable, and explain why it is desirable. If possible, use examples of your own experiences with immigrants.

2. How does Gilder support his claim that immigrants are necessary to America's technological dominance? What are the most effective forms of support? To what extent do the authors of the letters refute his claim? Be specific.

3. What does Brimelow mean by "The country is coming apart ethnically under the impact of the enormous influx" (paragraph 5)? What do other authors say about this possibility?

4. The Welds offer the most comprehensive argument in favor of immigration. List the "facts" that they refute. Do they respond to all the objections of Brimelow, Huddle, Coleman, and in the letters to the *Wall Street Journal?*

5. Summarize the issues in the debate over illegal immigration as expounded by Raspberry, Jordan, and Huddle.

6. Coleman's argument is more subjective in its approach than any of the other articles. Does this increase or decrease its effectiveness? Do you think there is any way of resolving the differences spelled out in this article?

7. The writers in this section make appeals to our heads and to our hearts. Describe briefly the two kinds of appeals (although there is overlap) and point out where they appear. Explain why you do or do not find one more effective than the other in supporting your own view of immigration policy.

8. Both the cartoon on page 534 and the article by the Welds make reference to lines from a famous poem by Emma Lazarus written in 1886 and

later inscribed at the base of the Statue of Liberty. These are the oft-repeated lines with which you may be familiar:

Give me your tired, your poor,
Your huddled masses yearning to breathe free,
The wretched refuse of your teeming shore.
Send these, the homeless, tempest-tost to me,
I lift my lamp beside the golden door!

Explain the cartoonist's reinterpretation of the poem.

Topics for Research

Cultural contributions by an immigrant group

An immigrant's story in my family history

History of an immigrant group in a selected community

Comparing and contrasting immigration in the early 1900s and the early 1980s

Immigration laws in the 1990s, state and/or federal

Chapter Sixteen

Punishment

When crime (or the perception of crime) mounts in the United States, the demand for punishment also increases. But even advocates of punishment disagree about both the goals and the kinds of punishment most likely to be fair and effective.

One view holds that the goal of punishment is rehabilitation or the return of the criminal to productive activity. Another sees the goal as retribution, a payment exacted from the criminal by an outraged society. Still another may regard punishment primarily as a deterrent, removing the criminal from activity and serving as a caution to would-be criminals. These goals are not, of course, necessarily exclusive of one another.

In recent years doubts about the success of rehabilitation and fear of revolving-door justice have resulted in support for changes in the criminal justice system. The demands for capital punishment — thirty-eight federal crimes are now punishable by death — more prisons, longer prison terms, tougher parole, trials of juveniles as adults, even the reappearance of chain gangs in at least three states, testify to the widespread belief that only harsher punishment can reduce the incidence of crime.

As a society we accept limits. These are broadly defined in the Eighth Amendment to the Constitution, which prohibits "cruel and unusual punishment." But a completely satisfactory definition of such punishment would be hard to find. The caning of Michael Fay, an eighteen-year-old American living in Singapore who was convicted of minor vandalism, occasioned a heated debate in this country between those who approved of the punishment and those who considered it barbarous.

Among those involved in the actual administration of criminal justice, including prison wardens and other correctional officials, a growing minority has begun to question the effectiveness of incarceration for nonviolent offenders. Some judges have introduced innovative penalties like public shaming — mandating a public show of remorse or posting the name of a criminal in a public place available to neighbors. But the questions to be asked about all punishments are the same. In the words of the well-known criminologist James Q. Wilson, "Is it useful? Is it just? Or is it only cruel?"

In a book first published in 1764 and considered to be the foundation of modern criminology, Italian philosopher Cesare Beccaria laid out the principles that ought to govern the administration of punishment:

> A punishment may not be an act of violence, of one, or of many against a private member of society; it should be public, immediate and necessary; the least possible in the case given; proportioned to the crime and determined by the laws.[1]

Therapy, Not Punishment

KARL MENNINGER

Since ancient times criminal law and penology have been based upon what is called in psychology the pain-pleasure principle. There are many reasons for inflicting pain — to urge an animal to greater efforts, to retaliate for pain received, to frighten, or to indulge in idle amusement. Human beings, like all animals, tend to move away from pain and toward pleasure. Hence the way to control behavior is to reward what is "good" and punish what is "bad." This formula pervades our programs of childrearing, education, and social control of behavior.

With this concept three out of four readers will no doubt concur.

"Why, of course," they will say. "Only common sense. Take me for example. I know the speed limit and the penalty. Usually I drive moderately because I don't want to get a ticket. One afternoon I was in a hurry; I had an appointment, I didn't heed the signs. I did what I knew was forbidden and I got caught and received the punishment I

---

[1] Cesare Beccaria, *An Essay in Crimes and Punishment,* London, 1770.

Karl Menninger (1893–1990) was a clinical professor of psychiatry at the University of Kansas and cofounder of the Menninger Foundation for Psychiatric Education and Research. This essay, originally titled "Verdict Guilty — Now What?," first appeared in *Harper's Magazine,* August 1959.

deserved. Fair enough. It taught me a lesson. Since then I drive more slowly in that area. And surely people are deterred from cheating on their income taxes, robbing banks, and committing rape by the fear of punishment. Why, if we didn't have these crime road blocks we'd have chaos!"

This sounds reasonable enough and describes what most people think — *part of the time.* But upon reflection we all know that punishments and the threat of punishments do *not* deter *some* people from doing forbidden things. Some of them take a chance on not being caught, and this chance is a very good one, too, better than five to one for most crimes. Not even the fear of possible death, self-inflicted, deters some speedsters. Exceeding the speed limit is not really regarded as criminal behavior by most people, no matter how dangerous and self-destructive. It is the kind of a "crime" which respectable members of society commit and condone. This is not the case with rape, bank-robbing, check-forging, vandalism, and the multitude of offenses for which the prison penalty system primarily exists. And from these offenses the average citizen, including the reader, is deterred by quite different restraints. For most of us it is our conscience, our self-respect, and our wish for the good opinion of our neighbors which are the determining factors in controlling our impulses toward misbehavior.

Today it is no secret that our official, prison-threat theory of 5 crime control is an utter failure. Criminologists have known this for years. When pocket-picking was punishable by hanging, in England, the crowds that gathered about the gallows to enjoy the spectacle of an execution were particularly likely to have their pockets picked by skillful operators who, to say the least, were not deterred by the exhibition of "justice." We have long known that the perpetrators of most offenses are never detected; of those detected, only a fraction are found guilty and still fewer serve a "sentence." Furthermore, we are quite certain now that of those who do receive the official punishment of the law, many become firmly committed thereby to a continuing life of crime and a continuing feud with law enforcement officers. Finding themselves ostracized from society and blacklisted by industry, they stick with the crowd they have been introduced to in jail and try to play the game of life according to this set of rules. In this way society skillfully converts individuals of borderline self-control into loyal members of the underground fraternity.

The science of human behavior has gone far beyond the common-sense rubrics which dictated the early legal statutes. We know now that one cannot describe rape or bank-robbing or income-tax fraud simply as pleasure. Nor, on the other hand, can we describe imprisonment merely as pain. Slapping the hand of a beloved child as he reaches to do a forbidden act is utterly different from the institutionalized process of official punishment. The offenders who are chucked into our county and state and federal prisons are not anyone's beloved children; they are usually unloved children, grown-up physically but still hungry for human concern which they never got or never get in normal ways. So they pursue it in abnormal ways — abnormal, that is, from *our* standpoint.

Why Our Crime Therapy Has Failed

What might deter the reader from conduct which his neighbors would not like does not necessarily deter the grown-up child of vastly different background. The latter's experiences may have conditioned him to believe that the chances of winning by undetected cheating are vastly greater than the probabilities of fair treatment and opportunity. He knows about the official threats and the social disapproval of such acts. He knows about the hazards and the risks. But despite all this "knowledge," he becomes involved in waves of discouragement or cupidity or excitement or resentment leading to episodes of social offensiveness.

These episodes may prove vastly expensive both to him and to society. But sometimes they will have an aura of success. Our periodicals have only recently described the wealth and prominence for a time of a man described as a murderer. Konrad Lorenz, the great psychiatrist and animal psychologist, has beautifully described in geese what he calls a "triumph reaction." It is sticking out of the chest and flapping of the wings after an encounter with a challenge. All of us have seen this primitive biological triumph reaction — in some roosters, for example, in some businessmen and athletes and others — *and* in some criminals.

In general, though, the gains and goals of the social offender are not those which most men seek. Most offenders whom we belabor are not very wise, not very smart, not even very "lucky." It is not the successful criminal upon whom we inflict our antiquated penal system. It is the unsuccessful criminal, the criminal who really doesn't know how to commit crimes, and who gets caught. Indeed, until he is caught and convicted a man is technically not even called a criminal. The clumsy, the desperate, the obscure, the friendless, the defective, the diseased — these men who commit crimes that do not come off — are bad actors, indeed. But they are not the professional criminals, many of whom occupy high places. In some instances the crime is the merest accident or incident or impulse, expressed under unbearable stress. More often the offender is a persistently perverse, lonely, and resentful individual who joins the only group to which he is eligible — the outcasts and the antisocial.

And what do we do with such offenders? After a solemn public ceremony we pronounce them enemies of the people, and consign them for arbitrary periods to institutional confinement on the basis 10 of laws written many years ago. Here they languish until time has ground out so many weary months and years. Then with a planlessness and stupidity only surpassed by that of their original incarceration they are dumped back upon society, regardless of whether any change has taken place in them for the better and with every assurance that changes have taken place in them for the worse. Once more they enter the unequal tussle with society. Proscribed for employment by most concerns, they are expected to invent a new way to make a living to survive without any further help from society.

Intelligent members of society are well aware that the present system is antiquated, expensive, and disappointing, and that we are wasting vast quantities of manpower through primitive methods of dealing with those who transgress the law. In 1917 the famous Wickersham report of the New York State Prison Survey Committee recommended the abolition of jails, the institution of diagnostic clearing houses or classification centers, the development of a diversified institutional system and treatment program, and the use of indeterminate sentences. *Forty-two years have passed.* How little progress we have made! In 1933 the American Psychiatric Association, the American Bar Association, and the American Medical Association officially and jointly recommended psychiatric service for every criminal and juvenile court to assist the court and prison and parole officers with all offenders.

That was twenty-six years ago! Have these recommendations been carried out anywhere in the United States? With few exceptions offenders continue to be dealt with according to old-time instructions, written by men now dead who knew nothing about the present offender, his past life, the misunderstandings accumulated by him, or the provocation given to him.

The sensible, scientific question is: What kind of treatment could be instituted that would deter him or be most likely to deter him? Some of these methods are well known. For some offenders who have the money or the skillful legal counsel or the good luck to face a wise judge go a different route from the prescribed routine. Instead of jail and deterioration, they get the sort of reeducation and redirection associated with psychiatric institutions and the psychiatric profession. Relatively few wealthy offenders get their "treatment" in jail. This does not mean that justice is to be bought, or bought off. But it does mean that some offenders have relatives and friends who *care* and who try to find the best possible solution to the problem of persistent misbehavior, which is NOT the good old jail-and-penitentiary and make-'em-sorry treatment. It is a reflection on the democratic ideals of our country that these better ways are so often — indeed, *usually* — denied to the poor, the friendless, and the ignorant.

Science versus Tradition

If we were to follow scientific methods, the convicted offender would be detained indefinitely pending a decision as to whether and how and when to reintroduce him successfully into society. All the skill and knowledge of modern behavioral science would be used to examine his personality assets, his liabilities and potentialities, the environment from which he came, its effects upon him, and his effects upon it.

Having arrived at some diagnostic grasp of the offender's personality, those in charge can decide whether there is a chance that he can be redirected into a mutually satisfactory adaptation to the world. If so, the most suitable techniques in education, industrial training, group administration, and psychotherapy should be selectively applied. All this may be best done extramurally or intramurally. It may require maximum "security" or only minimum "security." If, in due time, perceptible change occurs, the process should be expedited by finding a suitable spot in society and industry for him, and getting him out of prison control and into civil status (with parole control) as quickly as possible.

The desirability of moving patients out of institutional control swiftly is something which we psychiatrists learned the hard way, and recently. Ten years ago, in the state hospital I know best, the average length of stay was five years; today it is three months. Ten years ago few patients were discharged in under two years; today 90 percent are discharged within the first year. Ten years ago the hospital was overcrowded; today it has eight times the turnover it used to have; there are empty beds and there is no waiting list.

But some patients do not respond to our efforts, and they have to remain in the hospital, or return to it promptly after a trial home visit. And if the *prisoner*, like some of the psychiatric patients, cannot be changed by genuine efforts to rehabilitate him, we must look *our* failure in the face, and provide for his indefinitely continued confinement, regardless of the technical reasons for it. This we owe society for its protection.

There will be some offenders about whom the most experienced are mistaken, both ways. And there will be some concerning whom no one knows what is best. There are many problems for research. But what I have outlined is, I believe, the program of modern penology, the program now being carried out in some degree in California and a few other states, and in some of the federal prisons.

This civilized program, which would save so much now wasted money, so much unused manpower, and so much injustice and suffering, is slow to spread. It is held back by many things — by the continued use of fixed sentences in many places; by unenlightened community attitudes toward the offender whom some want tortured; by the prevalent popular assumption that burying a frustrated individual in a hole for a short time will change his warped mind, and that when he is certainly worse, he should be released because his "time" has been served; by the persistent failure of the law to distinguish between crime as an accidental, incidental, explosive event, crime as a behavior pattern expressive of chronic unutterable rage and frustration, and crime as a business or elected way of life. Progress is further handicapped by the lack of interest in the subject on the part of lawyers, most of whom are proud to say that they are not concerned with criminal law. It is handicapped by the lack of interest on the part of members of my own profession. It is handicapped by the mutual distrust of lawyers and psychiatrists.

The infestation or devil-possession theory of mental disease is 20 an outmoded, premedieval concept. Although largely abandoned by psychiatry, it steadfastly persists in the minds of many laymen, including, unfortunately, many lawyers.

On the other hand, most lawyers have no really clear idea of the way in which a psychiatrist functions or of the basic concepts to which he adheres. They cannot understand, for example, why there is no such thing (for psychiatrists) as "insanity." Most lawyers have no conception of the meaning or methods of psychiatric case study and diagnosis. They seem to think that psychiatrists can take a quick look at a suspect, listen to a few anecdotes about him, and thereupon be able to say, definitely, that the awful "it"— the dreadful miasma of madness, the loathsome affliction of "insanity"— is present or absent. Because we all like to please, some timid psychiatrists fall in with this fallacy of the lawyers and go through these preposterous antics.

As the Psychiatrist Sees It

It is true that almost any offender — like anyone else — when questioned for a short time, even by the most skillful psychiatrist, can make responses and display behavior patterns which will indicate that he is enough like the rest of us to be called "sane." But a barrage of questions is not a psychiatric examination. Modern scientific personality study depends upon various specialists — physical, clinical, and sociological as well as psychological. It takes into consideration not only static and presently observable factors, but dynamic and historical factors, and factors of environmental interaction and change. It also looks into the future for correction, reeducation, and prevention.

Hence, the same individuals who appear so normal to superficial observation are frequently discovered in the course of prolonged, intensive scientific study to have tendencies regarded as "deviant," "peculiar," "unhealthy," "sick," "crazy," "senseless," "irrational," "insane."

But now you may ask, "Is it not possible to find such tendencies in any individual if one looks hard enough? And if this is so, if we are all a little crazy or potentially so, what is the essence of your psychiatric distinctions? Who is it that you want excused?"

And here is the crux of it all. We psychiatrists don't want *anyone*   25
excused. In fact, psychiatrists are much more concerned about the protection of the public than are the lawyers. I repeat; psychiatrists don't want anyone excused, certainly not anyone who shows antisocial tendencies. We consider them all responsible, which lawyers do not. And we want the prisoner to take on that responsibility, or else deliver it to someone who will be concerned about the protection of society and about the prisoner, too. We don't want anyone excused, but neither do we want anyone stupidly disposed of, futilely detained, or prematurely released. We don't want them tortured, either sensationally with hot irons or quietly by long-continued and forced idleness. In the psychiatrist's mind nothing should be done in the name of punishment, though he is well aware that the offender may regard either the diagnostic procedure or the treatment or the detention incident to the treatment as punitive. But this is in *his* mind, not in the psychiatrist's mind. And in our opinion it should not be in the public's mind, because it is an illusion.

It is true that we psychiatrists consider that all people have potentialities for antisocial behavior. The law assumes this, too. Most of the time most people control their criminal impulses. But for various reasons and under all kinds of circumstances some individuals become increasingly disorganized or demoralized, and then they begin to be socially offensive. The man who does criminal things is less convincingly disorganized than the patient who "looks" sick, because the former more nearly resembles the rest of us, and seems to be indulging in acts that we have struggled with and controlled. So we get hot under the collar about the one and we call him "criminal" whereas we pityingly forgive the other and call him "lunatic." But a surgeon uses the same principles of surgery whether he is dealing with a "clean" case, say some cosmetic surgery on a face, or a "dirty" case which is foul-smelling and offensive. What we are after is results and the emotions of the operator must be under control. Words like "criminal" and "insane" have no place in the scientific vocabulary any more than pejorative adjectives like "vicious," "psychopathic," "bloodthirsty," etc. The need is to find all the *descriptive* adjectives that apply to the case, and this is a scientific job — not a popular exercise in name-calling. Nobody's insides are very beautiful; and in the cases that require social control there has been a great wound and some of the insides are showing.

Intelligent judges all over the country are increasingly surrendering the onerous responsibility of deciding in advance what a man's conduct will be in a prison and how rapidly his wicked impulses will evaporate there. With more use of the indeterminate sentence and the establishment of scientific diagnostic centers, we shall be in a position to make progress in the science of *treating* antisocial trends. Furthermore, we shall get away from the present legal smog that hangs over the prisons, which lets us detain with heartbreaking futility some prisoners fully rehabilitated while others, whom the prison officials know full well to be dangerous and unemployable, must be released, *against our judgment,* because a judge far away (who has by this time forgotten all about it) said that five years was enough. In my frequent visits to prisons I am always astonished at how rarely the judges who have prescribed the "treatment" come to see whether or not it is effective. What if doctors who sent their seriously ill patients to hospitals never called to see them!

The End of Taboo

As more states adopt diagnostic centers directed toward getting the prisoners *out* of jail and back to work, under modern, well-structured parole systems, the taboo on jail and prison, like that on state hospitals, will begin to diminish. Once it was a lifelong disgrace to have been in either. Lunatics, as they were cruelly called, were feared and avoided. Today only the ignorant retain this phobia. Cancer was then considered a *shameful* thing to have, and victims of it were afraid to mention it, or have it correctly treated, because they did not want to be disgraced. The time will come when offenders, much as we disapprove of their offenses, will no longer be unemployable untouchables.

To a physician discussing the wiser treatment of our fellow men it seems hardly necessary to add that under no circumstances should we kill them. It was never considered right for doctors to kill their patients, no matter how hopeless their condition. True, some patients in state institutions have undoubtedly been executed without benefit of sentence. They were a nuisance, expensive to keep and dangerous to release. Various people took it upon themselves to put an end to the matter, and I have even heard them boast of it. The Hitler regime had the same philosophy.

But in most civilized countries today we have a higher opinion 30 of the rights of the individual and of the limits to the state's power. We know, too, that for the most part the death penalty is inflicted upon obscure, impoverished, defective, and friendless individuals. . . .

Capital punishment is, in my opinion, morally wrong. It has a bad effect on everyone, especially those involved in it. It gives a false sense of security to the public. It is vastly expensive. Worst of all it beclouds the entire issue of motivation in crime, which is so importantly relevant to the question of what to do for and with the criminal that will be most constructive to society as a whole. Punishing — and even killing — criminals may yield a kind of grim gratification; let us all admit that there are times when we are so shocked at the depredations of an offender that we persuade ourselves that this is a man the Creator didn't intend to create, and that we had better help correct the mistake. But playing God in this way has no conceivable moral or scientific justification.

Let us return in conclusion to the initial question: "Verdict guilty — now what?" My answer is that now we, the designated representatives of the society which has failed to integrate this man, which has failed him in some way, hurt him and been hurt by him, should take over. It is *our* move. And our move must be a constructive one, an intelligent one, a purposeful one — not a primitive, retaliatory, offensive move. We, the agents of society, must move to end the game of tit-for-tat and blow-for-blow in which the offender has foolishly and futilely engaged himself and us. We are not driven, as he is, to wild and impulsive actions. With knowledge comes power, and with power there is no need for the frightened vengeance of the old penology. In its place should go a quiet, dignified, therapeutic program for the rehabilitation of the disorganized one, if possible, the protection of society during his treatment period, and his guided return to useful citizenship, as soon as this can be effected.

Punishment v. Rehabilitation

RICHARD WASSERSTROM

There is a view, held most prominently but by no means exclusively by persons in psychiatry, that we ought never punish persons who break the law and that we ought instead to do something much more like what we do when we treat someone who has a disease. According to this view, what we ought to do to all such persons is to do our best to bring it about that they can and will function in a satisfactory way within society. The functional equivalent to the treatment of a disease is the rehabilitation of an offender, and it is a rehabilitative system, not a punishment system, that we ought to have if we are to respond, even to criminals, in anything like a decent, morally defensible fashion.

Karl Menninger has put the proposal this way:

Richard Wasserstrom, who retired in 1994, was a professor of philosophy at the University of California at Santa Cruz. This selection is from *Philosophy and Social Issues: Five Studies* (1980).

If we were to follow scientific methods, the convicted offender would be detained indefinitely pending a decision as to whether and how to reintroduce him successfully into society. All the skill and knowledge of modern behavior science would be used to examine his personality assets, his liabilities and potentialities, the environment from which he came, its effects upon him, and his effects upon it.

Having arrived at some diagnostic grasp of the offender's personality, those in charge can decide whether there is a chance that he can be redirected into a mutually satisfactory adaptation to the world. If so, the most suitable techniques in education, industrial training, group administration, and psychotherapy should be selectively applied. All this may be best done extramurally or intramurally. It may require maximum "security" or only minimum "security." If, in due time, perceptible change occurs, the process should be expedited by finding a suitable spot in society and industry for him, and getting him out of prison control and into civil status (with parole control) as quickly as possible.[1]

It is important at the outset to see that there are two very different arguments which might underlie the claim that the functional equivalent of a system of treatment is desirable and in fact always ought to be preferred to a system of punishment.

The first argument fixes upon the desirability of such a system over one of punishment in virtue of the fact that, because no offenders are responsible for their actions, no offenders are ever justifiably punished. The second argument is directed toward establishing that such a system is better than one of punishment even if some or all offenders are responsible for their actions. A good deal of the confusion present in discussion of the virtues of a system of treatment results from a failure to get clear about these two arguments and to keep the two separate. The first is superficially the more attractive and ultimately the less plausible of the two. Each, though, requires its own explication and analysis.

One way in which the first argument often gets stated is in terms 5 of the sickness of offenders. It is, so the argument begins, surely wrong to punish someone for something that he or she could not help, for something for which he or she was not responsible. No one can help being sick. No one ought, therefore, ever be punished for being sick. As the Supreme Court has observed: "Even one day in prison would be cruel and unusual punishment for the 'crime' of having a common cold."[2] Now, it happens to be the case that everyone who commits a crime is sick. Hence, it is surely wrong to punish anyone who commits a crime. What is more, when a response is appropriate, the appropriate response to sickness is treatment. For

---

[1]Menninger, "Therapy, Not Punishment," reprinted in Murphy (ed.), *Punishment and Rehabilitation* (Belmont, Calif.: Wadsworth Publishing Co., 1973), p. 136.

[2]*Robinson v. California,* 370 U.S. 660 (1962).

this reason what we ought to do is to treat offenders, not punish them.

One difficulty with this argument is that the relevance of sickness to the rightness or wrongness of the punishment of offenders is anything but obvious. Indeed, it appears that the conclusion depends upon a non sequitur just because we seldom, if ever, seek to punish people for being sick. Instead we punish them for actions they perform. On the surface, at least, it would seem that even if someone is sick, and even if the person cannot help being sick, this in no way implies that none of his or her actions could have been other than what it was. Thus, if the argument against ever punishing the guilty criminal is to be at all persuasive, it must be shown that for one reason or another, the sickness which afflicts all criminals must affect their actions in such a way that they are thereby prevented ever from acting differently. Construed in this fashion, the argument is at least coherent and responsive. Unfortunately, there is now no reason to be persuaded by it.

It might be persuasive were there any reason to believe that all criminal acts were, for example, instances of compulsive behavior; if, that is, we thought it likely to be true that all criminals were in some obvious and distinguishable sense afflicted by or subjected to irresistible impulses which compelled them to break the law. For there are people who do seem to be subjected to irresistible impulses and who are thereby unable to keep themselves from, among other things, committing crimes. And it is surely troublesome if not clearly wrong to punish them for these actions. Thus, the kleptomaniac or the person who is truly already addicted to narcotics does seem to be suffering from something resembling a sickness and, moreover, to be suffering from something which makes it very difficult if not impossible for such a person to control the actions so compelled. Pity not blame seems appropriate, as does treatment rather than punishment.[3]

Now, the notion of compulsive behavior is not without difficulties of its own. How strong, for instance, does a compulsion have to be before it cannot be resisted? Would someone be a kleptomaniac only if such an individual would steal an object even though a policeman were known by the person to be present and observing every move? Is there anything more that is meant by compulsive behavior than the fact that it is behavior which is inexplicable or unaccountable in terms of the motives and purposes people generally have? More importantly, perhaps, why do we and why should we suppose that the apparently "motiveless" behavior must be the

---

[3] The Supreme Court has worried about this problem in, for example, the case of chronic alcoholism, in *Powell v. Texas,* 392 U.S. 514 (1968). The discussion in this and related cases is neither very clear nor very illuminating.

product of compulsions which are less resistible than those to which we all are at times subjected? As has been observed, " . . . it is by no means self-evident that [a wealthy] person's yearnings for valueless [items] are inevitably stronger or more nearly irresistible than the poor man's hunger for a square meal or for a pack of cigarettes."[4]

But while there are problems such as these, the more basic one is simply that there is no reason to believe that all criminal acts are instances of compulsive behavior. Even if there are persons who are victims of irresistible impulses, and even if we ought always to treat and never to punish such persons, it surely does not follow that everyone who commits a crime is doing a compulsive act. And because this is so, it cannot be claimed that all criminals ought to be exempted from punishment — treated instead — because they have a sickness of this sort.

It might be argued, though, that while compulsive behavior accounts only for some criminal acts, there are other sicknesses which account for the remainder. At this juncture the most ready candidate to absorb the remaining cases is that of insanity. The law, for example, has always been willing to concede that a person ought never be punished if the person was so sick or so constituted that he or she did not know the nature or quality of the act, or if this were known, that the person did not know that the act was wrong. And more recently, attempts have been made, sometimes successfully, to expand this exemption to include any person whose criminal action was substantially the product of mental defect or disease.[5]

Once again, though, the crucial point is not the formulation of the most appropriate test for insanity, but the fact that it is far from evident, even under the most "liberal" test imaginable, that it would be true that everyone who commits a crime would be found to be sick and would be found to have been afflicted with a sickness which in some sense rendered the action in question unavoidable. Given all of our present knowledge, there is simply every reason to suppose that some of the people who do commit crimes are neither subject to irresistible impulses, incapable of knowing what they are doing, nor suffering from some other definite mental disease. And, if this is so, then it is a mistake to suppose that the treatment of criminals is on this ground always to be preferred to their punishment.

There is, though, one final version of the claim that every criminal action is excusable on grounds of the sickness of the actor. And

---

[4] Barbara Wootton, *Social Science and Social Pathology* (London: G. Allen & Unwin, 1959), p. 235.

[5] See, e.g., *Durham v. United States,* 214 F. 2d 862 (D.C. Cir., 1954); *United States v. Brawner,* 471 F. 2d 969 (D.C. Cir., 1972); and Model Penal Code § 4.01.

this version does succeed in bringing all the remaining instances of criminality, not otherwise excusable, within the category of sickness. It does so only by making the defining characteristic or symptom of mental illness the commission of an illegal act. All criminals, so this argument goes, who are not insane or subject to irresistible impulses are sociopaths — people afflicted with that mental illness which manifests itself exclusively through the commission of antisocial acts. This sickness, like any other sickness, should be treated rather than punished.

Once this stage of the discussion is reached, it is important to be aware of what has happened. In particular, there is no longer the evidentiary claim that all criminal acts are caused by some sickness. Instead there is the bare assertion that this must be so — an assertion, moreover, of a somewhat deceptive character. The illness which afflicts these criminals *is simply* the criminal behavior itself. The disease which is the reason for not punishing the action is identical with the action itself. At this point any attempt to substantiate or disprove the existence of a relationship between sickness and crime is ruled out of order. The presence of mental illnesses of these kinds cannot, therefore, be reasons for not punishing, or for anything else.

Thus, even if it is true that we ought never to punish and that we ought always to treat someone whose criminal action was unavoidable because the product of some mental or physical disease — even if we concede all this — it has yet to be demonstrated, without begging the question, that all persons who commit crimes are afflicted with some disease or sickness of this kind. And, therefore, if it is always wrong to punish people, or if it is always preferable to treat them, then an argument of a different sort must be forthcoming.

In general form that different argument is this: The legal system 15 ought to abandon its attempts to assess responsibility and punish offenders and it ought instead to focus solely on the question of how most appropriately the legal system can deal with, that is, rehabilitate if possible, the person presently before the court — not, however, because everyone is sick, but because no good comes from punishing even those who are responsible.

One such proponent of this view is Lady Barbara Wootton.[6] Her position is an ostensibly simple one. What she calls for is the "elimination" of responsibility. The state of mind, or *mens rea,* of the actor at the time he or she committed the act in question is no longer to be determinative — in the way it now is — of how he or she shall be dealt with by society. Rather, she asserts, when some-

---

[6] Barbara Wootton, *Crime and the Criminal Law* (London: Stevens, 1963).

one has been accused of violating the law we ought to have a social mechanism that will ask and answer two distinct questions: Did the accused in fact do the act in question? If he or she did, given all that we know about this person (including his or her state of mind), what is the appropriate form of social response to him or her?

Lady Wootton's proposal is for a system of social control that is thoroughly forward-looking, and in this sense, rehabilitative in perspective. With the elimination of responsibility comes the elimination of the need by the legal system to distinguish any longer between wickedness and disease. And with the eradication of this distinction comes the substitution of a forward-looking, treatment system for the backward-looking, punitive system of criminal law.

The mental state or condition of the offender will continue to be important but in a different way. "Such conditions . . . become relevant, not to the question of determining the measure of culpability but to the choice of the treatment most likely to be effective in discouraging him from offending again. . . ."[7]

> One of the most important consequences must be to obscure the present rigid distinction between the penal and the medical institution. . . . For purposes of convenience offenders for whom medical treatment is indicated will doubtless tend to be allocated to one building, and those for whom medicine has nothing to offer to another; but *the formal distinction between prison and hospital will become blurred, and, one may reasonably expect, eventually obliterated altogether. Both will be simply "places of safety" in which offenders receive the treatment which experience suggests is most likely to evoke the desired response.*[8]

Thus, on this view even if a person was responsible when he or she acted and blameworthy for having so acted, we still ought to behave toward him or her in roughly the same way that we behave toward someone who is sick — we ought, in other words, to do something very much like treating him or her. Why? Because this just makes more sense than punishment. The fact that he or she was responsible is simply not very relevant. It is wrong of course to punish people who are sick; but even with those who are well, the more humane and civilized approach is one that concerns itself solely with the question of how best to effect the most rapid and complete rehabilitation or "cure" of the offender. The argument is not that no one is responsible or blameworthy; instead, it is that these descriptions are simply irrelevant to what, on moral grounds, ought to be the only significant considerations, namely, what mode of behavior toward the offender is most apt to maximize the likelihood that he or she will not in the future commit those obnoxious or dangerous

---

[7] Ibid., p. 77.
[8] Ibid., pp. 79–80 (emphasis added).

acts that are proscribed by the law. The only goal ought to be reha-bilitation (in this extended sense of "rehabilitation"), the only issue how to bring about the rehabilitation of the offender.

The moral good sense of this approach can be perceived most [20] clearly, so the argument goes on, when we contrast this thoroughly forward-looking point of view with punishment. For if there is one thing which serves to differentiate any form of punishment from that of treatment, it is that punishment necessarily permits the possibil-ity and even the desirability that punishment will be imposed upon an offender even though he or she is fully "cured"— even though there is no significant likelihood that he or she will behave improp-erly in the future. And, in every such case in which a person is pun-ished — in every case in which the infliction of the punishment will help the offender not at all (and may in fact harm him or her immea-surably) — the act of punishment is, on moral grounds, seriously of-fensive. Even if it were true that some of the people who commit crimes are responsible and blameworthy, and even if it were the case that we had meaningful techniques at our disposal for distin-guishing those who are responsible from those who are not — still, every time we inflict a punishment on someone who will not be ben-efited by it, we commit a seriously immoral act. This claim, or some-thing like it, lies, I think, at the base of the case which can be made against the punishment even of the guilty. For it is true that any sys-tem of punishment does require that some people will be made to suffer even though the suffering will help them not at all. It is this which the analogue to a system of treatment, a rehabilitative system such as Lady Wootton's, expressly prevents, and it is in virtue of this that such a system might be thought preferable.[9]

---

[9] There are some additional, more practical arguments that might be offered in support of such a proposal.

To begin with, by making irrelevant the question of whether the actor was re-sponsible when he or she acted, the operation of the criminal law could be greatly simplified. More specifically, by "eliminating" the issue of responsibility we thereby necessarily eliminate the requirement that the law continue to attempt to make those terribly difficult judgments of legal responsibility which our system of punishment re-quires to be made. And, as a practical matter, at least, this is no small consideration. For surely there is no area in which the techniques of legal adjudication have func-tioned less satisfactorily than in that of determining the actor's legal responsibility as of the time he violated the law. The attempts to formulate and articulate satisfactory and meaningful criteria of responsibility; the struggles to develop and then isolate specialists who can meaningfully and impartially relate these criteria to the relevant medical concepts and evidence; and the difficulties encountered in requiring the tra-ditional legal fact-finding mechanism — the jury — ultimately to resolve these issues — all of these bear impressive witness, it could plausibly be claimed, for the case for ceasing to make the effort.

In addition, it is no doubt fair to say that most people do not like to punish oth-ers. They may, indeed, have no objection to the punishment of others; but the actual task of inflicting and overseeing the infliction of an organized set of punishments is

There are, I think, both practical and theoretical objections to a proposal such as this. The practical objections concern, first, the possibility that certain "effective" treatments may themselves be morally objectionable, and, second, the possibility that this way of viewing offenders may create a world in which we all become indifferent to the characteristics that distinguish those who are responsible from those who are not. The ease, for example, with which someone like Menninger tends to see the criminal not as an adult but as a "grown-up child"[10] says something about the ease with which a kind of paternalistic manipulativeness could readily pervade a system composed of "places of safety."[11]

These are, though, contingent rather than necessary worries. A system organized in accordance with this rehabilitative ideal could have a view that certain therapies were impermissible on moral grounds, just as it could also treat all of the persons involved with all of the respect they deserved as persons. Indeed, it is important when comparing and contrasting proposals for rehabilitative systems with punishment to make certain that the comparisons are of things that are comparable. There are abuses present in most if not all institutional therapeutic systems in existence today, but there are also abuses present in most if not all institutional penal systems in existence today. And the practical likelihood of the different abuses is certainly worth taking seriously in trying to evaluate the alternatives. What is not appropriate, however, is to contrast either an ideal of the sort proposed by Wootton or Menninger with an existing penal one, or an ideal, just penal system with an existing therapeutic one.[12]

---

distasteful to most. It is all too easy, therefore, and all too typical, for society to entrust the administration of punishments to those who, if they do not actually enjoy it, at least do not find it unpleasant. Just as there is no necessary reason for punishments ever to be needlessly severe, so there is no necessary reason for those who are charged with the duty of punishing to be brutal or unkind. Nonetheless, it is simply a fact that it is difficult, if not impossible, to attract sensitive, kindly or compassionate persons to assume this charge. No such analogous problem, it might be argued, attends the call for treatment.

[10] "What might deter the reader from conduct which his neighbors would not like does not necessarily deter the grown-up child of vastly different background. . . .

"It is not the successful criminal upon whom we inflict our antiquated penal system. It is the unsuccessful criminal, the criminal who really doesn't know how to commit crimes, and who gets caught. . . . The clumsy, the desperate, the obscure, the friendless, the defective, the diseased — these men who commit crimes that do not come off — are bad actors, indeed. But they are not the professional criminals, many of whom occupy high places." Menninger, "Therapy, Not Punishment," supra note 1 [see p. 538 of this volume].

[11] These are discussed persuasively and in detail by Morris in his important article, "Persons and Punishment," *The Monist* 52 (1968): 476–490.

[12] I think that Morris at times indulges in an improper comparison of the two. Ibid.

These matters to one side, one of the chief theoretical objections to a proposal of the sort just described is that it ignores the whole question of general deterrence. Were we to have a system such as that envisioned by Lady Wootton or Menninger, we would ask one and only one question of each person who violated the law: What is the best, most efficacious thing to do to this individual to diminish substantially the likelihood that he or she will misbehave in this, or similar fashion, again? If there is nothing at all that need be done in order for us to be quite confident that he or she will not misbehave again (perhaps because the person is extremely contrite, or because we are convinced it was an impulsive, or otherwise unlikely-to-be-repeated act), then the logic of this system requires that the individual be released forthwith. For in this system it is the future conduct of the actor, and it alone, that is the only relevant consideration. There is simply no room within this way of thinking to take into account the achievement of general deterrence. H. L. A. Hart has put the matter this way in explaining why the *reform* (when any might be called for) of the prisoner cannot be the general justifying aim of a system of punishment.

> The objection of assigning to Reform this place in punishment is not merely that punishment entails suffering and reform does not; but that Reform is essentially a remedial step for which ex hypothesi there is an opportunity only at the point where the criminal law has failed in its primary task of securing society from the evil which breach of the law involves. Society is divisible at any moment into two classes: (i) those who have actually broken a given law and (ii) those who have not yet broken it but may. *To take Reform as the dominant objective would be to forgo the hope of influencing the second — and in relation to the more serious offenses — numerically much greater class. We should thus subordinate the prevention of first offenses to the prevention of recidivism.*[13]

A system of punishment will on this view find its justification in the fact that the announcement of penalties and their infliction upon those who break the laws induces others to obey the laws. The question why punish anyone at all *is* answered by Hart. We punish because we thereby deter potential offenders from becoming actual offenders. For Hart, the case for punishment as a general social practice or institution rests on the prevention of crime; it is not to be found either in the inherent appropriateness of punishing offenders or in the contingently "corrective" or rehabilitative powers of fines or imprisonments on some criminals.

Yet, despite appearances, the appeal to general deterrence is not as different as might be supposed from the appeal to a rehabili-

---

[13] H. L. A. Hart, *The Concept of Law* (Oxford: Clarendon Press, 1961), p. 181 (emphasis added).

tative ideal. In both cases, the justification for doing something (or nothing) to the offender rests upon the good consequences that will ensue. General deterrence just as much as rehabilitation views what should be done to offenders as a question of *social control*. It is a way of inducing those who can control their behavior to regulate it in such a way that it will conform to the dictates of the law. The disagreement with those who focus upon rehabilitation is only over the question of whose behavioral modification justifies the imposition of deprivations upon the criminals. Proponents of general deterrence say it is the modification of the behavior of the noncriminals that matters; proponents of rehabilitation say it is the modification of the behavior of the criminals that is decisive. Thus, a view such as Hart's is less a justification of punishment than of a system of threats of punishment. For if the rest of society could be convinced that offenders would be made to undergo deprivations that persons would not wish to undergo we would accomplish all that the deterrent theory would have us achieve through our somewhat more visible applications of these deprivations to offenders. This is so because it is the belief that punishment will follow the commission of an offense that deters potential offenders. The actual punishment of persons is on this view necessary in order to keep the threat of punishment credible. . . .

Justice Served or Medieval Sadism?

GREGORY P. HETTER and ALAN BUEL KENNADY

I was pleased to see an American, Jonathan Holburt, writing on your March 28 editorial page to defend the "Strong Arm of Singapore Law," in which "a young American who confessed to a ten-day spree of vandalism here has been sentenced to six strokes of the [bamboo] cane, a $1,400 fine, and four months in jail."

I have followed this story in the newspapers with progressively greater astonishment. Our State Department's charge d'affaires wastes America's good will and my tax dollars protesting the punishment of a young American vandal.

As America slides into social chaos at the hands of the lawyers, Singapore is an interesting lesson. In the span of the same fifty years that America has slipped into crime and disorder under an ever-

---

These letters appeared in the *Wall Street Journal* on April 12, 1994.

more incoherent set of legal manipulations that have deprived society of the right to protect itself, Singapore has risen from a seamy, corrupt seaport to an astonishingly productive, orderly multicultural society that lives in peace because of respect for and enforcement of high standards of civil behavior.

The lessons are clear. In America, the lawyers have control of the judiciary, the presidency, and the Congress. The hour is very late for America. Certainly no one in Washington seems aware, nor do the cultural radicals at the indoctrination centers which we still call universities.

I suspect if this vandal is caned it will turn out to be a seminal   5
moment in his life and may well save him from further destructive behavior. After having given Dr. Spock's teachings fifty years of trial and having seen the error, I feel we need to give caning a chance.

Gregory P. Hetter, M.D.

The apologia Mr. Holburt offered for Singapore's use of the rattan (a bamboo shaft) on a young American convicted of vandalism is casuistic in the extreme. He neglects to mention that the rattan is used for only three classes of offense: vandalism, murder, and rape.

No matter how traumatized a Singaporean may be to find his or her car spray-painted, no one who has not entirely lost touch with Western standards of justice would argue that vandalism is comparable to murder or rape, and merits a punishment normally accorded to these. In fact, the strokes of the rattan result in severe injury — it is no mere spanking. Anyone who has ever handled bamboo will know that, once snapped, it breaks into numerous longitudinal slats that splay when pressed against something and that pinch when retracted. Each stroke of the rattan will splay against the victim's buttocks, and with each recoil will lift off long, bloody strips of the victim's flesh. That is the reason the rattan is normally saved for murder and rape: After sixteen strokes (the maximum), the victim is not only scarred for life, but without prompt medical attention could die from shock or loss of blood.

I was in Singapore twice as a member of the U.S. Marines. We were all carefully briefed about this bizarre penalty when we took liberty there. And I have no sympathy for willful vandals. But this punishment is nothing less than a sadistic punishment that has no more place in the modern world than the Islamic practice of maiming thieves or the medieval European practice of frying religious and political dissidents on an enormous skillet. Indeed, Singapore uses the rattan as a punishment for vandalism, and equates it with murder or rape, primarily to suppress political dissent.

Alan Buel Kennady

Pain: The Forgotten Punishment

GRAEME NEWMAN

It is said that Brunelleschi, the great Italian artist, architect, and engineer of the Renaissance, had to reexamine Rome's Pantheon in order to learn how to build the great *Duomo* of Florence. The Pantheon was built in the second century A.D. Western Civilization had forgotten over a period of about one thousand years how to build a dome.

The same may be said of criminal punishment today. We have forgotten how to punish — although we are perhaps more fortunate in that our amnesia is only a couple of hundred years old.

If there is any doubt that we are in some kind of punishment crisis — perhaps confusion is a better word — the following examples, one from the everyday world of the criminal court, the other from the highest court in the land, easily illustrate the point.

In a park at Hillside Avenue and 20th Street in the Queens Village section of New York, a radio plays rock music and nineteen-year-old Robert Loftman relaxes, tapping out the rhythm on the grass.

Clifford Smith comes by. He's only sixteen, but he acts tough. He objects to Loftman playing the radio. "Get the . . . out of the park," he orders.

Loftman stands up. Smith warns:

"If you take another step, I'll blow you away."

Loftman takes another step.

Clifford Smith produces a .38 caliber handgun and pulls the trigger crazily. Twice the gun fails to fire. The third time it finds its mark, and Loftman is struck in the stomach.

Loftman subsequently dies.

Smith is found guilty of manslaughter and sentenced to five years probation by Justice Kenneth N. Browne of State Supreme Court.

D.A. John Santucci of Queens complains that the judge should have given a prison sentence.

Loftman's mother, on hearing the sentence, cries:

"There's no justice! He snuffed out my son's life for no reason. Why shouldn't he be made to suffer?"[1]

William James Rummel was convicted of theft for a third time, and was prosecuted under the Texas recidivist statute which mandates life imprisonment for anyone upon his third conviction of a felony. The

---

Graeme Newman, a professor of criminal justice at the State University of New York, Albany, is the author of *The Punishment Response* (1978), *Understanding Violence* (1979), and *Just and Painful* (1983), from which this excerpt is taken.

[1] Reported in *New York Times*, April 14, 1981.

total amount of goods and services Rummel stole came to $229.11. He appealed the conviction all the way to the United States Supreme Court on the grounds that the sentence amounted to cruel and unusual punishment. The court refused to rule that this punishment was grossly disproportionate to the offense. So, Mr. Rummel continues to serve his life sentence. (Decided March 18, 1980.)[2]

One can see that the sentences of probation for the murderer and life imprisonment for the three minor thefts are, to put it mildly, unjust. Judges are supposed to be among our more wise and well-informed people. How can they — especially in the highest court of the land — affirm punishments of such bizarre proportions?

The answer is that our legislators, our judges, our prosecutors have been thoroughly confused by the twentieth-century penologists, who have advocated one reform after another, each reform successively recognized as a failure.

The reformers have tried to water down criminal punishment into nonpunitive alternatives such as probation, halfway houses, or conjugal visits in prison. Or they have insisted that prison should be a "treatment" rather than a punishment. Indeed the more vocal of them, such as Dr. Karl Menninger in his book *The Crime of Punishment,* have argued that criminals are "sick," not bad.

There is now a virtual clamor of consensus that these "reforms" have been absolute failures. Prisons have failed to rehabilitate. Offenders have often been worse off "treated" rather than "punished."[3]

In the 1970s the prestigious Committee on Incarceration, chaired by Senator Charles Goodell, led a new wave of reform. This was to be a return to retribution and a strict reorientation of criminal punishment away from treatment and back to punishment.

But these reformers are now drowning in their own solution. Longer and more prison terms have been the logical result of their reforms which now face us with one of the most terrible social problems of today: a veritable archipelago of prisons overflowing with inmates. And they have produced a fiscal bind of considerable magnitude.

The Attorney General's Task Force on Violent Crime, chaired by former Attorney General Griffin Bell and Governor James Thompson (August 17, 1981), noted that as of January 1981:

Approximately 315,000 were incarcerated in all state and 51 federal correctional institutions. On any given day, an additional 158,000 persons are being held over in 3,000 jails.[4]

---

[2] *Rummel v. Estelle,* 63 LEd. 2d, 382 (1980).

[3] See D. Rothman, *Conscience and Convenience* (Boston: Little Brown, 1980); also Willard Gaylin et al., *Doing Good: The Limits of Benevolence* (New York: Pantheon, 1978).

[4] These statistics are reported annually in U.S. Department of Justice. *Prisoners in State and Federal Institutions.* Washington, D.C.: GPO, SD-NPS-PSF-5.

At a cost of roughly $20,000 per inmate per year, this amounts to a colossal annual expenditure of $10 billion. The *Task Force Report* adds that to accommodate the existing inmate population according to nationally recognized standards of square footage, it would cost an additional $10 billion.

A number of states have tried to address this problem by floating prison bond issues. In the November 1981 election in New York State, a $500 million bond issue was narrowly defeated. Perhaps this is a sign to the experts that the people are not prepared to spend so much money on this form of punishment.

Yet it is undoubtedly clear, when one reads of the many cases like that of Mrs. Loftman's son, that a punishment must be found that can meet with the philosophical challenge of just punishment and that can also go much of the way to solving the fiscal problem of criminal punishment.

The solution lies in the rediscovery of punishment in all its variety, for there are many punishments that do not need the expensive apparatus of prison and which will do the job of administering pain so much better than prison. The answer is really so simple, yet in this century has been lost. We must take seriously what the advocates of retribution have been saying for a long time, but not truly understanding:

Punishment must, above all else, be painful.

15

Indeed, pain is part of the definition of punishment. The origin of the word pain is the Latin *poena,* which meant in Roman times, punishment or penalty. Its meaning as a localized and acute sense experience is of relatively recent origin, probably of seventeenth-century England.[5]

In those days punishment was there for all to see. It was publicly intimate and largely physical. Ears were cut off, the whip was applied, and so was the death penalty. These were clear and concrete punishments; there could be no doubt that they were painful.

This is not the case today. We are simply told that so-and-so received "five years," another "two years." What do *these* punishments mean? What is the concrete difference between two years' and five years' punishment of prison? We shall see in this book that these

---

[5] See H. Fabregga and S. Tyma, "Culture, Language and the Shaping of Illness: An Illustration Based on Pain," *Journal of Psychosomatic Research* 20 (1976): 323–337. Scholars have traced the word back to about 400 B.C. when it referred to a penalty, specifically a fine. Around 500 A.D. it meant to inflict suffering, and in another sense the opposite of pleasure. Not until 1100 did it come to mean suffering in a general sense (that is, the suffering in hell), and eventually in 1400 to mean suffering of mental as well as physical pain (this no doubt, coinciding with the mental tortures of the Inquisition). The modern meaning of any mental or physical suffering, or that one specifically "had a pain" did not arise until after 1600.

sentences have no concrete meaning whatsoever either to the public or to the criminal who is punished.[6]

In other words, the punishment is *symbolic,* and the great problem is that the powerful need for punishment will not be adequately satisfied with symbolic punishments. They must be concrete. That is, they must clearly inflict pain. This means that we must return to truly painful punishment for crimes.

Does this mean: Bring back the whip and the lash? Let's start   20
cutting off the hand of a thief, the tongue of a blasphemer? Or turning back the clock to the tortures of two hundred years ago when criminals were whipped till blood gushed out of their backs and until they collapsed and died? How could any civilized person or society even contemplate such punishments?

If we are to rediscover the significance of pain in punishment we must be prepared to consider all kinds of punishment which clearly inflict pain. Yes, we must reconsider corporal punishment. We must reconsider the infliction of all punishments regardless of the kind of pain, whether mental or physical, that they produce.

Many of these kinds of pain already occur in our prisons. However, they occur by default rather than by design, and this is essentially what is wrong with them. The eminent historian David Rothman of Columbia University has claimed in his book *Conscience and Convenience* that this state of affairs exists because of lack of money to deal with them. But, while an important factor, this explanation fails to penetrate the veneer of excuses we have invented during the course of this century, for the failures of our correctional system.

The fundamental reason for the mess we are in is that there is no clear purpose to our use of punishment.[7] This is because we have lost the art of matching crimes to their punishments which our forefathers were most adept at doing. The reason we have lost this art is that the prime ingredient in translating the crime into its punishment has been cast aside.

That ingredient is pain.

We must see that pain is not only the prime ingredient of punish-   25
ment but it is also a necessary condition of justice. For without it there can be no punishment. And there can be no justice without punishment — which was the source of Mrs. Loftman's complaint.

It is also true that too much pain may make a particular punishment unjust. But we shall see that the cases in which too much of it

---

[6] Indeed, in this monograph, Professor Wilkins noted that it was not possible for his staff to agree upon what the difference between these sentences really meant. See L. T. Wilkins, *Principles of Guidelines for Sentencing: Methodological and Philosophical Issues* (Washington, D.C.: National Institute of Criminal Justice, 1981).

[7] See G. Newman, review of Rothman's *Conscience and Convenience* in *Crime and Delinquency* (July 1981): 422–428.

is used result from our failure to comprehend pain in a concrete way, a result, paradoxically, of our having "civilized" our punishments. Today these unjust punishments occur mostly in our irresponsible use of prison, without any clear idea of what kind of pain we wish to administer. The Supreme Court case of Mr. Rummel is a prime example.

This confusion about the use of pain in criminal punishment is well demonstrated by the following quotation from the 1976 Report of the Committee on Incarceration, *Doing Justice,* a committee comprised of a prestigious body of clerics, laymen, social scientists, and lawyers:

> One reason for preferring incarceration is simply that we have not found another satisfactory severe punishment. Historically, the alternative was corporal punishment, but that is worse. Incarceration at least can be divided into weeks, months, and years — and its duration prescribed by standards. Given the numerous possibilities that modern technology affords for inflicting pain and the difficulty of measuring degrees of subjective distress, effectively controlling the use of corporal punishment is virtually an impossible task.
>
> Beyond the question of effective control, corporal punishment poses disturbing ethical problems. Besides any physical pain involved, intentional corporal maltreatment evokes in its victim intense feelings of humiliation and terror.... Ought a civilized state ever to visit such mortifications? Might there not exist a right to the integrity of one's own body, that not even the state's interests in punishing may override?[8]

The confusion is clear. They call corporal punishment "maltreatment," but they do not call prison "maltreatment." They claim that corporal punishment causes humiliation and terror — yet we will see in this book that none of the research substantiates this claim. But it is well established that prison rests on a platform of humiliation and terror. Some criminals may deserve such punishment. Unfortunately, humiliation and terror in prisons occur by default not by design and therefore subject all inmates to such punishments regardless of their crimes.

Not one of the committee's factual claims is true. Corporal punishment *can* be controlled because of the very fact that it can be technologically and scientifically administered. It is prison that is out of control, not corporal punishment.

As for the claim that a criminal has the right of integrity over his own body: Who are they trying to fool? Such a right is worthless if

30

---

[8] A. Von Hirsch, *Doing Justice: The Choice of Punishments,* Report of the Committee for the Study of Incarceration. Preface by Charles Goodell, Chairman (New York: Hill and Wang, 1976).

that body is enclosed in a prison cell, especially if that cell contains other violent inmates who may attack each other at will.

Given this confusion of our experts about criminal punishment it seems perfectly reasonable for a civilized society to reconsider the painful possibilities of criminal punishment — *all* the possibilities, including various ways of inflicting pain. . . .

1. Acute corporal punishment should be introduced to fill the gap between the severe punishment of prison and the nonpunishment of probation.

2. For the majority of property crimes, the preferred corporal punishment is that of electric shock because it can be scientifically controlled and calibrated, and is less violent in its application when compared with other corporal punishments such as whipping.

3. For violent crimes in which the victim was terrified and humiliated, and for which a local community does not wish to incarcerate, a violent corporal punishment should be considered, such as whipping. In these cases, humiliation of the offender is seen as justifiably deserved.

4. Every effort should be made to develop a split system of criminal justice: one system for the punishment of *crimes,* and one for the punishment of *criminals.*   35

5. After an offender has committed a number of repeated offenses, or when the combined injury and damage of his crimes reach a certain amount, he will be treated as a criminal deserving of incarceration.

6. Only criminals should receive prison as a punishment, and only two prison sentences should be allowed: fifteen years for the first incarceration, and life if the individual recommits after his release. The fifteen-year term is the "warning" that the offender is close to the point of no return. There is no more getting off lightly with corporal punishment.

7. The decision to incarcerate will depend on many factors, but should especially depend on how much money the community is prepared to spend on incarcerating repeat offenders.

8. Before pronouncing either a fifteen-year or a life sentence, the judge should be required to seek a budgetary assessment of the cost of keeping this offender for the respective period. If such money is not approved beforehand by the Division of Budget, the sentence should be disallowed, and corporal punishment substituted.

9. A life sentence means life. If we truly believe that treatment or   40
rehabilitation no longer works, then there is no sense at all, especially from the point of view of incapacitation, in ever letting the "dangerous" criminal out.

10. The measure of the effectiveness of prison as a punishment should not be whether the offender recommits after release. Rather,

the notion of prison as retributive considers it entirely possible that a truly terrible offender may not have sufficient time in one life to work through the guilt of his crimes. Furthermore, even if he does work off his guilt, there is no expectation at all, according to the retributive philosophy, that the offender should have learned not to repeat his crime. What he *has* learned is that his crimes have a reciprocal cost to him in suffering. Thus, we do not speak of "rehabilitation" of the criminal, but of "redemption."

11. When corporal punishment is used, offenders should receive the same punishment for the same crime, whether it is their first offense or not. The only time an offender's entire record should be taken into account is when we decide to incarcerate. At that point an assessment of the dollar cost of the criminal's offenses may be considered, along with other individual background factors.

12. Because corporal punishment does not discriminate according to the offender's background, no distinction should be made according to age, sex, race, or any other social or psychological characteristic when deciding on the amount of deserved corporal punishment. Of course a medical examination will be required to establish the offender's fitness to receive punishment.

13. The scaling of corporal punishment will be tied to (1) the comparative seriousness of offense categories, and (2) the amount of injury and damage of the offense.

14. Corporal punishment may be applied according to intensity, frequency, and time, but should never exceed an eight-hour period. 45

15. Corporal punishment should be immediate: applied as soon as possible after the sentence (and preferably upon the finding of guilt).

16. All punishment should be public: Corporal punishment should be conducted in the presence of community representatives, including the press, and a description of the offender's crime or crimes should be graphically portrayed to the public at the time of the punishment. Prisons should also be opened to public tours.

17. Corporal punishment should never be used either in combination with prison or in order to "correct" the offender, because in these uses it comes too close to torture, which is barbaric and destructive.

18. Judges must be given more discretion not less. Corporal punishment, along with a "guidelines" model, is merely a first transitional step toward breaking down sentencing practices which at present are rigid and narrow. By using creative punishments judges will help free the higher courts to break with the purely quantitative notion of crime and punishment, and to begin thinking in terms of *appropriateness*.

19. Fines should be eliminated from the range of punishment alternatives unless they are part of a punishment that tries to reflect a particular offense. 50

20. When prisons are used as a chronic punishment we must take full responsibility for their harshness and put them to a clear retributive purpose. This means getting rid of the watered down versions of prisons, and making those few prisons that will exist extremely harsh places, reserved only for the terrible few.

21. A prison-intensive system will deemphasize prison as a form of punishment. The advantages of this strategy are obvious: a decrease in the number of people in prison, and a great savings in cost.

But by far the greatest consequence of this deemphasis in prisons is that fewer persons will come under the direct control of the State (which is what we mean by prisons), and that the major portion of criminal punishment (that is, corporal punishment) will be conducted with the view that it is not criminals per se who are being punished at all, but free citizens who have exercised their right to break the law.

In this way the most basic of all freedoms in a society is preserved: the freedom to break the law.

Let 'em Rot

JOHN J. DiIULIO, JR.

In his State of the Union address last night, President Clinton took a step in the right direction on crime. For example, the public wants thrice-convicted violent criminals locked up for good, and last night the president heeded their call. But who really speaks for this administration on crime, the president or Attorney General Janet Reno? Ms. Reno has challenged the need for mandatory minimum prison sentences, praised 1960s-style criminal rehabilitation programs that don't work, and mumbled about "prevention" even as violent crimes by juveniles have reached horrifying new heights. . . .

Solid Majorities

As the president's pollsters surely know, solid majorities of Americans, including overwhelming majorities of African Americans, believe that criminals who assault, rape, rob, burglarize, deal drugs, or murder should be arrested, prosecuted, and punished in a swift and certain fashion. They believe that violent and repeat criminals

---

John J. DiIulio, Jr., is a professor of politics and public affairs at Princeton University and a fellow in governmental studies at the Brookings Institution. This essay appeared in the *Wall Street Journal* on January 26, 1994.

should be imprisoned; that a prison sentence of X years should mean a prison sentence of X years (truth-in-sentencing); that criminals with multiple convictions should receive long prison sentences or life without parole (two- or three-time-loser laws); and that capital punishment is warranted on both social and moral grounds.

Among the liberal elite, however, only gun control is politically correct; criminal control isn't. For a generation now, the sorts of people who have been cheering Ms. Reno's speeches have been speaking condescendingly of the need to educate the public about the virtues of alternatives to incarceration, and lamenting the ostensible failure of policymakers to resist public pressures to lock up street predators.

By every measure, the anti-incarceration elite has been winning its tug-of-war with the public on crime. The so-called get-tough laws of the 1980s were filled with get-out-of-jail loopholes. Prison is now the alternative sentence: About three of every four convicted criminals (more than 3 million people) are on the streets without meaningful probation or parole supervision.

The average time served in confinement fell by several months 5 in the 1980s. Most convicted criminals spend only about one-third of their sentences in prison. On average, convicted rapists spend barely five years in prison; robbers spend 3.9 years; assaulters and burglars spend barely two years; and drug traffickers spend less than two years. Only 42 percent of reported murders result in a prison sentence; most convicted murderers spend well under ten years behind bars.

The Swiss cheese of mandatory sentencing laws has left little room behind bars for petty, first-time, or nonviolent criminals. More than 93 percent of state prisoners are violent criminals, repeat criminals (with two or more felony convictions), or violent repeat criminals. Most of the "property offenders" behind bars have long criminal histories and a propensity for violence. Within three years about two-thirds of all probationers get into serious trouble with the law again, and 20 percent of released property offenders are re-arrested for a *violent* crime.

It's true that, measured in relation to the country's total residential population, the rate of incarceration in the United States has been going up. But so has the rate of cereal consumption, bike-helmet wearing, and gasoline consumption. The relevant measure is the rate of incarceration relative to the number of serious crimes being committed. Today only some 7 percent of burglaries in the United States ever result in an arrest, and barely 1.2 percent ever result in imprisonment. And the probability that a violent criminal, or violent repeat criminal, will go to prison and serve most of his time behind bars in the United States is today only about one-fifth what it was in the early 1960s.

Even though crime has long been a leading public concern, barely a half cent of every government dollar (federal, state, and local) goes to keeping convicted criminals behind bars, and just over three cents goes to all criminal justice activities (cops, courts, and corrections). Indeed, American taxpayers spend about seven times more on transportation, twelve times more on public welfare programs, and twenty-seven times more on education and libraries than they do on prison and jails.

In short, the people know what the Renos deny: America has crime without punishment, and it has got to stop if we are ever going to rebuild public confidence in government, let alone our economically crime-ravaged inner cities.

But as years of public frustration with crime have begun to boil 10
over, the people are being subjected to a last-ditch anti-incarceration dodge: Even though public spending on prisons relative to other government activities is a pittance, it would "cost too much" (we are told) to imprison all violent repeat criminals for all or most of their terms; even if crime pays, stiffening sentences, abolishing parole, and adding prisons won't help.

The best available evidence, however, suggests that prison pays for most prisoners. In 1987 a Justice Department study analyzed the social costs and benefits of imprisonment. That study gave rise to a storm of criticism, most of it purely ideological. Since then a number of independent studies, including one by Harvard economist Ann Piehl and me (published in *The Brookings Review*), have been done. They suggest that, on average, it costs society about twice as much to let a criminal roam the streets as it does to keep him behind bars.

Prisoner self-report surveys conducted in New Jersey, Wisconsin, and other jurisdictions reveal that the typical street criminal commits more than a dozen serious crimes a year when free, excluding all drug crimes. Each crime imposes costs on its victims and on society — physical pain and suffering, hospital bills, days lost from work, psychological trauma (including the trauma of experiencing a "mere" property crime such as burglary). According to several studies, it costs society hundreds of billions of dollars each year to heal the economic and human wounds wrought by street crime.

Prison pays for chronic juvenile offenders, too. For example, in 1983 the federal government began a program for "serious habitual" juvenile criminals. In twenty cities law enforcement officials identified juveniles who had done three or more major crimes. These juveniles were targeted for arrest and prosecution, and they received the maximum penalties available under law. As a result of this program, a number of jurisdictions experienced sharp decreases in both violent and property crimes.

Stop the Cant

Get-tough politics *is* good crime policy. One can only hope that the president who delivered last night's speech will order his attorney general to publish a list of the federal and state prisoners who she believes ought never to have been incarcerated, complete with an objective account of their criminal histories — or insist that she stop spouting Waco-reasoned cant about mandatory prison terms. Let him further demand that she support new mandatory minimum sentences for violent and repeat criminals, or detail her fundamental disagreements with presidential policy and resign. And let him brook no nonsense from Democratic congressmen who demand more money for Great Society retreads as the price of their support for serious anticrime measures.

If the president breaks faith with the public on crime, he will be   15
a three-time loser — morally, intellectually, and politically. Let us hope that last night's words mean that, when it comes to the government's role in fighting crime, he's decided to go straight.

The Rush to Punish
JEROME MILLER

The Humanist [TH]: What do you think the purpose or philosophy of criminal justice is, or should be?

Jerome Miller: The purpose should be to bring some peace and calm to the community — but I don't think that is true any longer. There's been a real sea change in this country in our approach to criminal justice. For the most part, particularly in the past six to eight years, our "war on crime" has been focused on the poor and minorities, especially black men. It hasn't come back yet to bite the majority — but that will ultimately happen.

TH: Crime has become one of the most racially divisive issues in American society today. I recall a Florida woman calling in to a C-SPAN program you were on and saying, "I know you're not going to want to hear this, but nine out of ten people who are committing violent crimes are from the inner city. They are black . . . and nobody

Jerome Miller is the founder and executive director of the National Center for Institutions and Alternatives in Alexandria, Virginia. This interview originally appeared in the January–February 1994 issue of *The Humanist* and was adapted and updated for the September–October issue of *Utne Reader,* from which this excerpt is taken. [The title is the editor's.]

wants to face this problem. It's totally and completely out of hand, and it's a segment of our society that we better do something about."

Miller: Yes — "lock them away." And the genetic arguments put forth by neoconservatives like James Q. Wilson only encourage people like the Florida caller. In his book *Thinking about Crime,* which he wrote in the mid-1970s, Wilson openly disparaged the idea of root causes of crime. Then, in *Crime and Human Nature,* which he wrote with Harvard psychologist Richard Herrnstein — who in turn coauthored *The Bell Curve* with Charles Murray — Wilson talked about the genetic components of criminal behavior. And in his latest book, *The Moral Sense,* he suggests that some races inherit more of a moral sense than others. It's bizarre, but I think much of the liberal community is open to that sort of reasoning these days. We've turned away from looking at the social factors that create crime.

We don't want to talk about things like adequate income, em- 5
ployment, antipoverty programs — all of that is now passé. And so we're left with the idea that criminals therefore must somehow or other simply be wicked; if we can genetically define them, that's even easier.

I'm very pessimistic about where things are heading. We now have over a million people in prison, and if you include the jails we're at 1.5 million. Somewhere around 1984 or 1985 we reached the point where the absolute majority of men going into our prisons and jails were minorities, mostly black. Over 50 percent of the people in prison now are black. Including Hispanics adds another 17 to 19 percent, while slightly over 26 percent are white. So we're now at a point where over two-thirds of our prison populations are nonwhite minorities. That's the first time in our history that this has been the case.

The fact that something approaching three-fourths of those now going into our state and federal prisons are either black or Hispanic has changed the discussion. Now when we talk about building more prisons, when we talk about longer sentences, when we talk about cracking down on violent offenders, everyone knows that we're talking about men of color. And so, when it comes to proposing vicious anticrime policies, the sky is the limit.

TH: Do you agree with what I think is a recurrent conservative notion: that there's been a vast moral breakdown throughout our society, and that this is the source of our problems with crime?

Miller: No. As far as street crime is concerned, what we've seen is some class-crossing, if you will, that we didn't see before. Crime has spilled out of the restricted areas to which it used to be confined and has begun to affect middle-class people.

One thing we see in dealing with average offenders — the kind of 10
person who would be stereotyped as a serious, violent, savagelike street offender (and we see a lot of these young people here) — is

that their labelers have seldom spent any time with them finding out where they came from, what their life has been like, what's happened to them, why they would do what they did. Those are the kinds of things we not only do *not* want to know but from which we run in fear — because if we were to hear them, we'd all feel a little bit guilty. It's much easier to start talking about people in genetic terms.

There is no question that you're at much greater risk walking around a poor neighborhood at midnight in Washington, D.C., than you would be in some rural Iowa town. The question is whether we're going to address the causes of such environments. It is our belief that a significant percentage of the violence in our cities is being created by the criminal justice system itself. I'll use the District of Columbia as a prime example. It always has one of the top five murder rates among U.S. cities with populations over 100,000. The District of Columbia is also the incarceration capital of the nation, and has been for quite some time. It incarcerates somewhere around 2,400 people per 100,000 now; the national average is a little over 300 per 100,000. Even for most cities, the District of Columbia incarcerates both juveniles and adults at much higher rates than usual.

The city has succeeded in creating this huge alumni association on the streets consisting of people who have been run through one or another of D.C.'s reform schools, jails, and prisons. It's now a rite of passage for a young black male teenager to be arrested, handcuffed, and dragged off in police vans, to have a "mug shot" taken, to sit in jail until he's released — little of it having to do with serious or violent crime, most of it for very small-time stuff. These kinds of policies carry profound, unanticipated consequences. They've recreated the violent subculture of prison on the street.

If we are to successfully address violence in our cities, the criminal justice system needs to be *unwound;* it doesn't need to be intensified. We're running somewhere between 12 million and 14 million people a year through local jails — 80 percent for misdemeanors, though all acquire a "criminal record." We now maintain 50 million criminal records in this country. We have succeeded in criminalizing a large proportion of the nation, and among minority males we have given the majority a criminal label.

Now, I have no quarrel at all with those who want to get violent criminals off the street. But in the process of criminalizing such a large portion of nonviolent people we have set in place the conditions for more long-term violence. You do not willy-nilly arrest a father in front of a son, or break into someone's house looking for some kind of minor drug dealer and throw everyone onto the floor in front of screaming children and upset mothers, and drag people off the way we now do routinely in our inner cities, without having it come back at you. You create anger. You nurture alienation.

TH: Hubert Williams, president of the Police Foundation, has 15 pointed out that over the past decade the prison population in the United States has doubled. By the end of the 1990s, do you think it will actually have doubled again?

Miller: Researchers from the National Council on Crime and Delinquency have looked at some of the potential implications of both the Clinton anticrime proposals and those of the Republican leadership: such things as "three strikes and you're out" bills, mandatory sentences with no parole, heavier prosecution of drug crimes, 100,000 new police, increased use of the death penalty, and so on. They predict that within a relatively few years, we could find ourselves with 5 million to 7 million people in prison. Significantly, if current trends continue — and there's no reason to believe they won't — 2.5 million to 3.5 million of those inmates will be black. Well, there are only about 5.5 million black men between the ages of eighteen and thirty-nine in the whole nation. We will have put the absolute majority of black men in prison or camps. We're already at a point where in some cities most age-eligible black men are now either in prison or on probation or parole.

TH: What kind of alternatives are available for making the criminal justice system more just?

Miller: The best service you can do for anyone who finds himself caught up in the criminal justice system is to get him out of it as quickly as possible. There are some very dangerous and violent people who must be placed in it for public-safety reasons, but the majority of people in it should be under other sorts of supervision or receiving other kinds of human services. But I don't think that will happen. I think we will increasingly rely upon the criminal justice system as a means of managing the underclass.

TH: How long can that possibly go on?

Miller: It will go on until it changes the very nature of our soci- 20 ety. And when we reach a point where we have 5 million to 7 million people in our prisons and jails, we will be a very different society. As the eminent Norwegian criminologist Nils Christie comments, the United States will have become a "gulag society." I think that's precisely what will happen. I'm not suggesting that the prisons will become concentration camps. I think they'll be much more benign — although I don't think we should discount the possibility of some of them moving in that direction, especially when you look at the so-called supermax prisons like the U.S. Penitentiary in Marion, Illinois; Pelican Bay State Prison in California; and the Maryland Correctional Adjustment Center in Baltimore. A very eminent professor friend of mine, one of the premier sociologists in this country, visited the prison in Baltimore and told me that, were this prison discovered after World War II, the people running it would be up for war crimes. People are kept in isolation or with white light on them all the time;

they are subjected to sensory deprivation of the worst sort. These are facilities specifically designed to break people down. And not incidentally, of the 288 individuals in that prison when I last checked, 283 were black men.

TH: If you could address root causes, what would they be?

Miller: I will be very traditional, very conservative in answering that question. I think it has to do with the family. When you look into the individual cases of those relatively few kids who have participated personally in some horrific act of violence, the story is the same across the board for white, black, brown, whatever. They come from horrendous backgrounds; they've been subjected to gross personal violence in their own lives; they hold life at very little value, as their own lives have been held. This is not to excuse them but to suggest that we need to understand where this comes from and begin to deal with those kinds of problems.

However, I fear that in the current national mood, whatever social policies are proposed will be less than helpful. For example, we are on the verge of dealing with the single black mother in precisely the way we have dealt with the young black male — as expendable — and, as within the criminal justice system, there's very little subtlety to it. Armed with a meat ax, we are poised to cut, rip, and tear at the already fragile situation of many of these families with proposals from the theorists of the right to remove as many as half a million children to ersatz orphanages — and perhaps as Wilson has recently proposed, to place their teenage mothers in "resocialization" facilities.

I was trained in the Catholic tradition, and Saint Thomas Aquinas says at one point that of the so-called cardinal sins of the medieval era the worst is the sin of despair, of giving up hope, because that closes off the possibility that one can do better. That's what I struggle with as I watch the decisions that are made in this country.

The Chain Gang Show

BRENT STAPLES

Any animal with teeth enough will chew off its leg to escape a trap. Human beings behaved similarly when chain gang imprisonment — a successor to slavery — swept through the labor-starved South during Reconstruction. Beaten and driven like maltreated beasts, shackled to one another around the clock, prisoners turned to self-mutilation to make themselves useless for work. They slashed their bodies, broke their own legs, crippled themselves by cutting their tendons.

A public outcry beginning in the thirties gradually shamed even the most backward states into abolishing the gangs. Their return this spring to Alabama — followed by Florida and Arizona, with several other states mulling them over — signals an end to the fiction of rehabilitation and a resurgence of the American appetite for spectacles of punishment and humiliation. Calls for corporal punishment in schools and for the caning of petty criminals tell a similar story.

In Alabama, highway gangs were reinstated to great fanfare. The debut of its rock-breaking gangs at the Limestone Correctional Facility near Hunstville in August was staged like a Sunday picnic. A tent was erected where reporters could sip cold lemonade in shaded comfort while the prisoners struggled under ten-pound sledgehammers in the blazing sun. Mindful of the chain gangs' racist past — and the sight of white, shotgun-wielding guards in mirrored sunglasses lording over shackled black men — Governor Fob James, Jr., decreed that the gangs, which consist of five-man groups, would "reflect the demographics of the prison." The gangs are thus racially correct — three blacks and two whites apiece, where possible.

The prisoners were eager to be photographed, hoping that a shocked citizenry would rally to the rescue. The prison authorities were just as eager for publicity, given what one of Limestone's assistant wardens, Ralph Hooks, called "the perception that prison life was too easy." The prisoners spend one to three months on the gangs. To further combat the perception of easy living, the men are stripped of everything that makes prison life bearable: television, radio, smoking, and the right to make purchases (except for necessities like soap and deodorant) at the prison store. Worst of all, they are denied personal visits, even from family members. Public opinion is thus far on the side of the wardens.

Brent Staples is an editorial writer for the *New York Times;* this essay is from the October 15, 1995, issue of the *New York Times Magazine.*

The chain gangs will furnish a handy campaign commercial if 5
Governor James runs for reelection. But like most political symbols,
this one is not what it seems. The men in shackles and white suits
are medium-security prisoners — not quite the ax murderers, assas-
sins, and sundry death-row candidates that onlookers might wish to
imagine. The gangs are made up of nonviolent criminals only —
check forgers, deadbeat dads, safe crackers, parole violators.

The "work" the gangs do is valueless. The rock breaking is pure
photo opportunity. The highway crews allegedly clear weeds and
debris, but this is impossible to do on any useful scale with five men
chained eight feet apart, each stumbling when the next does. The
real reason for stretching legions of chained, white-suited men for a
mile or so along the highway is to let motorists gorge on a visible
symbol of punishment and humiliation. Hanging, too, was once a
public entertainment. No one should be surprised if some ambitious
politician suggests making it so again.

Many Alabamans delight in the chain gangs' reappearance. Drivers roll down their windows to taunt the prisoners, barking like
dogs. Others look on the predominantly black gangs and feel nostalgia for the South they knew as children. "I love seeing 'em in chains,"
one elderly white woman said. "They ought to make them pick cotton."

The warden thinks the experience of being trussed up in chains
and paraded before a scornful public will make inmates better citizens. Inmates see it differently. Louis Bennett, a twenty-five-year-old
serving time for burglary, said being chained "makes you start hat-
ing." Chris Davis, a twenty-six-year-old doing time for drug dealing,
put it more strongly: "It would make a person kill somebody to get
away, if the police were chasing him, to not come back to this."

Prison officials in other parts of the country should heed these
sentiments. Hard-core prisoners are bound to be less pliable, particularly in the Northern industrial states, where the history of prison
activism is strong, the grip of authority tenuous. In such places,
chain gangs might be more than morally repugnant. They could also
be self-defeating.

As Jails Overflow, Other Forms of Punishment Beckon

GEORGE F. WILL

A New Hampshire state legislator says of teenage vandals, "These little turkeys have got total contempt for us, and it's time to do something." His legislation would authorize public, bare-bottom spanking, a combination of corporal punishment and shaming — degradation to lower the offender's social status.

In 1972 Delaware became the last state to abolish corporal punishment of criminals. Most states abandoned such punishments almost 150 years ago, for reasons explained by Dan M. Kahan, a University of Chicago Law School professor, in an essay to be published in the spring issue of that school's Law Review. He also explains why Americans are, and ought to be, increasingly interested in punishment by shaming. Such punishment inflicts reputational harm to deter crime and perform an expressive function.

Around the United States, various jurisdictions are punishing with stigmatizing publicity (publishing in newspapers or on billboards or broadcasting the names of drug users, drunk drivers, or men who solicit prostitutes or are delinquent in child support); with actual stigmatization (requiring persons convicted of drunk driving to display license plates or bumper stickers announcing the conviction and requiring a woman to wear a sign reading "I am a convicted child molester"); with self-debasement (sentencing a slumlord to house arrest in one of his rat-infested tenements and permitting victims of burglars to enter the burglars' homes and remove items of their choosing); with contrition ceremonies (requiring juvenile offenders to apologize while on their hands and knees).

In "What Do Alternative Sanctions Mean?" Kahan argues that such penalties can be efficacious enrichments of the criminal law's expressive vocabulary. He believes America relies too heavily on imprisonment, which is extraordinarily expensive and may not be more effective than shaming punishments at deterring criminal actions or preventing recidivism.

There are many ways to make criminals uncomfortable besides 5 deprivation of liberty. And punishment should do more than make offenders suffer; the criminal law's expressive function is to articulate society's moral condemnation. Actions do not always speak louder than words but they always speak — and have meaning. Pun-

---

This piece by George F. Will, a syndicated columnist, appeared in the *Boston Globe* on February 2, 1996.

ishing by shaming is a powerful means of shaping social preferences by instilling in citizens an aversion to certain kinds of prohibited behavior.

For most violent offenses, incarceration may be the only proper punishment. But most of America's inmates were not convicted of violent crimes. Corporal punishment is an inadequate substitute for imprisonment because, Kahan says, of "expressive connotations" deriving from its association with slavery and other hierarchical relationships, as between kings and subjects.

However, corporal punishment became extinct not just because democratization made American sensibilities acutely uncomfortable with those connotations. Shame, even more than the physical pain of the lash and the stocks, was the salient ingredient in corporal punishment. But as communities grew and became more impersonal, the loosening of community bonds lessened the sting of shame.

Not only revulsion toward corporal punishment but faith in the "science," as it was called, of rehabilitation produced America's reliance on imprisonment. And shame — for example, allowing the public to view prisoners at work — occasionally was an additive of incarceration. It is so today with the revival of chain gangs.

Recent alternatives to imprisonment have included fines and sentencing to community service. However, both are inadequately expressive of condemnation. Fines condemn ambivalently because they seem to put a price on behavior rather than proscribe it. The dissonance in community-service sentences derives from the fact that they fail to say something true — that the offenders deserve severe condemnation — and that they say something false — that community service, an admirable activity which many people perform for pleasure and honor, is a suitable way to signify a criminal's disgrace.

Sentences that shame not only do reputational harm and lower 10 self-esteem, their consequences can include serious financial hardship. And Kahan argues: "The breakdown of pervasive community ties at the onset of the Industrial Revolution may have vitiated the stake that many individuals had in social status, but the proliferation of new civic and professional communities, combined with the advent of new technologies for disseminating information, has at least partially restored it for many others."

Today the United States has 519 people imprisoned for every 100,000 citizens. The figures for Mexico and Japan are 97 and 36, respectively. The United States needs all the prison cells it has and will need more. But policies of indiscriminate incarceration will break states' budgets: The annual cost of incarceration is upward of $20,000 per prisoner and $69,000 for those over age sixty. It would be a shame to neglect cheaper and effective alternatives.

THINKING AND WRITING ABOUT PUNISHMENT

Questions for Discussion and Writing

1. What reasons does Staples give for his objections to chain gangs? Which reasons seem most important? Do you think Will would agree or disagree with Staples?
2. What, according to Will, is the purpose of punishment? Why is shaming superior to incarceration in fulfilling that purpose? Why does he condemn community service as a punishment?
3. Explain the differences between Will and Newman regarding corporal punishment. What does Newman mean by symbolic punishment? Do his twenty-one rules for punishment fulfill the criteria of fairness and effectiveness for punishment? Are there portions of it with which you disagree? Defend your point of view.
4. Menninger's article was written almost forty years ago. Does any of it seem outdated? How much is still relevant? Be specific. To what extent would Miller agree with him? What warrants or assumptions underlie their claims about rehabilitation?
5. Summarize Wasserstrom's objections to both Menninger's and Wootton's arguments. What is his opinion of the deterrent factor in punishment? If you found one side of the debate between Menninger and Wasserstrom more persuasive, explain why.
6. Does Dilulio's get-tough policy answer the objections of Menninger and Miller? Which of his points seems strongest? Which weakest?

"LAST SPRING YOU ROBBED ME AND GOT 3 YEARS. LAST MONTH YOU NAILED ME AGAIN AND GOT 5 TO 10 ... HAVEN'T YOU LEARNED YOUR LESSON YET?"

7. How do you respond to the arguments about the caning of Michael Fay? Do you think that corporal punishment would be effective in reducing juvenile crime in the United States?
8. What is the cartoonist saying about prison terms as deterrents to crime?

Topics for Research

Alternatives to incarceration for petty crime

The reality of prison life

History of corporal punishment in the schools

Rehabilitation programs: What works?

CHAPTER SEVENTEEN

Sex Education

Sex education in school has always occasioned some controversy even when courses were devoted only to the facts of reproduction and boys and girls were instructed in separate classes. Although many parents may have been unable or unwilling to discuss such facts with their children, they were nevertheless convinced that home or church should be the place of instruction. And if values were to be taught, premarital chastity, marriage, and sexual fidelity in marriage were to be emphasized above all others. Now changing mores and increased sexual activity among teenagers have produced sweeping reforms in the subject matter of sex education courses, especially in big-city schools, and an ongoing debate between those who favor the reforms and those who oppose them. The debate about subject matter remains, however, essentially a debate about values: the freedom of teenagers to choose when and how they engage in sexual activity, the rights of parents and community to control the moral content of their children's education, the right of educators to introduce controversial material that reflects a changing society.

The advocates of the new curriculum argue that it is intended primarily to reduce an alarmingly high number of teenage pregnancies and to teach sexually active teenagers how to protect themselves against AIDS. Advocates are convinced that it is unrealistic to assume that teenagers will practice abstinence even when confronted by disease or unwanted pregnancy. For this reason they have supported the distribution of condoms and instruction in their use, sometimes in the classroom. Equally controversial is the inclusion in some school curricula of a "diversity" component that treats homosexuality as an acceptable alternative to heterosexuality and urges respect for gay families.

Those who oppose the distribution of the new materials believe that, however well intentioned, it will appear to sanction greater sexual activity and lead to further weakening of the traditional heterosexual family. They insist that the curriculum of a sex education course should emphasize abstinence as the only morally and medically acceptable approach. In part, parental and community objections to the changes are based on deeply held religious beliefs.

In addition to questions about the content of the curriculum, there are questions about the administration of the programs. Should sex education be mandatory? Or should parents have the option of withdrawing their children from some parts of the course? At what age should sex education begin? (According to the recent Roper Organization poll, the average recommended age was nine.) By whom should it be taught? (Peer education has proven effective in some schools. Would it be appropriate everywhere?)

One troubling aspect of the debate is that not much is known about the effectiveness of the proposed changes. Whether information alone will induce teenagers to refrain from risky sexual activity is doubtful. Both sides have offered data to support their claims that sex education does or does not work, but most studies have been inconclusive.

What They Want to Teach
Your Child about Sex
BARBARA DAFOE WHITEHEAD

What are kindergartners through third-graders learning in some of our public schools these days? Here's a sample:

"Grownups sometimes forget to tell children that touching can also give people pleasure, especially when someone you love touches you. You can give yourself pleasure, too, and that's okay. When you touch your own genitals, it's called masturbating."

"A clitoris is a small sensitive part that only girls have, and it sometimes makes you feel good."

"To have sex, the man and woman lie very close to each other so that their bodies are touching. Usually it happens in bed and they don't have any clothes on."

Barbara Dafoe Whitehead, a social historian, is author of the forthcoming book *The Divorce Culture* (Alfred A. Knopf, 1997). This selection, condensed from the October 1994 issue of the *Atlantic Monthly*, appeared in *Reader's Digest* in February 1995.

These quotes are from a textbook for elementary-school chil- 5
dren used by sixteen New Jersey school districts. The book is more
explicit than most texts for children of that age, but it does reflect
where some educators think sex education ought to go. Should it?

The question affects huge numbers of children. Sex education is
mandated in sixteen states and the District of Columbia and is recommended by the state legislature or state board of education in
thirty others.

Sex education is not new, of course, but never before has it attempted to expose children to so much so soon. Beginning as early
as kindergarten and continuing into high school, comprehensive
sex-ed programs generally cover the biology of reproduction, the
psychology of relationships, the sociology of the family, and even
the sexology of masturbation.

The textbook quoted earlier, *Learning about Family Life*, follows
a fictional class of primary-school children — "Class 203"— during a
school year. Stories include a teacher's pregnancy, a girl's trip to see
her divorced father, and the visit of a child's HIV-infected uncle.
These and other events lead to straight talk about a variety of subjects, including genitalia, intercourse, AIDS, sexual abuse, and alternative family structures. According to teachers who use the book,
students eagerly ask, "When are we going to talk about those kids in
Class 203 again?" Little wonder. This is sex education packaged like
"Sesame Street."

Modern sex education is not just a "plumbing lesson," says former Surgeon General Joycelyn Elders. She and others see it as a key
way to reduce illegitimacy and sexually transmitted diseases (STDs)
among teenagers. Each year, a million teenage girls, most of them
unmarried, become pregnant. Half give birth. And an estimated
three million teens contract an STD.

But is it appropriate — or effective — to teach elementary- 10
school children about masturbation and intercourse, as well as introducing them to the idea of contraception?

Yes, say proponents of the comprehensive approach, because
as children gain fluency and ease in talking about sexual matters,
they become more comfortable with their own sexuality and more
skillful in communicating their feelings and desires — and therefore
grow into teenagers who govern their own sexual behavior responsibly.

As they read about Class 203, children are encouraged to use
scientific terms — like *anus* and *buttocks* — instead of words that are
perfectly apt for a six-year-old's vocabulary. In a lesson on pregnancy, one boy talks about how his mother's tummy felt when the
baby was growing inside. Mrs. Ruiz, the Class 203 teacher, says, "I
know we are used to saying 'baby' and 'tummy.' But 'fetus' and
'uterus' are more accurate words."

The same book encourages straight talk about masturbation regardless of parents' feelings on the subject. "Masturbation is a topic that is viewed negatively in many families," notes the teachers' guide. "Assure parents that your approach will be low-keyed and will stress privacy, but make it clear that you will not perpetuate myths that can mar children's healthy sexual development."

As it turns out, though, early sex-ed is not *always* straight talk. Let's look at how *Learning about Family Life* deals with the gritty reality of illegitimacy and broken families. In the book, a seventeen-year-old girl has a child out of wedlock. The father had sex (apparently as an expression of love — just as *Learning about Family Life* described), but then he abandoned the girl. Though the story acknowledges some of the problems involved with teen pregnancy, the family rallies round and the girl returns to school while an aunt cares for the baby. There seem to be no long-term consequences for the sister or the baby.

As children approach adolescence, their sex education may take 15 a more technical turn. Middle-schoolers may learn not only about abstinence but also about condoms, other forms of contraception, and abortion. They may also learn about an alternative called "sexual expression without risk," which might include such topics as mutual masturbation.

Should teachers discourage such behavior? Many proponents of comprehensive sex-ed say no, a teacher should not impose his or her opinions. When asked "What is the right time to begin having sex?" teachers are usually advised by guides to turn the question back to the students: "How would you begin to make that decision?" Defending this approach, sex educators say that since grownups can't supervise teenagers every minute, the students must acquire the knowledge and skills to answer these questions for themselves.

Critics respond that public schools should give one clear message about sex: abstinence. When a student asks, "What is the best time to begin having sex?" they urge teachers to state unequivocally: "Not yet. You are not ready for sex."

Sex-education advocates agree that abstinence is the best way to avoid STDs and early pregnancy, but they reject teaching abstinence only. And many do not feel it is even necessary to send clear behavioral messages. They assume that once teenagers acquire a knowledge of sexuality and decision-making skills, they will behave responsibly.

How effective are these programs? Does early sex education affect sexual behavior later on?

In New Jersey, there is no definitive evidence that *Learning about* 20 *Family Life* or other early sex-education programs reduce teen sexual activity — or, in fact, that responsible sexual behavior depends on long years of sexual schooling. Indeed, sex education may be most effective in the relatively brief middle-school period, when teenagers are hormonally gearing up for sex but mainly uninitiated. And what about "sexual expression without risk"? Studies show no evidence that encouraging noncoital sex reduces the likelihood of coitus.

According to California health-education researcher Douglas Kirby, it's true that sex-ed students know more about contraception, pregnancy, and STDs — but knowledge and decision-making skills alone seem to have little effect on a teenager's decision to engage in or postpone sex, or on reducing teenage pregnancies or STDs. As Kirby puts it, "Ignorance is not the solution, but knowledge is not enough."

What are some other influences on children's sexual behavior? Parental supervision, researchers say. One study found that teenagers with moderately strict parents who enforced some dating rule (as reported by the teens) had the lowest level of sexual activity. Teens with very strict parents had higher levels, and those with permissive parents had the highest levels of all.

Family structure also influences early sexual activity. Daughters in single-parent families are more likely to engage in early sex than girls who grow up in two-parent families. Teens in divorced families have more permissive attitudes toward sexual intercourse outside marriage.

Religion matters too. Studies confirm that religiously observant teens have less permissive attitudes. And conversely, the highest level of premarital intercourse occurs among teens with no religious affiliation.

Kirby's research has found that effective programs give a clear behavioral message. One such program was begun by Grady Memorial Hospital in Atlanta and is now being used in a number of school systems around the country. In the Grady program, popular older teenagers teach eighth-graders to postpone sex by practicing resistance to peer pressure. 25

The Grady program has had encouraging results: A study of one group of high-risk students found that by the end of ninth grade, only 24 percent of the participants who had not already experienced intercourse had since begun having intercourse, compared with 39 percent of the nonparticipants. (And those who did fail to abstain were 50 percent more likely to use contraception than students who hadn't taken the course.)

The Grady program also indicates that formal sex-ed may be most successful when it reinforces abstinence among sexually inexperienced adolescents; the program was not effective for teenagers who were already engaging in sex.

Schools seem to have lost sight of their historical role in helping children through adolescence — a period for a moratorium on sexual activity, when young people should have a chance to grow into adulthood before they become parents. While adults' rules once safeguarded this special stage in life, too many sex educators now advocate equipping kids with condoms and sending them into the world to fend for themselves. The educators defend this as realism; in fact it is retreat.

Protect Our Children

CAROL F. ROYE

To the Editor:

The AIDS education battle in New York City is deeply disturbing. Our adolescents are contracting the human immunodeficiency virus, which causes AIDS, at an alarming rate. It is believed that at least 20 percent of new patients with AIDS were infected during teenage or early adult years.

Further, the male-to-female ratio of HIV seroprevalence in teenagers and young adults is much lower than for adults, emphasizing the heterosexual transmission in this age group. They will die from this disease. Yet, some of our school leaders are trying to foil AIDS education — the best means we have of preventing the disease among teenagers.

AIDS cannot be cured. Why then are we loath to teach our children how to prevent AIDS? We must get beyond our personal discomfort about discussing sexuality and get on with protecting our children.

Opponents of comprehensive AIDS education have not presented documentation showing that discussion of AIDS prevention leads to increased sexual activity. They just think it is so. The literature on adolescent sexuality suggests that frank discussion of sexuality and AIDS prevention, even in a setting where condoms and other forms of birth control are distributed, results in lower rates of sexual activity. Also, national surveys show that parents overwhelmingly want their children protected, and endorse education on sexuality and family life in schools. As a mother of five, I agree.

My experience as a nurse practitioner in New York City adoles- 5
cent clinics bears this out. When teenagers who are sexually active

Carol F. Roye is a nurse practitioner in New York City. This article appeared as an editorial in the September 12, 1992, *New York Times*.

or at high risk for sexual activity come to the clinic, I counsel them about all aspects of sexuality. Even those who are considered "problem children" listen wide-eyed to an honest, frank discussion of sexuality. They ask for clarification of potentially fatal misperceptions. And, of course, abstinence is presented as the safest option. However, abstinence is not a realistic option for many teenagers.

Yet after such a discussion and the dispensing of birth-control devices (or instructions on obtaining them, depending on the type of clinic), a number of patients come to their follow-up appointment and state that they have not been sexually active since their last clinic visit. Kids respond to honesty, respect, and genuine concern. They understand that teaching about AIDS prevention does not mean we condone their sexual activity, but that we care about them.

The rates of teenage pregnancy (approximately 1 million a year in the United States), sexually transmitted diseases (which are increasing at alarming rates with the highest rates for teenagers and young adults), and HIV seroprevalence in teenagers all attest to the prevalence of adolescent sexual activity in New York City and the country. Denying that social reality so that we adults can avoid facing uncomfortable discussions with our children will not protect them from AIDS.

Carol F. Roye

We've Educated Sex to Death

KAY S. HYMOWITZ

Teaching teenagers about masturbation, the issue that led to Joycelyn Elders's dismissal as surgeon general last week, is a howling example of bringing coals to Newcastle. But as the smoke clears from this latest skirmish in the culture wars, we would do well to rethink the terms of the debate. Condom distribution and "safe sex" curriculums that include explicit instruction in subjects like masturbation are only symptoms of a much deeper problem: the prevalent divorce of sex from deep feeling.

Critics have long assailed the media's fascination with images of cool, routine sex and fleeting infatuations in a consumer's paradise of abundance and variety. But what is perhaps less thoroughly understood is the way sex educators implicitly endorse this state of affairs. It's true that while Hollywood turns up the heat to a boil,

Kay S. Hymowitz is a contributing editor of the Manhattan Institute's *City Journal*. This article appeared in the *New York Times* on December 13, 1994.

educators scramble for ways to keep the lid on. But though they may call into question the brutal posturing of gangster rappers and warn of the dangers of serial encounters, their medical, bureaucratic, and legalistic assumptions add oxygen to the general atmosphere in which trivialized, deromanticized sex can thrive.

In the fifties, David Riesman wrote of young people who "take sex along with their vitamins." But today's chilly discourse makes the sex education manuals of those days look like "Romeo and Juliet."

Sex nowadays is defined as a healthy release of energy. It's good for you, like jogging. As Dr. Elders implies, sometimes it might even be healthier to do it alone. "Sex is too important to glop up with sentiment," shrugged a Planned Parenthood pamphlet for teens. "If you feel sexy, for heaven's sake admit it to yourself. If the feeling and tension bother you, you can masturbate." "Sex for Yourself" is the title of a chapter of "Girls and Sex," a self-help manual by Wardell B. Pomeroy, a coauthor of the Kinsey Report.

At its most sentimental, sex is only a method in an arid list of 5 ways of "sharing" or "showing feelings," which is healthy as long as you are "comfortable" or "relaxed" about it. And passionless, one might add. In today's sex education manuals, profound emotions like love, jealousy, possessiveness, and longing are conspicuous only in their absence.

Nothing better attests to this rationalized vision than the technical parlance that dominates sex education tracts. Curriculums are replete with the "skills" required by today's healthy teenager: refusal skills, communication skills, decision-making skills, condom skills, and, evidently, masturbation skills. "We taught them what to do in the front seat of a car," Dr. Elders once said, tritely comparing the taming of the rawest of human urges to learning to use a turn signal. "Now it's time to teach them what to do in the back seat."

Codes dealing with sexual harassment and with speech and sex on campus support a similar idea. Reducing the most intimate of human relations to the terms of an apartment lease, the infamous Antioch College sexual offense policy epitomizes the new bureaucratic, technical sexuality: "Obtaining consent is an ongoing process in any sexual interaction," the code asserts without irony. "Verbal consent should be obtained with each new level of physical and/or sexual conduct in any given interaction. . . . The request for consent must be specific to each act."

Deprived of any ideal by which to imagine sex except as a negotiated contract for mutual self-expression, kids today would seem to have only one reason to say no: health. In a 1993 poll for *Good Housekeeping* and CBS, teenagers were asked to give reasons not to have sex. Eighty-five percent mentioned fear of AIDS or pregnancy; 4

percent said "not being in love." "Doing it," the popular term for intercourse, is a perfect emblem for the ethos of deromanticized sex. The lover (a word that seems a senile, mumbling old lady in this brave new world) is reduced to a throwaway object for relief of an annoying itch. "Sex Is Mind over Matter," read a T-shirt popular a few years ago. "If She Doesn't Mind, It Doesn't Matter."

The better students have learned to ape their elders' lessons, with even more precision. According to Marian Jensen, dean of students at Antioch, wine and candlelight have been replaced by this seductive come-on: "Would you like to activate the policy?" In an article in the current *Vassar Quarterly*, one student explained that she was uneasy with the term *boyfriend*; she refers to "my special friend with whom I spent lots of quality physical time."

All societies have artificial moral codes to tame and describe   10 Eros. But surely this is the first generation in history to learn the lessons of love from lawyers, health professionals, and bureaucrats. Those lessons evoke a joyless and narcissistic sexuality — without romance, without imagination, without idealism, and without passion. "We in America have tried ignorance," said Dr. Elders. "Now it's time to try education." If this is education, I'll take ignorance.

School Birth-Control Clinics: A Necessary Evil

CHARLES KRAUTHAMMER

The latest outrage of American life: The pill goes to school. There are now seventy-two "comprehensive health clinics" in or near the nation's public high schools.

Very comprehensive. More than a quarter dispense and more than half prescribe birth-control devices. When the New York City Board of Education found out that two of its clinics were in the dispensing business, it ordered them to cease and desist.

Secretary of Education William Bennett has waxed eloquent on the subject. He is surely right that birth control in the schools makes sexual activity legitimate and represents an "abdication of moral authority." Clinics are not only an admission by adults that they can-

---

The former chief resident in psychiatry at Harvard Medical School, Charles Krauthammer is now a well-known writer on public policy and contributes regularly to such publications as *The New Republic* and *Time* magazine. This article is reprinted from the December 3, 1986, *Washington Post.*

not control teenage sexuality, but also tacit consent, despite that "just say no" rhetoric.

Unfortunately, there are two problems: not just sex, but pregnancy. As in all social policy, there is a choice to be made. Is it worth risking the implicit message that sex is OK in order to decrease pregnancies?

(Clinic opponents sometimes argue that birth-control dispensaries do not decrease the number of pregnancies, a contention that defies both intuition and evidence.)

Bennett is right about the nature of the message. But he vastly overestimates its practical effect. Kids do not learn their morals at school. (Which is why the vogue for in-school drug education will prove an expensive failure.) They learn at home. Or they used to.

Now they learn from the culture, most notably from the mass media. Your four-eyed biology teacher and your pigeon-toed principal say don't. The Pointer Sisters say do. To whom are you going to listen?

My authority for the image of the grotesque teacher and moronic principal is *Porky's*, the wildly popular teen sex flick that has spawned imitators and sequels. My authority for the fact that teenage sex control is an anachronism is Madonna. "Papa don't preach," she sings. "I'm gonna keep my baby."

The innocent in the song is months — nine months, to be precise — beyond the question of sex. Her mind is already on motherhood.

Kids are immersed in a mass culture that relentlessly says yes. A squeak from the schools saying no, or a tacit signal saying maybe, is not going to make any difference. To pretend otherwise is grossly to misread what shapes popular attitudes.

What a school can credibly tell kids depends a lot on whether they grew up on the Pillsbury dough boy or on a grappling group of half-nudes frenzied with Obsession.

Time to face facts. Yes, birth-control clinics are a kind of surrender. But at Little Big Horn, surrender is the only sound strategy. Sex oozes from every pore of the culture, and there's not a kid in the world who can avoid it. To shut down school birth-control clinics in order to imply the contrary is a high-minded but very costly exercise in message sending. Costly because the message from the general culture will prevail anyway, and sex without contraception means babies.

The sex battle is lost. The front-line issue is pregnancy. Some situations are too far gone to be reversed. They can only be contained. Containment here means trying at least to prevent some of the personal agony and social pathology that invariably issue from teenage pregnancy.

Not that the sexual revolution can never be reversed. It can, in principle. In our time, the vehicle might be AIDS. The association of sex and sin elicits giggles. The association of sex and death elicits terror. Nevertheless, the coming counterrevolution, like all cultural revolutions, will not be made in the schools. It will happen outside — in movies and the newsmagazines, on the soaps and MTV — and then trickle down to the schools. As usual, they will be the last to find out.

I am no more pleased than the next parent to think that in ten years' time my child's path to math class will be adorned with a tasteful display of condoms in the school's clinic window. But by then it will be old hat.

The very word "condom" has broken through into the national consciousness, i.e., network TV. It was uttered for the first time ever on a prime-time entertainment show, *Cagney and Lacey*. Condoms will now find their place beside bulimia, suicide, incest, and spouse murder in every child's mental world.

If the schools ignore that world, it will not change a thing. Neglect will make things worse. In a sex-soaked culture, school is no shelter from the storm. Only a monastery is, if it doesn't have cable.

The Case for Abstinence Doesn't Work

PHILIP ELMER-DeWITT

Amid all the anguish, confusion, and mixed signals surrounding teenage sexuality, the simplicity of one group's message is striking: Sex outside marriage is just plain wrong. To instruct children in the mechanics of birth control or abortion, it argues, is to lead them down the path of self-destruction. That's the philosophy of the abstinence-only movement, a coalition of conservative parents, teachers, and religious groups that, in the absence of any national sex-education consensus, has been remarkably successful in having its approach adopted as the official curriculum in schools across the United States.

But is it the best approach? Its adherents claim the message is both morally correct and demonstrably effective. Opponents argue that in an age in which most teenagers are already sexually active, preaching the case for chastity without teaching the case for condoms is dangerously naive. "All the parents I know are absolutely in favor of abstinence," says Carole Chervin, senior staff attorney for

Philip Elmer-DeWitt is a senior editor at *Time* magazine, where this article appeared on May 24, 1993.

the Planned Parenthood Federation. "It's the abstinence *only* approach that's bothersome. We believe sex education should be comprehensive."

The fight has moved into the courts. In what could become a landmark case, Planned Parenthood of Northeast Florida and twenty-one citizens in Duval County, Florida, have sued the local school board for rejecting a broad-based sex-education curriculum developed by the board's staff in favor of a controversial abstinence-only program from Teen-Aid, Inc., of Spokane, Washington. Planned Parenthood complains that the material in the text is biased, sensationalist, and, at times, misleading. Some school-board members argue that the real issue is whether the local community has the right to choose the sex-education curriculum it wants, however flawed

Late last week a similar case in Shreveport, Louisiana, went against the abstinence-only movement when a district judge ruled that a prochastity text called "Sex Respect" was biased and inaccurate and ordered it pulled from the Caddo Parish junior high schools. The court is scheduled to rule this week on the fate of the abstinence-only text still being used in the high schools.

Abstinence is hardly a new idea, but the organized abstinence-only movement dates back to a Reagan-era program that set aside $2 million a year for the development of classroom materials to teach adolescents to say no to sex. Today there are more than a dozen competing curriculums on the market, each offering lesson plans, activities, and workbook exercises designed to encourage abstinence among teenagers. 5

"Sex Respect," developed by Project Respect in Golf, Illinois, is one of the most widely used, having been adopted by a couple of thousand schools nationwide. Class activities include listing ways humans are different from animals, making bumper stickers that read CONTROL YOUR URGIN'/BE A VIRGIN, and answering multiple-choice test questions about what kinds of situations put pressure on teens to have sex. The teacher's manual features a section on sexual messages in the media, a list of suggested alternatives to sex when on dates (bicycling, dinner parties, playing Monopoly) and a chapter on "secondary virginity"— the decision to stop having sex until marriage, even if one is sexually experienced.

Missing from the Sex Respect curriculum is the standard discussion of the comparative effectiveness of various birth-control methods found in most sex-education courses. Furthermore, it fails to offer any follow-up programs, outside counseling or guidance for teens who might become pregnant or contract a sexually transmitted disease. Kathleen Sullivan, director of Project Respect, defends her program: "We give the students a ton of information," she says. "We point out, for example, the tremendous failure rate of condoms."

One argument put forward for abstinence-only programs is that they work. Sullivan cites a study conducted by Project Respect showing that pregnancy rates among students who have taken the course are 45 percent lower than among those who have not. But critics say none of these studies have been reviewed by outside scientists and wonder whether any will bear close scrutiny. The San Diego *Union* looked into one of the most widely reported success stories — that the Teen-Aid program lowered the rate of pregnancy at a San Marcos, California, high school from 147 to only 20 in two years — and reported that while the 147 figure was well documented, the number 20 had apparently been made up.

The argument most often used against abstinence-only programs is that they are a thinly disguised effort to impose fundamentalist religious values on public-school students and thus violate the constitutional separation of church and state. Some of the texts started out as religious documents and were rewritten to replace references to God and Jesus with nonsectarian words like goodness and decency. Still, it makes little sense to criticize the programs simply because they originate from a religious perspective; what matters is not where the courses came from but what they say.

That's the real issue with the Teen-Aid text at the center of the   10
Florida lawsuit. In making the case for chastity, Teen-Aid has asserted, among other things, that "the only way to avoid pregnancy is to abstain from genital contact" and that the "correct use of condoms does not prevent HIV infection but only delays it." Most teens don't need a school course to know that neither of those statements is correct. How are they going to believe in abstinence if those who preach don't have their facts straight?

Sex Is for Adults

ELLEN HOPKINS

Remember how drunken driving used to be kind of funny? Or if not funny, inevitable, especially for the young. When I was in high school (I'm thirty-five), only losers worried about the alcoholic consumption of the person behind the wheel. Fourteen years later, when my sister made her way through the same suburban high school, designated drivers had become the norm and only losers swerved off into the night.

I was reminded of this remarkable evolution in attitude when I began to explore the idea that teaching abstinence to teenagers

Ellen Hopkins is a contributing editor to *Rolling Stone*. This article appeared in the December 26, 1992, *New York Times*.

need not be the province of right-wing crazies. Could it be that teenage sex is no more inevitable than we once thought teenage drunken driving? Is it possible to make a liberal, feminist argument for pushing abstinence in the schools? I believe it is.

The argument goes like this:

Sex education doesn't work.

There are lots of nice things to be said for sex education. It makes kids more knowledgeable, more tolerant, and maybe even more skillful lovers. But it does not do the one thing we all wish it would: make them more responsible.

In a landmark study of ten exemplary programs published by the Centers for Disease Control in 1984, no evidence was found that knowledge influenced teenagers' behavior significantly. Supporters of sex education point to studies that show that educated teenagers are slightly more likely to use birth control. Opponents point to studies that show they are slightly more likely to have sex at a younger age. No one points to the many studies that compare the pregnancy rates of the educated and the ignorant: depressingly similar.

Even if sex education worked, birth control doesn't.

At least it doesn't work often enough. The Alan Guttmacher Institute, a research organization that specializes in reproductive health, estimates that up to 36 percent of women in their early twenties will get pregnant while relying on male use of condoms in the first year; and with the supposedly foolproof pill, up to 18 percent of teenage girls get pregnant in the first year. (The more effective and more expensive contraceptive Norplant is not widely available to young women.) If you project these failure rates a few years ahead, unintended pregnancy begins to look uncomfortably close to an inevitability.

So let's follow one sexually active teenager who does just what she's statistically likely to do. Her options are bleak.

If she wants an abortion, good luck to her if she's poor, under eighteen, or doesn't live near a big city. The simplest abortion costs about $300. Only twelve states have no laws requiring parental consent or notification for minors seeking an abortion. And 83 percent of America's counties don't even have an abortion provider.

What if our teenager chose to have the baby and give it up for adoption? While there's a dearth of solid follow-up research on birth mothers, surrendering the flesh of your flesh is obviously wrenching. Suppose our teenager keeps the baby. She may be ruining her life. Only 50 percent of women who have their first child at seventeen or younger will have graduated from high school by the age of thirty. And many of those who do have merely gotten a General Education Development degree, which is of such dubious worth that the army no longer accepts recruits with it.

Even a ruined life may be better than a life cut short by AIDS.

If condoms — or young condom users — are so unreliable that up to 36 percent of young women get pregnant in a single year of use, what does that say about our teenager's chances of being exposed to HIV as she "protects" herself with a latex sheath?

Our teenager, though, leads a charmed life. Or so she thinks. Even if she doesn't get pregnant and none of her boyfriends is HIV positive, she still puts herself at substantial risk for later infertility.

More than 12 million episodes of sexually transmitted diseases   15 occur each year in the United States, and two-thirds of those afflicted are under twenty-five. Most such diseases can damage the female and male reproductive systems. Infectious-disease experts estimate that after just one episode of pelvic inflammatory disease (a common result of contracting sexually transmitted disease), 35 percent of women become infertile. After three episodes, the odds of becoming infertile soar to more than 75 percent. Many infertility specialists believe that one of the prime causes of today's high infertility rate is that so many baby boomers had sex early and with multiple partners.

Current recommendations for "safer" sex are unrealistic.

Our teenager knows that before going to bed with someone, she and the guy are supposed to exchange detailed sexual histories. Tandem AIDS tests are next, and if both can forge a monogamy pact, they will use condoms (and a more reliable form of birth control like the pill) for six months and then get tested again.

Does our teenager hammer out these elaborate social contracts every time Cupid calls? Of course not.

I had always assumed that abstinence lessons were synonymous with Sex Respect, the religious right's curriculum that uses fear to pressure kids to avoid all sexual activity — including necking — until marriage. While supporters claim success, their evaluation techniques are problematic. Plus, imagine those poor kids having to chant silly Sex Respect slogans ("Control your urgin', be a virgin" is my favorite).

But studies of a program in Atlanta's public schools suggest that   20 promoting abstinence can be done intelligently and effectively. Eighth graders are taught by peer counselors (popular, reasonably chaste kids from the upper grades — kids who look like they *could* have sex if they wanted it). Their message is simple: Sex is for grown-ups. Weirdly, it works. By the end of the eighth grade, girls who weren't in the program were as much as fifteen times more likely to have begun having sex as those who were.

While the program in Atlanta is backed up by contraceptive counseling, kids who choose to have sex are erratic birth-control users and just as likely to get pregnant as sexually active kids who aren't in the program.

In other words, sex is for grown-ups. I feel strange writing this. Then I remember my first heady experimentations (at a relatively geriatric age) and contrast them with those of a sixteen-year-old girl who recently visited Planned Parenthood in Westchester county. Three boys were with her, their relationship to her unclear. On the admittance form, the girl wrote that she wasn't in a relationship and had been sexually active for some time. An exam proved her pregnant. Her entire being was joyless.

I once thought I'd tell my young son that anything goes — so long as he used condoms. Now I'm not so sure. Not only do I want my son to live, I don't want him to miss out on longing — longing for what he isn't yet ready to have.

Sex Education

WILLIAM KILPATRICK

There are two basic approaches to sex education. One view is that teenagers "are going to do it anyway," and the only thing adults can do is to encourage them to have sex safely (avoiding disease) and responsibly (avoiding pregnancy). The other view is that abstinence is the only appropriate course for unmarried teens and the only 100 percent safe approach to sex.

Until the late 1980s there was really no choice about which model a school would adopt. No abstinence-based curriculums had been developed before that point. Ever since the introduction of sex education on a large scale in the 1960s, the "responsible sex" approach had had the field all to itself. Let's start, then, by taking a look at that method and at the reasons why it came to be challenged.

The Day America Told the Truth, a 1990 survey of American beliefs and values, contains this scene from a California high school:

> It's Friday afternoon and the students are leaving a class in "social living." The teacher's parting words are, "Have a great weekend. Be safe.

William Kilpatrick is a professor of education at Boston College. This excerpt is from his book *Why Johnny Can't Tell Right from Wrong* (1993).

Buckle up. Just say 'No' . . . and if you can't say 'No,' then use a condom!"

The teacher explains her philosophy: "I try to give support to everyone's value system. So I say, 'If you're a virgin, fine. If you're sexually active, fine. If you're gay, fine.'"

Although the teacher in this example gives a nod in the direction of abstinence, her approach is basically of the "responsible sex" variety. Abstinence is fine, but so is sexual activity. So is gay sex. The teacher is committed to respecting and supporting whatever choices the students make. She just wants to encourage them to make their choices "responsibly."

If this sounds like an echo of the affective/nonjudgmental approach to drug education, there is no mistake. The type of sex education that has dominated the schools from the late sixties to the present is a product of the same nondirective school of thought. Like affective drug education, it serves up a blend of facilitation, values clarification, self-esteem, and choices. Students are encouraged to question, to explore options, and to develop more tolerant attitudes toward the sexual behavior of others. This approach also supplies information about pregnancy, venereal diseases, and birth control in the belief that informed students will make better decisions. Although this informational aspect is much stronger now than in the days before AIDS, decision making remains the key ingredient. Students have to decide for themselves what is right. Teachers, parents, and churches do not have the right to tell a youngster what to choose. *Changing Bodies, Changing Lives,* one of the most widely used texts in high school and junior high sex education, tells its readers: "If you feel your parents are overprotective . . . or if they don't want you to be sexual *at all* until some distant time, you may feel you have to tune out their voice entirely." Religious teachings come in for the same treatment. "Many Catholics, Protestants, Jews, and Muslims believe sex outside marriage is sinful," says *Changing Bodies.* "You will have to decide for yourself how important these messages are for you." In sex education, as in drug education, right and wrong is what you say it is.

How well has the nondirective approach worked?

In 1986 *Family Planning Perspectives*, a publication of Planned Parenthood's Alan Guttmacher Institute, published the results of two large studies, both of which failed to show any reduction in sexual activity for teenagers who had taken sex-education courses. The larger of the two studies found that for fifteen- and sixteen-year-old girls, participation in sex education slightly increased the odds of initiating sexual activity. In the same year (1986) a Lou Harris poll commissioned by Planned Parenthood revealed that teenagers who had had comprehensive sex education had significantly higher rates of sexual activity than their peers who had not had sex education. As a result of these and numerous other studies, proponents of "responsible" sex education no longer bother to claim that their programs reduce sexual activity. The *best* that is claimed is that the programs do not increase it.

How about pregnancies? In 1988 Douglas Kirby, research director of Education, Training and Research (ETR), an offshoot of Planned Parenthood, reported to the National Family Planning and Reproductive Health Association on the "Effectiveness of School-Based Clinics": "We find basically that . . . there is no measurable impact upon the use of birth control, nor upon pregnancy rates or birth rates. This is all based upon the survey data. There is no measurable impact." A subsequent study by the Guttmacher Institute showed that condom use had, indeed, increased among teens, but so also had the rate of sexual activity. The effect of these competing trends is that the overall pregnancy rate has remained the same, with one of every ten teenage girls becoming pregnant each year.

Compared to other assessments, however, these findings are on the optimistic side. In Virginia, for example, school districts that instituted comprehensive sex education showed a 17 percent increase in teen pregnancies, while schools that were *not* teaching it had an average 16 percent *decrease* during the same time period. Dr. Jacqueline Kasun of Humboldt State University found that in Humboldt County, California, with several model programs and higher than average funding of family planning, teenage pregnancy had increased at a rate of ten times the national average. At the same time, the increase in teenage abortions was fifteen times the national average.

One of the chief goals of "safe sex" education was to reduce the 10 number of sexually transmitted diseases — STDs for short. Yet over the last two decades, the incidence of STDs has dramatically increased — and nowhere more than in the teen population. Although AIDS has received the most attention, it actually represents only a small part of the problem.

- In 1950 genital herpes was a rare disease. It is now estimated to infect about 30 million Americans, with half a million new cases each year. The virus can cause problems during pregnancy and poses a serious threat to infants during childbirth. Herpes has no cure.

- *Chlamydia trachomatis*, an organism that is a major cause of pelvic inflammatory disease and sterility, infects about 2 million new victims each year. Girls fifteen to nineteen years old appear to have the highest infection rate.

- There are an estimated 1 million new cases of genital warts each year in the United States. Some studies suggest that a third of all sexually active teenagers have them.

- The risk of cervical cancer is dramatically increased by two factors: multiple sex partners and early involvement in sexual activity. According to an article in *Medical Aspects of Human Sexuality*, women who have venereal warts are 1,000 to 2,000 times more likely to develop cervical cancer than uninfected women. Physicians now talk about "an epidemic of cervical cancer."

- The incidence of gonorrhea has declined among teenagers over the last fifteen years, due largely to a national gonorrhea control program. Among young blacks, however, the infection rate increased dramatically in the 1980s.

- The rate of syphilis infection of teens aged fifteen to nineteen climbed 67 percent between 1984 and 1988.

- Each year more babies are born with birth defects caused by STDs than all the children stricken with polio in the decade of the fifties.

Linus Wright, former under secretary of education, had the following comments on these trends: "The permissiveness of American society over the past twenty years has exposed a generation of teenagers to a variety of medical dangers that were known in an earlier time only to the most jaded and irresponsible of adults."

The ironic fact is that a good deal of this permissiveness has been fostered in American classrooms.

Why has sex education been unable to curb sexual activity among American teens? One simple but often overlooked answer is that it never intended to do so. Nonjudgmental sex education does *not* frown on early sexuality — not in any way that a youngster would take seriously. The fact is, most classroom sex education is based on the expectation that youngsters *will* be sexually active.

A good example of the climate of expectancy can be found in a demonstration video produced a few years ago by the Massachusetts Department of Public Health and intended to serve as a model of exemplary AIDS education. Let's fast-forward to the last ten minutes.

Shoshona, a young nurse dressed in casual clothes, is nearing   15
the end of her presentation to a small group of suburban high school students. She has already covered a lot of ground. In the short space of forty minutes Shoshona has laid out the various sexual options, including man to man, woman to woman, woman to man, anal, oral, oral-anal, and vaginal. In addition, she has discussed several precautionary measures, including condoms, dental dams,

and Nonoxynol-9 — although, as Shoshona helpfully points out, "if you're using it for oral sex, you don't want to use a lubricated condom with Nonoxynol-9; it would taste pretty awful." With Shoshona's encouragement, the students have also discussed the best type of condoms (latex, not natural) and other highly practical matters such as who should pay for them and who ought to go to the pharmacy.

Shoshona's classroom manner is relaxed and friendly. Her rapport with these teens is at a level most parents could only envy. The discussion appears to be completely free and unscripted. One obvious advantage is her youth: Shoshona looks to be in her early twenties. Another advantage is her thoroughly nonjudgmental approach. Most parents would have difficulty in granting equal legitimacy to all sexual options. But Shoshona is above prejudice. Only when she speaks of society's "fear and oppression of gay people" does a judgmental tone come into her voice.

So far, the discussion has taken the prescribed nondirective path. Shoshona has encouraged the students to think about all the options, and she has been able to make most of her points in response to their questions. She has created an atmosphere in which, it seems, the discussion could go in any direction.

Some things, however, can't be left to chance. During the last ten minutes, Shoshona gives each student a large card — the kind that kindergarten teachers refer to as a flashcard. Unlike the kindergarten variety, however, each one of these cards denotes one of the fourteen steps of condom use. Shoshona asks the students to stand up, look at one another's cards, talk it over, and then try to line themselves up in the proper sequence. The cards in their proper order read: "talk with partner," "decision by both partners to have sex," "buy the condom," "sexual arousal," "erection," "roll condom on," "leave space at tip (squeeze out air)," "intercourse," "orgasm/ejaculation," "hold on to the rim," "withdraw the penis," "loss of erection," "relaxation," "throw condom out."

The students line up, but not quite in the correct sequence; Shoshona has to rearrange them. Once they have it right, she has each student display his or her card and read it aloud. "That's great!" she tells them. She seems genuinely proud. On their part, the students seem slightly embarrassed, but they all go about the exercise in a cooperative, good-humored way. Shoshona's sensitive, nonjudgmental manner has won them over.

I've shown this film to students in my adolescent psychology 20 class, and they respond favorably. They particularly like the way Shoshona allows her students to "think for themselves."

My own reaction is different. Although Shoshona's presentation exudes an atmosphere of nondirectiveness, it seems to me that there is no real intention of looking at all the options. One alternative that might be raised and explored in a sex education class is abstinence. In fact, it is one of the many alternatives offered by the teens in the videotape. One student mentions "not having sex" as an option. Shoshona reflects this back in good nondirective fashion and then they move on. It is all over in a matter of seconds, and the subject never comes up again during the hourlong session.

Why not?

One problem with the nondirective technique is that it can never be truly nondirective. In a counseling situation (the situation in which the technique was developed), a typical client will raise more issues than can be handled in a therapy session. Certain topics seem more fruitful than others to the therapist, and those are the ones he chooses to reinforce. If he pays more attention to issue A than to issues B, C, and D, the conversation will tend to go in the direction of issue A. Clients usually develop a sense of what the therapist is interested in, and that is the sort of material that tends to come up.

The students in this class quickly sense that Shoshona is interested not in abstinence but in safe sex, and so the discussion goes in the latter direction. One boy who mentions "massage" as a possible way of having body contact while avoiding AIDS gets a good deal more attention than the girl who mentioned abstinence. "That's a really good suggestion," says Shoshona of the massage prescription, and she refers to it favorably again five minutes later.

Just how nondirective is this?   25

When I bring up this objection, my students concede that I have a point. Maybe it's not as nondirective as they first thought. Still, they think it's a fairly open classroom (of the kind, I suspect, they wish I would conduct). I can usually win them over to my point of view, however, by posing a question. Do they think Shoshona has come prepared with an alternative set of flashcards displaying the proper sequence for practicing abstinence, in case the discussion should go in that direction? At this point they are usually willing to admit that the discussion is never intended to go very far in that direction.

Like most teachers in most parts of the world, Shoshona is doing what teachers have always done. She is creating a set of expectations. However, Shoshona's expectations are not those of a teacher in China or Japan or the Philippines. She expects youngsters to have sex and she expects them to use condoms when they do. The same expectation is created in sex education classrooms around the country where safe-sex instruction has become the order of the day. In addition, many schools are now establishing clinics where students can come for contraceptive information and devices. These "school-based clinics" are supposed to be only for the sexually active students, but it is difficult to imagine that their presence won't send a powerful message to the other students — namely, that the school accepts and sanctions sexual activity for teens. It is sometimes argued in defense of the clinics that students don't have to make use of them. But that seems beside the point. The courts, for example, have decided that school prayer is not permissible even if the students are not required to participate, because the very presence of prayer at school constitutes an implied endorsement of religion. In similar fashion, the presence of school-based clinics that pass out condoms would seem to lend legitimacy to sexual activity.

As the statistics show, American teenagers are living up to expectations. They are having more sex and they are using more condoms. Unfortunately, for those who believe that fewer pregnancies will result, the two activities cancel each other out. As the number of teens engaging in sex increases, the number who will "make mistakes" also increases.

Not that defenders of the safe-sex/nonjudgmental approach don't have a ready answer. They claim that without their curriculums, the situation might be much worse, and besides, they say, in what has become the most common defense of safe-sex education, "you have to be realistic."

The claim of realism, however, needs some examination. 30

It rests, in the first place, on the assumption that all teens are having sex. But the Lou Harris/Planned Parenthood poll of late 1986 revealed that of the twelve- to seventeen-year-olds sampled, 72 percent of the girls had not engaged in intercourse. A lot of teens are having sex, but a great many are not. And of those who are "sexually active," many are a long way from being habituated to sex. Statistics on sexually active teens include adolescents who in reality are not very active at all. For example, a national survey by Zelnick and Kantner found that 20 percent of "sexually experienced" teenagers aged fifteen to seventeen have had intercourse only once. According to Douglas Powell, chief of psychology services at Harvard and author of the book *Teenagers*, "it is not unusual for normal teenagers to become celibate after their initial sexual encounters." The question that then arises is whether schools should take the tack that teenage sex is inevitable or whether they should reinforce those who are trying to resist sexual involvement.

Another lapse in realism was revealed when, in the late 1980s, the term "safe sex" had to be scuttled in favor of the more realistic term "safer sex." Medical research simply would not support the original formulation. For example, a number of studies have shown that the rate of condom failure — that is, the rate of unplanned pregnancies when using condoms — is 10 percent for all age groups and 18 percent for women under eighteen (the failure rate for diaphrams for this age group is 32 percent; for spermicide, 34 percent). But these figures are only for the first year of use. Extrapolated over time, they mean that a sexually active fourteen-year-old girl who relies on condoms has a more than 50 percent chance of becoming pregnant before she graduates from high school, and a 70 percent chance before finishing college.

Bear in mind, however, that these statistics refer only to pregnancy rates. Condoms are much less effective in stopping the spread of the AIDS virus, which can be transmitted at any time and which is 410 times smaller than sperm. As a Department of Education position paper points out: "A woman is fertile roughly 36 days a year, but someone with AIDS can transmit it 365 days a year." Furthermore, in a 1987 study of seventeen homosexual couples using condoms "especially designed for the study," 15 percent of the condoms slipped off and 11 percent ruptured. A 1985 study published in the British medical journal *Lancet* reported condom breakage rates of up to 50 percent during anal intercourse.

In light of these statistics, it would appear that the nonjudgmental/safe-sex approach can add up to a dangerous combination. Dr. Theresa Crenshaw, a past president of the American Association of Sex Educators, Counselors and Therapists, in testimony before a House subcommittee in February 1987, said, "To say that the use of condoms is 'safe sex' is in fact playing Russian roulette. A lot of people will die in this dangerous game." Yet despite warnings like this, schoolteachers routinely present homosexuality to their students as just another option about which they must decide for themselves.

Still another failure of realism is the failure to understand teenage psychology. One of the distinctive features of adolescent psychology is a belief in personal invulnerability. Adolescents believe that pregnancy and disease are things that happen to others but "won't happen to me." Logically they know this is not true, but they believe it anyway and act accordingly. For this and other reasons, teens are notoriously poor users of contraceptives. Even when "it" does happen to them, teens have a hard time comprehending the long-range implications. Wanda Franz, a professor of child development who has worked extensively with teens, writes, "Many adolescents report being more upset about missing the prom because of pregnancy than of having a baby."

Many people think that the answer to this is more information. Lack of information is not the problem, however, but rather a lack of the ability to process it. A *New York Times* writer recounts, "I was sitting at a table with half a dozen sixteen-year-old girls, listening with some amazement as they showed off their knowledge of human sexuality. They knew how long a sperm lived inside the body and how many women out of 100 using a diaphragm were statistically likely to get pregnant . . . there was just one problem with this performance: Every one of the girls was pregnant." . . .

Although sex educators like to say that proponents of abstinence for teens are not realistic, the argument cuts two ways. One of the harsh realities that now confront us is that children from broken or single-parent homes have much higher rates of drug abuse, crime, alcoholism, school failure, and suicide. They also have a much higher rate of sexual activity, pregnancy, and out-of-wedlock births. A large part of their problem derives from the fact that their parents have been unable either to make or to keep commitments. But again, what sort of marriages will the current generation of desensitized children be able to make? In what way do courses that break down inhibitions and strip sex of any moral content constitute a preparation for a committed marriage? Or committed parenthood? Isn't it likely that youngsters trained in this way will only fuel the problem of irresponsible parenthood once they grow up? Someone no doubt will supply *their* children with condoms, but who will supply them with parents? T. S. Eliot once observed that modern thinkers have a habit of "dreaming of systems so perfect that no one will need to be good." That appears to have been the hope of Planned Parenthood and other groups involved in sex education. But in any long-term view, their technical/informational approach reveals itself to be extremely shortsighted.

At one time modesty, not a condom, was a young woman's protection against any hasty indulgence she might regret. Modesty, in turn, was linked to an understanding that the sexual act is by nature intimate, private, intensely personal, and connected to the deepest level of the soul. At the same time, it was understood that society has an interest in proper sexual conduct. The pleasure principle is not a very good rule for social order. Sooner or later, sexual irresponsibility, adulteries, diseases, neglected children, and abandoned families become everyone's problem.

One way that a breakdown of sexual restraint hurts society is in the educational sphere. There is abundant evidence that the more sexually active students do poorly in school and tend to drop out more frequently. Almost half of the teenage girls who drop out of school do so because of pregnancy. But that figure only suggests one dimension of the problem. The constant distraction caused by worries about sex and about relationships takes a toll on schoolwork. Harvard sociologist David Riesman says the problem is especially acute for girls: "I can't help thinking of all the fears girls have as teenagers, especially as young teenagers. Will they get pregnant if they sleep with a boy? Should they take precautions? If they do, will it show they were waiting for it? They have terrible anxieties about all this."

Riesman goes so far as to question the whole concept of coeducation. "If one looks over the globe, one sees very few places where boys and girls are thrown at each other the way they are here in American schools — with everything unchaperoned, unsupervised, and permissive," declared Riesman in a recent interview. He suggests that co- 40 education only works in societies that maintain high standards of sexual conduct. Several recent studies confirm that girls do learn better in single-sex environments on both the high school and college levels. How much of this is due to the absence of sexual distraction and how much to other factors is difficult to say, but the studies do provide correlational evidence of an inverse link between sexual stimulation and school achievement. Other evidence comes from a 1987 "Survey of High Achievers" for *Who's Who among American High School Students*. The survey found that 73 percent of the high-achieving students had never had intercourse. In Japan, where the general level of educational achievement is much higher than ours, only 17 percent of unmarried girls below the age of twenty have lost their virginity, compared to 65 percent of American girls.

It is difficult to concentrate on one's studies in a sex-saturated society, and even more so when the schools themselves become a source of erotic stimulation. During the same years that safe-sex education expanded throughout the nation's schools, scores on reading, math, science, history, and knowledge of geography declined steadily. Nine years ago, a presidential commission studying our education system titled its report "A Nation at Risk." "If an unfriendly foreign power had attempted to impose on America the mediocre educational performance that exists today," observed the panel, "we might well have viewed it as an act of war." I don't know if the remark was also meant to refer to our system of sex education, but it might well have.

In light of the foregoing, it is not surprising that a strong resistance eventually grew up against the "going-to-do-it-anyway" school of sex education. In 1981, with the passage of the Adolescent Family Life Act, federal funds became available for the development of abstinence-based curriculums. The bill was aimed at encouraging programs that would "clearly and unequivocally" promote abstinence. It also called for greater family involvement in the development of programs, since "prevention of adolescent sexual activity and adolescent pregnancy depends primarily upon developing strong family values and close family ties." . . .

Is abstinence a realistic expectation? Yes and no. No, if the expectation is that all youngsters will wait until marriage before having sex. Yes, if it means that a majority can be persuaded that postponing sex is the right thing to do. It is true that some will "do it anyway," no matter what. It is also true that actual behavior tends to fall below the cultural ideal. What this means in practice, however, is that the higher the cultural standard is set, the farther actual behavior rises to meet it. In turn, the lower the culture sets its standard, the farther below it actual behavior will sink.

If the culture upholds sex within marriage as the norm, it doesn't mean that everyone will wait until marriage, but it does mean that many will at least wait until they're engaged — a situation that seems to have prevailed in our culture until recent decades. But if society decides it has to be "realistic" and lowers the standard to "sex with commitment," actual behavior tends to fall to the next lowest level — let's call it "sex within the context of love." "We're not engaged," a couple will maintain, "but it's okay because we love each other." If society then decides it has to adjust to the new reality of many couples not waiting for engagement and lowers the norm to "sex with love," actual behavior again falls — this time to the level of what we might call "sex with like." Once the standard falls to the level of recreational sex — about where it is now — we shouldn't be surprised to find that exploitative sex has become the norm for many or that date rape has become a major problem.

We are all, to a great extent, creatures of our culture. By and large, we tend to conform to cultural expectations, even if not perfectly. Our present culture sends out confused and misleading messages about sex — messages that, in the long run, threaten our survival. But it's not inevitable that we remain in this state. Key cultural institutions — such as the schools — can make a difference if they are willing to take a clear stand. Some will say that you can't take such stands in a pluralistic society. And it's true that some people will undoubtedly take offense, as did a group of parents in Wisconsin who, together with the ACLU, recently filed a discrimination suit against the Sex Respect program because of its emphasis on two-parent, heterosexual families. It's futile to hope to please everyone. Most people, however, do not call for their lawyer when they hear the words "marriage" or "teen abstinence"— certainly not most parents. As William Bennett observed at the time he was secretary of education, "I have never had a parent tell me that he or she would be offended by a teacher telling a class that it is better to postpone sex. Or that marriage is the best setting for sex, and in which to have and raise children. On the contrary, my impression is that the overwhelming majority of parents would gratefully welcome help in transmitting such values."

A lot depends on marriage — not least the moral health of a society. And marriage, as we are once again coming to understand, depends to a large extent on a code of chastity outside of marriage. With the coming of the sexual revolution, men began to flee their homes in droves, leaving women with the children, with double the work, and with little time or energy to provide discipline or moral guidance. Many men, of course, never bother to get married in the first place, since there is little incentive to do so. But that doesn't prevent them from fathering children. The "safe sex" approach to sex education doesn't do anything to alleviate this situation; it only intensifies it. It should be obvious by now to all but the most obtuse that women are going to continue to have babies, safe sex or no. The

45

trouble with safe sex is that it accustoms young men to the idea that sex is something that can be had without commitment. And if they can have it without commitment, that is the way they would rather have it.

I've heard teachers complain that creating an expectation of abstinence and self-control would require going back to old-fashioned methods of education. But this is really a false premise; the fact is, teachers fall back on those "old-fashioned" methods all the time. Consider Shoshona's use of the flashcards. When it comes to teaching something she feels strongly about, she drops her nonjudgmental stance and switches to a highly directive method. It is only the values she regards lightly — such as premarital chastity — that can safely be left up to the "whatever-feels-right-for-you" process.

In trying to promote ideas about safe sex or to raise the students' consciousness about homosexuality, sex educators have no hesitation at all in using traditional methods. In the service of those causes, they are willing to employ rote learning, repetition, memorization, absolute and authoritative statements, posters, school assemblies (in which, for example, condoms are demonstrated and distributed), campaigns ("National Condom Week"), instructional films, "pregnancy prevention" fairs, pamphlets, essay contests, and yes, even flashcards.

In so doing, of course, they are paying an unintended compliment to the methods traditionally used in character education. All of which suggests there may be more to that approach than educators are currently willing to concede.

THINKING AND WRITING ABOUT SEX EDUCATION

Questions for Discussion and Writing

1. The writer Norman Cousins coined the term "cop-out realism" to describe our reluctant acceptance of antisocial behavior that seems difficult or impossible to control. Would this definition apply to the decision to distribute condoms in school? Do any of the writers in this chapter support such an interpretation?

2. How do the writers treat parental rights in the sex education debate? Specify the warrants on which the different claims are grounded. What is your own position on the degree to which parents should be involved?

3. What is Hymowitz's complaint against sex education? Is it justified? If you have taken a sex education course that fits her description, comment on her objections.

4. Does your own experience confirm Whitehead's opinions about the influences on sexual activity of children? What kind of sex education curriculum would she favor?

"Guess who's been made condom monitor?"

5. Roye says that "abstinence is not a reality." Elmer-DeWitt seems to agree with her. Do they make their reasons clear? Compare Hopkins's discussion of abstinence with theirs.
6. Educator Sarah Glazer says, "It is virtually impossible to teach sex education without discussing values. . . ." Do writers in this section agree with her? What values are mentioned? Are other values implicit in the arguments?
7. What different kinds of evidence does Kilpatrick use to bolster his claim? Do you think he is right in blaming coeducation for a role in promoting sexual activity among teenagers?
8. Do you think the cartoonist objects to all sex education in schools or only some aspects of it? How did you arrive at your interpretation?

Topics for Research

A sex education program in the United States that has worked

Why some sex education courses don't work

The conflict over values in the sex education debate

Sex education messages in the media

Reasons for the rise in sexual activity among children

CHAPTER EIGHTEEN

Sex and Violence
in Popular Culture

The ongoing controversy about explicit sex and violence in movies, television, and rap music has surfaced again with particular urgency. A 1995 *New York Times* article found that "nine out of ten of those polled could think of something bad to say about popular culture, with a large proportion mentioning too much sex, violence, and vulgar language."[1] The reasons for the renewed attacks are not hard to find. An explosion of crime and sexual activity among the young has energized the search for a cause, and popular culture is a perennial target. But the extraordinary accessibility of this culture raises new alarms. Never has commercial entertainment been so widely and easily available to the young, the population thought to be most susceptible to its influence.

The debate begins with claims about the nature and extent of that influence. Are some forms of popular entertainment necessarily dangerous and immoral? How much are viewers affected by continued exposure to depictions of explicit sex and violence? Researchers have argued the point for years, but today a majority consensus believes that long-term viewing does, in fact, alter the behavior of certain audiences. In recent years what appear to be copycat crimes have followed the showing of particularly violent films. Experts also debate the relative effects of fictional and real-life images: Which are more corrupting — the graphic creations in movies or the daily reports of real-life horrors in the news?

Not surprisingly, even where agreement exists on the nature of the problem, there is disagreement about solutions. However

---

[1] Elizabeth Kolbert, "Americans Despair of Popular Culture," *New York Times,* August 20, 1995, Sec. H, p. 1.

strongly some critics feel about the dangers of exposure, they argue that the dangers of government censorship may, in the long run, be greater. But if government intervention is rejected, can other solutions — a rating system for TV shows and music albums, a V-chip in the TV set allowing parents to block undesirable programs, respect by producers for the so-called family hour, and above all, closer monitoring by parents — guarantee that young people will be insulated from exposure to sex and violence in the media? Most Americans are not optimistic. The *New York Times* poll shows that 63 percent of those questioned believe that ratings alone, for example, will not "keep children from seeing or listening to inappropriate material."

Of course, popular culture is not the only source of exposure. Movies, television, and music reflect the activities, tastes, fantasies, and prejudices of a larger society. Reducing the amount of sex and violence in the media is certainly easier than reforming a whole society. Still, the question remains: To what extent can any reform in popular entertainment successfully address the problems of teenage crime and sexual activity?

Sex, Violence, and Videotape
IRVING KRISTOL

On March 31, Britain experienced an unexpected cultural shock. That was when Professor Elizabeth Newson, head of the child development unit at Nottingham University, issued a report on violence-rich videos (known in the United Kingdom as "video nasties") and their effect on children. The report was signed by twenty-five psychologists and pediatricians, all known to be of the liberal persuasion. Its gist is summed up by the following quotations:

"Many of us hold our liberal ideals of freedom of expression dear, but now begin to feel that we were naive in our failure to predict the extent of damaging material and its all-too-free availability to children."

It then went on: "By restricting such material from home viewing, society must take on a necessary responsibility in protecting children from this, as from other forms of child abuse."

A storm of controversy ensued, which the American press largely ignored. A Labour member of Parliament introduced legislation to limit the availability of such "video nasties." The movie in-

---

Irving Kristol, a fellow of the American Enterprise Institute, coedits *The Public Interest* and publishes *The National Interest*. This essay appeared in the May 31, 1994, issue of the *Wall Street Journal*.

dustry was naturally outraged, since so much of their profits come from the subsequent sale of videotapes, and they cried "Censorship!"— which, of course, is what was being advocated. More surprising was the reaction of the Tory Home Minister, Michael Howard, who turned out to be "wet" (we would say "soft") on this whole issue. He was very worried about all those households without children, whose freedom to watch "video nasties" would be circumscribed.

Both True and False

And then, inevitably, there were the unreconstructed liberal academics, who kept insisting that no one had ever proved a causal relation between TV violence and aggressive behavior by the young. This was both true and false. It was true in the sense that such clear-cut, causal relations are beyond the reach of social science — there are simply too many other factors that influence youthful behavior. It was false because there is an abundance of circumstantial evidence that points to the existence of such a relation — circumstantial evidence so strong as to raise no reasonable doubt in the minds of ordinary people, and of parents especially.

In the Spring 1993 issue of *The Public Interest,* Brandon Centerwall, a professor of epidemiology at the University of Washington, summarizes much of this circumstantial evidence. He focuses on research findings on the effect of television when it was introduced to rural, isolated communities in Canada and when English-language TV came to South Africa in 1975, having previously been banned by the Afrikaans-speaking government. In all such instances there was a spectacular increase in violent crime, most especially among the young.

Professor Centerwall also notes that when TV was introduced in the United States after World War II, the homicide rate among whites, who were the first to buy sets, began to rise, while the black homicide rate didn't show any such increase until four years later.

Statistical studies of the relation between youthful aggressiveness and TV can be deceptive, Professor Centerwall explains, if they focus on the overall, average response — which, indeed, seems weak. But aggressive impulses, like most human phenomena, are distributed along a bell-shaped curve, and it is at the margin where the significant effect is to be observed: "It is an intrinsic property of such 'bell curve' distributions that small changes in the average imply major changes at the extremes. Thus, if an exposure to television causes 8 percent of the population to shift from below-average aggression to above-average aggression, it follows that the homicide rate will double."

Professor Centerwall concludes that "the evidence indicates that if, hypothetically, television technology had never been developed, there would today be 10,000 fewer homicides each year in the United States, 70,000 fewer rapes, and 700,000 fewer injurious assaults. Violent crime would be half what it is."

So the evidence for some kind of controls over television (and 10 tapes) is strong enough to provoke popular and political concern. It is certainly true that any such controls will involve some limitations on the freedom of adults to enjoy the kind of entertainment they might prefer. But modest limits on adult liberties ought to be perfectly acceptable if they prevent tens of thousands of our children from growing up into criminal adults. And it is the children we should be focusing on. The violence-prone adults, especially at the pathological fringe, are beyond our reach and, in most cases, beyond all possibility of redemption. It is the young people — especially those who have not yet reached adolescence — who are most affected by television, as all the studies agree.

Something will surely be done about this problem, despite the American Civil Liberties Union and other extreme interpreters of the First Amendment. In Britain, Mr. Howard has reluctantly agreed to propose appropriate legislation, propelled by a powerful consensus among Tories, the Labour Party, the Liberal Party, the media, and popular opinion. There is little doubt that, in the United States, a momentum for similar action is building up. How politicians will respond to it remains to be seen. But the idea that our popular culture can have malignant effects upon our young, and upon our society in its entirety, seems to be an idea whose coming cannot be long delayed.

And if there is a connection between our popular culture and the plague of criminal violence we are suffering from, then is it not reasonable to think that there may also be such a connection between our popular culture and the plagues of sexual promiscuity among teenagers, teenage illegitimacy, and, yes, the increasing number of rapes committed by teenagers? Here again, we don't really need social science to confirm what common sense and common observations tell us to be the case.

Can anyone really believe that soft porn in our Hollywood movies, hard porn in our cable movies, and violent porn in our "rap" music is without effect? Here, the average, overall impact is quite discernible to the naked eye. And at the margin, the effects, in terms most notably of illegitimacy and rape, are shockingly visible.

Clearly, something must be done to lower the temperature of the sexual climate in which we live. And whatever is done, it will of necessity limit the freedoms of adults to indulge their sexual fantasies. Most of us will not mourn the loss of such freedoms, but — as with violence — there are those who will loudly protest any such rude "violation" of our "civil liberties."

Censorship, we will be told, is immoral — though no moral code 15 of any society that has ever existed has ever deemed it so. Besides, we will be told further, it is ineffectual. Well, those of us who have lived in a slightly chillier sexual climate have survived as witnesses to the fact that it is not so ineffectual after all. True, censorship makes a difference only at the margin. But, and this cannot be repeated too often, it is at the margin where the crucial action is. This is as true for sexual activity as it is for economic activity.

Invitation to Promiscuity

The most common (hypocritical and politically cowardly) response to the problems generated by our overheated sexual climate is that these are something parents have to do something about. But parents cannot do it on their own. They never have been able to do it on their own. Parents have always relied on churches, schools, and the popular culture for help. Today, no such reliance is possible.

The mainline churches, still intoxicated with a vulgarized Freudianism, have discovered that sex is good and repression is bad. The schools hand out condoms to adolescents while timidly suggesting that they ought to limit their activity to "responsible sex." This is nothing less than an official invitation to promiscuity. The culture, meanwhile, is busy making as much money as possible out of as much sex as possible.

No, the government, at various levels, will have to step in to help the parents. And it will do so despite the anticipated cries of outrage from libertarians, liberal or conservative. The question, and it is no easy question, is just how to intervene. That is the issue that is now up for serious discussion.

The Myth of Television Depravity

MICHAEL HIRSCHORN

A nationwide *New York Times* poll two Sundays ago reported that 21 percent of those surveyed blame television for teenage violence, compared with only 8 percent who believe the breakdown of the family is the cause of the trouble. To solve this putative problem, the Senate has passed legislation requiring violence-screening technology in all new television sets, and conservatives would like to see prime time declared a violence-and-sex free zone. As best I can tell, the effect of this radical change would be about . . . zero.

Michael Hirschorn is executive editor of *New York* magazine, where the essay from which this excerpt is taken appeared on September 4, 1995.

It is remarkable, in fact, how consistently prime-time television dwells on the very issues the conservatives complain are being ignored by Hollywood: how to raise children, how to keep families together, what to do with aging parents, how to construct a meaningful life when money is short and both parents must work. Have you seen MTV recently? The network considered literally satanic by many conservatives is now almost completely devoid of the T&A that made it so controversial a few years ago.

Watched as a block, prime-time TV shows yield a remarkably consistent message: They are dramas and comedies of coping, far from the merry subversion of families that top conservative media critic L. Brent Bozell III says is "all the rage" now. The harried Roseanne and husband Dan making do with little money and a touchingly infirm grasp on how best to be parents; Grace from *Grace under Fire* finding her way as a single mother; the cops on *NYPD Blue* (those butt shots are pretty much a thing of the past) earnestly dramatizing the conflicting demands of family and work, competence and ethics — *these are among the most popular shows in America,* and to accuse television of subverting family values without considering this mainstream programming means someone is either not doing his homework or just doesn't care.

Consider *ER*, the runaway hit of last season. In a single episode the following happens: overworked boyfriend worrying how to show a girlfriend's son that he cares; two doctors debating whether a patient should be given an expensive medical test; a brother and sister, amid many tears, telling their mother she must go into an old-age-home; a doctor telling a poor mom without health insurance that he'll treat the daughter anyway; an illegal immigrant worrying about being treated because she fears being deported; the poor mom watching her daughter almost die; a married fortyish woman desperately trying to get pregnant; a character taking in her troubled pregnant sister. At show's end, the black actor Eriq La Salle, playing the son who has put his mother in a home, is shown massaging her feet and looking over the family photo album. The old lady tells her doctor son: "Your talent is God's gift to you. What you do with it is your gift back to God." Could there be a purer family-values moment?

Family values make their way even into the single–New Yorker 5 sitcoms. On *Seinfeld,* where much of the comic frisson comes from the fact that every character on the show is venal, solipsistic Jerry helps his grandmother open a bottle of ketchup, then helps his mother get back $50 his bad uncle Leo has owed her for fifty years.

Ellen, a kind of distaff Seinfeld, opens with a fur protest that's played for anti-PETA ridicule. "Everyone here is passionately dedicated to the cause," Ellen says. "Could one of you introduce me to the girl without the bra?" counters the Arye Gross character. *Ba-dum*

dum. One guy has made sandwiches for the protest — "lettuce, tomato, and seal pup. I call 'em my club sandwiches." The self-righteous organizer slaps him. He retorts: "There's one thing I love about you political extremists. It's your ability to laugh at yourselves." Ellen gets arrested at the protest. Her friend never comes to help her because, she says, "I was on my way to the fur department, then I saw these great little shoes." After several wacky plot twists, thirtysomething Ellen ends up in the custody of her silly suburban parents, and there are jokes about eating your vegetables. It's a nightmare, and Ellen tries to sneak out with her parents' car. They call the police and have her arrested again. The judge is astonished. "You called the police on your own daughter?" he asks. Ellen stands up for her parents, and this time they all end up in jail. It turns out to be something of a bonding experience: They may quarrel, but they're all willing to go to jail for one another. Out the next day, they drive home singing Steppenwolf's "Born to be Wild" together.

On *Mad about You,* a popular (but not top ten) show about a prosperous, happily married Manhattan couple, Jamie learns that her mom was briefly on television and that her aunt Lolly consorted with a number of famous fifties comedians up in the Catskills. On *Grace under Fire,* Grace's father-in-law has a heart-bypass operation, and Grace must get the whole family, including her terrifying mother-in-law, through the ordeal. She promises Dad-in-law that if he dies, she'll let Mom-in-law live with her — even though Grace is no longer married to his son. Son and daughter-in-law exchange tearful professions of love. Meanwhile, the couple who are Grace's best friends decide whether to keep trying to have a baby or to adopt.

Is there a more wholesome group of kids than the cute boys and girls on *Friends*? They are all white and hetero; dress well; have nice haircuts; work hard; and rarely smoke, drink, or have sex. They are, as Michael Kinsley once said of Al Gore, an old person's idea of young people.

Dole Depravity Score

Casual sex — None; discussion on *Roseanne* of what to do about the fifteen-year-old D.J., whose trouble in school is caused, it turns out, by the fact that he gets spontaneous erections. *Gratuitous violence* — No violence of any sort. *Mainstreaming deviancy* — None; except for the singles on *Seinfeld* and *Friends,* virtually everyone else on the top ten is either conspicuously married or in a family (and Disney hasn't even taken over ABC yet). *Slurs against religion* — None. *E.T. syndrome (subverting parental authority)* — None. Kids do what Mama and Papa say in *Grace, Roseanne,* and *Home Improvement,* where zestily insensitive dad Tim Allen is clearly hipper than his three generi-boys. *Attacks on the free-enterprise system* — The

Roseanne episode ends postmodernistically with her talking to an actor playing the network censor, proposing a number of names for erections ("raising the drawbridge," "standing up for democracy") while the increasingly exasperated network official keeps repeating "No." She finally points to a camera, revealing to him that all her lines in fact are already being broadcast. He looks over his shoulder in shock and says, "Is that on? Aw, shit!" The expletive is beeped out and his mouth is pixelated. It's the funniest moment on prime time.

Pop Culture and Drugs
THE WALL STREET JOURNAL

A new national poll has just drawn an association between drug use and popular culture. TV, movies, magazines, and music encourage illegal use of drugs, say 67 percent of the adults surveyed. More interesting, though, is that the response of the MTV generation is even stronger: 76 percent of twelve- to seventeen-year-olds say pop culture encourages drug use. Insofar as these outlets have generally backed off the most explicit references to drug use, the young respondents seem to be saying that they understand that drugs are obviously part of the wide-open life-styles and behavior depicted in what they read or watch.

Since the days of "Lucy in the Sky with Diamonds," liberal sophisticates have smirked at conservatives for saying such things about contemporary American culture. The personal wreckage suggests it's time to stop laughing and get serious. Indeed, this survey comes from eminently mainstream Columbia University, not Bob Jones University. Maybe on this one the religious right was, well, right.

The sobering findings come from Columbia's Center on Addiction and Substance Abuse. The center's president, Joseph Califano, puts it succinctly: "Our children are crying out for help," he says. "They're telling us that drugs are by far the most important problem they face growing up."

Some 32 percent of the adolescents polled support that view of illegal drugs. No other problem even comes close. Crime and violence in the schools, certainly a related issue, comes in second at 13 percent. Social pressure is third, at 10 percent. Everything else is in single digits.

This editorial appeared in the *Wall Street Journal* on August 26, 1995.

In the hope of trying to figure out how to protect kids from 5 drugs, the survey also analyzed which children are most likely to resist. Race isn't a factor. Nor does it matter whether a child lives in the suburbs instead of the city or with one or both parents. Instead, the survey found that the children most apt to say no to drugs practice a religion, perform well at school, are hopeful about the future (expect to do as well or better than their parents), receive parental guidance, and think marijuana is dangerous.

So the good news seems to be that with the help of a good family and a religion, kids can resist the siren song of the pushers. The bad news is that most of our children don't live in that world anymore. The results of the Columbia poll, taken together with research by the Partnership for a Drug-Free America, the University of Michigan, and others, paint a stark picture of the world our children live in. Instead, it's an anything-goes social culture that discourages self-restraint; add in the easy availability of drugs and bad things happen to good children.

As this and other surveys suggest, parents are the first and best defense against drugs. But it certainly would help a lot if the entertainment industry recognized its responsibility for the effect on children of the trashy, morally slovenly life-styles it promotes. Something similar might be said for tobacco companies, since, as the Columbia poll found, kids who smoke are far more likely to move on to illegal drugs.

An important step toward solving any problem is to find out what's contributing to it. The Columbia survey's helpful contribution is to assert that even the kids now think the country's popular culture just doesn't get it.

TV Isn't Violent Enough

MIKE OPPENHEIM

Caught in an ambush, there's no way our hero (Matt Dillon, Eliot Ness, Kojak, Hoss Cartwright . . .) can survive. Yet, visibly weakening, he blazes away, and we suspect he'll pull through. Sure enough, he's around for the final clinch wearing the traditional badge of the honorable but harmless wound: a sling.

As a teenager with a budding interest in medicine, I knew this was nonsense and loved to annoy my friends with the facts.

"Aw, the poor guy! He's crippled for life!"

When this essay was published in the February 11, 1984, issue of *TV Guide,* Mike Oppenheim was a freelance writer and physician practicing medicine in California.

"What do you mean? He's just shot in the shoulder."

"That's the worst place! Vital structures everywhere. There's the blood supply for the arm: axillary artery and vein. One nick and you can bleed to death on the spot." 5

"So he was lucky."

"OK. If it missed the vessels it hit the brachial plexus: the nerve supply. Paralyzes his arm for life. He's gotta turn in his badge and apply for disability."

"So he's *really* lucky."

"OK. Missed the artery. Missed the vein. Missed the nerves. Just went through the shoulder joint. But joint cartilage doesn't heal so well. A little crease in the bone leaves him with traumatic arthritis. He's in pain the rest of his life — stuffing himself with codeine, spending his money on acupuncture and chiropractors, losing all his friends because he complains all the time. . . . Don't ever get shot in the shoulder. It's the end. . . ."

Today, as a physician, I still sneer at TV violence, though not be- 10 cause of any moral objection. I enjoy a well-done scene of gore and slaughter as well as the next viewer, but "well-done" is something I rarely see on a typical evening in spite of the plethora of shootings, stabbings, muggings, and brawls. Who can believe the stuff they show? Anyone who remembers high-school biology knows the human body can't possibly respond to violent trauma as it's usually portrayed.

On a recent episode, Matt Houston is at a fancy resort, on the trail of a vicious killer who specializes in knifing beautiful women in their hotel rooms in broad daylight. The only actual murder se-quence was in the best of taste: all the action off screen, the flash of a knife, moans on the sound track.

In two scenes, Matt arrives only minutes too late. The hotel is alerted, but the killer's identity remains a mystery. Absurd! It's im-possible to kill someone instantly with a knife thrust — or even ren-der him unconscious. Several minutes of strenuous work are required to cut enough blood vessels so the victim bleeds to death. Tony Perkins in *Psycho* gave an accurate, though abbreviated, demonstration. Furthermore, anyone who has watched an inexperi-enced farmhand slaughter a pig knows that the resulting mess must be seen to be believed.

If consulted by Matt Houston, I'd have suggested a clue: "Keep your eyes peeled for someone panting with exhaustion and covered with blood. That might be your man."

Many Americans were puzzled at the films of the assassination attempt on President Reagan. Shot in the chest, he did not behave as TV had taught us to expect ("clutch chest, stagger backward, col-lapse"). Only after he complained of a vague chest pain and was taken to the hospital did he discover his wound. Many viewers assumed Mr. Reagan is some sort of superman. In fact, there was nothing extraordinary about his behavior. A pistol is certainly a deadly weapon, but not predictably so. Unlike a knife wound, one bullet can kill instantly — provided it strikes a small area at the base of the brain. Otherwise, it's no different: a matter of ripping and tearing enough tissue to cause death by bleeding. Professional gangland killers understand the problem. They prefer a shotgun at close range.

The trail of quiet corpses left by TV's good guys, bad guys, and 15 assorted ill-tempered gun owners is ridiculously unreal. Firearms reliably produce pain, bleeding, and permanent, crippling injury (witness Mr. Reagan's press secretary, James Brady: shot directly in the brain but very much alive). For a quick, clean death, they are no match for Luke Skywalker's light saber.

No less unreal is what happens when T. J. Hooker, Magnum, or a Simon brother meets a bad guy in manly combat. Pow! Our hero's fist crashes into the villain's head. Villain reels backward, tipping over chairs and lamps, finally falling to the floor, unconscious. Handshakes all around.... Sheer fantasy! After hitting the villain, our hero would shake no one's hand. He'd be too busy waving his own about wildly, screaming with the pain of a shattered fifth metacarpal (the bone behind the fifth knuckle), an injury so predictable it's called the "boxer's fracture." The human fist is far more delicate than the human skull. In any contest between the two, the fist will lose.

The human skull is tougher than TV writers give it credit. Clunked with a blunt object, such as the traditional pistol butt, most victims would not fall conveniently unconscious for a few minutes. More likely, they'd suffer a nasty scalp laceration, be stunned for a second or two, then be extremely upset. I've sewn up many. A real-life, no-nonsense criminal with a blackjack (a piece of iron weighing several pounds) has a much better success rate. The result is a large number of deaths and permanent damage from brain hemorrhage.

Critics of TV violence claim it teaches children sadism and cruelty. I honestly don't know whether or not TV violence is harmful, but if so the critics have it backward. Children can't learn to enjoy cruelty from the neat, sanitized mayhem on the average series. There isn't any! What they learn is far more malignant: that guns or fists are clean, efficient, exciting ways to deal with a difficult situation. Bang! — you're dead! Bop! — you're unconscious (temporarily)!

"Truth-in-advertising" laws eliminated many absurd commercial claims. I often daydream about what would happen if we had "truth in violence"— if every show had to pass scrutiny by a board of doctors who had no power to censor but could insist that any action scene have at least a vague resemblance to medical reality ("Stop the projector! . . . You have your hero waylaid by three Mafia thugs who beat him brutally before he struggles free. The next day he shows up with this cute little Band-aid over his eyebrow. We can't pass that. You'll have to add one eye swollen shut, three missing front teeth, at least twenty stitches over the lips and eyes, and a wired jaw. Got that? Roll 'em . . .").

Seriously, real-life violence is dirty, painful, bloody, disgusting. It causes mutilation and misery, and it doesn't solve problems. It makes them worse. If we're genuinely interested in protecting our children, we should stop campaigning to "clean up" TV violence. It's already too antiseptic. Ironically, the problem with TV violence is: It's not violent enough.

20

Imagebusters

TODD GITLIN

I have denounced movie violence for more than two decades, all the way back to *The Wild Bunch* and *The Godfather*. I consider Hollywood's slashes, splatters, chain saws, and car crashes a disgrace, a degradation of culture, and a wound to the souls of producers and consumers alike.

But I also think liberals are making a serious mistake by pursuing their vigorous campaign against violence in the media. However morally and aesthetically reprehensible today's screen violence, the crusades of Senator Paul Simon and Attorney General Janet Reno against television violence are cheap shots. There are indeed reasons to attribute violence to the media, but the links are weaker than recent headlines would have one believe. The attempt to demonize the media distracts attention from the real causes of — and the serious remedies for — the epidemic of violence.

The sheer volume of alarm can't be explained by the actual violence generated by the media's awful images. Rather, Simon and Reno — not to mention Dan Quayle and the Reverend Donald Wildmon — have signed up for a traditional American pastime. The campaign against the devil's images threads through the history of

Todd Gitlin, professor of culture, journalism, and sociology at New York University, is the author of *The Sixties: Years of Hope, Days of Rage* (1987); *The Twilight of Common Dreams* (1995), and other books. This essay originally appeared in the Winter 1994 issue of *The American Prospect;* the excerpt reprinted here is from the May–June 1994 *Utne Reader.*

middle-class reform movements. For a nation that styles itself practical, at least in technical pursuits, the United States has always been remarkably quick to become a playground of moral prohibitions and symbolic crusades.

If today's censorious forces smell smoke, it is not in the absence of fire. In recent years, market forces have driven screen violence to an amazing pitch. But the question the liberal crusaders fail to address is not whether these violent screen images are wholesome but just how much real-world violence can be blamed on the media. Assume, for the sake of argument, that *every* copycat crime reported in the media can be plausibly traced to television and movies. Let us make an exceedingly high estimate that the resulting carnage results in 100 deaths per year that would not otherwise have taken place. These would amount to 0.28 percent of the total of 36,000 murders, accidents, and suicides committed by gunshot in the United States in 1992.

That media violence contributes to a climate in which violence is legitimate — and there can be no doubt of this — does not make it an urgent social problem. Violence on the screens, however loathsome, does not make a significant contribution to violence on the streets. Images don't spill blood. Rage, equipped with guns, does. Desperation does. Revenge does. As liberals say, the drug trade does; poverty does; unemployment does. It seems likely that a given percent increase in decently paying jobs will save thousands of times more lives than the same percent decrease in media bang-bang.

Now, I also give conservative arguments about the sources of violence their due. A culture that despises and disrespects authority is disposed to aggression, so people look to violence to resolve conflict. The absence of legitimate parental authority also feeds a culture of aggression. But aggression per se, however unpleasant, is not the decisive murderous element. A child who shoves another child after watching a fistfight on television is not committing a drive-by shooting. Violence plays on big screens around the world without generating epidemics of carnage. The necessary condition permitting a culture of aggression to flare into a culture of violence is access to lethal weapons.

It's dark out there in the world of real violence, hopelessness, drugs, and guns. There is little political will for a war on poverty, guns, or family breakdown. Here, under the light, we are offered instead a crusade against media violence. This is largely a feel-good exercise, a moral panic substituting for practicality. It appeals to an American propensity that sociologist Philip Slater called the Toilet Assumption: Once the appearance of a social problem is swept out of sight, so is the problem. And the crusade costs nothing.

There is, for some liberals, an additional attraction. By campaigning against media violence, they hope to seize "family values" from conservatives. But the mantle of antiviolence they wrap themselves in is threadbare, and they are showing off new clothes that will not stop bullets.

The symbolic crusade against media violence is a confession of despair. Those who embrace it are saying, in effect, that they either do not know how, or do not dare, to do anything serious about American violence. They are tilting at images. If Janet Reno cites the American Psychological Association's recently published report, *Violence and Youth,* to indict television, she also should take note of the following statements within it: "Many social science disciplines, in addition to psychology, have firmly established that poverty and its contextual life circumstances are major determinants of violence.... It is very likely that socioeconomic inequality — not race — facilitates higher rates of violence among ethnic minority groups.... There is considerable evidence that the alarming rise in youth homicides is related to the availability of firearms." The phrase "major determinant" does not appear whenever the report turns to the subject of media violence.

The question for reformers, then, is one of proportion and focus. 10 If there were nothing else to do about deadly violence in America, then the passionate crusade against TV violence might be more justifiable, even though First Amendment absolutists would still have strong counterarguments. But the imagebusting campaign permits politicians to fulminate photogenically without having to take on the National Rifle Association or, for that matter, the drug epidemic, the crisis of the family, or the shortage of serious jobs.

So let a thousand criticisms bloom. Let reformers flood the networks and cable companies and, yes, advertisers, with protests against the gross overabundance of the stupid, the tawdry, and the ugly.

But not least, let the reformers not only turn off the set, but also criticize the form of life that has led so many to turn, and keep, it on.

Voyeurism and Vengeance

WENDY KAMINER

It is virtually axiomatic that a strong consensus about the existence of a national problem is likely to generate a strong demand for the government to solve it. (This is not only an axiom for liberals: Conservatives who protest excessive reliance on government meddling in daily life would probably not oppose a federal education law providing incentives for prayer in school.) Given the widely shared belief that media violence causes crime, it seems possible, at least, to garner majority support for restrictive legislation. People may support a voluntary ratings system as a first step, but, according to Gallup, 61 percent believe that warnings do not "go far enough."

Public concern about TV violence has hardly been lost on Washington, which occasionally consummates its historic flirtation with censorship. Since the first federal obscenity law was passed in 1873, Congress has dipped in and out of the business of policing popular entertainments and "obscene" information (notably sex education and information about birth control, which were once proscribed by federal law). From the beginning, Congress has been alert to the alleged dangers of TV. In 1954, Republican Senator Robert Hendrickson proposed appointing a "TV czar" to monitor programs that might encourage juvenile delinquency. Historically, the American tradition of free speech has had to coexist, somehow, with a tradition of moral reform. . . .

Apart from genuine concern about violence in the media, there were obvious political reasons for congressional action. Many more Americans are exposed to violent media than violent crime, which tends to be concentrated in low-income urban neighborhoods. In New York City, for example, in 1993, the overall homicide rate declined, but the percentage of homicides occurring in depressed areas of the South Bronx, upper Manhattan, and Brooklyn, increased. Nearly half of the city's reported homicides took place in 16 percent of its precincts. Violence in the media is much more equitably distributed and affects many more middle-class suburbanites than gang wars and drive-by shootings.

So, if violence in the media is a less compelling problem than violence in the streets, it's more widespread and at the same time less intractable. Actual violence is more likely to generate despair and nihilism than TV violence, which often leads to activism, because TV violence seems amenable to control. In Colombia, where the murder

Wendy Kaminer is a contributing editor for *The Atlantic Monthly*. This excerpt is from her 1995 book, *It's All the Rage*. [Bibliographic citations have been cut.]

rate is eight times higher than in the United States, politicians and business people have crusaded against violence in the media. . . .

In this country, Congress can't summon all the violent felons or potentially violent felons in the nation to hearings on the effect of their antisocial behavior, but it can summon TV and movie executives to hearings on violence in the media and threaten them with regulation. And felons may be immune to social pressure, social critics, and consumer boycotts, but media moguls — public relations masters and slaves — are not. In fact, as the moguls always point out, they're in the business of giving the public what it wants. Action movies are produced because they're profitable. That studio executives don't spawn the desire for violence doesn't excuse them from so enthusiastically satisfying it. Still, they are no more than collaborators.

More worrisome than the public demand for violent feature films and action fantasies is the taste for sensational true crime stories, which have become primary sources of "information" about criminal justice. People who are spared firsthand experience with the system learn about it from docudramas about Amy Fisher (the Long Island teenager who shot her lover's wife), "reality-based" TV cop shows and crime stories, and talk shoe palaver about sensational cases. The most attention is paid to the least typical cases.

But at the same time that people draw misleading lessons about criminal justice in general from these cases assuming that they're educational, they also find them entertaining. That's what's most disturbing. People loved the Amy Fisher, Erik and Lyle Menendez, and O. J. Simpson cases, gorging themselves on TV movies, tabloids, and hours of boring televised courtroom proceedings, as if the victims in these cases were characters in B movies, not sentient human beings. If action movies desensitize people to violence, as critics charge, at least the violence they depict is fictional. We tend to forget or deny the difference between watching Clint Eastwood shoot blanks into an actor playing a character who never lived or died and watching a stand-in for Lyle Menendez shoot blanks into a stand-in for his mother.

This confusion about fact and fiction also distorts perceptions of the actual cases people follow. That was one of the lessons of the sympathetic response to murder suspect O. J. Simpson. Racial tensions, the pervasive fascination with celebrity, and the willingness to tolerate domestic crimes all contributed to the willingness to believe he was innocent. But it also reflected the influence of popular entertainments.

Televised, starring an established celebrity, the Simpson case seemed like popular genre fiction. He seemed less like a real-life defendant than a hero in a Scott Turow or John Grisham novel slated for the screen; and on screen the defendant, especially when played by a star, is usually an innocent man, "caught in a web of circumstance," if he hasn't been framed. The story of an innocent man on the run — Robert Donat in *The Thirty-Nine Steps* or Harrison Ford in *The Fugitive* — has been a Hollywood staple for years. The Simpson case seemed just another installment. It was as if people presumed Simpson's innocence not out of respect for his constitutional rights but in anticipation of a last-minute plot twist.

If people sometimes mistake real courtroom dramas for enter-   10
tainments, they may also relate to entertainment as if it were real life. (My grandmother seemed genuinely concerned about the characters on her favorite soaps.) Preschool children are particularly prone to confuse imaginary and actual violence, critics of TV charge. "In the minds of such young children, television is a source of entirely factual information regarding how the world works," Brandon Centerwall wrote, in a 1992 article in the *Journal of the American Medical Association.* They grow out of this confusion, but it can have a lasting impact on behavior, Centerwall asserted. "Serious violence is most likely to erupt at moments of severe stress — and it is precisely at such moments that adolescents and adults are most likely to revert to their earliest, most visceral sense of what violence is and what its role is in society."

This merger of fact and fantasy is particularly acute for children who live in violent homes and neighborhoods, Sissela Bok has observed. These children are "especially likely to conclude that television violence reflects real life." For them, "the violence that they witness around them reinforces the realism they attribute to the violence they see enacted on the screen; and their view of the world is in turn strongly influenced by what they see on television."

Children are instinctively imitative creatures, critics assert. Television teaches them how to behave. This argument has particular resonance in a culture that has become sensitized to child abuse. It is generally acknowledged that children who grow up in violent homes are at high risk of becoming violent partly in reaction to their own mistreatment and partly because they mirror the behavior of adults around them. If children do not distinguish between fact and fantasy, between entertainment and information, it follows that they may adopt the behavior they see on TV, as they adopt the behavior they see in the world. In other words, critics argue, children don't just watch TV, they experience it, the way they experience a day at school.

Statements about the effect of television violence on children are sometimes made with an air of discovery, but few of them are new. Since the early days of film and video, advocates for children, as well as moral reformers, have focused on the effects of screen violence. And intensified concern about media violence naturally accompanies intensified concern about crime. The first congressional hearings on TV violence took place in the early 1950s, when television was just beginning to take hold of American culture and youth crime was increasing, which in one view was no coincidence.

In 1954, a Senate Judiciary Committee convened a series of hearings on the effect of TV on "the shocking rise in our national delinquency rate." Television was characterized as "the most powerful force man has yet devised for planting and spreading ideas." The Senate took particular interest in "ideas that spring into the living room for the entertainment of the youth of America, which have to do with crime and horror, sadism, and sex."

Television was "mental poisoning," according to Clara Logan, 15 president of the National Association for Better Radio and Television. Toxic shows included *Roy Rogers, The Lone Ranger,* and *Captain Midnight.* Logan asserted that 40 percent of all children's programming focused on crime and violence, and she worried that TV might directly induce some young viewers to commit crimes. But, like many media critics today, Logan was most concerned about the indirect, brutalizing effect of TV violence. "How can a youngster see so many human beings killed each week without acquiring an indifference toward violent death?" she asked. "How can a child who sees countless incidents of sadism and meaningless violence keep from becoming callous and unconcerned toward human misery and suffering?"

James Bennett, director of the Federal Bureau of Prisons, suggested at the Senate hearings that TV violence was most harmful to troubled, unstable children, and Harvard psychologist Eleanor Maccoby essentially agreed. Her experiments indicated that the effects of TV on children varied with their moods and personalities ("a TV program can have one function for one child and an entirely different function for another"). In this view, media violence doesn't cause aggression but may exacerbate aggressive tendencies. The causes of delinquency were more difficult to quantify than the shootings and fistfights on TV, Bennett observed. They included "lack of affection, feelings of rejection in the home, hostilities, and anxieties." Bennett was also skeptical of anecdotal evidence of copycat crimes. He had conducted interviews of delinquents convicted of committing crimes that had been dramatized in the media. "It was not unusual for a boy to claim that he had gotten the idea for the offense out of some comic book or out of the radio. But there is a tendency for those people to rationalize their offense, to blame it on something else or not accept the responsibility for it themselves."

Opinion was divided on the effect of TV crime shows: NBC Vice President Joseph Heffernan cited J. Edgar Hoover's support for "anti-crime programs" that showed criminals "playing a losing game." Indeed, NBC programming standards decreed that "criminals are always punished . . . crime is not condoned . . . law enforcement is upheld and portrayed with respect and dignity."

Violence and villainy on TV could have positive effects on children, Captain Video (aka actor Al Hodge) pointed out. "We have to have violence. Otherwise, there is no excuse for a heroic character existing. He has to go after somebody." Hodge stressed, however, that when Captain Video "went after" a bad guy in his TV show, he was armed only with a stun-gun. "This gun merely immobilizes an adversary to the point where we can take whatever lethal weapon he may have away from him, even to the point where we can say that this action of being stunned is not painful." Hodge also noted that Captain Video did not indulge in the violence of capital punishment. Villains were never hung: "We never have a line in the program which says, 'You had better do what we say or you will swing.' We do what we think will happen in the future. We confine our criminals in what we call a rehabilitation center. Actually it is a penal center on a planet of Ganymede, if you are familiar with your science fiction."

Captain Video's hopeful vision of enlightened criminal justice in the future seems about as quaint today as this colloquy between the Senate subcommittee's Chief Counsel Herbert Beaser and NBC Vice President Joseph Heffernan, over a scene of cowboy Hopalong Cassidy bleeding to death:

> *Heffernan:* I would doubt [it showed] Hopalong Cassidy bleeding to death because the man never dies.
>
> *Beaser:* It looked like he was bleeding to death.
>
> *Heffernan:* It may have looked like he was bleeding.
>
> *Beaser:* He was bleeding.

To contemporary audiences concerned with carnage in the media, Hopalong Cassidy with a spot of ketchup on his shirt is an image of the good old days. But, perhaps forty years from now, today's media violence will seem tame. The capacity of violent imagery to shock or damage or titillate people is relative. The westerns and crime shows that the Senate pondered in the early 1950s were the action movies of their day, appealing to a similar desire for order, justice, or vengeance, or pleasure in celluloid mayhem.

Still, if our enjoyment of violence isn't new, opportunities for indulging in it have been greatly expanded by technology, along with possibilities for portraying it. The evolution of special effects has been stunning. Video games and music videos, cable TV and Hollywood movies serve as more "powerful sources for promoting and spreading ideas" than the Senate of 1954 could ever have imagined. A large body of social science studies suggests that the media provides much more than harmless entertainment.

Since the advent of television, numerous studies have considered the link between violent TV and violent behavior. Critics of TV often claim that there have been 3,000 studies of television violence; but, in an enlightening critique of the social science data, American Civil Liberties Union attorney Marjorie Heins points out that many of the 3,000 studies cited are secondary reviews of primary studies of TV violence, which number about 100, and many of the oft-cited studies focus expansively on television, in general, not just television violence. Studies that are said to prove that media violence causes actual violence also tend to rely on laboratory experiments, which cannot duplicate conditions in real life. Yet, the studies provide media critics with a lot of ammunition, because they are widely cited by critics (uncritically) and rarely read by the public at large. Most of us lack the patience to decipher dense academic studies or the training and skills to critique them. Many of us take on faith the proposition "studies show . . ." (as advertisers know). Nowadays, the proposition that violent media cause violent behavior is hardly considered open to question.

Are there reasonable doubts about the effect of TV violence and the compelling need to regulate it? A well-publicized study by the American Psychological Association reports that "the accumulated research clearly demonstrates a correlation between viewing violence and aggressive behavior — that is, heavy viewers behave more aggressively than light viewers." If you read that statement quickly on the front page of your local newspaper, it seems conclusive. But even if the statement is true, it doesn't justify regulating violence in the media, given the strong, practically irrefutable proof of harm (and causation) required to regulate speech. Television may correlate to rising violence without directly causing it. The popularity of TV may itself reflect other political and social changes that retard children's moral and emotional development. What if excessive, uncritical TV watching correlates to the dearth of decent day care or a decline in public education?

Defenders of TV violence also claim that it mirrors reality. That's not quite true. In reality, people hurled through plate glass windows do not get up, grimace, and walk away. Even TV news does not present a realistic view of the crime problem, considering the disproportionate coverage of violent crime, particularly random, stranger-to-stranger crime. (In general, you're less likely to be attacked by a stranger than by someone you know.) Indeed, when media moguls are not defending screen violence as realistic, they dismiss it as mere fantasy — harmless entertainment. But some evidence suggests that the demographic groups most attracted to violence in the media include people for whom it may seem most realistic, given the violence in their communities. According to the 1993 Times Mirror poll, reality-based TV crime and emergency shows "have their strongest following among the less educated, racial minorities, the young and the poor." Viewing of violent programming in general is highest among males, people under thirty, blacks, and urbanites.

Still, even if you believe that media violence contributes to violent behavior or exacerbates violent tendencies, particularly among children and adolescents (and I am willing to believe that it might), you may find the singular effect of the media virtually impossible to isolate and quantify (as James Bennett observed in his Senate testimony in the mid-1950s). How do we parse the environments of violent teenagers, putting aside questions about their physical and mental health? How do we separate on-screen violence from the actual violence a teenage boy may experience at home and in the streets and from cultural stereotypes of masculinity that long predate the movies?

The fact that the media is, at most, only one of many factors con-   25
tributing to violence is not an excuse for ignoring it, Sissela Bok has pointed out. Consider our approach to heart disease, she argues. "Few critics maintain, that just because a number of risk factors such as smoking or heredity contribute to the prevalence of the disease, there is reason not to focus on risk of any one of them." But there is also no reason to focus on any one risk factor exclusively. The trouble with campaigns against TV violence is that they tend to exaggerate its importance and distract us from other, more complicated and controversial causes of violence. Media violence seems cheaper and easier to address than, say, the deplorable state of many public schools or the social conditions that make television such an important presence in children's lives.

Television is watched most frequently by children in the inner cities, who are said to be most susceptible to its brutalizing effects because of the brutality that surrounds them. (According to the American Psychological Association, the average American child watches twenty-seven hours of television per week; inner city children watch as much as eleven hours per day.) If watching TV is making these kids more prone to violence, watching TV is also one of the safest things they can do, Sissela Bok observes. The streets are dangerous, community programs are sparse; they are hiding out with their TVs because there are no safe places to play. What if, instead of focusing on making television shows less violent, politicians focused on making TV watching less necessary, by funding after-school programs for kids?

There are obvious political and fiscal answers to this question. A Senate hearing on the need for after-school programs in the inner cities would not be front-page news, nor would it garner as much bipartisan support as a hearing on media violence, nor would its proposed solutions be cost-free. Politicians and the public at large are attracted to the problem of TV violence partly because what is in everyone's living room is hard to ignore but also because we can easily envision simple, reactive solutions to it, such as a ratings system or restrictions on material that may be shown to minors. Addressing TV violence doesn't seem to require much affirmative action from government, such as the establishment of new social programs; it doesn't seem to require us to rethink social policy.

The irony is that media violence is a social problem, not a legal one — at least, it's not amenable to legal solutions as long as we value free speech. The primary mistake we make in regard to media violence is not ignoring it (we pay a great deal of attention to it, as the polls show). The mistake we make is approaching it legalistically.

The list of nonlegalistic, public and private approaches to media violence is easy to devise (without a Senate hearing), although it isn't terribly dramatic. Let consumers who are concerned about violence apply pressure to the industry. (Some civil libertarians argue that consumer pressure groups threaten the First Amendment, and in a way, that may be true but also irrelevant. Consumer-imposed censorship is our natural state, given the role consumer preferences play in determining which books are published and which movies produced.) Let gratuitously violent films and videos become as socially unacceptable as smoking or drunk driving (which can't be eliminated by social pressure, but can be reduced). Let parents monitor their kids' habits, but let us also recognize that the children who watch the most TV and are most vulnerable to TV violence may enjoy the least parental supervision. Let schools teach children how to watch television critically. And, let media consumers confront their own predilections for violence.

One of the most remarkable findings of the 1993 Times Mirror 30 poll was that a majority of people who are considered heavy viewers of violent entertainment believe that TV violence is harmful to society (37 percent believe it is "very harmful"; 34 percent label it "somewhat harmful"). Nearly half of people surveyed who watch a lot of violent entertainment say that they are "bothered by" violence on TV. Sometimes the media seems like Dr. Frankenstein's monster; sometimes it seems like the stock market. We created it; we sustain it; yet the media controls us.

Like Ted Bundy we tend to blame the media for increasing violence in order to absolve ourselves. And we look to the law to save us. Despite all the commentary about America's historical romance with violence, we rarely confront the contradictions between our own violent impulses and our expectations that laws — penal codes and censorship — will quell the violence that surrounds us. Many of the same people who drive with their car doors locked, keep guns by their beds, and demand death sentences or "three time loser" laws or government regulation of whatever they consider harmful speech also revel in such spectacles as the Simpson or Menendez trials or a Diane Sawyer sweeps week interview with Charles Manson.

TV Causes Violence?
Try Again

IRA GLASSER

To the Editor:

In "Look to Television's Role in Youth Violence" (letter, June 1), Paul Kettl, a professor of psychiatry, cites research that shows a statistical correlation between the rise in the rate of homicide in the United States and the onset of television. He cites his own research, which shows, he states, that "Children who watch more than two hours of television a day are especially at risk" of having "behavioral problems."

He doesn't say if this finding applies to all children or what else may be going on in the lives of those children with behavioral problems. Nor does he say whether the research implicates all television watching or only certain programs or perhaps the news. Although never said explicitly, the implication is there to draw: Watching too much television may turn your kid into a killer. And indeed your headline draws that conclusion.

But such conclusions misuse and misunderstand the nature of such research. The kind of research Dr. Kettl cites is called epidemiological research. This consists of observing groups of people and then showing statistical associations between their life-styles or behavior and what happens to them later. Scientists know, as the public often does not, that such epidemiological research tells us nothing about cause and effect.

For example, some early epidemiologic research showed a statistical association between heart disease and the number of television sets a person owned. But this did not mean that owning more than one television set caused heart disease. Clinical trials demonstrated that cholesterol, but not the number of television sets one owned, was causally related.

Similarly, one could show that the rate at which grass grows corre- 5
lates with the number of drownings. As one increases, so does the other. But that's because both are caused by warm weather. One would not seek to reduce the number of drownings by buying lawn mowers.

Yet that is precisely what is being suggested to curb violence. "Television is the cause," many people will falsely conclude after reading about such statistical associations.

This letter from Ira Glasser, executive director of the American Civil Liberties Union, appeared in the *New York Times* on June 15, 1994.

Television? Not drug prohibition, or the easy availability of guns or the loss of hope or relentless deprivation? No, we don't want to address those intractable problems. But dealing with television is easy. We can censor it. We can threaten to pass laws regulating when certain programs can be shown. We can decide, as a Florida hotel chain did for its rooms, to block reception of local television news that covers crime zealously (news article, June 3).

Finding scapegoats and diverting our attention from real and difficult problems is not new. But as we are not so gullible as to believe that we can reduce drownings by cutting the grass or have healthier hearts by limiting ourselves to owning one television, let us also not leap to the conclusion that watching too much television makes people killers. No studies show such a cause-and-effect connection. Homicide is a tad more complicated.

Ira Glasser

A Desensitized Society Drenched in Sleaze

JEFF JACOBY

I was seventeen years old when I first saw an X-rated movie. It was Thanksgiving in Washington, D.C. My college dorm had all but emptied out for the holiday weekend. With no classes, no tests, and nobody around, I decided to scratch an itch that had long been tormenting me.

I used to see these movies advertised in the old *Washington Star,* and — like any seventeen-year-old boy whose sex life is mostly theoretical — I burned with curiosity. I wondered what such films might be like, what awful, thrilling secrets they might expose.

And so that weekend I took myself to see one. Full of anticipation, nervous and embarrassed, I walked to the Casino Royale at 14th Street and New York Avenue. At the top of a long flight of stairs, a cashier sat behind a cage. "Five dollars," he demanded — steep for my budget, especially since a ticket to the movies in the late seventies usually cost $3.50. But I'd come this far and couldn't turn back. I paid, I entered, I watched.

For about twenty minutes. The movie, I still remember, was called *Cry for Cindy,* and what I saw on the screen I'd never seen —

Jeff Jacoby is a columnist for the *Boston Globe,* where this essay appeared on June 8, 1995.

I'd never even imagined — before. A man and a woman, oral sex, extreme close-ups. The sheer gynecological explicitness of it jolted me. Was *this* the forbidden delight hinted at by those ads? This wasn't arousing, it was repellent. I was shocked. More than that: I was ashamed.

I literally couldn't take it. I bolted the theater and tumbled down 5 the steps. My heart was pounding and my face was burning. I felt dirty. Guilty. I was conscience-stricken.

All that — over a dirty movie.

Well, I was an innocent at seventeen. I was naive and inexperienced, shy with girls, the product of a parochial-school education and a strict upbringing. Explicit sex — in the movies, music, my social life — was foreign to me. Coming from such an environment, who *wouldn't* recoil from *Cry for Cindy* or feel repelled by what it put up on that screen?

But here's the rub: Dirty movies don't have that effect on me anymore. I don't make a practice of seeking out skin flicks or films with explicit nudity, but in the years since I was seventeen, I've certainly seen my share. Today another sex scene is just another sex scene. Not shocking, not appalling, nothing I feel ashamed to look at. Writhing bodies on the screen? Raunchy lyrics in a song? They may entertain me or they may bore me, but one thing they no longer do is make me blush.

I've become jaded. And if a decade and a half of being exposed to this stuff can leave *me* jaded — with my background, my religious schooling, my disciplined origins — what impact does it have on kids and young adults who have never been sheltered from anything? What impact does it have on a generation growing up amid dysfunctional families, broken-down schools, and a culture of values-free secularism?

If sex- and violence-drenched entertainment can desensitize me, 10 it can desensitize anyone. It can desensitize a whole society. It can drag us to the point where nothing is revolting. Where nothing makes us blush.

And what happens to an unblushing society? Why, everything. Central Park joggers get raped and beaten into comas. Sixth-graders sleep around. Los Angeles rioters burn down their neighborhood and murder dozens of their neighbors. The Menendez boys blow off their parents' heads. Lorena Bobbitt mutilates her husband in his sleep. "Artists" sell photographs of crucifixes dunked in urine. Pro-life fanatics open fire on abortion clinics. Daytime TV fills up with deviants. The U.S. Naval Academy fills up with cheaters. The teen suicide rate goes through the roof.

And we get used to all of it. We don't blush.

The point isn't that moviegoers walk out of Oliver Stone's latest grotesquerie primed to kill. Or that Geto Boys' sociopathic lyrics

("Leavin' out her house, grabbed the bitch by her mouth / Drug her back in, slam her down on the couch. / Whipped out my knife, said, 'If you scream I'm cutting,' / Open her legs and . . .") cause rape. The point is that when blood and mayhem and sleazy sex drench our popular culture, we get accustomed to blood and mayhem and sleazy sex. We grow jaded. Depravity becomes more and more tolerable because less and less scandalizes us.

Or course, the entertainment industry accepts no responsibility for any of this. Time Warner and Hollywood indignantly reject the criticisms heaped on them in recent days. We don't cause society's ills, they say, we only reflect them. "If an artist wants to deal with violence or sexuality or images of darkness and horror," said film director Clive Barker, "those are legitimate subjects for artists."

They are, true. Artists have dealt with violence and sexuality   15
and horror since time immemorial. But debauchery is not art. There is nothing ennobling about a two-hour paean to bloodlust. To suggest that Snoop Doggy Dogg's barbaric gang-rape fantasies somehow follow in the tradition of Sophocles' tragic drama, Chaucer's romantic poetry, or Solzhenitsyn's moral testimony is to suggest that there is no difference between meaning and meaninglessness.

For Hollywood and Time Warner, perhaps there no longer is. The question before the house is, what about the rest of us?

THINKING AND WRITING ABOUT
SEX AND VIOLENCE IN POPULAR CULTURE

Questions for Discussion and Writing

1. What evidence do you find in these essays that establishes a cause/effect relationship between TV violence and youthful crime? What fallacy does Glasser see in the arguments attempting to prove a relationship?
2. Several authors contend that TV or movie violence is not to blame for youthful crime. What causes do they suggest?
3. Although Jacoby is writing about sex and Oppenheim about violence, both their claims are based on a shared assumption. Explain it and decide whether it is valid.
4. Popular culture, says the *Wall Street Journal* editorial, encourages drug use. Can you think of examples that prove or disprove this claim?
5. Do you think Kaminer is right in her conviction that many people confuse real courtroom cases and dramas on TV or in the movies? If she is right, what are the dangers of such confusion? Be specific.
6. Hirschorn claims that prime-time TV shows reflect sound moral values. Do you agree? Are his examples typical? Can you think of popular TV shows that do not reflect these values? If so, what *do* they teach?
7. Kristol defends a limited censorship of popular culture. Summarize his reasons. Would any of the writers in the chapter on "Freedom of Speech" agree with him?

8. What ironic comment is the cartoonist making about studies of TV violence?

Topics for Research

Violence in selected TV shows: Justified or unjustified?

Sex on TV: What message?

The significance of Gangsta Rap

Survey of studies on the effect of TV and movie violence

Influence of music videos and sports events on youthful behavior

PART FOUR

Classic Arguments

From Crito

PLATO

Plato, who died in 347 B.C., was one of the greatest Greek philosophers. He was a student of the Greek philosopher Socrates, whose teachings he recorded in the form of dialogues between Socrates and his pupils. In the dialogue below, Crito visits Socrates in prison — condemned to death for corrupting the youth of Athens — and tries to persuade him to escape. Socrates, however, refuses, basing his decision on his definition of justice and virtue.

Socrates: . . . Ought a man to do what he admits to be right, or ought he to betray the right?

Crito: He ought to do what he thinks right.

Socrates: But if this is true, what is the application? In leaving the prison against the will of the Athenians, do I wrong any? Or rather do I not wrong those whom I ought least to wrong? Do I not desert the principles which are acknowledged by us to be just — what do you say?

Crito: I cannot tell, Socrates; for I do not know.

Socrates: Then consider the matter in this way: — Imagine that I 5 am about to play truant (you may call the proceeding by any name which you like), and the laws of the government come and interrogate me: "Tell us, Socrates," they say: "what are you about? Are you not going by an act of yours to overturn us — the laws, and the whole state, as far as in you lies? Do you imagine that a state can subsist and not be overthrown, in which the decisions of law have no power, but are set aside and trampled upon by individuals?" What will be our answer, Crito, to these and the like words? Any one, and especially a rhetorician, will have a good deal to say on behalf of the law which requires a sentence to be carried out. He will argue that this law should not be set aside; and shall we reply, "Yes, but the state has injured us and given an unjust sentence." Suppose I say that?

Crito: Very good, Socrates.

Socrates: "And was that our agreement with you?" the law would answer; "or were you to abide by the sentence of the state?" And if I were to express my astonishment at their words, the law would probably add: "Answer, Socrates, instead of opening your eyes — you are in the habit of asking and answering questions. Tell us, — What complaint have you to make against us which justifies you in attempting to destroy us and the state? In the first place did we not

From Plato's *Crito*, translated by Benjamin Jowett (3rd edition, 1982).

bring you into existence? Your father married your mother by our aid and begat you. Say whether you have any objection to urge against those of us who regulate marriage?" None, I should reply. "Or against those of us who after birth regulate the nurture and education of children, in which you also were trained? Were not the laws, which have the charge of education, right in commanding your father to train you in music and gymnastics?" Right, I should reply. "Well then, since you were brought into the world and nurtured and educated by us, can you deny in the first place that you are our child and slave, as your fathers were before you? And if this is true you are not on equal terms with us; nor can you think that you have a right to do to us what we are doing to you. Would you have any right to strike or revile or do any other evil to your father or your master, if you had one, because you have been struck or reviled by him, or received some other evil at his hands? — you would not say this? And because we think right to destroy you, do you think that you have any right to destroy us in return, and your country as far as in you lies? Will you, O professor of true virtue, pretend that you are justified in this? Has a philosopher like you failed to discover that our country is more to be valued and higher and holier far than mother or father or any ancestor, and more to be regarded in the eyes of the gods and of men of understanding? Also to be soothed, and gently and reverently entreated when angry, even more than a father, and either to be persuaded, or if not persuaded, to be obeyed? And when we are punished by her, whether with imprisonment or stripes, the punishment is to be endured in silence, and if she leads us to wounds or death in battle, thither we follow as is right; neither may any one yield or retreat or leave his rank, but whether in battle or in a court of law, or in any other place, he must do what his city and his country order him; or he must change their view of what is just: and if he may do no violence to his father or mother, much less may he do violence to his country." What answer shall we make to this, Crito? Do the laws speak truly, or do they not?

Crito: I think that they do.

Socrates: Then the laws will say, "Consider, Socrates, if we are speaking truly that in your present attempt you are going to do us an injury. For, having brought you into the world, and nurtured and educated you, and given you and every other citizen a share in every good which we had to give, we further proclaim to any Athenian by the liberty which we allow him, that if he does not like us when he has become of age and has seen the ways of the city, and made our acquaintance, he may go where he pleases and take his goods with him. None of us laws will forbid him or interfere with him. Any one who does not like us and the city, and who wants to emigrate to a colony or to any other city, may go where he likes, retaining his property. But he who has experience of the manner in which we order justice and administer the state, and still remains, has entered into an implied contract that he will do as we command him. And he who disobeys us is, as we maintain, thrice wrong; first, because in disobeying us he is disobeying his parents; secondly, because we are the authors of his education; thirdly, because he has made an agreement with us that he will duly obey our commands; and he neither obeys them nor convinces us that our commands are unjust; and we do not rudely impose them, but give him the alternative of obeying or convincing us; — that is what we offer, and he does neither.

"These are the sort of accusations to which, as we were saying, 10 you, Socrates, will be exposed if you accomplish your intentions; you, above all other Athenians." Suppose now I ask, why I rather than anybody else? They will justly retort upon me that I above all other men have acknowledged the agreement. "There is clear proof," they will say, "Socrates, that we and the city were not displeasing to you. Of all Athenians you have been the most constant resident in the city, which, as you never leave, you may be supposed to love. For you never went out of the city either to see the games, except once when you went to the Isthmus, or to any other place unless when you were on military service; nor did you travel as other men do. Nor had you any curiosity to know other states or their laws: your affections did not go beyond us and our state; we were your special favorites, and you acquiesced in our government of you; and here in this city you begat your children, which is a proof of your satisfaction. Moreover, you might in the course of the trial, if you had liked, have fixed the penalty at banishment; the state which refuses to let you go now would have let you go then. But you pretended that you preferred death to exile, and that you were not unwilling to die. And now you have forgotten these fine sentiments, and pay no respect to us the laws, of whom you are the destroyer; and are doing what only a miserable slave would do, running away and turning your back upon the compacts and agreements which you made as a citizen. And first of all answer this very question: Are we right in saying that you agreed to be governed according to us in deed, and not in word only? Is that true or not?" How shall we answer, Crito? Must we not assent?

Crito: We cannot help it, Socrates.

Socrates: Then will they not say: "You, Socrates, are breaking the covenants and agreements which you made with us at your leisure, not in any haste or under any compulsion or deception, but after you have had seventy years to think of them, during which time you were at liberty to leave the city, if we were not to your mind, or if our covenants appeared to you to be unfair. You had your choice, and might have gone either to Lacedaemon or Crete, both which states are often praised by you for their good government, or to some other Hellenic or foreign state. Whereas you, above all our Athenians, seemed to be so fond of the state, or, in other words, of us her laws (and who would care about a state which has no laws?), that you never stirred out of her; the halt, the blind, the maimed were not more stationary in her than you were. And now you run away and forsake your agreements. Not so, Socrates, if you will take our advice; do not make yourself ridiculous by escaping out of the city.

"For just consider, if you transgress and err in this sort of way, what good will you do either to yourself or to your friends? That your friends will be driven into exile and deprived of citizenship, or will lose their property, is tolerably certain; and you yourself, if you fly to one of the neighboring cities, as, for example, Thebes or Megara, both of which are well governed, will come to them as an enemy, Socrates, and their government will be against you, and all patriotic citizens will cast an evil eye upon you as a subverter of the laws, and you will confirm in the minds of the judges the justice of their own condemnation of you. For he who is a corrupter of the laws is more than likely to be a corrupter of the young and foolish portion of mankind. Will you then flee from well-ordered citizens and virtuous men? and is existence worth having on these terms? Or will you go to them without shame, and talk to them, Socrates? And what will you say to them? What you say here about virtue and justice and institutions and laws being the best things among men? Would that be decent of you? Surely not. But if you go away from well-governed states to Crito's friends in Thessaly, where there is a great disorder and licence, they will be charmed to hear the tale of your escape from prison, set off with ludicrous particulars of the manner in which you were wrapped in a goatskin or some other disguise, and metamorphosed as the manner is of runaways; but will there be no one to remind you that in your old age you were ashamed to violate the most sacred laws from a miserable desire of a little more life? Perhaps not, if you keep them in a good temper; but if they are out of temper you will hear many degrading things; you will live, but how? — as the flatterer of all men, and the servant of all men; and doing what? — eating and drinking in Thessaly, having gone abroad in order that you may get a dinner. And where will be your fine sentiments about justice and virtue? Say that you wish to live for the sake of your children — you want to bring them up and educate them — will you take them into Thessaly and deprive them of Athenian citizenship? Is this the benefit which you will confer upon them? Or are you under the impression that they will be better cared for and educated here if you are still alive, although absent from them; for your friends will take care of them? Do you fancy that if you are an inhabitant of Thessaly they will take care of them, and if you are an inhabitant of the other world that they will not take care of them? Nay: but if they who call themselves friends are good for anything, they will — to be sure they will.

"Listen, then, Socrates, to us who have brought you up. Think not of life and children first, and of justice afterwards, but of justice first, that you may be justified before the princes of the world below. For neither will you nor any that belong to you be happier or holier or juster in this life, or happier in another, if you do as Crito bids. Now you depart in innocence, a sufferer and not a doer of evil; a victim, not of the laws of men. But if you go forth, returning evil for evil, and injury for injury, breaking the covenants and agreements which you have made with us, and wronging those whom you ought least of all to wrong, that is to say, yourself, your friends, your country, and us, we shall be angry with you while you live, and our brethren, the laws in the world below, will receive you as an enemy; for they will know that you have done your best to destroy us. Listen, then, to us and not to Crito."

This, dear Crito, is the voice which I seem to hear murmuring in   15
my ears, like the sound of the flute in the ears of the mystic; that voice, I say, is humming in my ears, and prevents me from hearing any other. And I know that anything more which you may say will be vain. Yet speak, if you have anything to say.

Crito: I have nothing to say, Socrates.

Socrates: Leave me then, Crito, to fulfill the will of God, and to follow whither he leads.

Discussion Questions

1. What debt to the law and his country does Socrates acknowledge? Mention the specific reasons for which he owes obedience. Is the analogy of the country to parents a plausible one? Why or why not?
2. Explain the nature of the "implied contract" that exists between Socrates and the state. According to the state, how has Socrates forfeited his right to object to punishment?
3. What appeal does that state make to Socrates' sense of justice and virtue?

Writing Suggestions

4. Socrates bases his refusal to escape the death penalty on his definition of justice and virtue. Basing your own argument on other criteria, make a claim for the right of Socrates to try to escape his punishment. Would some good be served by his escape?
5. The analogy between one's country and one's parents is illustrated at great length in Socrates' argument. In the light of modern ideas about the relationship between the state and the individual in a democracy, write a refutation of the analogy. Perhaps you can think of a different and more fitting one.

The Passionate Shepherd to His Love

CHRISTOPHER MARLOWE

Christopher Marlowe (1564–1593) has been called the first major playwright of the English Renaissance, remembered especially for his "mighty line," the power of his blank verse. Among his memorable plays are Doctor Faustus, Tamburlaine, *and* The Jew of Malta. *Marlowe was murdered as the result of what was probably a political quarrel. "The Passionate Shepherd to His Love" was circulated posthumously in 1599.*

Come live with me and be my love,
And we will all the pleasures prove
That valleys, groves, hills, and fields,
Woods, or steepy mountain yields.

And we will sit upon the rocks, 5
Seeing the shepherds feed their flocks,
By shallow rivers to whose falls
Melodious birds sing madrigals.

And I will make thee beds of roses
And a thousand fragrant posies, 10
A cap of flowers, and a kirtle
Embroidered all with leaves of myrtle;

A gown made of the finest wool
Which from our pretty lambs we pull;
Fair lined slippers for the cold, 15
With buckles of the purest gold;

A belt of straw and ivy buds,
With coral clasps and amber studs:
And if these pleasures may thee move,
Come live with me, and be my love. 20

The shepherds' swains shall dance and sing
For thy delight each May morning:
If these delights thy mind may move,
Then live with me and be my love.

The Nymph's Reply
to the Shepherd

SIR WALTER RALEIGH

*Sir Walter Raleigh (1552?–1618) embodies the attributes of the
Renaissance man. He was a soldier, politician, explorer, poet,
historian, and essayist. He was several times condemned to death
and several times reprieved. Searching for gold in South America, he
was accused of destroying a Spanish settlement and, at the request of
the Spanish ambassador, arrested and executed. Although he is
thought to have written many poems, only thirty short pieces survive.
Written in 1600, this poem is a response to Christopher Marlowe's
"The Passionate Shepherd to His Love."*

If all the world and love were young,
And truth in every shepherd's tongue,
These pretty pleasures might me move
To live with thee and be thy love.

Time drives the flocks from field to fold   5
When rivers rage and rocks grow cold,
And Philomel¹ becometh dumb;
The rest complains of cares to come.

The flowers do fade, and wanton fields
To wayward winter reckoning yields;   10
A honey tongue, a heart of gall,
Is fancy's spring, but sorrow's fall.

Thy gowns, thy shoes, thy beds of roses,
Thy cap, thy kirtle, and thy posies
Soon break, soon wither, soon forgotten —   15
In folly ripe, in reason rotten.

Thy belt of straw and ivy buds,
Thy coral clasps and amber studs,
All these in me no means can move
To come to thee and be thy love.   20

But could youth last and love still breed,
Had joys no date nor age no need,
Then these delights my mind might move
To live with thee and be thy love.

---

¹ In Greek mythology, a princess who was changed into a nightingale. — ED.

Discussion Questions

1. What different kinds of appeals does Marlowe's shepherd make to his love?
2. Compare Marlowe's invitation to that of Andrew Marvell in "To His Coy Mistress" (p. 641). Point out the major differences between the appeals in these two poems.
3. Why does Raleigh's nymph refuse the shepherd's invitation? Does she suggest the circumstances that might cause her to change her mind?

Writing Suggestions

4. If you think that Marlowe's invitation was based on mistaken assumptions, write a criticism of it and suggest how he might have made a successful appeal.
5. Write another response to the shepherd by (a) developing in greater detail the reasons given by Raleigh's nymph, or (b) providing the reasons of a modern woman for refusing a would-be lover's invitation.

To His Coy Mistress

ANDREW MARVELL

Andrew Marvell (1621–1678) was a long-time member of the British Parliament and a writer of political satires. Today, however, he is remembered for two splendid poems, "The Garden" and the one that appears below. "To His Coy Mistress" is a noteworthy expression of an idea familiar in the love poems of many languages — carpe diem in Latin, meaning "seize the day," the idea that life is fleeting and love and other pleasures should be enjoyed while the lovers are still young and beautiful.

Had we but world enough, and time,
This coyness, lady, were no crime.
We would sit down, and think which way
To walk, and pass our long love's day.
Thou by the Indian Ganges' side   5
Should'st rubies find; I by the tide
Of Humber[1] would complain. I would
Love you ten years before the Flood;
And you should, if you please, refuse
Till the conversion of the Jews.   10
My vegetable love should grow
Vaster than empires, and more slow.
An hundred years should go to praise
Thine eyes, and on thy forehead gaze;
Two hundred to adore each breast;   15
But thirty thousand to the rest:
An age at least to every part,
And the last age should show your heart.
For, lady, you deserve this state,
Nor would I love at lower rate.   20
     But at my back I always hear
Time's wingèd chariot hurrying near;
And yonder all before us lie
Deserts of vast eternity.
Thy beauty shall no more be found,   25
Nor in thy marble vault shall sound
My echoing song; then worms shall try
That long-preserved virginity;
And your quaint honor turn to dust,
And into ashes all my lust.   30

---

[1] An estuary in England. — ED.

The grave's a fine and private place,
But none, I think, do there embrace.
  Now, therefore, while the youthful hue
Sits on thy skin like morning dew,
And while thy willing soul transpires   35
At every pore with instant fires,
Now let us sport us while we may;
And now, like amorous birds of prey,
Rather at once our time devour,
Than languish in his slow-chapped[2] power.   40
Let us roll all our strength and all
Our sweetness up into one ball;
And tear our pleasures with rough strife
Thorough[3] the iron gates of life.
Thus, though we cannot make our sun   45
Stand still, yet we will make him run.

Discussion Questions

1. One critic notes that "To His Coy Mistress" is an argument in the form of a poem, which can be outlined as a syllogism. What are the major and minor premises and the conclusion?
2. What witty images in the first half of the poem suggest "world enough, and time" for love?
3. There is a change in the tone of the lover's exhortation in the middle of the poem. At what point does it occur? What words and images convey a different mood?
4. Why is the *carpe diem* sentiment more likely to have been taken seriously in earlier times?

Writing Suggestions

5. Address a letter or an essay to Marvell, wherever he is, telling him how some circumstances surrounding love among the young have changed since he wrote his poem more than 300 years ago.
6. Look at some other poems that express the *carpe diem* idea — for example, Robert Herrick's "To the Virgins to Make Much of Time," Omar Khayyám's "The Rubáiyát," works by Catullus, a Latin Poet — and write a paper analyzing their concerns (what do they most wish to enjoy while they are young?) and their acceptance of or resistance to the end of youth and pleasure.

---

[2] Slow-jawed. — ED.
[3] Through. — ED.

A Modest Proposal

JONATHAN SWIFT

This essay is acknowledged by almost all critics to be the most power-
ful example of irony in the English language. (Irony means saying
one thing but meaning another.) In 1729 Jonathan Swift, prolific
satirist and dean of St. Patrick's Cathedral in Dublin, was moved to
write in protest against the terrible poverty in which the Irish were
forced to live under British rule. Notice that the essay is organized ac-
cording to one of the patterns outlined in Part Two of this book (see
"Presenting the Stock Issues," p. 318). First, Swift establishes the need
for a change, then he offers his proposal, and finally, he lists its
advantages.

It is a melancholy object to those who walk through this great town[1] or travel in the country, when they see the streets, the roads, and cabin doors, crowded with beggars of the female sex, followed by three, four, or six children, all in rags and importuning every passenger for an alms. These mothers, instead of being able to work for their honest livelihood, are forced to employ all their time in strolling to beg sustenance for their helpless infants, who, as they grow up, either turn thieves for want of work, or leave their dear native country to fight for the Pretender in Spain, or sell themselves to the Barbados.[2]

I think it is agreed by all parties that this prodigious number of children in the arms, or on the backs, or at the heels of their mothers, and frequently of their fathers, is in the present deplorable state of the kingdom a very great additional grievance; and therefore whoever could find out a fair, cheap, and easy method of making these children sound, useful members of the commonwealth would deserve so well of the public as to have his statue set up for a preserver of the nation.

But my intention is very far from being confined to provide only for the children of professed beggars; it is of a much greater extent, and shall take in the whole number of infants at a certain age who are born of parents in effect as little able to support them as those who demand our charity in the streets.

As to my own part, having turned my thoughts for many years upon this important subject, and maturely weighed the several

---

[1] Dublin. — ED.

[2] The Pretender was James Stuart, who was exiled to Spain. Many Irishmen had joined an army attempting to return him to the English throne in 1715. Others had become indentured servants, agreeing to work for a set number of years in Barbados or other British colonies in exchange for their transportation out of Ireland. — ED.

schemes of other projectors,[3] I have always found them grossly mistaken in their computation. It is true, a child just dropped from its dam may be supported by her milk for a solar year, with little other nourishment; at most not above the value of two shillings, which the mother may certainly get, or the value in scraps, by her lawful occupation of begging; and it is exactly at one year that I propose to provide for them in such a manner as instead of being a charge upon their parents or the parish, or wanting food and raiment for the rest of their lives, they shall on the contrary contribute to the feeding, and partly to the clothing, of many thousands.

There is likewise another great advantage in my scheme, that it 5 will prevent those voluntary abortions, and that horrid practice of women murdering their bastard children, alas, too frequent among us, sacrificing the poor innocent babes, I doubt, more to avoid the expense than the shame, which would move tears and pity in the most savage and inhuman breast.

The number of souls in this kingdom being usually reckoned one million and a half, of these I calculate there may be about two hundred thousand couples whose wives are breeders; from which number I subtract thirty thousand couples who are able to maintain their own children, although I apprehend there cannot be so many under the present distress of the kingdom; but this being granted, there will remain an hundred and seventy thousand breeders. I again subtract fifty thousand for those women who miscarry, or whose children die by accident or disease within the year. There only remain an hundred and twenty thousand children of poor parents annually born. The question therefore is, how this number shall be reared and provided for, which, as I have already said, under the present situation of affairs, is utterly impossible by all the methods hitherto proposed. For we can neither employ them in handicraft or agriculture; we neither build houses (I mean in the country) nor cultivate land. They can very seldom pick up a livelihood by stealing till they arrive at six years old, except where they are of towardly parts;[4] although I confess they learn the rudiments much earlier, during which time they can however be looked upon only as probationers, as I have been informed by a principal gentleman in the county of Cavan, who protested to me that he never knew above one or two instances under the age of six, even in a part of the kingdom so renowned for the quickest proficiency in that art.

I am assured by our merchants that a boy or a girl before twelve years old is no salable commodity; and even when they come to this age they will not yield above three pounds, or three pounds and a half a crown at most on the Exchange; which cannot turn to account

---

[3] Planners. — ED.
[4] Innate talents. — ED.

either to the parents or the kingdom, the charge of nutriment and rags having been at least four times that value.

I shall now therefore humbly propose my own thoughts, which I hope will not be liable to the least objection.

I have been assured by a very knowing American of my acquaintance in London, that a young healthy child well nursed is at a year old a most delicious, nourishing, and wholesome food, whether stewed, roasted, baked, or boiled; and I make no doubt that it will equally serve in a fricassee or a ragout.[5]

I do therefore humbly offer it to public consideration that of the 10 hundred and twenty thousand children, already computed, twenty thousand may be reserved for breed, whereof only one fourth part to be males, which is more than we allow to sheep, black cattle, or swine; and my reason is that these children are seldom the fruits of marriage, a circumstance not much regarded by our savages, therefore one male will be sufficient to serve four females. That the remaining hundred thousand may at a year old be offered in sale to the persons of quality and fortune through the kingdom, always advising the mother to let them suck plentifully in the last month, so as to render them plump and fat for a good table. A child will make two dishes at an entertainment for friends; and when the family dines alone, the fore or hind quarter will make a reasonable dish, and seasoned with a little pepper or salt will be very good boiled on the fourth day, especially in winter.

I have reckoned upon a medium that a child just born will weigh twelve pounds, and in a solar year if tolerably nursed increaseth to twenty-eight pounds.

I grant this food will be somewhat dear, and therefore very proper for landlords, who, as they have already devoured most of the parents, seem to have the best title to the children.

Infant's flesh will be in season throughout the year, but more plentiful in March, and a little before and after. For we are told by a grave author, an eminent French physician,[6] that fish being a prolific diet, there are more children born in Roman Catholic countries about nine months after Lent than at any other season; therefore, reckoning a year after Lent, the markets will be more glutted than usual, because the number of popish infants is at least three to one in this kingdom; and therefore it will have one other collateral advantage, by lessening the number of Papists among us.

I have already computed the charge of nursing a beggar's child (in which list I reckon all cottagers, laborers, and four-fifths of the farmers) to be about two shillings per annum, rags included; and I

---

[5] Stew. — ED.

[6] A reference to Swift's favorite French writer, François Rabelais (1494?–1553), who was actually a broad satirist known for his coarse humor. — ED.

believe no gentleman would repine to give ten shillings for the carcass of a good fat child, which, as I have said, will make four dishes of excellent nutritive meat, when he hath only some particular friend or his own family to dine with him. Thus the squire will learn to be a good landlord, and grow popular among the tenants; the mother will have eight shillings net profit, and be fit for work till she produces another child.

Those who are more thrifty (as I must confess the times require)   15
may flay the carcass; the skin of which artificially[7] dressed will make admirable gloves for ladies, and summer boots for fine gentlemen.

As to our city of Dublin, shambles[8] may be appointed for this purpose in the most convenient parts of it, and butchers we may be assured will not be wanting; although I rather recommend buying the children alive, and dressing them hot from the knife as we do roasting pigs.

A very worthy person, a true lover of his country, and whose virtues I highly esteem, was lately pleased in discoursing on this matter to offer a refinement upon my scheme. He said that many gentlemen of his kingdom, having of late destroyed their deer, he conceived that the want of venison might be well supplied by the bodies of young lads and maidens, not exceeding fourteen years of age nor under twelve, so great a number of both sexes in every county being now ready to starve for want of work and service; and these to be disposed of by their parents, if alive, or otherwise by their nearest relations. But with due deference to so excellent a friend and so deserving a patriot, I cannot be altogether in his sentiments; for as to the males, my American acquaintance assured me from frequent experience that their flesh was generally tough and lean, like that of our schoolboys, by continual exercise, and their taste disagreeable; and to fatten them would not answer the charge. Then as to the females, it would, I think with humble submission, be a loss to the public, because they soon would become breeders themselves; and besides, it is not improbable that some scrupulous people might be apt to censure such a practice (although indeed very unjustly) as a little bordering upon cruelty; which, I confess, hath always been with me the strongest objection against any project, how well soever intended.

But in order to justify my friend, he confessed that this expedient was put into his head by the famous Psalmanazar,[9] a native of the island Formosa, who came from thence to London above twenty

---

[7] With art or craft. — ED.

[8] Butcher shops or slaughterhouses. — ED.

[9] Georges Psalmanazar was a Frenchman who pretended to be Japanese and wrote an entirely imaginary *Description of the Isle Formosa.* He had become well known in gullible London society. — ED.

years ago, and in conversation told my friend that in his country when any young person happened to be put to death, the executioner sold the carcass to persons of quality as a prime dainty; and that in his time the body of a plump girl of fifteen, who was crucified for an attempt to poison the emperor, was sold to his Imperial Majesty's prime minister of state, and other great mandarins of the court, in joints from the gibbet, at four hundred crowns. Neither indeed can I deny that if the same use were made of several plump young girls in this town, who without one single groat to their fortunes cannot stir abroad without a chair, and appear at the playhouse and assemblies in foreign fineries which they never will pay for, the kingdom would not be the worse.

Some persons of a desponding spirit are in great concern about that vast number of poor people who are aged, diseased, or maimed, and I have been desired to employ my thoughts what course may be taken to ease the nation of so grievous an encumbrance. But I am not in the least pain upon that matter, because it is very well known that they are every day dying and rotting by cold and famine, and filth and vermin, as fast as can be reasonably expected. And as to the younger laborers, they are now in almost as hopeful a condition. They cannot get work, and consequently pine away for want of nourishment to a degree that if any time they are accidentally hired to common labor, they have not strength to perform it; and thus the country and themselves are happily delivered from the evils to come.

I have too long digressed, and therefore shall return to my subject. I think the advantages by the proposal which I have made are obvious and many, as well as of the highest importance.   20

For first, as I have already observed, it would greatly lessen the number of Papists, with whom we are yearly overrun, being the principal breeders of the nation as well as our most dangerous enemies; and who stay at home on purpose to deliver the kingdom to the Pretender, hoping to take their advantage by the absence of so many good Protestants, who have chosen rather to leave their country than to stay at home and pay tithes against their conscience to an Episcopal curate.

Secondly, the poorer tenants will have something valuable of their own, which by law may be made liable to distress,[10] and help to pay their landlord's rent, their corn and cattle being already seized and money a thing unknown.

Thirdly, whereas the maintenance of an hundred thousand children, from two years old and upwards, cannot be computed at less than ten shillings a piece per annum, the nation's stock will be thereby increased fifty thousand pounds per annum, besides the

---

[10] Subject to possession by lenders. — ED.

profit of a new dish introduced to the tables of all gentlemen of fortune in the kingdom who have any refinement in taste. And the money will circulate among ourselves, the goods being entirely of our own growth and manufacture.

Fourthly, the constant breeders, besides the gain of eight shillings sterling per annum by the sale of their children, will be rid of the charge of maintaining them after the first year.

Fifthly, this food would likewise bring great custom to taverns, where the vintners will certainly be so prudent as to procure the best receipts for dressing it to perfection, and consequently have their houses frequented by all the fine gentlemen, who justly value themselves upon their knowledge in good eating; and a skillful cook, who understands how to oblige his guests, will contrive to make it as expensive as they please.

Sixthly, this would be a great inducement to marriage, which all wise nations have either encouraged by rewards or enforced by laws and penalties. It would increase the care and tenderness of mothers toward their children, when they were sure of a settlement for life to the poor babes, provided in some sort by the public, to their annual profit instead of expense. We should see an honest emulation among the married women, which of them could bring the fattest child to the market. Men would become as fond of their wives during the time of their pregnancy as they are now of their mares in foal, their cows in calf, or sows when they are ready to farrow; nor offer to beat or kick them (as is too frequent a practice) for fear of a miscarriage.

Many other advantages might be enumerated. For instance, the addition of some thousand carcasses in our exportation of barreled beef, the propagation of swine's flesh, and improvements in the art of making good bacon, so much wanted among us by the great destruction of pigs, too frequent at our tables, which are no way comparable in taste or magnificence to a well-grown, fat, yearling child, which roasted whole will make a considerable figure at a lord mayor's feast or any other public entertainment. But this and many others I omit, being studious of brevity.

Supposing that one thousand families in this city would be constant customers for infants' flesh, besides others who might have it at merry meetings, particularly weddings and christenings, I compute that Dublin would take off annually about twenty thousand carcasses, and the rest of the kingdom (where probably they will be sold somewhat cheaper) the remaining eighty thousand.

I can think of no one objection that will possibly be raised against this proposal, unless it should be urged that the number of people will be thereby much lessened in the kingdom. This I freely own, and it was indeed one principal design in offering it to the world. I desire the reader will observe, that I calculate my remedy for this one individual kingdom of Ireland and for no other that ever was, is, or I think ever can be upon earth. Therefore let no man talk to me of other expedients: of taxing our absentees at five shillings a pound: of using neither clothes nor household furniture except what is of our own growth and manufacture: of utterly rejecting the materials and instruments that promote foreign luxury: of curing the expensiveness of pride, vanity, idleness, and gaming in our women: of introducing a vein of parsimony, prudence, and temperance: of learning to love our country, in the want of which we differ even from Laplanders and the inhabitants of Topinamboo:[11] of quitting our animosities and factions, nor acting any longer like the Jews, who were murdering one another at the very moment their city was taken:[12] of being a little cautious not to sell our country and conscience for nothing: of teaching landlords to have at least one degree of mercy toward their tenants: lastly, of putting a spirit of honesty, industry, and skill into our shopkeepers; who, if a resolution could now be taken to buy only our native goods, would immediately unite to cheat and exact upon us in the price, the measure, and the goodness, nor could ever yet be brought to make one fair proposal of just dealing, though often and earnestly invited to it.

Therefore I repeat, let no man talk to me of these and the like expedients, till he hath at least some glimpse of hope that there will ever be some hearty and sincere attempt to put them in practice. 30

But as to myself, having been wearied out for many years with offering vain, idle, visionary thoughts, and at length utterly despairing of success, I fortunately fell upon this proposal, which, as it is wholly new, so it hath something solid and real, of no expense and little trouble, full in our own power, and whereby we can incur no danger in disobliging England. For this kind of commodity will not bear exportation, the flesh being of too tender a consistence to admit a long continuance in salt, although perhaps I could name a country which would be glad to eat up our whole nation without it.

After all, I am not so violently bent upon my own opinion as to reject any offer proposed by wise men, which shall be found equally innocent, cheap, easy, and effectual. But before something of that kind shall be advanced in contradiction to my scheme, and offering a better, I desire the author or authors will be pleased maturely to consider two points. First, as things now stand, how they will be able to find food and raiment for an hundred thousand useless mouths and backs. And secondly, there being a round million of creatures in human figure throughout this kingdom, whose sole subsistence put into a common stock would leave them in debt two millions of pounds sterling, adding those who are beggars by profession to the bulk of farmers, cottagers, and laborers, with their

---

[11] District of Brazil. — ED.

[12] During the Roman siege of Jerusalem (A.D. 70), prominent Jews were charged with collaborating with the enemy and put to death. — ED.

wives and children who are beggars in effect; I desire those politicians who dislike my overture, and may perhaps be so bold to attempt an answer, that they will first ask the parents of these mortals whether they would not at this day think it a great happiness to have been sold for food at a year old in this manner I prescribe, and thereby have avoided such a perpetual scene of misfortunes as they have since gone through by the oppression of landlords, the impossibility of paying rent without money or trade, the want of common sustenance, with neither house nor clothes to cover them from the inclemencies of the weather, and the most inevitable prospect of entailing the like of greater miseries upon their breed forever.

I profess, in the sincerity of my heart, that I have not the least personal interest in endeavoring to promote this necessary work, having no other motive than the public good of my country, by advancing our trade, providing for infants, relieving the poor, and giving some pleasure to the rich. I have no children by which I can propose to get a single penny; the youngest being nine years old, and my wife past childbearing.

Discussion Questions

1. What implicit assumption about the treatment of the Irish underlies Swift's proposal? Do expressions such as "just dropped from its dam" and "whose wives are breeders" give the reader a clue?
2. In this essay Swift assumes a persona; that is, for the purposes of the proposal he makes, he pretends to be a different person. Describe the characteristics of that person. Point out the places in the essay that reveal them.
3. In several places, however, Swift reveals himself as the outraged witness of English cruelty and indifference. Note the language that seems to reflect his own feelings.
4. Throughout the essay Swift recites lists of facts, many of them in the form of statistics. How do these facts contribute to the persuasiveness of his argument? How do they affect the reader?
5. What social practices and attitudes of both the Irish and the English does Swift condemn?
6. Does Swift offer any solutions for the problems he attacks? How do you know?
7. When this essay first appeared in 1729, some readers took it seriously and accused Swift of monstrous cruelty. Can you think of reasons why these readers failed to recognize the ironic intent?

Writing Suggestions

8. Try an ironical essay of your own. Choose a subject that clearly lends itself to such treatment. As Swift did, use logic and restraint in your language.
9. Choose a problem for which you think you have a solution. Defend your solution by using the stock issues as your pattern of organization.

Civil Disobedience

HENRY DAVID THOREAU

Henry David Thoreau (1817–1862), philosopher and writer, is best known for Walden, *an account of his solitary retreat to Walden Pond, near Concord, Massachusetts. Here he remained for more than two years in an effort to "live deliberately, to front only the essential facts of life." "Civil Disobedience" was first given as a lecture in 1848 and published in 1849. It was widely read and influenced both Mahatma Gandhi in the passive-resistance campaign he led against the British in India and Martin Luther King, Jr., in the civil rights movement.*

I heartily accept the motto, — "That government is best which governs least"; and I should like to see it acted up to more rapidly and systematically. Carried out, it finally amounts to this, which also I believe, — "That government is best which governs not at all"; and when men are prepared for it, that will be the kind of government which they will have. Government is at best but an expedient; but most governments are usually, and all governments are sometimes, inexpedient. The objections which have been brought against a standing army, and they are many and weighty, and deserve to pre-vail, may also at last be brought against a standing government. The standing army is only an arm of the standing government. The gov-ernment itself, which is only the mode which the people have cho-sen to execute their will, is equally liable to be abused and perverted before the people can act through it. Witness the present Mexican war, the work of comparatively a few individuals using the standing government as their tool; for, in the outset, the people would not have consented to this measure.

This American government, — what is it but a tradition, though a recent one, endeavoring to transmit itself unimpaired to posterity, but each instant losing some of its integrity? It has not the vitality and force of a single living man; for a single man can bend it to his will. It is a sort of wooden gun to the people themselves. But it is not the less necessary for this; for the people must have some compli-cated machinery or other, and hear its din, to satisfy that idea of government which they have. Governments show thus how success-fully men can be imposed on, even impose on themselves, for their own advantage. It is excellent, we must all allow. Yet this govern-ment never of itself furthered any enterprise, but by the alacrity with which it got out of its way. *It* does not keep the country free. *It* does not settle the West. *It* does not educate. The character inherent in the American people has done all that has been accomplished; and it would have done somewhat more, if the government had not sometimes got in its way. For government is an expedient by which men would fain succeed in letting one another alone; and, as has been said, when it is most expedient, the governed are most let alone by it. Trade and commerce, if they were not made of India-rubber, would never manage to bounce over the obstacles which legislators are continually putting in their way; and, if one were to judge these men wholly by the effects of their actions, and not partly by their intentions, they would deserve to be classed and punished with those mischievous persons who put obstructions on the railroads.

But, to speak practically and as a citizen, unlike those who call themselves no-government men, I ask for, not at once no government, but *at once* a better government. Let every man make known what kind of government would command his respect, and that will be one step toward obtaining it.

After all, the practical reason why, when the power is once in the hands of the people, a majority are permitted, and for a long period continue, to rule, is not because they are most likely to be in the right, nor because this seems fairest to the minority, but because they are physically the strongest. But a government in which the majority rule in all cases cannot be based on justice, even as far as men understand it. Can there not be a government in which majorities do not virtually decide right and wrong, but conscience? — in which majorities decide only those questions to which the rule of expediency is applicable? Must the citizen ever for a moment, or in the least degree, resign his conscience to the legislator? Why has every man a conscience, then? I think that we should be men first, and subjects afterward. It is not desirable to cultivate a respect for the law, so much as for the right. The only obligation which I have a right to assume, is to do at any time what I think right. It is truly enough said, that a corporation has no conscience; but a corporation of conscientious men is a corporation *with* a conscience. Law never made men a whit more just; and, by means of their respect for it, even the well-disposed are daily made the agents of injustice. A common and natural result of an undue respect for law is, that you may see a file of soldiers, colonel, captain, corporal, privates, powder-monkeys, and all, marching in admirable order over hill and dale to the wars, against their wills, aye, against their common sense and consciences, which makes it very steep marching indeed, and produces a palpitation of the heart. They have no doubt that it is a damnable business in which they are concerned; they are all peaceably inclined. Now, what are they? Men at all? or small moveable forts and magazines, at the service of some unscrupulous man in power? Visit the Navy-Yard, and behold a marine, such a man as an American government can make, or such as it can make a man with its black arts, — a mere shadow and reminiscence of humanity, a man laid out alive and standing, and already, as one may say, buried under arms with funeral accompaniments, though it may be, —

> Not a drum was heard, nor a funeral note,
> As his corse to the rampart we hurried;
> Not a soldier discharged his farewell shot
> O'er the grave where our hero we buried.

The mass of men serve the state thus, not as men mainly, but as 5 machines, with their bodies. They are the standing army, and the militia, jailers, constables, posse comitatus, &c. In most cases there is no free exercise whatever of the judgment or of the moral sense; but they put themselves on a level with wood and earth and stones; and wooden men can perhaps be manufactured that will serve the purpose as well. Such command no more respect than men of straw, or a lump of dirt. They have the same sort of worth only as horses and dogs. Yet such as these even are commonly esteemed good citizens. Others, — as most legislators, politicians, lawyers, ministers, and office-holders, — serve the State chiefly with their heads; and, as they rarely make any moral distinctions, they are as likely to serve the Devil, without *intending* it, as God. A very few, as heroes, patriots, martyrs, reformers in the great sense, and *men,* serve the state with their consciences also, and so necessarily resist it for the most part, and they are commonly treated as enemies by it. A wise man will only be useful as a man, and will not submit to be "clay," and "stop a hole to keep the wind away," but leave that office to his dust at least: —

> I am too high-born to be propertied,
> To be a secondary at control,
> Or useful serving-man and instrument
> To any sovereign state throughout the world.

He who gives himself entirely to his fellow-men appears to them useless and selfish; but he who gives himself partially to them is pronounced a benefactor and philanthropist.

How does it become a man to behave toward this American government today? I answer that he cannot without disgrace be associated with it. I cannot for an instant recognize that political organization as *my* government which is the *slave's* government also.

All men recognize the right of revolution; that is, the right to refuse allegiance to, and to resist, the government, when its tyranny or its inefficiency are great and unendurable. But almost all say that such is not the case now. But such was the case, they think, in the Revolution of '75. If one were to tell me that this was a bad government because it taxed certain foreign commodities brought to its ports, it is most probable that I should not make an ado about it, for

I can do without them. All machines have their friction; and possibly this does enough good to counterbalance the evil. At any rate, it is a great evil to make a stir about it. But when the friction comes to have its machine, and oppression and robbery are organized, I say, let us not have such a machine any longer. In other words, when a sixth of the population of a nation which has undertaken to be the refuge of liberty are slaves, and a whole country is unjustly overrun and conquered by a foreign army, and subjected to military law, I think that it is not too soon for honest men to rebel and revolutionize. What makes this duty the more urgent is the fact, that the country so overrun is not our own, but ours is the invading army.

Paley, a common authority with many on moral questions, in his chapter on the "Duty of Submission to Civil Government," resolves all civil obligation into expediency; and he proceeds to say, "that so long as the interest of the whole society requires it, that is, so long as the established government cannot be resisted or changed without public inconveniency, it is the will of God that the established government be obeyed, and no longer.... This principle being admitted, the justice of every particular case of resistance is reduced to a computation of the quantity of the danger and grievance on the one side, and of the probability and expense of redressing it on the other." Of this, he says, every man shall judge for himself. But Paley appears never to have contemplated those cases to which the rule of expediency does not apply, in which a people, as well as an individual, must do justice, cost what it may. If I have unjustly wrested a plank from a drowning man, I must restore it to him though I drown myself. This, according to Paley, would be inconvenient. But he that would save his life, in such a case, shall lose it. This people must cease to hold slaves, and to make war on Mexico, though it cost them their existence as a people.

In their practice, nations agree with Paley; but does any one think that Massachusetts does exactly what is right at the present crisis? 10

> A drab of state, a cloth-'o-silver slut,
> To have her train borne up, and her soul trail in the dirt.

Practically speaking, the opponents to a reform in Massachusetts are not a hundred thousand politicians at the South, but a hundred thousand merchants and farmers here, who are more interested in commerce and agriculture than they are in humanity, and are not prepared to do justice to the slave and to Mexico, *cost what it may.* I quarrel not with far-off foes, but with those who, near at home, cooperate with, and do the bidding of, those far away, and without whom the latter would be harmless. We are accustomed to say, that the mass of men are unprepared; but improvement is slow, because the few are not materially wiser or better than the many. It is not so important that many should be as good as you, as that there be some absolute goodness somewhere; for that will leaven the whole lump. There are thousands who are *in opinion* opposed to slavery and to the war, who yet in effect do nothing to put an end to them; who, esteeming themselves children of Washington and Franklin, sit down with their hands in their pockets, and say that they know not what to do, and do nothing; who even postpone the question of freedom to the question of free-trade, and quietly read the prices-current along with the latest advice from Mexico, after dinner, and, it may be, fall asleep over them both. What is the price-current of an honest man and patriot today? They hesitate, and they regret, and sometimes they petition; but they do nothing in earnest and with effect. They will wait, well disposed, for others to remedy the evil, that they may no longer have it to regret. At most, they give only a cheap vote, and a feeble countenance and God-speed, to the right, as it goes by them. There are nine hundred and ninety-nine patrons of virtue to one virtuous man; but it is easier to deal with the real possessor of a thing than with the temporary guardian of it.

All voting is a sort of gaming, like checkers or backgammon, with a slight moral tinge to it, a playing with right and wrong, with moral questions; and betting naturally accompanies it. The character of the voters is not staked. I cast my vote, perchance, as I think right; but I am not vitally concerned that that right should prevail. I am willing to leave it to the majority. Its obligation, therefore, never exceeds that of expediency. Even voting *for the right* is *doing* nothing for it. It is only expressing to men feebly your desire that it should prevail. A wise man will not leave the right to the mercy of chance, nor wish it to prevail through the power of the majority. There is but little virtue in the action of masses of men. When the majority shall at length vote for the abolition of slavery, it will be because they are indifferent to slavery, or because there is but little slavery left to be abolished by their vote. *They* will then be the only slaves. Only *his* vote can hasten the abolition of slavery who asserts his own freedom by his vote.

I hear of a convention to be held at Baltimore, or elsewhere, for the selection of a candidate for the presidency, made up chiefly of editors, and men who are politicians by profession; but I think, what is it to any independent, intelligent, and respectable man what decision they may come to? Shall we not have the advantage of his wisdom and honesty, nevertheless? Can we not count upon some independent votes? Are there not many individuals in the country who do not attend conventions? But no: I find that the respectable man, so called, has immediately drifted from his position, and despairs of his country, when his country has more reason to despair of him. He forthwith adopts one of the candidates thus selected as the only *available* one, thus providing that he is himself *available* for any purposes of the demagogue. His vote is of no more worth than that of any unprincipled foreigner or hireling native, who may have been bought. O for a man who is *a man,* and, as my neighbor says, has a bone in his back which you cannot pass your hand through! Our statistics are at fault: The population has been returned too large. How many *men* are there to a square thousand miles in this country? Hardly one. Does not America offer any inducement for men to settle here? The American has dwindled into an Odd Fellow, — one who may be known by the development of his organ of gregariousness, and a manifest lack of intellect and cheerful self-reliance; whose first and chief concern, on coming into the world, is to see that the Almshouses are in good repair; and, before yet he has lawfully donned the virile garb, to collect a fund for the support of the widows and orphans that may be; who, in short, ventures to live only by the aid of the Mutual Insurance company, which has promised to bury him decently.

It is not a man's duty, as a matter of course, to devote himself to the eradication of any, even the most enormous wrong; he may still properly have other concerns to engage him; but it is his duty, at least, to wash his hands of it, and, if he gives it no thought longer, not to give it practically his support. If I devote myself to other pursuits and contemplations, I must first see, at least, that I do not pursue them sitting upon another man's shoulders. I must get off him first, that he may pursue his contemplations too. See what gross inconsistency is tolerated. I have heard some of my townsmen say, "I should like to have them order me out to help put down an insurrection of the slaves, or to march to Mexico; — see if I would go"; and yet these very men have each, directly by their allegiance, and so indirectly, at least, by their money, furnished a substitute. The soldier is applauded who refuses to serve in an unjust war by those who do not refuse to sustain the unjust government which makes the war; is applauded by those whose own act and authority he disregards and sets at nought; as if the State were penitent to that degree that it hired one to scourge it while it sinned, but not to that degree that it left off sinning for a moment. Thus, under the name of Order and Civil Government, we are all made at last to pay homage to and support our own meanness. After the first blush of sin, comes its indifference; and from immoral it becomes, as it were, *un*moral, and not quite unnecessary to that life which we have made.

The broadest and most prevalent error requires the most disinterested virtue to sustain it. The slight reproach to which the virtue of patriotism is commonly liable, the noble are most likely to incur. Those who, while they disapprove of the character and measures of a government, yield to it their allegiance and support, are undoubtedly its most conscientious supporters, and so frequently the most serious obstacles to reform. Some are petitioning the State to dissolve the Union, to disregard the requisitions of the President. Why do they not dissolve it themselves, — the union between themselves and the State, — and refuse to pay their quota into its treasury? Do not they stand in the same relation to the State, that the State does to the Union? And have not the same reasons prevented the State from resisting the Union which have prevented them from resisting the State?

How can a man be satisfied to entertain an opinion merely, and 15 enjoy *it?* Is there any enjoyment in it, if his opinion is that he is aggrieved? If you are cheated out of a single dollar by your neighbor, you do not rest satisfied with knowing that you are cheated, or with saying that you are cheated, or even with petitioning him to pay you your due; but you take effectual steps at once to obtain the full amount, and see that you are never cheated again. Action from principle, the perception and the performance of right, changes things and relations; it is essentially revolutionary, and does not consist wholly with anything which was. It not only divides states and churches, it divides families; ay, it divides the *individual,* separating the diabolical in him from the divine.

Unjust laws exist: Shall we be content to obey them, or shall we endeavor to amend them, and obey them until we have succeeded, or shall we transgress them at once? Men generally, under such a government as this, think that they ought to wait until they have persuaded the majority to alter them. They think that, if they should resist, the remedy would be worse than the evil. But it is the fault of the government itself that the remedy *is* worse than the evil. *It* makes it worse. Why is it not more apt to anticipate and provide for reform? Why does it not cherish its wise minority? Why does it cry and resist before it is hurt? Why does it not encourage its citizens to be on the alert to point out its faults, and *do* better than it would have them? Why does it always crucify Christ, and excommunicate Copernicus and Luther, and pronounce Washington and Franklin rebels?

One would think, that a deliberate and practical denial of its authority was the only offence never contemplated by government; else, why has it not assigned its definite, its suitable and proportionate penalty? If a man who has no property refuses but once to earn nine shillings for the State, he is put in prison for a period unlimited by any law that I know, and determined only by the discretion of those who placed him there; but if he should steal ninety times nine shillings from the State, he is soon permitted to go at large again.

If the injustice is part of the necessary friction of the machine of government, let it go, let it go: Perchance it will wear smooth, — certainly the machine will wear out. If the injustice has a spring, or a pulley, or a rope, or a crank, exclusively for itself, then perhaps you may consider whether the remedy will not be worse than the evil; but if it is of such a nature that it requires you to be the agent of injustice to another, then, I say, break the law. Let your life be a counter friction to stop the machine. What I have to do is to see, at any rate, that I do not lend myself to the wrong which I condemn.

As for adopting the ways which the State has provided for remedying the evil, I know not of such ways. They take too much time, and a man's life will be gone. I have other affairs to attend to. I came into this world, not chiefly to make this a good place to live in, but to live in it, be it good or bad. A man has not everything to do, but something; and because he cannot do *everything*, it is not necessary that he should do *something* wrong. It is not my business to be petitioning the Governor or the Legislature any more than it is theirs to petition me; and, if they should not hear my petition, what should I do then? But in this case the State has provided no way: Its very Constitution is the evil. This may seem to be harsh and stubborn and unconciliatory; but it is to treat with the utmost kindness and consideration the only spirit that can appreciate or deserves it. So is all change for the better, like birth and death, which convulse the body.

I do not hesitate to say, that those who call themselves Abolitionists should at once effectually withdraw their support, both in person and property, from the government of Massachusetts, and not wait till they constitute a majority of one, before they suffer the right to prevail through them. I think that it is enough if they have God on their side, without waiting for that other one. Moreover, any man more right than his neighbors, constitutes a majority of one already. 20

I meet this American government, or its representative, the State government, directly, and face to face, once a year — no more — in the person of its tax-gatherer; this is the only mode in which a man situated as I am necessarily meets it; and it then says distinctly, Recognize me; and the simplest, the most effectual, and, in the present posture of affairs, the indispensablest mode of treating with it on this head, of expressing your little satisfaction with and love for it, is to deny it then. My civil neighbor, the tax-gatherer, is the very man I have to deal with, — for it is, after all, with men and not with parchment that I quarrel, — and he has voluntarily chosen to be an agent of the government. How shall he ever know well what he is and does as an officer of the government, or as a man, until he is obliged to consider whether he shall treat me, his neighbor, for whom he has respect, as a neighbor and well-disposed man, or as a maniac and disturber of the peace, and see if he can get over this obstruction to his neighborliness without a ruder and more impetuous thought or speech corresponding with his action? I know this well, that if one thousand, if one hundred, if ten men whom I could name, — if ten *honest* men only, — aye, if *one* HONEST man, in this State of Massachusetts, *ceasing to hold slaves,* were actually to withdraw from this copartnership, and be locked up in the county jail therefor, it would be the abolition of slavery in America. For it matters not how small the beginning may seem to be: What is once well done is done forever. But we love better to talk about it: That we say is our mission. Reform keeps many scores of newspapers in its service, but not one man. If my esteemed neighbor, the State's ambassador, who will devote his days to the settlement of the question of human rights in the Council Chamber, instead of being threatened with the prisons of Carolina, were to sit down the prisoner of Massachusetts, that State which is so anxious to foist the sin of slavery upon her sister, — though at present she can discover only an act of inhospitality to be the ground of a quarrel with her, — the Legislature would not wholly waive the subject the following winter.

Under a government which imprisons any unjustly, the true place for a just man is also a prison. The proper place today, the only place which Massachusetts has provided for her freer and less desponding spirits, is in her prisons, to be put out and locked out of the State by her own act, as they have already put themselves out by their principles. It is there that the fugitive slave, and the Mexican prisoner on parole, and the Indian come to plead the wrongs of his race, should find them; on that separate, but more free and honorable ground, where the State places those who are not *with* her, but *against* her, — the only house in a slave State in which a free man can abide with honor. If any think that their influence would be lost there, and their voices no longer afflict the ear of the State, that they would not be as an enemy within its walls, they do not know by how much truth is stronger than error, nor how much more eloquently and effectively he can combat injustice who has experienced a little in his own person. Cast your whole vote, not a strip of paper merely, but your whole influence. A minority is powerless while it conforms to the majority; it is not even a minority then; but it is irresistible when it clogs by its whole weight. If the alternative is to keep all just men in prison, or give up war and slavery, the State will not hesitate which to choose. If a thousand men were not to pay their tax-bills this year, that would not be a violent and bloody measure, as it would be to pay them, and enable the State to commit violence and shed innocent blood. This is, in fact, the definition of a peaceable revolution, if any such is possible. If the tax-gatherer, or any other public officer, asks me, as one has done, "But what shall I do?" my answer is, "If you really wish to do any thing, resign your office." When the subject has refused allegiance, and the officer has resigned his office, then the revolution is accomplished. But even suppose blood should flow. Is there not a sort of blood shed when the conscience is wounded? Through this wound a man's real manhood and immortality flow out, and he bleeds to an everlasting death. I see this blood flowing now.

I have contemplated the imprisonment of the offender, rather than the seizure of his goods, — though both will serve the same

purpose, — because they who assert the purest right, and consequently are most dangerous to a corrupt State, commonly have not
spent much time in accumulating property. To such the State ren-
ders comparatively small service, and a slight tax is wont to appear
exorbitant, particularly if they are obliged to earn it by special labor
with their hands. If there were one who lived wholly without the use
of money, the State itself would hesitate to demand it of him. But the
rich man, — not to make any invidious comparison, — is always
sold to the institution which makes him rich. Absolutely speaking,
the more money, the less virtue; for money comes between a man
and his objects, and obtains them for him; and it was certainly no
great virtue to obtain it. It puts to rest many questions which he
would otherwise be taxed to answer; while the only new question
which it puts is the hard but superfluous one, how to spend it. Thus
his moral ground is taken from under his feet. The opportunities of
living are diminished in proportion as what are called the "means"
are increased. The best thing a man can do for his culture when he
is rich is to endeavor to carry out those schemes which he enter-
tained when he was poor. Christ answered the Herodians according
to their condition. "Show me the tribute-money," said he; — and one
took a penny out of his pocket; — if you use money which has the
image of Cæsar on it, and which he has made current and valuable,
that is, *if you are men of the State,* and gladly enjoy the advantages of
Cæsar's government, then pay him back some of his own when he
demands it; "Render therefore to Cæsar that which is Cæsar's, and
to God those things which are God's,"— leaving them no wiser than
before as to which was which; for they did not wish to know.

When I converse with the freest of my neighbors, I perceive that,
whatever they may say about the magnitude and seriousness of the
question, and their regard for the public tranquility, the long and the
short of the matter is, that they cannot spare the protection of the
existing government, and they dread the consequences to their
property and families of disobedience to it. For my own part, I
should not like to think that I ever rely on the protection of the State.
But, if I deny the authority of the State when it presents its tax-bill, it
will soon take and waste all my property, and so harass me and my
children without end. This is hard. This makes it impossible for a
man to live honestly, and at the same time comfortably, in outward
respects. It will not be worth the while to accumulate property; that
would be sure to go again. You must hire or squat somewhere, and
raise but a small crop, and eat that soon. You must live within yourself, and depend upon yourself always tucked up and ready for a
start, and not have many affairs. A man may grow rich in Turkey
even, if he will be in all respects a good subject of the Turkish government. Confucius said: "If a state is governed by the principles of
reason, poverty and misery are subjects of shame; if a state is not

governed by the principles of reason, riches and honors are the subjects of shame." No: Until I want the protection of Massachusetts to be extended to me in some distant southern port, where my liberty is endangered, or until I am bent solely on building up an estate at home by peaceful enterprise, I can afford to refuse allegiance to Massachusetts, and her right to my property and life. It costs me less in every sense to incur the penalty of disobedience to the State, than it would to obey. I should feel as if I were worth less in that case.

Some years ago, the State met me in behalf of the Church, and 25 commanded me to pay a certain sum toward the support of a clergyman whose preaching my father attended, but never I myself. "Pay," it said, "or be locked up in the jail." I declined to pay. But, unfortunately, another man saw fit to pay it. I did not see why the schoolmaster should be taxed to support the priest, and not the priest the schoolmaster; for I was not the State's schoolmaster, but I supported myself by voluntary subscription. I did not see why the lyceum should not present its tax-bill, and have the State to back its demand, as well as the Church. However, at the request of the selectmen, I condescended to make some such statement as this in writing: — "Know all men by these presents, that I, Henry Thoreau, do not wish to be regarded as a member of any incorporated society which I have not joined." This I gave to the town clerk; and he has it. The State, having thus learned that I did not wish to be regarded as a member of that church, has never made a like demand on me since; though it said that it must adhere to its original presumption that time. If I had known how to name them, I should then have signed off in detail from all the societies which I never signed on to; but I did not know where to find a complete list.

I have paid no poll-tax for six years. I was put into a jail once on this account, for one night; and, as I stood considering the walls of solid stone, two or three feet thick, the door of wood and iron, a foot thick, and the iron grating which strained the light, I could not help being struck with the foolishness of that institution which treated me as if I were mere flesh and blood and bones, to be locked up. I wondered that it should have concluded at length that this was the best use it could put me to, and had never thought to avail itself of my services in some way. I saw that, if there was a wall of stone between me and my townsmen, there was a still more difficult one to climb or break through, before they could get to be as free as I was. I did not for a moment feel confined, and the walls seemed a great waste of stone and mortar. I felt as if I alone of all my townsmen had paid my tax. They plainly did not know how to treat me, but behaved like persons who are underbred. In every threat and in every compliment there was a blunder; for they thought that my chief desire was to stand the other side of that stone wall. I could not but smile to see how industriously they locked the door on my meditations, which followed them out again without let or hindrance, and *they* were really all that was dangerous. As they could not reach me, they had resolved to punish my body; just as boys, if they cannot come at some person against whom they have a spite, will abuse his dog. I saw that the State was half-witted, and it was timid as a lone woman with her silver spoons, and that it did not know its friends from its foes, and I lost all my remaining respect for it, and pitied it.

Thus the State never intentionally confronts a man's sense, intellectual or moral, but only his body, his senses. It is not armed with superior wit or honesty, but with superior physical strength. I was not born to be forced. I will breathe after my own fashion. Let us see who is the strongest. What force has a multitude? They only can force me who obey a higher law than I. They force me to become like themselves. I do not hear of *men* being *forced* to live this way or that by masses of men. What sort of life were that to live? When I meet a government which says to me, "Your money or your life," why should I be in haste to give it my money? It may be in a great strait, and not know what to do: I cannot help that. It must help itself; do as I do. It is not worth the while to snivel about it. I am not responsible for the successful working of the machinery of society. I am not the son of the engineer. I perceive that, when an acorn and a chestnut fall side by side, the one does not remain inert to make way for the other, but both obey their own laws, and spring and grow and flourish as best they can, till one, perchance, overshadows and destroys the other. If a plant cannot live according to its nature, it dies; and so a man.

The night in prison was novel and interesting enough. The prisoners in their shirt-sleeves were enjoying a chat and the evening air in the doorway, when I entered. But the jailer said, "Come, boys, it is time to lock up"; and so they dispersed, and I heard the sound of their steps returning into the hollow apartments. My roommate was introduced to me by the jailer, as "a first-rate fellow and a clever man." When the door was locked, he showed me where to hang my hat, and how he managed matters there. The rooms were whitewashed once a month; and this one, at least, was the whitest, most simply furnished, and probably the neatest apartment in the town. He naturally wanted to know where I came from, and what brought me there; and, when I had told him, I asked him in my turn how he came there, presuming him to be an honest man, of course; and, as the world goes, I believe he was. "Why," said he, "they accuse me of burning a barn; but I never did it." As near as I could discover, he had probably gone to bed in a barn when drunk, and smoked his pipe there; and so a barn was burnt. He had the reputation of being a clever man, had been there some three months waiting for his trial to come on, and would have to wait as much longer; but he was quite domesticated and contented, since he got his board for nothing, and thought that he was well-treated.

He occupied one window, and I the other; and I saw, that if one stayed there long, his principal business would be to look out the window. I had soon read all the tracts that were left there, and examined where former prisoners had broken out, and where a grate had been sawed off, and heard the history of the various occupants of that room; for I found that even here there was a history and a gossip which never circulated beyond the walls of the jail. Probably this is the only house in the town where verses are composed, which are afterward printed in a circular form, but not published. I was shown quite a long list of verses which were composed by some young men who had been detected in an attempt to escape, who avenged themselves by singing them.

I pumped my fellow-prisoner as dry as I could, for fear I should never see him again; but at length he showed me which was my bed, and left me to blow out the lamp. 30

It was like travelling into a far country, such as I had never expected to behold, to lie there for one night. It seemed to me that I never had heard the town-clock strike before, nor the evening sounds of the village; for we slept with the windows open, which were inside the grating. It was to see my native village in the light of the Middle Ages, and our Concord was turned into a Rhine stream, and visions of knights and castles passed before me. They were the voices of old burghers that I heard in the streets. I was an involuntary spectator and auditor of whatever was done and said in the kitchen of the adjacent village-inn, — a wholly new and rare experience to me. It was a closer view of my native town. I was fairly inside of it. I never had seen its institutions before. This is one of its peculiar institutions; for it is a shire town. I began to comprehend what its inhabitants were about.

In the morning, our breakfasts were put through the hole in the door, in small oblong-square tin pans, made to fit, and holding a pint of chocolate, with brown bread, and an iron spoon. When they called for the vessels again, I was green enough to return what bread I had left; but my comrade seized it, and said that I should lay that up for lunch or dinner. Soon after, he was let out to work at haying in a neighboring field, whither he went every day, and would not be back till noon; so he bade me good-day, saying that he doubted if he should see me again.

When I came out of prison, — for some one interfered, and paid that tax, — I did not perceive that great changes had taken place on the common, such as he observed who went in a youth, and emerged a tottering and gray-headed man; and yet a change had to my eyes come over the scene, — the town, and State, and country, — greater than any that mere time could effect. I saw yet more distinctly the State in which I lived. I saw to what extent the people among whom I lived could be trusted as good neighbors and friends; that their friendship was for summer weather only; that they did not greatly propose to do right; that they were a distinct race from me by their prejudices and superstitions, as the Chinamen and Malays are; that, in their sacrifices to humanity, they ran no risks, not even to their property; that, after all, they were not so noble but they treated the thief as he had treated them, and hoped, by a certain outward observance and a few prayers, and by walking in a particular straight though useless path from time to time, to save their souls. This may be to judge my neighbors harshly; for I believe that many of them are not aware that they have such an institution as the jail in their village.

It was formerly the custom in our village, when a poor debtor came out of jail, for his acquaintances to salute him, looking through their fingers, which were crossed to represent the grating of a jail window, "How do ye do?" My neighbors did not thus salute me, but first looked at me, and then at one another, as if I had returned from a long journey. I was put into jail as I was going to the shoemaker's to get a shoe which was mended. When I was let out the next morning, I proceeded to finish my errand, and having put on my mended shoe, joined a huckleberry party, who were impatient to put themselves under my conduct; and in half an hour, — for the horse was soon tackled, — was in the midst of a huckleberry field, on one of our highest hills, two miles off, and then the State was nowhere to be seen.

This is the whole story of "My Prisons."

35

I have never declined paying the highway tax, because I am as desirous of being a good neighbor as I am of being a bad subject; and, as for supporting schools, I am doing my part to educate my fellow-countrymen now. It is for no particular item in the tax-bill that I refuse to pay it. I simply wish to refuse allegiance to the State, to withdraw and stand aloof from it effectually. I do not care to trace the course of my dollar, if I could, till it buys a man, or a musket to shoot one with, — the dollar is innocent, — but I am concerned to trace the effects of my allegiance. In fact, I quietly declare war with the State, after my fashion, though I will still make what use and get what advantage of her I can, as is usual in such cases.

If others pay the tax which is demanded of me, from a sympathy with the State, they do but what they have already done in their own case, or rather they abet injustice to a greater extent than the State requires. If they pay the tax from a mistaken interest in the individual taxed, to save his property or prevent his going to jail, it is because they have not considered wisely how far they let their private feelings interfere with the public good.

This, then, is my position at present. But one cannot be too much on his guard in such a case, lest his action be biased by obstinacy, or an undue regard for the opinions of men. Let him see that he does only what belongs to himself and to the hour.

I think sometimes, Why, this people mean well; they are only ignorant; they would do better if they knew how: why give your neighbors this pain to treat you as they are inclined to? But I think again, this is no reason why I should do as they do, or permit others to suffer much greater pain of a different kind. Again, I sometimes say to myself, When many millions of men, without heat, without ill will, without personal feelings of any kind, demand of you a few shillings only, without the possibility, such is their constitution, of retracing or altering their present demand, and without the possibility, on your side, of appeal to any other millions, why expose yourself to this overwhelming brute force? You do not resist cold and hunger, the winds and the waves, thus obstinately; you quietly submit to a thousand similar necessities. You do not put your head into the fire. But just in proportion as I regard this as not wholly a brute force, partly a human force, and consider that I have relations to those millions as to so many millions of men, and not of mere brute or inanimate things, I see that appeal is possible, first and instantaneously, from them to the Maker of them, and, secondly, from them to themselves. But, if I put my head deliberately into the fire, there is no appeal to fire or to the Maker of fire, and I have only myself to blame. If I could convince myself that I have any right to be satisfied with men as they are, and to treat them according, and not according, in some respects, to my requisitions and expectations of what they and I ought to be, then, like a good Mussulman and fatalist, I should endeavor to be satisfied with things as they are, and say it is the will of God. And, above all, there is this difference between resisting this and a purely brute or natural force, that I can resist this with some effect; but I cannot expect, like Orpheus, to change the nature of the rocks and trees and beasts.

I do not wish to quarrel with any man or nation. I do not wish to 40 split hairs, to make fine distinctions, or set myself up as better than my neighbors. I seek rather, I may say, even an excuse for conforming to the laws of the land. I am but too ready to conform to them. Indeed, I have reason to suspect myself on this head; and each year, as the tax-gatherer comes round, I find myself disposed to review the acts and position of the general and State governments, and the spirit of the people, to discover a pretext for conformity.

> We must affect our country as our parents;
> And if at any time we alienate
> Our love or industry from doing it honor,
> We must respect effects and teach the soul
> Matter of conscience and religion,
> And not desire of rule or benefit.

I believe that the State will soon be able to take all my work of this sort out of my hands, and then I shall be no better a patriot than my fellow-countrymen. Seen from a lower point of view, the Constitution, with all its faults, is very good; the law and the courts are very respectable; even this State and this American government are, in many respects, very admirable and rare things, to be thankful for, such as a great many have described them; but seen from a point of view a little higher, they are what I have described them; seen from a higher still, and the highest, who shall say what they are, or that they are worth looking at or thinking of at all?

However, the government does not concern me much, and I shall bestow the fewest possible thoughts on it. It is not many moments that I live under a government, even in this world. If a man is thought-free, fancy-free, imagination-free, that which *is not* never for a long time appearing *to be* to him, unwise rulers or reformers cannot fatally interrupt him.

I know that most men think differently from myself; but those whose lives are by profession devoted to the study of these or kindred subjects, content me as little as any. Statesmen and legislators, standing so completely within the institution, never distinctly and nakedly behold it. They speak of moving society, but have no resting-place without it. They may be men of a certain experience and discrimination, and have no doubt invented ingenious and even useful systems, for which we sincerely thank them; but all their wit and usefulness lie within certain not very wide limits. They are wont to forget that the world is not governed by policy and expediency. Webster never goes behind government, and so cannot speak with authority about it. His words are wisdom to those legislators who contemplate no essential reform in the existing government; but for thinkers, and those who legislate for all time, he never once glances at the subject. I know of those whose serene and wise speculations on this theme would soon reveal the limits of his mind's range and hospitality. Yet, compared with the cheap professions of most reformers, and the still cheaper wisdom and eloquence of politicians in general, his are almost the only sensible and valuable words, and we thank Heaven for him. Comparatively, he is always strong, original, and, above all, practical. Still his quality is not wisdom, but prudence. The lawyer's truth is not Truth, but consistency, or a consistent expediency. Truth is always in harmony with herself, and is not concerned chiefly to reveal the justice that may consist with wrong-doing. He well deserves to be called, as he has been called, the Defender of the Constitution. There are really no blows to be given by him but defensive ones. He is not a leader, but a follower. His leaders are the men of '87. "I have never made an effort," he says, "and never propose to make an effort; I have never countenanced an effort, and never mean to countenance an effort, to disturb the arrangement as originally made, by which the various States came into the Union." Still thinking of the sanction which the Constitution gives to slavery, he says, "Because it was a part of the original compact, — let it stand." Notwithstanding his special acuteness and ability, he is unable to take a fact out of its merely political relations, and behold it as it lies absolutely to be disposed of by the intellect, — what, for instance, it behooves a man to do here in America today with regard to slavery, but ventures, or is driven, to make some such desperate answer as the following, while professing to speak absolutely, and as a private man, — from which what new and singular code of social duties might be inferred? "The manner," says he, "in which the governments of those States where slavery exists are to regulate it, is for their own consideration, under their responsibility to their constituents, to the general laws of propriety, humanity, and justice, and to God. Associations formed elsewhere, springing from a feeling of humanity, or any other cause, have nothing whatever to do with it. They have never received any encouragement from me, and they never will."[1]

They who know of no purer sources of truth, who have traced up its stream no higher, stand, and wisely stand, by the Bible and the Constitution, and drink at it there with reverence and humility; but they who behold where it comes trickling into this lake or that pool, gird up their loins once more, and continue their pilgrimage toward its fountainhead.

No man with a genius for legislation has appeared in America. They are rare in the history of the world. There are orators, politicians, and eloquent men, by the thousand; but the speaker has not yet opened his mouth to speak, who is capable of settling the much-vexed questions of the day. We love eloquence for its own sake, and not for any truth which it may utter, or any heroism it may inspire. Our legislators have not yet learned the comparative value of free-trade and of freedom, of union, and of rectitude, to a nation. They have no genius or talent for comparatively humble questions of taxation and finance, commerce and manufactures and agriculture. If we were left solely to the wordy wit of legislators in Congress for our guidance, uncorrected by the seasonable experience and the effectual complaints of the people, America would not long retain her rank among the nations. For eighteen hundred years, though perchance I have no right to say it, the New Testament has been written; yet where is the legislator who has wisdom and practical talent enough to avail himself of the light which it sheds on the science of legislation?

The authority of government, even such as I am willing to submit to, — for I will cheerfully obey those who know and can do bet-

45

---

[1] These extracts have been inserted since the Lecture was read.

ter than I, and in many things even those who neither know nor can do so well, — is still an impure one: To be strictly just, it must have the sanction and consent of the governed. It can have no pure right over my person and property but what I concede to it. The progress from an absolute to a limited monarchy, from a limited monarchy to a democracy, is a progress toward a true respect for the individual. Even the Chinese philosopher was wise enough to regard the individual as the basis of the empire. Is a democracy, such as we know it, the last improvement possible in government? Is it not possible to take a step further towards recognizing and organizing the rights of man? There will never be a really free and enlightened State, until the State comes to recognize the individual as a higher and independent power, from which all its own power and authority are derived, and treats him accordingly. I please myself with imagining a State at last which can afford to be just to all men, and to treat the individual with respect as a neighbor; which even would not think it inconsistent with its own repose, if a few were to live aloof from it, not meddling with it, nor embraced by it, who fulfilled all the duties of neighbors and fellowmen. A State which bore this kind of fruit, and suffered it to drop off as fast as it ripened, would prepare the way for a still more perfect and glorious State, which also I have imagined, but not yet anywhere seen.

Discussion Questions

1. Summarize briefly Thoreau's reasons for arguing that civil disobedience is sometimes a *duty*.
2. Thoreau, like Martin Luther King, Jr., in "Letter from Birmingham Jail" (p. 693), speaks of "unjust laws." Do they agree on the positions that citizens should take in response to these laws? Are Thoreau and King guided by the same principles? In Plato's "Crito" (p. 633), what does Socrates say about obedience to unjust laws?
3. What examples of government policy and action does Thoreau use to prove that civil disobedience is a duty? Explain why they are — or are not — effective.
4. Why do you think Thoreau provides such a detailed account of one day in prison? (Notice that King does not give a description of his confinement.) What observation about the community struck Thoreau when he emerged from jail?

Writing Suggestions

5. Argue that civil disobedience to a school policy or action is justified. (Examples might include failure to establish an ethnic studies department, refusal to allow ROTC on campus, refusal to suspend a professor accused of sexual harassment.) Be specific about the injustice of the policy or action and the values that underlie the resistance.

6. Under what circumstances might civil disobedience prove to be dangerous and immoral? Can you think of cases of disobedience when *conscience,* as Thoreau uses the term, did not appear to be the guiding principle? Try to identify what you think is the true motivation for the resistance.

Declaration of Sentiments and Resolutions, Seneca Falls

ELIZABETH CADY STANTON

Elizabeth Cady Stanton (1815–1902) was an early activist in the movement for women's rights, including the right to vote and the freedom to enroll in college and to enter professions that were closed to women. She was also active in the campaign to abolish slavery. In 1848 the first women's rights convention was held in her home in Seneca Falls, New York, where the "Declaration of Sentiments and Resolutions" was issued.

When, in the course of human events, it becomes necessary for one portion of the family of man to assume among the people of the earth a position different from that which they have hitherto occupied, but one to which the laws of nature and of nature's God entitle them, a decent respect to the opinions of mankind requires that they should declare the causes that impel them to such a course.

We hold these truths to be self-evident: that all men and women are created equal; that they are endowed by their Creator with certain inalienable rights; that among these are life, liberty, and the pursuit of happiness; that to secure these rights governments are instituted, deriving their just powers from the consent of the governed. Whenever any form of government becomes destructive of these ends, it is the right of those who suffer from it to refuse allegiance to it, and to insist upon the institution of a new government, laying its foundation on such principles, and organizing its powers in such form, as to them shall seem most likely to effect their safety and happiness. Prudence, indeed, will dictate that governments long established should not be changed for light and transient causes; and accordingly all experience hath shown that mankind are more disposed to suffer, while evils are sufferable, then to right themselves by abolishing the forms to which they were accustomed. But when a long train of abuses and usurpations, pursuing invariably the same object evinces a design to reduce them under absolute despotism, it is their duty to throw off such government, and to provide new guards for their future security. Such has been the patient sufferance of the women under this government, and such is now the necessity which constrains them to demand the equal station to which they are entitled.

The history of mankind is a history of repeated injuries and usurpations on the part of man toward woman, having in direct object the establishment of an absolute tyranny over her. To prove this, let facts be submitted to a candid world.

670

He has never permitted her to exercise her inalienable right to the elective franchise.

He has compelled her to submit to laws, in the formation of which she had no voice.

He has withheld from her rights which are given to the most ignorant and degraded men — both natives and foreigners.

Having deprived her of this first right of a citizen, the elective franchise, thereby leaving her without representation in the halls of legislation, he has oppressed her on all sides.

He has made her, if married, in the eye of the law, civilly dead.

He has taken from her all right in property, even to the wages she earns.

He has made her, morally, an irresponsible being, as she can commit many crimes with impunity, provided they be done in the presence of her husband. In the covenant of marriage, she is compelled to promise obedience to her husband, he becoming, to all intents and purposes, her master — the law giving him power to deprive her of her liberty, and to administer chastisement.

He has so framed the laws of divorce, as to what shall be the proper causes, and in case of separation, to whom the guardianship of the children shall be given, as to be wholly regardless of the happiness of women — the law, in all cases, going upon a false supposition of the supremacy of man, and giving all power into his hands.

After depriving her of all rights as a married woman, if single, and the owner of property, he has taxed her to support a government which recognizes her only when her property can be made profitable to it.

He has monopolized nearly all the profitable employments, and from those she is permitted to follow, she receives but a scanty remuneration. He closes against her all the avenues to wealth and distinction which he considers most honorable to himself. As a teacher of theology, medicine, or law, she is not known.

He has denied her the facilities for obtaining a thorough education, all colleges being closed against her.

He allows her in Church, as well as State, but a subordinate position, claiming Apostolic authority for her exclusion from the ministry, and, with some exceptions, from any public participation in the affairs of the Church.

He has created a false public sentiment by giving to the world a different code of morals for men and women, by which moral delinquencies which exclude women from society, are not only tolerated, but deemed of little account in man.

He has usurped the prerogative of Jehovah himself, claiming it as his right to assign for her a sphere of action, when that belongs to her conscience and to her God.

He has endeavored, in every way that he could, to destroy her confidence in her own powers, to lessen her self-respect, and to make her willing to lead a dependent and abject life.

Now, in view of this entire disfranchisement of one-half the people of this country, their social and religious degradation — in view of the unjust laws above mentioned, and because women do feel themselves aggrieved, oppressed, and fraudulently deprived of their most sacred rights, we insist that they have immediate admission to all the rights and privileges which belong to them as citizens of the United States.

In entering upon the great work before us, we anticipate no 20 small amount of misconception, misrepresentation, and ridicule; but we shall use every instrumentality within our power to effect our object. We shall employ agents, circulate tracts, petition the State and National legislatures, and endeavor to enlist the pulpit and the press in our behalf. We hope this Convention will be followed by a series of Conventions embracing every part of the country.

Resolutions

WHEREAS, The great precept of nature is conceded to be, that "man shall pursue his own true and substantial happiness." Blackstone in his Commentaries remarks, that this law of Nature being coeval with mankind, and dictated by God himself, is of course superior in obligation to any other. It is binding over all the globe, in all countries and at all times; no human laws are of any validity if contrary to this, and such of them as are valid, derive all their force, and all their validity, and all their authority, mediately and immediately, from this original; therefore,

Resolved, That such laws as conflict, in any way, with the true and substantial happiness of woman, are contrary to the great precept of nature and of no validity, for this is "superior in obligation to any other."

Resolved, That all laws which prevent woman from occupying such a station in society as her conscience shall dictate, or which place her in a position inferior to that of man, are contrary to the great precept of nature, and therefore of no force or authority.

Resolved, That woman is man's equal — was intended to be so by the Creator, and the highest good of the race demands that she should be recognized as such.

Resolved, That the women of this country ought to be enlight- 25 ened in regard to the laws under which they live, that they may no longer publish their degradation by declaring themselves satisfied with their present position, nor their ignorance, by asserting that they have all the rights they want.

Resolved, That inasmuch as man, while claiming for himself intellectual superiority, does accord to woman moral superiority, it is preeminently his duty to encourage her to speak and teach, as she has an opportunity, in all religious assemblies.

Resolved, That the same amount of virtue, delicacy, and refinement of behavior that is required of woman in the social state, should also be required of man, and the same transgressions should be visited with equal severity on both man and woman.

Resolved, That the objection of indelicacy and impropriety, which is so often brought against woman when she addresses a public audience, comes with a very ill-grace from those who encourage, by their attendance, her appearance on the stage, in the concert, or in feats of the circus.

Resolved, That woman has too long rested satisfied in the circumscribed limits which corrupt customs and a perverted application of the Scriptures have marked out for her, and that it is time she should move in the enlarged sphere which her great Creator has assigned her.

Resolved, That it is the duty of the women of this country to se- 30 cure to themselves their sacred right to the elective franchise.

Resolved, That the equality of human rights results necessarily from the fact of the identity of the race in capabilities and responsibilities.

Resolved, therefore, That, being invested by the Creator with the same capabilities, and the same consciousness of responsibility for their exercise, it is demonstrably the right and duty of woman, equally with man, to promote every righteous cause by every righteous means; and especially in regard to the great subjects of morals and religion, it is self-evidently her right to participate with her brother in teaching them, both in private and in public, by writing and by speaking, by any instrumentalities proper to be used, and in any assemblies proper to be held; and this being a self-evident truth growing out of the divinely implanted principles of human nature, any custom or authority adverse to it, whether modern or wearing the hoary sanction of antiquity, is to be regarded as a self-evident falsehood, and at war with mankind.

[At the last session Lucretia Mott offered and spoke to the following resolution:]

Resolved, That the speedy success of our cause depends upon the zealous and untiring efforts of both men and women, for the overthrow of the monopoly of the pulpit, and for the securing to woman an equal participation with men in the various trades, professions, and commerce.

Discussion Questions

1. Are all the grievances listed in the document of equal importance? If not, which seem the most important? Why?

2. What is the great precept of nature on which the resolutions are based? How does this compare to the motivating principle of the Declaration of Independence?
3. What characteristics of male thinking and behavior are attacked in the Declaration at Seneca Falls?
4. Does the Declaration at Seneca Falls anywhere suggest that women have gifts superior to those of men? Does it suggest that equal rights for women bestow benefits on others as well?

Writing Suggestions

5. Is it necessary today to call attention to some of the old grievances or to suggest new ones? Pick out one or two old issues and offer examples to show that such a need no longer exists. Or argue that women are still being deprived of their right to their own "true and substantial happiness."
6. Most newspapers and journals treated the Declaration at Seneca Falls with contempt and ridicule. What attitudes and convictions in the mid-nineteenth century could have caused such a reaction?

Professions for Women

VIRGINIA WOOLF

*Virginia Woolf (1882–1941) was a novelist and essayist and a leading
member of the Bloomsbury group, a celebrated circle of writers,
artists, and intellectuals that flourished in London in the early part of
the century. Her novels, among them* Mrs. Dalloway, To the
Lighthouse, *and* The Waves, *were brilliant technical experiments.
Her essays and literary criticism were highly original, distinguished by
wit and spontaneity. All her life she suffered from nervous depression,
and in 1941 she committed suicide. "Professions for Women" was a
paper read to the Women's Service League in London in 1931.*

When your secretary invited me to come here, she told me that
your Society is concerned with the employment of women and she
suggested that I might tell you something about my own professional experiences. It is true I am a woman; it is true I am employed;
but what professional experiences have I had? It is difficult to say.
My profession is literature; and in that profession there are fewer experiences for women than in any other, with the exception of the
stage — fewer, I mean, that are peculiar to women. For the road was
cut many years ago — by Fanny Burney, by Aphra Behn, by Harriet
Martineau, by Jane Austen, by George Eliot — many famous women,
and many more unknown and forgotten, have been before me, making the path smooth, and regulating my steps. Thus, when I came to
write, there were very few material obstacles in my way. Writing was
a reputable and harmless occupation. The family peace was not broken by the scratching of a pen. No demand was made upon the family purse. For ten and sixpence one can buy paper enough to write
all the plays of Shakespeare — if one has a mind that way. Pianos
and models, Paris, Vienna, and Berlin, masters and mistresses, are
not needed by a writer. The cheapness of writing paper is, of course,
the reason why women have succeeded as writers before they have
succeeded in the other professions.

But to tell you my story — it is a simple one. You have only got
to figure to yourselves a girl in a bedroom with a pen in her hand.
She had only to move that pen from left to right — from ten o'clock
to one. Then it occurred to her to do what is simple and cheap
enough after all — to slip a few of those pages into an envelope, fix a
penny stamp in the corner, and drop the envelope into the red box
at the corner. It was thus that I became a journalist; and my effort
was rewarded on the first day of the following month — a very glori-

---

From *The Death of the Moth and Other Essays* (1942).

ous day it was for me — by a letter from an editor containing a check for one pound ten shillings and sixpence. But to show you how little I deserve to be called a professional woman, how little I know of the struggles and difficulties of such lives, I have to admit that instead of spending that sum upon bread and butter, rent, shoes, and stockings, or butcher's bills, I went out and bought a cat — a beautiful cat, a Persian cat, which very soon involved me in bitter disputes with my neighbors.

What could be easier than to write articles and to buy Persian cats with the profits? But wait a moment. Articles have to be about something. Mine, I seem to remember, was about a novel by a famous man. And while I was writing this review, I discovered that if I were going to review books I should need to do battle with a certain phantom. And the phantom was a woman, and when I came to know her better I called her after the heroine of a famous poem, the Angel in the House. It was she who used to come between me and my paper when I was writing reviews. It was she who bothered me and wasted my time and so tormented me that at last I killed her. You who come of a younger and happier generation may not have heard of her — you may not know what I mean by the Angel in the House. I will describe her as shortly as I can. She was intensely sympathetic. She was immensely charming. She was utterly unselfish. She excelled in the difficult arts of family life. She sacrificed herself daily. If there was a chicken, she took the leg; if there was a draft she sat in it — in short she was so constituted that she never had a mind or a wish of her own, but preferred to sympathize always with the minds and wishes of others. Above all — I need not say it — she was pure. Her purity was supposed to be her chief beauty — her blushes, her great grace. In those days — the last of Queen Victoria — every house had its Angel. And when I came to write I encountered her with the very first words. The shadow of her wings fell on my page; I heard the rustling of her skirts in the room. Directly, that is to say, I took my pen in my hand to review that novel by a famous man, she slipped behind me and whispered: "My dear, you are a young woman. You are writing about a book that has been written by a man. Be sympathetic; be tender; flatter; deceive; use all the arts and wiles of our sex. Never let anybody guess that you have a mind of your own. Above all, be pure." And she made as if to guide my pen. I now record the one act for which I take some credit to myself, though the credit rightly belongs to some excellent ancestors of mine who left me a certain sum of money — shall we say five hundred pounds a year? — so that it was not necessary for me to depend solely on charm for my living. I turned upon her and caught her by the throat. I did my best to kill her. My excuse, if I were to be had up in a court of law, would be that I acted in self-defense. Had I not killed her she would have killed me. She would have plucked the heart out of my writing. For, as I found, directly I put pen to paper, you cannot review even a novel without having a mind of your own, without expressing what you think to be the truth about human relations, morality, sex. And all these questions, according to the Angel of the House, cannot be dealt with freely and openly by women; they must charm, they must conciliate, they must — to put it bluntly — tell lies if they are to succeed. Thus, whenever I felt the shadow of her wing or the radiance of her halo upon my page, I took up the inkpot and flung it at her. She died hard. Her fictitious nature was of great assistance to her. It is far harder to kill a phantom than a reality. She was always creeping back when I thought I had dispatched her. Though I flatter myself that I killed her in the end, the struggle was severe; it took much time that had better have been spent upon learning Greek grammar; or in roaming the world in search of adventures. But it was a real experience; it was an experience that was bound to befall all women writers at this time. Killing the Angel in the House was part of the occupation of a woman writer.

But to continue my story. The Angel was dead; what then remained? You may say that what remained was a simple and common object — a young woman in a bedroom with an inkpot. In other words, now that she had rid herself of falsehood, that young woman had only to be herself. Ah, but what is "herself"? I mean, what is a woman? I assure you, I do not know. I do not believe that you know. I do not believe that anybody can know until she has expressed herself in all the arts and professions open to human skill. That indeed is one of the reasons why I have come here — out of respect for you, who are in process of showing us by your experiments what a woman is, who are in process of providing us, by your failures and successes, with that extremely important piece of information.

But to continue the story of my professional experiences, I made 5 one pound ten and six by my first review; and I bought a Persian cat with the proceeds. Then I grew ambitious. A Persian cat is all very well, I said; but a Persian cat is not enough. I must have a motor car. And it was thus that I became a novelist — for it is a very strange thing that people will give you a motor car if you will tell them a story. It is a still stranger thing that there is nothing so delightful in the world as telling stories. It is far pleasanter than writing reviews of famous novels. And yet, if I am to obey your secretary and tell you my professional experiences as a novelist, I must tell you about a very strange experience that befell me as a novelist. And to understand it you must try first to imagine a novelist's state of mind. I hope I am not giving away professional secrets if I say that a novelist's chief desire is to be as unconscious as possible. He has to induce in himself a state of perpetual lethargy. He wants life to proceed with the utmost quiet and regularity. He wants to see the same faces, to read the same books, to do the same things day after day, month after month, while he is writing, so that nothing may break the illusion in which he is living — so that nothing may disturb or disquiet the mysterious nosings about, feelings round, darts, dashes, and sudden discoveries of that very shy and illusive spirit, the imagination. I suspect that this state is the same both for men and women. Be that as it may, I want you to imagine me writing a novel in a state of trance. I want you to figure to yourselves a girl sitting with a pen in her hand, which for minutes, and indeed for hours, she never dips into the inkpot. The image that comes to my mind when I think of this girl is the image of a fisherman lying sunk in dreams on the verge of a deep lake with a rod held out over the water. She was letting her imagination sweep unchecked round every rock and cranny of the world that lies submerged in the depths of our unconscious being. Now came the experience, the experience that I believe to be far commoner with women writers than with men. The line raced through the girl's fingers. Her imagination had rushed away. It had sought the pools, the depths, the dark places where the largest fish slumber. And then there was a smash. There was an explosion. There was foam and confusion. The imagination had dashed itself against something hard. The girl was roused from her dream. She was indeed in a state of the most acute and difficult distress. To speak without figure she had thought of something, something about the body, about the passions which it was unfitting for her as a woman to say. Men, her reason told her, would be shocked. The consciousness of what men will say of a woman who speaks the truth about her passions had roused her from her artist's state of unconsciousness. She could write no more. The trance was over. Her imagination could work no longer. This I believe to be a very common experience with women writers — they are impeded by the extreme conventionality of the other sex. For though men sensibly allow themselves great freedom in these respects, I doubt that they realize or can control the extreme severity with which they condemn such freedom in women.

These then were two very genuine experiences of my own. These were two of the adventures of my professional life. The first — killing the Angel in the House — I think I solved. She died. But the second, telling the truth about my own experiences as a body, I do not think I solved. I doubt that any woman has solved it yet. The obstacles against her are still immensely powerful — and yet they are very difficult to define. Outwardly, what is simpler than to write books? Outwardly, what obstacles are there for a woman rather than for a man? Inwardly, I think, the case is very different; she has still many ghosts to fight, many prejudices to overcome. Indeed it will be a long time still, I think, before a woman can sit down to write a book without finding a phantom to be slain, a rock to be dashed against. And if this is so in literature, the freest of all professions for women, how is it in the new professions which you are now for the first time entering?

Those are the questions that I should like, had I time, to ask you. And indeed, if I have laid stress upon these professional experiences of mine, it is because I believe that they are, though in different forms, yours also. Even when the path is nominally open — when there is nothing to prevent a woman from being a doctor, a lawyer, a civil servant — there are many phantoms and obstacles, as I believe, looming in her way. To discuss and define them is I think of great value and importance; for thus only can the labor be shared, the difficulties be solved. But beside this, it is necessary also to discuss the ends and the aims for which we are fighting, for which we are doing battle with these formidable obstacles. Those aims cannot be taken for granted; they must be perpetually questioned and examined. The whole position, as I see it — here in this hall surrounded by women practicing for the first time in history I know not how many different professions — is one of extraordinary interest and importance. You have won rooms of your own in the house hitherto exclusively owned by men. You are able, though not without great labor and effort, to pay the rent. You are earning your five hundred pounds a year. But this freedom is only a beginning; the room is your own, but it is still bare. It has to be furnished; it has to be decorated; it has to be shared. How are you going to furnish it, how are you going to decorate it? With whom are you going to share it, and upon what terms? These, I think are questions of the utmost importance and interest. For the first time in history you are able to ask them; for the first time you are able to decide for yourselves what the answers should be. Willingly would I stay and discuss those questions and answers — but not tonight. My time is up; and I must cease.

Discussion Questions

1. How does Woolf explain the attraction of writing as a profession for women in the eighteenth and nineteenth centuries?
2. Who is the Angel in the House? What advice did she give to Woolf? Why did Woolf think it necessary to kill her?
3. What other experience constituted an adventure in her professional life? Is such an experience relevant for women writers today?
4. What questions does Woolf pose at the end to her audience of professional women? Why does she leave them vague and undefined?

Writing Suggestions

5. Woolf says, "Even when the path is nominally open — when there is nothing to prevent a woman from being a doctor, a lawyer, a civil servant — there are many phantoms and obstacles . . . looming in her way." Choose a specific profession, describe it, and try to explain the

"many phantoms and obstacles" in it for women. Or make a case for an opposing view — that women no longer experience the problems described by Woolf in 1931.

6. Some critics argue that men entering professions generally practiced only by women suffer the same "phantoms and obstacles." Choose one or more vocations and spell out the prejudices that such men might encounter. Or, if you disagree with the critics, argue that these men do not experience difficulties.

Politics and the English Language

GEORGE ORWELL

This essay, written after World War II, develops George Orwell's claim that careless and dishonest use of language contributes to careless and dishonest thought and political corruption. Political language, he argues, is "largely the defense of the indefensible." But Orwell, novelist, critic, and political satirist — best known for his book 1984 — believes that bad language habits can be reversed, and he lists rules for getting rid of some of the most offensive.

Most people who bother with the matter at all would admit that the English language is in a bad way, but it is generally assumed that we cannot by conscious action do anything about it. Our civilization is decadent and our language — so the argument runs — must inevitably share in the general collapse. It follows that any struggle against the abuse of language is a sentimental archaism, like preferring candles to electric light or hansom cabs to aeroplanes. Underneath this lies the half-conscious belief that language is a natural growth and not an instrument which we shape for our own purposes.

Now, it is clear that the decline of a language must ultimately have political and economic causes: It is not due simply to the bad influence of this or that individual writer. But an effect can become a cause, reinforcing the original cause and producing the same effect in an intensified form, and so on indefinitely. A man may take to drink because he feels himself to be a failure, and then fail all the more completely because he drinks. It is rather the same thing that is happening to the English language. It becomes ugly and inaccurate because our thoughts are foolish, but the slovenliness of our language makes it easier for us to have foolish thoughts. The point is that the process is reversible. Modern English, especially written English, is full of bad habits which spread by imitation and which can be avoided if one is willing to take the necessary trouble. If one gets rid of these habits one can think more clearly, and to think clearly is a necessary first step towards political regeneration: So that the fight against bad English is not frivolous and is not the exclusive concern of professional writers. I will come back to this presently, and I hope that by that time the meaning of what I have said here will have become clearer. Meanwhile, here are five specimens of the English language as it is now habitually written.

From *Horizon*, April 1946.

These five passages have not been picked out because they are especially bad — I could have quoted far worse if I had chosen — but because they illustrate various of the mental vices from which we now suffer. They are a little below the average, but are fairly representative samples. I number them so that I can refer back to them when necessary:

(1) I am not, indeed, sure whether it is not true to say that the Milton who once seemed not unlike a seventeenth-century Shelley had not become out of an experience ever more bitter in each year, more alien *[sic]* to the founder of that Jesuit sect which nothing could induce him to tolerate.

Professor Harold Laski (Essay in *Freedom of Expression*)

(2) Above all, we cannot play ducks and drakes with a native battery of idioms which prescribes such egregious collocations of vocables as the Basic *put up with* for *tolerate* or *put at a loss* for *bewilder.*

Professor Lancelot Hogben *(Interglossa)*

(3) On the one side we have the free personality: By definition it is not neurotic, for it has neither conflict nor dream. Its desires, such as they are, are transparent, for they are just what institutional approval keeps in the forefront of consciousness; another institutional pattern would alter their number and intensity; there is little in them that is natural, irreducible, or culturally dangerous. But *on the other side,* the social bond itself is nothing but the mutual reflection of these self-secure integrities. Recall the definition of love. Is not this the very picture of a small academic? Where is there a place in this hall of mirrors for either personality or fraternity?

Essay on psychology in *Politics* (New York)

(4) All the "best people" from the gentlemen's clubs, and all the frantic fascist captains, united in common hatred of Socialism and bestial horror of the rising tide of the mass revolutionary movement, have turned to acts of provocation, to foul incendiarism, to medieval legends of poisoned wells, to legalize their own destruction of proletarian organizations, and rouse the agitated petty-bourgeoisie to chauvinistic fervor on behalf of the fight against the revolutionary way out of the crisis.

Communist pamphlet

(5) If a new spirit *is* to be infused into this old country, there is one thorny and contentious reform which must be tackled, and that is the humanization and galvanization of the BBC. Timidity here will bespeak cancer and atrophy of the soul. The heart of Britain may be sound and of strong beat, for instance, but the British lion's roar at present is like that of Bottom in Shakespeare's *Midsummer Night's Dream* — as gentle as any sucking dove. A virile new Britain cannot continue indefinitely to be traduced in the eyes or rather ears, of the world by the effete languors of Langham Place, brazenly masquerading as "standard English." When the Voice of Britain is heard at nine o'clock, better far and infinitely less ludicrous to hear aitches honestly dropped than the present priggish, inflated, inhibited, school-ma'amish arch braying of blameless bashful mewing maidens!

Letter in *Tribune*

Each of these passages has faults of its own, but, quite apart from avoidable ugliness, two qualities are common to all of them. The first is staleness of imagery: The other is lack of precision. The writer either has a meaning and cannot express it, or he inadvertently says something else, or he is almost indifferent as to whether his words mean anything or not. The mixture of vagueness and sheer incompetence is the most marked characteristic of modern English prose, and especially of any kind of political writing. As soon as certain topics are raised, the concrete melts into the abstract and no one seems to think of turns of speech that are not hackneyed: Prose consists less and less of *words* chosen for the sake of their meaning, and more and more of *phrases* tacked together like the sections of a prefabricated hen-house. I list below, with notes and examples, various of the tricks by means of which the work of prose-construction is habitually dodged:

Dying metaphors.   A newly invented metaphor assists thought   5
by evoking a visual image, while on the other hand a metaphor which is technically "dead" (e.g., *iron resolution*) has in effect reverted to being an ordinary word and can generally be used without loss of vividness. But in between these two classes there is a huge dump of worn-out metaphors which have lost all evocative power and are merely used because they save people the trouble of inventing phrases for themselves. Examples are: *ring the changes on, take up the cudgels for, toe the line, ride roughshod over, stand shoulder to shoulder with, play into the hands of, no axe to grind, grist to the mill, fishing in troubled waters, rift within the lute, on the order of the day, Achilles' heel, swan song, hotbed.* Many of these are used without knowledge of their meaning (what is a "rift," for instance?), and incompatible metaphors are frequently mixed, a sure sign that the writer is not interested in what he is saying. Some metaphors now current have been twisted out of their original meaning without those who use them even being aware of the fact. For example, *toe the line* is sometimes written *tow the line.* Another example is *the hammer and the anvil,* now always used with the implication that the anvil gets the worst of it. In real life it is always the anvil that breaks the hammer, never the other way about: A writer who stopped to think what he was saying would be aware of this, and would avoid perverting the original phrase.

Operators or verbal false limbs.   These save the trouble of picking out appropriate verbs and nouns, and at the same time pad each sentence with extra syllables which give it an appearance of symmetry. Characteristic phrases are: *render inoperative, militate against, make contact with, be subjected to, give rise to, give grounds for, have the effect of, play a leading part (role) in, make itself felt, take effect, exhibit a tendency to, serve the purpose of,* etc., etc. The keynote is the elimination of simple verbs. Instead of being a single word, such as *break, stop, spoil, mend, kill,* a verb becomes a *phrase,* made up of a noun or adjective tacked on to some general-purpose verb such as *prove, serve, form, play, render.* In addition, the passive voice is wherever possible used in preference to the active, and noun constructions are used instead of gerunds (*by examination of* instead of *by examining*). The range of verbs is further cut down by means of the *-ize* and *de-* formation, and the banal statements are given an appearance of profundity by means of the *not un-* formation. Simple conjunctions and prepositions are replaced by such phrases as *with respect to, having regard to, the fact that, by dint of, in view of, in the interests of, on the hypothesis that;* and the ends of sentences are saved from anticlimax by such resounding commonplaces as *greatly to be desired, cannot be left out of account, a development to be expected in the near future, deserving of serious consideration, brought to a satisfactory conclusion,* and so on and so forth.

Pretentious diction.   Words like *phenomenon, element, individual* (as noun), *objective, categorical, effective, virtual, basic, primary, promote, constitute, exhibit, exploit, utilize, eliminate, liquidate,* are used to dress up simple statements and give an air of scientific impartiality to biased judgments. Adjectives like *epoch-making, epic, historic, unforgettable, triumphant, age-old, inevitable, inexorable, veritable,* are used to dignify the sordid processes of international politics, while writing that aims at glorifying war usually takes on an archaic color, its characteristic words being: *realm, throne, chariot, mailed fist, trident, sword, shield, buckler, banner, jackboot, clarion.* Foreign words and expressions such as *cul de sac, ancien régime, deus ex machina, mutatis mutandis, status quo, gleichshaltung, weltanschauung,* are used to give an air of culture and elegance. Except for the useful abbreviations *i.e., e.g.,* and *etc.,* there is no real need for any of the hundreds of foreign phrases now current in English. Bad writers, and especially scientific, political, and sociological writers, are nearly always haunted by the notion that Latin or Greek words are grander than Saxon ones, and unnecessary words like *expedite, ameliorate, predict, extraneous, deracinated, clandestine, subaqueous,* and hundreds of others constantly gain ground from their Anglo-Saxon opposite numbers.[1] The jargon peculiar to Marxist writing (*hyena, hangman, cannibal, petty bourgeois, these gentry, lackey, flunkey, mad dog, White Guard,* etc.) consists largely of words and phrases trans-

---

[1]An interesting illustration of this is the way in which the English flower names which were in use till very recently are being ousted by Greek ones, *snapdragon* becoming *antirrhinum, forget-me-not* becoming *myosotis,* etc. It is hard to see any practical reason for this change of fashion: It is probably due to an instinctive turning-away from the more homely word and a vague feeling that the Greek word is scientific. [All notes are Orwell's.]

lated from Russian, German, or French; but the normal way of coining a new word is to use a Latin or Greek root with the appropriate affix and, where necessary, the *-ize* formation. It is often easier to make up words of this kind (*deregionalize, impermissible, extramarital, nonfragmentatory,* and so forth) than to think up the English words that will cover one's meaning. The result, in general, is an increase in slovenliness and vagueness.

Meaningless words. In certain kinds of writing, particularly in art criticism and literary criticism, it is normal to come across long passages which are almost completely lacking in meaning.[2] Words like *romantic, plastic, values, human, dead, sentimental, natural, vitality,* as used in art criticism, are strictly meaningless in the sense that they not only do not point to any discoverable object, but are hardly ever expected to do so by the reader. When one critic writes, "The outstanding feature of Mr. X's work is its living quality," while another writes, "The immediately striking thing about Mr. X's work is its peculiar deadness," the reader accepts this as a simple difference of opinion. If words like *black* and *white* were involved, instead of the jargon words *dead* and *living,* he would see at once that language was being used in an improper way. Many political words are similarly abused. The word *fascism* has now no meaning except insofar as it signifies "something not desirable." The words *democracy, socialism, freedom, patriotic, realistic, justice,* have each of them several different meanings which cannot be reconciled with one another. In the case of a word like *democracy,* not only is there no agreed definition, but the attempt to make one is resisted from all sides. It is almost universally felt that when we call a country democratic we are praising it: Consequently the defenders of every kind of regime claim that it is a democracy, and fear that they might have to stop using the word if it were tied down to any one meaning. Words of this kind are often used in a consciously dishonest way. That is, the person who uses them has his own private definition, but allows his hearer to think he means something quite different. Statements like *Marshal Pétain was a true patriot, The Soviet Press is the freest in the world, The Catholic Church is opposed to persecution,* are almost always made with intent to deceive. Other words used in variable meanings, in most cases more or less dishonestly, are: *class, totalitarian, science, progressive, reactionary, bourgeois, equality.*

---

[2] Example: "Comfort's catholicity of perception and image, strangely Whitmanesque in range, almost the exact opposite in aesthetic compulsion, continues to evoke that trembling atmospheric accumulative hinting at a cruel, an inexorably serene timelessness . . . Wrey Gardiner scores by aiming at simple bull's-eyes with precision. Only they are not so simple, and through this contended sadness runs more than the surface bittersweet of resignation" (*Poetry Quarterly*).

Now that I have made this catalog of swindles and perversions, let me give another example of the kind of writing that they lead to. This time it must of its nature be an imaginary one. I am going to translate a passage of good English into modern English of the worst sort. Here is a well-known verse from *Ecclesiastes:*

> I returned and saw under the sun, that the race is not to the swift, nor the battle to the strong, neither yet bread to the wise, nor yet riches to men of understanding, nor yet favor to men of skill; but time and chance happeneth to them all.

Here it is in modern English:

> Objective consideration of contemporary phenomena compels the conclusion that success or failure in competitive activities exhibits no tendency to be commensurate with innate capacity, but that a considerable element of the unpredictable must invariably be taken into account.

This is a parody, but not a very gross one. Exhibit (3), above, for 10 instance, contains several patches of the same kind of English. It will be seen that I have not made a full translation. The beginning and ending of the sentence follow the original meaning fairly closely, but in the middle the concrete illustrations — race, battle, bread — dissolve into the vague phrase "success or failure in competitive activities." This had to be so, because no modern writer of the kind I am discussing — no one capable of using phrases like "objective consideration of contemporary phenomena"— would ever tabulate his thoughts in that precise and detailed way. The whole tendency of modern prose is away from concreteness. Now analyze these two sentences a little more closely. The first contains forty-nine words but only sixty syllables, and all its words are those of everyday life. The second contains thirty-eight words of ninety syllables: Eighteen of its words are from Latin roots, and one from Greek. The first sentence contains six vivid images, and only one phrase ("time and chance") that could be called vague. The second contains not a single fresh, arresting phrase, and in spite of its ninety syllables it gives only a shortened version of the meaning contained in the first. Yet without a doubt it is the second kind of sentence that is gaining ground in modern English. I do not want to exaggerate. This kind of writing is not yet universal, and outcrops of simplicity will occur here and there in the worst-written page. Still, if you or I were told to write a few lines on the uncertainty of human fortunes, we should probably come much nearer to my imaginary sentence than to the one from *Ecclesiastes.*

As I have tried to show, modern writing at its worst does not consist in picking out words for the sake of their meaning and inventing images in order to make the meaning clearer. It consists in gumming together long strips of words which have already been set in order by someone else, and making the results presentable by sheer humbug. The attraction of this way of writing is that it is easy. It is easier — even quicker once you have the habit — to say *In my opinion it is a not unjustifiable assumption that* than to say *I think.* If you use ready-made phrases, you not only don't have to hunt about for words; you also don't have to bother with the rhythms of your sentences, since these phrases are generally so arranged as to be more or less euphonious. When you are composing in a hurry — when you are dictating to a stenographer, for instance, or making a public speech — it is natural to fall into a pretentious, Latinized style. Tags like *a consideration which we should do well to bear in mind* or *a conclusion to which all of us would readily assent* will save many a sentence from coming down with a bump. By using stale metaphors, similes, and idioms, you save much mental effort, at the cost of leaving your meaning vague, not only for your reader but for yourself. This is the significance of mixed metaphors. The sole aim of a metaphor is to call up a visual image. When these images clash — as in *The Fascist octopus has sung its swan song, the jackboot is thrown into the melting pot* — it can be taken as certain that the writer is not seeing a mental image of the objects he is naming; in other words he is not really thinking. Look again at the examples I gave at the beginning of this essay. Professor Laski (1) uses five negatives in fifty-three words. One of these is superfluous, making nonsense of the whole passage, and in addition there is the slip *alien* for akin, making further nonsense, and several avoidable pieces of clumsiness which increase the general vagueness. Professor Hogben (2) plays ducks and drakes with a battery which is able to write prescriptions, and, while disapproving of the everyday phrase *put up with,* is unwilling to look *egregious* up in the dictionary and see what it means. (3), if one takes an uncharitable attitude towards it, is simply meaningless: Probably one could work out its intended meaning by reading the whole of the article in which it occurs. In (4), the writer knows more or less what he wants to say, but an accumulation of stale phrases chokes him like tea leaves blocking a sink. In (5), words and meaning have almost parted company. People who write in this manner usually have a general emotional meaning — they dislike one thing and want to express solidarity with another — but they are not interested in the detail of what they are saying. A scrupulous writer, in every sentence that he writes, will ask himself at least four questions, thus: What am I trying to say? What words will express it? What image or idiom will make it clearer? Is this image fresh enough to have an effect? And he will probably ask himself two more: Could I put it more shortly? Have I said anything that is avoidably ugly? But you are not obliged to go to all this trouble. You can shirk it by simply throwing your mind open and letting the ready-made phrases come crowding in. They will construct your sentences for you — even think your thoughts for you, to a certain extent — and at need they will perform the important service of partially concealing your meaning even from yourself. It is at this point that the special connection between politics and the debasement of language becomes clear.

In our time it is broadly true that political writing is bad writing. Where it is not true, it will generally be found that the writer is some kind of rebel, expressing his private opinions and not a "party line." Orthodoxy, of whatever color, seems to demand a lifeless, imitative style. The political dialects to be found in pamphlets, leading articles, manifestos, White Papers, and the speeches of undersecretaries do, of course, vary from party to party, but they are all alike in that one almost never finds in them a fresh, vivid, home-made turn of speech. When one watches some tired hack on the platform mechanically repeating the familiar phrases — *bestial atrocities, iron heel, bloodstained tyranny, free peoples of the world, stand shoulder to shoulder* — one often has a curious feeling that one is not watching a live human being but some kind of dummy; a feeling which suddenly becomes stronger at moments when the light catches the speaker's spectacles and turns them into blank discs which seem to have no eyes behind them. And this is not altogether fanciful. A speaker who uses that kind of phraseology has gone some distance towards turning himself into a machine. The appropriate noises are coming out of his larynx, but his brain is not involved as it would be if he were choosing his words for himself. If the speech he is making is one that he is accustomed to make over and over again, he may be almost unconscious of what he is saying, as one is when one utters the responses in church. And this reduced state of consciousness, if not indispensable, is at any rate favorable to political conformity.

In our time, political speech and writing are largely the defense of the indefensible. Things like the continuance of British rule in India, the Russian purges and deportations, the dropping of the atom bombs on Japan, can indeed be defended, but only by arguments which are too brutal for most people to face, and which do not square with the professed aims of political parties. Thus political language has to consist largely of euphemism, question-begging, and sheer cloudy vagueness. Defenseless villages are bombarded from the air, the inhabitants driven out into the countryside, the cattle machine-gunned, the huts set on fire with incendiary bullets: This is called *pacification.* Millions of peasants are robbed of their farms and sent trudging along the roads with no more than they can carry; this is called *transfer of population* or *rectification of frontiers.* People are imprisoned for years without trial, or shot in the back of the neck, or sent to die of scurvy in Arctic lumber camps: This is called *elimination of unreliable elements.* Such phraseology is needed if one wants to name things without calling up mental pictures of them. Consider for instance some comfortable English professor defending Russian totalitarianism. He cannot say outright, "I believe in killing off your opponents when you can get good results by doing so." Probably, therefore, he will say something like this:

> While freely conceding that the Soviet régime exhibits certain features which the humanitarian may be inclined to deplore, we must, I think, agree that a certain curtailment of the right to political opposition is an unavoidable concomitant of transitional periods, and that the rigors which the Russian people have been called upon to undergo have been amply justified in the sphere of concrete achievement.

The inflated style is itself a kind of euphemism. A mass of Latin words fall upon the facts like soft snow, blurring the outlines and covering up all the details. The great enemy of clear language is insincerity. When there is a gap between one's real and one's declared aims, one turns as it were instinctively to long words and exhausted idioms, like a cuttlefish squirting out ink. In our age there is no such thing as "keeping out of politics." All issues are political issues, and politics itself is a mass of lies, evasions, folly, hatred, and schizophrenia. When the general atmosphere is bad, language must suffer. I should expect to find — this is a guess which I have not sufficient knowledge to verify — that the German, Russian, and Italian languages have all deteriorated in the last ten or fifteen years, as a result of dictatorship.

But if thought corrupts language, language can also corrupt 15 thought. A bad usage can spread by tradition and imitation, even among people who should and do know better. The debased language that I have been discussing is in some ways very convenient. Phrases like *a not unjustifiable assumption, leaves much to be desired, would serve no good purpose, a consideration which we should do well to bear in mind,* are a continuous temptation, a packet of aspirins always at one's elbow. Look back through this essay, and for certain you will find that I have again and again committed the very faults I am protesting against. By this morning's post I have received a pamphlet dealing with conditions in Germany. The author tells me that he "felt impelled" to write it. I open it at random, and here is almost the first sentence that I see: "(The Allies) have an opportunity not only of achieving a radical transformation of Germany's social and political structure in such a way as to avoid a nationalistic reaction in Germany itself, but at the same time of laying the foundations of a cooperative and unified Europe." You see, he "feels impelled" to write — feels, presumably, that he has something new to say — and yet his words, like cavalry horses answering the bugle, group themselves automatically into the familiar dreary pattern. This invasion of one's mind by ready-made phrases *(lay the foundations, achieve a radical transformation)* can only be prevented if one is constantly on guard against them, and every such phrase anesthetizes a portion of one's brain.

I said earlier that the decadence of our language is probably curable. Those who deny this would argue, if they produced an argument at all, that language merely reflects existing social conditions, and that we cannot influence its development by any direct tinkering with words and constructions. So far as the general tone or spirit of a language goes, this may be true, but it is not true in detail. Silly words and expressions have often disappeared, not through any evolutionary process but owing to the conscious action of a minority. Two recent examples were *explore every avenue* and *leave no stone unturned,* which were killed by the jeers of a few journalists. There is a long list of flyblown metaphors which could similarly be got rid of if enough people would interest themselves in the job; and it should also be possible to laugh the *not un-* formation out of existence,[3] to reduce the amount of Latin and Greek in the average sentence, to drive out foreign phrases and strayed scientific words, and, in general, to make pretentiousness unfashionable. But all these are minor points. The defense of the English language implies more than this, and perhaps it is best to start by saying what it does *not* imply.

To begin with it has nothing to do with archaism, with the salvaging of obsolete words and turns of speech, or with the setting up of a "standard English" which must never be departed from. On the contrary, it is especially concerned with the scrapping of every word or idiom which has outworn its usefulness. It has nothing to do with correct grammar and syntax, which are of no importance so long as one makes one's meaning clear, or with the avoidance of Americanisms, or with having what is called a "good prose style." On the other hand it is not concerned with fake simplicity and the attempt to make written English colloquial. Nor does it even imply in every case preferring the Saxon word to the Latin one, though it does imply using the fewest and shortest words that will cover one's meaning. What is above all needed is to let the meaning choose the word, and not the other way about. In prose, the worst thing one can do with words is to surrender to them. When you think of a concrete object, you think wordlessly, and then, if you want to describe the thing you have been visualizing you probably hunt about till you find the exact words that seem to fit. When you think of something abstract you are more inclined to use words from the start, and unless you make a conscious effort to prevent it, the existing dialect will come rushing in and do the job for you, at the expense of blurring or even changing your meaning. Probably it is better to put off

---

[3] One can cure oneself of the *not un-* formation by memorizing this sentence: *A not unblack dog was chasing a not unsmall rabbit across a not ungreen field.*

using words as long as possible and get one's meaning as clear as one can through pictures or sensations. Afterwards one can choose — not simply *accept* — the phrases that will best cover the meaning, and then switch round and decide what impression one's words are likely to make on another person. This last effort of the mind cuts out all stale or mixed images, all prefabricated phrases, needless repetitions, and humbug and vagueness generally. But one can often be in doubt about the effect of a word or a phrase, and one needs rules that one can rely on when instinct fails. I think the following rules will cover most cases:

(i) Never use a metaphor, simile, or other figure of speech which you are used to seeing in print.
(ii) Never use a long word where a short one will do.
(iii) If it is possible to cut a word out, always cut it out.
(iv) Never use the passive where you can use the active.
(v) Never use a foreign phrase, a scientific word, or a jargon word if you can think of an everyday English equivalent.
(vi) Break any of these rules sooner than say anything outright barbarous.

These rules sound elementary, and so they are, but they demand a deep change in attitude in anyone who has grown used to writing in the style now fashionable. One could keep all of them and still write bad English, but one could not write the kind of stuff that I quoted in those five specimens at the beginning of this article.

I have not here been considering the literary use of language, but merely language as an instrument for expressing and not for concealing or preventing thought. Stuart Chase and others have come near to claiming that all abstract words are meaningless, and have used this as a pretext for advocating a kind of political quietism. Since you don't know what Fascism is, how can you struggle against Fascism? One need not swallow such absurdities as this, but one ought to recognize that the present political chaos is connected with the decay of language, and that one can probably bring about some improvement by starting at the verbal end. If you simplify your English, you are freed from the worst follies of orthodoxy. You cannot speak any of the necessary dialects, and when you make a stupid remark its stupidity will be obvious, even to yourself. Political language — and with variations this is true of all political parties, from Conservatives to Anarchists — is designed to make lies sound truthful and murder respectable, and to give an appearance of solidity to pure wind. One cannot change this all in a moment, but one can at least change one's own habits, and from time to time one can even, if one jeers loudly enough, send some worn-out and useless phrase — some *jackboot, Achilles' heel, hotbed, melting pot, acid test, veritable inferno,* or other lump of verbal refuse — into the dustbin where it belongs.

Discussion Questions

1. Orwell disagrees with a common assumption about language. What is it? Where in the essay does he attack this assumption directly?
2. What faults do his five samples of bad language have in common? Select examples of these faults in each passage.
3. What "tricks" for avoiding good prose does Orwell list? Do you think that some are more dangerous or misleading than others? Explain the reasons for your answer.
4. What different reasons does Orwell suggest for the slovenliness of much political writing and speaking? What examples does he give to support these reasons? Are they persuasive?
5. How does Orwell propose that we get rid of our bad language habits? Do you think his recommendations are realistic? Can the teaching of writing in school assist in the remedy?
6. Why does Orwell urge the reader to "look back through this essay" to find "the very faults I am protesting against"? Can you, in fact, find any?

Writing Suggestions

7. Choose a speech or an editorial whose meaning seems to be obscured by pretentious diction, meaningless words, euphemism, or "sheer cloudy vagueness." Point out the real meaning of the piece. If you think that its purpose is deceptive, expose the unpleasant truth that the author is concealing. Use Orwell's device, giving concrete meaning to any abstractions. (One source of speeches is a publication called *Vital Speeches of the Day*. Another is the *New York Times,* which often prints in full, or excerpts major portions of, speeches by leading figures in public life.)
8. Orwell's essay appeared before the widespread use of television. Do you think that TV makes it harder for politicians to be dishonest? Choose a particular public event — a war, a street riot, a terrorist activity, a campaign stop — and argue either for or against the claim that televised coverage makes it harder for a politician to engage in "sheer cloudy vagueness." Or does it make no difference at all? Be specific in your use of evidence.

Letter from Birmingham Jail
MARTIN LUTHER KING, JR.

Martin Luther King, Jr., (1929–1968) was a clergyman, author, distinguished civil rights leader, and winner of the Nobel Peace Prize in 1964 for his contributions to racial harmony and his advocacy of nonviolent response to aggression. He was assassinated in 1968. In the following selections we meet King in two of his various roles. In "Letter from Birmingham Jail," he appears as historian and philosopher. He wrote the letter from a jail cell on April 16, 1963, after his arrest for participation in a demonstration for civil rights for blacks. The letter was a reply to eight Alabama clergymen who, in a public statement, had condemned demonstrations in the streets.

My dear Fellow Clergymen,

While confined here in the Birmingham city jail, I came across your recent statement calling our present activities "unwise and untimely." Seldom, if ever, do I pause to answer criticism of my work and ideas. If I sought to answer all of the criticisms that cross my desk, my secretaries would be engaged in little else in the course of the day, and I would have no time for constructive work. But since I feel that you are men of genuine good will and your criticisms are sincerely set forth, I would like to answer your statement in what I hope will be patient and reasonable terms.

I think I should give the reason for my being in Birmingham, since you have been influenced by the argument of "outsiders coming in." I have the honor of serving as president of the Southern Christian Leadership Conference, an organization operating in every southern state, with headquarters in Atlanta, Georgia. We have some eighty-five affiliate organizations all across the South — one being the Alabama Christian Movement for Human Rights. Whenever necessary and possible we share staff, educational, and financial resources with our affiliates. Several months ago our local affiliate here in Birmingham invited us to be on call to engage in a nonviolent direct-action program if such were deemed necessary. We readily consented and when the hour came we lived up to our promises. So I am here, along with several members of my staff, because we were invited here. I am here because I have basic organizational ties here.

Beyond this, I am in Birmingham because injustice is here. Just as the eighth-century prophets left their little villages and carried

From *A Testament of Hope* (1986).

their "thus saith the Lord" far beyond the boundaries of their hometowns; and just as the Apostle Paul left his little village of Tarsus and carried the gospel of Jesus Christ to practically every hamlet and city of the Graeco-Roman world, I too am compelled to carry the gospel of freedom beyond my particular hometown. Like Paul, I must constantly respond to the Macedonian call for aid.

Moreover, I am cognizant of the interrelatedness of all communities and states. I cannot sit idly by in Atlanta and not be concerned about what happens in Birmingham. Injustice anywhere is a threat to justice everywhere. We are caught in an inescapable network of mutuality, tied in a single garment of destiny. Whatever affects one directly affects all indirectly. Never again can we afford to live with the narrow, provincial "outside agitator" idea. Anyone who lives in the United States can never be considered an outsider anywhere in this country.

You deplore the demonstrations that are presently taking place 5 in Birmingham. But I am sorry that your statement did not express a similar concern for the conditions that brought the demonstrations into being. I am sure that each of you would want to go beyond the superficial social analyst who looks merely at effects, and does not grapple with underlying causes. I would not hesitate to say that it is unfortunate that so-called demonstrations are taking place in Birmingham at this time, but I would say in more emphatic terms that it is even more unfortunate that the white power structure of this city left the Negro community with no other alternative.

In any nonviolent campaign there are four basic steps: (1) collection of the facts to determine whether injustices are alive, (2) negotiation, (3) self-purification, and (4) direct action. We have gone through all of these steps in Birmingham. There can be no gainsaying of the fact that racial injustice engulfs this community.

Birmingham is probably the most thoroughly segregated city in the United States. Its ugly record of police brutality is known in every section of this country. Its unjust treatment of Negroes in the courts is a notorious reality. There have been more unsolved bombings of Negro homes and churches in Birmingham than any city in this nation. These are the hard, brutal, and unbelievable facts. On the basis of these conditions Negro leaders sought to negotiate with the city fathers. But the political leaders consistently refused to engage in good faith negotiation.

Then came the opportunity last September to talk with some of the leaders of the economic community. In these negotiating sessions certain promises were made by the merchants — such as the promise to remove the humiliating racial signs from the stores. On the basis of these promises Reverend Shuttlesworth and the leaders of the Alabama Christian Movement for Human Rights agreed to call a moratorium on any type of demonstrations. As the weeks and months unfolded we realized that we were the victims of a broken promise. The signs remained. Like so many experiences of the past we were confronted with blasted hopes, and the dark shadow of a deep disappointment settled upon us. So we had no alternative except that of preparing for direct action, whereby we would present our very bodies as a means of laying our case before the conscience of the local and national community. We were not unmindful of the difficulties involved. So we decided to go through a process of self-purification. We started having workshops on nonviolence and repeatedly asking ourselves the questions, "Are you able to accept blows without retaliating?" "Are you able to endure the ordeals of jail?" We decided to set our direct-action program around the Easter season, realizing that with the exception of Christmas, this was the largest shopping period of the year. Knowing that a strong economic withdrawal program would be the by-product of direct action, we felt that this was the best time to bring pressure on the merchants for the needed changes. Then it occurred to us that the March election was ahead and so we speedily decided to postpone action until after election day. When we discovered that Mr. Connor was in the run-off, we decided again to postpone action so that the demonstrations could not be used to cloud the issues. At this time we agreed to begin our nonviolent witness the day after the run-off.

This reveals that we did not move irresponsibly into direct actions. We too wanted to see Mr. Connor defeated; so we went through postponement after postponement to aid in this community need. After this we felt that direct action could be delayed no longer.

You may well ask, "Why direct action? Why sit-ins, marches, 10 etc.? Isn't negotiation a better path?" You are exactly right in your call for negotiation. Indeed, this is the purpose of direct action. Nonviolent direct action seeks to create such a crisis and establish such creative tension that a community that has constantly refused to negotiate is forced to confront the issue. It seeks so to dramatize the issue that it can no longer be ignored. I just referred to the creation of tension as a part of the work of the nonviolent resister. This may sound rather shocking. But I must confess that I am not afraid of the word tension. I have earnestly worked and preached against violent tension, but there is a type of constructive nonviolent tension that is necessary for growth. Just as Socrates felt that it was necessary to create a tension in the mind so that individuals could rise from the bondage of myths and half-truths to the unfettered realm of creative analysis and objective appraisal, we must see the need of having nonviolent gadflies to create the kind of tension in society that will help men to rise from the dark depths of prejudice and racism to the majestic heights of understanding and brotherhood. So the purpose of the direct action is to create a situation so crisis-packed that it will inevitably open the door to negotiation. We, therefore, concur with you in your call for negotiation. Too long has our beloved Southland been bogged down in the tragic attempt to live in monologue rather than dialogue.

One of the basic points in your statement is that our acts are untimely. Some have asked, "Why didn't you give the new administration time to act?" The only answer that I can give to this inquiry is that the new administration must be prodded about as much as the outgoing one before it acts. We will be sadly mistaken if we feel that the election of Mr. Boutwell will bring the millennium to Birmingham. While Mr. Boutwell is much more articulate and gentle than Mr. Connor, they are both segregationists, dedicated to the task of maintaining the status quo. The hope I see in Mr. Boutwell is that he will be reasonable enough to see the futility of massive resistance to desegregation. But he will not see this without pressure from the devotees of civil rights. My friends, I must say to you that we have not made a single gain in civil rights without determined legal and nonviolent pressure. History is the long and tragic story of the fact that privileged groups seldom give up their privileges voluntarily. Individuals may see the moral light and voluntarily give up their unjust posture; but as Reinhold Niebuhr has reminded us, groups are more immoral than individuals.

We know through painful experience that freedom is never voluntarily given by the oppressor; it must be demanded by the oppressed. Frankly, I have never yet engaged in a direct-action movement that was "well-timed," according to the timetable of those who have not suffered unduly from the disease of segregation. For years now I have heard the words "Wait!" It rings in the ear of every Negro with a piercing familiarity. This "Wait" has almost always meant "Never." It has been a tranquilizing thalidomide, relieving the emotional stress for a moment, only to give birth to an ill-formed infant of frustration. We must come to see with the distinguished jurist of yesterday that "justice too long delayed is justice denied." We have waited for more than 340 years for our constitutional and God-given rights. The nations of Asia and Africa are moving with jetlike speed toward the goal of political independence, and we still creep at horse and buggy pace toward the gaining of a cup of coffee at a lunch counter. I guess it is easy for those who have never felt the stinging darts of segregation to say, "Wait." But when you have seen vicious mobs lynch your mothers and fathers at will and drown your sisters and brothers at whim; when you see hate-filled policemen curse, kick, brutalize, and even kill your black brothers and sisters with impunity; when you see the vast majority of your 20 million Negro brothers smothering in an airtight cage of poverty in the midst of an affluent society; when you suddenly find your tongue twisted and your speech stammering as you seek to explain to your six-year-old daughter why she can't go to the public amusement park that has just been advertised on television, and see tears welling up in her little eyes when she is told that Funtown is closed to colored children, and see the depressing clouds of inferiority begin to form in her little mental sky, and see her begin to distort her little personality by unconsciously developing a bitterness toward white people; when you have to concoct an answer for a five-year-old son asking in agonizing pathos: "Daddy, why do white people treat colored people so mean?"; when you take a cross-country drive and find it necessary to sleep night after night in the uncomfortable corners of your automobile because no motel will accept you; when you are humiliated day in and day out by nagging signs reading "white" and "colored"; when your first name becomes "nigger" and your middle name becomes "boy" (however old you are) and your last name becomes "John," and when your wife and mother are never given the respected title "Mrs."; when you are harried by day and haunted by night by the fact that you are a Negro, living constantly at tiptoe stance never quite knowing what to expect next, and plagued with inner fears and outer resentments; when you are forever fighting a degenerating sense of "nobodiness"; then you will understand why we find it difficult to wait. There comes a time when the cup of endurance runs over, and men are no longer willing to be plunged into an abyss of injustice where they experience the blackness of corroding despair. I hope, sirs, you can understand our legitimate and unavoidable impatience.

You express a great deal of anxiety over our willingness to break laws. This is certainly a legitimate concern. Since we so diligently urge people to obey the Supreme Court's decision of 1954 outlawing segregation in the public schools, it is rather strange and paradoxical to find us consciously breaking laws. One may well ask, "How can you advocate breaking some laws and obeying others?" The answer is found in the fact that there are two types of laws: There are *just* and there are *unjust* laws. I would agree with Saint Augustine that "An unjust law is no law at all."

Now what is the difference between the two? How does one determine when a law is just or unjust? A just law is a man-made code that squares with the moral law or the law of God. An unjust law is a code that is out of harmony with the moral law. To put it in the terms of Saint Thomas Aquinas, an unjust law is a human law that is not rooted in eternal and natural law. Any law that uplifts human personality is just. Any law that degrades human personality is unjust. All segregation statutes are unjust because segregation distorts the soul and damages the personality. It gives the segregator a false sense of superiority, and the segregated a false sense of inferiority. To use the words of Martin Buber, the great Jewish philosopher, segregation substitutes an "I-it" relationship for the "I-thou" relationship, and ends up relegating persons to the status of things. So segregation is not only politically, economically, and sociologically unsound, but it is morally wrong and sinful. Paul Tillich has said that sin is separation. Isn't segregation an existential expression of man's tragic separation, an expression of his awful estrangement, his terrible sinfulness? So I can urge men to disobey segregation ordinances because they are morally wrong.

Let us turn to a more concrete example of just and unjust laws.   15 An unjust law is a code that a majority inflicts on a minority that is not binding on itself. This is difference made legal. On the other hand, a just law is a code that a majority compels a minority to follow that it is willing to follow itself. This is sameness made legal.

Let me give another explanation. An unjust law is a code inflicted upon a minority which that minority had no part in enacting or creating because they did not have the unhampered right to vote. Who can say that the legislature of Alabama which set up the segregation laws was democratically elected? Throughout the state of Alabama all types of conniving methods are used to prevent Negroes from becoming registered voters, and there are some counties without a single Negro registered to vote despite the fact that the Negro constitutes a majority of the population. Can any law set up in such a state be considered democratically structured?

These are just a few examples of unjust and just laws. There are some instances when a law is just on its face and unjust in its application. For instance, I was arrested Friday on a charge of parading without a permit. Now there is nothing wrong with an ordinance which requires a permit for a parade, but when the ordinance is used to preserve segregation and to deny citizens the First Amendment privilege of peaceful assembly and peaceful protest, then it becomes unjust.

I hope you can see the distinction I am trying to point out. In no sense do I advocate evading or defying the law as the rabid segregationist would do. This would lead to anarchy. One who breaks an unjust law must do it *openly, lovingly* (not hatefully as the white mothers did in New Orleans when they were seen on television screaming, "nigger, nigger, nigger"), and with a willingness to accept the penalty. I submit that an individual who breaks a law that conscience tells him is unjust, and willingly accepts the penalty by staying in jail to arouse the conscience of the community over its injustice, is in reality expressing the very highest respect for law.

Of course, there is nothing new about this kind of civil disobedience. It was seen sublimely in the refusal of Shadrach, Meshach, and Abednego to obey the laws of Nebuchadnezzar because a higher moral law was involved. It was practiced superbly by the early Christians who were willing to face hungry lions and the excruciating pain of chopping blocks, before submitting to certain unjust laws of the Roman Empire. To a degree academic freedom is a reality today because Socrates practiced civil disobedience.

We can never forget that everything Hitler did in Germany was "legal" and everything the Hungarian freedom fighters did in Hungary was "illegal." It was "illegal" to aid and comfort a Jew in Hitler's Germany. But I am sure that if I had lived in Germany during that time I would have aided and comforted my Jewish brothers even though it was illegal. If I lived in a Communist country today where certain principles dear to the Christian faith are suppressed, I believe I would openly advocate disobeying these antireligious laws. I must make two honest confessions to you, my Christian and Jewish brothers. First, I must confess that over the last few years I have been gravely disappointed with the white moderate. I have almost reached the regrettable conclusion that the Negro's great stumbling block in the stride toward freedom is not the White Citizen's Councilor or the Ku Klux Klanner, but the white moderate who is more devoted to "order" than to justice; who prefers a negative peace which is the absence of tension to a positive peace which is the presence of justice; who constantly says, "I agree with you in the goal you seek, but I can't agree with your methods of direct action"; who paternalistically feels that he can set the timetable for another man's freedom; who lives by the myth of time and who constantly advises the Negro to wait until a "more convenient season." Shallow understanding from people of good will is more frustrating than absolute misunderstanding from people of ill will. Lukewarm acceptance is much more bewildering than outright rejection.

I had hoped that the white moderate would understand that law and order exist for the purpose of establishing justice, and that when they fail to do this they become dangerously structured dams that block the flow of social progress. I had hoped that the white moderate would understand that the present tension of the South is merely a necessary phase of the transition from an obnoxious negative peace, where the Negro passively accepted his unjust plight, to a substance-filled positive peace, where all men will respect the dignity and worth of human personality. Actually, we who engage in nonviolent direct action are not the creators of tension. We merely bring to the surface the hidden tension that is already alive. We bring it out in the open where it can be seen and dealt with. Like a boil that can never be cured as long as it is covered up but must be opened with all its pus-flowing ugliness to the natural medicines of air and light, injustice must likewise be exposed, with all of the tension its exposing creates, to the light of human conscience and the air of national opinion before it can be cured.

In your statement you asserted that our actions, even though peaceful, must be condemned because they precipitate violence. But can this assertion be logically made? Isn't this like condemning the robbed man because his possession of money precipitated the evil act of robbery? Isn't this like condemning Socrates because his unswerving commitment to truth and his philosophical delvings precipitated the misguided popular mind to make him drink the hemlock? Isn't this like condemning Jesus because His unique God-consciousness and never-ceasing devotion to His will precipitated the evil act of crucifixion? We must come to see, as federal courts have consistently affirmed, that it is immoral to urge an individual to withdraw his efforts to gain his basic constitutional rights because the quest precipitates violence. Society must protect the robbed and punish the robber.

I had also hoped that the white moderate would reject the myth of time. I received a letter this morning from a white brother in Texas which said: "All Christians know that the colored people will receive equal rights eventually, but it is possible that you are in too great of a religious hurry. It has taken Christianity almost two thousand years to accomplish what it has. The teachings of Christ take time to come to earth." All that is said here grows out of a tragic misconception of time. It is the strangely irrational notion that there is something in the very flow of time that will inevitably cure all ills. Actually time is neutral. It can be used either destructively or constructively. I am coming to feel that the people of ill will have used time much more effectively than the people of good will. We will have to repent in this generation not merely for the vitriolic words and actions of the bad people, but for the appalling silence of the good people. We must come to see that human progress never rolls in on wheels of inevitability. It comes through the tireless efforts and persistent work of men willing to be co-workers with God, and without this hard work time itself becomes an ally of the forces of social stagnation. We must use time creatively, and forever realize that the time is always ripe to do right. Now is the time to make real the promise of democracy, and transform our pending national elegy into a creative psalm of brotherhood. Now is the time to lift our national policy from the quicksand of racial injustice to the solid rock of human dignity.

You spoke of our activity in Birmingham as extreme. At first I was rather disappointed that fellow clergymen would see my nonviolent efforts as those of the extremist. I started thinking about the fact that I stand in the middle of two opposing forces in the Negro community. One is a force of complacency made up of Negroes who, as a result of long years of oppression, have been so completely drained of self-respect and a sense of "somebodiness" that they have adjusted to segregation, and of a few Negroes in the middle class who, because of a degree of academic and economic security, and because at points they profit by segregation, have unconsciously become insensitive to the problems of the masses. The other force is one of bitterness and hatred, and comes perilously close to advocating violence. It is expressed in the various black nationalist groups that are springing up over the nation, the largest and best known being Elijah Muhammad's Muslim movement. This movement is nourished by the contemporary frustration over the continued existence of racial discrimination. It is made up of people who have lost faith in America, who have absolutely repudiated Christianity, and who have concluded that the white man is an incurable "devil." I have tried to stand between these two forces, saying that we need not follow the "do-nothingism" of the complacent or the hatred and despair of the black nationalist. There is the more excellent way of love and nonviolent protest. I'm grateful to God that, through the Negro church, the dimension of nonviolence entered our struggle. If this philosophy had not emerged, I am convinced that by now many streets of the South would be flowing with floods of blood. And I am further convinced that if our white brothers dismiss us as "rabble-rousers" and "outside agitators" those of us who are working through the channels of nonviolent direct action and refuse to support our nonviolent efforts, millions of Negroes, out of frustration and despair, will seek solace and security in black nationalist ideologies, a development that will lead inevitably to a frightening racial nightmare.

Oppressed people cannot remain oppressed forever. The urge 25 for freedom will eventually come. This is what happened to the American Negro. Something within has reminded him of his birthright of freedom; something without has reminded him that he can gain it. Consciously and unconsciously, he has been swept in by what the Germans call the *Zeitgeist,* and with his black brothers of Africa, and his brown and yellow brothers of Asia, South America, and the Caribbean, he is moving with a sense of cosmic urgency toward the promised land of racial justice. Recognizing this vital urge that has engulfed the Negro community, one should readily understand public demonstrations. The Negro has many pent-up resentments and latent frustrations. He has to get them out. So let him march sometime; let him have his prayer pilgrimages to the city hall; understand why he must have sit-ins and freedom rides. If his repressed emotions do not come out in these nonviolent ways, they will come out in ominous expressions of violence. This is not a threat; it is fact of history. So I have not said to my people "get rid of your discontent." But I have tried to say that this normal and healthy discontent can be channelized through the creative outlet of nonviolent direct action. Now this approach is being dismissed as extremist. I must admit that I was initially disappointed in being so categorized.

But as I continued to think about the matter I gradually gained a bit of satisfaction from being considered an extremist. Was not Jesus an extremist in love — "Love your enemies, bless them that curse you, pray for them that despitefully use you." Was not Amos an extremist for justice — "Let justice roll down like waters and righteousness like a mighty stream." Was not Paul an extremist for the gospel of Jesus Christ — "I bear in my body the marks of the Lord Jesus." Was not Martin Luther an extremist — "Here I stand; I can do none other so help me God." Was not John Bunyan an extremist — "I will stay in jail to the end of my days before I make a butchery of my conscience." Was not Abraham Lincoln an extremist — "This nation cannot survive half slave and half free." Was not Thomas Jefferson an extremist — "We hold these truths to be self-evident, that all men are created equal." So the question is not whether we will be extremist but what kind of extremist will we be. Will we be extremists for hate or will we be extremists for love? Will we be extremists for the preservation of injustice — or will we be extremists for the cause of justice? In that dramatic scene on Calvary's hill, three men were crucified. We must not forget that all three were crucified for the same crime — the crime of extremism. Two were extremists for immorality, and thusly fell below their environment. The other, Jesus Christ, was an extremist for love, truth, and goodness, and thereby rose above his environment. So, after all, maybe the South, the nation, and the world are in dire need of creative extremists.

I had hoped that the white moderate would see this. Maybe I was too optimistic. Maybe I expected too much. I guess I should have realized that few members of a race that has oppressed another race can understand or appreciate the deep groans and passionate yearnings of those that have been oppressed and still fewer have the vision to see that injustice must be rooted out by strong, persistent, and determined action. I am thankful, however, that some of our white brothers have grasped the meaning of this social revolution and committed themselves to it. They are still all too small in quantity, but they are big in quality. Some like Ralph McGill, Lillian Smith, Harry Golden, and James Dabbs have written about our struggle in eloquent, prophetic, and understanding terms. Others have marched with us down nameless streets of the South. They have languished in filthy roach-infested jails, suffering the abuse and brutality of angry policemen who see them as "dirty nigger-lovers." They, unlike so many of their moderate brothers and sisters, have recognized the urgency of the moment and sensed the need for powerful "action" antidotes to combat the disease of segregation.

Let me rush on to mention my other disappointment. I have been so greatly disappointed with the white church and its leadership. Of course, there are some notable exceptions. I am not unmindful of the fact that each of you has taken some significant stands on this issue. I commend you, Reverend Stallings, for your Christian stance on this past Sunday, in welcoming Negroes to your worship service on a nonsegregated basis. I commend the Catholic leaders of this state for integrating Springhill College several years ago.

But despite these notable exceptions I must honestly reiterate that I have been disappointed with the church. I do not say that as one of the negative critics who can always find something wrong with the church. I say it as a minister of the gospel, who loves the church; who was nurtured in its bosom; who has been sustained by its spiritual blessings, and who will remain true to it as long as the cord of life shall lengthen.

I had the strange feeling when I was suddenly catapulted into   30 the leadership of the bus protest in Montgomery several years ago that we would have the support of the white church. I felt that the white ministers, priests, and rabbis of the South would be some of our strongest allies. Instead, some have been outright opponents, refusing to understand the freedom movement and misrepresenting its leaders; all too many others have been more cautious than courageous and have remained silent behind the anesthetizing security of the stained-glass windows.

In spite of my shattered dreams of the past, I came to Birmingham with the hope that the white religious leadership of this community would see the justice of our cause, and with deep moral concern, serve as the channel through which our just grievances would get to the power structure. I had hoped that each of you would understand. But again I have been disappointed. I have heard numerous religious leaders of the South call upon their worshipers to comply with a desegregation decision because it is the *law*, but I have longed to hear white ministers say, "Follow this decree because integration is morally *right* and the Negro is your brother." In the midst of blatant injustices inflicted upon the Negro, I have watched white churches stand on the sideline and merely mouth pious irrelevancies and sanctimonious trivialities. In the midst of a mighty struggle to rid our nation of racial and economic injustice, I have heard so many ministers say, "Those are social issues with which the gospel has no real concern," and I have watched so many churches commit themselves to a completely otherworldly religion which made a strange distinction between body and soul, the sacred and the secular.

So here we are moving toward the exit of the twentieth century with a religious community largely adjusted to the status quo, standing as a taillight behind other community agencies rather than a headlight leading men to higher levels of justice.

I have traveled the length and breadth of Alabama, Mississippi, and all the other southern states. On sweltering summer days and crisp autumn mornings I have looked at her beautiful churches with their lofty spires pointing heavenward. I have beheld the impressive outlay of her massive religious education buildings. Over and over again I have found myself asking: "What kind of people worship here? Who is their God? Where were their voices when the lips of Governor Barnett dripped with words of interposition and nullification? Where were they when Governor Wallace gave the clarion call for defiance and hatred? Where were their voices of support when tired, bruised, and weary Negro men and women decided to rise from the dark dungeons of complacency to the bright hills of creative protest?"

Yes, these questions are still in my mind. In deep disappointment, I have wept over the laxity of the church. But be assured that my tears have been tears of love. There can be no deep disappointment where there is not deep love. Yes, I love the church; I love her sacred walls. How could I do otherwise? I am in the rather unique position of being the son, the grandson, and the great-grandson of preachers. Yes, I see the church as the body of Christ. But, oh! How we have blemished and scarred that body through social neglect and fear of being nonconformists.

There was a time when the church was very powerful. It was 35 during that period when the early Christians rejoiced when they were deemed worthy to suffer for what they believed. In those days the church was not merely a thermometer that recorded the ideas and principles of popular opinion; it was a thermostat that transformed the mores of society. Wherever the early Christians entered a town the power structure got disturbed and immediately sought to convict them for being "disturbers of the peace" and "outside agitators." But they went on with the conviction that they were "a colony of heaven," and had to obey God rather than man. They were small in number but big in commitment. They were too God-intoxicated to be "astronomically intimidated." They brought an end to such ancient evils as infanticide and gladiatorial contest.

Things are different now. The contemporary church is often a weak, ineffectual voice with an uncertain sound. It is so often the archsupporter of the status quo. Far from being disturbed by the presence of the church, the power structure of the average community is consoled by the church's silent and often vocal sanction of things as they are.

But the judgment of God is upon the church as never before. If the church of today does not recapture the sacrificial spirit of the early church, it will lose its authentic ring, forfeit the loyalty of millions, and be dismissed as an irrelevant social club with no meaning for the twentieth century. I am meeting young people every day whose disappointment with the church has risen to outright disgust.

Maybe again, I have been too optimistic. Is organized religion too inextricably bound to the status quo to save our nation and the world? Maybe I must turn my faith to the inner spiritual church, the church within the church, as the true *ecclesia* and the hope of the world. But again I am thankful to God that some noble souls from the ranks of organized religion have broken loose from the paralyzing chains of conformity and joined us as active partners in the struggle for freedom. They have left their secure congregations and walked the streets of Albany, Georgia, with us. They have gone through the highways of the South on tortuous rides for freedom. Yes, they have gone to jail with us. Some have been kicked out of their churches, and lost support of their bishops and fellow ministers. But they have gone with the faith that right defeated is stronger than evil triumphant. These men have been the leaven in the lump of the race. Their witness has been the spiritual salt that has preserved the true meaning of the gospel in these troubled times. They have carved a tunnel of hope through the dark mountain of disappointment.

I hope the church as a whole will meet the challenge of this decisive hour. But even if the church does not come to the aid of justice, I have no despair about the future. I have no fear about the outcome of our struggle in Birmingham, even if our motives are presently misunderstood. We will reach the goal of freedom in Birmingham and all over the nation, because the goal of America is freedom. Abused and scorned though we may be, our destiny is tied up with the destiny of America. Before the Pilgrims landed at Plymouth we were here. Before the pen of Jefferson etched across the pages of history the majestic words of the Declaration of Independence, we were here. For more than two centuries our foreparents labored in this country without wages; they made cotton king; and they built the homes of their masters in the midst of brutal injustice and shameful humiliation — and yet out of a bottomless vitality they continued to thrive and develop. If the inexpressible cruelties of slavery could not stop us, the opposition we now face will surely fail. We will win our freedom because the sacred heritage of our nation and the eternal will of God are embodied in our echoing demands.

I must close now. But before closing I am impelled to mention 40 one other point in your statement that troubled me profoundly. You warmly commended the Birmingham police force for keeping "order" and "preventing violence." I don't believe you would have so warmly commended the police force if you had seen its angry violent dogs literally biting six unarmed, nonviolent Negroes. I don't believe you would so quickly commend the policemen if you would observe their ugly and inhuman treatment of Negroes here in the city jail; if you would watch them push and curse old Negro women and young Negro girls; if you would see them slap and kick old Negro men and young boys; if you will observe them, as they did on two occasions, refuse to give us food because we wanted to sing our grace together. I'm sorry that I can't join you in your praise for the police department.

It is true that they have been rather disciplined in their public handling of the demonstrators. In this sense they have been rather publicly "nonviolent." But for what purpose? To preserve the evil system of segregation. Over the last few years I have consistently preached that nonviolence demands that the means we use must be as pure as the ends we seek. So I have tried to make it clear that it is wrong to use immoral means to attain moral ends. But now I must affirm that it is just as wrong, or even more so, to use moral means to preserve immoral ends. Maybe Mr. Connor and his policemen have been rather publicly nonviolent, as Chief Pritchett was in Albany, Georgia, but they have used the moral means of nonviolence to maintain the immoral end of flagrant racial injustice. T. S. Eliot has said that there is no greater treason than to do the right deed for the wrong reason.

I wish you had commended the Negro sit-inners and demonstrators of Birmingham for their sublime courage, their willingness to suffer, and their amazing discipline in the midst of the most inhuman provocation. One day the South will recognize its real heroes. They will be the James Merediths, courageously and with a majestic sense of purpose facing jeering and hostile mobs and the agonizing loneliness that characterizes the life of the pioneer. They will be old, oppressed, battered Negro women, symbolized in a seventy-two-year-old woman of Montgomery, Alabama, who rose up with a sense of dignity and with her people decided not to ride the segregated buses, and responded to one who inquired about her tiredness with ungrammatical profundity: "My feet is tired, but my soul is rested." They will be the young high school and college students, young ministers of the gospel, and a host of their elders courageously and nonviolently sitting-in at lunch counters and willingly going to jail for conscience's sake. One day the South will know that when these disinherited children of God sat down at lunch counters they were in reality standing up for the best in the American dream and the most sacred values in our Judeo-Christian heritage, and thusly, carrying our whole nation back to those great wells of democracy which were dug deep by the Founding Fathers in the formulation of the Constitution and the Declaration of Independence.

Never before have I written a letter this long (or should I say a book?). I'm afraid that it is much too long to take your precious time. I can assure you that it would have been much shorter if I had been writing from a comfortable desk, but what else is there to do when you are alone for days in the dull monotony of a narrow jail cell other than write long letters, think strange thoughts, and pray long prayers?

If I have said anything in this letter that is an overstatement of the truth and is indicative of an unreasonable impatience, I beg you to forgive me. If I have said anything in this letter that is an understatement of the truth and is indicative of my having a patience that makes me patient with anything less than brotherhood, I beg God to forgive me.

I hope this letter finds you strong in the faith. I also hope that   45
circumstances will soon make it possible for me to meet each of you, not as an integrationist or a civil rights leader, but as a fellow clergyman and a Christian brother. Let us all hope that the dark clouds of racial prejudice will soon pass away and the deep fog of misunderstanding will be lifted from our fear-drenched communities and in some not too distant tomorrow the radiant stars of love and brotherhood will shine over our great nation with all of their scintillating beauty.

Yours for the cause of Peace and Brotherhood,

Martin Luther King, Jr.

Discussion Questions

1. As in "I Have a Dream" (p. 708), King uses figurative language in his letter. Find some particularly vivid passages and evaluate their effect in the context of this letter.
2. Explain King's distinction between just and unjust laws. Are there dangers in attempting to make such a distinction?
3. What characteristics of mind and behavior does King exhibit in the letter? Select the specific passages that provide proof.
4. Why does King say that "the white moderate" is a greater threat to Negro progress than the outspoken racist? Is his explanation convincing?
5. How does King justify his philosophy of nonviolence in the face of continued aggression against the Negro?

Writing Suggestions

6. Can you think of a law against which defiance would be justified? Explain why the law is unjust and why refusal to obey is morally defensible.
7. In paragraph 12 King lists the grievances of Negroes in this country. King's catalog is similar to the lists in the Declaration of Independence. Can you think of any other group who might compile a list of grievances? If so, choose a group and draw up such a list, making sure that your list is as clear and specific as those you have read.

I Have a Dream

MARTIN LUTHER KING, JR.

In the widely reprinted "I Have a Dream" speech, Martin Luther King, Jr., appears as the charismatic leader of the civil rights movement. This inspirational address was delivered on August 28, 1963, in Washington, D.C., at a demonstration by two hundred thousand people for civil rights for blacks.

Five score years ago, a great American, in whose symbolic shadow we stand, signed the Emancipation Proclamation. This momentous decree came as a great beacon light of hope to millions of Negro slaves who had been seared in the flames of withering injustice. It came as a joyous daybreak to end the long night of captivity.

But one hundred years later, we must face the tragic fact that the Negro is still not free. One hundred years later, the life of the Negro is still sadly crippled by the manacles of segregation and the chains of discrimination. One hundred years later, the Negro lives on a lonely island of poverty in the midst of a vast ocean of material prosperity. One hundred years later, the Negro is still languishing in the corners of American society and finds himself an exile in his own land. So we have come here today to dramatize an appalling condition.

In a sense we have come to our nation's capital to cash a check. When the architects of our republic wrote the magnificent words of the Constitution and the Declaration of Independence, they were signing a promissory note to which every American was to fall heir. This note was a promise that all men would be guaranteed the unalienable rights of life, liberty, and the pursuit of happiness.

It is obvious today that America has defaulted on this promissory note insofar as her citizens of color are concerned. Instead of honoring this sacred obligation, America has given the Negro people a bad check; a check which has come back marked "insufficient funds." But we refuse to believe that the bank of justice is bankrupt. We refuse to believe that there are insufficient funds in the great vaults of opportunity of this nation. So we have come to cash this check — a check that will give us upon demand the riches of freedom and the security of justice. We have also come to this hallowed spot to remind America of the fierce urgency of *now*. This is no time to engage in the luxury of cooling off or to take the tranquilizing drugs of gradualism. *Now* is the time to make real the promises of

---

From *A Testament of Hope* (1986).

Democracy. *Now* is the time to rise from the dark and desolate valley of segregation to the sunlit path of racial justice. *Now* is the time to open the doors of opportunity to all of God's children. *Now* is the time to lift our nation from the quicksands of racial injustice to the solid rock of brotherhood.

It would be fatal for the nation to overlook the urgency of the moment and to underestimate the determination of the Negro. This sweltering summer of the Negro's legitimate discontent will not pass until there is an invigorating autumn of freedom and equality. Nineteen sixty-three is not an end, but a beginning. Those who hope that the Negro needed to blow off steam and will now be content will have a rude awakening if the nation returns to business as usual. There will be neither rest nor tranquillity in America until the Negro is granted his citizenship rights. The whirlwinds of revolt will continue to shake the foundations of our nation until the bright day of justice emerges.

But there is something that I must say to my people who stand on the warm threshold which leads into the palace of justice. In the process of gaining our rightful place we must not be guilty of wrongful deeds. Let us not seek to satisfy our thirst for freedom by drinking from the cup of bitterness and hatred. We must forever conduct our struggle on the high plane of dignity and discipline. We must not allow our creative protest to degenerate into physical violence. Again and again we must rise to the majestic heights of meeting physical force with soul force. The marvelous new militancy which has engulfed the Negro community must not lead us to a distrust of all white people, for many of our white brothers, as evidenced by their presence here today, have come to realize that their destiny is tied up with our destiny and their freedom is inextricably bound to our freedom. We cannot walk alone.

And as we walk, we must make the pledge that we shall march ahead. We cannot turn back. There are those who are asking the devotees of civil rights, "When will you be satisfied?" We can never be satisfied as long as the Negro is the victim of the unspeakable horrors of police brutality. We can never be satisfied as long as our bodies, heavy with the fatigue of travel, cannot gain lodging in the motels of the highways and the hotels of the cities. We cannot be satisfied as long as the Negro's basic mobility is from a smaller ghetto to a larger one. We can never be satisfied as long as a Negro in Mississippi cannot vote and a Negro in New York believes he has nothing for which to vote. No, no, we are not satisfied, and we will not be satisfied until justice rolls down like waters and righteousness like a mighty stream.

I am not unmindful that some of you have come here out of great trials and tribulations. Some of you have come fresh from narrow jail cells. Some of you have come from areas where your quest for freedom left you battered by the storms of persecution and staggered by the winds of police brutality. You have been the veterans of creative suffering. Continue to work with the faith that unearned suffering is redemptive.

Go back to Mississippi, go back to Alabama, go back to South Carolina, go back to Georgia, go back to Louisiana, go back to the slums and ghettos of our northern cities, knowing that somehow this situation can and will be changed. Let us not wallow in the valley of despair.

I say to you today, my friends, that in spite of the difficulties and 10 frustrations of the moment I still have a dream. It is a dream deeply rooted in the American dream.

I have a dream that one day this nation will rise up and live out the true meaning of its creed: "We hold these truths to be self-evident; that all men are created equal."

I have a dream that one day on the red hills of Georgia the sons of former slaves and the sons of former slaveowners will be able to sit down together at the table of brotherhood.

I have a dream that one day even the state of Mississippi, a desert state sweltering with the heat of injustice and oppression, will be transformed into an oasis of freedom and justice.

I have a dream that my four little children will one day live in a nation where they will not be judged by the color of their skin but by the content of their character.

I have a dream today. 15

I have a dream that one day the state of Alabama, whose governor's lips are presently dripping with the words of interposition and nullification, will be transformed into a situation where little black boys and black girls will be able to join hands with little white boys and white girls and walk together as sisters and brothers.

I have a dream today.

I have a dream that one day every valley shall be exalted, every hill and mountain shall be made low, the rough places will be made plain, and the crooked places will be made straight, and the glory of the Lord shall be revealed, and all flesh shall see it together.

This is our hope. This is the faith with which I return to the South. With this faith we will be able to hew out of the mountain of despair a stone of hope. With this faith we will be able to transform the jangling discords of our nation into a beautiful symphony of brotherhood. With this faith we will be able to work together, to pray together, to struggle together, to go to jail together, to stand up for freedom together, knowing that we will be free one day.

This will be the day when all of God's children will be able to 20 sing with new meaning

My country, 'tis of thee,
Sweet land of liberty,
  Of thee I sing:
Land where my fathers died,
Land of the pilgrims' pride,
From every mountain-side
  Let freedom ring.

And if America is to be a great nation this must become true. So let freedom ring from the prodigious hilltops of New Hampshire. Let freedom ring from the mighty mountains of New York. Let freedom ring from the heightening Alleghenies of Pennsylvania!

Let freedom ring from the snowcapped Rockies of Colorado!

Let freedom ring from the curvaceous peaks of California!

But not only that; let freedom ring from Stone Mountain of Georgia!

Let freedom ring from Lookout Mountain of Tennessee!   25

Let freedom ring from every hill and molehill of Mississippi. From every mountainside, let freedom ring.

When we let freedom ring, when we let it ring from every village and every hamlet, from every state and every city, we will be able to speed up that day when all of God's children, black men and white men, Jews and Gentiles, Protestants and Catholics, will be able to join hands and sing in the words of the old Negro spiritual, "Free at last! free at last! thank God almighty, we are free at last!"

Discussion Question

1. King's style alternates between the abstract and the concrete, between the grandiloquent and the simple, with abundant use of metaphors. Find examples of these qualities. Are all the stylistic strategies equally effective? Explain your answer.
2. What specific injustices suffered by black people does King mention? Why does he interrupt his series of "Let freedom ring" imperatives at the end with the statement, "But not only that"?
3. What values does the speech stress? Would these values be equally appealing to both blacks and whites? Why or why not?
4. More than thirty years later, how much of King's indictment of conditions remains true? Mention specific changes or lack of changes. If conditions have improved, does that make his speech less meaningful today?

Writing Suggestions

5. Using the same material as the original, rewrite this speech for an audience that is not impressed with the inspirational style. Think carefully about the changes in language you would make to convince this audience that, despite your dispassionate treatment, injustices exist and should be rectified.

6. Choose another highly emotional subject — for example, women's rights, child pornography, nuclear power — and write an inspirational speech or advertisement urging your audience to change their views. Be passionate, but try to avoid sentimentality or corniness. (You may want to look at other examples of the inspirational or hortatory style in a collection of speeches, among them speeches made in favor of the abolition of slavery and women's suffrage, declarations of war, and inaugural addresses.)

Arguing about Literature

Writing a paper about a work of literature — a novel, a short story, a poem, or a play — is not so different from writing about matters of public policy. In both cases you make a claim about something you have read and demonstrate the validity of that claim by providing support. In papers about literature, support consists primarily of evidence from examples and details in the work itself and your own interpretation of the language, the events, and the characters. In addition, you can introduce expert scholarly opinion and history and biography where they are relevant.

First, a note about the differences between imaginative literature and argumentative essays. Although the strategies for writing papers about them may be similar, strategies for reading and understanding the works under review will be different. Suppose you read an essay by a psychologist who wants to prove that lying to children, even with the best intentions, can have tragic consequences. The claim of the essay will be directly stated, perhaps even in the first sentence. But if an author writes a short story or a play about the same subject, he or she will probably not state the central idea directly but will *show* rather than *tell*. The theme will emerge through a narrative of dramatic events, expressions of thoughts and feelings by the characters, a depiction of relationships, descriptions of a specific setting, and other elements of fiction. In other words, you will derive the idea or the theme indirectly. This is one reason that a work of fiction can lend itself to multiple interpretations. But it is also the reason that literature, with its evocation of the mysteries of real life, exerts a perpetual fascination.

Different kinds of literary works emphasize different elements. In the following discussion the elements of fiction, poetry, and drama are briefly summarized. The discussion will suggest ways of reading imaginative literature for both pleasure and critical analysis.

THE ELEMENTS OF FICTION

The basic elements of imaginative prose — a short story, a novel, or a play — are *theme, conflict,* and *character.* Other elements such as language, plot, point of view, and setting also influence the effectiveness of any work, but without a central idea, a struggle between opposing forces, and interesting people, it's unlikely that the work will hold our attention. (On the other hand, literature is full of exceptions, and you will certainly find examples that defy the rules.)

The theme is the central idea. It answers the question, What is the point of this story or play? Does the author give us some insight into a personal dilemma? Does he or she show how social conditions shape human behavior? Do we learn how certain traits of character can influence a human life? The answers to these questions apply not only to the specific situation and invented characters in a particular story. In the most memorable works the theme — the lesson to be drawn, the truth to be learned — embodies an idea that is much larger than the form the story assumes. For example, in "The Use of Force," the short story by William Carlos Williams at the end of this appendix, the title refers to the *subject* but not the theme. The author wanted to say something *about* the use of force. His theme is a complicated and unwelcome insight into human nature, with implications for all of us, not just the doctor who is the principal actor in the story.

Conflict is present in some form in almost all imaginative writing. It creates suspense and introduces moral dilemmas. External conflicts occur between individuals and between individuals and natural forces. Internal conflicts take place in the minds and hearts of the characters who must make difficult choices between competing goals and values — between right and wrong, pleasure and duty, freedom and responsibility. These two kinds of conflict are not exclusive of each other. A story of war, for example, will include suspenseful physical encounters between opposing forces, but the characters may also be compelled to make painful choices about their actions. In the best works, conflicts are important, not trivial. They may reveal uncommon virtues or shortcomings in the characters, alter their relationships with other people, and even change the course of their lives.

Conflicts exist only because characters — human beings, or in some satires, animals — engage in them. In contests with forces of nature, as in Hemingway's *The Old Man and the Sea,* it is the courage and persistence of a human being that gives meaning to the story.

Memorable fictional characters are not easy to create. As readers we demand that characters be interesting, plausible, consistent, and active, physically and mentally. We must care about them, which is not the same as liking them. To care about characters means retaining enough curiosity about them to keep reading and to regret their departure when the story has come to an end. However different and unfamiliar their activities, we should feel that the characters are real. Even in science fiction we insist that the creatures exhibit human characteristics that we can recognize and identify with. But fictional characters should also be distinguishable from one another. Stereotypes are tiresome and unconvincing.

We learn about characters primarily from their speech and their actions but also from what the author and other characters reveal about them. Remembering that characters often withhold information or conceal their motives, even from themselves, we must often depend on our own knowledge and experience to interpret their behavior and judge their plausibility.

THE ELEMENTS OF DRAMA

Drama shares with fiction the elements we have discussed earlier — theme, conflict, and character. But because a play is meant to be performed, it differs from a written story in significant ways. These differences impose limits on the drama, as opposed to the novel, which can do almost anything.

First, stage action is restricted. Violent action — a war scene, for example — must usually take place offstage, and certain situations — such as the hunt for Moby Dick in Melville's novel — would be hard to reproduce in a theater. This means that a play emphasizes internal rather than external conflict.

Second, the author of a play, unlike the author of a short story or a novel, cannot comment on the action, the characters, or the significance of the setting. (It is true that a narrator sometimes appears on stage as a kind of Greek chorus to offer observation on the action, but this is uncommon.) A much greater burden must therefore rest on what the characters say. They must reveal background, explain offstage events, interpret themselves and others, and move the plot forward largely through speech. If the author of a novel lacks skill in reproducing plausible speech, he can find ways to avoid dialogue, but the playwright has no such privilege. She must have an ear for the rhythms and idioms of language that identify particular characters.

Another element which assumes more importance in a play than in a novel is plot. The dramatist must confine an often complicated and event-filled story to two or three hours on the stage. And, as in any listening experience, the audience must be able to follow the plot without the luxury of going back to review.

As you read a long play, you may find it helpful to keep in mind a simple diagram that explains the development of the plot, whether comedy or tragedy. The Freytag pyramid, created in 1863 by a German critic, shows that almost every three- or five-act play begins in a problem or conflict which sets in motion a series of events, called *the rising action.* At some point there is a *climax,* or turning point, followed by *the falling action,* which reverses the fortunes of the main characters and leads to a conclusion that may be happy or unhappy.

Shakespeare's *Macbeth* is an almost perfect example of the pyramid. The rising action in this tragedy is one of continued success for the main characters. The climax is a crisis on the battlefield, after which the fortunes of Macbeth and Lady Macbeth decline, ending in failure and death. In a comedy, the developments are reversed. The rising action is a series of stumbles and mishaps; then in the climax the hero finds the money or rescues the heroine and the falling action ushers in a number of welcome surprises that culminate in a happy ending. (Think of a Jim Carrey adventure.) Typically the rising action in any play takes longer and thus creates suspense.

Reading a play is not the same as seeing one on stage. Many playwrights, like novelists, describe their settings and their characters in elaborate detail. In *Long Day's Journey Into Night,* Eugene O'Neill's autobiographical play, descriptions of the living-room in which the action occurs and of the mother and father, who appear in the first act, cover more than three pages in small print. When you read, you fill the imaginary stage with your own interpretations of the playwright's descriptions, derived perhaps from places or persons in your own experience. You may forget that the playwright is dependent on directors, set designers, and actors, with other philosophies and approaches to stagecraft, to interpret his or her work. It can come as a surprise to see the stage version of the play you have read and interpreted very differently.

All playwrights want their plays to be performed. Still, the best plays are read far more frequently than they are produced on stage. Fortunately, reading them is a literary experience with its own rewards.

THE ELEMENTS OF POETRY

There are several kinds of poetry, among them epic, dramatic, and lyric. Epic poetry celebrates the heroic adventures of a human or superhuman character in a long, event-filled narrative. Milton's *Paradise Lost* is the preeminent example in English, but you may also be familiar with *The Iliad, The Odyssey,* and *The Aeneid,* the epics of ancient Greece and Rome. Dramatic poetry also tells a story, sometimes through monologue, as in Robert Browning's "My Last Duchess," where the Duke recounts the reasons why he murdered his wife; sometimes through dialogue, as in Robert Frost's "The Death of the Hired Man." These stories are often told in blank verse, unrhymed five-beat lines. Playwrights of the past, Shakespeare among others, adopted this poetic form.

Modern poems are much more likely to be lyrics — poetry derived from song. (The term *lyric* comes from the word for an ancient musical instrument, the lyre.) The lyric is most frequently an expression of the poet's feeling rather than an account of events. The characteristics that make poetry harder to read than prose are the very characteristics that define it: compression and metaphor. A lyric poem is highly concentrated. It focuses on what is essential in an experience, the details that illuminate it vividly against the background of our ordinary lives. Metaphor is a form of figurative language, a way of saying one thing to mean something else. It is a simile which omits the "like" or "as": for example, "A mighty fortress is our God." The poet chooses metaphoric images that appeal to our senses in order to reinforce the literal meaning. In a famous poem Thomas Campion compared the beauty of his sweetheart's face to that of a garden.

> There is a garden in her face
> Where roses and white lilies grow,
> A heavenly paradise is that place,
> Wherein all pleasant fruits do flow.

A poem, like an essay, tries to prove something. Like a short story, its message is indirect, expressed in the language of metaphor. It seldom urges a practical course of action. What it tries to prove is that a feeling or a perception — a response to love or death, or the sight of a snowy field on a dark night — is true and real.

The lyric poet's subjects are common ones — love, joy, sorrow, nature, death — but he or she makes uncommon use of words, imagery, and rhythm. These are the elements you examine as evidence of the poet's theme and depth of feeling.

Precisely because the poem will condense her experience, the poet must choose words with immediate impact. For example, in a poem about an encounter with a snake, Emily Dickinson writes,

> But never met this Fellow
> Attended, or alone
> Without a tighter breathing
> And Zero at the bone —

Although we have never seen this use of "zero" before, it strikes us at once as the perfect choice to suggest a kind of chilling fear.

In the best poems images transform the most commonplace experiences. Here is the first quatrain of Shakespeare's sonnet number 73, about loving deeply what will not live forever.

> That time of year thou mayest in me behold
> When yellow leaves or none or few do hang
> Upon those boughs which shake against the cold
> Bare ruined choirs where late the sweet birds sang.

Nowhere does Shakespeare mention that he is growing old. Instead, here and in subsequent stanzas he creates images of dead or dying things — autumn trees, the coming of night, dying fires — that convey feelings of cold and desolation. The final couplet expresses the theme directly:

> Thus thou perceivs't, which makes thy love more strong,
> To love that well which thou must leave ere long.

It is the imagery, however, that brings the theme to life and enables us to understand and share the poet's feeling.

Rhythm, defined as measured and balanced movement, is almost as important as language. As children, even before we fully understand all the words, we derive pleasure from the sounds of Mother Goose and the Dr. Seuss rhymes. Their sound patterns reflect the musical origin of poetry and the fact that poetry was meant to be chanted rather than read. Listen to the rhythm of these opening lines from Andrew Marvell's "To His Coy Mistress" — "Had we but world enough and time, / This coyness, lady, were no crime" — and hear the lilting four-beat meter that suggests song. If you look through an anthology of poetry written before the twentieth century, you will see even from the appearance of the poems on the page that the cadence or rhythm of most poems creates an orderly pattern. Edgar Allan Poe's "The Raven" is a familiar example of poems in which rhyme and rhythm come together to produce a harmonious design.

Measured movement in poetry is less common today. Free verse breaks with this ancient convention. (The very regularity of "The Raven" is now a subject for parody.) The poet of free verse invents his own rhythms, governed by meaning, free association, and a belief in poetry as a democratic art, one capable of reaching all people. In "Song of Myself," Walt Whitman (1819–1892), one of America's most influential poets, writes in a new voice that resembles the sound of spoken language:

> A child said *What is the grass?* fetching it to me with
>   full hands,

How could I answer the child? I do not know what it is
    any more than he.
I guess it must be the flag of my disposition, out of hopeful
    green stuff woven.

Notice, however, that the phrase "out of hopeful green stuff woven"
is the language of poetry, not prose.

Much modern poetry dispenses altogether with both rhyme and
formal rhythms, but the lyric remains unmistakably alive. Perhaps
you have read poems by William Carlos Williams or e. e. cummings,
who have used new rhythms to create their own distinctive versions
of the lyric.

THE CULTURAL CONTEXT

Even those works that are presumed to be immortal and universal are products of a particular time in history and a particular social and political context. These works may therefore represent
points of view with which we are unsympathetic. Today, for
example, some women are uncomfortable with Shakespeare's *The
Taming of the Shrew,* which finds comic possibilities in the subjuga-
tion of a woman to her husband's will. Jews may be offended by the
characterization of Shylock in *The Merchant of Venice* as a Jewish
money-lender who shows little mercy to his debtor. Some African
Americans have resented the portrayal of Jim, the slave in *Huckleberry Finn.* Even *Peter Pan* has provoked criticism for its depiction of
American Indians. In your own reading you may find fault with an author's attitude toward his subject; defending your own point of view
against that of the author can be a satisfying literary exercise. To
bring fresh, perhaps controversial, interpretations into an analysis
may, indeed, enliven discussion and even revive interest in older
works that no longer move us. But remember that the evidence will
be largely external, based on social and political views that will
themselves need explanation.

There is, after all, a danger in allowing our ideas about social
and political correctness to take over and to impose our values on
those of another time, place, or culture. Literature, like great historical writing, enables us to enter worlds very different from our
own. The worlds we read about in novels and plays may be governed by different moral codes, different social conventions, different religious values, many of which we reject or don't understand.
Characters in these stories, even those cast as heroes and hero-
ines, sometimes behave in ways we consider ignorant or self-
serving. (Russell Baker, the humorist, observed that it was unfortunate that the writers of the past were not so enlightened as we are.)
But reading has always offered an experience otherwise unavail-

able, a ready escape from our own lives into the lives of others, whose ways, however strange, we try to understand, whether or not we approve.

CHOOSING WHAT TO WRITE ABOUT

Your paper can take one of several different approaches. It is worth emphasizing that comedy and tragedy generally share the same literary elements. A tragedy, of course, ends in misfortune or death. A comedy typically ends with a happy resolution of all problems.

1. You may analyze or explain the meaning or theme of a work that is subject to different interpretations. For example, a famous interpretation of *Hamlet* in 1900[1] suggested that Hamlet was unable to avenge his father's murder because of guilt over his own Oedipal love for his mother. Or, having seen a distorted movie version of a familiar book (unfortunately, there are plenty of examples) you can explain what you think is the real theme of the book and how the movie departs from it.

Some stories and plays, although based in reality, seem largely symbolic. "The Lottery," a widely read short story by Shirley Jackson, describes a ritual that hints at other meanings than those usually attributed to lotteries. *Waiting for Godot,* a play by Samuel Beckett, is a work that has inspired a dozen interpretations; the name *Godot,* with the embedded word *God,* suggests several. But exercise caution in writing about symbols. Saul Bellow, the Nobel Prize–winning novelist, has written an essay, "Deep Readers of the World, Beware!" that explains the dangers. He reminds us that "a true symbol is substantial, not accidental. You cannot avoid it, you cannot remove it."

2. You may analyze the conflicts in a story or play. The conflicts that make interesting papers are those that not only challenge our understanding (as with Iago's villainy in *Othello*) but encourage us to reflect on profound moral issues. For example, how does Mark Twain develop the struggle in Huckleberry Finn between his southern prejudices and his respect for Jim's humanity? How does John Proctor, the hero of Arthur Miller's *The Crucible,* resolve the moral dilemmas that lead him to choose death rather than a freedom secured by lies?

3. You may choose to write about an especially vivid or contradictory character, describing his traits in such a way as to make clear why he is worth a detailed examination. The protagonist of *The Stranger* by Albert Camus, for example, is a murderer who, although

---

[1] By Ernest Jones, a Freudian analyst.

he tells us little or nothing about himself and is therefore difficult to understand, eventually earns our sympathy.

4. You may concentrate on the setting if it has special significance for the lives of the characters and what they do, as in Joseph Conrad's *Heart of Darkness* and Tennessee Williams's *A Streetcar Named Desire*. Setting may include time or historical period as well as place. Ask if the story or play would have taken shape in quite the same way in another time and place.

5. You may examine the language or style. No analysis of a poem would be complete without attention to the language, but the style of a prose work can also contribute to the impact on the reader. Hemingway's clean, economical style has often been studied, as has Faulkner's dense, complicated prose, equally powerful but very different. But you should probably not attempt an analysis of style unless you are sure you can discuss the uses of diction, grammar, syntax, and rhythm.

GUIDELINES FOR WRITING THE PAPER

1. Decide on a limited topic as the subject for your paper. The most interesting topics, of course, are those that are not so obvious: original interpretations, for example, that arise from a genuine personal response. Don't be afraid to disagree with a conventional reading of the literary work, but be sure you can find sufficient evidence for your point of view.

2. Before you begin to write, make a brief outline of the points that will support your thesis. You may find that you don't have enough evidence to make a good case to a skeptical reader. Or you may find that you have too much for a short paper and that your thesis, therefore, is too broad.

3. The evidence that you provide can be both internal and external. Internal evidence is found in the work itself: an action that reveals motives and consequences, statements by the characters about themselves and others, comments by the author about her characters, and interpretation of the language. External evidence comes from outside the work: a comment by a literary critic, information about the historical period or the geographical location of the work, or data about the author's life and other works he has written.

If possible, use more than one kind of evidence. The most important proof, however, will come from a careful selection of material from the work itself.

4. One temptation to avoid is using quotations from the work or from a critic so abundantly that your paper consists of a string of quotations and little else. Remember that the importance of your

paper rests on *your* interpretations of the evidence. Your *own* analysis should constitute the major part of the paper. The quotations should be introduced only to support important points.

5. Organize your essay according to the guidelines you have followed for an argumentative essay on a public issue (see Chapter 9, pp. 315–21). Two of the organizational plans that work best are defending the main idea and refuting the opposing view — that is, a literary interpretation with which you disagree. In both cases the simplest method is to state your claim — the thesis you are going to defend — in the first paragraph and then line up evidence point by point in order of importance. If you feel comfortable beginning your paper in a different way, you may start with a paragraph of background: the reasons that you have chosen to explore a particular topic or a description of your personal response to the work — for example, where you first saw a play performed, how a story or poem affected you. (H. L. Mencken, the great American social critic, said discovering *Huckleberry Finn* was "the most stupendous event of my whole life!" What a beginning for an essay!)

It is always useful to look at book or movie reviews in good newspapers and magazines for models of organization and development that suggest a wide range of choices for your own paper.

SAMPLE STORY AND ANALYSIS

Read the following short story and reflect on it for a few moments. Then turn back to the following questions. Were you surprised at the actions of the doctor? What is the author saying about the use of force? Do you agree? What kinds of conflicts has he dramatized? Are some more important than others? How do the characterizations of the people in the story contribute to the theme?

Thinking about the answers to these questions will give you a clearer perspective on the essay written by a student that follows the story. After reading the essay, you may see other elements of fiction that might have been analyzed in a critical paper.

The Use of Force

WILLIAM CARLOS WILLIAMS

They were new patients to me, all I had was the name, Olson. Please come down as soon as you can, my daughter is very sick.

When I arrived I was met by the mother, a big startled looking woman, very clean and apologetic who merely said, Is this the doctor? and let me in. In the back, she added, You must excuse us, doctor, we have her in the kitchen where it is warm. It is very damp here sometimes.

The child was fully dressed and sitting on her father's lap near the kitchen table. He tried to get up, but I motioned for him not to bother, took off my overcoat and started to look things over. I could see that they were all very nervous, eyeing me up and down distrustfully. As often, in such cases, they weren't telling me more than they had to, it was up to me to tell them; that's why they were spending three dollars on me.

The child was fairly eating me up with her cold, steady eyes, and no expression to her face whatever. She did not move and seemed, inwardly, quiet; an unusually attractive little thing, and as strong as a heifer in appearance. But her face was flushed, she was breathing rapidly, and I realized that she had a high fever. She had magnificent blonde hair, in profusion. One of those picture children often reproduced in advertising leaflets and the photogravure sections of the Sunday papers.

She's had a fever for three days, began the father and we don't 5 know what it comes from. My wife has given her things, you know, like people do, but it don't do no good. And there's been a lot of sickness around. So we tho't you'd better look her over and tell us what is the matter.

As doctors often do I took a trial shot at it as a point of departure. Has she had a sore throat?

Both parents answered me together, No . . . No, she says her throat don't hurt her.

Does your throat hurt you? added the mother to the child. But the little girl's expression didn't change nor did she move her eyes from my face.

Have you looked?

I tried to, said the mother, but I couldn't see. 10

As it happens we had been having a number of cases of diphtheria in the school to which this child went during that month and we

---

"The Use of Force," William Carlos Williams, *The Farmers' Daughters* (1938).

were all, quite apparently, thinking of that, though no one had as yet spoken of the thing.

Well, I said, suppose we take a look at the throat first. I smiled in my best professional manner and asking for the child's first name I said, come on, Mathilda, open your mouth and let's take a look at your throat.

Nothing doing.

Aw, come on, I coaxed, just open your mouth wide and let me take a look. Look, I said opening both hands wide. I haven't anything in my hands. Just open up and let me see.

Such a nice man, put in the mother. Look how kind he is to you. 15 Come on, do what he tells you to. He won't hurt you.

At that I ground my teeth in disgust. If only they wouldn't use the word "hurt" I might be able to get somewhere. But I did not allow myself to be hurried or disturbed but speaking quietly and slowly I approached the child again.

As I moved my chair a little nearer suddenly with one cat-like movement both her hands clawed instinctively for my eyes and she almost reached them too. In fact she knocked my glasses flying and they fell, though unbroken, several feet away from me on the kitchen floor.

Both the mother and father almost turned themselves inside out in embarrassment and apology. You bad girl, said the mother, taking her and shaking her by one arm. Look what you've done. The nice man . . .

For heaven's sake, I broke in. Don't call me a nice man to her. I'm here to look at her throat on the chance that she might have diphtheria and possibly die of it. But that's nothing to her. Look here, I said to the child, we're going to look at your throat. You're old enough to understand what I'm saying. Will you open it now by yourself or shall we have to open it for you?

Not a move. Even her expression hadn't changed. Her breaths 20 however were coming faster and faster. Then the battle began. I had to do it. I had to have a throat culture for her own protection. But first I told the parents that it was entirely up to them. I explained the danger but said that I would not insist on a throat examination so long as they would take the responsibility.

If you don't do what the doctor says you'll have to go to the hospital, the mother admonished her severely.

Oh yeah? I had to smile to myself. After all, I had already fallen in love with the savage brat, the parents were contemptible to me. In the ensuing struggle they grew more and more abject, crushed, exhausted while she surely rose to magnificent heights of insane fury of effort bred of her terror of me.

The father tried his best, and he was a big man but the fact that she was his daughter, his shame at her behavior and his dread of hurting her made him release her just at the critical moment several times when I had almost achieved success, till I wanted to kill him. But his dread also that she might have diphtheria made him tell me to go on, go on though he himself was almost fainting, while the mother moved back and forth behind us raising and lowering her hands in an agony of apprehension.

Put her in front of you on your lap, I ordered, and hold both her wrists.

But as soon as he did the child let out a scream. Don't, you're 25 hurting me. Let go of my hands. Let them go I tell you. Then she shrieked terrifyingly, hysterically. Stop it! Stop it! You're killing me!

Do you think she can stand it, doctor! said the mother.

You get out, said the husband to his wife. Do you want her to die of diphtheria?

Come on now, hold her, I said.

Then I grasped the child's head with my left hand and tried to get the wooden tongue depressor between her teeth. She fought, with clenched teeth, desperately! But now I also had grown furious — at a child. I tried to hold myself down but I couldn't. I know how to expose a throat for inspection. And I did my best. When finally I got the wooden spatula behind the last teeth and just the point of it into the mouth cavity, she opened up for an instant, but before I could see anything she came down again and gripping the wooden blade between her molars she reduced it to splinters before I could get it out again.

Aren't you ashamed, the mother yelled at her. Aren't you 30 ashamed to act like that in front of the doctor?

Get me a smooth-handled spoon of some sort, I told the mother. We're going through with this. The child's mouth was already bleeding. Her tongue was cut and she was screaming in wild hysterical shrieks. Perhaps I should have desisted and come back in an hour or more. No doubt it would have been better. But I have seen at least two children lying dead in bed of neglect in such cases, and feeling that I must get a diagnosis now or never I went at it again. But the worst of it was that I too had got beyond reason. I could have torn the child apart in my own fury and enjoyed it. It was a pleasure to attack her. My face was burning with it.

The damned little brat must be protected against her own idiocy, one says to one's self at such times. Others must be protected against her. It is social necessity. And all these things are true. But a blind fury, a feeling of adult shame, bred of a longing for muscular release are the operatives. One goes on to the end.

In a final unreasoning assault I overpowered the child's neck and jaws. I forced the heavy silver spoon back of her teeth and down her throat till she gagged. And there it was — both tonsils covered with membrane. She had fought valiantly to keep me from knowing her secret. She had been hiding that sore throat for three days at least and lying to her parents in order to escape just such an outcome as this.

Now truly she *was* furious. She had been on the defensive before but now she attacked. Tried to get off her father's lap and fly at me while tears of defeat blinded her eyes.

Jennifer Rampolla
Professor Harrington
English 102-C
May 2, 19--

Conflicts in "The Use of Force"

"The Use of Force" tells us something about human nature that probably comes as no surprise: The impulse to
use violence against a helpless but defiant opponent can be
thrilling and irresistible. But the conflict which produces
this insight is not a shoot-out between cops and robbers,
not a fight for survival against a dangerous enemy, but a
struggle between a grown man and a sick child.

In this story two major conflicts are dramatized, one
external or physical, the other internal or psychological.
The conflicts seem obvious. Even the blunt, unadorned
language means to persuade us that nothing is concealed.
But below the surface, some motives remain unacknowledged, and we guess at them only because we know how
easily people deceive themselves.

The external conflict is vividly depicted, a physical
struggle between doctor and child, complete with weapon--
a metal spoon. The outcome is hardly in doubt; the doctor
will win. One critic calls this story primarily "an
accomplishment (external conflict) story" (Madden 16). But
the internal conflict that accompanies a difficult choice is
the real heart of the story. The doctor must decide between
waiting for a more opportune time to examine the child or
exercising brute force to subdue her now. When he decides
on brute force, he seems aware of his motives.

> But the worst of it was that I too had got beyond
> reason. I could have torn the child apart in
> my own fury and enjoyed it. It was a pleasure
> to attack her.

This shocking revelation is not, however, the whole
story. Why has he got beyond reason? Why does he take
pleasure in attacking a child? The answer lies not only in
what we know about the antagonists but in what we can assume about their relationship to each other.

Title indicates
subject

Introduction
|
The theme
|
Theme emerges
through conflicts

|

Naming the
major conflicts
(external and
internal)
|
A concealed
conflict (to be
explained later)
|
Body
External conflict
developed

|

Evidence: com-
ment from a
critic
|
Internal conflict
developed

|

Evidence:
Quotation

|

Concealed con-
flict, based on the
characters and
their relationship

Rampolla   2

Description
of the child

The child is brilliantly portrayed in a few grim encounters with the doctor. She is strong, stubborn, secretive, and violent. Despite her size and age, she is a match for the doctor, a challenge that at first excites him.

Evidence:
Quotation

> I had to smile to myself. After all, I had already fallen in love with the savage brat. . . . In the ensuing struggle . . . she surely rose to magnificent heights of insane fury. . . .

Description
of the doctor

The picture of the doctor is somewhat harder to read. Sixty years ago (when this story was written) the doctor in a working-class community occupied a position of unusual power and authority. He would not be accustomed to challenges at any level. Clearly the differences in social and economic status between the doctor and his clients are another source of conflict that influences his use of force.

Unexpressed
social conflict

Evidence: External, from history

Like many people in positions of power, the doctor is torn by contradictory emotions toward those below him. On the one hand, he despises those who are deferential to him, in this case the child's parents. On the other hand, it is unthinkable that a child should dare to oppose him, not only in refusing to obey his instructions but in trying, like a desperate small animal, to attack him. It is even more unthinkable that she should prevail in any contest. He confesses to "a feeling of adult shame." If we look for it, there is also a hint of sexual conflict. The child is blond and beautiful; the doctor says he is in love with her. (Would this story have worked in quite the same way if the child had been a boy?) The doctor attempts to rationalize his use of force, but he knows that it is not the child's welfare that finally compels him to overcome her resistance. In the end, reason gives way to pride and vanity.

Evidence:
Quotation

Perhaps another
concealed
conflict?

The doctor's
real motivation

Conclusion

Most of us respond to this story with a mixture of feelings--anger at the pleasure the doctor takes in his use of force, confusion and even fear at the realization that doctors may not always behave like gentle and loving helpers, and pity for the little girl with whom it is easy to identify. The author doesn't spell out the moral implications of the doctor's internal conflict. But perhaps it is significant

The reader's
mixed reaction

Rampolla   3

that the author gives the last words to the little girl: "Tears   Sympathy for
of defeat blinded her eyes." I think he has chosen this   the child
ending in order to direct our sympathy to the victim, an
unhappy child who struggled hopelessly to protect herself.
Although we know that the doctor has performed a   Reaction to
necessary and merciful act, we are left to wonder if it   the theme
matters that he has done it for the wrong reason.

Rampolla   4
Works Cited
Madden, David. Studies in the Short Story. New York: Holt,
    1980.

ACKNOWLEDGMENTS (continued from page iv)

". . . Back to Square One." Drawing by Walt Handelsman. Copyright © 1995 Handelsman–Times-Picayune. Reprinted by permission of Tribune Media Services.

John Perry Barlow, "Is There a There in Cyberspace?" From *The Utne Reader,* March/April 1995. Reprinted by permission of the author.

Mike Barnicle, "Heroes on Our Doorstep." From the *Boston Globe,* June 21, 1994. Reprinted courtesy of The Boston Globe.

Bostongas advertisement, "Perhaps the most beautiful thing about using energy more efficiently isn't the fuel it can save." Illustrator: Suzanne Barnes. Reprinted by permission of Bostongas and the illustrator.

Ellen Bravo and Ellen Cassedy, "What Sexual Harassment Is — And Is Not." From *The 9 to 5 Guide to Combatting Sexual Harassment: Candid Advice from 9to5, the National Association of Working Women.* Copyright © 1992 John Wiley & Sons, Inc. Reprinted by permission of John Wiley & Sons, Inc.

Peter Brimelow, "Unchecked Immigration." Reprinted from *Commentary,* November 1995, by permission, all rights reserved; and by permission of the author.

Armin A. Brott, "Not All Men Are Sly Foxes." From *Newsweek,* June 1, 1992. Reprinted by permission of the author.

Warren E. Burger, "The Right to Bear Arms." From *Parade,* January 14, 1990. Reprinted with permission from Parade, copyright © 1990, and the author.

Edmund B. (Peter) Burke, "Net.Censor: Who's to Say What We Should See or Hear?" Copyright © 1995 by the author. Reprinted by permission. This article appeared in *Educom Review,* November/December 1995.

Peggy Carlson, "Why We Don't Need Animal Experimentation." From the *Wall Street Journal,* November 7, 1995. Reprinted with permission of The Wall Street Journal © 1995 Dow Jones & Company, Inc. All rights reserved.

Stephen L. Carter, "Racial Justice on the Cheap." From *Reflections of an Affirmative Action Baby* by Stephen L. Carter. Copyright © 1991 by Stephen L. Carter. Reprinted by permission of HarperCollins Publishers, Inc.

Cease Fire advertisement, "A gun in the home is much more likely to kill a family member than to kill an intruder." Reprinted courtesy of Cease Fire, Inc.

Wanda Coleman, "Get Out of Dodge!" From the February 15, 1993, issue of *The Nation.* Reprinted with permission from *The Nation* magazine. © 1993 The Nation Company, L.P.

John P. Conrad, "Against the Death Penalty." From *Death Penalty: A Debate* by John P. Conrad and Ernest van den Haag. Copyright © 1983 Plenum Publishing Corporation. Reprinted by permission of Plenum Publishing Corporation and the authors.

Louis L. Cregler and Herbert Mark, "Cocaine Is Even Deadlier Than We Thought." From the *New York Times,* July 30, 1986. Reprinted by permission of the authors.

Mandalit del Barco, "Affirmative Action: A Tale of Two Women." From *Sí,* Fall/Winter 1995. Reprinted by permission of the author.

Alan Dershowitz, "The Case for Medicalizing Heroin" and "Tragic Mercy Killing Case Didn't Belong in Court." From *Contrary to Popular Opinion* by Alan Dershowitz. Copyright © 1992 United Feature Syndicate, Inc. Reprinted by permission of United Feature Syndicate, Inc.

John Diebold, "What Are We Waiting For?" Reprinted with permission from the April 1994 *Reader's Digest.* Copyright © 1994 by The Reader's Digest Assn., Inc.

John Patrick Diggins, "The Pursuit of Whining: Affirmative Action circa 1776." From the *New York Times,* September 25, 1995. Copyright © 1995 by The New York Times Co. Reprinted by permission.

John J. DiIulio, Jr., "Let 'em Rot." From the *Wall Street Journal,* January 26, 1994. Reprinted with permission of The Wall Street Journal © 1994 Dow Jones & Company, Inc. All rights reserved.

1994. Reprinted with the permission of The Wall Street Journal © 1994 Dow Jones & Company, Inc. All rights reserved.

Land's End advertisement, "Numbers don't lie." Reprinted courtesy of Land's End Direct Merchants.

"Last spring you robbed me and got 3 years. Last month you nailed me again and got 5 to 10 . . . Haven't you learned your lesson yet?" Drawing by Wayne Stayskal. Copyright © 1993 Stayskal–Tampa Tribune. Reprinted by permission of Tribune Media Services.

Charles R. Lawrence III, "On Racist Speech." From *The Chronicle of Higher Education,* October 25, 1989. Reprinted by permission of the author.

Michael Levin, "The Case for Torture." Reprinted by permission of the author.

Steven Levy, "Indecent Proposal: Censor the Net." From *Newsweek,* April 3, 1995. Copyright © 1995 Newsweek, Inc. All rights reserved. Reprinted by permission.

John E. Mack, "UFO Abductions: An Introduction." Reprinted with the permission of Scribner, a Division of Simon & Schuster from *Abduction: Human Encounters with Aliens* by John E. Mack. Copyright © 1994 by John E. Mack, M.D.

Catharine MacKinnon, Floyd Abrams, and Anthony Lewis. "The First Amendment under Fire from the Left." From the *New York Times Magazine,* March 13, 1994. Copyright © 1994 by The New York Times Co. Reprinted by permission.

Karl Menninger, "Therapy, Not Punishment." Original title: "Verdict Guilty — Now What?" Copyright © 1959 by *Harper's Magazine.* All rights reserved. Reproduced from the August issue by special permission.

Metropolitan Energy Council advertisement, "Gas heat makes me nervous." Reprinted by permission of the Metropolitan Energy Council.

Jerome Miller [interview with], "The Rush to Punish." From *The Humanist,* January/February 1994. Copyright © 1994 Jerome Miller. Reprinted by permission of the author.

Nicholas Negroponte, "Don't Dissect a Frog, Build One." From *Being Digital* by Nicholas Negroponte. Copyright © 1995 Nicholas Negroponte. Reprinted by permission of Alfred A. Knopf, Inc.

Jacob Neusner, "The Speech the Graduates Didn't Hear." Copyright © 1983 by Jacob Neusner. Reprinted from the [Brown University] *Daily Herald,* June 12, 1983. Used by permission of the author.

Newman, Graeme, "Pain: The Forgotten Punishment." From *Just and Painful* (Macmillan, 1983). Copyright © Graeme Newman. Used by permission of the author.

Mike Oppenheim, "TV Isn't Violent *Enough.*" From *TV Guide,* February 11, 1984. Reprinted with permission from TV Guide. Copyright © News America Publications, Inc. [TV Guide]

George Orwell, "Politics and the English Language." Copyright © by Sonia Brownell Orwell, renewed 1974 by Sonia Orwell. Reprinted from his volume *Shooting an Elephant and Other Essays* by permission of Harcourt Brace & Company and the Estate of the late Sonia Brownell Orwell and Martin Secker & Warburg Ltd.

David M. Oshinsky and Michael Curtis, "Freedom of Speech and Holocaust Revisionism." From the *New York Times,* December 11, 1991. Copyright © by The New York Times Co. Reprinted by permission.

Mortimer Ostow, "That Right Belongs Only to the State." Reprinted by permission of the author.

Tony Parker and Hank Sullivan, "People Like Me." From *The Violence of Our Lives: Interviews with American Murderers* edited by Tony Parker. Copyright © 1995 by Tony Parker. Reprinted by permission of Henry Holt and Co., Inc.

Curtis Peebles, "Abductions and Abductionists." Reprinted from *Watch the Skies! A Chronicle of the Flying Saucer Myth* by Curtis Peebles (Washington, DC: Smithsonian Institution Press), pages ix–x, 234–41, by permission of the publisher. Copyright © 1994.

Stanton Peele, "Addiction Is Not a Disease." Reprinted with permission from *Diseasing of America: Addiction Treatment Out of Control* by Stanton Peele. Copyright © 1989 Stanton Peele. First published by Lexington Books. All correspondence should be sent to Jossey-Bass Inc., Publishers, San Francisco. All rights reserved.

"Plastic That Goes to Waste," pie chart. From the *Wall Street Journal,* February 2, 1990. Reprinted by permission of The Wall Street Journal © 1990 Dow Jones & Company, Inc. All rights reserved worldwide.

Neil Postman, "Virtual Students, Digital Classroom." From the October 9, 1995, issue of *The Nation.* Reprinted with permission from *The Nation.* © The Nation Company, L.P.

James Rachels, M.D., "Active and Passive Euthanasia." From *The New England Journal of Medicine,* Vol 292 (1975), pp. 78–80. Copyright © 1975 Massachusetts Medical Society. Reprinted by permission. All rights reserved.

David Rakoff, "A Former Smoker Cheers." From the *New York Times,* April 14, 1995. Copyright © 1995 by The New York Times Co. Reprinted by permission.

William Raspberry, "Immigration Straight-talk." Copyright © 1995 Washington Post Writers Group. Reprinted by permission.

William Rathje and Cullen Murphy, "The Landfill Excavations." From *Rubbish! The Archaeology of Garbage* by William Rathje and Cullen Murphy. Copyright © 1992 by William Rathje and Cullen Murphy. Reprinted by permission of HarperCollins Publishers, Inc.

Jonathan Rauch, "In Defense of Prejudice." Copyright © 1995 by *Harper's Magazine.* All rights reserved. Reproduced from the May issue by special permission.

Heloisa Sabin, "Animal Research Saves Human Lives." From the *Wall Street Journal,* October 18, 1995. Reprinted with permission of The Wall Street Journal © 1995 Dow Jones & Company, Inc., all rights reserved, and by permission of Americans for Medical Progress Educational Foundation.

Franklin Saige, "Mega Buys." From *Plain,* Spring 1994. Reprinted by permission of *Plain* Magazine.

Saturn advertisement, "Cheryl Silas had a highway collision, was hit twice from behind, and then sold three cars for us." Reprinted by permission of the Saturn Corporation.

Lisa Schiffren, "Penalize the Unwed Dad? Fat Chance." From the *New York Times,* August 10, 1995. Copyright © 1995 by The New York Times Co. Reprinted by permission.

Albert Shanker, "The Real Victims." Copyright © 1995 by Albert Shanker and reprinted with his permission.

Joseph P. Shapiro and Andrea R. Wright, "Sins of the Fathers." From *U.S. News & World Report,* August 14, 1995. Copyright, Aug. 14, 1995, U.S. News & World Report. Reprinted by permission.

Brent Staples, "The Chain Gang Show." From the *New York Times Magazine,* September 17, 1995. Copyright © 1995 by The New York Times Co. Reprinted by permission.

Shelby Steele, "Affirmative Action Must Go." From the *New York Times,* March 1, 1995. Copyright © 1995 by The New York Times Co. Reprinted by permission.

Clifford Stoll, "On Classrooms, with and without Computers." From *Silicon Snake Oil* by Clifford Stoll. Copyright © 1995 by Clifford Stoll. Used by permission of Doubleday, a division of Bantam Doubleday Dell Publishing Group, Inc.

Deborah Tannen, "Talking Up Close." From *Talking 9 to 5* by Deborah Tannen, Ph.D. Copyright © 1994 by Deborah Tannen, Ph.D. By permission of William Morrow & Co.

"This is a surprise — he doesn't want any extraordinary measures taken to resuscitate him." Drawing by Ed Fisher. Copyright © 1992 The New Yorker Magazine, Inc. Reprinted by permission.

Kathleen Kennedy Townsend, "Not Just Read and Write, but Right and Wrong." From *The Washington Monthly,* January 1990. Reprinted with permission from *The*

Glossary and Index of Terms

Abstract language: language expressing a quality apart from a specific object or event; opposite of *concrete language* *223–27*

Ad hominem: "against the man"; attacking the arguer rather than the *argument* or issue *267–68*

Ad populum: "to the people"; playing on the prejudices of the *audience* *271*

Appeal to tradition: a proposal that something should continue because it has traditionally existed or been done that way *271–72*

Argument: a process of reasoning and advancing proof about issues on which conflicting views may be held; also, a statement or statements providing *support* for a *claim* *3–24*

Audience: those who will hear an *argument;* more generally, those to whom a communication is addressed *13–14*

Authoritative warrant: a *warrant* based on the credibility or trustworthiness of the source *186*

Backing: the assurances upon which a *warrant* or assumption is based *180–81*

Begging the question: making a statement that assumes that the issue being argued has already been decided *269–70*

Claim: the conclusion of an argument; what the arguer is trying to prove *10–11*

Claim of fact: a *claim* that asserts something exists, has existed, or will exist, based on data that the *audience* will accept as objectively verifiable *10, 47–53*

Claim of policy: a *claim* asserting that specific courses of action should be instituted as solutions to problems *11, 62–72*

Claim of value: a *claim* that asserts some things are more or less desirable than others *10, 54–62*

Hasty generalization: drawing conclusions from insufficient evidence *264*

Induction: reasoning by which a general statement is reached on the basis of particular examples *249–50*

Inference: an interpretation of the *facts* *11, 50–51*

Major premise: see *syllogism*

Minor premise: see *syllogism*

Motivational appeal: an attempt to reach an *audience* by recognizing their *needs* and *values* and how these contribute to their decision making *11*

Motivational warrant: a type of *warrant* based on the *needs* and *values* of an *audience* *187*

Need: in the hierarchy of Abraham Maslow, whatever is required, whether psychological, or physiological, for the survival and welfare of a human being *155–57*

Non sequitur: "it does not follow"; using irrelevant proof to buttress a *claim* *271*

Picturesque language: words that produce images in the minds of the *audience* *221–23*

Policy: a course of action recommended or taken to solve a problem or guide decisions *11, 62–64*

Post hoc: mistakenly inferring that because one event follows another they have a causal relation; from *post hoc ergo propter hoc* ("after this, therefore because of this"); also called "doubtful cause" *264–66*

Proposition: see *claim*

Qualifier: a restriction placed on the *claim* to state that it may not always be true as stated *48, 182*

Refutation: an attack on an opposing view in order to weaken it, invalidate it, or make it less credible *316–17*

Reservation: a restriction placed on the *warrant* to indicate that unless certain conditions are met, the warrant may not establish a connection between the *support* and the *claim* *182*

Slanting: selecting *facts* or words with *connotations* that favor the arguer's bias and discredit alternatives *218–21*

Slippery slope: predicting without justification that one step in a process will lead unavoidably to a second, generally undesirable step *268–69*

Slogan: an attention-getting expression used largely in politics or advertising to promote support of a cause or product *230–34*

Statistics: information expressed in numerical form *141–42, 148–50*

Stipulative definition: a *definition* that makes clear that it will explore a particular area of meaning of a term or issue *99–100*

Straw man: disputing a view similar to, but not the same as, that of the arguer's opponent *270*

Style: choices in words and sentence structure that make a writer's language distinctive *324*

Substantive warrant: a *warrant* based on beliefs about the reliability of *factual evidence* *186–87*

Support: any material that serves to prove an issue or *claim;* in addition to *evidence,* it includes appeals to the *needs* and *values* of the *audience* *11, 138–60*

Syllogism: a formula of deductive *argument* consisting of three propositions: a major premise, a minor premise, and a conclusion *254–58*

Thesis: the main idea of an essay *261–63*

Toulmin model: a conceptual system of argument devised by the philosopher Stephen Toulmin; the terms *claim, support, warrant, backing, qualifier,* and *reservation* are adapted from this system *261–63*

Two wrongs make a right: diverting attention from the issue by introducing a new point, e.g., by responding to an accusation with a counteraccusation that makes no attempt to refute the first accusation *270–71*

Values: conceptions or ideas that act as standards for judging what is right or wrong, worthwhile or worthless, beautiful or ugly, good or bad *158–60*

Warrant: a general principle or assumption that establishes a connection between the *support* and the *claim* *11–13, 179–87*

Index of Authors
and Titles